W9-BLL-616

ENCOUNTERS WITH KIERKEGAARD

ENCOUNTERS

—»•· WITH ·•«—

KIERKEGAARD

A Life as Seen by His Contemporaries

Collected, Edited, and Annotated by

BRUCE H. KIRMMSE

Translated by

Bruce H. Kirmmse *and* Virginia R. Laursen

PRINCETON UNIVERSITY PRESS • PRINCETON, NEW JERSEY

WESTPORT PUBLIC LIBRARY
WESTPORT, CONNECTICUT

Copyright © 1996 by Princeton University Press

eet,

B K5466E KIERKE- GAARD,
Encounters with Kierkegaard
: a life as seen by his

.... Reserved

Library of Congress Cataloging-in-Publication Data

Encounters with Kierkegaard : a life as seen by
his contemporaries / collected, edited, and
annotated by Bruce H. Kirmmse; translated by
Bruce H. Kirmmse and Virginia R. Laursen.

p.   cm.

Includes bibliographical references (p.   ) and index.

ISBN 0-691-01106-0 (cl : alk. paper)

1. Kierkegaard, Søren, 1813–1855.   2. Philosophers—Denmark—
Biography.   3. Authors, Danish—Denmark—Biography.
4. Theologians—Denmark—Biography.
I. Kirmmse, Bruce H.

B4376.E43   1996

198'.9—dc20   [B]   95-43183

This book has been composed in Bembo

Princeton University Press books are printed on
acid-free paper and meet the guidelines for permanence
and durability of the Committee on Production
Guidelines for Book Longevity of the
Council on Library Resources

Printed in the United States of America

1   3   5   7   9   10   8   6   4   2

3 4015 06730 0747

Søren Kierkegaard was not so inscrutable and mysterious. Indeed, everyone who came into close contact with him was able to see something of the reality of his spiritual essence. Some people can surely still remember him as a young man, when he was feisty and combative and used the keen-edged weapons of dialectic and irony to fight for poetic ideals against prosaic mediocrity. Others will remember him a bit older, when, with the highest of goals before him, he worked "in the service of divinity" with an energetic will, undaunted by physical weakness, compressing into a few short years the substance of a long and fruitful life. Still others, perhaps only a few, will remember him during his final years. They will recall that during his earnest struggle—when "his wish was death, his longing the grave, his desire that this wish and this longing might soon be fulfilled"—he retained a loving concern for others, even for life's smallest details; that he retained gentleness, friendliness, even playfulness; that he retained an even-tempered spirit and clarity of thought; and that he retained above all peace and repose in the faith which he had won for himself with great efforts and which never failed him, even during the severe suffering of his deathbed. Different people may well have seen different sides of his personality, some his strengths, some his failings, but no one who was close to him failed to receive an impression of a markedly artistic life, which in pain or in joy was in the service of the Idea and was sacrificed for it.

From "Søren Kierkegaards literaire Efterladenskaber" [Søren Kierkegaard's Literary Remains], a review of *SKEP 1833–43* by an anonymous reviewer who was actually Christian Frederik Molbech (see the notes to the Brøchner-Molbech correspondence in chapter 11 of this book); the review appeared in *Dagbladet* [The Daily News], no. 46 (February 24, 1870). Molbech drew much of the present text from a letter to him from Hans Brøchner, dated February 17, 1856; see the Brøchner-Molbech correspondence in chapter 11 of this book.

Contents

—————>◦<——————

List of Illustrations	ix
Preface and Acknowledgments	xi
Maps	xv
Abbreviations and Editor's Remarks	xix

Chapter One
"The Fork": Childhood and School   3

Chapter Two
A Young Intellectual: The University Years   19

Chapter Three
Søren and Regine: The Engagement and Afterward   33

Chapter Four
The Young Writer (ca. 1840–1845)   55

Chapter Five
Goldschmidt and the *Corsair* Affair   65

Chapter Six
After *The Corsair*: The Peripatetic and Controversialist
of the Later 1840s   89

Chapter Seven
The Moment Comes: Final Opposition   99

Chapter Eight
Illness, Death, and Burial   116

Chapter Nine
Søren and the Family   137

Chapter Ten
Five Portraits by Contemporaries   193

Chapter Eleven
Hans Brøchner on Kierkegaard   225

Appendix A
The Kierkegaard Family Tree   253

Appendix B
Peter Christian Kierkegaard on Søren Kierkegaard 256

Notes 269

Bibliography 343

Index 353

Illustrations

Painting of Michael Pedersen Kierkegaard   4

Painting of Ane Sørensdatter Kierkegaard, *née* Lund   5

Manuscript facsimile of Søren Kierkegaard's school report,
with English translation   16

Drawing of Søren Kierkegaard at age twenty-four   21

Drawing of Søren Kierkegaard as a university student   22

Manuscript facsimile of Prof. J. N. Madvig's remarks on
Søren Kierkegaard's dissertation, with English translation   30

Photograph of Regine Schlegel, *née* Olsen   34

Photograph of Meïr Aron Goldschmidt   66

Lithograph of Peter Christian Kierkegaard   122

Photograph of Emil Boesen   123

Lithograph of mid-nineteenth-century view of Gammeltorv   155

Drawing of Peter Tutein's house   156

Photograph of (Anna) Henriette Lund   174

Daguerreotype of Troels Frederik Troels-Lund   176

Lithograph of Hans L. Martensen   197

Watercolor of Nørreport with the ramparts   198

Retouched daguerreotype of Israel Levin   206

Print of Grib Forest, with a view over Esrøm Lake   209

Drawing of Frederik C. Sibbern   214

Lithograph of Henrik Hertz   219

Drawing of Hans Brøchner at age twenty-five   227

Preface and Acknowledgments

SØREN KIERKEGAARD (1813–55) left neither memoirs nor an autobiography. In addition to his vast body of published work, which runs to twenty volumes in the latest Danish edition and which will run to twenty-six volumes in English translation upon completion of the new Princeton University Press edition, Kierkegaard left an even larger corpus of unpublished papers and journals, which constitutes twenty-two large volumes in the current Danish edition. Included in this enormous mass of materials, published and unpublished, are several highly tendentious essays in self-interpretation, including most notably *The Point of View for My Activity as an Author* and *On My Activity as an Author*, but nothing like the memoirs left by other nineteenth-century writers.

Kierkegaard was viewed in his time as a mysterious personage. Indeed, some thought that he deliberately cultivated an air of mystery and eccentricity. He was an odd though familiar figure to many people, some of whom remembered their encounters with Kierkegaard and subsequently wrote them down. Although a difficult writer in a minor language and the resident of a small city, Kierkegaard eventually became world-famous. By the time of his early death in 1855, he had already achieved a remarkable fame (or notoriety) in his native Denmark, where he was engaged in a furious assault upon the established Church. Several thousand people attended his funeral service, and it was feared that a riot might break out at his burial, where an illegal and incendiary speech was in fact delivered.

Kierkegaard immediately became a cult figure, and the Kierkegaard biography industry was launched soon after his death, with no end in sight. In the absence of a proper autobiography, and spurred on by the enormous and baffling maze of his published works and (especially) by his unpublished papers, which appear to contradict one another on a number of points and in which researchers have been able to find just about any Kierkegaard they were looking for, a considerable body of myth has developed around the enigmatic Danish genius.

Much of what has been written about Kierkegaard goes well beyond all available evidence. All that we really have, in addition to Kierkegaard's own writings, is a rather slender stock of accounts by those who had or claimed to have had direct knowledge of him. Most of these accounts by his contemporaries are not contemporary in the strictest sense, but were written down ten, twenty, or more years after Kierkegaard's death. The publication in 1869 of the first volume of Kierkegaard's unpublished papers, the *Efterladte Papirer* [Posthumous Papers], edited by H. P. Barfod, set off a new wave of interest in

Kierkegaard. Now many relatives, friends, acquaintances, schoolmates, university colleagues, opponents, and even those who had had more casual contact with him on the street or in the chance encounters of daily life rushed to put their reminiscences on paper. By the turn of the century or soon thereafter, the final chance had come for reports from all who could claim to have known Kierkegaard, even as children.

While there are quite a number of individual accounts by those who knew Kierkegaard, or who claimed to have known him, the total size of this fund of information is rather modest. The individual reports vary considerably in length, in style, and—undoubtedly—in reliability. There can be no doubt that many individual accounts may have been colored by the passage of time after the events they claim to portray, influenced, for example, by Kierkegaard's writings themselves, his publicly known traits and eccentricities, his attack on the Church, and especially by the myths which grew up around him after his death and after the publication of his posthumous papers. While some of these accounts may expose the sources of the myths which surround Kierkegaard, there is also the danger that they may to some extent reinforce those myths rather than act as an external check upon them. Nonetheless, they are the only sources—other than Kierkegaard's own writings—that we have, and they are very much worth reading. While the individual reports often tend to contradict one another in details, they also tend to point in the same direction and to reinforce one another, so that a collective and identifiable portrait emerges. For the general reader, who has perhaps read a bit of Kierkegaard, this collection forms an intriguing "do-it-yourself" biography of the great thinker, while for the scholar it is an indispensable resource. The present work is intended as a convenient sourcebook of all putative firsthand accounts of Søren Kierkegaard, as complete as possible and accompanied by explanatory commentary. In the future, as additional material comes to light, it can be added to the present collection. The intention of this collection is to include all contemporary accounts of a biographical nature, but not the scholarly and critical reception of Kierkegaard's works themselves. It has occasionally been difficult to draw this line, and in doubtful cases inclusion has generally been the rule; thus, although they do not strictly fit the category of biographical materials, a number of letters containing comments on Kierkegaard's attack on the Church have been included. A more comprehensive view of the contemporary critical reception of Kierkegaard's writings will be the subject of future work. The first eight chapters of the present work cover Kierkegaard's life in chronological order. The final three chapters contain lengthier accounts, covering broader segments of time, by family members and others who knew Kierkegaard.

The accounts collected and translated here were originally scattered through a wide range of memoir literature and correspondence, both published and unpublished. The late Steen Johansen, a research librarian at the Royal Library in Copenhagen, originally published some of this material, and his collection forms the original core of the present collection, which, however, is more than twice the size of Johansen's. Where they were deemed helpful, Johansen's notes have been utilized, but since they assume a rather thorough knowledge of Danish cultural history, they are usually too brief and telegraphic for the non-Danish reader, so the entire scholarly apparatus has been reworked. All entries, both those which were in Johansen's collection and those which are new to the present volume, are based upon the editor's reading of original manuscripts or, when these were lacking, upon the earliest printed version of each account. All the sources for each entry are provided at the beginning of the note for that entry.

Approximately one-third of the translated material is the work of Virginia R. Laursen, and the remaining two-thirds of the translated material is the work of Bruce H. Kirmmse, though we each have read and corrected one another's work. The research behind the present volume—that is, the collecting and editing of the source materials and the writing of the notes—are the work of Bruce H. Kirmmse. It is impossible to thank individually all the many people who have been of assistance in this project, but we would like specifically to express our thanks and appreciation to Diane Tyburski Birmingham, Morten Brøgger, Andrew Burgess, Helen E. Kirmmse, Iben Thranholm Madsen, Alastair McKinnon, and Rita Smith for help with proofreading and for comments upon all or portions of the manuscript; to Stéphane Hogue and Karsten Kynde for technical assistance; to Johnny Kondrup and Jette Knudsen for advice about the scholarly apparatus; to Dawne Roberge for secretarial help; to Helen K. Aitner and Ashley B. P. Hansen of the Interlibrary Loan Office at Connecticut College, New London, Connecticut; to Hanne Caspersen of the Danish Loan Centre, State and University Library, Aarhus, Denmark for supplying photocopies of hard-to-find materials; to the Royal Library (Copenhagen) and its Picture Collection for help in locating many of the illustrations used in this volume; to Erland Kolding Nielsen, Director-General of the Royal Library (Copenhagen) for generously donating photographic work in connection with the illustrations supplied by the Royal Library; to Thorkild Kjærgaard and Erik Vestergaard of the Danish National Historical Museum at Frederiksborg for permission to reproduce the portrait of Hans Brøchner; to Marianne Saabye of the Hirschsprung Collection and the helpful personnel of the Royal Museum of Fine Arts for providing assistance in choosing some of the illustrations used in this volume; to the Royal Museum of Fine Arts for supplying the portrait of F. C. Sibbern and for permission to reproduce it; to Joakim Garff, Hans Raun Iversen, Grethe Kjær, Kjeld Bagger Laursen, Tinne Vammen, and Julia Watkin for help with translation and in tracking down sources; to Margaret Ryan Hellman for help with translation and for editorial assistance with the final manuscript; to Louise Arnheim and Birgit Christensen for help in deciphering difficult passages in Henrik Hertz's notebooks; to Kenneth H. Ober for help in deciphering difficult passages in M. A. Goldschmidt's correspondence; to Anna Bojsen-Møller for permission to publish material from the original manuscript of Eline Heramb Boisen's memoirs; to Knud Arne Jürgensen for permission to use material he unearthed in his research for his forthcoming book on Bournon-ville; to Anders Monrad Møller for permission to publish material from the original manuscript of C. J. Brandt's diary; to Svend Olufsen of C. A. Reitzel's Press, Copenhagen, for his friendly cooperation and assistance; to the friendly and helpful personnel of the Danish National Archives, the Reading Room and the Manuscript Department of the Royal Library (Copenhagen), the Depart-ment of Søren Kierkegaard Research at the Institute for Systematic Theology of the University of Copenhagen, and the Howard and Edna Hong Kier-kegaard Library at St. Olaf College, Northfield, Minnesota, for providing mate-rials and fine and hospitable work environments; and to the Fulbright Commis-sion, the National Endowment for the Humanities, the R. Francis Johnson Fund of Connecticut College, and the Scandinavian-American Foundation for the support that made this book possible.

Bruce H. Kirmmse
Virginia R. Laursen

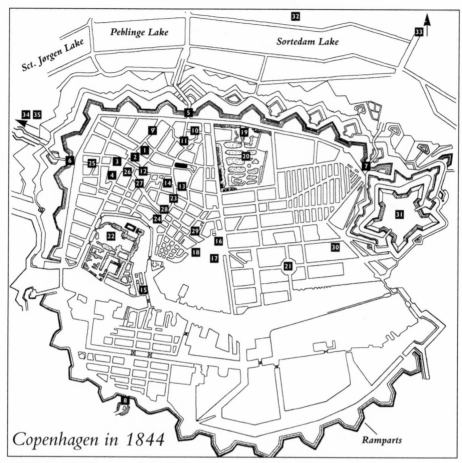

Copenhagen in 1844

Ramparts

1. *University of Copenhagen*
2. *Church of Our Lady*
3. *Gammeltorv*
4. *Nytorv*
   [Kierkegaard lived at Nytorv 2, now torn down, until September 1837, and from October 1844 to April 1848]
5. *Nørreport*
6. *Vesterport*
7. *Østerport*
8. *Amagerport*
9. *Nørregade*
   [Kierkegaard lived at Nørregade 230A, now no. 38, from April/October 1840 to October 1844, and at Nørregade 43, now no. 35, from April 1850 to April 1851]
10. *Rosenborggade*
    [Kierkegaard lived at Rosenborggade 156A, now no. 9, from April 1848 to April 1850]
11. *Kultorvet*
    [Kierkegaard lived at Kultorvet 132, now no. 11, from late 1839/early 1840 to April/October 1840]
12. *Klædeboderne*
    [Kierkegaard lived at Klædeboderne 5–6, now Skindergade 38/Dyrkøb 5 (he lived on the Dyrkøb side, with a view of the Church of Our Lady), from April/October 1852 to October 1855]
13. *Borgerdyd School*
14. *Løvstræde*
    [Kierkegaard lived at Løvstræde 7 (the probable location; it is now torn down) from September 1837 to an unknown date]
15. *Olsen family home*
16. *Kongens Nytorv*
17. *Charlottenborg*
18. *Royal Theater*
19. *Rosenborg Castle*
20. *Royal Gardens*
21. *Amalienborg Castle*
22. *Christiansborg Castle*
23. *Købmagergade*
24. *Højbro Plads*
25. *Frederiksberggade*
26. *Nygade*
27. *Vimmelskaftet*
28. *Amagertorv*
29. *Østergade*
30. *Frederik's Hospital*
31. *Citadel*
32. *Blegdamsvej*
33. *Østerbro*
    [Kierkegaard lived at Østerbro 108A (at the site where Willemoesgade enters Østerbrogade; it is now torn down) from April 1851 to April/October 1852]
34. *Hill House*
    [Bakkehus]
35. *Frederiksberg Gardens*

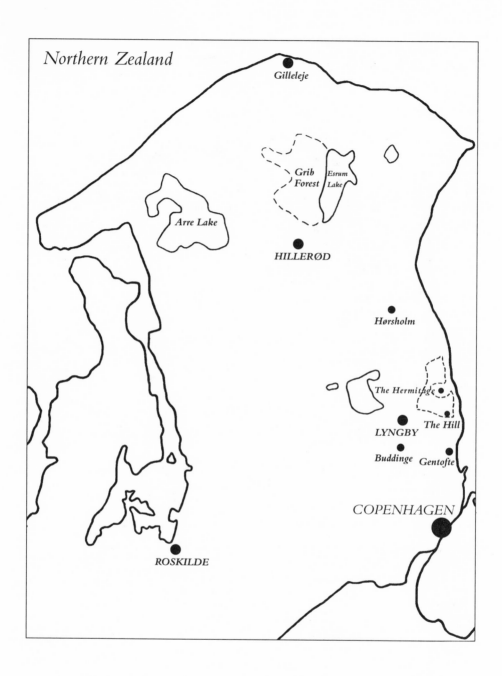

Northern Zealand

Gilleleje

Grib
Forest

Esrum
Lake

Arre Lake

HILLERØD

Hørsholm

The Hermitage

The Hill

LYNGBY

Buddinge   Gentofte

COPENHAGEN

ROSKILDE

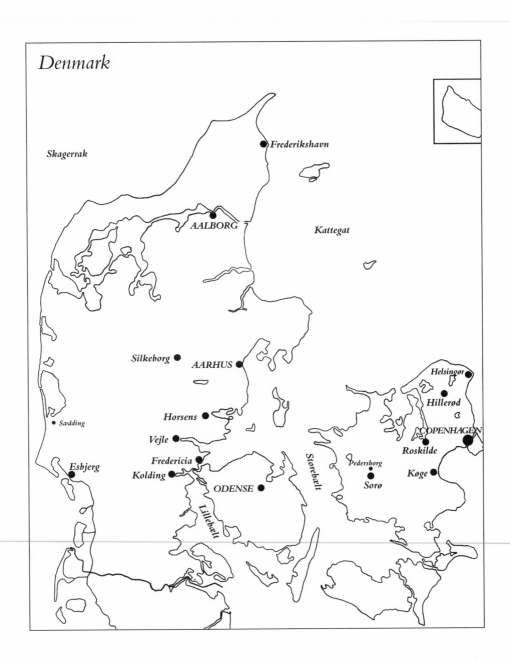

Denmark

Skagerrak

Frederikshavn

AALBORG

Kattegat

Silkeborg   AARHUS

Helsingør

Hillerød

Sædding

Horsens

COPENHAGEN

Vejle

Roskilde

Fredericia

Pedersborg

Køge

Esbjerg   Kolding

ODENSE

Storebælt

Sorø

Lillebælt

Abbreviations and Editor's Remarks

———❧•❧———

B&A = *Breve og Aktstykker vedrørende Søren Kierkegaard* [Letters and Documents Pertaining to Søren Kierkegaard], I–II, ed. Niels Thulstrup (Copenhagen: Munksgaard, 1953–54)

KBHA = Det kongelige Bibliotek, Håndskriftafdeling [Manuscript Department of the Royal Library (Copenhagen)]

KW = *Kierkegaard's Writings*, I–XXVI, ed. Howard V. Hong (Princeton: Princeton University Press, 1978–). 19 vols. published as of September 1995

NBD = Nyere Brevsamling Dansk [New Collection of Danish Letters] in the Manuscript Department of the Royal Library (Copenhagen)

NkS = Ny kongelige Samling [New Royal Collection] in the Manuscript Department of the Royal Library (Copenhagen)

Pap. = *Søren Kierkegaards Papirer* [The Papers of Søren Kierkegaard], I–XVI, ed. P. A. Heiberg, V. Kuhr, and E. Torsting; 2d augmented ed., ed. Niels Thulstrup; index by N. J. Cappelørn (Copenhagen: Gyldendal, 1968–78)

RA = Rigsarkivet [National Archives] (Copenhagen)

SKA = Søren Kierkegaard Arkiv [Søren Kierkegaard Archive] in the Manuscript Department of the Royal Library (Copenhagen)

SKEP = *Søren Kierkegaards Efterladte Papirer* [The Posthumous Papers of Søren Kierkegaard], I–VIII, ed. H. P. Barfod and H. Gottsched (Copenhagen: Reitzel, 1869–81)

SKJP = *Søren Kierkegaard's Journals and Papers*, I–VII, ed. and trans. Howard V. Hong and Edna H. Hong (Bloomington, Indiana: 1967–78)

SV = *Søren Kierkegaards Samlede Værker* [The Collected Works of Søren Kierkegaard], I–XIV, 1st ed., ed. A. B. Drachmann, J. L. Heiberg, and H. O. Lange (Copenhagen: Gyldendal, 1901–6)

Italic type has been employed to represent all forms of emphasis in the original text, for the titles of published works, and for Latin, French, and German words and phrases.

Square brackets have been employed to indicate editorial additions to the original text and for dates and other components of letters and journal entries.

All footnotes in this volume also appear as footnotes in the original source materials. All explanatory notes by the editor are printed as endnotes, which are grouped and numbered by chapter at the end of the volume. Each entry is accompanied by a numbered endnote, which begins with source information for that entry and which often will also include explanations of various details in that entry; the details explained in each entry are highlighted in **boldface type** in the endnote.

In the nineteenth century, standardized spelling had not yet been introduced in the Danish language, and the name "Søren Aabye Kierkegaard" was thus spelled and abbreviated in many different ways. These variants have been retained in the present volume in order to preserve some of the flavor of the original documents.

ENCOUNTERS WITH KIERKEGAARD

Chapter One

"THE FORK": CHILDHOOD
AND SCHOOL

Troels Frederik Troels-Lund[1]

IT IS POSSIBLE that it was the first, childish expressions of that sort of attitude which earned him his pet name as a child in the family home. He was called "the Fork." According to his sister's account this stems from an incident in which he was asked what he would most like to be, and he answered, "A fork." "Why?" "Well, then I could 'spear' anything I wanted on the dinner table." "But what if we come after you?" "Then I'll spear you."

Frederik Hammerich[2]

At the Boesens' house we played and spoke our childhood slang with *Søren Kierkegaard*, who was quite a little wildcat. He was very fond of my cousin, Emil Boesen, now an archdeacon, who later became his best friend. When he was near death, Boesen was the only pastor with whom he would talk.

He took us to his house one time, and there we saw his strangely gifted parents. The old Jutland hosier was a man who was always reading. He could work his way through philosophical systems but nonetheless made the family's daily purchases at the market himself. I can still see him on his way home from the market, carrying a fat goose. When one of his daughters lay near death, and people were trying to conceal the truth from her, he exclaimed: "No, my children have not been brought up like that!" And he went to her bed and told her the plain truth. Søren told me about his father's mood in 1848, when he was a worn-out old man: "Oh, to be young at a time like this!" he cried. "I feel things stirring in me, and I could take up a sword to punish the traitors!" In every other way he was in all respects a part of the old world. He had a double respect for Uncle Boesen, both as a man and as a Councillor of Justice.

Christian Julius Svendsen and
Thomas Wilhelm Severin Svendsen[3]

As usual, Søren sat in a corner and sulked.

Michael Pedersen Kierkegaard. Painting by unknown artist. The original is in the National Historical Museum at Frederiksborg. From a photograph of the original in the Picture Collection of the Royal Library. Reproduced courtesy of the Royal Library.

Frederik Meidell[4]

[*F. Meidell to H. P. Barfod, November 7, 1869*]

Søren was a rather ill-tempered child. He was not well liked by his cousins, who generally fled when he came for a visit with one of his parents. He was not without a certain teasing mischievousness, and this malady developed further when he started attending school, particularly after he became a student at the Borgerdyd School [literally, "The School of Civic Virtue"]. One of his classmates, Councillor of Justice Thorup, the district judge of Sunds-Gudme, who is now living in Svendborg, has told me that Søren's classmates resented the clever dialectical argumentation with which he triumphed over everyone, and that they therefore decided to give him a spanking.

Ane Sørensdatter Kierkegaard, *née* Lund. Painting by unknown artist. The original is in the National Historical Museum at Frederiksborg. From a photograph of the original in the Picture Collection of the Royal Library. Reproduced courtesy of the Royal Library.

Consequently, one day, when school was over, Søren was forced up onto a table, where two of his classmates held him by the arms, two by the legs, and the rest gave his behind a vigorous working-over with rulers, book straps, etc. He thus had firsthand knowledge of what it means to take a beating.

Harald Peter Ipsen[5]

[*H. P. Ipsen to H. P. Barfod, September 24, 1869*]

It is true that I went to the Borgerdyd School with him, but he was two classes ahead of me and entered the university in 1830, whereas I entered in 1832. I can indeed still remember my impression of the rather thin, light-haired boy's appearance and behavior among us on the playground. I also met him subsequently, both as a university student and after I had completed my studies; I walked and talked with him, and I have retained impressions and expressions from the things he said.

F. L. Liebenberg[6]

Among those of my schoolmates who subsequently became well known, I will mention . . . the famous Søren Kierkegaard, whose renown did not begin in school, however—not, at any rate, while we were there on the treadmill together, from February 1823 to February 1827—where he was a quiet, peaceable, industrious boy who drew little attention to himself.

Peter Munthe Brun[7]

When Peter Brun was nine years old he entered the Borgerdyd School, where the strict headmaster, Prof. Michael Nielsen, who has a widely varied reputation, was not very nice to him. In his later years, Brun always remembered a statement of Prof. Nielsen to the effect that boys should tremble when they walked through Klædeboderne, the street on which stood the Gyldendal building, where the school was then located. He sat on a school bench together with the strange, precocious child who later became the century's greatest thinker and philosopher, Søren Kierkegaard. And he also went home with Søren to his father's house. He was attracted by the odd, old hosier and the serious, somber, but also loving tone which characterized the relationship between him and his sons. The old man suffered from insomnia, and he once remarked to fourteen-year-old Brun: "When I can't sleep, I lie down and talk with my boys, and there are no better conversations here in Copenhagen." This statement accords well with Søren Kierkegaard's story of how he and his father walked around the living room of their house and fantasized that they were taking the most splendid walks outside the city gates, down along the shore, or through the city streets.

One day one of the big boys was sitting and crying. The teacher asked what was wrong and received the answer, "Søren is teasing me." But the teacher gave him scant comfort when he said: "So what? You could easily put him in your pants pocket."

Frederik Welding[8]

[F. Welding to H. P. Barfod, September 3, 1869]

I don't know when S.K. entered the Borgerdyd School. When I entered the second form—the first form is the highest—in 1826, I met S.K. there. I had the impression that S.K. had been at the school for a long time and was quite at home there, so he had surely started out in one of the school's lowest forms. I never heard him speak of having attended any other school. He was always number two or number three in the various classes in which we were students until we were graduated in 1830. If he was number one in the class, it was only for a few short periods of time. In addition to Prof. M. Nielsen, the best of our teachers were Boiesen, Bindesbøll, Prof. Warnecke in history and geography, and Martensen in mathematics. Profs. Nielsen and Bindesbøll had particular influence on Kierkegaard, who at an early age produced work in Latin composition and in Danish which showed signs of such unusual maturity and meticulous preparation that we others found it odd and eccentric without being able to appreciate it. I was often surprised by his work, but did not really understand why the teachers were pleased with his written compositions. As boys and youths, many of the other students and I found Kierkegaard's work, like his handwriting, quite peculiar. There were surely only a very few classmates who understood Kierkegaard or came to be on close terms with him in the way typical of others of that age. S.K. did not reveal his character in the way that boys and young people of school age usually do. He went his own way, almost self-contained, never spoke of his home, and neither brought classmates home with him nor visited them in their homes. To the rest of us, who knew and lived a more genuinely boyish life, S.K. was a stranger and an object of pity, especially because of his clothing, which was always the same, of rough dark tweed fabric with an odd cut, a jacket with short tails, and always with shoes and woolen stockings, never boots, as far as I can remember. This earned him the nickname "the Choirboy," because of the similarity of his clothing to that worn by choirboys in the cathedral schools. This name also alternated with the name "Søren Sock," which was an allusion to his father's earlier occupation, which we believed to have been a hosier. We all viewed S.K. as someone whose home was shrouded in mysterious shadows of strictness and eccentricity. S.K.'s school days passed quietly and, it seemed, without joy. He worked more out of fear and compulsion than out of desire or any happy industriousness. He never helped his classmates nor asked for any help from them. Not infrequently he could be seen making use of his position behind the professor's chair, which stood in front of the first two or three desks, in order to cheat or peek, as it was called in the jargon of the school. He resorted to this especially in history and geography. Grades were very important to him. As far as I can remember, he was not friends with any of the other boys. Although we were often together, and although S.K. was very fond of the baked goods I occasionally gave him at school—my father was a baker—when we were boys, I was never close to him as I was to others in the class. In most of his contacts with us he showed that he was so foreign to our interests that we quickly broke off contact with him, and he often displayed a superior and teasing attitude, which made it clear that he was always a source of the unexpected. He was a skinny boy, always on the run, and he could never keep from giving free rein to his whimsy and from teasing others with nicknames he had heard, with laughter, and with funny faces, even though it often earned him a beating. I do not recall that his language was ever genuinely witty or cutting, but it was annoying and provocative, and he was aware that it had this effect even though he was often the one who paid for it.

These outbursts of his passion for teasing seemed to be absolutely unconnected with the rest of his otherwise silent and unspeaking existence among us, with the withdrawn and introverted character he displayed the rest of the time. During these outbursts his most remarkable talent was the ability to make his target appear ridiculous, and it was especially the big, tall, and powerfully built boys whom he chose as the objects of his derision. In the more advanced classes, he regularly assumed another role in this drama, and he thus became even stranger and isolated from most of us. When he was a boy and a youth, I doubt that his teachers—it would have been Bindesbøll in religion and in Danish— saw in him the great powers which he later developed. It was a surprise to all of us, his peers, when he eventually made his appearance as a fully developed and unusually gifted person.

As a boy, he did not have the least trace of the great poetic gifts he later developed. Now and then, when our classmate H. P. Holst would read us his attempts at poetry, S.K. was always one of the first to interrupt his reading by throwing a book at his head.

In the second form S.K.'s Greek teacher was his brother, the [later] bishop. It was clear and often striking to us that he [Søren] deliberately made things difficult by bringing his relationship to his brother into the classroom situation on various occasions, and it seemed to us that he was teasing him.

As a boy and a youth, in the years before he became a university student, he was a strangely dressed fellow, small for his age, thin and freckled, and his most striking characteristic was his oddness, his peculiarity. But there was also something unusual in his quiet nature, which bore the stamp of the customs of his home and of his own inner self, secrets which were never revealed. All this was combined with abilities which, although apparently not extraordinary, were always steady and consistent, and this must certainly have impressed the teachers, in whose presence S.K. always behaved quietly and never broke the school's rules. It would be interesting to learn of the impression S.K. made on Bindesbøll and on Scharling, later a professor of theology, who was also our Latin teacher for a time. Prof. Warnecke worked diligently with us but had a weak personality and had to make a real effort to assert himself. S.K. would frequently make fun of him—when he was not there. When I look back on things, it seems to me that, in general, as a boy S.K. usually had a good eye for people's weak points, for the incoherent and offensive features of their behavior. He therefore pounced upon tall fellows who were intellectual midgets, upon those who were heavyweights only in the physical sense, and in general upon those who were quick to develop physically, but slower intellectually. I myself belonged to this latter group. I reached my full height as a sixteen- or seventeen-year-old boy but really grew intellectually only after I graduated from school. For this reason I was surely in no position to judge S.K.

After I left the university, S.K. visited me frequently in the summer at Frederiksborg. On these trips, which he made on a momentary whim, he drove out with a man who was a charcoal-burner. On these trips he found it amusing to

Peter Engel Lind[10]

[P. E. Lind to H. P. Barfod, September 16, 1869]

I will answer your questions in the order in which you ask them.

S.K. was viewed by his fellow students as a witty fellow with whom it was dangerous to quarrel, because he knew how to make his opponent appear ridiculous. They also viewed him as a fundamentally good boy, religious and moral, and they did not tease him about this.

It was clear that he was very capable because he read only sparingly but in general managed quite well by picking up things from context and from what he learned from others. When it was time for him to give recitations which he was to have learned by heart, he was unusually talented in reading with his book concealed under his desk, without attracting the notice of his teachers, and he learned quite a bit in this way. No one knew anything about his *unusual* talents. His answers in religion class were like those of many other students, and his Danish compositions were no better (though probably more detailed) than those of other good students. His teacher, Bindesbøll (now a bishop), claimed that one of his compositions had been plagiarized from Mynster's sermons.

We did not have the least suspicion that he would one day come forth as a great opponent of his times. He seemed to be very conservative, to honor the king, love the Church, and respect the police.

He of course preferred some boys in the school to others, but he did not seem to have friends. As a boy it was not easy for him to come to someone's home. But outside of school hours I believe he was friends with Boesen (archdeacon in Aarhus).

The teachers acknowledged that S.K. was unusually gifted, but were not always satisfied with him. They believed him lacking in diligence, and he sometimes treated them with impudence. One time, the late L. C. Müller, our Hebrew teacher, corrected him rather sharply, and when S.K. broke out into loud laughter, Müller, who knew him from the family home, buttoned up his coat and said with great anger, "Either you leave or I will." After a moment's consideration S.K. replied, "Well, then, it's best that I leave." And he left. S.K. had unconditional respect for Prof. Nielsen, the headmaster of the school.

Martin Attrup[11]

When he had concluded a successful visit [to the school where Attrup was a teacher] and was therefore in a good mood, the dean told us grownups of an educational experience from his school days: "I was a pupil at *the Metropolitan School* in *Copenhagen*, where the respected Jutlander professor *Mikael Nielsen* was the headmaster. He established so strict a discipline that we boys held him in great respect." (Here I thought of a sturdy Jutlander, Svenningsen, the school inspector of Christianshavn, who had the same qualities.)

The discipline was relaxed only when there was a thunderstorm, which made the headmaster anxious, so that he folded his hands and said:

"When God speaks, I keep silent!"

He had a special talent for recounting things in a lively and graphic manner and with great authority.

One day he had spoken with special warmth about the famous naval battle at *Salamis*, ca. 500 B.C., when the brave little *Greeks* defeated the mighty Persian fleet.

The next day he examined us boys on the *Battle of Salamis*.

Peter Christian Kirkegaard—afterward bishop of Aalborg—was the number-one student in the headmaster's class.

I, *Peder Ravn*, was his number-two student, and number three was *Søren Kirkegaard*, who later became a famous author.

First he asked number one: "Were you there at the Battle of *Salamis*?" But when P.C.K. answered, "No!" he got a well-directed slap on the head.

As number two I was asked the same question and answered with a nervous "Yes!" in order to avoid *P.C.K.*'s fate. But the headmaster queried me further, "Did you have your father's permission?" and when I answered "No!" to that question, I received the same punishment as number one.

The question then passed to number three.

"Were you there at the Battle of Salamis?" to which *Søren Kirkegaard* answered, "Yes! I was there in spirit, Herre Professor!"

The strict headmaster smiled, stroked him on the chin, and exclaimed: "You will be a source of joy and honor to me."

H. P. Holst[12]

[*H. P. Holst to H. P. Barfod, September 11, 1869*]

It is undoubtedly true that the article "Literary Quicksilver" is by S. Kjerkegaard, with whom I was on very intimate terms in my younger days. I literally *rewrote* his first written work on Andersen—or rather, I translated it from Latin to Danish. It was quite natural that he turned to me for this help, because at the Borgerdyd School we had a regular practice whereby I wrote the Danish essays for him and he wrote the Latin ones for me. It is strange that he, who ended up writing such excellent Danish, had absolutely no grasp of it in his youth, but wrote a Latin-Danish, which was crawling with participials and the most complexly punctuated sentences.

[*H. P. Holst to H. P. Barfod, September 13, 1869*]

If I were able, I would gladly fulfill your wishes and give you more items about S.K.'s childhood, but boys of school age do not attribute much importance to one another and consequently do not pay one another much notice. With respect to S.K., I remember that he was physically delicate and small, very industrious and always well regarded by the school's headmaster, Prof. Michael Nielsen. I was his classmate for many years, and I conclude from this that he must have entered the Borgerdyd School around 1820. Wouldn't Bishop P. C. Kierkegaard be able to give you somewhat more certain information? He [P. C. Kierkegaard] in fact was a teacher in the school while we were still students, and, as far as I can remember, he wrote his dissertation *de mendacio* at that very time. In his boyhood years S.K. was not the object of great expectations. I don't think he was even seen as especially bright. After a while he got the reputation of being a good Latinist, and Prof. Nielsen made use of him to review and correct the Latin compositions in the classes in which he [Nielsen] was the teacher. From Prof. N.'s point of view this was a post of extraordinary trust, and it was also viewed as such by others in the school. In his school days, he [Kierkegaard] was closest to the late I. E. Damkier (the attorney) and myself. In those days he was jovial and good-natured. He displayed neither any symptoms of becoming an author nor any passion for dispute and philosophizing, and was without any trace of the sharp dialectics that later became his forte. In his earliest days as a university student he was especially attracted by the *idea of wit* (à la I. L. Heiberg), and it would surprise me very much if his desire to present himself as an author was not first kindled by some witty and amusing articles in *Den flyvende Post* [The Flying Post]. I remember how in those days he frequently composed articles in that spirit about various things, and, displaying an admirable capacity for memory, he would recite them to me on the street. And I remember how he would walk in the street in this same manner—he was already a peripatetic at that time—and plan more articles of the same sort. On the other hand, in later years, if a larger body of material had to be thought through, he liked to sit alone in a landau and drive through the woods, which surprised his peers, who could not understand how he could permit himself such extravagances. He was quite depressed by the fact that Heiberg would never really involve himself with his [Kierkegaard's] writings or recognize him as a philosopher, and this supposed failure to appreciate him was a constant theme of our conversations during the years when I was a frequent guest of Heiberg and Mrs. Gyllembourg. I will not conclude these aphoristic remarks without mentioning a rejoinder from his later years that has just come to mind. As you of course know, for many years he went to church every Sunday (just as he never missed a performance of *Don Giovanni*). One day I met him as he was walking with a hymnal in his hand. I don't know how it came to me, but I asked him which of the city's pastors he preferred to hear. He answered instantly: "Visby, and I will tell you why. When one of the other pastors has written his sermon counting on sunshine, he will talk about sunshine, even if it pours rain, but when Visby preaches, and a ray of sunshine comes into the church, he grasps that ray and speaks about it at such length, and so beautifully and edifyingly, that you leave with a ray of sunshine in your heart. He is the only improviser of them all."

Frederik Hammerich[13]

The brother, *Søren* Kierkegaard, was still too young to associate with us. In other respects he seemed to be a very promising if somewhat unsteady person whom it was difficult to keep focused on his reading for the examinations, because his mind was interested in so many other things. "Hebrew Müller," who read [Hebrew] with him, often exclaimed half in jest: "But what in the world are we going to do with that Søren?"

Juliane and Christiane Rudelbach[14]

[*J. and C. Rudelbach to A. G. Rudelbach, June 5, 1830*]
  Incidentally, I must greet you from the entire Kierkegaard family. They hope and expect that their youngest son will become a university student in October.

[*C. and J. Rudelbach to A. G. Rudelbach, July 9, 1830*]
  Their youngest son will matriculate into the university in October, and his mother cannot help but be a bit uneasy until the examinations are over, especially because, as she says, "The young man is a bit too free and easy about it."

School Report[15]

2. Søren Aabye Kierkegaard, son of the merchant Michael Pedersen Kierkegaard, born May 5, 1813 (Baptismal Certificate number 2), entered the school's preparatory class in 1821.
  A good mind, open to everything that requires first-rate attention, but for a long time he was very childish and quite lacking in seriousness. He had a desire for freedom and independence, which was expressed in his behavior in the form of a good-natured, sometimes amusing lack of constraint, which prevented him from getting too involved with anything or from showing any greater interest in things than would keep him from being able to withdraw into himself again. His irresponsibility rarely permitted him to bring his good intentions to fruition or to pursue a definite goal in a sustained manner. When, in time, this trait diminishes, allowing his character to take on more seriousness—and recognizable progress has been made in this direction in the past year—and his fine intellectual abilities are able to develop more freely and unconstrainedly at the university, he will certainly be among the more capable students and in many ways will come to resemble his oldest brother. His character is lively, like that of Anger's, but even more cheerful and, although more clever, nonetheless open and uncorrupted. He is the youngest of a large group of siblings who have all had the benefit of an excellent upbringing. Two years before he entered the school he lost his next-to-youngest brother, whose illness was perhaps caused when his head struck that of another boy while at play in the schoolyard. This

event, coupled with the fact that he [Søren Kierkegaard] was small for his age, may well have had an influence on his upbringing over the following several years.

He has read and presents for examination the following works:

IN LATIN

by Cicero, *de Oratore*, the first two books; *The Letters*, the first forty, in Weiske's edition. In other respects, excepting for *Amicitia* and *de Senectute*, the same as no. 1.

IN GREEK

by Homer: *Odyssey*, books 3, 4, 5, 8, 9, 10, 11, 12, and 22, and the first seven books of the *Iliad*. In other respects, the same as no. 1.

IN HEBREW

Genesis and fifteen chapters of Exodus.

Copenhagen, July 29, 1830
Most respectfully, M. NIELSEN

School Testimony[16]

Rector Magnificus!
Illustrious and excellent professors!

Cicero says that citizens ought to be convinced first and foremost that the gods govern and direct all things; that all events come to pass by virtue of divine power; that the gods are also the benefactors of the human race; that they keep watch over every person's character, his actions, errors, and piety with respect to the external worship of the gods; and that they reward the good and punish the wicked. The annals of the Roman people and the other monuments of antiquity witness to the fact that people whose minds were steeped in these thoughts never strayed from true and useful wisdom, and that those who obeyed the gods enjoyed all sorts of good fortune, while on the other hand, those who defied them were struck with misfortune. The estimable young Severinus Aabye Kierkegaard was from an early age accustomed to seeking the basis of his life in this conviction and to judging the outcome of events in accordance with it. From the very beginning he was steeped in his parents' seriousness and in the good example of their strong sense of religious reverence, devotion to God, and moral responsibility, and this was subsequently nourished in early childhood with instruction provided by teachers who had been carefully chosen with this goal in mind. Thus when he was entrusted to our care at the age of nine he did not permit himself to be confused by those who are ignorant of how they should act and who are like those who swim into a strong current and are swept along with bad companions as if by a powerful river. On the contrary, he showed all of us his talent and his eagerness for learning, and especially his ready obedience and his entirely moderate and moral attitude toward life, so that one

Manuscript facsimile of school report by M. A. Nielsen of the Borgerdyd School, July 29, 1830. From the original in the Danish National Archives (Københavns Universitet, Det filosofiske Fakultet. KU. 35.20.03).

2. Søren Aabye Kierkegaard, Søn af Kjøbmand Michael Petersen Kierkegaard, fød d. 5te Mai 1813 (Døbeattest N^0 2), kom i Skolens Forberedelsesklasse 1821.—

Et godt Hoved, aabent for Alt, hvad der gjør Fordring paa fortriinlig Interesse, men han var længe i høj Grad barnagtig og uden al Alvor, og en Lyst til Frihed og Uafhængighed, der ogsaa i hans Opførsel viser sig i en godmodig, undertiden pudseerlig Ugeneerthed, hindrede ham fra at indlade sig videre i nogen Ting og omfatte den med større Interesse end at han itide kunde drage sig tilbage igjen. Naar hans Letsindighed, der sjeldent tillod ham at bringe sine gode Forsætter til Modenhed eller stadigt at forfølge et vist Maal, med Tiden tager af, der kommer mere Alvor i hans Charakteer,

may certainly hope that he will be his brother's equal, since he is his equal in talent.

The root of these virtues is the pure devotion to God that was implanted in his character from the very beginning of his life. Indeed, his father has conducted his business in accordance with the precepts of philosophy, and he has united his business life with the reading of works of theology, philosophy, and literature. His [father's] wisdom and goodness can be seen in all of his circumstances, and especially in child rearing, from which he [the father] himself derived great benefit in the cultivation of his mind and in intellectual enjoyment. Because his father's home is thus such a model of industriousness, patience, and moderation, and is arranged in conformity with the principles by which children are trained in virtue and in the wisdom which is given by God, he has enjoined his son to view all things in the light of the fear of God and a sense of duty, and to seek the source of all things in God as the fount of all wisdom. He has taught him, on the one hand, that God does not listen to the prayers of do-nothings and, on the other hand, that acumen without prayer can achieve nothing except to ensnare the mind in error. And he has done everything to

---

hvortil der især i det sidste Aar er gjort en kjendelig Fremgang, og hans gode Aandsevner faae Raadighed til mere frit og ugeneert at udvikles ved Universitetet, vil han sikkert blive blandt de dygtige, og i Meget komme til at ligne sin ældste Broder. Hans Charakter er, som Angers, levende og endnu muntrere, og, skjøndt snildere, dog aaben og ufordærvet. Blandt flere Søskende, der alle have nydt en meget fortriinlig Opdragelse, er han den yngste; . . .

2. Søren Aabye Kierkegaard, son of the merchant Michael Pedersen Kierkegaard, born May 5, 1813 (baptismal certificate number 2), entered the school's preparatory class in 1821.

A good mind, open to everything that requires first-rate attention, but for a long time he was very childish and quite lacking in seriousness. He had a desire for freedom and independence, which was expressed in his behavior in the form of a good-natured, sometimes amusing lack of constraint, which prevented him from getting too involved with anything or from showing any greater interest in things than would keep him from being able to withdraw into himself again. His irresponsibility rarely permitted him to bring his good intentions to fruition or to pursue a definite goal in a sustained manner. When, in time, this trait diminishes, allowing his character to take on more seriousness—and recognizable progress has been made in this direction in the past year—and his fine intellectual abilities are able to develop more freely and unconstrainedly at the university, he will certainly be among the more capable students and in many ways will come to resemble his oldest brother. His character is lively, like that of Anger's, but even more cheerful, and, although more clever, nonetheless open and uncorrupted. He is the youngest of a large group of siblings who have all had the benefit of an excellent upbringing. . . .

awaken the boy's love for scholarly culture, which is the foundation of all praiseworthy endeavors. This young man, who has thus been raised and educated in this manner, in keeping with the customs of our forebears and with the discipline that will promote the welfare of the state—and not in the rash and rebellious spirit of the times—I recommend to you, learned men, in the highest fashion.

Copenhagen, September 29, 1830
M. NIELSEN
Headmaster of the Borgerdyd School

Chapter Two

A YOUNG INTELLECTUAL: THE UNIVERSITY YEARS

Juliane and Christiane Rudelbach[1]

[*J. and C. Rudelbach to A. G. Rudelbach, May 7, 1831*]

I found the Doctor much more handsome than the first time I saw him, and he is certainly a worthy and God-pleasing young man. At the table it pleased me to hear him cut his somewhat conceited brother and—I dare say—stupid brother-in-law down to size for their arrogant and dull remarks. But he did it with so much good nature and gentleness that the brother-in-law, at least, never even understood him.

Augusta Sibbern Møller[2]

[*A. S. Møller to Harald Høffding, November 20, 1912*]

I have remembered S.K. for my whole life. When I was a child he visited Father [Prof. F. C. Sibbern] and liked to sit in our parlor at dusk, when the fire gleamed in the stove.

[*A. S. Møller to Harald Høffding, December 7, 1912*]

I know a little about the walks the two men took together. One of my childhood memories is of walking and holding my father's hand while S. Kierkegaard was on the other side of us, talking eagerly and stopping now and again in order to speak clearly about things that were important to him.

Niels Lindberg[3]

[*Niels Lindberg to P. C. Kierkegaard, March 14, 1866*]

I can remember him well from my childhood, when, on his walks through Frederiksberg Allé, he [Søren Kierkegaard] always had a friendly word for us children, or when (most likely on an errand from Father to Your Reverence) we came to Nytorv 2, where he often gave us prunes or a shilling for a pastry.

Peter Rørdam[4]

[P. Rørdam to Hans Rørdam, December 4, 1834]

There has recently been a rather serious scene here between the theological students and Prof. Clausen. The fact is that now that the new university building—which is a very splendid structure, in every respect the equal of the Church of Our Lady— has been completed, and use of the new auditorium is to begin, the theological faculty insisted that each student have a numbered seat and sit in the same seat for the entire semester so that the faculty can more easily keep an eye on the diligence of every student. One [student] speaker after another stood up [to oppose this]. A young student named Krøyer and the younger Kierkegaard were particularly notable for their sober but serious opposition. The consistory has now decided the case; nothing further will be done, and the old arrangement will continue.

Vilhelm Birkedal[5]

Later, of course, he [Prof. H. N. Clausen] lectured on dogmatics and published a volume on the subject. With his biting mockery S. Kierkegaard characterized the book as follows: "The author follows the custom of the king of the Persians when he went into battle against the Egyptians. He placed their [the Egyptians'] sacred animals in front of his army because he believed it would paralyze the enemy. Prof. Clausen places a host of sacred scriptural passages in front of every paragraph of his dogmatics, in the belief that by presenting his version of dogma from behind these scriptural passages he can gain acceptance for his views, for he thinks that all this array of holy scripture will terrify people, who will quietly allow him and his views to triumph."

Johannes A. Ostermann[6]

[J. A. Ostermann to H. P. Barfod, May 28, 1867]

I will immediately have the honor of replying to your letter, which I received this morning, to the extent that my memory serves me. You are completely on the right track with respect to the essay by Kierkegaard. In those days, the movements of the times tore some of us young people out of our poetic dreams and hurled us into political life, because in those days only a few individuals—at least among the trend-setting group in the Student Union—were taken with the idea [of politics]. But the alpha and omega of politics in those days was freedom of the press, which was exposed to persecution from above and to grumbling criticism from the public. Under these conditions I read my essay to a large crowd. It attracted a bit of attention, and I was immediately requested to turn it over to Joh. Hage, who printed it in *Fædrelandet* [The Fatherland] in unedited form, except that the introduction, which had had a comic form, now took on more serious dress. In those days, or just before then, I was often (almost

Søren Kierkegaard, age twenty-four, dated January 15, 1838. Drawing by Niels Christian Kierkegaard. The original is in the Danish National Historical Museum at Frederiksborg, Hillerød. From a photograph of the original in the Picture Collection of the Royal Library (Copenhagen). Reproduced courtesy of the Royal Library.

daily, in fact) in the company of Kjerk., who was as little interested in politics then as he would be later. But his lively intellect took hold of any issue in those days, and he exercised his brilliant dialectical skill and wit upon it, without bothering himself much about the reality of the matter. The fact that my defense [of freedom of the press] was met with sympathy pushed him into the opposite camp, where he allied himself more or less as a matter of indifference. He borrowed my essay after having informed the leadership of the Student Union that he wanted to "give a reading," and the manuscript which you have found can scarcely be—indeed, I would say it is impossible that it can be—anything other than the essay which he read aloud at the Student Union shortly thereafter, perhaps fourteen days after I did. There was a very large crowd present. People had expected a debate between us on the issue. But for one

Søren Kierkegaard as a university student. First published in *Ny illustrerad Tidning* [New Illustrated Times] (Stockholm) in 1876. From a photograph in the Picture Collection of the Royal Library. Reproduced courtesy of the Royal Library.

thing, I had only fleetingly heard him read his essay; and for another, as an eager politician I had no desire to take on such an opponent, whom I knew had only a slight interest in the reality of the matter. As far as I can remember it, Kierkegaard's essay was rather ponderous; it bore the hallmark of his unique intellectual talents and was received with great applause. *The essay was read aloud*, but it was not given as a talk, because in accordance with the customs of those times it would have been impudent and shameless to have offered it as a talk to such a learned public. If I remember correctly, it was a couple of years later, after an agreement with Lehmann, that such informal talks were given.

Peter Rørdam[7]

[P. Rørdam to Hans Rørdam, February 23, 1836]
   There has also been a change in the Student Union. Their chief and leader, Lehmann, has fallen, totally defeated: "Homeward went brave Peter with his kettle upon his back." With him has fallen *Kjøbenhavns-Posten* [The Copen-

hagen Post], for which he had recently been writing. And the victor is the younger Kierkegaard, who now writes in *Flyvende Post* under the pseudonym B.

Johan Hahn[8]

[*J. Hahn to P. C. Kierkegaard, May 17, 1836*]
I hear from many quarters that your brother Søren has made a witty and powerful appearance in *Flyveposten*. I would be happy to read it. But where can it be had?

Benjamin Feddersen[9]

The annual school examination took place at the beginning of July.

On the way to school I bought a very beautiful cut rose. It was stupid, because what did a flower have to do with a serious examination?

In class the school benches were arranged along the four walls, allowing for an empty space in the middle of the floor. Here an oblong table was placed, where the trial took place, a procedure to which I looked forward without the least bit of fear, even though today the examination dealt in fact with Latin.

The examiner was none less than *Søren Kierkegaard*, who usually served as a teacher in the higher classes and whom I therefore knew only from the schoolyard. But because I had the feeling that there was something unusual about that man, I would stake my life on the fact that I have never laughed at his narrow and uneven trouser legs.

He had come before anyone else and had taken a place at the end of the table, where I was near him, sitting with my rose in my hand.

As a sign of politeness to the examiner, we had all stood up when he entered, and, when I was about to sit down again, I was met by his penetrating gaze.

After careful consideration, I am unable to explain to myself what happened next. It was as if a magnetic force drew me away from my seat and toward that singular man, and because his eyes continued to rest upon me, I gave him my rose.

He accepted it with a smile, put his arm around my neck and whispered in my ear:

"My friendly boy, you will certainly get an A!"

And I got one.

Holger Lund[10]

Many of those who had studied with him have said that he was an extraordinarily capable teacher, who understood how to interest pupils in their work. He was very amusing, though occasionally somewhat teasing or irritating. Once in a while he would let his mind wander and be lost entirely in his thoughts,

apparently pursuing some intellectual problem. Such digressions often concluded with him bursting into hearty laughter, but the students never found out
what it was that was so funny.

J. H. Lorck[11]

At the above-mentioned performance on Weyse's birthday, a number of people
expressed dismay about the unfortunate situation in which our composers
found themselves, for it was practically impossible for them to get their works
published. It was therefore suggested that we should try to form a society for the
publication and distribution of such works. This suggestion immediately met
with approval, and that very same evening, when a number of theatergoers
were gathered at the Student Union, ten of them signed up as potential members of such a society. The number of members increased rapidly over the
following days, particularly because of the efforts of E. Collin and myself. Then
one evening the two of us met at my place together with Søren Kjerkegaard—
whom we had invited, though I cannot really remember why—where we
wrote the draft of the by-laws for the society. On March 16, only eleven days
after the idea was first thought of, the number of members had increased to 141,
and the first general meeting was held. I presented the draft of the by-laws,
which were then discussed and adopted.

Angul Hammerich[12]

The newly elected steering committee quickly went to work. The immediate
task was one of internal organization, by-laws, etc. At this point an odd coincidence brought one of the great intellects of the day into contact with the
[Music] Society. After the first draft of the by-laws had been adopted by the
general meeting, it became the task of *Collin* and *Lorck* to work out the final
version. In their efforts to cast these regulations into the tightest possible form,
they did not depend upon their own talents but turned to *Søren Kierkegaard*,
who was a friend and associate of those whose dialectical acumen they trusted
most. No one less would do. One evening they gathered with the author of
Either/Or at Lorck's place and, over a glass of punch, they presented him with
the rough draft. Søren Kierkegaard apparently took the matter very seriously
and engaged in discussion about the details. But soon his skills at dialectical
dissection took the wind out of the sails of the two legislators, who had hardly
considered the consequences discovered in their by-laws by the philosopher
they had summoned. With heads swimming, they left their adviser.

Eline Heramb Boisen[13]

Other members of Bojsen's circle of acquaintances during these years included
the two brothers *Peter and Søren Kierkegaard* and *Peter Rørdam*. He was occasion-

ally witness to the well-known debates between old [Michael Pedersen] *Kierkegaard* and his two sons. Peter [Kierkegaard] was (or became) his [Pastor Boisen's] brother-in-law, of course. And it was interesting, Eline Heramb writes, to hear the skill with which old Kierkegaard (who had originally been a wool dealer from Jutland and was now a well-to-do merchant) could join in the debate with his two gifted sons and always have a ready answer, even though the discussions concerned heaven and earth and everything imaginable in between. The old mother listened to this with admiration, but occasionally she would interrupt to calm things down when it seemed to her that they were getting too excited.

Jakob Knudsen[14]

As soon as you turned into the Deer Park you could see the Hermitage sitting in the sunshine at the end of a rather straight forest road which was a good half-mile long. It looked as if it were so far away and yet could be seen so clearly; it was like looking through a reversed telescope.

The road was so little traveled that it looked in places almost overgrown with grass. There was absolutely no dust. Everything one saw was exactly as though in a fairy tale. On either side there were new leaves on the beech trees—the trees were quite young for a good part of the way—like airy billows of green, untouched, like the mountains of water in the sea. And above all this green, the equally pure but light blue sky. It was so strangely unearthly: it resembled the sea or the sky, as though one were driving through a tunnel up into some cloud landscape.

Old Mrs. Nielsen [i.e., Mrs. Knudsen] noticed how these surroundings freed her mind completely from her customary thoughts and how her thoughts came to drift like clouds across the sky and were able to assume any shape or color. But they did not as yet have any definite shape or color, and what passed through her consciousness was so indistinct that she didn't think about it at all.

Not until she had traveled the length of the forest road and it became clear that the Hermitage was not right at the end of the road, and that the large, open, sun-drenched plain extended another good half-mile, from the forest gate to the lodge—not until then did old Mrs. Nielsen sense that her mind was about to grasp something definite, that she was giving birth to a memory. She could not yet say what it was. But this was something that she had noticed over the last ten years: her memories came to her with strange slowness; they could be sensed far in advance, and they revealed themselves only gradually. She felt that it was an important memory, this one, an experience that had been of great significance to her. It built up almost like thunder, but she still didn't know what it was. Suddenly there was a little flash, as if of far-off lightning. She thought of Hans Husby's talk about his temptations, and she immediately knew that there had been talk of temptation during the episode which was now coming back to her in memory. Yes, now she *saw* the whole thing!

Now she saw the carriage, which was traveling across the Hermitage Plain. But it was a tall Holstein coach with wicker sides and very wide seats, which could seat three in the back and two in front. Now one thing comes after another, one person after another becomes visible, very clearly visible, in the transient gleam of memory, which illuminates areas that haven't been seen in more than fifty years. They stand before her in the light of memory almost with the excitement of something new. More than fifty! Yes, it's probably closer to sixty years ago. She was certainly not more than fourteen years old then. She lived with her grandmother, the bishop's wife, in Copenhagen, and it was in the days when Aunt Marie was engaged to the man who later became so famous. They were engaged for ten years, and then she died a few months after the wedding. It was Aunt Marie and Grandmother who sat on either side of her. And *he* sat on the front seat, on the right-hand side, and drove the horses himself, because he had had the coachman stay in Lyngby. Next to him sat his brother Søren, who also became famous later on and whom the people at Grandmother's house liked to call Magister Søren.

Now not only did she *see* them clearly, she could also sense the mood of the moment and the situation among the various people. It was such a difficult time for Aunt Marie, of course, because her sweetheart was so strange, in a way, despite the fact that he was also a good and pleasant man. And in that moment of recollection old Mrs. Nielsen discovered that even as early as that coach ride she had suspected what the problem was between Aunt Marie and her sweetheart—and this in spite of the fact that she came to know it only many, many years later, from her husband. That was it, of course: he could never be sure if he loved Aunt Marie enough, her sweetheart couldn't, nor did he know whether she was religious enough.

But there was also something else that had been unpleasant on that ride. Yes, because it had certainly been an unpleasant ride, in spite of the fact that the weather was so lovely, just as it is now. Oh, and it had also been exactly the same time of year! Of course, it must have been. She had traveled home again to Lolland on June 14, and that had been just a couple of days before. She had been confirmed that spring. To think: sixty-one years since she had last driven here! It was just as if the Now of the present moment became unreal: Hans Husby, who sat up there on the driver's seat instead of Uncle Peter, whom she had called Aunt Marie's sweetheart in those days. It was as if the present had become a picture, a painting, and as if she saw it by lamplight. And the past—that she saw in daylight.

Yes, it had been the loveliest June sunshine; now she remembered it well. But it had also been unpleasant that the younger brother sat up there, in front, next to the driver's seat, and sort of teased Uncle Peter. And she could remember that she had heard him do it before. To be sure, relations between the two brothers were not very good, but this was certainly Magister Søren's fault, because Uncle Peter was an exceptionally pleasant person. Whenever he wasn't sitting there and teasing his brother that day, Søren was constantly humming an aria from *Don Giovanni*, an aria that she knew well. It was "Wenn Du fein fromm bist." Yes, or perhaps he whistled it: the three identical notes with which the melody begins and which recur so often—she remembered that they had reminded her of the song of the thrush.

Yes, there had been something about temptation and something about the weather that the two brothers talked about, and also something about driving a carriage. Søren had certainly made fun of Uncle Peter for wanting to drive by himself and for having had the coachman remain in Lyngby.

Uncle Peter had surely said something about how Danish this sort of weather was—or even that it was Scandinavian: it was so light and so bright and so fine; there was no wilderness or heath; it was almost childlike in its purity.

But the younger brother had replied that such weather was perfectly suited to conceal the Eternal. It was a *temptation*—he had said that many times—it tempted the mind to dream and to wander. Who could keep hold of a serious thought while enjoying that smooth, billowing grass? Either one had to let one's mind billow and dream like the grass, or one had to surrender to one's thoughts, but in that case all this bright, transient lushness became painful. The whole thing was a quaking bog, he had said. Of course it looked as if that green, open plain was solid ground, but the entire thing was a bog, you know. It quaked and quaked, and Eternity lay beneath. He couldn't imagine how his brother could want to be a coachman for so many people across such dangerous ground. And then he had laughed and hummed the aria and looked around at those sitting behind. She of course had believed that he had said the part about the land they drove across being a bog only in order to scare her, but in spite of the fact that she had thought this, she *became* frightened just the same, because it was as though he in fact believed it. Yes, of course he had believed it, she thought now, because his brother had indeed said something quite similar many years later. But the first time she simply hadn't understood it correctly—she had been frightened that the carriage might actually sink in. Uncle Peter hadn't really contradicted him. He had only said that for him there was something other than the green of springtime that covered over anxiety about Eternity, and that was the word of God.

Then Magister Søren had laughed and said something in German, which he repeated two times: "Da stellt ein Wort zur rechten Zeit sich ein."

Yet I think that all that about sinking through because there was nothing to bear one's weight, sinking through and disappearing—which Uncle Peter used to talk about so often years later, when they became reacquainted with him in the Kjettrup period, when he had become bishop of Aalborg—she had most probably heard it for the first time during that carriage ride. That was undoubtedly why there had been all those unpleasant feelings about the trip: springtime and calamity, merriment that was bright and cheerful, but un-reliable.

Hans Christian Andersen[15]

For a short time the novel *Only a Fiddler* engrossed one of the brilliant young men of our country. This was *Søren Kierkegaard*. When we met on the street he told me that he would write a review of it and that I would surely be more satisfied with it than with earlier reviews, since, he granted, I had been misunderstood! A long time passed. He read the book again, and his first good impression was obliterated. I must assume that the more seriously he considered the composition, the more faulty it became. When the review appeared I could not be pleased with it. It was an entire book (the first, I believe, that *Kierkegaard* wrote), and somewhat difficult to read with its heavy *Hegelian* style. It was said in jest that only *Kierkegaard* and *Andersen* had read the whole book. Its title was *From the Papers of One Still Living*. At that time this is what I got out of it: that I was no writer but a fictitious character who had slipped out of his category, and that it would be the task of some future writer to put me back into it or to use me as a character in a work in which he would create a supplement to me! Later I better understood this author, who has obliged me along my way with kindness and discernment.

Michael Nielsen[16]

Mr. S. Abye Kirkegaard, *candidatus theol.*, excelled as a student in this school because of his hard work and intelligence and his brilliant understanding of the subjects taught in general and of the form and spirit of languages in particular. Even as a student he gave us cause to expect great things of his integrity, self-reliance, and ability; his clear, acute, and comprehensive vision; his profound, lively, and serious mind; and his generally excellent gift for exposition, which he has subsequently demonstrated.

He has not been compelled to teach by circumstances, but he has nonetheless frequently felt a need to do so. At my request he has therefore helped me for several years with students who were weak in Latin composition, and he has successfully motivated them to do the sort of thinking that is not merely directed at passing the examination but that will continue to have an effect in their later lives. For a couple of years, when my own weak eyesight prevented me from correcting the essays of the most advanced class, he did this in my stead, displaying, now in a more mature fashion, the insight into language that I had recognized in him when he was a student at this school. In accordance with his request, during one academic year he taught Latin to the students in the second form and helped them progress a great deal, both in their Latin and in their general intellectual development. Several of them were graduated this year, when during my busiest time he again was kind enough to assist me with Latin and composition for the advanced class, and he performed just as well as I would have.

As far as I can judge, he has an unusual command of the Latin language, both orally and in writing.

Borgerdyd School in Copenhagen
M. Nielsen
Nov. , 1840

Emil Boesen[17]

[*E. Boesen to H. P. Barfod, May 22, 1868*]
He generally did not write letters, or at any rate only little notes whose contents were carefully considered. The style seemed easy, but it had been carefully scrutinized, and he could usually remember them for a long time. When he received letters he generally destroyed them soon afterward. . . . This must have been very important to him, and when he destroyed them he did so with great agitation. If he feared that the least written scrap of paper had escaped destruction, he could search after it with great zeal—though most often in vain, because it had been burned with the rest. . . .

In the days when he frequented my parents' house, he brought wit and irony, though always affectionately and with great respect for the adults in the house, and my mother was very fond of him. When he came up to my room, his disposition would vary, and he did not conceal what he felt, though I think that he revealed his feelings most clearly during our long walks in the evening on the outskirts of town. It was, however, years later—most probably while he was writing *On the Concept of Irony* and then during the period of his engagement, in particular—that he first gained a clear understanding of what he himself wanted to do and what his abilities were.

Comments on Kierkegaard's Dissertation,
On the Concept of Irony[18]

[*Prof. Frederik Christian Sibbern, June 16, 1841*]
Indeed, one might wish that our author's idea were carried through with more precision than seems to me to have been the case with all these efforts at bringing forth everything in order to clarify it—which is what we see here in our author, whose work has thereby taken on large proportions. With respect to various details, it would certainly be desirable that in the final revision of the dissertation a few things that are appropriate to a lower sort of genre could be trimmed away as luxuriant growths. But for the rest, *from the point of view of style*, the dissertation reads easily.

[*Prof. Johan Nicolai Madvig, June 20, 1841*]
With respect to the dissertation itself (of which I had earlier seen a large portion), it is characterized by such a stamp of intellectual liveliness and fresh

Manuscript facsimile of remarks by Prof. J. N. Madvig on Kierkegaard's dissertation, June 20, 1841. From the original in the Danish National Archives (Københavns Universitet. Det filosofiske Fakultet. KU. 35.02.17).

Hvad Afhandlingen selv angaaer, af hvilken jeg kjender et stort Partie tidligere, da bærer den saadant Præg af aandeligt Liv og frisk Tankebevægelse og af fleersidige Studier baade af græsk Litteratur og af nyere Philosophie og æsthetik, at den forekommer mig fuldkommen at qvalificere Forf. til Magistergraden; men paa den anden Side laborerer den ikke blot i Compositionen af en vis bred og magelig Løshed, men i selve Begrebsudviklingen af Mangel paa videnskabelig Orden, Form og concentreret Fasthed, der ikke mindst viser sig i Anordningen og Forbindelsen af Afhandlingens to Hovedbestanddele. Fremstillingen lider af en selvbehagelig Jagen efter det Piqvante og Vittige, der ikke saa sjelden slaaer over i det reentud Plat-Smagløse. (En lille Prøve kan

thought, and by multi-faceted studies, both of Greek literature and of modern philosophy and aesthetics, that it seems to me entirely to qualify the author for the degree of magister. But on the other hand, not only is it burdened with a certain free and easy carelessness of composition, but even its exposition of concepts lacks scholarly order, form, and firmness. This is particularly clear in the arrangement of the dissertation's two principal parts and the connection between them. The exposition suffers from a self-satisfied pursuit of the piquant and the witty, which not infrequently lapses into the purely vulgar and taste- less. . . . One could be tempted to make the removal of the [crossed out: "crud- est"] worst of these excrescences a *condition* for acceptance, were it not for the fact that negotiations about this would be difficult and awkward. Given the particular nature of the author and his preference for these elements, it would be fruitless to express a *wish* about this if not even the dean will see the disserta- tion after it has been trimmed a bit in this respect.

---

den af Decanus med Blyant mærkede Anmærkning i 5te H. S. 17 fra Enden give og en ditto kan sees 6. H. S. 10, hvor Skjæbnen har villet, at Forf. giver denne Skildring af et stagnerede "Stilleben" for en Tid, der af den franske Revolution allerede var rystet ret vel ud af de gamle Folder). At de ~~plumpeste~~ værste af disse Udvexter borttages, kunde man være fristet til at gjøre til **Betingelse** for Antagelsen, naar ikke Forhandlingen herom var besværlig og kjedsommelig. At yttre et **Ønske** herom vil efter Forf[.]ens Individualitet og Forkjerlighed for disse Ingredientser, være forgjæves, naar ikke i det Ringeste Decanus seer Afhandlingen efterat den er beskaaren lidt i denne Henseende.

With respect to the dissertation itself (of which I had earlier seen a large portion), it is characterized by such a stamp of intellectual liveliness and fresh thought, and by multifaceted studies, both of Greek literature and of modern philosophy and aesthetics, that it seems to me entirely to qualify the author for the degree of magister. But on the other hand, not only is it burdened with a certain free and easy carelessness of composi- tion but even its exposition of concepts lacks scholarly order, form, and firmness. This is particularly clear in the arrangement of the dissertation's two principal parts and the connection between them. The exposition suffers from a self-satisfied pursuit of the piquant and the witty, which not infrequently lapses into the purely vulgar and tasteless. (A little sample of this can be seen in the remarks—marked by the dean in pencil— seventeen pages from the end of the fifth fascicle, as well as in the sixth fascicle, p. 10, where, as chance would have it, the author describes a period which had already been shaken out of its old ways by the French Revolution as a stagnant "still life.") One could be tempted to make the removal of the ~~crudest~~ worst of these excrescences a **condition** for acceptance, were it not for the fact that negotiations about this would be difficult and awkward. Given the particular nature of the author and his preference for these ele- ments, it would be fruitless to express a **wish** about this if even the dean will not see the dissertation after it has been trimmed a bit in this respect.

[Prof. Frederik Christian Petersen, July 4, 1841]

This piece would profit a great deal from a reworking in the direction of increased order and compression. But since I, too, share the view that this probably cannot be attained because, given his personality, the author neither can nor will undertake such a change, we must limit ourselves to suggesting that various excesses of the sarcastic or mocking sort be removed as inappropriate in a piece of academic writing. Conferring with the author about this could certainly be left to the dean, who has already noted in the margins the worst instances of this sort of thing.

[Prof. Peder Oluf Brøndsted, July 7, 1841]

I cannot, however, refrain from expressing the same wish as my colleagues have already uttered, that Amplissimus Decanus [the most excellent dean] will endeavor to have the author trim away certain excrescences, which indeed in some places—e.g., the passage pointed out by Prof. Madvig on pp. 10–11 in the sixth fascicle—burgeon into quite large growths and testify to the author's occasional inability to resist the internal temptation to leap over the boundary that separates both genuine irony and reasonable satire from the unrefreshing territory of vulgar exaggeration. Passages of this sort are frequent and coarse. If a personal preference for tidbits of this sort prevents the author from following advice in this regard, we can certainly take comfort in the fact that it is the task of the faculty *only* to recognize *knowledge* and *proficiency* but *not in any way* to bring about better taste in those who, in keeping with their knowledge and their proficiency, *ought* to have better taste.

[Rector Hans Christian Ørsted, undated (early July 1841)]

Despite the fact that I certainly see in it the expression of significant intellectual strengths, I nevertheless cannot deny that it makes a generally unpleasant impression on me, particularly because of two things, both of which I detest: verbosity and affectation.

Chapter Three

SØREN AND REGINE: THE ENGAGEMENT AND AFTERWARD

Regine Schlegel
(as told to Hanne Mourier in 1896)[1]

To Regina Schlegel:

In accordance with your wishes I have summarized what you told me. I have tried to reproduce your own words, together with my own impressions, as reliably as possible, though this was not originally done with any intention of publishing what I wrote down. However, since you have been disturbed by the idea that after your death there might appear inaccurate accounts of your own and your husband's attitudes toward, and views of, Søren Kierkegaard, I know you will find it reassuring now to read a faithful version of your own words, which can serve as a full explanation should the need arise.

After the death of your husband, interest in the story of your youth, of your engagement to Søren Kierkegaard, has again surfaced. There have been many direct appeals to you regarding this matter. At first you felt overwhelmed by this and had to force yourself to speak of it, since during the many years of your life of perfect intimacy and happiness with your husband virtually no one had dared to approach you with indiscreet questions. Now, however, it is clear to you that it is your duty to give an account of what only you can tell: the views you and your husband had of S. Kierkegaard. Your wishes are that future generations should know about S. Kierkegaard and your noble husband, about their relationship to you, and that they should be seen in the true and beautiful light in which you knew both of them. It must be said and affirmed that S. Kierkegaard never misused your love to torment you or to carry out spiritual experiments on you, as has been commonly but incorrectly assumed. It was his serious intention to marry you when he became engaged. In recent years you have spoken of this relationship with a number of people with whom you have contact, because you want it to be understood that S. Kierkegaard's life was not in conflict with his activity as a religious author. For over fifty years your husband was your only confidant in this matter; he knew and understood completely what you had suffered. During your engagement [to Schlegel] he [Schlegel] helped you with his gentle and reasonable conversation—on the basis of complete mutual confidence and honesty—to talk about everything that had so distressed you, and so

Regine Schlegel, *née* Olsen. Photograph. From a photograph in the Picture Collection of the Royal Library. Reproduced courtesy of the Royal Library.

helped you regain your peace and happiness. He had been your teacher in school and consequently had known you from your earliest youth and had your welfare at heart.

You remember having seen S. Kierkegaard for the first time when you were somewhere between fourteen and sixteen years old. You met him at the home of the widowed Mrs. Rørdam (mother of the well-known pastor Peter Rør-dam) where you had been invited as company for a girl of the same age who was there as a houseguest (Thrine Dahl from Roskilde). Kierkegaard called on the family, and the liveliness of his intellect made a very strong impression on you, which you did not reveal, however. You remember that he spoke unceasingly, that his speech practically poured forth and was extremely captivating; but after the passage of so many years you no longer remember its content. You believe that perhaps the lines in the *Posthumous Papers: 1833–1843* [*SKEP 1833–1843*], p. 123 (May 8 [1837]) [cf. *Pap*. II A 68 (*SKJP* 5220)], "My God, why should this tendency awaken just now? Oh, how I feel *that I am alone!* etc." refer to this meeting with you, when he received his first impression of you, as you did of him. You do not remember at what point or on what occasion Kierkegaard first had himself introduced at your home, since it was only later, after you yourself were married, that your parents had open house one evening a week for your family and friends.* Kierkegaard gave you sheet music but must otherwise not have paid you any conspicuous attention, since when he met you on the street one day and wanted to accompany you home, you hardly noticed that he ignored your reply that no one was home and followed along with you. On arrival at home you suggested playing for him. You were used to doing this, since he loved music; but after a short time he closed the book of music in front of you and declared that that was not why he had come. When he then confessed to you his love, you were struck completely speechless, and, without a single word or any explanation, but only by gesture, you ushered him out the door as quickly as possible! Your singular reaction disquieted Kierkegaard concerning you; so he immediately visited your father at his office and related the whole scene to him. Your father mentioned nothing to you, but on the next day, when Kierkegaard returned, you gave him your consent, though not before you had mentioned that there was a teacher from your school days of whom you were very fond, and whom you believed was also fond of you [cf. Kierkegaard's version in *Pap.* X⁵ A 149:5, p. 160 (*SKJP* 6472, p. 192)]. This, however, did not bother Kierkegaard in the least, for he later said: "You could have talked about Fritz Schlegel until Doomsday—it would not have helped you at all, because I *wanted* you!" [not found in *Pap.* or *B&A*]. You were then eighteen years old.

You have told me that while you were still a child, your mother took you with her to the "gathering of the Holy" (The Moravians?) in Stormgade; and, as was she, you too were by nature religiously inclined. You found it satisfying to read *The Imitation of Christ* by Thomas á Kempis, and you sought your refuge in God. It was evidently your healthy, straightforward nature that had made such a deep impression on Kierkegaard that he could not but love you! But when he writes of you, in one of his diary entries, that "she was not religiously inclined" [not found in *Pap.* or *B&A*, but cf. *Pap.* X¹ A 24, p. 18 (*SKJP* 6304), and IV A 142, p. 54 (*SKJP* 5689)], this must have been based on a passing impression of you, perhaps because it was not in your nature to carry on profound conversations about your relationship to God, out of a reluctance to cause the very best in a person to vanish, as it were, through overmuch talk about it. But in relation to these questions you were the listener, the one seeking to apprehend. You were happy and glad, and surely expressed this in an innocent and charming way; you were a young girl with both enthusiasm and imagination; and you still clearly remember from before your engagement how your heroine was Joan of Arc, and how for a number of months you had dreamed of a similar task for yourself. You felt that Kierkegaard understood you, but the two of you did not have profound religious conversations; however, the fact

---

* Here you make a correction: even while you still lived at home with your parents, these open house evenings took place, as your family had a large circle of acquaintances. [Hanne Mourier]

that he dedicated the whole of his religious works to you, notwithstanding the preceding quote from his diary, indicates that he must have regarded you as religious. He was exceedingly different from you! Though he himself was not "the most simply constructed sundial, that tells the hour exactly, granted only that the sun's rays are permitted to shine upon it" [*SV* IV 158 (*KW* V 276)]—this dialectician loved and admired the immediate, the shortest path to God. Kierkegaard understood that "every holy feeling which in its most profound depth is good, is silent . . . since the lips are closed and only the heart is opened" [*SV* V 144 (*KW* V 370)]. He understood and loved you as though you were an expression of this truth. His spiritual contact with you, of which you were unaware at the time, inspired him and emerges in his writings in numerous passages and in a great variety of forms, but *embellished by his own rich imagination*, so that it is in no way justifiable to conclude or to assume that the various passages in his writings have direct reference to his actual relationship to you (with the exception of the *Posthumous Papers*). Kierkegaard recommended that you attend the church services of Paulli (b. 1809, then catechist at the Church of the Holy Spirit, later archdeacon). Paulli was an excellent preacher, and Kierkegaard said that his preaching was just the thing for you. Kierkegaard visited your home several times a day during the period of the engagement. He also spent much time in conversation with your father. But it was not long before you became acquainted with his deep melancholia; he poured out his troubles to you and always reproached himself over his relationship to his deceased father. Your own father suffered from melancholia, so that when Kierkegaard was beside himself with sorrow and self-accusation, his mental state was not unfamiliar to you. Therefore, when after a few months he began to have scruples with regard to his relationship to you, you thought that if you allowed him to release you, then he would surely become truly unhappy and despairing with self-reproach. That you one day should marry Kierkegaard was actually quite foreign to your thoughts; the thought occurred to you quite briefly and only once; but you loved him and were captivated by his spirit. When he sent you his letter breaking off the engagement, it was clear to you that it was a consequence of his melancholia and nothing else. You therefore asked him to retract his decision, and he willingly did so for the time being—so much the more, he said, because he was writing his doctoral dissertation. He then asked you if you would bear with him until that was finished. This happened three months later. You had continually struggled with him during this difficult period, but when it was over, you said to him: "Now I can bear it no longer; kiss me one last time and then have your freedom!" [not found in *Pap.* or *B&A*]. These words and the impression they made on Kierkegaard are recorded in his diary from this period. You felt no bitterness, anger, or reproach against him, but sorrow and pain. Kierkegaard's motivation for the break was his conception of his religious task; he dared not bind himself to anyone on earth in order not to be obstructed from his calling. He had to sacrifice the very best thing he owned in order to work as God demanded of him: therefore he sacrificed his love for you for the sake of his writing. Kierkegaard continued to keep track of you and sent you his first religious discourses through F. C. Sibbern, another visitor in your home, who had been a frequent guest on your carriage rides with Kierkegaard.

For some time after the engagement was broken off, you were ill; it was feared that your lungs were affected. At your young age, the tension and sorrow you had experienced were too great and too heavy a burden for you.

You have related to me that Schlegel bore his sorrow over your engagement to Kierkegaard quietly and with good grace. But when you were free again and had regained your health he approached you, and he proposed to you about two years after the hard blow. You were received by his relations lovingly and with the greatest joy, since, despite his quiet, reserved bearing, his parents and sisters had understood what he was experiencing during the time that he knew you were engaged to someone else. Your late sister-in-law, Mrs. Emma Nansen (née Schlegel), in particular, made it clear to you how hard his parents and sisters took the sorrow of their son and brother. Even in your eightieth year you can still exclaim to me: "Oh, that he could forgive me for being a little scoundrel, for becoming engaged to the other one!" But your beloved Fritz was not just any ordinary person. When you became engaged to him, he not only accepted your love but also took upon himself to help you to bear all the sorrow and pain you had experienced. He had a rare sense of delicacy; he did not pass judgment on Kierkegaard, nor did he harbor any petty resentment against him, but read Kierkegaard's writings with you in the parlor when you visited his parents' home in the evenings. Your husband's letters, both from the time of your engagement and afterward, as well as a couple of your own, bear witness beautifully to the true confidence and love you had for each other, combined with the most complete understanding. You have also described many small details of your life together in the same vein. You, for your part, had promised yourself, with God as your witness, to do everything in your power to make your husband happy! You did not overtax his love for you by plaguing him with constant references to the Kierkegaard affair, but occasionally, when overwhelmed by thoughts of the past, you confidently approached your husband about it. For example, when the *Posthumous Papers* were published you were able to ask your husband to buy the book, and he fulfilled your wish immediately, the very same day. But after having read the first volume you asked your husband not to purchase the rest, since what you had read of the first volume touched too closely upon personal topics.

You were married on November 3, 1847, and two years later your father died. His death made a deep impression on Kierkegaard, who had been very fond of your father from the times he had frequented his house. He felt a desire to see you and speak with you again, and he wrote to your husband on that occasion with the thought that it would be good, both for you and for him, to meet again. A letter to you was enclosed; but your husband replied to this with a written, polite but definite refusal [for Kierkegaard's version, see *Pap.* X² A

210, p. 162 (*SKJP* 6538), and *B&A* I 253–64 (*KW* XXV 322–37)]. He showed you Kierkegaard's letter and his own answer, and you were in complete agreement with him. This answer, however, could hardly please Kierkegaard, who gave vent to his displeasure in his diary. Seven years after your marriage, your husband was named to the governorship of the West Indies, and on the day of your departure, you saw Kierkegaard for the last time by purposely meeting him in the street. As he passed you, you said quietly to him: "God bless you— may all go well with you!" [not found in *Pap.* or *B&A*]. He seemed to retreat a step and greeted you for the first time since the break, and for the last time here on earth!

You saw the loving hand of God in the fact that you and your husband were so far away during the whole of the intense reaction elicited by Kierkegaard's *Moment* pamphlets and his subsequent death. But he, for his part, was happy that his "little governess" [not found in *Pap.* or *B&A*, but cf. Kierkegaard's hospital conversations with Emil Boesen in chapter 8 of this book] (as he referred to you after your husband became governor) was not there during all the strife. In his will he left to you the remainder of his fortune—you never asked whether it was a lot or a little—but you and your husband refused to take it. Insofar as I have understood you, as the motive for this bequest Kierkegaard mentioned that he had never felt himself unengaged from you. You accepted your own few letters, which you burned, and Kierkegaard's diaries. These latter, together with his letters to you, are preserved, sealed until after your death, at the University Library. Among Kierkegaard's belongings was found a package for you which contained some of his writings, bound in pale calf with gilt edges, which you still have. You know that Kierkegaard approved of your marriage to your husband from the letter in which he wrote to you, "Thank you for having married, but especially for having married Schlegel!" (he whom you in fact loved from the very first!) [for Kierkegaard's version, cf. e.g., *B&A* I 261 (*KW* XXV 333)]. Another written message to you from Kierkegaard read: "You see, Regina, in eternity there is no marriage; there, both Schlegel and I will happily be together with you" [not found in *Pap.* or *B&A*].

You informed me of an opinion regarding Kierkegaard expressed by your husband in his response to a remark made by Inspector Ottesen at Refsnæs, on whose wall portraits of Grundtvig and Kierkegaard hung side by side. When Ottesen remarked that he owed his spiritual development exclusively to Kierkegaard, your husband pointed his finger at the picture of Kierkegaard and replied: "Long after Grundtvig's influence is over and done, his [Kierkegaard's] will still be alive!"

What continually strikes me first and last in every piece of information you give me from times past is this: your intense love for and admiration of your husband, who was such a noble, unselfish person. He did not wear his heart on his sleeve, but he had profound, heartfelt, and loyal feelings. He was a good son to his parents and his country; he was forthright, just, and never petty; he was sincere, wise, sensitive, and kind. But neither are there any dark shadows on the memories you have about S. Kierkegaard's relationship to you. You have assured me that "he was good and kind to me!" You were also able to say that "the pain he was forced to cause himself and me was inexpressibly difficult and burdensome and left its lifelong mark; my life has not been easy, but happy!"

March 1, 1902

I have achieved what I set out to do with the present brief notes of these memories, which have become sacred and valuable to me through your account of them. This is because you have told me that you are satisfied with the present version of your report, inasmuch as I have succeeded in reproducing them in complete agreement with what you have told me.

Regine Schlegel
(as told to Raphael Meyer in 1898–99)[2]

As long as Schlegel was alive (he died June 18, 1896), Mrs. Schlegel had been left in peace. Only once, on a social occasion, some clergyman from Copenhagen had got her off into a corner and wanted to converse with her on the subject of her first engagement; I have no doubt that she had not been at a loss for an answer. But scarcely was Schlegel dead before people began to approach her; scholarly inquiries were even enclosed in letters of condolence. In the beginning she found it distressing, but gradually she became convinced that she had survived longest of the three of them in order that she should have the last word. She had therefore taken this opportunity to disseminate, in places she viewed as secure, information about her youthful relationship, and thus she corresponded with Prof. Rudin in Uppsala.

She remembered having seen Søren Kierkegaard for the first time when quite a young girl, as yet unconfirmed. On that day she was visiting with young people of her own age at the home of Mrs. Catrine Rørdam (the widow of Dean Thomas Schatt Rørdam, who died in 1831) in Frederiksberg when Kierkegaard chanced to pay a visit. He immediately made a very strong impression on her, though she gave no sign of this. She could still remember that he spoke unceasingly, that his speech practically poured forth and was highly captivating, but after so many years she was unable to remember the substance. She believed that the statements in the *Posthumous Papers: 1833–1843* [*SKEP 1833–1843*, p. 123 (May 8 [1837]); cf. *Pap.* II A 68 (*SKJP* 5220)], "My God, why should this tendency awaken just now? Oh, how I feel *that I am alone!* Oh, damned be this proud satisfaction with standing alone—thou, oh God, do not remove thy hand from me!" referred to this initial meeting at which he received his first impression of her, as well as she of him.

There was no difficulty in being introduced at the Olsens'. The family held open house one evening a week. Kierkegaard sought out the young girl more and more. He paid attention to her reading and her piano playing, lent her books, and gave her music. She had to confess to herself that he gained great power over her. And yet she was quite overwhelmed when he proposed, so that through her bearing, quite speechless, and without giving him any explanation or saying a single word, she ushered him out the door as quickly as possible. When he renewed his proposal two days later, she frankly and honestly responded that there was a teacher from her school days to whom she was much attached, and she believed that he also cared for her [for Kierkegaard's version, see *Pap.* X⁵ A 149:5, p. 160 (*SKJP* 6472, p. 192)]. But Kierkegaard persevered. "You could have talked about Fritz Schlegel until Doomsday—it would not have helped you at all, because I *wanted* you!" he told her later [not found in *Pap.* or *B&A*], after she had said yes to him.

Kierkegaard suffered frightfully from melancholia; many a time he sat by her and wept. He was tormented by the thought that he had been inadequate [as a son] to his father, whom he had loved so much. But even this increased his power over her. Melancholia was nothing new to her; she had experienced it in her own home. She hoped to be able to overcome it, but it was not to be exorcized from him. He was physically affected by it and his appearance altered. He suffered so much that when they met on a local street a week after his declaration, she did not recognize him.

Her love for Kierkegaard was, as it had been from the very beginning, a spiritual love. This love she sustained all her life. It had always pleased her when she noted an interest in Kierkegaardian thought. She was delighted about the interest in him that now reigned in Germany. The French would never understand him. But to the same extent she resented the Danish clergymen who had rejected him and who had failed to appreciate his greatness or significance for the inner religious life. Once she had actually become angry with a clergyman from Copenhagen who was her close friend, when she discovered that he was totally devoid of knowledge concerning Kierkegaard. "That is unacceptable in an educated man in the country where Kierkegaard was born and worked, and especially so in a pastor in the Danish Church," she had said and clenched her fist. She believed that the pastor most likely had made a start on his reading after that.

She was also unwilling to allow Kierkegaard's oft-repeated judgment of her—"She was not religiously inclined" [not found in *Pap.* or *B&A*, but cf. *Pap.* X¹ A 24, p. 18 (*SKJP* 6304), and IV A 142, p. 54 (*SKJP* 5689)]—to pass unopposed. In her home she had had a profoundly religious upbringing; at an early age her mother had taken her to "the gatherings of the holy" in Stormgade; the Bible and Thomas à Kempis's *Imitation of Christ* had been her preferred reading from an early age and had remained so all through her life. But she had lacked the ability and the desire to carry on detailed conversations about her relationship with God and had almost had a sort of fear of thereby causing what was best in her to disappear. Vis-à-vis Kierkegaard she had been the listener, the receiver. He had, of course, dedicated his writings to her, in particular the religious discourses, which she loved more than all the rest.

When Kierkegaard sent her the letter in which he broke off the engagement, she felt that it was a result of his melancholia, against which she had so long struggled in vain with her love and cheerfulness. She asked him to keep his promise to her for his late father's sake—at least for the time being, until his doctoral defense had taken place. After two months of fervent struggle they separated as good friends and without bitterness. At their last meeting she said, "No, now I cannot go on; we must separate; now you are free; do not visit me again" [not found in *Pap.* or *B&A*]. They shook hands and gave each other a last kiss. Even so, the next day Kierkegaard's servant brought her a letter from him.*

Schlegel had endured his sorrow in a quiet and fine manner when he saw her engaged to Kierkegaard, but after she had recovered from the state into which she had been cast by the sorrow and tension of her struggle and break with Kierkegaard, he again approached her. Two years later they became engaged. Through his sister, the late Mrs. Emma Nansen, Mrs. Schlegel later learned how hard Schlegel's parents and closest family—who now received her with love and gladness—had taken his sorrow. Even at the age of eighty, Mrs. Schlegel could cry out: "Oh, that he could ever forgive me for being such a little scoundrel that I became engaged to the other one." And his forgiveness was not based on any demand that she now had to forget the "other one," as Mrs. Schlegel generally referred to Kierkegaard in her old age.

Whereas Kierkegaard had earlier desired that her relationship with Schlegel, which was in fact older than her relationship with him, should be regarded as merely a parenthesis in her life, Schlegel allowed the parenthesis—*Søren Kierkegaard–Regine Olsen*—to remain open. He harbored no petty distrust of her old memories, even though he had firsthand knowledge of how strained she had been by the first engagement. It was no easy matter either to be engaged or to have been engaged to Søren Kierkegaard, but she found in her husband the best support for overcoming all the difficulties with which life had confronted her in this connection and all the doubts with which she still had to contend. Only he understood what she felt and what she suffered from time to time. His chivalry, his rare sensitivity, and his sensible conversation had always been her sole help.

Schlegel did not pass judgment on Kierkegaard and bore no rival's hatred toward him. She always remembered with pleasure a remark that Schlegel made to Inspector Ottesen at Refsnæs, who had pictures of Grundtvig and Kierkegaard hanging on the wall: "Long after Grundtvig's influence is over and done, Kierkegaard's will still be alive." Naturally, Kierkegaard had not been an item of their daily conversation, but Schlegel had never evaded discussing the matter with her in his clear and loving manner when she felt a need for it—discussions that she could scarcely have done without. And it was not only in later years, when the difficult memories were at a safe distance, that the Schlegels shared

---

* It must be mentioned that she had the impression that she had broken off the engagement with him, and not the other way around, as it appears from Kierkegaard's correspondence with his intimate friend Emil Boesen at roughly the same time and as is reflected at numerous points in his writings. [Raphael Meyer]

their interest in this issue. Even as a newly engaged couple, they could be seen sitting together in Schlegel's room in the evening and reading Kierkegaard's works aloud to one another. And of course, one after another, his writings contained bits of her past, memories of the engagement period, studies of him and of her—a reality that Kierkegaard's poetic spirit had transformed into "Dichtung und Wahrheit." And this reading continued throughout all their younger days. When the first volume of the *Posthumous Papers* appeared in 1869, at her request Schlegel bought the book immediately. But she was upset by its personal connection to her, and she refrained from reading the other volumes. That Schlegel, with her complete agreement, had replied with a refusal to Kierkegaard's wish for a renewal of their acquaintance two years after their wedding was exclusively due to his desire to protect the peace she had now found with him [for Kierkegaard's version, cf. *Pap.* X² A 210, p. 162 (*SKJP* 6538), and *B&A* I 253–64 (*KW* XXV 322–37)].

In the spring of 1855, Schlegel was named governor of the Danish West Indies. On March 17, the day of their departure, Mrs. Schlegel deliberately encountered Kierkegaard on the street, and as she passed close by him, she said in a low voice: "God bless you—may all go well with you" [not found in *Pap.* or *B&A*]. He seemed to retreat a step and returned her wish with a greeting.

In December of 1854, the first of Kierkegaard's newspaper articles on the occasion of Martensen's eulogy of Bishop Mynster appeared. By the time the Schlegels departed, the fierce battle against official Christianity and the paid professional clergy, which was to be Kierkegaard's last message to the public, had already flared up. But they did not witness the publication of the violent broadsheets and *The Moment.* According to what Kierkegaard said to his nephew Henrik Lund on his deathbed, this was a great comfort to him: "Oh, how glad I am that my little governess is away from all this; oh, how glad I am that she is married, and to Fritz Schlegel" [not found in *Pap.* or *B&A*, but cf. Kierkegaard's hospital conversations with Emil Boesen in chapter 8 of this book].

Now the old lady herself has passed away; lonesome as she was, she often longed for an end to her life. She had a simple youthful longing to see her Fritz again, and yet she repeated with sincere conviction Kierkegaard's words to her: "You see, Regine, in eternity there is no marriage; there, both Schlegel and I will happily be together with you" [not found in *Pap.* or *B&A*].

Regine Schlegel
(as told to Peter Munthe Brun in 1902)[3]

Mrs. Schlegel recounted [in the autumn of 1902] that one evening Søren Kierkegaard had heard her sing and play a particular piece of music, and that she had noticed that it made a certain impression on him. He said nothing that evening, however, but the next morning he came back again, despite the fact that her father, with whom Kierkegaard usually spoke, was out. Then he asked her to perform the same piece of music, and immediately thereafter he proposed to her. She was so surprised and astounded that she rushed out of the room and slammed the door without answering a word. Then S.K. went to her father at his office and proposed that he marry the daughter. The father made the matter dependent upon his daughter's decision. When the father came home, however, not a word was spoken about the matter that day. He expected that she would speak about it, but she couldn't [cf. Kierkegaard's account in *Pap.* X⁵ A 149:5, p.160 (*SKJP* 6472, p. 192)].

It was of course S.K. who broke off the engagement. Mrs. S. said nothing about the much-discussed and painful "experiments" during the time of her engagement. The reason S.K. gave for breaking off the engagement was that he did not feel himself sufficiently worthy. Afterward he sent her several letters, which she and Schlegel read together. From what she said it was very clear that her understanding of the matter was that it had been a genuinely profound and personal matter for S.K., and that he had suffered greatly in breaking off the engagement.

Henriette Lund[4]

After finishing his degree in the summer of 1840, however, Kierkegaard made a visit to the [Olsen family] house quite as a matter of course. Next he made a trip to Jutland to visit his father's birthplace; but first he attempted to establish a tie by lending some books to the daughters of the house while he was away, even making a suggestion that they read a particular passage in one of the books. In August he returned to Copenhagen, and according to his own account, the days that passed from the beginning of that month and on into September could in the strict sense be called the period in which he made his advances to her. On September 8, he went out, resolved to bring the matter to a conclusion. They met on the street just outside the house in which she lived. She said that no one was at home, and he says of himself that he was fool-headed enough to view this as the invitation he needed. Shortly thereafter the two of them were sitting alone in the parlor. He asked her to play for him, which she had done previously. But he rather quickly interrupted the music himself by proclaiming what was in his heart. "Moreover," he says, "I did nothing to deceive her; I even warned her against myself—against my melancholia." She fell silent; and soon afterward he said goodbye. He was afraid, in fact, that he might have overwhelmed her and was also averse to their being found alone together. He went directly up to the councillor. Though Kierkegaard got the impression that he was very willing, he did not give a definite answer, either. He requested and was granted an interview with the daughter on the 10th, and she said: yes! [for Kierkegaard's account, see *Pap.* X⁵ A 149:5, p. 160 (*SKJP* 6472, p. 192)]. And thus he took the step from the kingdom of fantasy, where thought is mighty, into the world of reality, a place where, despite all his excellent wit and external liveliness, he was less well suited.

Nevertheless, his entrance into these new circumstances hardly presented a great outward change. Her father, of whom Kierkegaard was always very fond, had a serious disposition. In his official capacity he served directly under old Privy Councillor Collin, so well known for success in business and who directed so much of the interconnected financial world of the period, so her father can hardly have been idle, either. In keeping with the modest circumstances of the times, the family led a rather quiet life. A party held some time after the engagement for a group of young people, mostly Kierkegaard's nieces and nephews, was thus by no means an ordinary event.* Later in the summer, when the crown prince, later Frederik VII, brought his young consort to Copenhagen, a good number of young ladies, the contemporaries of the Olsen daughters and other friends, gathered at the house to see the festive procession pass right by their windows on the way from the harbor to Christiansborg Palace. This same occasion gives an impression of the sympathy and understanding between Kierkegaard and his [prospective] father-in-law, since both of them, by taking a walk together in the open air, had preferred the solitude of the woods on a day when the whole population of the capital had turned out to see all the finery and the new princess.

He quickly got on equally good footing with the other members of the family, since he had a unique ability to establish rapport with whomever he wished and thereby to control the situation. . . .

Mrs. Schlegel has related how she met him in the arched passageway of the palace riding ring shortly after the engagement, and that it had been as if he were completely changed—absent and cold! Her youthful pride felt wounded by this; this may in turn have manifested itself in a brief period of arrogance, which he mentions specifically. In contrast to his own doubts and scruples he says of her: "She did not seem to notice anything; on the contrary, she became at last so arrogant that she even declared that she would break off the engagement if she believed that I was visiting her out of mere habit. This became, in one sense, something dangerous. If she does not get too upset, then I will be well served. Thus I regained my composure" [cf. a slightly different version in *Pap*. X⁵ A 149:5, p. 161 (*SKJP* 6472, p. 193)].

Shortly after this, however, a decisive change took place in her. Since, as she has said, melancholia was hardly an unknown factor in her family, it soon be-

---

* While the party was at its liveliest, however, Kierkegaard was taken ill, to the point of spitting up blood. His fiancée, who had become very frightened, went to his house several days later to hear how he was. But according to Mrs. Schlegel, this did not suit his taste, since he strictly observed the proprieties in such situations. Even so, he tried to calm her fears (and afterward he was so touched by her concern that he even thanked her in a letter). He told her, further, that the attack was surely connected to back pains from which he often suffered and which were the result of a fall from a tree that had happened when he was a boy. [Henriette Lund]

came evident to her that his behavior of this sort stemmed from that source. Her love for him thus took on a stronger and more conscious character, because it seemed to her that he must need it all the more. For his part, Kierkegaard, in discussing this change from haughtiness to a devotion that appeared to him almost to be worship, remarks: "I am myself to some degree responsible for, or guilty of, this, because—seeing only too clearly the difficulties of the relationship and having the insight that the greatest strength had to be used, in order, if possible, to gain the upper hand over my melancholia—I had said to her: surrender! Your pride will make it easy for me. Thoroughly true words, sincerely said to her and depressingly treacherous to myself" [cf. a slightly different version in *Pap*. X^5 A 149:5, p. 161 (*SKJP* 6472, p. 193)]. Because her complete devotion has the effect of placing the responsibility back on him, thereby rekindling his depression with renewed strength. . . .

As alluded to earlier, instead of scaring away his fiancée, this insight into the power that melancholia exercised over Kierkegaard's soul had in fact increased her sensitivity, so that she felt the need to make every effort to remain with him—precisely for his sake. At the same time, she made no secret of the fact that in addition to this motive there was a quite natural fear of loss of self-esteem if she should lose him. But the result of these feelings was so powerful and the desperation so apparent that Kierkegaard went back to her—not to remain with her, but, as he himself says, "to repel" [*Pap*. X^5 A 149:10 (*SKJP* 6472, p. 194)], thereby helping her, insofar as possible, to pull herself together in confronting their separation.

In these hard days of deception he sought to detach her with all his strength by, among other methods, pretending that he no longer cared for her.* By his own account, he observed the cautionary solicitude of saying directly to her at intervals: "Give in, let me go! You will not be able to endure it" [*Pap*. X^5 A 149:11 (*SKJP* 6472, p. 194)]. To this she answered passionately that she would rather endure anything than abandon him. In order to avoid injuring her honor he also suggested that the matter should be made to look as if it were she who broke the engagement. She would not hear of this, either, but merely answered that if she could endure the rest of it then she could also endure that. "Besides," she said, "there is certainly no one who would make anything of this in my presence, and what they may say in my absence hardly matters" [ibid.].

He was similarly touched, indeed impressed, by a statement from one of her sisters. When aspects of his strange behavior during this period leaked out in many ways and became known to the friends and acquaintances of the family— and when, in his own words, "All the clever people easily understood that I was a villain, and every clever person flattered himself that he could surely under-

---

* Cf. *Eftl. Pap. 1841* [i.e., *SKEP 1833–43*], p. 294 [*recte* p. 295]: "I am not in the custom of shaming my honor [omitted by Henriette Lund: "I have always found honor in faithfulness"], but I must appear to her as a deceiver, and this is the only way I can right the wrong I have done" [cf. *Pap*. III A 172]. [Henriette Lund]

stand that"—then she [Regine's sister] merely remarked quietly: "I do not understand Magister Kierkegaard, but I nonetheless believe that he is a good person!" [cf. a slightly different version in *Pap.* X^5 A 149:30, pp. 170–71 (*SKJP* 6472, p. 200].

He himself exclaims: "It was a frightfully agonizing time—to have to be cruel like that, and then to love as I did. She struggled like a lioness; had I not believed that I had a divine defense, she would have prevailed" [*Pap.* X^5 A 149:10, p. 163 (*SKJP* 6472, p. 194)].

"It collapsed," he continues, "about two months later. She despaired. For the first time in my life I quarreled. It was the only thing to do" [*Pap.* X^5 A 149:12, p. 163 (*SKJP* 6472, p. 195)].

One evening, in order to meet his friend Boesen, whom he knew to be attending a play and with whom he wanted to have a talk that very evening, Kierkegaard went directly from Regine's home to the theater. From this incident arose the story, which for a while circulated around town, that Kierkegaard had said to the family, as he removed his watch from his pocket, that if they had anything more to say they had better hurry, since he wanted to go to the theater!

But at the theater he chanced to meet someone else whom he had not expected to see: her old father, who again sought him out to plead his daughter's case. "I am a proud man," he said. "It is not easy for me to come to you like this; but I beg of you, do not leave her! It will be the death of her!" She herself had hinted of precisely this latter possibility in the days of their parting, and the extent to which this shook Kierkegaard became apparent later. Nonetheless, at this point he answered merely that he would calm her down but that the matter was settled. Then he accompanied her father home and spent the evening with the family. The next morning he got a letter with a request that he visit her. He came but consistently maintained the character that he had assumed. There was nothing further to be done. At their parting she asked him to remember her once in a while [for Kierkegaard's account, see *Pap.* X^5 A 149:12, pp. 163–64 (*SKJP* 6472, p. 195)]. . . .

Opinion was heavily against him, and gossip circulated around the town unceasingly. A letter he sent to the councillor was returned unopened [cf. *Pap.* X^5 A 149:17 (*SKJP* 6472, p. 196)]. His brother, Peter Kierkegaard, was moved and wanted to approach the family in order to protest against Søren being viewed as a wicked or irresponsible person. But S. Kierkegaard forbade this emphatically [ibid.]. For her sake, it was exactly in this light that he wanted to be viewed. . . .

From time to time, Mrs. Schlegel encountered him on familiar streets. They never spoke and only rarely greeted one another.* But of course the unrest of

---

* Mrs. Schlegel remembered that she met him quite accidentally just a short time after the engagement was broken. He was walking together with Cand. Brandt, later the pastor at Vartov, who knew her and greeted her, and then Kierkegaard also greeted her. In the emotional agitation

a soul can reveal itself in a glance and without a word. She could be beset by these feelings even after her marriage, when her loving husband, who knew what was in her soul, stood by her side. And the *Posthumous Papers* testify to the fact that these meetings always made a powerful impression on Kierkegaard [for Kierkegaard's accounts of these encounters, see *Pap.* X³ A 769 and 770 (*SKJP* 6713 and 6714); X⁴ A 540, p. 359 (*SKJP* 6800, p. 443) ("I have never exchanged a word with her"); X⁵ A 21, p. 26 (*SKJP* 6826); 59, p. 64 (*SKJP* 6835)]. In his papers he imagines that by getting married she may have thought of the possibility of establishing a friendly relationship with him, and he is therefore surprised that she makes no overtures in this direction. Because she does know him, after all, and so she knows that for him everything depends upon responsibility, which is why things would have been much easier if it had been she who had wished to break off the engagement. "This does not occur to her, however, so I must certainly give up [the idea of reestablishing friendly relations]," he adds [*Pap.* X⁵ A 149:25 (*SKJP* 6472, p. 199)].

In the summer of 1849 Councillor Olsen died, however, and the sad memories that assaulted Kierkegaard finally made him decide to take the decisive step: to write and tell her what was on his mind and to enclose the letter in a note to Schlegel, who could then decide whether he wanted her to see it or not [for Kierkegaard's account of this, see *Pap.* X² A 210 (*SKJP* 6538), and *B&A* I 253–64 (*KW* XXV 322–37)]. . . .

According to Mrs. Schlegel's account, in the spring of 1855, when Schlegel had been appointed governor of the West Indies, and they were both to travel there, Mrs. Schlegel tried to meet him [Kierkegaard] to say goodbye, and on this occasion she greeted him in passing. Apparently not aware of their departure, he tore off his hat with an extremely startled expression as he walked past.

That was their last meeting in this life. When the Schlegels returned from the West Indies, Kierkegaard had already been dead for many years, and Mrs. Schlegel had already received the package with the letters.

Søren Kierkegaard's Will and Correspondence Regarding It[5]

To: Reverend Dr. [Peter Christian] Kierkegaard
To be opened after my death.
Dear Brother:

It is naturally my will that my former fiancée, Mrs. Regine Schlegel, should inherit unconditionally what little I leave behind. If she herself refuses to accept it, it is to be offered to her on the condition that she act as trustee for its distribution to the poor.

---

of the moment, however, she turned her head aside, only to feel both intensely distressed and ashamed afterward. [Henriette Lund]

What I wish to express is that for me an engagement was and is just as binding as a marriage, and that therefore my estate is to revert to her in exactly the same manner as if I had been married to her.

Your brother,
S. Kierkegaard

St. Croix, January 14, 1856
The Reverend Mr. Parish Priest, Dr. Kierkegaard,

On New Year's Day I received Your Reverence's honored letter of November 23 of last year, and I am using the first departing steamship in order to send you my reply.

First and foremost, on behalf of my wife and myself, I wish to thank you and your honorable relatives for the discretion you have observed in a matter that, for many reasons, we do not wish to become an object of public discussion.

Next, with respect to the surprising information contained in your letter, I have the following to say to Your Reverence:

In the beginning my wife had some doubt as to whether, for her part, she had an obligation to fulfill with respect to the sort of thing implied in the second portion of the declaration of the deceased's will [i.e., the passage in which Kierkegaard requests that Regine assume responsibility for distributing his estate to the poor], which you have brought to our notice. She has given up this doubt, however, in part because of the great difficulties occasioned by our absence from home, and in part because of a consideration that both of us view as decisive: namely, that she absolutely does not dare to consider herself justified in accepting an offer that, according to what has been said, is motivated by views she finds totally unacceptable. This has been made even clearer in the private note you included for me, a note with which I acquainted her, because I believed that I ought to leave the decision in this matter entirely in my wife's own hands. She therefore has asked me to request that you and your co-heirs proceed entirely as if the above-mentioned will did not exist; the only wish she has expressed is that she retain some letters and several small items found among the property of the deceased, which she assumes formerly belonged to her, concerning which she has written to Dr. Henrik Lund.

I have directly informed attorney Maag of my wife's decision.

With the greatest of esteem, I remain Your Reverence's

Most respectful
F. Schlegel

Dear Henrik, *Whitmonday, May 12, 1856*
He (who was the occasion for you and I having first become acquainted, and who has now again become the occasion for our finally entering into correspondence) once attributed to you a very fine character trait: faithfulness. That was many years ago! In addition to everything else, these many years have taught me through experience that those words about you were true. I was very

young then, and had only very little confidence in myself. I remember clearly having thought, concerning myself, "Would that those words could some day be said about me." Now I do not know whether anyone has had occasion to say those words about me, but I will nonetheless say them about myself, because my friendship for you and your brothers and sisters has really been faithful. I hope, however, that this does not sound like self-praise but that what I say expresses your thoughts about me. Can you remember when I lived in Bredgade, when you visited me after a lapse of many years in order to tell me that you had done very well on your professional examinations and that you were about to travel abroad? I hope that you remember the friendly memories that brought you to me in order to tell me of the important events in your life, and that in me you encountered equally warm feelings. I thought I could read from your dear letter that you are still inspired by these same feelings, and I hope that my letters demonstrate to you that the same is also the case with me. I thank you many times for the manner in which you fulfilled my wishes. The two brooches had been mine, and I was happy to receive them. I have not seen the third one before, but you are right in saying that they cannot be returned from such a great distance, so I shall certainly keep it. The rings were the right ones. The one with the clear stone had been changed into the form of a cross, which is certainly not without significance. But it hurts me to think that by receiving all of them I have perhaps deprived you of a cherished memento. With the help of God, I also believe that it was right for you to send me all the letters, both those that were supposed to be burned and the rest, because if it was his will that after his death I was to receive everything, he definitely knew that it was precisely this portion of his papers that I would scrutinize. And therefore, with a humble prayer to God beseeching his blessing in this matter, I have done so, and thus I hope that this did me more good than harm. With this same conviction I ask again that you hold *nothing* back from me, whether it is in writing or an oral communication. I believe I understood that some of his writings were preserved for me in a rosewood cabinet, though perhaps I have not understood this correctly. It was surely proper that you sent me the posthumous note "in accordance with orders." God tempts no one, so if it were not his will that I should have come to know what I now know, it would not have happened. Despite the fact that he made no explanation concerning us after he said goodbye to me—in accordance with the best convictions of my conscience at that time [November 1849] and in agreement with my husband, I had returned unopened the letter that you found—I certainly expected some explanation after his death, although I must admit I did not expect it in quite the form in which I received it.

If I were not afraid that this letter would become too long, *even* for your patience, I would like to tell you a little about our life out here, though perhaps I can do it in a couple of words. Life out here is very monotonous, but thank God we both tolerate the climate very well. Schlegel has a great deal to do and I have nothing whatever. And you certainly know that too little or too much ruins everything in this world, so it is important to manage this without being harmed by it. Who knows but whether these many serious thoughts, which I have recently had in my head, are destined to save me from becoming lost in the petty things that are a part of small-town life—and that is what life out here really ought to be called. At least it is my judgment of myself—after everything I have experienced and will perhaps come to experience in the future as a result of my husband's talents—that I am permitted less than any other woman to lose myself in petty things.

Dear Henrik,   *September 10 [1856]*
    You must absolutely not think that I have allowed your letter of June 11 to lie about unanswered because I was not thankful for receiving it. No, on the contrary, I have thanked you for it many times in my heart, and now I send you my thanks today in words. It is always a rule with me to answer every letter by the next post, but of course there is no rule without an exception, and I have made yours such an exception, in part because we probably will not have any regular correspondence, so that a little pause of course does not make any difference—and in part because I have both something to ask you about and something to say to you that I wanted to consider quite carefully. I have not been well recently. I do not tolerate the very hot weather well, and it has been particularly weakening to my nerves. But because I have recently had some boils, which are very healthful out here, I feel healthier, and am therefore in a better condition to write letters. You say that you almost regret that you did not come out to St. Jean, etc. [the letter is illegible at this point] Søllerød, etc. Thank you for the books you are sending me. If they haven't already been sent, and if it doesn't cause you too much inconvenience or even sacrifice, I would also like to request that you send me some of his theological writings. I have some of them, especially the later works. That is what I wanted to ask you for. Now to what I wanted to question you about: you wrote that he mentioned me in his final illness, and I would so very much like to know what he said about me. Of course it is true that I have received information about our relationship from his posthumous papers, which places our relationship in a different light, a light in which I myself have sometimes seen it. But I don't know if you will understand me when I add that my modesty frequently forbade me to see things in that light—a light to which, however, my unshakable faith in him repeatedly led me back. You see, it was an uncertainty, but on the other hand, what that uncertainty led me to feel was that there was an unsettled issue between us, which some day would have to be cleared up. Shortsighted person that I was, I assigned this task to the peaceful time of old age, and because of a remarkable thoughtlessness [on my part] it never occurred to me that he might die. His death came to me all the more unexpectedly, and filled me not only with sorrow but also with regret, as if by putting things off I had seriously wronged him. It was in connection with this that I hoped to be able to come to conclusions by hearing what his last words about me were, because as far as I can see,

his papers were all written a number of years ago, and of course the years were accompanied by great changes. Among his papers I found a sealed document in which the *only* thing written was: "It is my will that my writings be dedicated to my late father and to her" [cf. *Pap.* X^5 A 149:25, p. 169 (*SKJP* 6472, p. 199)]. How strange, that the first time I saw the dedication to "An Unnamed Person" which precedes a small volume containing three discourses [actually, the *Two Discourses at the Communion on Fridays, SV* XII 265], I believed that it referred to me. I also want to ask you whether you can give any information about this matter. His intention at the time was to make me happy, to honor me, because it was of course his famous name. And to that extent I can, in a way, be at peace, because I have received both of them [the happiness and the honor] in equal measure, as if the entire world shared them with me—despite the fact that no one is able to share this with me. Because I have always had a fearful feeling with respect to all publicity—a feeling I especially have out here, where I am so very exposed and therefore feel this fear of publicity very strongly. Therefore, as far as I was concerned, there could never be any possibility except that I would renounce it. But since his death things have come to me from another point of view: as though it were out of cowardice that I was neglecting a duty not only to him but to God, to whom he sacrificed me—whether it was due to an innate tendency toward self-torture (a doubt that he himself had) or whether it was an inner call from God (which I believe has been demonstrated by the times and by the results of his actions). All the same, for the time being, whatever information you might be able to provide for me will not change my decision—which you can also surely understand with respect to my husband and his position. But I feel a need to have it cleared up for myself. I will no longer postpone it in silence. I have done enough of that in this life. I have something else to explain to you. (Note how unhesitatingly I attribute to you the deepest interest in me, in that I reveal my innermost doubts to you. But isn't it true that I can rely on you?) You write that you can see from my letter that I am not really satisfied, and you are perhaps correct in drawing that conclusion from the letter you received at that time, because you know well enough from experience that people are subject to moods. But I would be very ungrateful if I did not call myself happy—yes, indeed, happy as very few are happy. [The fact that] a happy marriage is the main thing in life has of course been often repeated, and Schlegel and I are so much to one another that we mutually enrich each other. In a way, I also owe him this [here the letter breaks off].

Georg Brandes[6]

If one went to Nørrebro [in 1867] there was a house where one was welcome on the first floor and where an attractive and distinguished couple held a weekly reception for young men on behalf of Mrs. Schlegel's young niece, her brother's daughter. The master of the house was a quiet, slender man whose appearance was always proper and dignified. He had served with honor in a high post in the government. In her youth, the wife had been very captivating and while still quite young had become white-haired. Now she was pretty, with snow-white curls and a fresh face. To me it was as though she bore an invisible mark, because as a very young woman she had been loved by a great man. She showed true kindness and was sincerely accommodating. But there was no great profit in getting to know her; company made her much too restless for that. When there was an evening reception at the house, she did not remain standing with any group long enough really to grasp what was being discussed. After a minute she rushed over to the other corner of the room, said a couple of words there, half listened to the topic of conversation, and went off to take care of tea.

Julius Clausen[7]

She [Regine Schlegel] has written no books, yet she has won a place in the history of Danish literature. Regine Olsen's name has become widely known as Søren Kierkegaard's fiancée.

A rather small, white-haired old lady with the friendliest of expressions opens the door for me the first time I ring the doorbell at the corner house at Nørrebrogade and Sortedamsdossering. She is dressed in a black silk dress and wears a fringed cap. Just about a year ago she was left the widow of Privy Councillor *Schlegel*, a highly respected civil servant, who was most recently prefect in Copenhagen, and formerly the governor of the Danish West Indies. The councillor has left a very large library—a sort of universal library including all sorts of books—the type of library established before this era of specialized knowledge. Mrs. Schlegel's agent has asked me to organize and catalog this library before it is sent to auction. That is why I am here.

This work lasted through a whole series of brightly sunlit summer evenings in the year 1896. Toward nine o'clock Mrs. Schlegel generally approached me: "You must be tired now. You could certainly use a little something cool to drink." She still had supplies of guava rum from her days in the West Indies, and she mixed it with ice water.

And so we sat there in the large rooms, warm from the summer heat, while the cool of the evening fell and the conversation began. I, of course, knew who she was but naturally did not presume to make any allusions. But the old lady was less reticent. It always began with Schlegel, whose excellent qualities she praised in high-toned fashion, but it always ended with—Kierkegaard. The dream of her young days had arrived at her armchair.

She had met *Kierkegaard* for the first time, and frequently thereafter, at the home of the Rørdam family in Frederiksberg. He had accompanied her home "behind the Stock Exchange" where her home was. One day he overtook Regine as she returned from her piano lesson, followed her uninvited into the house, and proposed. She was surprised and dumbfounded, and mentioned something about the fact that one of her former schoolteachers, Candidat Schlegel, was evidently fond of her [for Kierkegaard's account, see *Pap.* X^5 A 149:5,

p. 160 (*SKJP* 6472, p. 192)]. Kierkegaard ignored this; later, after they were engaged, he said with an arrogant smile: "Schlegel could have proposed to you a hundred times—I was determined to have you" [not found in *Pap.* or *B&A*]. Regine's days slipped by in a state of astonishment and admiration. She felt instinctively that she was faced with something unusual and worthy of respect, but the youthful woman could not cope with his temperament. He was always kind and friendly, and she became very fond of him. Mrs. Schlegel asserted firmly that all the many rumors that circulated after Kierkegaard had broken off the engagement—about how he had experimented with her—were groundless. I then asked whether there was any truth in the well-known story about Kierkegaard having invited his fiancée to *Don Giovanni* and then, after the overture, standing up and saying, "Now we are leaving. You have had the best, the expectation of pleasure!" Mrs. Schlegel collected her thoughts for moment, and then said: "Yes, I remember that evening well; but it was after the first act, and we left because he had a bad headache."

An informative example of how rumors arise. Somebody in the theater saw them leave. This was then distorted, given an interpretation, and made piquant.

After the break, Kierkegaard continued to send Regine his writings, at any rate the religious ones, with dedications. She took them out of her bureau drawer. They were bound in deep violet morocco and gilt-edged.

A couple of years after her marriage to Schlegel she received a letter from Kierkegaard. He asked for permission to visit her. She showed the letter to her husband—a husband was still a woman's "master" in those days—and Schlegel himself undertook to answer the letter. Up to a point he admired Kierkegaard, but he had no desire to have this great spiritual agitator in his home. Consequently, he wrote a very polite but definite refusal [see *Pap.* X^2 A 210, p. 162 (*SKJP* 6538), and *B&A* I 253–64 (*KW* XXV 322–37)].

That Kierkegaard made this attempt at an approach—that *he* could not forget either—has hardly been known to more than a few intimates. I cannot say whether this played a role in Schlegel's seeking the post in the West Indies. His wife said nothing about that. On the other hand she strongly emphasized how good it had been for her to be "out there" in the years of Kierkegaard's crises, 1854–55. It would have been painful for her, the wife of a proper civil servant, to have experienced at close hand all the invective aimed at him [Kierkegaard] from the clergy because of his attack on the Church, as well as his sorrowful death. He had once been her beloved.

Kierkegaard's fortune was nearly all used up when he died. He did, however, leave a large book collection and his copyrights, and in his will it was all left to Regine. But her husband refused the inheritance on her behalf—it would have made too much of a sensation.

When the auction [of Schlegel's books] was completed, Mrs. Schlegel moved out to Alhambra Road to live with an elderly brother. I visited her there often; and now she no longer spoke of Schlegel but only of Kierkegaard. It of course often happens that old people are absorbed by memories of their childhood and youth, while the more recent years slip out of recollection. She was now up in her eighties, and the contours were becoming blurred. One day she asked me: "Aren't you the one I gave that ring to, the one I got from Søren?" Unfortunately I was not.

Regine never forgot the great experience of her early youth. Even though it to some extent had been over her head, the sense of having been face to face with the exceptional, the rare, was never extinguished.

Robert Neiiendam[8]

Mrs. Regine Schlegel was a small, amiable, and very attractive lady with kind eyes, which must once have been full of life. Despite her age it was obvious that in her youth she would have fallen into the category of a lovely young girl with a sensitive temperament. Her husband's official positions had given her speech a stamp of correct and tactful conversation. But it was not the late excellent civil servant and art collector Fritz Schlegel who was of interest, but a memory that went back some sixty years: her engagement to Søren Kierkegaard. Time had smoothed away the pain, and what remained was the memory of *the experience* of her life. At the time spoken of here Kierkegaard's letters to her had not yet been published, and people were curious as to whether it was appropriate to speak to her of him. It was said that it was not. But after the privy councillor's death, a change took place in her mind regarding this subject. Now, on the contrary, she was pleased that young people were interested in Søren Kierkegaard. One day I showed her a picture of him in a volume of literary history and asked if it was a good likeness. "Both yes and no," she answered. "Kierkegaard's external appearance was easy to caricature, and people exploited that." When I said that in pictures he always looked so stiff in the back, she answered: "Yes, he was somewhat high-shouldered and his head tilted forward a bit, probably from all that reading and writing at his desk." We also talked about his deep interest in the theater and of his talent for depicting theatrical themes in his works. "He certainly did not go to the theater in order to kill an evening," she said. On the other hand, she did not relate an experience that I later heard through one of her family: that on one evening, when they sat in the theater, he got up after the overture and said, "Now we are leaving. We have had the pleasure of expectation, and that is the best part." He was suffering at that time from his painful melancholia, which not even she was capable of alleviating. She spoke only handsomely of him, and the years had clarified her relationship to him. It had become a mission from God, who had used her as an instrument to lead Kierkegaard to produce the great religious works, which would assume so much significance. She was at that time one of the few who were acquainted with his letters, and she knew *"that he took her with him into history."* And this thought made up for what she had suffered.

Chapter Four

THE YOUNG WRITER (CA. 1840–1845)

Elise Lindberg[1]

A small farewell party was held for [Peter Rørdam] at our house. I don't remember how many guests there were, or who else was there, but Søren Kierkegaard was there, and he was very lively and talked a lot. Speeches were made
at the table, but suddenly Søren Kierkegaard said to Rørdam: "Now be careful,
Rørdam, when you get to Mæhren [Mern]. There are so many members of the
nobility in that area." "Ah," answered Rørdam in a raised voice, "the aristocracy is a rotten tree that must be felled at the root," and continued in that vein.
Apart from this, the evening was an enjoyable occasion. Rørdam then departed,
but six months later we heard the remarkable news that he, who was not exactly
youthful, had become engaged to a girl he had prepared for confirmation, a
Countess Knuth. Christensen met Søren Kierkegaard in the Allé when this
piece of news was going the rounds and said to him: "Well, whatever do you
think of Rørdam, after the way he spoke of the aristocracy that evening at the
Lindbergs'?" "Ah," answered Kierkegaard with his satirical smile, "he has behaved completely consistently, since the surest way of eliminating the aristocracy is for countesses to marry into the bourgeoisie."

Holger Frederik Rørdam[2]

In her later years [my grandmother, Catrine Rørdam] lived in the town of
Frederiksberg. She lived out her remaining years quietly and in the fear of God,
and it was a joy for her to attend the pretty little church in Frederiksberg. In fact
she kept to her parish church, to which she had been accustomed since childhood. Her youngest son, Peter R., a recent theological graduate who was serving as teacher (with a speciality in religion) in several of the larger schools in
Copenhagen, lived with her until he became pastor in Mern in 1841. As time
went on, his liveliness and winning personality put him on friendly terms with
many of the most well-known men in Copenhagen of that time, who thereby
also came to make the acquaintance of his mother, who hospitably opened her
house to them. She of course delighted and interested them with her cheerful
faith and unaffected piety, which were united with a loving temperament, cultivated morals, and the ability to converse reasonably on every subject then topi-
cal in the intellectual world. Grundtvig, Sibbern, Søren Kierkegaard, Gold-

schmidt, Fr. Barfod, and others often came by to say hello to her, particularly in the summer, when their walks led them to Frederiksberg.

[I] remember having seen Søren Kierkegaard at the home of my old grandmother in Frederiksberg when I was a child. At that time he made an impression on me because of his zeal and his strident tone in debate; his hair, which stood on end; and finally, what touched upon me the most, and which I found unpleasant, was the fact that he made fun of my Jutland dialect.

A. D. Jørgensen[3]

[June 14, 1885]

Today Giödvad told me that he first made *Sören Kierkegård's* acquaintance when he [Kierkegaard] came to him to ask that he publish *Either/Or*. The reason for this was that he (G.) had given a firm rebuff to someone who had wanted to know who had written an anonymous article in *Fædrelandet*. The publication of *Either/Or* was rushed to such an extent that he received thirty-two pages of proofs daily; as far as G. could remember, they began on December 23 [1842] (the book was published on February 15 [1843]).

Hother Ploug[4]

But in addition to this, the office of *Fædrelandet* became a kind of club for Giødwad's more personal circle of friends. As the eldest and most experienced, Giødwad was a sort of "housemother of the Danish press" and the real host of the office, and he was visited by many who really had no particular relationship to the newspaper but who liked to stop by in the morning and strike up a conversation with him. Among these friends can be named the brothers *Carl and Ernst Weis, Christian Winther*, and finally *Søren Kierkegaard*. Kierkegaard came there daily, and in the winter of 1843 [i.e., 1842–43] the proofreading of *Either/Or* took place, so to speak, in the offices of *Fædrelandet*, a situation that was partially responsible for the fact that [Carl] Ploug never entered into any relation of personal friendship with the famous thinker. One must imagine what it is like to have to have a newspaper ready at a definite time—and in those days it was early in the afternoon, because the police inspector had to look at the issue before it could be distributed—and to have an impractical and very self-absorbed man sitting in the office, ceaselessly lecturing and talking without the least awareness of the inconvenience he is causing. However captivating Ploug found him, and however often he might have felt an urge to sit and listen, he nonetheless had to leave the room and go into his own cubicle in order to carry out his thankless daily task, while Giødwad reverently sat listening at the master's feet. Kierkegaard who, as is known, had his petty side, did not appreciate people taking leave of a conversation with him, and must surely have nourished a private disdain for Ploug as a philistine who devoted himself to the nonsense of daily existence. The personal relationship between them was certainly very

cool, and Ploug subsequently resented Kierkegaard because he had comman-
deered his co-worker in such an inconsiderate fashion and had made him his
audience all morning long, which cannot fail to have influenced Giødwad's
interest in the routine drudgery of the office.

Henriette Wulff[5]

[*Henriette Wulff to Hans Christian Andersen, February 20, 1843*]
   Recently a book was published here with the title *Either/Or*! It is supposed
to be quite strange, the first part full of Don Juanism, skepticism, etc., and the
second part toned down and conciliating, ending with a sermon that is said to
be quite excellent. The whole book has attracted much attention. It has not yet
been discussed publicly by anyone, but it surely will be. It is actually supposed
to be by a Kirkegaard who has adopted a pseudonym: do you know him?

Signe Læssøe[6]

[*Signe Læssøe to Hans Christian Andersen, April 7, 1843*]
   A new literary comet (I think it looks like I wrote "camel," but I mean a
comet) has soared in the heavens here—a harbinger and a bringer of bad fortune. It is so demonic that one reads and reads it, puts it aside in dissatisfaction,
but always takes it up again, because one can neither let it go nor hold onto it.
"But what is it?" I can hear you say. It is *Either/Or* by Søren Kierkegaard. You
have no idea what a sensation it has caused. I think that no book has caused such
a stir with the reading public since Rousseau placed his *Confessions* on the altar.
After one has read it one feels disgust for the author, but one profoundly recognizes his intelligence and his talent. We women have to be especially angry with
him: like the Mohammedans, he assigns us to the realm of finitude, and he
values us only because we give birth to, amuse, and *save* menfolk. In the first
part (this is a work of 864 octavo pages) he is aesthetic, that is, evil. In the second
part he is ethical, that is, a little less evil. Everyone praises the second part
because it is his alter ego, the better half, which speaks. The second part only
makes me the angrier with him—it is *there* that he ties women to finitude. In fact
I only understand a small fraction of the book; it is altogether too philosophical.
For example, he says, "There is no bliss except in despair; hurry up and despair,
you will find no happiness until you do." At another point he says, "One's
happiness can consist only in choosing oneself." What does that mean? The
entire book contains a dissatisfaction with life that can only be the product of a
warped life. A gifted young man ought not say: "Happy the man who dies;
happier still the child who dies; happiest of all he who is never born." At first
Heiberg wrote a glowing review in the *Intelligensblade* [Intelligenser], but I think
that his eyes have now been opened after further reflection and rereading. I
expect a critique to appear in his newspaper in the middle of the month; therefore we did not receive anything on April 1, when it is usually 16 quarto pages

long. I am looking forward to it. He deserves rough treatment. Only someone who has contempt for everyone can express himself as he has done. Poor wretch, it is worst for him himself! Another book has appeared here—you see, we are productive, even though it is not the literary season—which is just as lovable as *Either/Or* is unlovable, namely, the third part of Poul Møller's *Works*.

Hans Christian Andersen[7]

[*Hans Christian Andersen to Signe Læssøe, April 21, 1843*]
What you have sent me about Kierkegaard's book does not exactly excite my curiosity. It is so easy to seem ingenious when one disregards all considerations and tears to pieces one's own soul and all holy feelings! But this sort of thing has an effect. It is reasonable to assume that Heiberg has for the time being been dazzled by the philosophical brilliance!

Caspar Wilhelm Smith[8]

[*C. W. Smith to his mother, Cathrina Fibiger, from Berlin, December 28, 1841*]
[The philosophical enthusiasms of Johannes Fibiger] sound as though they are compounded of various parts of *ignorantia plebeia, philisterium crassum, essentia reflexionis communis*, and numerous other such substances, which, it cannot be denied, might have a certain reality to them. Søren Kierkegaard said much the same thing to me a few days ago with respect to drinking binges, to which I replied in the same exalted tone: "Yes, they of course have the same reality as all everyday phenomena." He replied in turn with a shrug of his shoulders, answering, "Ah, yes," and went into Spargnapani to drink a cup of philosophical chocolate and meditate undisturbed upon Hegel. This same Søren Kierkegaard is the queerest bird of those we know: a brilliant head, but extremely vain and self-satisfied. He always wants to be different from other people, and he himself always points out his own bizarre behavior.

[*C. W. Smith to his mother, from Berlin, March 14, 1842*]
That you must have an answer to your letter is self-evident, as Søren Kierkegaard says more than twenty times in his monster of a book on Socrates, or rather, on Søren Kierkegaard. However, after having written this, I now see that this quotation is not really apt because of this strange disparity: he makes this remark about everything that most needs to be proven, whereas I of course say it about something that requires no proof.

[*C. W. Smith to Christian Fibiger, from Kraków, September 5, 1842*]
[My room in Kraków] is very large, but with the exception of the above-mentioned effects ["an old chest of drawers," "a bed, which is perfectly rotten and rickety, filled with straw," and "a pillow for my head"] it is completely empty. But every guest who visits me assures me that my abode is, for Kraków,

a good one. . . . The whole typical situation amuses me unspeakably, and I am far from losing my good humor because I lack a few conveniences. I almost laughed myself silly when I saw the whole arrangement. But I would like to see Søren Kierkegaard in such a situation.

[*C. W. Smith to his mother, from Berlin, August 3, 1845*]
Another Danish book I have recently read is the first part of *Either/Or*. On this occasion it occurred to me how exceedingly offensive I have always found Kierkegaard's personality, from the very first time I made his acquaintance. Since then this impression has been renewed on acquaintance with his first writings, because this singular personality is the sole content of these varied works. I did not put aside the book on Socrates or irony, however, but on the contrary read it with great eagerness. The reason for my hatred is now clear to me: this singular personality is my own caricature. It is obvious that his talent is not itself a part of the composition, since I would by no means attempt to present reality as he presents his caricature, and even if I could, I would not view the matter as worth making so much of. Nevertheless it is obvious that since I discovered this I am completely reconciled with him. I am most eager to get acquainted with the other things he has written in recent years.

C. J. Brandt[9]

[*September 1, 1843*]
This evening I had a conversation with Magister Søren Kierkegaard, and despite the fact that he is not exactly the person with whom one finds tranquility, it just so happened—as often happens—that his words made clear to me precisely what I have recently been thinking about so often. He had come to the conclusion that from now on he was going to read only "writings by men who have been executed." Strange as it sounds, it is nonetheless based on the truth that there is something to be learned only from those who have offered their lives for their convictions. At the time it sounded so paradoxical to me that I was compelled to laugh. Now I am annoyed with myself for not having pursued the ironist into more serious territory. In this connection it is of course quite obvious to think of Christianity: all the way from our Savior himself to the least of the martyrs, they indeed offered their lives for what they said. And oddly enough, moved obscurely by this same notion, I had in my hands at that very moment a book I had purchased, Rudelbach's volume of Christian consolation, drawn from the writings of pious confessors of the faith.

Frederik Benedikt Møller[10]

What occupied me intellectually most of all during that year was Søren Kierkegaard. I had got hold of *Either/Or*. His pen had placed him in the first class among the knights of literature. It was especially "The Diary of the Seducer" that fascinated me; I had no understanding of the rest—the aesthetic and the ethical views of life; nor did I understand the structure and meaning of the whole work. But what the seducer sketched—was it something actually experienced, or just something thought?

In those days the following story was told: Kierkegaard was a guest on a number of occasions at the home of a widow who had only one daughter, who was beautiful and engaged. There was a ball one evening. Kierkegaard stands in the recess of a window, concealed by drapery. Couples get up to dance. The daughter of the house stands next to the window with her sweetheart. She says to him: "Do you know Mr. Kierkegaard? I absolutely detest that man!" He hears this. All evening and all night he broods upon what he had heard, and now he formulates his battle plan. He will win her love, so that she will come to love him instead of detesting him. First he must see to getting the engagement broken off, and it must be she who breaks it, so that she can preserve her self-assertiveness. In order for this to happen, her fiancé must begin to lead a life that makes him despicable in her eyes. Kierkegaard establishes a friendship with him, gains his confidence, and uses it to lead him to places that call forth her contempt when she hears of the life he now leads. So she breaks off the connection. "The first act," Kierkegaard thinks. He visits her widowed mother often. He talks with her about the high cost of living, difficulties with the servants, etc. such as old women like to talk about. "My, but isn't he a reasonable person," she says to the daughter. And when the daughter is there he entertains her by talking about the theater, about literature, and by telling about his travels in foreign countries. She enjoys his interesting conversation and is completely conquered, so that she becomes his. But he wants only to carry out aesthetic experiments with her love, so that it becomes pain and agony for her. Then she breaks off this relationship as well and is later married to a respectable man.

In accordance with this, Kierkegaard was for us a heartless Don Juan, who deserved to be held in contempt. But on the other hand the rest of his writings, which were seriously Christian, spoke against this understanding of him.

Hans Brøchner[11]

[*H. Brøchner to H. P. Barfod, November 10, 1871*]

It is in fact true that I played the role of *Søren Kirk* in the first two performances of *Gjenboerne* [The Neighbors across the Way]. I played it two times in the beginning of 1844 and once again a bit later, probably in 1845. If the piece was performed on July 12, 1847, someone else must have played the role because I was abroad at the time and had been away since the spring of 1846. Most probably this is where there has been some confusion with the earlier performances.

I remember *with certainty* that for the performances in which I played, the placards bore no other name than Søren *Kirk*. I cannot say whether any of the papers added any interpretation to the name in their reviews, but I do not believe that they did. And just as Søren Kierkegaard's "full name" did not appear on the placard, he was not "put on the stage" in the sense that there was any intent to copy his personality in the presentation of the role. The speech that constitutes almost the entirety of Søren Kirk's role in *Gjenboerne* contains themes from the Diapsalmata in the first part of *Either/Or*. However, at least as far as I was concerned, I was very far from identifying the fictive author of the first part of *Either/Or* with the actual Kierkegaard, and in any case the personal relationship which I had to Søren Kierkegaard would have made it impossible for me to present him in a comic light. It was certainly the case that Søren Kirk's speech in general tended to focus the attention of the audience on the word-playing dialectics which at the time were pretty much the only yield harvested by university students who were immersed in a rather shallow study of philosophy. In any case, the fact that the name of the role brought Kierkegaard's name to mind served only to remind us that he *could* use this sort of dialectics—when he wanted to—far more capably than anyone else.

I remember that one evening, when I was on my way to a rehearsal for the play, I met Kierkegaard on Højbroplads and spoke with him. He said to me in a joking tone: "Well, so you are going to play me in Hostrup's comedy?" I related the contents of the role to him and told him my understanding of it. At that time I had no impression that Hostrup's joke affected him, although I later heard that it had done so. With K. it frequently happened that when he reflected on some minor matter, he could make it into a little piece of world history. His sense of reality did not always keep pace with his expertise at reflection, and he therefore came to view facts oddly displaced or transformed to abnormal dimensions. This may have happened with him in the case in question. He never again mentioned it to me, by the way.

Julie Weber Sødring[12]

One day, after I had a played a new role at the theater the evening before, Father came to me, put a rixdollar bill on the table in front of me, and said, "This is for you, because Søren Kierkegaard, with whom I was just talking, praised your performance of last evening."

Carl Brosbøll[13]

P. L. Møller . . . exclaimed:

"Listen, Goldschmidt, what did *Søren Kierkegaard* want with you the other day? I saw that you let him sit and wait in the anteroom over on Købmagergade before he was granted an audience. The little man became completely nervous and took at last to shuffling back and forth in the room."

"What he wanted was a matter between him and myself," Goldschmidt answered with an ironic smile. "Perhaps he wanted a poem like the one you printed about him in *Gæa*:

> Once a hunchback asked a poet
> To have an album verse written for him,
> Not long, but with a wealth of contents.
> He wrote: 'Your back affronts you, dear sir!'"

The host recited the verse with false pathos.

"He wrote that," said P. L. Møller, indicating me [Brosbøll] with his pipe.

"Søren Kierkegaard asked me [Brosbøll] about an album verse, because he had read my epigrams in *Gæa*. I was to send it to him at his place on Nørregade if I could write that sort of verse. I was insulted by that remark, and I fulfilled his wish. He didn't really like it."

W. I. Karup[14]

In that occupation [working in a bookshop] I became acquainted with *Søren Kierkegaard*, and it was partly because of him that I left it. He often came into the bookshop. One day he encountered me alone and began a conversation with me.

"Tell me, now, are you a Jew or a Christian?" he asked, while he fixed his penetrating gaze upon me.

"I am a Christian," was my answer.

"Yes, I certainly thought so," he continued. "But why, then, are you working for a Jew?"

"Because he can use me," I answered.

"Oh, so that's the reason," he exclaimed, and broke into a sarcastic smile. "The Devil can also use you. Thus you would also enter his service, isn't that true?"

"But," I objected, "there is a great difference, however, between the Devil and a Jew."

"Yes, certainly," answered Søren Kierkegaard, "but your position is nonetheless very dangerous. You stand on the brink of going to hell."

"Why so?" I asked, amazed.

"You are in the service of someone who is on the way there," he answered.

At that instant my employer came into the bookshop, and Søren Kierkegaard pointed out to him the perilousness of my situation, because he was a Jew.

"It's all the same whether one is a Jew or a Christian," said the insulted book dealer, "as long as one gives everyone his due and does justice to one's fellow men."

"It's all the same," repeated Søren Kierkegaard and burst into mocking laughter. "Yes, you are right. One is not thrown into jail by the police because of it, but if one is and remains a Jew, then one will in the end go straight to hell anyway! Adieu!"

Søren Kierkegaard went his way and slammed the door behind him. My employer assured me that *that man* was completely full of crazy ideas and that one ought not pay attention to his talk. But a couple of days later, however, I left that "perilous position."

Nanna Videbech[15]

At "The Dodecagon" Father met *Søren Kierkegaard*, whose sister was married to the owner of the estate, Agent Lund. (His other sister was married to the agent's brother Ferdinand, department head in the National Bank.) Søren Kierkegaard liked to talk to Father, and when they returned from one of their long walks he liked to talk with Mother, who was a bright, clear spirit. I can only vaguely remember him, but I can distinctly recall one evening when he was there. Father had then bought the country place, and all those present came up with suggestions of what it should be named: "Vilhelm's Peace," "Johanne's Delight," etc. Next Uncle Gottlieb Bindesbøll suggested that it should be called *"Enough,"* and then Søren Kierkegaard said, "Enough! That's too much. I would call it *Always Something!*" I can remember that I thought that it was a pity to call the country place that, and that is probably why I have retained the memory of that remark.

Vilhelm Birkedal[16]

At that time Sorø was full of intellectual life and activity. Ingemann, Hauch, Wilster, Hjort, and many other teachers or lecturers from the Academy were there, playing their roles on Parnassus and in the world of learning, and having more influence upon one another than was perhaps good for them. Søren Kierkegaard once said, with respect to this community of aesthetes, "They destroy themselves and each another by constantly having to be clever and interesting. They compel themselves to adopt piquant points of view and have no taste for ordinary everyday conversation. But there is a danger that this rotation of crops could cause sterility of the soul." There was certainly some truth in that observation.

Johannes A. Ostermann[17]

[*J. A. Ostermann to H. P. Barfod, April 25, 1868*]

Even while still a youth he [Søren Kierkegaard] was known by many people. When you met him he was usually in the company of somebody; he was on the same footing—equally close or distant—with most of these companions. We met often at the Student Union or at tearooms, and we frequently went on from there to take walks out around the lakes. Despite all his work, he was constantly on the street or in public places. Thus oral communication was so easy and convenient that it was unnecessary to write. Occasionally emotional subjects came up: he could complain of his nerves, or speak with a certain degree of admiration of one or another who was dear to him, e.g., his brother.

I think he was fond of J. F. Gjødvad, who, if I am right, had been involved with the proofreading of his writings. I can't say whether Gjødvad might possibly have materials pertaining to Kierkegaard's later period. I could of course mention others, many of them, with whom he conversed—students, scholars, actors; but it is highly uncertain, or unreasonable, to expect that there is anything to be gained from them with regard to the project you have in mind. It is not impossible that a person like "Danish Levin" may recollect characteristic traits and sayings of K.'s, but in Levin's mouth Kierkegaard might take on a somewhat foreign coloration or an entertaining yet spurious polish.

The possibility exists that in some corner somewhere there may be something that records interesting and characteristic traits. Why don't you indicate in the foreword that you would be grateful to receive such contributions? They could then be included in the later installments.

I no longer remember what I wrote in my letter of last year; but I think I remarked that in the early years of his youth, as he developed, he carried on a witty dialectical game on all fronts, and no one noticed that anything beyond the game itself and cleverness really interested him. He was definitely capable of admiring Mozart's *Don Giovanni*, and could speak of our prosaic era, in which the passions were stepchildren (cf. the motto in *Either or Or* [*sic*]), but the impression he gave was more that of a man who was amusing himself with a mixture of ingenious and witty expressions than that of a man whose words came from the depths of his heart. He was also pleased and surprised when other people displayed traits that testified to a certain superiority. He told me with considerable delight what [Bishop J. P.] Mynster had replied, when a pastor from Southern Zealand heatedly and bitterly complained that the police dragged [Baptist] children from their parents in order to baptize them. Mynster had laughed heartily and said, "Yes! Does the rogues good," whereupon the poor pastor left, crestfallen. Did K. approve of forcible baptism? Not a word was heard about that. Later on he certainly knew what he was about and spoke more openly about everything. I recollect that once, when both the bishop and I were attending the Rigsdag, Kierkegaard declared to me: it is a shame that my brother is a member of the Rigsdag; he could do something better.

A little story occurs to me that is hardly appropriate for publication. One day I was walking down Østergade with K.; suddenly he stopped by a gate where a man was standing. They carried on the following conversation, both parties quite serious: K.: "Are you no longer staying at the hotel?" "I am out in town, but will be moving back there again." K.: "How are the furnishings?" "Not bad under the circumstances." K.: "But the food probably hasn't improved." (With a laugh) "No! Not at all." At this we walked off. "Who was that?" I asked. "That was Goldschmidt, who is in prison on bread and water—quite a fine fellow."

Chapter Five

GOLDSCHMIDT AND THE *CORSAIR* AFFAIR

Henriette Collin[1]

[*Henriette Collin to Hans Christian Andersen, February 2, 1846*]

What stirs the greatest interest right now in the literary world is *The Corsair*'s sustained attack on Søren Kierkegaard, and the poor victim is not enough of a philosopher to ignore this annoyance, but is occupied with it day and night and talks about it with everyone. He called this fate down upon his own head, however, because he attacked *The Corsair* in an odd and farfetched article in *Fædrelandet*.

V. Fohlmann[2]

[*V. Fohlmann to P. L. Møller, June 3, 1846*]

This spring I read your new *Gæa* with enjoyment. And despite the fact that I believe he has been treated a bit too roughly, I was pleased that you have chased Sören philosophus into exile—in Berlin he will probably gather witty insults to heap upon *The Corsair*. It cannot be denied that his philosophical writings have yielded much interesting information from the land of madness and have demonstrated that it is by no means the deserted and trackless waste that is commonly supposed.

Meïr Aron Goldschmidt

1.[3]

It was during my time as an editor, in the summer of 1837—and should therefore have been discussed earlier—that I first met S. Kierkegaard. I met my former teacher P. Rørdam and he invited me to his home, or rather to the home of his mother, who lived in Frederiksberg. Among those present was Søren Kierkegaard. I was certainly not a calm, attentive observer, but I still have a mental photograph of him. He was about seven years older than I. In those days he had fresh color in his face but was thin, with his shoulders hunched forward a bit. His eyes had an intelligent, lively, and superior look, with a mixture of good nature and malice. Afterward I walked back with him along Gamle Kongevej, and he asked me if I had read a book he had recently published, *From the Papers of One Still Living, Published against His Will*. I had read it and

Meïr Aron Goldschmidt. Photograph. From a photograph in the Picture Collection of the Royal Library. Reproduced courtesy of the Royal Library.

remembered best something about Hans Christian Andersen, but I had not understood it to the extent that he desired. When he explained it and asked me about it, however, I was not intimidated, but said yes and yes. It surprised me that he talked so much about his own book, but doing so did not make him ridiculous, because he remained quite superior to me. There was a long pause, and he suddenly took a little hop and struck himself on the leg with his thin cane. There was something jaunty about it, although it was completely different from the sort of jauntiness one usually sees in the world. The movement was peculiar and seemed almost painful. I am very much aware that I am in danger of remembering that scene with an admixture of knowledge from a later period, but I am sure that there was something painful in it, something of the following sort: it was the fact that this learned, thin man wanted to be a part of the joys of life but felt himself either unable or not permitted to do so. I later heard that people in the Lyngby area believed that he was in love with, or was quite taken with, a young lady (who later married one of his cousins). He visited the Rørdam family often and liked to attend their dances, which he enjoyed, but he himself did not dance. Perhaps he had in mind a happy thought about the Lyngby area when he made that movement.

2.[4]

At that time I was brought together with *S. Kierkegaard* for the second time.

A review was sent to me of [Søren Kierkegaard's] doctoral thesis, *On the Concept of Irony with Continual Reference to Socrates.* Or really it was not a review, but an ironic thank-you that used Kierkegaard's own striking, mannered language. The article was well written, but I nonetheless wanted to see the book itself. I read it and found that justice required that I express reservations with respect to the content of the review. This I did in a short postscript, but I lacked the ability to write a witty, superior appreciation; however, I did manage to express my reservations (*The Corsair*, no. 51). At that point I did not know that this was the same Kierkegaard that I had met at the home of Madame Rørdam, the wife of Dean Rørdam. But immediately thereafter he met me on the street and said that I had now got hold of him in *The Corsair*, but that he didn't have any grounds for complaint. On the other hand, he felt that the article was weak in its composition: I ought to apply myself to comic composition; that was my task. I accepted his words as good and well-intentioned advice, which they undoubtedly were. Thus he consigned me to the comic alone and denied that I had the talent or the calling to show seriousness, respect, or reverence. But what was this task, comic composition, that he proposed for me? I really couldn't ask him about this, and I myself didn't know. Well, I had neglected aesthetics as a discipline, as a science, and I couldn't see the shortcomings of the article— specifically its raw mixture of jest and seriousness—and I knew nothing that could serve as a model for me. The term "comic composition" shone before me as something that, while certainly not connected with Lessing or with justified praise or blame, was nonetheless something of considerable importance. What was it, then? After the powerful flash of illumination he had given, I stood in the dark. There is something odd about the fact that it was he who should set forth the magazine or its supposed spirit as my law and purpose, rather than propose something in me as the law for the magazine. But it is certainly also true that, without either of us suspecting it, this was the day he sharpened the point on which he himself was later impaled.

I can report here on two additional encounters I had with him at that time.

I had ordered a winter coat at Fahrner's, the fashionable tailor of the day, and because I was uncertain about how it really ought to look, Fahrner said, "Would you do me the favor of leaving it to me? I will sew you the most beautiful coat in all of Copenhagen." I went along with that, and when it was finished it was indeed a very beautiful coat, of fine dark blue cloth with a fur collar, and instead of buttons with loops it had a luxuriant black braid on the breast. It pleased me, because it had a fine military touch that appealed to my fantasies about weaponry. But it was precisely this detail that frightened me about it as an article of clothing for the everyday world. If, as the tailor surely assumed, I had had a desire to arouse attention regarding my person, to be jaunty or a braggart, the coat would have been incomparable. Now, under the circumstances, it was not possible to criticize it because in its way it was a masterpiece, and Fahrner was very proud of it and wanted me to put it on right away and walk down Østergade. I didn't want to, however, and was satisfied with a tentative walk down Købmagergade, where the "establishment" [Fahrner's shop] was located, and when people along the way apparently took no notice of me—because that is the way people are; you can't see by looking at them what they are going to say after they have passed by—I began to gain confidence in the coat. Then I came up Amagertorv and Vimmelskaftet, and there I met Kierkegaard. He turned around and walked with me, talking at first of one or another thing that I cannot remember, and then he said quietly but with an unmistakable expression of good will, "Don't walk around in a coat like that. You are not a riding instructor. One ought to dress like other people." I did not tell him that this was the first time I had worn the coat and with what feelings I had done so, but I went home, sent it back, and had the fur collar and braid removed. The only thing that caused me pain was that Kierkegaard had thought that I was really pleased with the coat.

Something he did on another occasion pained me in a similar—or rather, more definite—way. One time, without betraying any curiosity but still with a certain inquisitiveness, he asked me how each issue of *The Corsair* took shape, and I told him quite simply. It seemed to surprise him that there was absolutely nothing secretive about it, and he asked, "But how do you have such good information about what is going on around town?" I answered that the truth was that I knew absolutely nothing more than everyone else, that I only read the newspapers and based my remarks on them. "But don't you receive a lot of anonymous contributions?" he asked. "Yes, but only a very few are any good, and most of them are quite terrible." "How so?" "Because they are a private sort of information. It's quite unpleasant to be the recipient of this sort of information, which deals with even intimate family relationships. I have even had a case in which a man and his wife denounced each other to me." "I don't want to hear about it!" Kierkegaard shouted. It hurt me, as if he were accusing me of having intended to betray some secret to him, as if I were of a coarser nature than he. This did not prevent him from later making use of me again in order to tell him about something in *The Corsair*, specifically about something that had happened to me and Pastor *Visby*. Visby had published a prayer book for prisoners at the penal institution, and I had been sharply critical of it. After a while he [Visby] came to me and said, "But, in God's name, how can you attack me like that? You don't even know me!" I answered that I attacked only his name, which was printed on the title page of the book, just as in other circumstances I had attacked others whose names I had found in the newspapers or in books. "Do you know that that's an amusing story?" Kierkegaard asked. I didn't know that.

During these encounters, the questions "What is the task you have assigned me? What is comic composition?" were always on the tip of my tongue. I was unable to pose the question, nor did his personality facilitate such an approach. The moment one encountered him, one was under pressure, one was being examined, while he himself was quite reserved.

In a novel, where one has the liberty of compressing things and making them striking, the next thing would be to tell how the hero, having met a learned man on the street and having been given the task of seeking after comic composition, went forth like a Japhet in search of a father and finally found it. But neither in great things nor in small does reality often follow such rules.

3.[5]

Then *P. L. Møller* loomed up.

4.[6]

It came over me like a fairy tale, like a miracle. That which had previously seemed to be something unattainable—despite the fact that, properly viewed, the germ of it lay in the first issue of *The Corsair*—I had now suddenly attained without knowing it: like a sleepwalker I had solved the Kierkegaardian problem and had produced a comic composition!

"God be praised!" I exclaimed.

5.[7]

S. Kierkegaard published *Either/Or* under the name Victor Eremita. I cannot say how P. L. Møller read and understood the book, and I have difficulty remembering my own understanding of it. But it seems to me that both of us more or less viewed Victor Eremita as a modern resurrection of the brilliant Hellene. There was a wealth of ideas, wit, irony, and brilliant superiority—especially this latter. He was superior to everything and was able—if not with his personality, then with his thought—to be Either-Or and Both-And. I have an obscure recollection that even at that point Møller had reservations and that he said it consisted more of intellectual web spinning than of flesh and blood. But this was something I really couldn't understand, and I left it for the genuine and proper masters to decide. I myself wrote a rather foggy and stilted but also enthusiastic encomium on the book in *The Corsair* of March 10, 1843.

At that time I had been given a bottle of rare Italian wine, and I wrote an invitation to Victor Eremita and P. L. Møller to come and drink it with me. Naturally, the letter to Eremita could not be sent because he was at that point a persona whom S. Kierkegaard had not officially acknowledged and whom I myself had not clearly identified with him, but had done so more by way of poetic reconstruction. But I included the invitation to Eremita with the invitation to Møller, so that he would know which guests would be present, despite invisibility, and in order that he himself would arrive "garlanded in the Greek fashion and in a festive spirit." Well, I was so young that I had had scant opportunity to combine enthusiasm with reality. And then Møller showed up in the appropriate mood. Never before or since did we ever converse like that—as though under sun-dappled grape leaves by the shore of the Ionian Sea—but I cannot recollect any of the details with the exception of the conclusion, because Møller had stood up and said: "Now I will conclude a pact with you: we must both remain in the service of literary truth, and, in the event that it is required, we will blindly oppose anyone whatsoever, including one another, without cliquish friendship or making deals—and as a reward we will remain imperishably young."

We shook hands on this pact, apparently in full seriousness on both sides, and I, at any rate, was deeply moved. Of course this was not really anything genuinely new for me. The foundation for taking this sort of isolated stand had certainly been laid down in my past. But what had previously been something external and accidental was now elevated to something internal and obligatory, and it seems to me that I may permit myself to believe that I have never abandoned that youthful moment, just as I have similarly failed to escape from the imperfections, the fraudulence, and the unpleasantness with which that pledge was carried out.

6.[8]

The slogan about the fundamental injustice of society accorded well with an obscure, youthful notion that one's own individuality had a unique and absolute right vis-à-vis all other people, the bourgeois philistines, and that when such an individuality strove for poetry and produced intellectual fireworks, it was blessed with favor and was wedded to good fortune. Without either knowing it or willing it, S. Kierkegaard also contributed to this, specifically by having broken off his engagement. That event stood as an illustration of the proposition concerning the artistic rights of the [individual] personality in the face of every constraint. It was like the case of Goethe, who had cast aside Frederikke in Sesenheim, and her reward for the sacrifice and the loss of [her] life was that she then lived eternally in literature or in literary history. Mysterious, perhaps untrue, things were also said about Kierkegaard, but they were recounted with, and had the appearance of, probability. Thus he was once supposed to have taken his fiancée to the theater to hear Mozart's *Don Giovanni*, and, after a couple of measures of the overture, to have led her away again with the remark that this was enough—that those measures contained the true conception of the entire opera, or were sufficient to establish the appropriate mood. The mood, to attain the correct mood—that seemed to be the main thing in life! Kierkegaard became the leader of this aesthetic view of life—not he himself, by means of his own personality, certainly, but by means of the poetic reconstructions produced by Victor Eremita, "the victorious hermit," and by himself.

7.[9]

A renewal of our acquaintance or a new encounter of especial significance was occasioned by the book and by S. *Kierkegaard*, who again showed himself on the streets. I use this expression because in those days it was as if he would disappear and then return to carry out a particular thought experiment, and disappear again. He asked me which character in the book I myself viewed as the best delineated, and when I said I thought it was the hero, he said, "No, it is the mother." "I hadn't even thought about her at all in writing the book." "I thought so!" he said, delighted. He continued, "Naturally, you have read the criticism in *Fædrelandet*, what do you think the point of it is?" "It was of course quite simply intended to praise the book." "No, the point is that there are people who want to see you as the author of *A Jew*, but not as the editor of *The Corsair*; *The Corsair* is P. L. Møller."

I almost cried aloud in terror on Møller's behalf, because I knew both how unjust this was and how unpleasant and damaging such opinions would be for him. I objected and reminded Kierkegaard of what I had told him about *The Corsair*, long before I had come to know Møller, but he smilingly shook his head and left me.

Møller was dejected when I told him about it, and he made me promise on my honor to repeat the truth to Kierkegaaard over and over again, which I did as soon as I had the opportunity. But the philosopher was unyielding and merely said that there are reports in the world that are more accurate than any police report. I asked, "How can you have any report in this matter that is more reliable than mine?" Then he laughed in his odd way, and I was tempted to treat the entire matter as a joke. But when I reported to Møller about my unsuccessful mission he took the matter more seriously and said that it would be a great problem for him just now if that opinion became general. He said that it would therefore be better if we broke off our association for a while, which he did, but not entirely, as will later be seen, and he was unable to avoid a collision with Kierkegaard.

8.[10]

The leading strings by which one is solemnly drawn forward on such occasions are so concealed that everything seems to be mysterious. And therefore the fact that the business in which Møller was engaged at that very moment would lead him, or would allow him to lead himself, into a collision with S. Kierkegaard can also be viewed as mysterious. Nonetheless, the principal threads can be more or less exposed. And, finally, some light can be shed on the case when it is said—and now I am saying something that applies to myself just as much as it does to many others— that the most profound reason that Møller was broken by his collision with S. Kierkegaard was that Kierkegaard's attitude with respect to woman was more beautiful, purer, and loftier. I assume that this—his

relationship to happiness, or grace, or, as I prefer to call it, his Nemesis-relation-
ship, plus whatever other unique characteristics in his organism to which that
relationship was connected—was the basis and not the consequence of his enthusiasm (this includes his religious enthusiasm). We are what we essentially are
by virtue of what has been asserted or preserved in us in this respect.

But what was it that led Møller to do battle with S. Kierkegaard, and not in
an ordinary article or an essay, but in a critical presentation that had the appearance of a manifesto issued from, or supported by, Sorø Academy? First and
foremost there was naturally an inner impulse, an antipathy, a disagreement
with S. Kierkegaard and a conviction that he could refute him by means of some
Hegelian philosophy and some proficiency in practical thought. But the issue of
the professorship also played a role, not only in the sense that a coming university teacher should indeed be able to demonstrate his superiority on some significant issue, but also in a unique manner. When Møller emerged from his resig-
nation and loneliness—when, with the vitality and hope one has at the age of
thirty, he put aside the notion of being a cast-off proletarian—he reached for the
world with both hands and wanted to appear worldly-wise. He did not want to
give the appearance of standing alone, but of being surrounded by friends like
other intelligent people, and thus have a claim to respect. With the plan for his
Gæa—the annual journal that was supposed to have formed the literary throne
from which his move to the professorship was to have been facilitated—and
with several contributions, especially from Øehlenschlæger, he traveled to Sorø
and encountered what seemed a favorable reception. From Copenhagen it
would therefore look as if his principal strength lay in Sorø. It was a sort of
cunning that perhaps only poets have; they are so simple in their craftiness that
they become both ridiculous and pathetic. Without committing any real indis-
cretion by mentioning the Sorø professors by name, Møller created the impression that those gentlemen lent their authority to his undertaking, and the entire
essay was in many respects first-rate, perhaps the most lively and energetic thing
he had ever written. But he had met his match.

S. Kierkegaard pounced on him with such vehemence, used such peculiar
words, had, or seemed to have, such an effect on the public that the professorship, instead of having been brought closer by *Gæa*, was placed at an immeasur-
able distance. And even while the dispute was still going on, Møller was seized
by a longing to leave Denmark, a longing that he satisfied shortly thereafter.

9.[11]

S. Kierkegaard was again "visible on the street" immediately following the
publication of *Gæa*, and when he met me he took me by the arm to accompany
him, as was his custom. I still hadn't read the entire book, and in particular not
the essay on him, and without ulterior motive I asked him whether he had seen
the new book and what he thought of it. What I really wanted to know, of
course, was what he thought of "Min Onkels Tømmerplads" [My Uncle's

Lumberyard]. "Oh, yes," he answered, and spoke of my story with some praise. But beyond this he was quieter than usual, apparently with his thoughts elsewhere. Perhaps he also thought that my naiveté was feigned.

Evidence of what had been occupying his thoughts soon came in the form of his extremely vehement article in *Fædrelandet*, directed against *The Corsair* and P. L. Møller, and signed by "Frater Taciturnus." Møller's essay in *Gæa* was called, among other things, "a disgusting *Corsair* attack," and Møller himself was called a tramp and was presented, with extreme recklessness, as the real *Corsair* and as the evil element in it: "Where P. L. Møller is, there is *The Corsair.*"

At that time people were not accustomed to seeing certain rules of literary honor set aside, and not a few people were taken aback by this outburst, which was either an arbitrary accusation or an impetuous, arbitrary breach of anonymity. But it was most striking to me because I had so clearly and repeatedly explained to Kierkegaard the way things actually were and had so earnestly pleaded with him not to cling to his view, which both was unjust to Møller and could do him damage.

I soon met him again, but now he had taken a peculiar position, which was, however, necessary under the circumstances: he held strictly to anonymity. Just as I, of course, neither would nor dared to say that he was Frater Taciturnus, he was equally unwilling to admit any knowledge that I was connected with the editorship of *The Corsair*. We could talk about P. L. Møller and *The Corsair* as though these were things that had absolutely nothing to do with us, and the fact that he sided with Frater Taciturnus and I took the other side had absolutely nothing to do with personal preferences. This tone was immediately established by the manner in which he initiated our conversations. I understood this and followed along; it was as if we were playing a light little comedy. But the consequence of this impersonal situation was that I could not come to him and say: "I told you thus and such. Why, despite this, have you made this accusation against P. L. Møller?" On the other hand, I could and did say, with respect to Frater Taciturnus, that however right he might be with respect to other matters, on this point he [Frater Taciturnus] had committed an injustice and an injury. Kierkegaard replied to this that Frater Taciturnus's right must be judged from a higher point of view. I said that I could not see this higher point of view, and then we spoke for a moment about other things.

Naturally, I, too, had to write on this matter. A hard blow such as this could not be directed against *The Corsair* without also "taking the gloves off," and thus a certain amount of roughness was bound to arise of itself, because in his personal meetings, Kierkegaard had made everything so impersonal—but I am not going to press this issue. What weighed most heavily on my heart at the time was to demonstrate to him that I had managed to solve the problem that he had set for me, to produce comic compositions. Even now, my opinion is still that the problem had been successfully solved because I had strictly limited the question and had given a jovial explanation of the fact that *The Corsair*'s secret editor had now finally been discovered. This editor in fact resembled the famous Venetian bandit Coronato the Frightful because, despite the fact that he carried out his actions with the greatest of daring, practically in broad daylight, even the famous Venetian police force had been unable to track him down or even to form the slightest notion of his identity. But one moonlit evening, sharing a glass of punch with "the silent brother," Frater Taciturnus, he had opened his heart and had confided his secret in him, though on the condition that he must tell no one else, and the silent brother had taken an oath to keep silence. But now Coronato had written a criticism of him, and so Frater Taciturnus did not feel obligated to keep silent any longer, but had gone up to *Fædrelandet* and had told everything: "Now I am publicly naming Coronato, and at the same moment I will destroy *The Corsair*." *Fædrelandet* was delighted with this, and Frater Taciturnus was delighted and said: "I am so happy that I will imagine giving a poor man a dollar."

When I took another look at that last sentence in the galley proofs, it seemed foreign to me, almost like something that had slipped off my pen without my knowing it. But I let it stand, because it seemed to me both witty and accurate; it had the look of truth. It corresponded to the opinion current at the time, that Kierkegaard lacked any genuine, personal relationship to his works or his life but carried out everything as a thought experiment. Was this really the case? The answer is not easy. From the ordinary, casual point of view this had been the likely opinion ever since the publication of *Either/Or*. In the years since the publication of that work, he more and more had something about him that gave him the appearance of someone who stands at a distance as an ironical observer, someone with a self-conscious superiority—a superiority that seemed to emanate both from his intellect and from his supposed wealth. He seemed to be someone who could understand everything, all worry and sorrow, and who could utter words of counsel, but could not share in that sorrow. Of course, this could well have been an illusion that would have disappeared if one followed him into his private little space, but who could have known this, and how much do we humans really trouble ourselves about one another before it is too late? As a rule, we are preoccupied with our own egos, and we accept prevailing opinions, which we ourselves create in our arbitrary and superficial interactions with one another. In keeping with the saying "Where there's smoke, there's fire," these opinions do contain a certain kind of truth, and they perform the service of providing every individual with his pain. With some malice, I accepted these views as true, and on my own responsibility I became the spokesman for this indistinct, hovering rumor and derived some joy from doing so. I have subsequently noticed that other people, who have written about me or against me, have in similar fashion served as the organs for something just-unjust that hovered in the atmosphere.

At that time the caustic qualities I have just touched upon seemed to me to be eclipsed by the playful fiction concerning Coronato and Frater Taciturnus, and I was so satisfied with it [this article]—childishly so, one might say—that the next time I met Kierkegaard I asked him if the article in *The Corsair* was in fact comic composition. He answered with a long, drawn-out "no." "Why not?" "Because the question cannot even be asked. For the first, it is lacking in respect." "Respect for what?" "For Frater Taciturnus's higher right." Once again we stranded on this point, and after a few words about other matters we parted.

His real answer came in *Fædrelandet*: a new, violent article in which, among other things, he called *The Corsair* "a prostitute." When the paper [*Fædrelandet*] arrived, Møller himself was with me. I read the article and burst into laughter. Møller took the paper, read it, and said, very pale: "You can laugh at what you please! I would never have had this disastrous business, this mixing of my *Gæa* with *The Corsair*, if I had not been involved with you."

The entire matter took an unexpectedly bitter turn. But nonetheless I could not get beyond what seemed to me to be comic in Kierkegaard's exaggeration and in the passion with which he asserted not only that he was a martyr to *The Corsair*, but that this had always been his intention. If the affair is to be judged as an ordinary literary quarrel, in accordance with the humor and the imagination contained in the articles, I would still dare to submit the case to a jury.

After the replies I myself wrote, some of which were accompanied by drawings, came those of others, and the affair was continually raked over, with slashing attacks against him [Kierkegaard]. I am unable to say how unpleasant it was for me. Not until a decisive moment did I really have a clear sense of the entire matter.

There was still an impersonal atmosphere over the dispute, in that the name Kierkegaard was never mentioned. He himself wrote anonymously, and he was attacked under one of the many names he had invented. Thus he was unable to emerge from the fiction with which he had surrounded our conversations, and when he met me—which now occurred rarely—it was with the same politeness as before, although neither he nor I showed any desire for conversation.

But then he identified himself publicly as Victor Eremita, Frater Taciturnus, etc., etc., and immediately thereafter he encountered me in Myntergade and walked past me with an intense and extremely embittered look, without wanting either to greet me or to be greeted.

In the bitterness of that look, as in Kierkegaard's entire personal bearing, there was something that touched upon the comic. But this gave way to something uplifting and ideal that his personality also contained. There was something in that intense, wild look that, as it were, removed the veil from the higher right upon which Kierkegaard had previously insisted, and which I had been unable (but had also been unwilling) to see, despite the fact that I certainly sensed its presence. I felt accused and oppressed: *The Corsair* had triumphed in the battle, yet I myself had acquired a false sense of being number one. But my spirit felt yet another protest arise during that burden-filled moment: I was not the sort of person to be looked down upon, and I could prove it. Walking through the streets, and before I reached home, I arrived at a firm decision to give up *The Corsair*. When I announced it at home they said Thank God!—so happy, but only a little surprised, as if they had known about the matter before I did.

It so happened that the first stranger to whom I reported my decision was the same person with whom I had spoken on the top of Skamlingsbanke, and who had made a wager with me, a reasonable, practical man some years older than myself. He reminded me of the proverb that one should not throw away dirty water until one has obtained clean water. But there exists a form of youthfulness (which need not perish with age) that manifests itself, for example, by throwing the water away as soon as it seems dirty. In fact, the misgivings he had on my behalf were well founded in several respects. *The Corsair* had earned four thousand rixdollars in the previous year, but I had not saved any of it. In addition to a good library I had, at most, a few hundred [rix]dollars. *The Corsair* itself was not really saleable. As soon as I left it, anyone could take the name and continue it. The xylographer Flinch, however, thought that if I would turn it over to him, he could give me ca. fifteen hundred rixdollars for it. Reitzel purchased a volume of short stories I had written, and thus I scraped together approximately four thousand rixdollars, which I divided into two equal portions. I used one portion to travel abroad "in order to be done with witticisms and to learn something."

I was then going on twenty-seven years of age and had been publishing *The Corsair* for six years.

10.[12]

At that time Møller was about to leave on his travels. We had not seen very much of each other since that evening during the dispute with Kierkegaard. Naturally, however, I looked him up on my arrival home [from abroad], and because we had, of course, not personally or deliberately done anything to hurt each other, everything was fine between us, even though a bit cooler and more distant than previously.

On one of the last days of the year, I went out to his place to say goodbye—because his departure, which for quite some time had been put off day after day, seemed to be finally approaching—and on that day he was in his own special sort of ill humor. At that time I still knew very little about him and had very little understanding of his temperament; however, it was he who took the lead in our conversation.

He congratulated me that I could now be cited by Bishop Mynster. Indeed, in time, I might be canonized, and—who knows?—the faithful would make pilgrimages to the shrine that contained my Christian-spirited bones. It is difficult to protect oneself against this sort of congratulation—I myself knew this from the *Corsair* period—and when I tried to defend myself all the same, he said that it was of no use: that in giving up *The Corsair* I had abandoned myself; that it was unnatural for me to desire any "positive good" in public life here in this country; that the corrosive Jewish nature required hatred, and that it was in hatred that I had my strength. His words bore no traces of any vulgar hatred of Jews—that was completely foreign to Møller—but it was a sort of private, comradely conversation, which seemed, in its quiet bitterness, to base itself on an irrefutable fact of world history. Those notions were not really very novel at that time, nor have they become particularly antiquated. When confronted with such an opinion, one can feel embarrassed, as though one were justly accused, because it may contain a certain plausibility, indeed even a bit of truth, but a truth that on the whole and in general must become untruth.

In order to free myself from the weight with which his assertion oppressed me, I changed tactics and asked him: "What have you yourself accomplished by not wanting to do anything positive? What has your aesthetics managed to accomplish for poetry, even if in a merely literary sense? Where are the things we hoped for in times past?" "What do you have against my poetry?" So then I came forward with criticisms of what I could remember, all the way from "Arion" to his recently published poems. It is much worse to criticize a poet verbally than in print; it more readily makes for bad blood. One word led to another, and we were a hair's breadth away from becoming out-and-out bourgeois philistine enemies. Fortunately, at the last instant I reminded him of a pact that we had made to the effect that, for the sake of literature we would, if necessary, oppose one another, thereby keeping ourselves young and strong. With this memory of our shared youth, a youth unusual yet genuine, the storm dissipated, and in a sort of elation he said to me: "Oh, let's fight! I will have the opportunity to say a great deal based on this. Come on!"

I went home and wrote down what I had said, just about as harshly, but with the added prospect of a bright, happy future as a consequence of his journey, and I sent it to him. He sent it back to me, and it was printed in *Nord og Syd* [North and South] (vol. 1, p. 166), with a note that it had been sent to him before his departure.

11.[13]

SELECTIONS FROM GOLDSCHMIDT'S CORRESPONDENCE
CONCERNING KIERKEGAARD

[*M. Goldschmidt to H. P. Barfod, February 28, 1870*]

Shortly after you published the first part of S. Kierkegaard's posthumous papers, I began a letter to you with the intention of debating, in an entirely friendly fashion, your right to revive the "stinging bitterness" of the deceased in that old dispute. But I abandoned it, because I did not want to appear to be placing any obstacles in your path. On other hand, it seems to me that I may dare to ask you where "the challenge to Goldschmidt" (on page xiii, with your quotation marks) is to be found? I would very much like to know, because in the notes I have preserved—a contribution to a sketch of S.K., which I read to Prof. Rasmus Nielsen as much as ten years ago—there is nothing of that sort. There, the entire dispute is seen to stem from P. L. Møller's criticism in *Gæa*, S.K.'s anger at being criticized, the reference to P.L.M. as the real editor of *The*

Corsair, and *The Corsair's* reply. Did you have information to the effect that K. had challenged me? I do not mean to a duel, of course. I can demonstrate that K. personally expressed himself to me in quite another fashion—but that is of course my affair, in the event that I ever wish to do so, and, like this letter, it is an entirely private communication with you, entirely unrelated to the material that you have solicited in your appeal to people who knew the deceased. If you wish, the reply—which I hope you will be kind enough to send me—will also be viewed as entirely confidential.

[*M. Goldschmidt to H. P. Barfod, March 9, 1870*]

Whoever would speak ill of S. Kierkegaard commits a sin of the sort the ancients called *nefas*. Despite his flaws, there was about him a certain inhuman loftiness and also something quite moving—yes, in the deepest sense, something tragic. Anyone who would accuse him of "villainy"—I am using your words, and even with that justification, unwillingly—is either not of sound mind, like an animal, or is a vicious, fanatical theologian. The fact that at a certain moment I wrote about him in a hostile fashion, or aroused his anger, or caused him any suffering, is something that lies outside of and beyond all regret. For one thing, at that time he had not yet grown into being what he later became, and for another, at that time I had within myself a principle—tightly folded together as in the greenest and most unripe of buds—which is utterly opposed to S.K.'s and for which it is my life's task to struggle. For my part, were I to demand leniency where light and shadow are otherwise distributed fairly, it would require a great deal of thoughtlessness (particularly toward myself), and it would thus also be foolish. Therefore I can only reiterate that neither my earlier letter nor this one has any connection whatever with any thought of hindering you. But when everything is clarified you will see how oddly unfair and self-contradictory your words are: "S.K. was extremely fond of you, but he was very displeased with your relation to *The Corsair* or at any rate with that topic in *The Corsair*."

Now we will drop the matter.

[*H. P. Barfod to M. Goldschmidt, May 18, 1872*]

It is almost seven years since I first had the pleasure of meeting you. At that time, I prepared you for the fact that when S. Kierkegaard's papers were published, they would contain fierce attacks on your connection with *The Corsair* and on your relation to S.K.'s activity as an author. At that time, you said that you would therefore have to prepare yourself and take measures to defend yourself against hostile views that might arise in the literary world. To treat S.K.'s "Posthumous Papers" as though they did not contain these pages seemed to me untruthful and impossible. And it also seems to me that your situation is more advantageous if you yourself are able to reply to the deceased than it would be if these portions [of Kierkegaard's papers] first saw the light of day after you had departed from the field of battle!

[M. Goldschmidt to F. Hendriksen, March 18, 1878]

Since I have occasion to write, I will add the remark that I now assume it is settled that it will be not Borchsenius but L[udvig] S[chrøder] who will write about me in *Ude og hjemme* [Abroad and at Home], and thus I would hope, among other things, that S. does not identify me entirely with *The Corsair*, as B[orchsenius] has done. Because, despite the fact that I bear the moral responsibility for everything that appeared in that journal, I by no means wrote it all, and it is thus wrong—both from the point of view of the history of literature and from the biographical point of view—to attribute it all to me. Similarly, I may assume that the relationship to S. Kierkegaard will be presented not simply in accordance with S.K.'s violent and abusive language but also in accordance with the presentation that I myself have given in my autobiography. It is also possible that I will soon publish a little comment on B.'s unexplained—and for me inexplicable—use of the above-mentioned abusive language, although it goes without saying that my comment will not be needed by anyone who will open his eyes to all the material that is available.

[M. Goldschmidt to O. Borchsenius, March 25, 1878]

But now I come to the worst part—or I will touch upon the detail in the book where in my opinion *the facts* are wrong. It is a fact that *The Corsair* did battle with S. Kierkegaard and that K. abused me frightfully. It is furthermore a fact that many of those still living have an incorrect understanding of the dispute. Later developments have been transferred to an earlier period, and people imagine that in those days S.K. stood in a religious nimbus and, with his halo over his head, passed judgment upon *The Corsair*—and that I, consequently, attacked him like a demon. You do not really contribute to clearing this matter up. You say that S.K. was unable to understand the significance of *The Corsair*. He was able to understand it very well, or he was able to remain personally friendly with me for five years. And then came the moment when he *did not want to* understand. So, with his personality and his passionate feelings, and because [he had been the target] of a literary critique, he labeled P. L. Møller a tramp, and he named him as the real editor of *The Corsair*—*and this was the source of the entire dispute.* All the articles against Kierkegaard in *The Corsair* stem from this unjust action of his. And all the artistry with which S.K. desired to give the affair the appearance that he sought "martyrdom" for purely ideal reasons, that he *wanted* to be attacked by *The Corsair*, cannot outweigh the simple, clear truth. Having called P. L. Møller the evil genius behind *The Corsair*, S.K. did not want to get involved with the question of his own wrongdoing, but said that I was in it for the money, that I was cowardly, and left it at that. All of S.K.'s abusive epithets are variations on this theme, while he also shrewdly protested against the idea that he was accusing me *as a Jew*! Why can the affair not be presented with this factual simplicity and truth (cf. my autobiography), without thereby denying in any way that S.K. was a remarkable genius of a man and in many ways a fine person? My lips are sealed with respect to his errors and his shortcomings. I cannot be forced to be an unwilling witness, and I have no desire to criticize the dead. The only thing I want to emphasize in this private letter is that I have been astounded by his inextinguishable hatred and resentment. He was a "Christian religious genius," and he could not even manage to forgive in a dispute in which nothing was said that touched upon his honor and in which no private matters were brought forth. It was not enough for him that I rid myself of *The Corsair*. He demanded that I put my neck under his foot, and his bitterness seemed even to increase. The Christians seem to be able to look upon such an Indian-style sort of hatred without amazement. I am afraid of sounding pharisaical, and yet I *must* say that when one views things in the light of the idea of Nemesis, one can no longer hate. Apropos of that, I must add that it pained me to see that at one point you use the word "Nemesis" about me—in its old, vulgar meaning. I ask that when you speak of me in the future you would do me the kindness either of using "N." in the sense that I have assigned the word or of using another word with which to express your thoughts. Is this not a reasonable request, and can you not forgive me for making it?

Finally, I come to the abusive language itself, which you copy down and reprint repeatedly with a certain literary relish. For you it is a *fact* that I have been abused so "mightily" and "violently." You seem to forget that I am alive, and that the renewed brutality can inflict injury. *You* have not *wanted* to cause injury—I assume that quite definitely. But you have neglected to make an argument that I would make as follows:

You have of course been paid royalties for the articles when they appeared in *Nær og Fjern* [Near and Far] and in book form. You were not unaware that the abusive language and that sort of thing were spicy and could attract readers. But you would be completely correct in feeling that it was a grievous injustice if someone said that you had repeated that mass of abuse only in order to make money by doing so. I therefore think that you have forgotten to express your displeasure that this sort of unruliness had been expressed. And this is not to mention that S.K.'s words could of course also be read as an accusation against me for having accepted money in order to attack or refrain from attacking people. If this latter were the case, then the brutality of the abusive language goes beyond the bounds of all propriety, and indeed becomes as vile as the alleged actions of *The Corsair* would have been if they in truth had actually taken place. I thus reproach you for having dipped your pen a little too much into that—passion.

It seems to me that wherever you cite my words they sound either gentle or cultivated, which corresponds to the fact that I have practically never brought charges of libel against the many people who have abused me. Attorneys have said that I could easily have won cases against those concerned, but I held to the old principles from the 1840s, namely, that the press and that freedom in general must themselves heal the wounds that they cause. Must this now appear as a great error on my part? Have I been wrong, for example, in not holding Barfod responsible for what he allowed to be published? And what should I do in the future? You seem, with a sort of literary delight, to be awaiting new outbursts against me in S.K.'s journals, and must these be printed and reprinted again and again, merely because they are a "fact"?

You see, a fact is not always so entirely simple to deal with. Now, there is one fact that I don't know but that I would like to take this occasion to discover: are you thin-skinned, or are you not? Can you bear it that I have dared to make these comments instead of saying some general words of thanks for this book? In any case, remember that I was compelled to reply as I have done here because if I had remained silent you would later be able to say that I had conceded everything.

I also point out that, although I am writing this letter as an entirely private matter, I of course reserve the right to make use of its contents at some point.

[*M. Goldschmidt to O. Borchsenius, April 22, 1878*]

Not even two literary people such as you and I can write to one another without generating misunderstandings that disturb the good will with which we approached one another. The greatest misunderstanding, which I therefore will address immediately, is that you believe that in my last letter I accused you of publishing your literary sketches, or even of writing them, with an eye to financial gain. I wrote that you could *rightly* call it a *grievous injustice* if anyone said that you had collected and published the abusive language for the sake of gaining readers with that spicy material, i.e., for the sake of money. But I also said, just as firmly, that you should feel, and that you should have said, that Kierkegaard committed a grievous injustice when he said that *The Corsair* was written for the sake of making money and insinuated the vile notion that by paying money, people could protect themselves from being attacked or could cause someone else to be attacked. I intended no insinuations against you; the whole tone of my letter testifies sufficiently to the fact that I regard you as an honorable man. But, just as you have the right to earn greater or lesser royalties for your work without anyone being entitled to yell Hep! Hep! Tradesman! at you, so ought I— especially in view of the information I have provided about the origins of *The Corsair*—to be safe from such name calling and from having to defend myself from it, whether it comes from the living or from the dead.

This point was the point of my letter. This was my real criticism or objection to the completeness with which you included various sorts of abusive language. And I still believe that you have instinctively adopted the view that it was really for religious reasons, to become a "martyr," that Kierkegaard hurled himself against *The Corsair*, and that his "mightiness" is thus encircled with a halo. Against this I cite the simple facts, in which K.'s extraordinary irritability, vanity, etc., play a role. Privately, I may permit myself to dwell on K.'s darker side; I would never do so publicly, and even privately it would be difficult for me to abandon my evenhandedness and refuse to acknowledge K.'s shining qualities.

I must add that if I had thought for an instant of letting my previous letter to you *appear in print*, I would have published it *immediately*. I will make use of its *contents*, but in a different fashion from what you imagine. I will explain this to you when we can talk.

On the whole, I think it would be best if we continued and concluded this discussion by talking to each other. I will soon return home, and I will take the liberty of visiting you.

[*M. Goldschmidt to O. Borchsenius, December 25, 1878*]

What is it that I want you to "correct" and "take back" concerning S. Kierkegaard and me? It is difficult to answer that question in the form in which it is put because any genuine retraction is and ought to be out of the question.

But here is a little comment.

What has pained me in what has happened, and what has—against your will—also injured me, was the repetition of S.K.'s abusive language and his accusations. Naturally, you cannot make what has been printed become unprinted, but neither do you need to print any more of that sort of thing.

Next, concerning *the issue* itself, I believe that K. understood *The Corsair* very well. It seems to me that one powerful bit of evidence is that he counseled me and assigned to me, as my task, to produce "comic composition." In my autobiography I have emphasized how he understood the mission of *The Corsair* in those days; how he adopted an aesthetic posture, quite indifferent to his soul and his personality; and how he thus came to "sharpen the point upon which he was later impaled."

This is of course inseparable from the fact that in those days, despite misunderstandings, for us younger people K. really was the chief representative of the aesthetic understanding of life.

Then he became angry with *The Corsair* because the journal, or I myself, had taken arms against the injustice he had committed, because of some literary criticism, in going after P. L. Møller so violently and attacking him as the real *Corsair*. *The entire dispute of course revolved around this.*

S.K. is dead. In the eyes of many people he stands as something of a saintly figure with a halo around his head. Because of this, many people cannot understand that in 1845 he was a simple mortal who could err, who had in fact a strong streak of egoism or vanity, and that he deservedly brought upon himself the harsh attacks, which for their part went beyond reasonable limits—although people now believe that they were worse than they actually were. Nothing evil or touching upon his honor was printed about him. I have tried to sketch this myself, of course, and I did it in so gentle a fashion that it surprised you. Someone else could perhaps do it equally gently, but in another sense better, more comprehensively, and with more insight.

S.K. became for me at first a means of "comic composition," and then—when I had practiced my art on him—he became the major cause of my ridding myself entirely of *The Corsair*. In that significant moment of my life I arrived at a painful ideality, which many years later cast a sort of brilliant illumination into my soul. It was a part of the development of the idea of Nemesis—which of course is at work in its own way in each person's existence.

[*M. Goldschmidt to O. Borchsenius, January 8, 1879*]

Many people live like animals, merely subjected to their fates. Our true, human task should be to tear ourselves and others out of that existence and make ourselves subject to "Nemesis"—that is, "*to acknowledge* the order of things and to bring ourselves to order."

Now this is of course precisely what I have attempted to do in my portrayal of my birth, my childhood, my youth, *The Corsair*, P. L. Møller, S. Kierkegaard, and in the Nemesis essay itself. I have demonstrated, or have wanted to demonstrate, the common development of the idea of Nemesis in an individual as paradigmatic. It is a nondogmatic religiousness, supported by universal human testimony. By avoiding tendentiousness I have shown how the idea grew up from its origins: from my blood and my race; from my father's talk about the secret law (at the burning field of rape plants); from my father's love, which was able to give me things he himself did not possess; from the [signal] bells that rang out along the path (the threads of Nemesis, by which the world is woven together); from the way in which *The Corsair* came into being; from the editors who bore legal responsibility for it, and from the backlash against it; from P.L.M. and S.K., who called me to aesthetics and to comic composition; from the collision with S.K., which led me to give up the *The Corsair* and gain a larger life.

12.[14]
P.L.M. AND S.K.

Both were so unhappy that when one considers their fates, the anxiety one has with regard to the enormous gravity of life sometimes becomes intensified to a terror that is greater than anxiety because it contains an admixture of unclarity. . . . The unhappiness of each of them was in its own way total, but there was no similarity, either in content or in origin.

M.'s [unhappiness] stemmed from the fact that he was immersed too firmly or too deeply in sensual existence and lacked the great and saving assistance that, under certain conditions, wealth can confer on a person. Later, more was required, and it did not come—love. K.'s unhappiness gradually emerged from the circumstance that his involvement in sensual existence lacked sufficient firmness or depth, and the central point was his engagement and the end of that engagement. Had K. become a married man, life would have given him troubles enough—yes, unhappiness—but not despair.

The difference between them was not that between an aesthete and an ethicist. P.L.M. was not entirely an aesthete. He did not act in accordance with a system. He was led to the decisive issues of his life by that which was within him. And he succumbed in a uniquely characteristic struggle with ethics, in hand-to-hand combat with the ethical, because he was incapable of embracing [the ethical] so that he was purified by it. S.K. was much more of an aesthete than P.L.M. Life's either/or was extraordinarily clear to him, and if he had had the natural strength to do so, he would have been able to carry out the aesthetic; he would have taken up life as a task of beauty and would have broken himself upon it. He chose "or," but he did so fully as much in his capacity as an author as he did as a person. He took up the entirety of ethics and everything connected with it, as a problem of knowledge; it could never become a question for his personality so simply and completely that it was a source of peace to him, because passage through the natural bliss and woe of life is a part of life and of life's peace. One might be tempted to say that if he had not been born wealthy but had been forced at an early age to battle against financial worries, it would have been his salvation not as an author but as a human being. This is because he was endowed with an idealistic tendency that, however, when all is said and done, is more profound and complete when it is divorced from materialism.

Both died in anger. I do not mean the moment of death itself, but the visible transition to death. I confess that I get a feeling as if the hair were about to rise on the back of my neck when I think of P.L.M.—there in that foreign land and entirely alone, in a perpetual, ill-tempered, misanthropic battle with his fate— meeting that fate one night on the highway and being killed by it. How extremely different this was from K.'s end. He [Kierkegaard] raised himself up for the last time with all his spiritual power in order to make demands of others on behalf of the idea or the ideal. He did not claim that what he demanded *could* be met by humanity, but that it *should*. He asserted this with an anger that was mixed with the feelings of a wounded personality. He elevated spiritual ecstasy and renunciation to such heights that the pain still quivers in the spirits of many. And then he went to the hospital, to his deathbed.

13.[15]

ON S.K.'s PHYSIOGNOMY

It is not my task to give a rounded picture of Kierkegaard or to pronounce any judgment on what he was. I am presenting only what he appeared to be at the time.

He looked like a person who was elevated above many or most of the ordinary conditions and temptations of life, though not in such a way that he seemed enviable or happy. The shape of his body was striking, not really ugly, certainly not repulsive, but with something disharmonious, rather slight, and yet also weighty. He went about like a thought that had got distracted at the very moment at which it was formed. According to what one generally heard about him and saw of him, he seemed to live only as a thought and to concern himself with human beings only insofar as they were the objects of thought. There was a sort of unreality about him. I cannot, of course, know how he was viewed by the very few who were intimately connected with him, but for myself and for the others who saw him "in his salon on the street," he was the sort of person to whom one could tell one's sorrows, not in order for him to feel them and share them but in order for him to investigate them. The result would nonetheless be a certain comfort, because his "unreality" was not so much dead cold or stone cold but was the coolness of the higher regions, of the starry heavens. Very often he was superior and ironic by means of the slightest bit of contrariness, so that one felt it as arrogance and mockery, but one also felt that there was a vast background that justified it. He could make one [feel] very small, but in that crushing experience there was finally something uplifting, if one could stand being uplifted in that manner. One of K.'s contemporaries, a very gifted attorney, now deceased, who practiced before the Supreme Court and who needed all his strength and self-confidence in order to maintain himself in his work, once said to me: "I cannot endure K.'s arrogance. He leads one into problems with which he has the time to concern himself, but which we others have had to give up for the sake of living, and then he leaves one standing there, naked, as it were, and despondent. . . . And then he [Kierkegaard] conclude[s] by saying: 'The others can entrust their ideas to me; I cannot use them, and I will not use them. I can also entrust my ideas to them; they would like to use them, but they cannot.' One must not be so arrogant, even if one is a genius— because that he is."

It was either the above-cited person or another of K.'s contemporaries who told me that he [Kierkegaard] used a considerable portion of his large inheritance in order to purchase an annuity, and that he used the rest in publishing his books, independent of the public. I do not know whether that part (about the annuity) is true, but even his supposed fortune helped to intensify the aura of "unreality." He was lifted up over the burdens and urges of material life. He contained his own motive force. He served the Idea as the freest of volunteers. He had no need to curb any eccentricity if it suited his personal whims. He could even lift himself above the secret jury that, for us others, stands in the background and helps us, in our efforts to please, to seek only to please the best. But, nonetheless, there is still room for doubt as to whether he was any less a member of the genus *irritabile poetæ* than other people.

I did not really like him, even though he was always attractive. Even his speech repelled me, because it was forced and mannered, and because its "manner" was colored by egoism and vanity. And yet I was sometimes completely transported by admiration, for example, of *Stages on Life's Way*. I particularly read his book *Repetition*, perhaps because it is the most comprehensible. How uncomfortable I could feel every time he gave a description of reality. It was deceptively realistic, but never completely so. The real freshness of life was missing. Everything was produced by thought. But it was well done. The flower was imitated so deceptively that one wished to smell it—and then the disappointment! This defect or this characteristic irritated me, and I felt that I sensed another, greater defect every time I had read a section and paused: he had no love in his heart; he did not love people, and therefore he was neither gentle nor humble in his heart. Suppose (on p. 96) instead of "mentally disordered" it were to read "un-loving." But after all this and despite all this, gradually a feeling emerges with great clarity. He was part of an enormous, shining world of thought. He carried it within himself. There was a sort of Olympus in his head—clear, blessed gods of thought. There was interest not in an individual but in all of humanity. There was a strange purity and consequently a strange power. And when he stood before me in that form, I realized that he was the sort of person to whom one must really give way with hat in hand, taking no notice of his minor weaknesses. And when I suddenly remembered that I was precisely the person who had been fatally led to attack his weaknesses, a veil descended, something both pleasant and unpleasant, in which I could wrap myself and shield myself from the thought [that I had been led to attack him]: [this veil consisted in the fact that] he himself took it so jovially, was not wounded, did not suffer from it.

I certainly admire S.K. for his gifts and for a purity that was surely connected to a certain lack of physical health and strength. What I felt repelled by was the quality or qualities that characteristically emerged in his language or style. It was not individual words or sentences, not the structure of his paragraphs, but the innermost tone of his language, which, when compared to its wealth and color, is nervous and overbearing. It does not stem from loving obedience to his mother tongue but is marked by the fact that he loved his language because it bore witness to his intellectual superiority, so that he could gambol about with its idioms in his own unique manner. In this, his two principal failings—lack of gentle, simple love and lack of humility—combine with his ideal love of hu-manity and his religious idealism. His style is so pronounced as to be unmistak-able. It is as though he were afraid to allow any truth to go forth into the world without the stamp "S.K." upon it, and it is the effort to produce that stamp which makes his style displeasing to me. This emphatic urge to put his stamp on things also contributed to the breakdown of his health. I can understand his extraordinary significance as a Christian thinker, and perhaps I can dare to say—of course, as part of a thought experiment in which I adopt a Christian stand-point—that I am able to admire it. But my blood, my nature, my thought processes, my will place me in an extremely antagonistic relation to "the Para-dox." And when I say this, I am consequently subject to Nemesis because either I am in error and ought therefore to atone for my error until I have corrected it, or I am right and must then substantiate my case to the best of my ability.

In relation to the notion of Nemesis I believe that there was something in S.K.'s existence that occasioned and required that he have such a collision and suffer the remarkable, irritating pain that it is clear he suffered. But it was up to him to make use of the pain itself, to respond to it, in the manner he wished. And it was I—not by chance, but as though prepared for this from the very begin-ning—who was to be the instrument by means of which this happened to him. And it was I—in some senses a blind instrument, and in other senses a responsible instrument—who was to experience all the consequences that resided in my nature as possibilities. It was I who was to be lifted by him and who would in later years be confronted by that being who—in dying and after his death—continued, as an idea, to grow toward me and watch over me. And as a consequence of this, it was also I who would at first come to suffer—blind suffering, like an animal that is beaten. But it was likewise I who would thereafter be able to make use of this suffering, in relation to this and to a great many other things, in order to gain insight into the justice of existence and to come to understand why I did not become "number one" in life—the possibility had hovered before me—and had to look to something different.

Now, that something lies concealed in these words, that I am aiming at something other and greater than what is presented here, is of course clear enough and could not be otherwise. This is so because what I have presented here did not extend beyond my twenty-sixth year, and because there is no way that the relationship to Kierkegaard could in itself have been decisive for my existence, but only [a] small part of a coherent whole, a paradigm in accordance with which the word is declined and conjugated.

14.[16]

ON S.K., AESTHETICALLY-CRITICALLY

The difference between the aesthetic and the ethical views of life is often stated thus: that the former views life as an object of enjoyment, whereas the latter sees life as a means or an instrument in service of something higher, as a prelude to death and immortality. This is correct enough, but it does not prevent us from viewing the activity of a life, which essentially moves in solitude, in fantasy, in poetry, or speculation (philosophy)—however much it may emphasize the ethical and proceed from an ethically determined personality—as profoundly colored by aesthetics and by what is pleasing to the self. This is especially clear when that life is compared with the life that connects itself actively and lovingly with society and that has a greater or lesser circle of reality to which it personally sacrifices itself for the sake of a goal.

My task is not to judge S.K. in any way or to provide a sketch of his existence as a person or as an author, but only to reproduce as completely as possible the impression he made upon me, and this must include the fact that he awakened the most distinct sense that, whatever profound and painful sacrifice he had achieved in his life, he nonetheless had not directed his intellect and his will toward the sacrifice that makes one humble and gentle. For him, both his philosophical and his actual personality stood in an extraordinary nimbus. Indeed, one could say what I once in fact said to one of his friends, who agreed with me, namely that for him [Kierkegaard] the Christianity that he confessed was not something of which he had a small part but something that was a part of him. There is undeniably something proud and brilliant about being such a personality, having such a sense of oneself, standing with one's consciousness elevated over the entire world. But it is an aesthetic sort of pride, and properly understood it was therefore not such a great misunderstanding when, in those days, we—or I—instinctively looked up to S.K. as the great aesthete, as the person who had achieved what we ourselves, with our coarser personalities, wanted to achieve, namely the highest spiritual egotism, the highest self-enjoyment.

Naturally, this last point must not be overemphasized. There are people who will find great joy in saying that a single genuine ethical deed is greater than writing a hundred ethical books. Yes, but where do these ethical books come from? Don't people think that they are the result of a feat that the personal self remembers having performed, a feat that not only makes possible the ideas contained in the books but also gives those ideas the power with which to seize hold of the readers' spirits?

Chapter Six

AFTER *THE CORSAIR*: THE PERIPATETIC AND CONTROVERSIALIST OF THE LATER 1840S

Anna Brosbøll[1]

Hansine Thorbjørnsen had another—not very pleasant—experience shortly after her engagement to Carl Brosbøll. While on a walk they met Magister Søren Kierkegaard. When Brosbøll presented his fiancée, Kierkegaard said only: "Well, oh yes, you have got engaged to this little girl, Brosbøll!"

To Hansine Thorbjørnsen's surprise, Carl Brosbøll became upset both with her and with Søren Kierkegaard, because he had called her—she was scarcely seventeen years old—a "little girl" and not "a lady."

Frederik Nielsen[2]

It was still in the period of pseudonyms although everyone knew who the author was, and the thin little man, whom you could meet one moment at Østerport and the next on the entirely opposite side of town, apparently a carefree peripatetic, was recognized by everyone.

Arthur Abrahams[3]

One day we met *Søren Kierkegaard*. It was outside of town, and we took a long walk with him on the paths by the lakes. I naturally have no notion of what he and my father spoke about, and even if I had listened I would scarcely have understood any of it. But what I do remember clearly is that, as I walked along, all the while I kept looking to see whether he really had one short and one long trouser leg. I had of course seen him depicted like that many times in *The Corsair*, which we often received on loan and which I used for "looking at pictures." When I come to think of it, his entire person comes into clear focus for me: the high shoulders; the restless, somewhat hopping gait; and the little, thin cane with which he flicked off the tips of the plants and blades of grass along the edge of the path. When, at a more mature age, I read *Either/Or* and *Stages on Life's Way* and came across Kierkegaard's repeated accounts of the many observations he made on his wanderings through the streets of Copenhagen, that walk was fixed forever as a living memory.

Willy Schorn[4]

Søren Kierkegaard was a pseudonymous author with whom I never had a close association except when I walked alongside of him. What I mean by this is that when I was a boy and my father and I took walks together we sometimes met the doctor [Søren Kierkegaard], who would then accompany us. I trotted alongside and of course did not understand a word of the grownups' conversation. I knew only that it concerned serious matters. I had often heard my father say that he [Kierkegaard] sought enlightenment with respect to [the] most profound spiritual questions, sometimes with Sibbern, sometimes with Mynster, and I felt that something similar was taking place in these conversations. However, I had often seen Søren Kierkegaard's likeness in *The Corsair*, where he was of course always depicted with the one trouser leg shorter than the other. Therefore, on these walks it was more important for me to observe his remarkable trouser leg than his remarkable face.

August Bournonville[5]

An excellent Danish philosopher has written a lengthy dissertation on the concept of irony. In all modesty, I confess that I have not yet read it, just as I have only read and digested very little else by that author. On the other hand, I often had the pleasure of walking with him and of refreshing myself from his inexhaustible font of wit and perspicacity. I learned this much: that *irony* is not synonymous with ridicule, mockery, or bitterness, but is on the contrary an important element in our spiritual existence—the fortification with alcohol that takes away the sickly sweetness of the grapes, the jet of cold water that cools the fever—in brief, the smile through the tears, which prevents us from becoming lachrymose.

Frederik Hammerich[6]

During the time that he [Kierkegaard] deliberately arranged his personal life so as to counteract his writings, like so many people in Copenhagen I regularly ran into him on the street and on the promenade atop the ramparts of the city. Then he would take me by the arm, as though he had no other use for his time. While he walked, he of course thought up the words for other things, which he subsequently wrote down. How words could pour forth from him, now profound thoughts, now humorous whimsy!

One afternoon, I remember, I was going for a walk in the woods with my father, and he [Søren Kierkegaard] met us and his brother out near Bellevue. The weather was lovely. The sun played with the leaves, and the shadows were doubly dark in contrast to the clear, green light that shone through the leaves. I said something about it. "Oh yes, you know," he said, "it's pretty enough, but you get bored with that sort of soulless beauty. Do you think that's why I come here? No. I have to take a bath, and in Copenhagen, of course, it's swarming all over with Jew-boys. So I took a coach and got my bath, and now I'm finished and I'm driving right home again."

When his brother later became pastor at Pedersborg-by-Sorø, he [Søren] could behave in the same fashion on the rare occasions when he thought of going out there. He rented a coach all for himself, rode ten miles on the dusty country road, stayed at his brother's for a couple of hours, gave his best wishes to his sister-in-law, ate dinner, and immediately thereafter drove back to Copenhagen. "Such an odd fellow," they said about him and laughed, which is exactly what he wanted at that point in order to scare off everyone except "that individual." At home in his hermitage he almost never saw anyone; only poor people and my nephew Emil Boesen had access to him.

When I walked with him I heard him talk about his writings in terms that practically overflowed with hubris. Was it meant sincerely, or was it to be understood dialectically, spoken as pretense? Of all the pastors in Copenhagen, there was none he would rather hear than Visby, and once again I had to ask him if he was serious about this or not. When you are dealing with an ironist, an "observer," you never really know: he wants to have the run of you; you are to be pumped and used. That is the only thing you can figure out, and it most definitely repels you.

Nor was I attracted very much to those writings, despite their dazzling brilliance. For me they were too dialectically involved, too twisted, and I therefore preferred to satisfy myself by browsing through them. The life-contrasts portrayed in *Either/Or* I myself had experienced more profoundly and completely, albeit without the passionate strength with which they appear in that book. At that time I had found my peace in my faith in Jesus Christ as Redeemer—but also as he who makes the world complete—and that was better than the peace to be found in *Either/Or*. With the pseudonyms I was again most struck by the passion, the religious passion. I was not unappreciative of the position that S. Kierkegaard took "in existence" vis-à-vis the arrogance of thought. Nor did I fail to appreciate his wonderfully sharp sense for spiritual things or the voice that emanated from the depths of conscience, which resounded mightily and has captivated so many people. But I had no use for a Christianity that was solitary and overwrought, oppressively melancholic, full of delusions and legalistic demands, and bitter toward society. I had too historical a nature for that sort of thing.

Julie Weber Sødring[7]

Along with his work in the theater, Father always had time to continue his studies, not only of his beloved Latin writers but also of the works of more recent authors, especially historical and philosophical works. During the period I am here discussing, it was specifically Søren Kierkegaard to whom he felt attracted. As mentioned earlier, he knew Kierkegaard personally, and they often took long walks together. It was impossible not to turn around and look when one met these two peculiar figures: Father in his large greatcoat, which he liked so much, "because," as he said, "when I pull it up around my ears no one recognizes me"—and Kierkegaard, limping along with his short trouser legs and swinging his little cane. The point of contact between Father and Kierkegaard was their common joy in experimentation. Together they experienced an uncountable number of curious little events. This is the source of the stories about the time that Father went to a poor woman and gave her a five-rixdollar bill, whereupon he and Kierkegaard delighted in her surprise, and about the time that they found a two-rixdollar coin and gave it to a rascal, politely saying, "Wouldn't you be good enough to drop this off if you should *by chance* go past a police station?"

Father had come from his home in order to congratulate me [on my wedding day]. On the way he met Søren Kierkegaard who fell into conversation with him. They stopped outside my uncle's house in Kronprinsessegade. Then Father pointed up to the windows and said, "Can you see? Something moved up there." "Yes," answered Kierkegaard, observing the windows carefully, "isn't it a bride?" "It's my daughter!" said Father, and a moment later he put his head in the door and nodded to me.

F. L. Liebenberg[8]

If I did not benefit much from my old classmate Søren Kierkegaard's famous product *Either/Or*, published in 1843, it was certainly because of my own inadequacies. The same goes for the publications that teemed from him over the next ten years. It was not that I was blind to the dazzling brilliance of this author's work, but its true significance was not clear to me, and I allowed myself to be put off by the style. Chiefly, I was irritated here, as in his theological works, by being continually confronted with "the paradox" and with "belief by virtue of the absurd." It seemed to me that every idea was pushed to the extreme. The fictitious characters failed to come to life for me, and the frequent pretentious lectures seemed so tiresomely lengthy that I could not bear to get very involved with these books. But I had liked Søren himself from our boyhood years, and when I met him on the street and walked a bit with him, which happened not infrequently, I always found him just as friendly and amiable as he was entertaining. Unfortunately I now only remember three somewhat atypical remarks from these occasions, but perhaps they are worth reading. We spoke one day about typographical errors. "One must not be very angry at the typesetters," he said. "Their misreadings may often suggest to authors significant thoughts that would not otherwise have occurred to them." I could not exactly agree with this, though they no doubt did the author a service from time to time by the chance typesetting of the proper, natural word, which he had missed. Another time, when I complained about being disturbed by some building construction next to and across from my house, he said: "And yet, if you found a home where it was as silent as a tomb, you would not be able to stand it." Once he said, "Now I must go home and write; I work certain definite hours every day." "But can you always be ready at a particular hour?" I asked. "If I am not when I sit down," he answered, "it comes quite soon."

Carl Koch[9]

There was someone who told me that he had once seen Grundtvig and Søren Kierkegaard walking together on Østergade. Grundtvig strode along, big and calm. Kierkegaard hopped about restlessly, now on the one side of his companion, now on the other, all the while engaged in lively discussion. Then they came to the gate at which Grundtvig was to enter. He promptly tipped his hat; Kierkegaard bowed deeply and removed his hat with great deference.

O. P. Sturzen-Becker[10]

S. *Kierkegaard* is an author who cannot really be called a poet—particularly because the necessary hallmark of a poet is of course that he understands the noble art of rhyme—but he at any rate has at least one foot within the domain of aesthetic literature. He first appeared in the year 1843 under the pseudonym "Victor Eremita" with his *Either/Or*, a work that, despite its essentially speculative subject matter, nonetheless contains episodes that employ the conventions of the novel. It has attracted a great deal of attention from the Danish literary world. Since then, with incredible productivity—and in this respect he constitutes a genuinely striking exception to the general remark I made about the relatively limited productivity of Danish writers—and under constantly changing pseudonyms, he has produced to date an entire little library, constituted primarily of large, thick, octavo volumes crammed with fine print. One month he has the name "Johannes de Silentio," another month "Constantin Constantius," next "Vigilius Haufniensis," then "Nicolaus Notabene," "Johannes Climacus," and "Hilarius Bookbinder." All these works could be viewed as speculative fantasies of a sort, of greater or lesser extent, even including entire symphonies, as it were. Kierkegaard himself calls them "thought experiments," his favorite term, and, with a truly remarkable talent, he discusses almost everything in the world at once—topics of a metaphysical nature as well as aesthetic, psychological, and social themes—holding it all together by means of the bass melody provided by dialectics as well as the incessant piping of "Socratic irony." In truth, Kierkegaard is the [Johann] Sebastian Bach of dialectics. No less true, however, is the fact that these clever, profound, ironic, and sophistical fantasies—which certainly do contain bits of real poetry here and there, but whose meaning and tendency are not always easy to understand—are pretty much inaccessible to the general public. And this raises the important question of whether—if one excepts *Either/Or*, which is indisputably Kierkegaard's most

human work—the actual works of this entire pseudonymous "Eremita" literature are more famous than they are read. But Kierkegaard happens to be a
wealthy man, and he can afford to continue these thought experiments—which
are all formed by his unusual genius, and the publication of which would bank-
rupt another author—for as long as he likes, even if only for his private enjoyment. Everyone has his own sort of luxury.

Kierkegaard's private life is just as unique as his writing. He cannot be said to
associate with anyone in the ordinary sense of the term, and he is a complete
peripatetic who wanders around the streets of Copenhagen without any goal at
all, from morning until late at night, in all weather and all seasons. But if he
meets anyone he knows during these walks, he unhesitatingly brings him along
and immediately gets involved in a conversation into which he always easily
mixes all sorts of profound and clever remarks on all manner of things, and in
this fashion he "associates" with quite a number of people. If, by means of this
endless peripateticism, it has been his intention to provoke people into posing
the question, "But, my God! How does this man find time to write all the thick
volumes he publishes?" he has fully accomplished this goal, and it cannot be
denied that the works themselves look a bit incomprehensible. At certain times
he disappears for a week or two from Østergade or from the arcades of Christiansborg Castle. Then we know that he is staying in Greifswald or Stettin—I
don't know exactly which city—where he supposedly has a strong preference
for one particular room in a certain hotel, and is therefore willing and ready to
take the room as soon as it is available. Other people add other, no less English,
eccentricities. One can believe as much of this as one wishes, and most of it may
be nothing but sheer hoax. Still, we are left with the fact that the man is in every
respect a very peculiarly secretive person and certainly one of the most interesting people Copenhagen has within its walls.

Frederikke Bremer[11]

Whereas the brilliant Martensen, from his central standpoint, sheds light upon
the entire sphere of existence and upon all the phenomena of life, *Sören Kierkegaard* stands on his isolated pillar like a Simeon Stylites, his gaze fixed un-
interruptedly on a single point. He places his microscope over this point, carefully investigating the tiniest atoms, the most fleeting motions, the innermost
alterations. And it is about this that he speaks and writes endless folios. For him,
everything is to be found at this point. But this point is—the human heart.
And—because he unceasingly has this changeable heart reflect itself in the Eternal and Unchangeable that "became flesh and dwelt among us"; because he says
divine things in the course of his exhausting wanderings—he has gained a not
inconsiderable audience in happy, pleasant Copenhagen, particularly among
ladies. The philosophy of the heart must be of importance to them. Concerning
the philosopher who writes on these matters—people speak well and ill, and
strangely. He who writes for "that single individual" lives alone, inaccessible

and, when all is said and done, known by no one. During the daytime one sees him walking in the midst of the crowd, up and down the busiest streets of Copenhagen for hours at a time. At night his lonely dwelling is said to glow with light. The cause of this [behavior] seems to be less his wealth and independence than a sickly and irritable nature, which can find occasion to be displeased with the sun itself when its rays shine in a direction other than what he wishes. Something like the transformation about which he writes so often seems to have taken place within him, however, and it has led him from being the doubt-plagued author of *Either/Or*, via *Anxiety and Trembling* [*sic*], to the brilliant heights from which he speaks with inexhaustible bombast about *The Gospel of Sufferings*, about *Works of Love*, and about "the mysteries of the inner life." S. Kierkegaard is one of the rare, involuted types who have been found in Scandinavia (more frequently in Sweden than in Denmark) since the earliest days, and it is to like-minded spirits that he speaks of the sphinx within the human breast and of the quiet, mysterious, and all-powerful heart.

Camilla Collett[12]

[After discouraging receptions from both Christian Winther and Hans Christian Andersen], things went no better with Søren Kierkegaard. When she [Camilla Collett] went to visit him, filled with naive enthusiasm, he was proclaimed to be not at home. When she reached the street, she glanced up at the building one more time and was very surprised to see the philosopher standing by his window, very much at home. Unaccustomed to visits by ladies, he nonetheless wanted to have a look at this pushy person. Their gazes met, and they involuntarily nodded to one another in surprise.

Andrew Hamilton[13]

There is a man whom it is impossible to omit in any account of Denmark, but whose place it might be more difficult to fix; I mean Søren Kierkegaard. But as his works have, at all events for the most part, a religious tendency, he may find a place among the theologians. He is a philosophical Christian writer, evermore dwelling, one might almost say harping, on the theme of the human heart. There is no Danish writer more in earnest than he, yet there is no one in whose way stand more things to prevent his becoming popular. He writes at times with an unearthly beauty, but too often with an exaggerated display of logic that disgusts the public. All very well, if he were not a popular author, but it is for this he intends himself.

I have received the highest delight from some of his books. But no one of them could I read *with pleasure* all the way through. His *Works of Love* has, I suppose, been the most popular, or perhaps, his *Either/Or*, a very singular book. A little thing published during my stay, gave me much pleasure, *Sickness unto Death*.

Kierkegaard's habits of life are singular enough to lend a (perhaps false) interest in his proceedings. He goes into no company, and sees nobody in his own house, which answers all the ends of an invisible dwelling; I could never learn that anyone had been inside of it. Yet his one great study is human nature; no one knows more people than he. The fact is *he walks about town all day*, and generally in some person's company; only in the evening does he write and read. When walking, he is very communicative, and at the same time manages to draw everything out of his companion that is likely to be profitable to himself.

I do not know him. I saw him almost daily in the streets, and when he was alone I often felt much inclined to accost him, but never put it into execution. I was told his "talk" was very fine. Could I have enjoyed it, without the feeling that I was myself being mercilessly pumped and sifted, I should have liked [*sic*] very much.

William and Mary Howitt[14]

Sören Aaby Kierkegaard, "the solitary philosopher," has also probed the depths of the same metaphysic systems in the society of the great advocates of them, having especially devoted himself to the study of Schelling; and in his singular but remarkable works, "Enten-Eller"; that is, "Either-Or," a Life's Fragment by Victor the Hermit; "Reiteration," "An Attempt in Experimental Psychology," "Fear and Trembling," a Dialectic Lyric, by John de Silentio; and his "Instructive Tales," dedicated *To That Individual*, has with wonderful eloquence, and with the warmth of an actual experience of the "Fear and Trembling" and the "Gospel of Suffering" of which he speaks, proclaimed his firm adhesion to the true spirit of the North, which of old saw, in the myth of Valhalla, combat and death as leading only to victory and life.

Otto Zinck[15]

Aside from my parents, among those who resided at number 37 in Nørrebro was a Councillor of Justice Lund, who was department head in the National Bank. He was married to a sister of Søren Kierkegaard, who often visited the family when he was a young student. I met him many times down in the large, shared garden and ultimately became very good friends with him. We remained acquaintances, and I can remember having visited him several times many years later, when he lived on Nørregade. One evening, when I came by, I found that the rooms that fronted on the street were brightly illuminated, and that he himself was dressed as though for a party. I wanted to leave right away, but he asked me to stay and chat. When I asked if he expected others, he answered, "No, I never have parties, but once in a while it occurs to me to pretend that I am having one, and so I walk to and fro through the rooms, mentally entertaining my imagined guests." I found this explanation rather peculiar, but I endured an hour with him; he was very charming and sometimes uncontrollably amusing. I heard him preach one morning at the Church of Our Lady, but this had less appeal for me, especially because his speaking voice was thin and weak.

Georg Brandes[16]

My earliest recollection of Kierkegaard is that when, as a child, I failed to pull my trousers down carefully and evenly over my boots, which in those days were serviceably long, the nurse would admonish me, saying: "Søren Kierkegaard!" This was how I first heard spoken the name that also echoed so strongly in the ears of the grownups. The caricature drawings in *The Corsair* had made Kierkegaard's legs known in circles where his genius had not penetrated. His trousers had achieved a fame with us that paralleled that achieved ten years earlier in France by Théophile Gautier's red vest.

In Copenhagen this curious man was known as a street eccentric. The externals of his life were bizarre and routinized. One could meet him in the early morning hours on the out-of-the-way paths along the city moat, where, comically enough, he had taken out a fishing license in order to be able to think and compose undisturbed. In *Repetition*, he has sketched such wanderings in the damp morning fogs, in the dew-covered grass, at the hour when nature shakes with the cold shudder that announces sunrise. One could see him ride alone in his hired coach, flying along the country roads of north Zealand or at a slow trot through the woods of north Zealand on one of his frequent drives, which lasted at least an entire day, and often several days. He took a couple of such trips every month during the winter and six or seven such trips each summer month. He stayed variously at the Kongelund on Amager, or at Lyngby, Frederiksborg, Fredensborg, Hørsholm, Roskilde. In Grib Forest he sought out his beloved Corner of the Eight Roads, the name of which was in itself appealing to him—the self-contained person whom everyone knew and spoke with—because of the contradiction contained in the notion that a place where eight roads meet could be said to form a corner. He sat there, and it seemed to him as if an entire people had migrated along the eight roads and had only forgotten one person, as if the eight roads had led all people away from him, only to bring him back to his own thoughts. He, who had such difficulty forgetting himself, could not lose himself entirely in nature, the study of which he disdained; never in history, which he, the great philosophical talent, lacked sense for; scarcely in music, in which he sought only his own ideals; even here in isolation he liked to feel himself as the midpoint.

On other days, in the crowd on Østergade around dinnertime, between two and four o'clock, one could follow the slight, thin form with the drooping head and with an umbrella under an arm. He was almost invariably to be found here on the so-called Strøg, which is the Corso of the upper-middle class in Copenhagen. He was constantly greeting people, and was seen in conversation first

with one person, then with another. On one occasion he would hear a little
street urchin shout "Either/Or!" after him. He would engage himself with anyone and everyone, just as accessible to everyone on the street as he was inaccessible in his home, just as profligate with his person here as he was protective of
it elsewhere. Here he apparently squandered his time, as if to make up for the
fact that when he was at home, he always stubbornly refused to admit that he
was in.

But if one went past his house on a winter evening and glanced at the long
row of lighted windows, which gave the floor on which he lived the appearance
of being illuminated for a celebration, one could get a glimpse, or a sense, of a
series of beautifully furnished and heated rooms in which the strange thinker
walked to and fro in a silence broken only by the scratching of pen on paper
when he would stop to jot down an idea in his manuscript or to make a notation
in his journal. Because in every room there was pen, paper, and ink.

That was how he lived: walking, riding in carriages, conversing, and above
all writing, always writing. He was diligent as few are, and his entire diligence
consisted in writing. With the help of his pen he conversed not only with his
times but with himself. In few human lives has ink played so large a role. At his
death he left about thirty printed volumes, which taken together constitute
almost (as he called it) a literature within literature, and he left equally many
volumes of handwritten journals. And almost all this was written during the
final twelve years of his life. Such was the odd and drab external appearance of
the life of one the most inwardly agitated lives that has ever been lived here in
Denmark.

Chapter Seven

THE MOMENT COMES: FINAL OPPOSITION

Johannes C. Barth[1]

[J. C. Barth to H. P. Barfod, undated (1870)]

S.K. and my father (retired Colonel Barth, then First Lieutenant Barth) often met each other at the Spangs' home, and as one often saw in S.K., he took an interest in people who were completely his opposite not only in their intellectual gifts but also in their intellectual interests. Thus K seemed to favor Lt. B, who was a dyed-in-the-wool military type but who was also well known for being of a quite practical turn of mind. Even in those days S.K.'s health was rather poor—he complained in particular about stomach pains—so, like a true cavalry officer, Father advised him to get himself a horse to ride and to ride properly. Then his stomach would certainly be all right again. S.K. answered that he thought Father might very well be right and that he would consider it.

Then many years passed during which they did not see each other, until Father came into town here in the summer of 1855. And he tells us that one day, when he was very busy running to and fro reporting to this person and to that, he espied S.K. on the street, but busy as he was, he tried to avoid him. This did not succeed, however, because S.K. had already noticed him and had signaled to him. So they greeted one another, and Father asked, perhaps a bit brusquely or without warning, "Well, Doctor, how is your stomach doing?" Then S.K. eyed him with an infinitely searching, investigative look, a look that, when I later heard the story, I understood to have signified something like, "What! Is he thinking or insinuating that all my recent actions and my sharp polemic against the Established Church at bottom are occasioned only by a bad stomach!" But probably this look at my father quickly convinced him of my father's complete innocence, and he simultaneously recalled the origin of my father's question and answered: "Oh! Yes, I really ought not say, but Kotzebue (?) says somewhere that angels manage easily because they have no stomachs."

I must permit myself to tell one more little anecdote in which even my own insignificance plays a role. As is certainly the case with most people who have the required sense for the ideal, during a certain period of my life I enthusiastically read *E/O*, a book that—called forth as it had been by an enthusiasm that, as K. himself says, bordered on "madness"—also came pretty near to "making me crazy." Naturally, therefore, for me the thought of seeing my idol and talking with him was the greatest possible good fortune. (Do you remember what S.K. says about the significance that many people attribute to having stood face to face with a world-historical personality?) And luckily I remembered that Father had spoken of him as an acquaintance, so I therefore sought his permission to go and say hello to the man. My knees shook under me as I rang the bell, and when the little man stood before me I was on the verge of fainting. With difficulty I stammered out the purpose of my visit. K. naturally saw the whole situation clearly right away. But he made one error, and that was when he assumed that I was a "student at the university." I am in fact a graduate of the Polytechnic Institute, and therefore in relation to him I am really "a beggar at the temple door." Despite the fact that during the fifteen minutes my audience lasted I didn't do anything except stare at him, I remember nothing else about his personality besides that enormously demonic look with which he seemed to read a person's soul. We walked through some very uncomfortable rooms and came to a room in which there stood—make no mistake about it—a desk with drawers in it! It is the one he bought from the secondhand furniture dealer, I thought: oh, if I could just dare ask him if I might see the place in which *E/O* was found. He asked me to sit down and did so himself. Now comes my actual story. "I have noted with pleasure that the government of Saxony has rewarded your father for his honorable work by giving him the Order of Albrecht. But tell me, wouldn't he rather have money?" You must certainly admit that this was a very insidious question, calculated to test me a bit. But you must also hear how the innocent can walk unharmed amid serpents. I answered: "I don't know, but it seems to me that a government cannot offer an officer money on such an occasion." "Naturally not," K. answered, in such a way as to indicate more or less that he had posed a rather stupid question. And he began to talk about other things, about Plato, Mrs. Gyllembourg, etc., etc. I sat there, and because of nervousness (and not because I was incapable of having understood him) I was

> so dumm,
> Als ging mir ein Mühlrad im Kopf herum.

> *With respect, faithfully yours,*
> J. C. BARTH, *cand. polyt.*

Apropos of this: Do you know the following anecdote? A.: "Well, Kierkegaard, now you can get out of studying for your examinations because you no longer have your father urging you all the time." K.: "No. Don't you see, my friend, that now I can no longer put off the old man with talk?"

Emil Boesen[2]

[*E. Boesen to L.S.C.H. Boesen, Autumn 1851*]

Yesterday I visited Søren K. out in Østerbro. It was evening, but as far as I could see, he has fine lodgings. He was as usual and behaved the way he generally does. In accordance with his usual custom, he gave me a copy of *For Self-*

Examination, so now you can lend out the copy you have over there if you like. He asked me to visit him often, but he lives so far away. Still, I will go there several times.

[*E. Boesen to L.S.C.H. Boesen, Autumn 1851, two days after previous letter*]
Yesterday evening I was at Søren's again for a long visit.

[*E. Boesen to L.S.C.H. Boesen, Autumn 1851, two days after previous letter*]
Yesterday evening with Søren, who talked to me for a long time.

August Bournonville[3]

[*Bournonville's diary, December 29, 1854*]
Evening party, *Høedt, Paullis*, S. Phiseldeck. We had a pleasant time, but Høedt displeases me by defending Søren Kjerkegaard's vile attack on Münster.

Petronella Ross[4]

[*Petronella Ross to F. C. Sibbern, January 6, 1855*]
For Christmas a cousin gave me Arndt's *Betrachtungen* and Blædel's most recently published sermons. . . . I have Mynster's earlier volumes of sermons. N.B.: Kirkegaard's *Christian Discourses* and [I] believe that his writings are my favorite reading—of the religious sort. And now that I have become used to him—such as he is—the preaching style and discourses of others do not satisfy me easily. The man himself must be very peculiar. With that article of his in *Fædrelandet* about Bishop Mynster, he has certainly made a good whip for himself; may he be whipped with a vengeance if he deserves it. But who can fell him? His wings do seem to need to be clipped a little, and perhaps not so very little. He has himself remained pretty flippant and in his own philosophical sphere, and the extravagant idioms in his logic are often as unattractive as possible. But nevertheless his works seem to be permeated by a life and a spirit of a better nature. I have read only a few—a little of him—on the whole, but a little of that sort of thing is a lot for me.

Bernhard Severin Ingemann[5]

[*B. S. Ingemann to J. Paludan-Müller, January, 15 1855*]
What you wrote in defense of Mynster's reputation against the master sophist of our Athens was true and just, worthy of both a pastor and a theologian.
. . . As far as Søren Sophist is concerned, I have never believed that the truth was in him; with his brilliant dialectics, he has always seemed to me to be a sleight-of-hand artist who plays hocus-pocus with the truth and with Christianity, letting it appear and disappear under his shells. Meanwhile he plays first

Simeon Stylites then Mephistopheles, and is himself fundamentally a hollow character who has in a way sold both his heart and his reason for a double portion of brilliant wit—without, however, having had the sense to conceal the hollowness from which a boundless vanity, pride, an unloving spirit, and a great many other sorts of wretchedness constantly peer forth. His brother is at heart sincere with regard to truth and Christianity, but though unable and unwilling to defend his brother [Søren] in full, he is tempted to agree with him in part—he refuses to consider Mynster a true witness to the truth (because of the weaknesses he supposedly had with respect to power and position and because of his opposition to "freedom of belief").

[*B. S. Ingemann to H. L. Martensen, January 28, 1855*]

I have been greatly angered and offended by Søren Sophist's unseemly antics on Mynster's grave. Your rebuke was harsh, but just and fitting. The only part of it that I would have hesitated to cite was Jacobi's phrase about a "thrashing," because opponents will take it in a vulgar physical fashion. In other respects, I think he fully deserves that sort of treatment—if it were not for the fact that such well-deserved punishment would make him into a martyr and *eo ipso* into a "witness to the truth" in his own imagination. He is a hollow, dialectical sleight-of-hand artist, who permits the truth to show itself and then disappear under a monk's cowl, which is really a clown's hat. In my view, unbounded pride and vanity and a great deal of other baseness peep out through the aesthetic rags and holes with which he adorns himself—and meanwhile he deepens and deepens the gulf between himself (together with his admirers) and the Christianity he preaches. It is a shame that his talent made it impossible to ignore the scandal in the graveyard! The most painful punishment for him would have been to have taken no notice of it.

Hans Rørdam[6]

[*Hans Rørdam to Peter Rørdam, February 28, 1855*]

Naturally, Kierkegaard's battle against the late bishop also has all of us agitated. Whether Mynster was a witness to the truth and belonged to the Lord ("I know my own and my own know me"), has long since been decided in Heaven, so it is not worth the trouble of arguing about it here on earth, but in my view there is something inhuman and demonic in Kierkegaard's behavior toward the deceased. This man, Mynster, to whom Kierkegaard was close until the end and about whom he spoke with the deepest veneration—now this same Kierkegaard drags his corpse through the most disgusting filth. It is villainous. And it confirms what I have always believed, or rather suspected, namely that S.K. stood outside of Christianity and spoke with the greatest virtuosity about the beauty of heavenly things—things that God has concealed from the wise and the prudent but has revealed to little children, Matthew 11.25—just as in the case of the young man who spoke with delight of the loveliness of the sunrise, but when he was asked about when he had seen the sun come up, had to answer, "I have not seen it myself, but I have read about it."

Bernhard Severin Ingemann[7]

[B. S. Ingemann to Carsten Hauch, March 9, 1855]
The little war around here, which is probably over by now—the graveyard scandal on Mynster's grave—has made me very angry, mostly because of the support that the impudence and shamelessness of this sophistry has found among young people, to whom this cruel clowning with the truth seems brilliant.

Petronella Ross[8]

[Petronella Ross to F. C. Sibbern, March 20, 1855]
I have been looking for a word from the councillor of state in the matter of the witness to truth. But since I do not receive the papers regularly I may well miss quite a bit. I read his *Christian Discourses* with such pleasure. The positive in Kierkegaard is so beneficial for the weak spirit, and through his words I can hear Novalis's good hymn "I know on whom I build."

Carsten Hauch[9]

[Carsten Hauch to B. S. Ingemann, March 25, 1855]
I am in complete agreement with your judgment of Kierkegaard's behavior. And it is remarkable how quickly unbelief and leveling sansculottism have used him in support of their views about tearing down what rises above the level of the ordinary. All reverence is to be uprooted from the heart: if nothing on earth be respected, nothing in heaven need be respected either. How unfortunate is the younger generation, which is educated and grows up under these auspices. But one may yet take comfort in the fact that there is a higher spirit from which salvation can come even when the prospects look dark from the human point of view.

Frederik Christian Sibbern[10]

[F. C. Sibbern to Petronella Ross, March 26, 1855]
At first I had thought of speaking out publicly against Kierkegaard. But then so much came out against him from every quarter, and just about everything that there was to say was said. So I gave up the notion of joining in, especially because I soon realized that it would be best to write a whole essay on the question of what a "witness to the truth" is—and then to let it be published without any specific reference to Kierkegaard's attack. Now, afterward, in

everything that he has subsequently produced, I can see only a sectarian, whose attacks resemble those made by the Baptists and the Mormon preachers: our Christianity, such as it is preached and furthered here in Denmark, is not Christianity at all. Mynster had to hear this sort of thing a long time ago when the Lindbergians attacked him.

As for the phrase "witness to the truth," I think it is very incorrect to wish to emphasize that it involves undergoing martyrdom. Many fanatics have been through the greatest of sufferings for the sake of false teachings. That a person clings to such teachings rather than abandon them testifies to the strength and power of his *conviction*, but it does not testify to the *truth* of it. There are proofs of how Indian women have tried with all their strength to ascend the funeral pyres on which their husbands' corpses lay; in so doing they testified to the strength of their faith, but not at all to its legitimacy or validity. India could provide many examples of this sort. True and false doctrine can equally well give birth to such martyrs. But part of being a witness to the truth is that his preaching must contain *truth*. And how can it best be recognized? By its *fruits*, which, of course, is what Christ himself teaches. Thus after I have acknowledged the truth that it contains, if I see that a person's preaching has a beneficial effect on the souls of many people, so that they are ennobled by it, warmed and edified by it, and if I see that they then praise and thank him for it, then I may be most likely to see this as a proof of the fact that he is a witness to the truth. On the other hand, if his sermon had the effect of stirring up malice against him, I do not see how this could be taken as evidence that he had been called by God to be a preacher of the truth. It testifies to the wickedness of the world. But if, in spite of this, he were praised by many as their benefactor because he had been so in a spiritual sense, I would view this as testimony to the power of truth in his preaching. The Christians have always seen the greatest testimony for Christ not in his crucifixion but because he rose up from the dead and was glorified, and because countless people have praised him since his departure. As far as Paul is concerned, I see much greater testimony to the truth in him when I read his letters, which speak so powerfully to the soul and the spirit—and in viewing the many congregations he founded, that is, the many adherents who loved him—than in the persecution he suffered.

I see an awful proof of the arrogance and ingratitude that rules the world, if a man who has exercised such a great and beneficial effect upon so many people by his preaching—which truly was based on a spirit that became and remained Christian—if he is now to be attacked because someone else has got another notion of Christianity into his head. Indeed, must not Kierkegaard himself thank Mynster for a great deal of what is good in his own writings? As for yourself, cling fast to what you have found to be beautiful and good in Kierkegaard's earlier writings; among the things to be regretted is also *this*, namely that, in his attack on Mynster, he has greatly impaired the effect of his own previous writings.

When Kierkegaard recently declared in *Fædrelandet* that the Christianity we have in this country, compared to the New Testament, is not genuine Christianity, he did nothing other than what every sect has always accused other sects of doing. Each one emphasizes its own one-sidedness and wants to make *that* into the main thing. But the ways of the Lord are manifold, and gifts are distributed in many different ways. In its type and spirit, Mynster's Christianity was closest to that of Melanchthon, even though he could also be quite outspoken. No one can deny that he worked zealously in the vineyard of the Lord. Kierkegaard has done so in another fashion, but with a certain one-sidedness. *Now* his one-sidedness is to be everything! If he has had a beneficial effect upon many people, that is a good testimony in his favor. But if he is now to be viewed and spoken of negatively by many people because of his attacks on Mynster, I do not see how *that* can make him a witness to the truth. On the contrary, I would instead view the anger he has stirred up against himself as a good testimony to the Danish people's sense of truth, justice, and gratitude.

C. T. Engelstoft[11]

[C. T. Engelstoft to Ludvig Müller, March 30, 1855]
Naturally I have looked upon the beginning of the Kierkegaardian battle with great indignation, but I immediately saw that it was only a beginning. One of the reasons this was an easy conclusion to draw was that he had said to me a number of years ago that as soon as M[ynster] was dead he would blow the trumpet loudly.

Hans Rørdam[12]

[Hans Rørdam to Peter Rørdam, May 4, 1855]
Søren Kierkegaard, who shouts that the Church of Christ has perished, is for me like a bogey who screeches to terrify the unbelieving and superstitious children of this world. But a Christian laughs at him. If he went to the ends of the earth like the Shoemaker of Jerusalem, shouting that the Church of Christ has perished, I would ask that I might be permitted to walk behind him and say: "You are lying, Søren! According to the testimony of Christ and the Spirit of God, you are a great liar!"

Frederik Christian Sibbern[13]

When Kierkegaard calls upon us to refrain entirely from attending church, it is as if, because of the abuses of bakers or butchers, he wishes to advise us to buy nothing from bakers or butchers; or to refuse to rent rooms because of the landlords; to refrain from purchasing groceries because of the adulteration of food.

Magdalene Hansen[14]

[*Magdalene Hansen to Elise Stampe, June 20, 1855*]

I have not yet received *The Moment*, but Constantin has now definitely promised to obtain it for me. He has read some of it, . . . and while he does not share Mrs. Monrad's opinion, her comments have at any rate not encouraged him to obtain it for me. But now I will certainly obtain it soon. It has also been a continuing source of sorrow to me to hear people tear S.K. apart and, so to speak, diligently deafen themselves to the truth in his conduct in order to be able to discern his own human weaknesses all the more distinctly—as if the question were, What sort of a person is S.K.? and not, Am I a Christian?

Vilhelm Birkedal[15]

I had only fleeting contact with *Søren Kierkegaard*. I saw him when I came to his brother to study moral doctrine [Christian ethics]. He liked to sit in the next room and would read when we left. But I did not speak to him at that time. Only during my later years as a student did we have some conversations with each other at the Student Union and on the street while we walked together out to the customs house or other places. His fine, expressive face and especially the brightness of his eyes led me to suspect that his soul concealed something out of the ordinary, but our conversations gave no indication of what it was or of what would later reveal itself. On only one occasion did he come forth with an expression that showed that he was in disagreement with his brother or with the Grundtvigian circle to which his brother adhered. His words were more or less as follows: "I can understand that they believe that in their understanding of Christianity they have found its substance and the key to its secret. In the middle of all this nonsense about Christianity with which we are surrounded, I can understand that. But it is nonetheless a misunderstanding." At that time I myself did not understand the distinctively Grundtvigian point of view, and I therefore had nothing to reply. This was in the 1830s, that is, twenty years before the final great explosion took place. In the meanwhile I became a pastor, and when I met S. Kierkegaard on the street during a visit to Copenhagen he took me by the arm and followed along with me, as was his custom with everyone. But I sensed that he only wanted to pump me and experiment with me psychologically, even though I never had happen to me what was said to have happened to the man who had stood by the railing at the customs office, staring darkly down into the water. S.K. stood next to this person, a stranger to him, and came closer and closer to him, with the notion that the man was contemplating jumping off and ending it all. The experimenting psychologist wanted to read the man's face in order to see how the idea of suicide expressed itself there—in order to see how a person looked at such a decisive moment. The stranger, who had never contemplated doing anything of the sort, noticing this, and tiring of being the object of that investigative gaze, suddenly turned and asked: "Mr. Magister!

What did you mean when you wrote that it's a blessing to have corns?" "I'll tell you," answered K., while he took the man by the arm and walked with him through the streets of the city, lecturing and gesticulating.

As I mentioned, when I met S.K. like this, I was afraid of becoming more deeply involved than necessary with him. I did not want to be pumped. He could cause the most ridiculous situations. One time I was walking along Øster-gade and suddenly heard a voice from the sidewalk on the other side: "Birke-dal!" It was S.K. who was walking with Cand. Gjødwad on his arm. I crossed the street diagonally toward him, while he and G. did the same, and we met in the middle of the street, where we found ourselves standing in a pile of mud. "May I present messieurs to one another," said K., "Pastor B. and Cand. G." Then we immediately said goodbye. On another occasion I met him in a restaurant. He sat in front of no small portion of food fit for a king and a very large goblet of sparkling wine. At that point he had begun his stern polemic against "official Christianity," and I then saw for myself that he did not apply to himself this "dying away from the world" or this (at any rate bloodless) martyrdom, which he continually preached for us others and which he made the hallmark of the genuine Christian witness—because what he had prepared for himself here was a quite generous enjoyment of the world. He immediately called over to me, involved as I was in a fierce battle for the Church: "Hello, B., you look good. Yes, you who are persecuted are getting fat." I answered: "Yes, and you who persecute are getting thinner." Because despite his high living he was only skin and bones. Thus our chance meetings were the occasion for only playful volleying without deeper significance, and I never came to discuss anything of a more serious content with him. But I have had to include him in my sketches because he was significant for my spiritual life at that time. This is because for a rather short period he intervened seriously in my life and occasioned no small amount of struggle in my soul. This was when his *Moment* also spoke to me. I was then a pastor on Funen, and the strong words cast a very profound shadow over me. I could not just take it lightly. The questions he raised: "The Christian testimonies given in our time, are they true or not? Is this a faded-out Christianity that now asks to be accepted as the complete and pure preaching but that wants to *fool* not only human beings but also God himself? Are we pastors hirelings, or can we, despite feebleness, measure up to the comparison to honest witnesses to the truth?" I couldn't shake off these questions but had to subject my entire spiritual posture to renewed testing, and I will not deny that I had to fight my way through no minor scruples in order to attain light and cheerfulness. Then, as if in a vision, I saw our Lord Jesus standing on the mountain *crying* over Jerusalem and the sinners in the city, and next to him I saw S.K. standing and *laughing* at all of us, condemning us to the abyss of hell—because that is obviously what he did. Then I was struck with the irrefutable certainty that these two could not be in agreement, that there must be a huge distance between them. And then I immediately emerged from my melancholy thoughts.

He was a strange mixture of belief and unbelief. He was, as I have previously called him, a spiritual *bachelor* without hearth or home, a bird of the spirit with-out a nest. And naturally there could be no offspring from this bachelor. This nestless bird could not hatch a flock to sing to the Lord with childlike sweetness.

Meïr Aron Goldschmidt[16]

[*April 15, 1855, published in* Nord og Syd *(North and South), September 15, 1855*]
    Herre Dr. S. Kierkegaard still continues (since December of last year) to write newspaper articles and even pamphlets on the real Christianity and the official Christianity, etc. If one compares the tone of these piquant and nervous articles with, for example, R. Nielsen's fine work, *Om Skjæbne og Forsyn* [On Fate and Providence], one can clearly see that even when Herre Dr. S. Kier-kegaard speaks the truth, he uses it as a diadem for *his own* brow.

[*September 1, 1855, published in* Nord og Syd, *September 15, 1855*]
    A retrospective historical examination of the Kierkegaardian dispute gives a dismal result. It was striking enough in itself when K. attacked the late Mynster and labeled as an orator the person for whom he had until then nourished great reverence—indeed, in whom he believed he had seen his "only one." It was also striking when Bishop Martensen replied and the personal and extraordinary hatred between him and K. became apparent. At that point, however, there was still something lofty about the dispute. What appeared wrong or unpleasant had slipped in as human weakness, which cannot always be avoided in vehement but important disputes about major questions. But then Kierkegaard displayed a nervous, hysterical ferocity, which combined odd confessions with character-istically beautiful, idealistic outbursts. Among these confessions is the remark on p. 4 of the first issue of *The Moment*: "I am by nature so polemical that I really feel that I am in my element only when I am surrounded by human mediocrity and meanness" [*SV* XIV 106]. This was not said as something he regretted or for which he apologized, but was said with unmistakable satisfaction, and thus it became a confession. Therefore, when everything is made clear, this new Reformer—who would like even to be called a Hero of the Faith or a Martyr for the Faith—absolutely cannot work with love and disinterestedness for the improvement of the world. He requires the wicked and the petty for his well-being; he must have publicans so that he can beat his breast and feel himself to be good! The remark [cited in the preceding] is a profound illumination. Until now it has not been clear whether or not K. was a noble character. He lived in the world without participating in the business of the world. He took no ac-tions, he was free of visible flaws but also of the temptations of the world, because he didn't concern himself with them, he didn't struggle. On the con-trary, he was viewed as a noble thinker. But can a person who thinks the sort of thing mentioned above really be called a noble thinker? Rather, it can be said—truly, without bitterness, perhaps bluntly (but he himself has served as an exam-ple of bluntness)—that he is an unhappy thinker. Many of the outbursts issuing

from him testify to sufferings that his pride will not confess. The life that desires to be great in the absence of other people is a personally wasted life, however. There is a vast desert where there are no other flowers than pride in one's own thoughts. In comparison with a fact such as this, other things become insignificant, though perhaps the following ought to be emphasized. In issue seven of *The Moment* there is "a sort of novella" with the title "First the Kingdom of God" [*SV* XIV 248–51] that shows the efforts a person makes before he obtains first his theological degree and then a call to a parish—how he has to keep busy, work, seek, be careful with his money, and only when he has done all this, only then does the wretched person remember God. One could reply to this that even S. Kierkegaard took earthly things into account and waited a long time before serving God's kingdom against Mynster. This is not the main thing, however. According to [Kierkegaard's] presentation of things, that person apparently cannot become blessed because he has the characteristic of not being rich. Thus, what official Christianity says is absolutely not true, that a camel will be able to pass through the eye of a needle before a rich man can inherit the Kingdom of God. On the contrary, it is the poor who cannot inherit the Kingdom of God. If someone lacks the characteristic of being the heir to pretty near a barrel of gold, and of investing it carefully in five-percent and three-percent bonds or in real property, then that person is a part of that human pettiness which, in order not to beg or steal, must seek an official position instead taking care of "the Kingdom of God."

In order to vindicate this obsession, K. even rewrites the lives of the apostles. On p. 4 of his piece "Brief and to the Point" [*SV* XIV 217–19] the following is written: "'Did the Apostle Paul have any official position?' No, Paul had no official position. 'Did he make a lot of money in some other way?' No, he did not earn a lot of money at all. 'Was he at least married?' No, he was not married. 'But then Paul is of course not a serious man!' No, Paul is not a serious man."

But God knows and everyone knows that K. here says something untrue about Paul. He earned money, and did so with his work. As the rabbinical authorities had prescribed (and as Spinoza, for example, did later), in addition to his scriptural studies with the Pharisees, he learned a craft, and when he became an apostle of Christ, he made use of that craft; he was a tent-maker by profession. Kierkegaard kicks against the pricks in vain. His attempt to banish the healthy, hearty, industrious life from the kingdom of true seriousness is in vain.

H. C. Rosted[17]

For many years *Søren Kierkegaard* was a frequent guest at the mailcoach inn [in Hørsholm]. In the summer he liked to come a couple of times a month. Sometimes he hired a coach for twenty rixdollars and rode to Hørsholm, where he would spend the entire day. Everyone out here knew "the magister," as he was called. He had a special ability to talk with ordinary people, and they liked having conversations with him. Often he stood out in the cow barn and chatted with the herdsman, and sometimes he could be seen sitting out by the road with an old stone breaker. He talked especially with the stone breaker a good deal, and when the latter met people from the inn he would always ask, "When is the magister coming?"—and he liked to add that the magister was such a fine man to talk with.

But Kierkegaard set greatest store by Miss *Regine Reinhard*, or *Tagine*, as Hvidberg's children had dubbed her. She directed the household and was an extraordinarily splendid person. Everyone looked up to Tagine, and she also took special care of Søren Kierkegaard. She roasted the wild fowl he sometimes brought with him, and she understood how to prepare roast veal the equal of which he could not find anywhere. She made sure that there was always a supply of the Rhine wine he liked best, and when he was finished eating she herself brought him the twelve boiled prunes he required for his stomach.

She always received copies of the writings he published. One day, when one of Hvidberg's sons saw her sitting and reading *The Moment*, he asked her whether she understood what she was reading.

Miss Reinhard took offense. "Do I understand it? Yes, you can believe I understand every word."

She was very religious, and she and Søren Kierkegaard often had long conversations together about religious questions. The family sometimes teased her and called Søren Kierkegaard her infatuation. And she did concede that she thought extraordinarily highly of him.

Otto B. Wroblewski[18]

The peculiar figure of *Søren Kierkegaard* is the sort one does not forget even if one has seen it really only once—even more unlikely that we would, we who saw him so regularly in the bookshop. He wasn't very forthcoming. With Reitzel, of course, he spoke only about press business, and with us at the bookshop only about buying books. But I, at any rate, was strangely moved by a friendly smile from the deep blue, melancholy eyes with which he could look at you, a look that occasionally was coupled with a satirical line near his mouth when a remark amused him or prompted him in this direction. And young and untutored as I was, I had but little sense of the vast and profound problems that were being worked on behind the brow of the great thinker.

The last time I saw Søren Kierkegaard was in the summer of 1855 during the harrowing battle he carried on in newspaper articles and in *The Moment* against the official state religion and its defenders. I was then living in Roskilde but had come to town one Sunday to visit Theodor Reitzel in Løvstræde. Shortly thereafter S.K. arrived, and I wanted to leave, but he wouldn't permit it. He spoke further with R., and we left and walked down the street together. Gripped as I was by that heaven-shaking battle in which he was involved—standing alone—at that very moment, and gripped by the movement he had called into being, I was incapable of talking about ordinary things. But I didn't need to. He asked me in a friendly way about how things were going for me in Roskilde and about what people were saying about *The Moment*, etc., and was quite his usual self in conversation, even though his voice was weaker and his glance sadder. As is well known, he died in November of that year.

Tycho E. Spang[19]

I was of course only a boy at the time, but I have preserved a clear memory of S.K. from the period in the early 1840s when he frequently came to my parents' house. He generally came in the evening to fetch my father for a walk. We were usually sitting at the table for tea. He joined us but didn't take anything. On the other hand, with his quite remarkable and unusual talent for talking to people of every age and from every walk of life, he was always a lively participant in conversation. It is certainly beyond doubt that on occasions like this he was also conducting his studies. Frequently, when the conversation was in full swing, S.K. could break off in midsentence with the words, "Shouldn't we take this occasion to go for a walk?" And then he went. If our father's aged father was there, S.K. was able to address him in a manner so plain and straightforward that it was as though Grandfather were talking with one of his peers. As for us children—he could joke and laugh so heartily with us and at us. He prepared food with my sister, tasted the children's food, and was so happy and merry that one could be tempted to think that he was a very happy person with easygoing, hilarious spirits. Then, during this happy, delighted laughter his head could sink way down between his shoulders while he leaned back in his chair and rubbed his hands so that the diamond in his ring would sparkle so much that it rivaled his deep, soulful eyes, which were blue and gentle. We delighted in that ring, and when we improvised our little comedies in the doll theater, it always had to be arranged so that *it* could play a role in the piece. We *all* liked him, and an old aunt often said to us, "My, but isn't that S.K. a truly nice person!" We had an eccentric in the house, a serving girl of the genuine Copenhagen type, a real character. S.K., who of course liked to talk with all sorts of people, continually amused himself by talking with her and getting her to say what was on her mind. He often had a good chat with her down in the courtyard, which he then recounted in the parlor to the delight of us children. Once he was particularly delighted when she said, "Don't you know, Mr. Magister! Every proper girl ought to have two sweethearts. Carpenters are of course the nicest in the summer, but cobblers hold the best balls in the winter."

A beautiful and precious memory that we children gratefully preserve is the time [1846] when he became a part of our circle after the death of my father, when he strengthened my mother very much with his great sympathy. For quite a while, he now came to visit us very frequently. After having a conversation with all of us, he generally went alone with Mother into a room where they could sit in peace, and where he could properly speak comforting words to her.

We could clearly tell what a blessing his words must have been to her during these quiet hours, how much she benefited from them, and how deeply she missed him when he was away longer than usual. He was, in the best sense of the term, the widow's friend and comforter, and he also helped her in purely practical things (with minor money matters, purchase of bonds, etc.). But finally he stopped coming entirely, giving as his reason, "Now, dear lady, you have again regained peace and equilibrium. You have renewed strength, and now you can do without me. Now you must become accustomed to standing on your own feet. In addition, everyone I come into contact with thereby comes into the public spotlight, and this is not good for your daughters who are now growing up." But he still continued to write to Mother, and we never encountered him on the street without his coming back home with us. Then, when we left him, we (and especially my sister) were often amazed that we had dared to talk with him the way we had—his eyes had now taken on a very strangely penetrating gray glint instead of the mild blue spark we had known in our childhood. On the other hand, I do have a clear memory from my home of the satirical smile and look with which he could greet people who insistently sought to become personally acquainted with him and who bothered him with their self-important worship of a great man. How he loved spring flowers, especially lily of the valley! Every spring we would pick him a large bouquet from the parsonage garden in Taarnby, and one of my sisters, a little girl, would bring them to his home. Then he became happy, rubbed his hands together, paced up and down the room, and said, "Now let me just see. If only I had a lump of sugar —I don't have one, but perhaps my housekeeper has." Then he laughed and the sack of sugar was produced, and she went away happy.

I have preserved memories of several aspects of S.K.'s peculiarities from some of his best years, but these are presumably known by everyone. He lived in a large elegant apartment with a series of furnished rooms which in winter were heated and illuminated, and in which he did a good deal of pacing back and forth. As best I can remember, in each room there was ink, pen, and paper, which he used during his wanderings to fix an idea by means of a few quick words or a symbol. He had a difficult time putting up with visitors, and to everyone except a very few individuals his servant had to deny that he was home. When he felt a need to be with people, he sought them out, and it was also for the sake of his health that he liked to spend several hours a day in the open air, either on his famous walks through the busiest streets in the most various humors (with the inevitable umbrella under his arm) or on his even more famous carriage rides. Sometimes he drove all night—in order to conquer the insomnia from which he suffered, I believe. His body was frail, but was sustained by enormous spiritual strength. We were told that he often had powerful attacks from his ailments when he was with G., so that he would fall to the floor, but he fought the pain with clenched hands and tensed muscles, then took up the broken thread of the conversation again, and often said, "Don't tell about this. What use is it for people to know about what I must bear?"

He never denied his old friendship with my parents, but always said a few words to us children in later years whenever he met us. Thus as a young university student I met him on the street one time. He was in his humorous, arrogant mood at the time, and perhaps he wanted to sound me out; he said, "Yes, you see. Well, Denmark has had its greatest sculptor in Thorvaldsen, its greatest poet in Oehlenschläger, and now its greatest prose stylist in me. Denmark won't last long now!"

In his later and final years, he was noticeably transformed by illness. True, he still walked in the streets a good deal, but I don't think he had his earlier delight in talking with people. At any rate, he never gave me an opportunity to exchange words with him in those days.

Peter Christian Zahle[20]

Hardly anyone can congratulate himself on having letters from K., but on the other hand there are few among Copenhagen's eminent figures who have not walked arm in arm with K. on his many walks. Statesmen, actors, philosophers, poets, old and young—in brief, the most various sorts of people—can pride themselves on having known Søren Kierkegaard, if from nowhere else then from Mini's, where he used to eat stewed prunes every evening for his weak stomach. On the other hand, he had close friendships only with very few. . . .

With respect to a permanent position, there was once a rumor that he had offered to serve as university pastor, a position that first had to be created. . . .

K. almost resembled a caricature. Under the low-crowned, broad-brimmed hat one saw the big head with the coarse, dark brown hair; the blue, expressive eyes; the pale yellow color of his face and the sunken cheeks, with many deep wrinkles down the cheeks and around a mouth that spoke even when it was silent. He frequently carried his head tilted a little to one side. His back was a bit curved. He had a cane or an umbrella under his arm. The brown coat was tight and snugly buttoned around the thin body. The weak legs seemed to bear their burden uncertainly, but for a long time they served to carry him from the study out into the open air, where he took his "people bath." Perhaps an all-too-strenuous use of the brain had damaged the spinal meninges, thereby paralyzing the lower body. After several weeks in a hospital sickbed, where he distinguished himself by bearing great pains without complaint, he died, prepared for death, to which the physician's journal could indeed also testify. . . .

At present no [portrait] of K. exists, but his contemporaries will not forget how Søren Kierkegaard looked. And in particular no one who has heard him preach will forget that extremely weak, but wonderfully expressive voice. Never have I heard a voice that was so capable of inflecting even the most delicate nuances of expression. . . .

It is said that a number of spiritual counselors and religious quacks privately turned to K. and pointed out to him what enormous perils were to be feared for the Established Church if he continued his activities in this manner. Free-thinkers, Mormons, and Catholics would break into the preserves of the Folke-kirke [literally, "People's Church"], and the confusion would be without end. He is said to have replied that he knew very well what he was doing and that he had clearly foreseen the consequences, but that it was necessary.

Mogens Abraham Sommer[21]

In 1855, when Dr. S. Kierkegaard's activities were known to everyone, I felt an irresistible urge to talk with that man. I had written many letters to him and had not received an answer. I then traveled over there and visited him. I had time to tell him what I felt about him. He listened and answered only: "That is good, my friend! Just keep to the New Testament and you will not go wrong. Go with God!" Tears ran down my cheeks. My heart said "Amen!"

Niels Johansen[22]

[Brevbærer mellem Kristne *(Letter Carrier among Christians), June 17, 1855*]
     Since he [Kierkegaard] is writing *The Moment*, I therefore thought that this might be the right moment to go and speak with him himself. And I went. But no, he answered, he did not involve himself with anyone concerning spiritual or godly things and never read what others wrote.

[Brevbærer mellem Kristne, *February 2, 1859*]
     My conversation with S. Kierkegaard. When the articles in *Fædrelandet* appeared, I was still living in the country. In the spring of 1855 I moved to Copenhagen, because I had begun publishing the *Brevbærer* [Letter Carrier]. . . . I then went up to where S.K. lived. I looked at the door. It was the wrong hour to come for a visit, but I considered, "Perhaps you will forget, or be prevented from returning." S.K. himself opened the door, because, as I learned, he was expecting the return from town of his servant, who arrived while I was there. "May I ask if this is S. Kierkegaard. I would very much like to have a word with him." "Yes, it is, and what do you wish to talk with me about?" "About spiritual and religious things." "I never speak with anyone about these things." "That is a mistake, then. You have said many strong things that people indeed need to hear. But you in turn need to listen to the people, and if you will not listen to people or go among them, your words will not have the effect they otherwise would have." "Who gives you the right to say this to me?" Here I had to soften my tone: "This is how I feel things." "Yes, but you must not say this. If this generation will not listen to my words, there will come another one after this, which perhaps will. It is possible that I might go among the people another time. I do not think that now is the time, and since I have refused to talk with others, I must consequently also refuse to do so with you." I said goodbye and was naturally offended.

Kristian Arentzen[23]

I spoke with Søren Kierkegaard, whose writings had a powerful effect upon me, only once, shortly before his death in 1855. One Sunday morning I went to the Athenæum Society reading room—where Kierkegaard was demonstratively spending the church hour in those days—in order to thank him for *The Moment*, the pamphlets he was then publishing, which were remarkable for their pathos and wit. He led me to a window recess and exchanged some friendly words with me. His powers were visibly waning, but his eyes glowed with a quiet glow of love, which I can still recall and which still moves me deeply. Only forty-two years old, this δοῦλος Χριστοῦ ᾽Ιησοῦ fell in the battle for the truth about Christianity, a battle that he had led with surprising endurance and brilliance. I was there by the casket in the Church of Our Lady where his brother Peter [Christian] Kierkegaard spoke. And I was at the cemetery where a relative, a young physician, visibly upset and with a New Testament in his hand, mocked the clergy represented by P. Kierkegaard and by Tryde, who had buried with full pomp a man who had renounced all fellowship with "the play-Christianity of the pastors." That distasteful scene still lives in my memory.

Chapter Eight

ILLNESS, DEATH, AND BURIAL

Mathilde Reinhardt[1]

MRS. B. occupied a very large apartment in Klædeboderne, and for many years she rented out blocks of three or four connected rooms, often to young men who later attained important positions. . . . Among those people who looked at the apartment in 1849, there was one person whom she quickly and quietly vowed was not to have it. This was Magister Søren Kierkegaard, of whose work she can scarcely have read anything, because that sort of thing was beyond her sphere of interest, at least at that time. But she had perhaps heard that he had made it his business to "create difficulties." Naturally, he was received politely, and after having inspected the rooms he sat on the sofa with her, looked around, and said, "Yes, I will stay here." And then he spoke in such a winning fashion, with such remarkable eyes and with a voice that reminded her of her late friend Rosenvinge, that he not only was permitted to take the rooms but also received a promise that she would arrange for service, which she otherwise did not do. For this servant she chose one of her former housemaids, a working-class widow in difficult economic circumstances, who was very trustworthy and capable, but slow-witted and extremely fussy. When the move was completed and all the magister's requirements were fulfilled, he was never seen again, and his sanctuary would have been completely inviolate were it not for the reports on his domestic existence by the shoemaker's widow. What she related was mostly concerned with her own relationship to him, however, and because she had absolutely no concept of "the concept of irony," she suffered greatly from his sarcastic remarks, which she took as serious insults. On the other hand, though, she could see the weaknesses that no one can conceal in his daily affairs. When the bombs [launched] from that protected tranquility started to strike at the things she held most holy, Mrs. B. became terrified at the explosive power she had in residence. But she soon sensed that as his intellectual powers strained to the limit, his physical powers were failing. K. subscribed to the newspapers in which he had begun [his attack], and he also read the other papers in which the raging battle continued. His "lady" told of a little incident from that time that confirms this: she had his permission to bring one of [his] newspapers each day to a woman in another part of the house, but always the day after the paper came out. In one of these newspapers—it must have been the *Berlingske Tidende* [Berling's Times]—the day after the appearance of a particularly harsh reply from Martensen, which he himself mentions in his autobiography, the lady searched for the paper in vain and found it on his floor, torn into little bits. So he was not entirely invulnerable. After the newspaper articles came the issues of *The Moment*, which we managed to read only now and then, and gradually the storm died down, like so many others. But things became more and more subdued with Kierkegaard, and toward the summer Mrs. B. (whose indignation had long since been replaced by sympathy) heard that he would be going to the hospital. On the day on which he was supposed to depart, Mrs. B. wanted to go out before the appointed time in order to avoid disturbing him with saying farewell. But just as she opened her door, his was opened on the other side of the stair, and he stood in the doorway, erect, though supported by someone else, and took off his hat to her with a look that was just as charming as the one with which he had previously conquered her. I, who knew *her* look, can understand that these two said a great deal to one another in that brief encounter.

Carsten Hauch[2]

[Carsten Hauch to B. S. Ingemann, October 6, 1855]

In these times, when an acute but ice-cold spirit whose words are as sharp as icicles loudly proclaims that he is more or less the only person who can see what true Christianity is, and bluntly declares that God hates people (even though it is merely people's impure and sinful nature that he hates and even though it is written that God is love, and that he who remains in love remains in him); in these times, when a false prophet comes forth like this with great gifts but with a heart so hollow that he plainly says that it really makes no difference to him whether the world is Christian or not, while he also pronounces the judgment of hatred and condemnation upon everything alive; in these times, I say, it is certainly a good thing when a nobler, milder spirit speaks up for once, a spirit in which love is still alive, even toward those who for the time being are lost in the abyss. . . .

Just recently Søren Kierkegaard is said to have been stricken with an attack of apoplexy, of which death is the likely consequence. Most likely illness, nervous stress, and a sort of convulsive irritability have played a large role in his bitter and negative activities, during which he displayed to the entire world his face, marked as it was by hatred of humanity. This is of course a sort of excuse for him, but he will certainly be called to account quite strictly for the passionate desire to be noticed, which is the root cause of this illness and which misled him into playing the role of a false prophet and into giving support to the most ferocious unbelief. To be consistent, Kierkegaard ought also to declare Christ to be un-Christian, because Christ, of course, says, "Go forth and teach and baptize all people," but Kierkegaard declares that it is unreasonable to baptize large numbers of people, because it is impossible for Christianity to reach more than a very few. Thus not only is it the Apostles who are in error, which he says quite straightforwardly, but, to be consistent, Christ himself is also in error.

Thus Christ himself is not a real Christian. Only Kierkegaard has got it right. But then, since according to his own admission he is not a Christian either, Christianity really does not exist. Thus unbelief is correct in rejecting it, because it is really only a phantom and is not suited for human beings. This is where hair splitting and the desire to come up with striking paradoxes have brought him. And now, in the midst of his hope of disrupting everything that has been established over the centuries and of casting everything back into chaos, from which only some undefined new arrangement will emerge—in the midst of his efforts to cast the teachers of the Church down into the dust, he is reminded that he himself is dust, and that all this activity based upon hatred and spiritual pride is just as perishable as dust.

H. P. Kofoed-Hansen's Account of His Friend
Johan Nikolai Lange[3]

Even though at that point Lange did not know S. Kierkegaard personally, he nonetheless went to him after he [Kierkegaard] had directed his most violent blows against the Church and against worship services, in order, if possible, to learn something with respect to Kierkegaard's real ideas and opinions. Kierkegaard recognized Lange and received him in a friendly fashion. But Lange received no other answer to his questions than a reference to something that he was already quite capable of considering—that is, in understanding Kierkegaard's conduct, Lange was referred "to himself," in accordance with his conscience and his intellectual capacities. Naturally, this did not lead to any further contact between the two of them, though Lange was one of the very few who were permitted access to him during his final illness, and he stood next to his deathbed, where at the end Lange addressed him with heartfelt words, to which Kierkegaard replied with a friendly handshake.

Hans Christian Andersen[4]

[*Hans Christian Andersen to Henriette Wulff, October 10, 1855*]
   Kirkegaard is very sick. They say the entire lower part of his body is paralyzed, and he is in the hospital. A theologian named Thura has written a *coarse* poem against him.

Hansine Andræ[5]

[*Diaries, October 18, 1855*]
   Søren Kierkegaard lies in the hospital . . . very sick—paralysis of the legs as a consequence of tuberculosis of the spine marrow. This awakens concern doubly at this time, because, with his writings against Mynster, Martensen, and the clergy—or, perhaps to express it better, against the whole outer form of the

worship of God—he has aroused a great sensation, and it is certain that his writings, which have a large readership, including many theologians, will sooner or later have a revolutionary impact upon matters concerning the Church.

Michael Lund[6]

[M. Lund to P. C. Kierkegaard, October 7, 1855]

Father has surely informed you how things are with Uncle Søren. It is really very distressing, most probably an infection of the spinal cord, with paralysis of both legs, so that he cannot support himself on them or hold himself upright. He is now a patient at Frederik's Hospital and, under the circumstances, is satisfied with being there and with the care he is receiving. At this point it is not clear whether the illness is curable, but one probably ought not hope for too much on this score—without abandoning hope, however.

Johan Christian Lund[7]

[J. C. Lund to P. C. Kierkegaard, October 10, 1855]

Things are only so-so with your brother, and I doubt very much that he will recover. I believe that both Henrik and Michael also share this view, though today Peter reportedly heard a more favorable prognosis.

[J. C. Lund to P. C. Kierkegaard, October 16, 1855]

My intention in sending you these lines is to tell you about your brother in a bit more detail, and therefore I must unfortunately report that his condition is quite feeble. Henrik and Michael, who visit him every day, seem to have given up the thought that he can hold out much longer. I myself have not seen him since last Sunday, when I visited him with Sophie, and today, when I was turned away by the nurse's orderly with the remark that he was feeling quite unwell and did not want any visitors, I confined myself to asking that they greet him from me. At that time I had the impression that he was worse off than what I have subsequently learned from my sons, which is why I intend to try to visit him again tomorrow. If you want to do so yourself, I'm afraid that you had better not hesitate too long.

Henrik Ferdinand Lund[8]

[H. F. Lund to P. C. Kierkegaard, October 23, 1855]

This afternoon I was with Søren, who was in a worse state than when I last saw him. I was hurt, for his sake, that when you were last here he would not permit you to come in to see him. I said to him that I wished to write to you and that I had come to ask him if I might convey to you a brotherly greeting from him. He had absolutely nothing against that, as long as it was not connected with your literary dispute. It is with joy that I hereby send you a friendly and brotherly greeting from him. When we said goodbye he was deeply moved, took my hand, and said, "God be with you."

I am obligated to tell you this right away, because I know that you were distressed that he could make a decision like that. He probably does not have very many days remaining. God grant him peace!

Carl Lund[9]

[C. Lund to P. C. Kierkegaard, October 24, 1855]

As I promised, I am now writing you to report how I found Uncle Søren. I was out to see him on Monday afternoon, after having inquired in the morning whether he would see me. As usual, Michael and Henrik had taken turns being with him that morning, and he was then quite lively and cheerful, having dismissed Michael with the words: "Here comes the relief detachment! March!" I was therefore rather surprised to find him as weakened and broken-down as he was when I came in to him. He was sitting in a reclining chair wearing a robe, but bent over, with his head fallen forward, and was totally unable to help himself. His hands trembled a great deal, and at times he coughed. I was with him for a while, and he complained in particular about his weakness and about the fact that he couldn't sleep at night. When I said that, now that we were finished with sowing, I was able to get away from the farm for a little while, he replied that he, too, would soon be getting away from here. I understood him very well: he had been expecting to die soon and was resigned to it. Now he had become weaker, and in a way stronger, because he could sense that now it was attacking his strength and that it would not last much longer. I parted from him with the thought that he did not have many days left here on this earth. But of course things go up and down with people when they are sick, and they did with him, because when I met him today he was much more energetic. He read the newspapers and was better able to use his hands, but the insomnia continued, and he suffered from pains in his buttocks from so much sitting and lying. But, according to what Henrik says, I do not think that we should permit ourselves to hope that he will live. His chest is also under attack by consumption, which is at work in his lungs, spine, and other places. So I do not know what to do other than to hope that in these, his last, days the Lord will graciously prepare him for his final journey! Amen!

Peter Severin Lund[10]

[P. S. Lund to P. C. Kierkegaard, October 25, 1855]

Uncle's Søren's condition is unchanged, that is, there has been no decisive change, while his powers are continually failing. . . . You wouldn't believe how happy I was to learn, as soon as I arrived home, that most likely that very morning you had received a letter from Father, and so good a letter. I was happy both on your behalf—because it was just the sort of news you needed—and on Uncle Søren's behalf, since it was surely a reply from the depths of his heart. Unfortunately, Uncle Søren's spirits are badly depressed, although things were a bit better in recent days. Sometimes he is lively in his old manner, but naturally his lack of sleep crushes him.

Emil Boesen[11]

FROM BOESEN'S LETTERS TO HIS WIFE

[E. Boesen to L.S.C.H. Boesen, October 15, 1855]

I was out to see Søren K. yesterday. The sight of him made a strong impression on me, but he was glad that I came, and he thanked me for doing so. We talked a little about his most recent affairs. He is gentle and at peace, and he said that now that he has become ill, he wishes for death. The lower part of his body is paralyzed because of his spinal cord. Today he was very much burdened physically, and I made only small talk with him. He won't see anyone aside from me. I spoke with Emil Fenger yesterday morning. He said that his [Kierkegaard's] life is in serious danger, although there is a possibility that he could recover. That prompted me to go visit him, both yesterday and today. I really cannot carry on any lengthy, serious conversation with him.

[E. Boesen to L.S.C.H. Boesen, October 17, 1855]

It seemed as though he wanted me to come so that he could say something. How strange it is now, when he is perhaps going to die, that I, who was his confidant for many years and was then separated from him, have come here almost to be his father confessor. . . . The visits make a strong impression on me in other ways. Incidentally, it seems that they are well disposed toward him in Martin Hammerich's and E. Fenger's circle and that they are quite interested in his cause. But much of what he talks about I may not report.

BOESEN'S ACCOUNT OF HIS HOSPITAL CONVERSATIONS
WITH KIERKEGAARD

[The first section appears to be a combined account of the first two visits, which took place on October 14 and 16, 1855]

How is it going?

"Badly. It's death. Pray for me that it comes quickly and easily. I am depressed. I have my thorn in the flesh, as did St. Paul, so I was unable to enter into ordinary relationships. I therefore concluded that it was my task to be extraordinary, which I then sought to carry out as best I could. I was a plaything of [divine] Governance, which cast me into play, and I was to be used. Then several years went by. Then flip, flop!—and Governance reaches forth its hand and takes me aboard the ark. This is always the existence and the fate of a special messenger. And that was also what was wrong with my relationship to Regine.

Peter Christian Kierkegaard. Lithograph by F. E. Bording, 1862. From a photograph in the Picture Collection of the Royal Library. Reproduced courtesy of the Royal Library.

I had thought that it could be changed, but it couldn't, so I dissolved the relationship. How strange. The husband became Governor. I don't like that. It would have been better if it had happened quietly. It was the right thing that she got Schlegel, that had been the earlier understanding, and then I came in and disturbed things. She suffered a great deal because of me." (And he spoke about her lovingly and sadly.) "I was afraid that she would become governess. She didn't, however, but now she is governess in the West Indies."

Have you been angry and bitter?

"No, but sad, and worried, and extremely indignant, e.g., with my brother Peter. I did not receive him when he last came to me after his speech in Roskilde. He thinks that as the elder brother, he must have priority. He played schoolmaster, when I was still being caned on my a——. I wrote a piece against him, very harsh, which is lying in the desk at home."

"Have you made any decisions about your papers?"

"No. That will have to be as it may. It depends upon Providence, to which

Emil Boesen. Photograph from a visiting card. From the original in the Picture Collection of the Royal Library. Reproduced courtesy of the Royal Library.

I submit. But in addition to this is the fact that I am financially ruined, and now I have nothing, only enough to pay the expenses of my burial. I began with a little, twenty-some thousand, and I saw that that amount could last for a certain amount of time—ten to twenty years. It has now been seventeen years, that was a great thing. I could have sought an appointment. As a veteran theological graduate, it would have been possible for me to obtain one, but I could not accept it—my thorn in the flesh prevented me—so the matter was decided. Suddenly, I understood it. What matters is to get as close to God as possible. There are those who have need of others, the many, all that nonsense about large numbers of people. There is someone who has need of only one. He stands highest among those who need anyone; he who needs most stands lowest. Only one person is needed to say this."

Miss Fibiger had sent him flowers, which he had put away in a cabinet. It seemed that he wanted to talk with me about his strange thorn in the flesh.

"The doctors do not understand my illness. It is psychical [*psychisk*], and now they want to treat it in the usual medical fashion. It's bad. Pray for me that it will soon be over."

He looked at the flowers that Miss Fibiger had sent him, but he did not want them put in water: "It is the fate of flowers that they must bloom and give off a scent and die." If he were able to believe that he could live, it would happen. He could go home if he had a glass of water and put his boots on, and then perhaps he would get out of here and not be in the hospital. Nonetheless, it was quite appropriate that he should die on ordinary terms, since he had lived as an exception. He began to think about whether it was not thus a sort of suicide to remain out there, but when I said that in the final analysis it did not depend on him, he was entirely in agreement with me.

[*Thursday, October 18, 1855*]

He was very weak. His head hung down on his chest and his hands trembled. He dozed off and was awakened by coughing. He sometimes took a nap in the daytime, especially after he had eaten.

"Now I have eaten, and everything is ready to receive you, which I am now doing with open arms."

I asked him if he could gather his thoughts, or if everything was confused for him. Most of the time he could think clearly; sometimes they were a bit confused at night. Whether he could pray to God in peace. "Yes, that I can do!" Whether there was anything he still wanted to say? "No. Yes, greet everyone for me, I have liked them all very much, and tell them that my life is a great suffering, unknown and inexplicable to other people. Everything looked like pride and vanity, but it wasn't. I am absolutely no better than other people, and I have said so and have never said anything else. I have had my thorn in the flesh, and therefore I did not marry and could not accept an official [ecclesiastical] position. I am of course a theological graduate; I was publicly qualified and enjoyed private favor. Of course I could have had it [a position] if I had wanted it, but I became the exception instead. The day went by in work and excitement, and in the evening I was put aside—that was the exception."

Then I asked if he could pray in peace: "Yes, I can do that. So I pray first for the forgiveness of sins, that everything might be forgiven; then I pray that I might be free of despair at the time of my death, and I am often struck by the saying that death must be pleasing to God. And then I pray for something I very much want, that is, that I might be aware a bit in advance of when death will come."

It was beautiful weather that day, and I said, When you sit and talk like that you look as healthy as if you could stand up and walk outside with me.

"Yes, there is only one thing wrong. I am unable to walk. But there is another method of transport, however. I can be lifted up. I have had the feeling of becoming an angel, of getting wings, and that is of course what will happen: to straddle a cloud and sing, Hallelujah, Hallelujah, Hallelujah. Any fool can say this, but it depends on how it is said."

And all that, of course, is because you believe in Christ and take refuge in him in God's name?

"Yes, of course, what else?"

About whether he would change anything of what he said? His words, of course, did not correspond to reality, but were more stringent.

"That is how it is supposed to be, otherwise it does no good. I certainly think that when the bomb explodes it has to be like this! Do you think I should tone it down, by speaking first to awaken people, and then to calm them down? Why do you want to bother me with this!"

He did not want Gjødwad to visit him: "He did favors for me in private and disavowed me publicly. I don't like that. You have no idea what sort of a poisonous plant Mynster was. You have no idea of it; it is staggering how it has spread its corruption. He was a colossus. Great strength was required to topple him, and the person who did it also had to pay for it. When hunters go after the wild boar they choose a certain dog and know very well what will happen: the wild boar will be trapped, but the dog who gets him will pay for it. I will gladly die. Then I will be certain that I accomplished the task. Often people would rather hear what a dead person has to say than someone who is alive."

I would prefer that you live a while longer. You have been so stringent, and you have gone so far, that there must be something left for you to say.

"Yes, then I wouldn't die. I have had to forget all the *Moments* and the other things in order to find peace, and I think I have had a task that was sufficiently appropriate, important, and difficult. You must take note of the fact that I have seen things from within the innermost center of Christianity, that everything is procrastination, pure procrastination. Things have certainly been pretty hot for you because of your association with me, haven't they?"

Yes, but I haven't talked about it, and in the places where it was known and talked about, it was respected.

"Well, is that so! I am pleased that you came. Thank you, thank you."

[*Friday, October 19, 1855*]

He had slept a couple of hours the evening before and was in good spirits. His brother had been there but had not been permitted to come in. S.K. said that he [Kierkegaard's brother, Peter Christian] could be stopped not by debate but by action, and in this manner he had taken action and stopped him.

Won't you take Holy Communion?

"Yes, but not from a pastor, from a layman."

That would be quite difficult to arrange.

"Then I will die without it."

That's not right!

"We cannot debate it. I have made my choice. I have chosen. The pastors are civil servants of the Crown and have nothing to do with Christianity."

But that is not true, of course. It is not in accord with truth and reality.

"Yes, you see, God is sovereign, but then there are all these people who want to arrange things comfortably for themselves. So they get Christianity for everybody, and there are the thousand pastors, so that no one in the country can die a blessed death without belonging to it. Then they are the sovereign, and God's sovereignty is finished. But he must be obeyed in all things."

Then he fell asleep. His voice became weak and he was having physical difficulties, so I soon left. I was worried. If he takes a layman [i.e., accepts the Eucharist from a layman], a definite step will have been taken, and it could easily be subject to great abuse by a layman. There would be a great temptation to do so, because then a layman would be [called] a good Christian—because he is not a pastor.

Miss Fibiger's flowers made him happy: "At night she is the supervisor [of the hospital]. In the daytime she supervises me." And, the woman attendant said to him, She *also* weeps for you.

[*Saturday, October 20, 1855*]

Two women attendants carried him from the one chair to the other. He was entirely without strength. His head hung down on his chest, and he quickly dozed off. He said that his entire illness was now a death struggle. He asked me to hold his head, and for a while I stood and held his head up. When I wanted to leave, I said that I would see him again the next day.

"Yes," he answered, "you do that, but no one knows, and we might as well say goodbye to one another right now."

God bless you, and thanks for everything!

"Goodbye. Thank you. Forgive me for involving you in difficulties you would otherwise have been spared."

Goodbye. Now repose in the peace of God until Our Lord calls you. Goodbye!

[*Sunday, October 21, 1855*]

I was in with him only for a moment. He said that it was an inconvenient time. He spoke about Thurah and Martensen.

[*Monday, October 22, 1855*]

You should have a little better view from your room. You could see out to the gardens.

"What good can it do to fool oneself like that? Things are different now. Now it is self-torment. That sort of an idea is now torture. No, when one is to suffer, one must suffer."

[*Tuesday, October 23, 1855*]

What beautiful flowers!

"Yes, she outdoes herself in inventiveness."

But he complained about how fatigued he was.

[*Thursday, October 25, 1855*]

"I become weaker every day, and my hands and my body tremble."

He looked dubiously for a moment at Fenger's farewell sermon, which I had brought him. Then he said, "Send it back to him. I will not accept it."

It was not for you to read, but he does think kindly of you.

"He has spoken publicly. Now he wants to send me this privately, and then it is supposed to be as if it were nothing—approaching me privately, and yet there is such a great difference."

Your brother Peter was there on his journey back.

"So the fact that I would not receive him is well known, and people were quite scandalized over it?"

No, I cannot say that. They really think of you with great sympathy. You should really not be surprised that they have said what they have. It was all only in self-defense, and we are all entitled to defend ourselves. For all that, they are still really quite capable of thinking of you with great sympathy.

"Believe me, this is the sort of thing of which Christ says, 'Get thee behind me Satan, for you are a stumbling block to me! You think only of earthly things and have no sense for that which is above.'"

No, they speak as they do because they are convinced that they are right and that your sort of attack on existing conditions is wrong. It is possible, of course, that there is a way to salvation that leads through the Established Church.

"I cannot stand talking about this. It is too much of a strain on me."

Was there bad air in the bedroom you had before?

"Yes. I get very irritated when I think about it. I certainly noticed it."

Then why didn't you move?

"I was under too much strain to do it. I still had several issues of *The Moment* that I had to get out and several hundred rixdollars left to be used for that purpose. So I could have set it aside and spared myself, or I could continue and then fall. I rightly chose the latter; then I was finished."

Then you got out the issues of *The Moment* that you wanted to?

"Yes!"

How strange that so many things in your life have just sufficed!

"Yes. And I am very happy about it, and very sad, because I cannot share my joy with anyone."

[*Friday, October 26, 1855*]

He kept the women attendants with him, and there was talk about only insignificant things.

[Saturday, October 27, 1855]

Just the same. His head hung down, and he felt himself burdened. There were larger crowds than usual in the street.

"Yes, that [crowds in the street] was what used to agree with me so much."

You never came to visit me in Horsens.

"No. Where would I have found the time for it!"

The last time I saw him he was lying down and was nearly incapable of speaking. I had to leave town, and he died shortly thereafter.

Peter Severin Lund[12]

[P. S. Lund to P. C. Kierkegaard, November 4, 1855]

In my last letter I promised to write you if there were any decisive change in Uncle Søren's condition. This has not happened, but because it has been a long time since I last wrote you, and because I don't know whether you have heard from anyone else in the meantime, I thought I ought to write you anyway, even though I don't have the pleasure of bringing you better news. On the contrary, things have gone rather downhill in recent days, so that Uncle is now lying down, and at the very least his situation is such that, for the first time, he has no hope of sitting up again. Since I last wrote you I have been out to visit him once with Jette. He was sitting up but was so weak that he could scarcely talk, and we therefore stayed with him for only a moment. Today I went out there with Father but did not go in with him [to see Uncle Søren]. He was lying down and was very weak. He himself had hopes of being able to sit up again, however. But I hardly think that we dare share that hope. Naturally, he is often in bleak spirits, but he did get some sleep in the last few days. You see, I am bringing you only bad news, but I expect that it will do you good to hear something from the city.

Johan Christian Lund[13]

[J. C. Lund to P. C. Kierkegaard, November 10, 1855]

Since it is all too likely that there is no longer any hope for an improvement in your brother's condition and that, on the contrary, we must expect instead that his powers will not endure much longer, I thought that you ought not be unprepared for the sorrowful news that can scarcely be delayed any further. Given the situation, just in case, I must not neglect to inquire whether you have the deed to the family burial plot, or if you know where it is. Henrik and Michael, who have attended to him every day, find him in such a state of decline that, judging from his condition during the last few days, he cannot last long, inasmuch as he is lying there more or less unconscious, and he was unable to eat or drink anything today. I saw him yesterday, and I must unfortunately confirm his nurse's inauspicious prognosis.

Henrik [Sigvard] Lund[14]

[*H. Lund to E. Boesen, November 11, 1855*]

You will remember that when we last spoke to one another about the illness of our mutual friend Dr. S. Kierkegaard, I promised to keep you informed if there was any change in the course of that illness. Now that this has indeed happened, I will not neglect to keep my promise, even though the only thing I have to report is saddening. I must beg for your forgiveness if I shrink from going into the details—which I find very painful—to the degree that you might wish because of your friendship with my uncle, intensified as it has been by absence and separation. I will therefore only give a short account of these details.

You know what my uncle's condition was like when you departed, and how little hope I (and probably you) entertained concerning changes in the course of his illness toward a direction that, from the human point of view, would be most desirable, i.e., toward a healthy recovery.

Unfortunately, these sad premonitions of ours were only all too true. Shortly after your departure it was necessary for him to remain in bed, in part because of increasing weakness, and especially because of the loss of skin on his body from sitting so long in the same position in the reclining chair, and for other reasons. Thereafter his condition worsened very much, because he was unable to bear lying in bed all day, and this then interfered with his sleep at night. He therefore became weaker and weaker, and subsequently became less and less aware of things going on around him. He recognized no one, made no replies, and fell at last into a comatose state, in which sad condition he remained, without regaining consciousness, until nine o'clock Sunday evening, the eleventh of November, when God, in his infinite mercy and grace, took him away to his eternal blessedness and peace, for which he had striven during his entire life— and away from the afflictions and troubles of the world, by which he was tried during his entire life.

He is no more. You have lost a friend of your youth, but I have lost my only and best friend, a tried and faithful counselor, an experienced and certain guide! Let us lament, but not be sorry for him!

I have now kept my promise with a heavy heart, and I ask you to forgive the fact that I have kept it only imperfectly. I ask you also to accept a wish for the true consolation of God and an assurance of the most sincere sympathy in your loss.

Michael Lund[15]

[*M. Lund to J. C. Lund, November 12, 1855*]

What we have foreseen for so long has now taken place: our good Uncle Søren died at nine o'clock yesterday evening, and his sufferings are now over, thank God. All yesterday he continued to lie in the same somnolent and unconscious state as in the days immediately preceding, excepting that his powers gradually faded away until the peaceful arrival of the death for which he himself had longed so much.

Uncle Ferdinand has been notified of the death, and we should now join forces and endeavor to make the necessary arrangements concerning both the burial and the probate court. I am also writing Uncle Peter and Carl today in order to inform them of the death, and we should inform the rest of the family here in town about it as well.

[*M. Lund to P. C. Kierkegaard, November 12, 1855*]

What we have long expected—and what you have probably also been prepared for by a letter from Father, sent the day before yesterday—has now happened, and it is my sad duty to inform you that your brother, our good Uncle Søren, ended his earthly life yesterday at nine o'clock in the evening with a peaceful death. In a way, his death struggle can be said to have lasted a long time, inasmuch as he lay completely unconscious, in a comatose state, for the last two days, without recognizing anyone, without being able to talk, swallow, etc. But precisely because of this unconsciousness, his sufferings were probably not so great, either, and after a gradual decrease in his powers, came the death for which he himself had longed so much.

Frederik Hammerich[16]

Søren Kierkegaard burned the last bridge between himself and the Church—as it had developed for worse or for better over the course of its history. He raged against it wildly in his *Moments* and was just on the verge of madness when he was called away by death.

Meïr Aron Goldschmidt[17]

[Nord og Syd, *November 15, 1855*]

After an illness of several weeks, Dr. S. Kierkegaard died on Sunday at Frederik's Hospital. When he fell ill right in the midst of his polemical activity, there were not a few people who said that this was the finger of God, a punishment for his merciless attack on "official Christianity" and the clergy. It would be closer to the truth if it were acknowledged that the peculiarities, the bitterness, and the passion in his most recent works stemmed from the illness that was already affecting his extraordinary talents. He was without doubt one of the greatest intellects Denmark has produced, but he died a timely death because his most recent activities had begun to gain him precisely the sort of popularity that he could never have harmonized with his personality. The most dangerous part of his actions against the clergy and the official Church is now only just beginning, because his fate undeniably has something of the martyr about it: the sincerity of his passion helped hasten the course of his illness and bring about his death.

Henrik Ferdinand Lund[18]

[H. F. Lund to V. N. Lund, November 16, 1855]

I am writing these lines mostly to inform you and Christiane of the latest information concerning your uncle's death and the decisions that have been made concerning his burial.

You are perhaps already aware that God called him away from the temporal world last Sunday evening, the 11th, at approximately nine o'clock. In the final days, sleep came and the paralysis in his lower body disappeared, but he could not take anything, because he could no longer swallow. He faced his final moments with peace and tranquility. He was faithful to his idea to the end, and God took him to himself, away from a world that was hostile to him because he had said what he believed to be the truth. Now he stands before his Judge, and we must all keep silent.

Even now, the world is judging him differently from when he was alive. They are willing to acknowledge his remarkable intellectual and spiritual gifts, and there is an excitement in the city, with people wanting to know when he will be buried.

Yesterday evening Uncle Peter and Cousin Carl came to town, and we gathered at Uncle Christian's, where we decided that the burial would take place [after a funeral service] at the Church of Our Lady at 12:30 P.M. on Sunday the 18th. I said that you were unable to be a part of the proceedings, because the sexton had to have a definite list. In fact, only eight pairs of pallbearers are permitted.

You know that I had the pleasure of bringing a loving greeting from the deceased to his brother. It was a significant greeting at that grave moment.

If anyone talks about the great fortune that he left behind, just let them talk. But the truth is this, that while he was alive he disposed of his money in such a way—in part on his writings, in part on living expenses, and in part on the poor—that he leaves nothing except his library, etc. This is a sign of God's great goodness toward him, in that he was spared from suffering need or dependency upon the goodwill of others.

Frederik Benedikt Møller[19]

After he became ill, Kierkegaard was admitted to the hospital, where he died without allowing his brother Peter Christian to visit him, because "then my heart will run away with me," he said. When he died soon thereafter, I was in the funeral cortège. His coffin lay in the Church of Our Lady. His brother, kneeling, offered a moving prayer for him. At the graveside, his sister's son, a medical graduate named Lund, stepped forth and protested against the fact that the Folkekirke had buried him [Kierkegaard] despite his declaration that he did not want to be buried with its ceremonies and by its pastors. Lund had to pay a fine for his actions.

Several days later I was with some medical students who were indignant because an autopsy had not been performed on Kierkegaard, and his brain had not been examined. They thought that the hospital had the right and even the obligation to do so on behalf of science, but that the hospital had yielded to the wishes of the family. I thought it was decent of the hospital, but those who were enthusiasts of science did not think that sort of thing should be taken into consideration.

F. Sodemann[20]

[F. Sodemann to P. M. Barfod, November 18, 1855]

Today I must unfortunately tell you about a scandal that scarcely has its equal in recent Danish history. Yesterday our famous man Søren Kirkegaard was buried after a funeral at the Church of Our Lady. There was an enormous crowd present. Church was full to bursting; it was all I could do to get a spot upstairs by one of the columns in the back, from which I could see the coffin. Rumor has it that the clergy had refused to speak, some say at the suggestion of Bishop Martensen, because if they spoke of him [Søren Kierkegaard] in an unkindly way, it would be speaking ill of the dead, and if they praised him, it would seem as if they either approved of Søren's actions or were eager for a good fee. No clergy wearing vestments were present other than Archdeacon Tryde and Dr. Kierkegaard, and the latter gave the eulogy. Of course, from way up where I was standing I could not hear everything he said; but he was moved and inspired. I shall give you what I can remember of the speech, though it will be most incomplete and inexact. First, he explained the family relationships, how their father, who had once herded sheep on the moors of Jutland, had loved the children most intensely; that gradually all but the two of them had departed this life; and now that his brother had also left him, he alone remained behind. Next, he said that this was not the time or place to discuss Søren's actions; that we neither dared to nor could accept much of what Søren had said; but that his true intention had been to clear away much of the rubble that had collected at the door of the Church; that he [Søren] himself had not been conscious of how far he had gone; and that he had gone too far. He could not thank this great gathering on behalf of his deceased brother, since the latter had always withdrawn into solitude, and it was in conflict with his principles and opinions to be surrounded by a crowd. Nor could he thank the crowd on his own or his family's behalf, since the crowd had been lured there by various motives of which he would not speak more specifically. He finished with a fervent prayer that Søren's endeavors and efforts not be misunderstood but that the truth in them might become apparent and have a positive influence in the service of Christ.

Then the body was carried away, and since I thought everything was over I was foolish enough not to go along out to the cemetery; but it was out there that things really came to a head. The archdeacon carried out the graveside service quite simply, with the casting on of earth. When this was finished, Dr. Lund from Frederik's Hospital, a son of Kierkeg.'s sister, stepped forth and declared that he and Søren were one. The archdeacon pointed out that since he was not ordained he was not allowed to speak at the graveside, but with shouts of "Bravo!" the crowd indicated that it wanted Lund to speak. He then continued and said that he had waited until now in order to see how far the clergy would go in their lip service. They thought they could earn a good fee, because they thought Søren was rich. Had he been poor, on the other hand, then we would have seen what would have become of him. Jews are not buried by official Christendom, nor are Muhammedans, Catholics, Mormons, etc. But here could be seen the clearest proof of the lukewarm state of affairs. Then he read a section of Revelations 3 (Laodicea), which he applied to the clergy.* Then he read something from *The Moment* (no. 2, "To Bury with Full Honors") and declared that he and Søren had placed themselves outside the Church. The crowd yelled "Bravo!" and voices were heard to call, "Down with the clergy." Prof. Clausen was in truth right yesterday, when he pointed out to the younger theology students that these were dangerous times for theologians, and if they felt the call to theology they had better keep their hands on the plow. Yes, it is important to stand fast on the foundation of the Gospel and protect it against violence and harm!†

Henrik [Sigvard] Lund's Speech at Kierkegaard's Burial[21]

[*November 18, 1855, published in* Fædrelandet, *November 22, 1855*]
   In the name of God.
   One moment, gentlemen, if you will permit me!
   I am the son of the sister of the deceased, and therefore I believe that I ought to be permitted to *speak* a few words.‡ I am bound to him by blood ties. I am bound to him even more closely by the memory of my mother, who died young, and it was only through him that I believed I had a living image of my mother. Over the years I became bound to him by the ties of a faithful friendship, a friendship that survived the test on his side and that I, for my part, hope that I will uphold until the end. I am tied to him, finally, by agreement with his views and opinions, and this is perhaps the strongest tie. I therefore believe that

---

   * The Established Church was equated with Babylon, *Apoc. 18*! [F. Sodemann]
   † The papers have referred to this affair very carefully and briefly, as if they were afraid of getting their fingers burned. *Dagbladet*, however, has a slightly snide tone and says that a person stepped forward from among the mourners and protested against the service that had been performed as having been against the wishes of the deceased. [F. Sodemann]
   ‡ I regret, and I am bound to say, that I misunderstood His Reverence Archdeacon *Tryde* in thinking that he had given me permission to speak, which I later discovered was not the case. If I had known, I would have obeyed him to the letter, even though I would have said in another place and on another occasion—e.g., here and now—what I believed I ought to say and must say. Because one must "be subject to the powers that be" [Romans 13.1], but nonetheless "fear God rather than men" [Acts 5.29]. [Henrik Lund]

I may speak here. He, my deceased friend, stands and falls with his writings and the opinions and views that he presents in those writings. But I have not heard them mentioned with a single word. On the contrary, I have heard only long-winded beating around the bush. Therefore let us investigate here whether his views are true or not!

His articles in *Fædrelandet* and the entire course of the battle are all too fresh in our memory for it to be necessary to recapitulate them here. I will therefore limit myself to reading the passage in which I have found them in the Bible, which of course is the book that must serve as the guide for all of us—namely the Revelation of St. John 3.14–end. In that passage all of his [Søren Kierkegaard's] views are set forth, and his views must thus be accepted as in accord with the word of Scripture. But perhaps people will say that the various issues of *The Moment*, on the other hand, were too exaggerated, too "overwrought," to have presented a true description of the way things are. Let us take a look. As an example let us choose the sixth article in the second issue of *The Moment*, entitled "We Are All Christians" [*SV* XIV 129]—though one could just as easily have chosen any other passage. Isn't this description of the situation correct? Is not what we are all witnessing today—namely, that this poor man, despite all his energetic protests in thought, word, and deed, in life and death, is being buried by "the Official Church" as a beloved member of same—isn't this in accordance with his words? It would never have happened in a Jewish society, and never among the Turks and Mohammedans: that a member of their society, who had left it so decisively, would, after his death and without any prior recantation of his views, nevertheless be viewed as a member of that society. That was something reserved for "official Christianity" to commit. Can this be "God's true Church," then? No! "God's Church" or a truly Christian society would never have served "Mammon!" Or it would never, at least, have done so to that extent, or so flagrantly! It would never have acted in such a manner that—for the sake of money, or perhaps for the sake of the reputation of his family—it set aside considerations of "God's Kingdom and His Righteousness!" Never would it have embraced, without further ado and by means of a public burial ceremony, *this sort* of antagonist and opponent as a faithful member of its society and treated him as such! Never!

What is this "official Christianity," then? If it isn't the true Church of Christ—which after these actions it cannot be—it must be what the deceased said it was, a "falling away from God." Or in other words, it is "the great whore, Babylon, with whom all the kings of the earth have fornicated, the wine of whose whoredom has made drunk all the peoples of the earth." But today the Church has laid violent hands upon him [Kierkegaard]. It has condemned itself by regarding him as "a Christian," i.e., as a member of the "official Christian Church." As is written in chapter 18 of the Revelation of St. John, it has "fallen; it has fallen and become the dwelling place of the devils, a prison for every unclean spirit, a prison for every unclean and loathsome bird." Therefore the deceased was also right when, at the end of his life, he so urgently and incisively said "what must be said," namely "that everyone, by ceasing to participate (if he does) in the official worship of God as it currently is (with its claim to being the Christianity of the New Testament), will always have one sin fewer, and a great sin, namely the sin of participating in making a fool of God by calling the Christianity of the New Testament what is not the Christianity of the New Testament." Because, as is indeed said later on in the Scriptures, "Come out of her, my people, lest you take part in her sins, lest you share in her plagues!"

Therefore, both on his behalf and on my own, I protest viewing our presence here as participation in the worship of God sponsored by "official Christianity," because he has been brought here against his repeatedly expressed will, and has in a way been violated. And I have come along only in order to ascertain what has now taken place. In any other case, after having understood what "official Christianity" is, neither I nor he would have been present at any "officially Christian" action.

I have spoken and freed my spirit!

Hans Lassen Martensen[22]

[*H. L. Martensen to L. Gude, November 18, 1855*]

Today, after a service at the Church of Our Lady, Kierkegaard was buried; there was a large cortège of mourners (in grand style, how ironic!). We have scarcely seen the equal of the *tactlessness* shown by the family in having him buried on a *Sunday*, between two religious services, from the nation's *most important church*. It could not be prevented by law, however, although it could have been prevented by *proper conduct*, which, however, Tryde lacked here as he does everywhere it is required. Kierkegaard's brother spoke at the church (as a brother, not as a pastor). At this point I do not know anything at all about what he said and how he said it. The newspapers will soon be running a spate of these burial stories. I understand the cortège was composed primarily of young people and a large number of obscure personages. There were no dignitaries, unless one wishes to include R. Nielsen and Magister Stilling in this category. . . . I have just learned that there was a great scandal at the grave; after Tryde had cast earth upon the grave, a son of the Kierkegaard's sister, a student named Lund, stepped forth with *The Moment* and the New Testament as a witness for the truth against the Church, which had buried S. Kd. "for money," etc. I still have not been informed about this through official channels, but it has caused great offense, which as far as I can see must be met with *serious* steps.

Hansine Andræ[23]

[*Diaries, November 18, 1855*]

Last Sunday *Søren Kierkegaard* died. Today, Sunday, he has been buried; a large number of people turned out. It has been announced that next Wednesday Martensen will deliver a memorial address for Bishop Mynster.

Hans Christian Andersen[24]

[Hans Christian Andersen to August Bournonville, November 24, 1855]

Søren Kierkegaard was buried last Sunday, following a service at the Church of Our Lady. The parties concerned had done very little. The church pews were closed, and the crowd in the aisles was unusually large. Ladies in red and blue hats were coming and going; item: a dog with a muzzle. At the gravesite itself there was a scandal: when the whole ceremony was over out there (that is, when Tryde had cast earth upon the casket), a son of a sister of the deceased stepped forward and denounced the fact that he had been buried in this fashion. He declared—this was the point, more or less—that Søren Kierkegaard had resigned from our society, and therefore we ought not bury him in accordance with our customs! I was not out there, but it was said to be unpleasant. The newspapers say a little about it. In *Fædrelandet*'s issue of last Thursday this nephew has published his speech along with some concluding remarks. To me, the entire affair is a distorted picture of Søren K.; I don't understand it!

Frederikke Bremer[25]

[Frederikke Bremer to Hans Christian Andersen, December 14, 1855]

God's will be done, I say, along with S. Kierkegaard. Would that we might have a sense of assurance that we are following his [God's] exhortation and carrying out his commandment to us! With respect to your Danish Simeon Stylites, he has awakened a great deal of interest, even here. Most people— myself included—know that he was *right in much and wrong in much*. He is no pure manifestation of the truth, and his sickly bitterness has certainly stood in the way of clarity and reasonableness in the judgments reached about him.

Chapter Nine

SØREN AND THE FAMILY

Eline Heramb Boisen[1]

WHILE I was out at the Boisens, before Aunt Würzen came to town, we also visited a sister of Kierkegaard, married to a Lund. She had recently had a baby and lay there like a princess, but she died a few days later.

Out there Kierkegaard was a completely different person. He played with the children and was an indulgent brother in every respect. He loved his sister terribly much; losing her was hard for him. An older sister had been married to this Lund's brother and had also died, so now only Søren and Peter were left. During that time, before he became a university student, Søren wrote some articles against Orla Lehmann.

That winter I was also a visitor several times at the home of the elder Kierkegaards, and those were interesting hours. It was very intriguing to hear the old man debate with the sons, with none of them giving in, and to see the quiet activity of the old mother, and how she would sometimes listen in admiration and sometimes interrupt to calm things down when they became too heated.

Søren was rather more likely to involve himself with a person than was Peter, and we had many amusing clashes with one another, mostly, however, when he met me on the street. It always pleased me to speak with him, but it did annoy me to be the focus of attention, and that was what one was when one walked with him, because he fenced so strangely with his cane and very often stood still in the street, gesticulating and then laughing quite loudly.

Once, before I moved out of town, I saw him court with great seriousness a little girl who had not even been confirmed yet. She subsequently became his fiancée—she, with whom he played such a shameless game for so many years and from whom he finally parted—without breaking off the relationship and without saying where he was going. I saw her only one time, at a little ball at the home of the widowed Mrs. Teilmann. I had more frequently met her older sisters Marie and Olga Olsen (I think those were their names), and they were very nice girls.

In the book *Repetition*, which in other respects testifies to his remarkable abilities as a writer, Søren attempts in vain to move the reader to feel some sympathy for him. Instead, he serves as a terrifying example of how easily a person who has not learned how to control his vanity and egoism—and who does not wish to learn how to do so—falls prey to fantastic dreams and, as a result of his capricious, hard-hearted, and untrustworthy character, becomes a burden to himself and to others.

In his autobiography (which was published by his brother after his death) he wishes to present himself as if *all* his endeavors had the intention of surreptitiously confronting people with the Gospel. This *cannot* be true with respect to the first part of his life, however. He did *not* honor his father and mother, and therefore things did not go well for him in the land. When the heart finally wanted to claim its own, he was not constant in his love but sacrificed the innocent young girl on the altar of vanity.

I did not know her so well, of course, but I knew that she was from a serious and not untalented family. Perhaps she was not intelligent enough for him, and perhaps she had wanted to assist his heart in clipping a bit off the wings of his high-flown ambition. But she had to give way to the sin that dominated him. Or perhaps it was not a sin to make use of all her struggles, all the sorrow and the tears he extorted from her, as a setting that would make his conceited little self noteworthy and interesting? How can such conduct be in the service of the Gospel? If it was calculated behavior, then he was certainly more a devil than a Christian. In the end, however, I would very much like to think well of him, even though I must condemn his early behavior as sheer perdition—despite the fact that he knew how to cover it over as dazzlingly as if he had been taught by the Devil himself.

One time he came to see us, not long after we had been married, but when Boisen came into town one day and went up to him in order to find out when he would come [to visit], he [Kierkegaard] excused himself and gave Boisen all the illustrations in his fancy Bible as a present for me. He wanted to keep one for himself, namely the picture of Jacob and Rachel, but he gave me that one as well. Most likely he thought of himself in looking at Jacob, because it was just at that time that he was intoxicated with love, and he became engaged shortly thereafter. That was probably the reason that he did not come to see us as we had arranged.

Boisen once visited him many years later, when he complained a great deal about the persecution he had had to suffer for the sake of the good cause. When Boisen asked about this persecution, however, he could mention only the taunts of boys in the street and some newspaper articles, particularly in *The Corsair*, in which he was shown standing and strutting in the middle of a room with his notorious cane. That was indeed a rather small martyr's crown! And when one considers it more carefully, the taunts of the street boys stemmed from his odd way of dressing.* And he himself roared his way into becoming "the rocket." This was the only thing he achieved in his mighty efforts to show himself everywhere, now at Gammel Strand among the fishmongers, now at Holmensgade. He places great emphasis on this in his writings, as if people were really supposed to care about where he showed himself. The only people, of

---

* Even before he became a university student, he wore a shirt frill. [Eline Boisen]

course, for whom it could have meant anything were those in his family, and he had, of course, long since spurned them.

In other respects, in those days he lived as a rich man in wealth and merriment, indulging even the most insignificant of his whims, admired by the general public, even though he was spoken of as an eccentric. Yes, he was an eccentric, that much is certain. But that was the fault of his own sins and his egoism. I would *prefer to believe* that in the final part of his life he cast himself into the arms of the Lord and devoted the rest of his life to him, which caused many people to oppose him. This is what I would prefer to believe, even though he wounded people (including myself) indiscriminately and went further than he was justified in going, further even than *he himself knew*—that is the truth.

Poor Søren! You were trapped for so long in the net of an evil bird catcher— in the net of your own spectacular natural talents. But I cannot believe otherwise than that you finally came to work in the service of the Lord and that you have also done good for people, even if you were not capable of seeing the fruit of these labors, but had to be called away. In any case, the pictures you gave me have done good things in my home and have served as the occasion for many good conversations with the children. And your fate has elicited many quiet tears from me and has provided the material for many reflections about God. For me you represent a *great* sinner who nonetheless found grace for the sake of Jesus Christ! Your reflections upon the theme of "being *alone* with our Lord" and about letting him judge one to the marrow—they have been a great blessing and comfort for me and have helped me to rely not upon my own strength but to fetch the oil of life from the source itself.

Søren Kirkegaard renewed his old acquaintance with Boisen on that occasion, and he came out to see us. And he gave Boisen all the little illustrations in his [Kierkegaard's] Bible to give to me. At first he [Kierkegaard] wanted to keep the one of Jacob and Rachel, but he gave it anyway. Perhaps he was thinking of himself in connection with that Jacob, because he was occupied with thoughts of marriage in those days, and it was his engagement that prevented him from carrying out his intention to visit us.

Vilhelm Birkedal[2]

Here in Kristiania [Oslo] I lived at the home of the noble Wexel family together with him [Peter Christian Kierkegaard]. When he was in good health I had many fine conversations with him, and in one of these in particular he gave a sketch of his home and his old father in Copenhagen and of the relationship of the sons to that Christian man. He said that [his] brother Søren had often had heated clashes with the father and that, on Søren's side, the relationship between the two of them was far from being so full of pious devotion as one might believe, judging from the way he speaks of his father in his writings.

Marguerite Løfting[3]

One of Søren Kierkegaard's female cousins was very sweet and very annoying. She was very much taken with her new apartment, and he finally promised to come and have a look at it. When he came back he said, "Now I have seen Augusta's apartment. It was small, but ugly."

Once, when he heard that a lady had a slightly unfortunate reputation, he said, "Yes, I have always had a hunch that there was something historic about her."

Hans Peter Kierkegaard
(as told to Frederik Meidell)[4]

At a certain time of day [Hans Peter Kierkegaard had] the right to visit Dr. S. K., who otherwise, of course, had a house rule that kept him a flight of stairs away from all would-be visitors.

Dr. Søren Kierkegaard was not merely his relative, who occasionally brought little gifts for the sake of family ties, but over a long period he demonstrated a fraternal concern for Peter; he viewed Peter and his situation as entirely worthy objects of conversation, neither too lofty to speak of nor beneath notice. If it occasionally happened that Peter traveled [to Søren's] in vain, he could be sure that before long he would receive a characteristically brief note of apology, delivered by Dr. S. K.'s messenger—because it was only very rarely that the doctor himself came to the house where Peter lived. Peter preserved these little notes for his personal enjoyment. The notes pleased him because they testified simultaneously to a warm and careful regard and to an extreme carelessness with respect to the choice of writing materials. He enjoyed them as he enjoyed the memory of the hours he spent with his relative, the doctor, when he [Hans Peter] would listen with the receptivity of a child, while at the same time his [Hans Peter's] heart yielded up treasures that were of proven value and that bore comparison with those of the master himself. One day I heard an echo of some of the hearty and liberating humor with which he viewed his relationship to "His Philosophical Majesty" when he [Hans Peter] answered my question, "What do you two talk about up there?" "Mostly about things pertaining to the Kingdom of God," was the answer, and then, after a little pause: "He is so unspeakably loving and understands me so well, but I am really afraid to make use of his arm when he offers it to me to help me into my carriage. Usually we also talk about the family and my situation at home, as well; then it is just as if he had lived here with me for a long time." "But don't you talk about books, then, about his work as an author?" "Oh, yes. One time, right after I received it, I thanked him for one of his edifying discourses, which really seemed to have been written specifically for me. Once in a while we certainly also spoke about new books 'and such and things,' as old Father says."

Peter Christian Kierkegaard

[*M. P. Kierkegaard to P. C. Kierkegaard, July 29, 1826*][5]
Nothing has changed with us since you left, so our health and situation are about the same now as then. . . . As usual, Søren is spending his vacations in Frederiksborg.

[*P. C. Kierkegaard's journal, April 20, 1828*][6]
Søren was confirmed on the 20th and received my watch; I [received] Father's.

[*P. C. Kierkegaard to H. F. Lund, January 2, 1829*][7]
The fact that Søren is not growing is just as inconceivable to me as the fact that he does not write—or rather, the latter is explained by the former.

[*T. V. Oldenburg to P. C. Kierkegaard, May 17, 1829*][8]
When I last visited your parents, they were doing very well. I exhorted your brother to write you. He promised to do so; I cannot say whether he kept his promise.

[*P. C. Kierkegaard to H. F. Lund, July 3–4, 1829*][9]
I received a letter from Christian the day before yesterday, and I have also received one from Wilhelm, which has been replied to. On the other hand, neither Niels nor Søren nor my dear sisters have been heard from in a long time. It is true that I owe them some letters, but I will probably have to continue owing them for the time being.

[*M. P. Kierkegaard to P. C. Kierkegaard, July 15, 1829*][10]
I don't know how things are with Søren. I cannot induce him to write to you. Is it intellectual poverty, so that he cannot think of anything to write? Or childish vanity, so that he is unwilling to write anything for which he cannot expect to be praised, and, since he is unsure of himself in this respect, he would thus prefer to write nothing at all?

[*N. A. Kierkegaard to P. C. Kierkegaard, February 26, 1833*][11]
If you could get Søren to write in the same fashion, it would please me. He has a good head and has used his talents better than I have thus far.

[*P. C. Kierkegaard's journal, February 1834*][12]
Incidentally, the last half of the month was not very happy. Because, after I had decided to take communion, first on the 14th and then on the 21st, I was prevented from doing so—the first time by chance events, the second time because of doubt and anxiety (in part because of Matthew 5.23–24 and because

of the impossibility, as far as I could judge and in the light of my earlier request for his forgiveness, of becoming truly reconciled with Søren). And so this mood increasingly gained control over me.

[P. C. Kierkegaard's journal, March 1834][13]
   The young Bornemann, who has imposed his company upon Søren, really seems to be interested in me, which offends Søren without pleasing me. A conceited chatterbox, *ni fallor* [if I am not mistaken].

[P. C. Kierkegaard's journal, late July 1834][14]
   Despite the fact that there was really no significant improvement with Mother, Søren finally set out for Gilleleje on the 26th [of July] in order to spend two weeks there for the sake of his health. . . . On the morning of Wednesday the 30th [of July] things were significantly worse with Mother, so that I feared a stroke. One of Christian Lund's office employees was sent to Gilleleje after Søren, but he could only come home the next morning.

[P. C. Kierkegaard's journal, January 1835][15]
   Nevertheless, praise God, on the 16th I did take communion with Father, after I had tried to make my peace with Søren, with whom I have recently got along reasonably well, inasmuch as we have each kept to ourselves. I have also got along reasonably well with Father, who often enough must endure my depressed and irritable humor, which has been intensified by illness this month.

[P. C. Kierkegaard's journal, March 1835][16]
   Søren does not seem to be studying for his examinations *at all* now. May God help him to find a good way out of all this inner ferment and to the salvation of his soul.

[P. C. Kierkegaard's journal, July 1835][17]
   To judge from his letters, Søren is now well and busy with his studies.

[M. P. Kierkegaard to P. C. Kierkegaard, July 15, 1836][18]
   I think that Søren will write you by this same post. I have asked him to do so and have shown him your letter, but he is busy these days because the examinations begin at the Borgerdyd School today, and he has something to do there.
   I have no news, and therefore—praise God!—have no bad luck or misfortunes to report to you. Søren and I and all our other friends and relations are in reasonably good health and are well, as usual.

[P. C. Kierkegaard's journal, August 1837][19]
   Lately Søren has been depressed perhaps more than ever by brooding, most likely over his health, but it makes him unhappy and unfit, and it is close to

making him mad. To judge from recent days, when things really began to go wrong, the pleasure trip he took on the very day of the burial did not benefit him at all.

[*P. C. Kierkegaard's journal, February 1838*][20]
Søren has recently become more and more sickly, vacillating, and dejected. And my conversations with him, which I generally have to initiate, do not produce any perceptible difference.

[*P. C. Kierkegaard's journal, May 1838*][21]
P. Købke has had a relapse and is very weak. Søren is also very weak but, praise God, he is now beginning to come closer not only to individual Chrs. [Christians] (e.g., Lindberg) but also to Christianity.

[*P. C. Kierkegaard's journal, August 1838*][22]
It was also very comforting to me that he [Michael Pedersen Kierkegaard] had just been to church with me on the 5th and, as he had longed, he saw me take communion after M.'s death. I also found it comforting that on Monday evening he was very well satisfied with Søren and was in agreement with him, despite the fact that he had scolded Søren during the day and had refused him something.

[*J. Hahn to P. C. Kierkegaard, August 18, 1838*][23]
And now the only member of your family whom you have left is your own brother. Poor Søren! May not this blow strike him down, shake him out of his torpor, so that he does not long for the vanity of the world but gains the desire and the strength to search after the one thing needful, thereby putting to shame all those who—perhaps now, especially—doubt his seriousness and his integrity, doubt his efforts to achieve peace and reconciliation with God. Make his salvation your vital concern. Work for him and work with him, in prayer and exhortation, so that he might become your brother in spirit. Do not fail to seize this opportunity, but make use of it in accordance with the Lord's will, that you may be a tool in the hand of God and serve for his [Søren's] awakening. I feel the difficulty and the burden of this very clearly, as I myself have until now neglected my suffering brother, but nonetheless I know that it is a duty to remind you, so that you will not have to reproach yourself—as I, unfortunately, must do often.
Live well, dearest friend! Greet your brother and think of us out here.

[*P. Hansen to P. C. Kierkegaard, November 7, 1867*][24]
I beg you to forgive me for resorting to a letter as a substitute for conversation. And in this letter I make bold to approach you and the gentleman who was your blessed brother: him—our dear Nathanael (because God granted him to us!), the name of an Israelite, indeed of a man of Israel (because he was God's

true warrior!) without falseness—with whom I once (1839 and 1840) lived together in a house on Kultorvet, much to my own spiritual awakening.

[*P. C. Kierkegaard's journal, October 1841*][25]
    October: On the 10th (?), after a long period of struggle and dejection, Søren
broke off his connection with Miss Olsen (Regina). . . . On the 25th [of Octo-
ber] Søren traveled to Berlin, seen off by Em. Boesen and myself.

[*P. C. Kierkegaard's journal, November 1841*][26]
    On the 30th [of November] I received the first proper letter from Søren since
his departure.

[*P. C. Kierkegaard's journal, March 1842*][27]
    March: On the 1st and 2d I wrote Søren in Berlin a detailed reply to his letter
of January 27, in which I impressed upon him, as seriously as I could, that he
should not eat into the capital of his assets. In his letter he had suggested that I
sell off [some of his] securities in order to cover what he borrowed from me
while abroad. I pointed out to him that I could cover the amounts he had
borrowed up to now without having to resort to such means, and I counseled
him (also via letters to others) to consider things carefully and to be cautious.
And I offered in any case to lend him in my own name any amount that he
could repay within a year. But I requested that under any circumstances he give
me *formal orders* if I was to do anything that I might regard as disadvantageous
to him.

[*Else Pedersdatter Kierkegaard to P. C. Kierkegaard, July 1, 1842*][28]
    With confidence in the goodness of your heart I do not neglect to inform you
about how happy a letter from you would make me, inasmuch as I could obtain
information about the health of your dear wife and your brother; for I have also
feared for him because you hinted that his health was weakened. One dare not
expect that his engagement will be reinstated now that it has been broken off?
If you or your dear brother could convince yourselves to travel over here, it
would make us eminently happy.

[*P. C. Kierkegaard to Henriette (Jette) Glahn Kierkegaard, December 11, 1842*][29]
    Say hello to Søren, and ask him to write to me sometime *à la fortune du pôt.*

[*P. C. Kierkegaard's journal, February 1843*][30]
    I hear today in Sorø that Søren's work *Either/Or* has been published, but
under the pseudonym Victor Eremita.

[*C. Lund to P. C. Kierkegaard, January 12, 1850*][31]
    I can send you greetings from Uncle Søren. I spoke with him today and
found him very well.

[*J. C. Lund to P. C. Kierkegaard, May 2, 1851*][32]
Your brother is now living in Østerbro in the nice new building where General Bylov lived last summer. Fond of peace and quiet as he is, it is certainly a good choice for him.

[*C. Lund to P. C. Kierkegaard, May 20, 1851*][33]
Uncle Søren has also half-moved out into the country. He has left the city and now lives out in Østerbro, on the right-hand side as you leave the city, at the end of the lake, near Tutein's. He has taken lodgings there on the second floor of a large new building, with an entrance and a view facing a pretty garden and the lake.

[*C. Lund to P. C. Kierkegaard, February 2, 1855*][34]
For the first time, Uncle Søren's battle now seems to be dying down.

[*P. C. Kierkegaard's journal, June 1855*][35]
Søren's "This Must Be Said" and *The Moment*, nos. 1 and 2, are from the previous month; I occupied myself with them (N.B.: in my thoughts), after a fleeting glance at them and at many (but not all) of his articles in *Fædrelandet*.

[*P. C. Kierkegaard's journal, July–August 1855*][36]
Spoke against the pseudonymous (Sørenish) literature and theory at the Roskilde Convention on July 5.

[*C. Lund to P. C. Kierkegaard, July 9, 1855*][37]
Now that, as I hope, you have come back to home and to peace after the business at the convention, I want first to thank you for your hospitality and then to convey to you my heartfelt congratulations on the occasion of your birthday, as well as my wish that your new year might be full of joy, strength, and peace, the peace that passeth all understanding, and that we might all be permitted to sense the power of God's word in its ability to conquer lies . . . and awaken life where there was sleep and death.

[*P. C. Kierkegaard's journal, October 1855*][38]
I learned of Søren's sickness here (after September 26, most likely collapsed between the 27th and the 29th). Consequent to a letter from J. C. Lund, was in Cph [Copenhagen] from the 18th to the 20th [of October], and on the 19th tried to see him at Frederik's Hospital, but in vain.

[*Obituary, published in the "Supplement" to* Berlingske Tidende, *November 16, 1855*][39]
On the evening of Sunday, the eleventh of this month, after an illness of six weeks, Dr. *Søren Aaby Kierkegaard* was taken from this earthly life, in his forty-

third year, by a calm death, which hereby is sorrowfully announced on his own behalf and on behalf of the rest of the family by his brother

P. CHR. KIERKEGAARD

(The funeral will take place on Sunday the 18th at 12:30 in the Church of Our Lady.)

[*P. C. Kierkegaard's Statement Regarding His Public Utterances Concerning His Brother: Written March 14–16, 1881, published in* Dansk Kirketidende *(Danish Church Times), May 29, 1881*][40]

Since the death of my famous brother *Søren* I have frequently been asked whether I do not feel myself called upon to communicate to a broader public the external facts, at least, concerning the *three occasions*—during the period of his work and immediately after his death—on which I came to speak publicly concerning him and his work. And people have thought that I should see myself as in some degree called upon, and practically obligated, to come forth with some definite information concerning this aspect of his affairs, in order to prevent posterity from perpetuating, without correction or opposition, all the loose and confused explanations that abounded in the newspapers in the period immediately following *Søren's* death. In the very tumultuous time right after his death, I myself certainly felt impelled to attempt this sort of communication. But I soon learned that I must give up and abide by the words of the Psalmist: "But I was like a deaf man, who cannot hear, and like the man who has no reply in his mouth." Because every time I began such an attempt I felt more strongly, or at any rate more definitely, that, confronted with the reports and judgments that emerged in the literature surrounding *The Moment*, with which I had only partially and reluctantly acquainted myself, it would be impossible for me to give the requisite explanation in a more or less objective, brief, and circumscribed fashion. Becoming involved in a dispute about the correctness of my report would certainly have been something more than I could have borne. Subsequently many obstacles arose that need not be touched upon here. But now that fully twenty-five years have elapsed since *Søren's* death, and since the complete publication of his literary remains in their entirety—in the form in which they will come to be known and used by posterity—draws toward its conclusion, I am again faced with a request, now almost a summons, which I no longer dare to refuse or evade. So let the attempt be made, and let me emphasize that what will be presented are the plain facts, in the strictest possible objectivity.

The *first* time I came to speak publicly on the already quite voluminous literature with which *Søren* had enriched the Danish world of letters was at the meeting of the Roskilde Ecclesiastical Convention at Ringsted on October 30, 1849. And, as can be seen in more detail from the account in *Dansk Kirketidende* for 1850, cols. 171–93, on that occasion it was an almost extemporaneous lecture. Its *intention* was to be at once both an interpretation of II Corinthians 5.13, in the context of the passages that precede and follow it, and an application of that text with respect to the relation between *Søren's* works and Martensen's *Dogmatics*, taking into account each author's principal characteristics. No reader could mistake that, in the liveliness and detail of its presentation, as well as in its tendency (if I may use that word), the lecture was strongly and decisively on the side of *Søren's* works. Rather, one might be tempted to believe that Martensen's *Dogmatics* was mentioned and included more in order to have a foil—something that was current and known to everyone—than in order really to make use of it or evaluate it. But on the basis of his spoken remarks at that time, I knew well that *Søren* was nevertheless displeased with that lecture as soon as it appeared in print and he thereby really became acquainted with it for the first time. This, of course, is something that I now understand more completely in the context of his entire stance and his efforts. I do not, however, remember that we ever had any real discussion about it, because even then our relationship had long been such that when we visited each other we did not touch upon his writings or upon the degree to which I was in agreement with what he argued for in them. It became clear quite early on that there was a definite difference between us on various points. Thus from then on it was clear to both parties that my silence did not indicate approval or consent, and he came to realize that I kept silent about what he told me, with respect to plans, intentions, personal relationships, etc. Thus he expressed himself many times and in a lively and detailed fashion about all these matters, unburdened himself to a confidant, so to speak. And yet one of the conditions of confidentiality, namely accord, was missing, and only the other condition, silence, was present. I, at least (I am indeed not a particularly acute observer),* did not recognize that he had perhaps terminated this sort of confidential communication after feeling displeased with my above-mentioned public pronouncement. Indeed, when I reflect back upon the years immediately thereafter, it seems to me that I can remember even more detailed private interviews, as it were, with him, concerning intentions, clandestine resistance to his efforts, etc., than from earlier years.

Then came the end of 1854 and the year 1855, with his direct and express attack on Martensen and Mynster and his *Moments*. As best I can remember, when, on a visit to Copenhagen in the summer of 1855, I made a suggestion to the effect that he should travel for a while, he brushed it aside curtly and emphatically with the words, "Is this the time to travel?" And to some extent he was justified in saying this, because the custom of excluding things from discussion, which we had long since adopted, had indeed prevented me from including, in the presentation of my advice, a complete and bold statement of the premise on which it was based—and of course without that premise it must have appeared to be a counsel to flee from battle. I made another suggestion to him afterward, and said that it had of course been clear to both of us how far I was from agreeing with his views and with a great many of his statements, and

* In col. 191 of my above-mentioned lecture, it can be seen from the manner in which I discuss the article published under the initials "H.H." that I did not know that it was by him. [Peter Christian Kierkegaard]

that we thus had been able, without any dishonesty, to allow these things between us to remain unspoken—but that I was *now* willing to debate with him
concerning various of the principal points concerning which his efforts seemed
to me to be in error. This suggestion, however, was also rejected, with—as it
later seemed to me, although I did not notice it right then—a sense of exhaus-
tion on the part of that dialectician who had always been so quick-witted. At
the summer meeting of the Roskilde Convention, July 5, 1855, the chairman
(Lic. Ferdinand Fenger) brought up *Søren's* most recent activities, and, after
some brief remarks by Dr. Andersen (now dean at Ringsted), the convention
seemed to be of a mind not to deal with the topic in any detail. Nonetheless,
after the urgent request of Gunni Busck, in which the convention joined, I did
give a talk about my views concerning some of the principal features of the
trend that runs through the entirety of *Søren's* work as an author, which at that
point was just about finished. There was a promise in *Dansk Kirketidende* (1855),
col. 592, to publish this *second* lecture, which I never wrote down; nor, as far as
I know, was it ever published anywhere in summary form by any of those who
heard it. I had only begun an attempt to jot down the contents when I fell into
a lengthy illness during which I learned that *Søren* had come down with his final
illness. It is thus impossible for me to reproduce it, even in the form in which
I otherwise am able to reproduce from memory, sometimes long afterward,
what I have said on a particular occasion. I believe that I am able to mention
only two points with some degree of certainty. *First of all*, just as the 1849 lecture
began with a passage in II Corinthians and expanded upon it, I have no doubt
that this time I began with the passage in I Corinthians (1.22–24) about the Jews
who seek signs and the Greeks who seek wisdom, while the Apostle proclaims
the Crucified, the power of God, and the wisdom of God. And expanding upon
this, I tried to say what it was that for some time had seemed to me to be not
quite right and to be troubling in *Søren's* way of understanding and applying his
two principal assertions—the one concerning the paradox of faith and the one
concerning suffering as the way—and how I could not but think that these
features had emerged more noticeably in his later writings.* And *next*, I ended

---

* I must omit any further sketch—even the briefest—of what I tried to discuss there. Not only
because—as I mention above—I underwent a period of physical and mental pain and tension
before I could put my remarks into written form, and because it was so very long ago, but also for
another reason: in the latter part of 1842 (November 11), when Bishop *Mynster* ordained me as a
pastor, I had in fact used the passage from I Cor. 1.22–25 as the text for my sermon (not without
reference to Hegelianism, which was then rampant). And during the time from then until 1855—
and especially during the time from 1855 to the present—[this passage] has so often been in my
thoughts, and I have spoken of it so frequently, that it would be completely impossible (without
the addition of some material, perhaps a great deal of material, that was not a part of that talk and
which I had perhaps not even thought about at all) for me to indicate how I treated it in the talk
in question. Curiously, by the way—something that occurs to me only now that I think about
it—it was precisely during that tumultuous period which began after Mynster's death (and which
in a way was surrounded by that event) that for the second time I came to preach publicly on the
text from my ordination sermon. (Mynster had found it necessary to tell me, with respect to that

the entire lecture with a statement to the effect that, of course, in large measure, what *Søren* had given us and had argued for so ably in his writings was in the form of statements by various different, quite distinct, and characteristic persons or points of view—and that one could indeed almost come to imagine the possibility that even that which appeared with the signature "Søren Kierkegaard," might not unconditionally be his last word (but a point of view).

Apart from the small card on which, according to my habit, I had suggested to myself something of the elements to be included, I do not have any notes from the *third* statement to be touched on here, my speech at *Søren's* coffin in the Church of Our Lady. I do think, however, that from these notes, from what was in fact a slightly hostile or clumsy summary that appeared in a newspaper, and from my memory, I am able to state the contents *more or less* as follows. It began with an immediate expression of the feeling by which I was seized, and by which I had to be seized, when I now saw called away the last man of that relatively numerous family in which I had grown up, and of whom all but one had survived to maturity. But this, I then stated, was not to be dwelt on under these circumstances and before this group to whom I now spoke, no matter how much interest the person and writings of the deceased surely must be presumed to have stirred among a great many of those present—if not an interest in the children [of Michael Pedersen Kierkegaard], then in the old man and his spiritual influence, the head of the family, he who had stood at the graves of all his other children with the exception of the one now deceased and the one now speaking. It was in any case unthinkable at that point for me to make a statement about the *activities* of my now-deceased brother, a statement that could be thought of as in any way giving voice to an understanding of him and an assessment of his work that might be shared by the enormous crowd that was present. Because if anything was clear, it was that there were certainly many people present here, from all classes of society, who recognized that it was to him that they owed their Christian awakening or their further development in making Christianity a part of themselves. Similarly, there were many others who, though unable to admit it, had nonetheless been jolted by him into great spiritual movements and struggles. Finally, there were certainly more than a few people who believed that they had learned from him that everything that for generations had claimed to be Christianity was pretense and illusion. And there were also some who felt that they had learned that Christianity was in fact something so inordinately exalted that its reality was in any case not for them and that its demands had no claim on them. But there were such conflicting views among those present; some of them probably even stood by the coffin of the deceased in the belief that he, like a John the Baptist, had given a sign of the coming of the Lord with a winnowing fan to cleanse his threshing floor, and that he had done so with such power that even his [Søren Kierkegaard's] sign

---

ordination sermon, that I had spoken so rapidly that he had not understood a word of it.) [Peter Christian Kierkegaard]

had already demonstrated some of the effect of a winnowing fan. Another group must almost have imagined him as a Samson who had fallen, and in his fall had brought down among the Danish people a false Christian Church. In these circumstances, at any rate, the speaker felt himself unable to express what he perhaps would have and could have dared to say in particular to each of the different groups—if he had not been under the overwhelming impression of his brother's funeral—in the hope, at least, of sympathy and understanding from some of them. Nevertheless he [P. C. Kierkegaard, the speaker] would dare to express this much here—and in this he knew himself to be in full agreement with the deceased, who had long been thankful for everything he [Søren Kierkegaard, the deceased] had learned and suffered and accomplished throughout his life—namely, that for us, and for large numbers of the Danish people, there is a powerful summons *to thank* God the Almighty for what heaven granted him [Søren Kierkegaard] to bear witness to and to accomplish among us for the sake of the truth and for the sake of the seriousness of eternity. And to this he [P. C. Kierkegaard] would then add on his own behalf (and possibly on behalf of many others, especially among the Danish clergy) the *confession* that he not only had profound regrets but also felt a sincere shame and remorse, because during recent years none of us had understood that the vision of the deceased had become partially darkened and distorted from exertions and suffering in the heat of battle, causing his blows to fall wildly and blindly, as did Ølver's in the Norwegian saga; and that we should have acted as did Ølver's friends, and, with the confident gaze and the mild embraces of love, lured him or compelled him to take a long and quiet rest and to collect himself calmly after the excessive stress. But in connection with this he [P. C. Kierkegaard] would therefore conclude by *praying* to God the Father in the name of Jesus, that he would guide us with his spirit in the proper use of that to which the now-deceased, in accordance with God's will, had vividly witnessed among us—though without permitting ourselves to be hindered by fixing our gaze on that which is incorrect and misleading. (Naturally, no one will expect that I include my prayer itself, even if it were possible.)

[*P. C. Kierkegaard's journal, February 24, 1883*][41]

Wrote to the probate court out of sheer impulse on the 24th; started with I John 3.15; sent off the 27th; opened there, but by Dahlstrøm, who came to me right away; against my consent it [the letter] was given back to him and from him to me.

Henriette Lund[42]

Living outside of town in isolation agreed well with both Father and Mother. Both of them loved nature, both of them had a certain tendency to romanticizing, and both had been brought up in quiet, serious homes. In particular, the last years spent at home with Grandmother must have been very lonely for Father; as the youngest, he was the only one of the children still at home, and Grandfather had died years earlier. Mother had also experienced the separations that time and the vicissitudes of life bring about among brothers and sisters; her only sister, Nicoline, who was a few years older, had married Father's brother Christian a few years earlier. But she still had three brothers at home. Peter Kierkegaard, the only one of them still alive now, and until recently bishop of Aalborg, was the oldest. Next came Niels, who died at an early age on a trip to America. Last came the subsequently famous author, Søren Kierkegaard. He was then not much more than a boy, and of a slight and delicate appearance. He went around in a coat the color of red cabbage, and his father usually called him "the Fork," because of his precocious tendency to make satirical remarks.

Even though there was a serious, almost strict tone in the Kierkegaard home, I still have the impression that there was room for youthful liveliness, though perhaps of a more sober, homemade sort than is usual today. In the same way the house was also open, with an old-fashioned kind of hospitality. Most of the young men, probably primarily Uncle Peter's guests, were budding theologians. They also saw a good deal of the Boesens, who came from proper clerical stock. Grandfather [Kierkegaard]'s acquaintance with Councillor Boesen (the father of a numerous flock of both sons and daughters, several of whom were of the same ages as the children in the Kierkegaard home) stemmed from their common membership in the "Congregation of Brothers" in Stormgade. Both Councillor Boesen himself, who lived to a very old age, and his excellent wife survived long after the breakup of Grandfather's household. Councillor Boesen's wife was born a Hammerich and was the aunt of the two professors of that name. Later on I continued visiting them for many years.

Aunt Nicoline Kierkegaard's engagement to Uncle Christian Lund introduced them [the Kierkegaards] to a large family whom they had not previously known. The Lunds were different from their own family in so infinitely many ways, without, however, being any less endowed with marked peculiarities. Many a time I have marveled at the thought of the joining of these two families. Eccentricities thrived in quite another way in those days, when each was allowed to remain undisturbed in his little spot, whereas the increasing travel and easy social contacts of our era jumble individuals together and smooth away many angularities without anyone noticing. On the other hand, much originality and freshness is lost in this all-leveling cultural current.

When I think of life as it went on in Grandfather Kierkegaard's house, I feel as if I were carried so far back along the stream of time that not even the most distant sound from the hustle and bustle of today with its trainlike speed can reach back there. No, haste was not known in that house. Quite the reverse, one settled one's affairs sedately. Thus there might have been some truth in Uncle Søren's teasing remark that in his home the fine pastries were bought a fortnight before a party. Another illustration of the prevailing prudence and

spirit of uniformity can be found in the custom of buying and cutting the clothing for the second child's confirmation when the first child started preparation
for confirmation.

At that time it was considered good order—good order in which Grandfather concurred—that insofar as possible, sons were to enter into different live-
lihoods: i.e., not all would choose to study at the university, but one would go
into commerce, another to sea, a third into a bank, etc. Once Grandfather had
adopted a view, he was the sort who carried it out. Therefore, since Uncle Peter
was studying at the university, Uncle Niels was supposed to go into commerce
and indeed was compelled to do so, even though his heart was set on books.
This was a continual source of sorrow throughout the remainder of his rather
brief life, since he never felt he had found his proper niche.

Nor were the daughters especially favored in such an old-fashioned home.
According to Grandfather's views, daughters did not need much learning; quite
the contrary, at an early age they were to get used to attending to their more
learned brothers and to helping around the house. Fortunately, they were both
so intelligent and endowed with so much natural charm that any possible defi-
ciencies in general knowledge were never noticed. But it really must have been
a great change for Mother to wield such complete sway at Father's side—as
complete, at least, as was compatible with her own mild and slightly melancholy
nature. Later on in life, when, with her intellectually curious and striving mind,
she complained of the gaps she perceived in her book learning, Father perpetu-
ally replied that he was pleased that she had not learned everything she had
wished to, since in that case she perhaps would have paid him no notice, and
they would then not be so happy. Throughout his life Father also believed that
it was most fortunate, and in every way most appealing, if a lady was not very
well acquainted with her husband's fields of knowledge. Perhaps it was this
particular recollection [of my mother] that he vaguely kept in mind. At any rate,
it is hardly an everyday occurrence that giftedness and natural intellect make up
for what is missing.

Grandfather and Grandmother Kierkegaard had had two children in addition
to the ones mentioned here. The elder, a daughter, had died as an adult, but I
do not recall ever having heard of what illness; the younger, a half-grown and
robust boy, died of a blow on the head received in play at school; and of this
whole flourishing flock only Uncle Peter and Uncle Søren survived their aged
father. Grandmother must also have died during the years in which the daughters and Uncle Niels were snatched away at such close intervals. I do not remember her at all, but she was referred to in the family as a kind little woman
with an unpretentious and cheerful turn of mind. Her sons' development was
a bit over her head; their high-flying appeared to her worried heart to be a flight
away from the level on which she felt comfortable, and on which she would so
much have preferred to have kept them. And she was therefore never more in
her element than when a passing illness forced them ever so slightly back under

her jurisdiction. She was especially gratified when she could get them peacefully into bed, since she then wielded her scepter with delight, cosseted them, and protected them like a hen her chicks. Her motherly inclinations also agreed with the grandchildren in the family. Her plump little figure often had only to appear in the doorway of the nursery, and the cries and screams would give way to a hush; the rebellious young boy or girl soon fell sweetly asleep in her soft embrace.

When Mother was taken from us, the last in that sorrowful sequence of deaths, I had just turned five. Nevertheless, I do not remember her. Yet a little evening prayer, which she had taught me, was for a long time my only refuge when I wanted to turn to the Father who dwells in heaven, where now Mother, too, was. In addition, I have a vague impression of her presence on particular occasions, as when the letter arrived telling of Uncle Niels's death, which I believe that I remember, or when she taught me that it was pointless to rip toys to pieces in order to search for a soul. I did not understand her words, but I comforted myself nevertheless by finding a soul in a quill pen, which seemed to me to have something of the transparency and delicacy that my thoughts connected with this mysterious entity.

My brother Vilhelm, one year my junior, believes, however, that he can remember a lady with long, blonde hair, who was sitting up in bed when he was led into her bedroom, probably to see her for a moment when she had regained consciousness. But during her last illness I was sent away from the house; otherwise, such a farewell would also have imprinted itself on my memory. On the occasion of another farewell—my parting from my childhood home— I was reminded of the long, blonde hair: a long golden lock, still as fresh as if it had just been clipped off, lay hidden there. The days of her life were so few that the first golden gleam had not yet been darkened with the dimmer hue painted by time, until at last both sheen and color are stolen, and the difference between blonde and dark is erased. And yet it was just those days of which Father had often dreamed with pleasure—the time when they would live together, gray with age, and finally accompany each other in death as in life. For the rest, Mother was tall and slender; her figure is referred to as very beautiful, as were her eyes. Small hands and feet were characteristic of the family, and her whole appearance, like that of her sister (who, however, was smaller, more buxom, and both livelier and more determined in manner) is said to have been attractive and sensible. A picture of Aunt Nicoline exists; admittedly, it was drawn after her death by Christian Kierkegaard, the son of one of Grandfather's cousins; but unfortunately there is no portrait at all of either my first or my second mother.

Grandfather survived all these deaths by more than four years. We children often visited him, in particular after we moved into Father's place on Gammeltorv, since Grandfather lived in his old apartment at the location on Nytorv between the apothecary and the City Hall where a memorial plaque to Uncle Søren was later put up.

I have the most vivid recollection of the aged, venerable figure of Grand-father in a long beige coat, his trousers stuffed into the tops of his narrow boots, a sturdy cane with a gold head in his hand, and, not least interesting to us children, his pockets filled with Pfeffernüße. His build was powerful, his fea-tures firm and determined; he carried his head bent slightly forward, while his eyes had an expression as if they were dreaming, still staring out over the moors of Jutland, where he had herded sheep as a child. But the dreams now seemed to go much farther afield, beyond the narrow limits of this earth, toward the longed-for goal of eternity, which the old man yearned for with all his soul. It was as if a quiet homesickness held sway over him and made his last days into the wandering of a pilgrim in foreign lands. But by no means should this give the impression that his character was sad or morbid; his speech was too lively and clear and his whole bearing too forceful for that. Rather, his calmness in sorrow might be found astonishing by those to whom his mode of thought was unfamiliar, although he may perhaps have seemed less than sympathetic because he had become accustomed to viewing the sorrows and pains of life with eyes other than those of more worldly types. Yet at the same time he was always ready to help with word and deed, whenever he could.

When he lost his two beloved daughters in rapid succession, he of course bowed his old gray head even lower, but nonetheless he folded his hands and praised God, who both gives and takes away. And when his house was engulfed in flames, and he was suddenly and unexpectedly presented with *that* spectacle, he placed his worldly welfare in God's hands with this same calmness: he went about doing what could be done with an almost festive heartiness. On the other hand, sometimes he let himself be vexed by petty aggravations and then his natural melancholia emerged. Melancholia was in truth his daily burden. More than most he knew the truth of Goethe's words: "We all suffer in life." But unlike that great poet, he had grasped hold of the faith that both comforts and gives to the poorest person a greatness that is far greater than that attained in the richest of earthly lives.

Grandfather had retired from trade in his fortieth year, and after that had primarily occupied himself with reading philosophy. In particular, the German philosopher Wolff was the object of his studies. And since he was thorough in everything he did (almost to the point of painful scrupulousness and exactitude), his reading was definitely not merely skimming over the surface. If I had not known the details of the story, I would have found it inconceivable that he, a poor boy who had come over here [from Jutland to Copenhagen] penniless, had succeeded in laying the foundation of a fortune that was quite sizable for those days. Indeed, I could not imagine him as possessing that sort of talent, and his honesty was almost of an overly conscientious sort. Order and frugality, even though the latter bordered on the severe, were hardly a sufficient explanation. Good fortune—great good fortune—must have played a role, and it did. That good fortune came in a form that spelled misfortune and ruin for most others: the decree of January 1813, which in one blow turned many a rich man into a

View of Gammeltorv as it looked in the middle of the nineteenth century. Part of the Nytorv is also included in the picture, and the Kierkegaard family home at number 2 Nytorv can be seen on the left-hand side of the picture, next to the courthouse. The towers of the Church of Our Lady and of St. Peter's Church can be seen at the right and left, respectively. Lithograph by Em. Bærentzen. From a photograph in the Picture Collection of the Royal Library. Reproduced courtesy of the Royal Library.

beggar by transforming fortunes in both money and bonds into mirages. Royal bonds were the only securities left untouched, and Grandfather was among the fortunate who owned them. Not only did he avoid losing his own modest fortune, but it grew proportionally as everything around him fell, and the continually rising market in the years afterward completed the task. In those days, all that was required to make a fortune grow on its own was to sit back calmly and hold on to what one had acquired.

When we [grand]children, both from Kjøbmagergade and Gammeltorv, spent an evening at Grandfather's, much was made of us, and great delights were always prepared for us. A long dinner table—well supplied in accordance with the standards of the time—awaited us, and afterward we played (not music but card games, old maid or twenty-one, and other games). To be sure, my brother and I had to pass up a good many of the pleasures of the table: the head cheese and other pickled or rich things that looked especially interesting were strictly forbidden to us by the instructions we brought from home. Miss Møller, Grandfather's proper, stiff, but exceedingly good-hearted housekeeper, shook her head in exasperation and remarked: "There are always so many things that the children from Gammeltorv aren't permitted." But Grandfather merely obeyed orders. His was no milquetoast good-nature! To him, obedience was

Peter Tutein's house, number 42 Købmagergade, at the corner of Klareboderne. Johan Christian Lund and his family lived in this house in Kierkegaard's time. The Borgerdyd School can be glimpsed on the left-hand side of Klareboderne. Sepia drawing by H.G.F. Holm, 1823. Owned by Copenhagen City Museum. Reproduced by permission of the Copenhagen City Museum.

not merely one of several fundamental principles; I think it was *the* principle itself. If he could raise his gray head above the earth once more to look at the family, he would probably apply Pascal's words to them and sorrowfully cry out: "It is so difficult to obey, and that is why it is so difficult to believe."

Uncle Peter was almost never present at these dinner parties, but Uncle Søren almost always turned up, at least toward the end of the evening. My memories of him actually begin at just about that time. In fact, it even seems to me that they date from one particular moment, when I saw him step inside the doorway and remove his hat from his shock of blond hair, all the while nodding to us with pleasure. And here I cannot avoid adding a little comment: it is of course not so strange that the younger generation, who hardly know his looks from any source other than the drawings in *The Corsair* or, at most, from having seen him only toward the end, just before he gave way to a degenerating illness, should think of him almost as a caricature. But I remember that I was most surprised a few years ago to see signs of a similar, though not so extreme, view in an otherwise most beautifully written article, which at the time was generally ascribed to Prof. Brøchner.

How could anyone who had ever spoken with him at close quarters, who had seen his intelligent face and the whole of his fine figure, exclaim ironically: "His physical attractions were rather few"? Indeed, I do not share the older view of things, when people preferred to believe that his body was broken in order to let his spirit shine in full glory; that was an aspect of the genius-worship of the times and was not without affectation. But however much one respects harmony and the eternal laws of beauty—or as an even more extreme opposite [to Kierkegaard], if one idolizes the athletic body type—still, this does not necessitate closing one's eyes completely to the beauty to be found in the type that is delicate and fine, and to the piquancy born of the contrast when such a body type is coupled with a spirit and an intellectuality that are anything but fragile.

On the little pencil drawing of him that I own, the nose has been given a somewhat too elegant and aristocratic turn, which brings to mind a portrait of Lytton Bulwer [sic] in his youth. Uncle Søren's nose, though crooked, was bolder and more substantial. On the other hand, the mouth, eyes, the entire form of the head, and the abundance of the hair are a splendid likeness. His posture is also typical. His mouth was large, but at the same time, what a range of different moods found expression in its curves and lines, all the way from soft sadness and tenderness to spirited contrariness or refined irony—and this latter was not the least dominant trait! And then his eyes, which lost nothing over the years; on the contrary, their naturally soulful expression gained such an intensified brilliance that they shone like stars when I took leave of him out at the hospital.

One pleasure that I also remember from Grandfather's house was watching the opening of the Supreme Court; since he lived right next to the City Hall and Court House, it was indeed almost as if the whole show were put on in our honor. We stood at the window and watched the two heralds in velvet capes, mounted on magnificent horses in the middle of the square, while the whole of the splendid Horse Guard formed a half circle around them. The message proclaimed by the herald also promised delight for the next day, when from our own windows we could see the king ride by in the golden carriage in a truly dignified parade to open the Supreme Court.

Grandfather was eighty-four years old and still so strong that nothing suggested that he might soon depart this life. Even so, the doctor no longer thought it advisable that Grandfather follow his old habit of taking an emetic once a year. But Grandfather liked old habits and would not follow his advice. It turned out, however, that the doctor was right, because he [Grandfather Kierkegaard] died, calmly and quietly, a few days afterward from the strain it entailed. Uncle Søren bought the place after Grandfather's death, and for a number of years he lived in part of the old apartment, while Uncle Peter used the other wing, at least for occasional lengthy stays. He [Uncle Peter] lived here during the years when his first wife, Marie Boisen, the daughter of Bishop Boisen of Lolland, was alive, and later on, during the first years of his marriage to Henriette Glahn, one of the daughters of Pastor Glahn at the Garrison Church, until he was called to the little parish of Pedersborg and Kindertofte near Sorø and moved away from Copenhagen for good.

Since Mother and her brothers and sisters were the same ages as the children in the Agerskov family, they of course spent time together. But it was especially Uncle Søren who, as a boy, visited the family repeatedly. During a visit there, while they were staying at Buddinge Mark, he fell out of a tree and hit his back so hard that (at least he himself believed) it influenced his health for the rest of his life—the first link in a series of painful events that would lead him down his lonely path. He himself once told me how old Madame Agerskov had impressed him on that occasion when, deeply distressed and in her sober manner, she said: "Dear child, will you ever in your life give me as much joy as the sorrow you have given me today?"

Mother, then a young married woman, was present when it happened and had to drive home, leaving the pale, suffering boy, whose tears fell slowly but unceasingly, as if from an inexhaustible well. She pressed a small purse of money into his hand as a salve for the wound. Immediate and effective medical attention would probably have been more appropriate. But no one thought of that at the time.

A summer stay with Cille's parents in Lyngby stands out in my memory as a refreshing, brief episode from the time during which I had been taken out of Miss Zeuthen's School, partly to have a holiday after scarlet fever but partly also because my second mother did not like girls' schools. At this point the new arrangement, whereby my brother and I were to study at home with Miss Lindbom, had not yet been put into effect.

During the last years of their lives, they [Cille Agerskov's parents] had established a laundry and bleaching works on a rather extensive plot of land with gardens and meadows that went right down to the stream by Sorgenfri Forest. That year, while they rented out the side wings of the equally extensive buildings (which still bear the name "Bleach Farm"), they themselves lived in the main building, which had many rooms as well as an old-fashioned, spacious veranda and the largest of the gardens, which sloped down toward the bleaching green. Since there was also plenty of space inside, they had taken Uncle Christian's children as boarders, my girl cousin and the "big boy cousins," as we called them, as well as Miss Dencker, the housekeeper. Some rooms in one of the side wings were rented out to Uncle Søren, who lived there for a couple of the summer months. Thus I found a large company there on the lovely day when I, too, was sent out there with permission to stay for a while. I took no little delight in running in the beautiful forest, romping among the stretched-out linens on the green slopes, building forts by the creek and ships to sail out into the wide world; I would lose myself scrutinizing the secret life that stirred down there, where the sticklebacks, water beetles, or whatever there might be slipped out of their hidden chambers and then, after a moment, disappeared again without a trace.

Uncle Søren, whom otherwise I now saw only rarely, eagerly entertained us during this holiday period. Even though, at least in my case, this often meant some teasing—so that at first I would even think, "Oh, no more peace!" as soon as I caught a glimpse of his slight figure and heard his short, half-choked laugh, which appeared to shake his entire body—it didn't take long before I guessed that a hidden partiality and tenderness lay behind this teasing manner, and my spirit, as well as my pleasure at seeing him, returned. The more clever our repartée, the more Uncle Søren enjoyed himself, and his chuckling little laugh was positively infectious. Once, in the heat of battle, when at my wit's end for lack of a bright reply, I was so quick with my hands that I slapped him instead of answering back. Uncle Søren could, with good cause, have responded as did the man whose opponent in court had spit in his face: "Yes, but this proves nothing." For a moment it looked as if an even sharper remark than this was hovering over my head, but my obvious perplexity evidently changed his mind, because a kindhearted, irresistible laughter immediately resolved the affair. Nor could he have been angry very long at "Madame Spectacles," as he usually called me, making fun of my tendency to sit and stare, while forgetting the whole external world—a tendency that he himself certainly had to an even greater degree.

Despite Mother's antipathy toward girls' schools, I went back to school again when I was about ten years old. This came about because Uncle Søren, who was otherwise loath to interfere in any way in the plans of parents, put the whole weight of his influence on the scales, as it seemed to him that I had too melancholy a nature to cope with the additional loneliness that results from being taught at home. I don't know if it was to celebrate the happy result of his negotiations concerning this matter, but shortly afterward he invited me to drive out to Lyngby with him. I do remember, though, that the trip was on a lovely autumn day, and that both my girl cousin and the big boy cousins were included. The trip out was very lively, and many stories were told about school and the approaching beginning of school. With horror I heard various examples of how difficult things could be, and this feeling hardly diminished on hearing Uncle Søren's well-orchestrated finale, in which my name was to remain on the blackboard for a full fourteen days [prior to my arrival at school], so that the others could get used to it before the actual person became subject to inspection! But as tireless as he was in teasing us, he was equally loving as well, and equally excellent at taking care of us. He wrapped me in his big traveling cape

on the drive home, which took place in deep silence, since Uncle Søren immediately fell into daydreams, while we children were probably nodding a bit
sleepily or were busy watching the sky and its ever-changing physiognomy.

In the late summer of 1838 Grandfather Kierkegaard died. I remember very
clearly that one day, during the time he was ill, we were on a visit at Uncle
Christian's and that Uncle Søren, who took it all very lightly and viewed it as
a bagatelle, arrived at the same time that we did. How difficult the transition had
been for him, and the extent of his sorrow at the loss of his father, became clear
to me only later. Mixed with this sorrow there was also perhaps some regret,
beyond that which we always must feel when we lose those who are dear to us,
since we are forever in their debt. And perhaps we are never more painfully
reminded of the insufficiency of the whole of our frail nature than when we are
separated from our parents. We understand their love only when we ourselves
must assume the position of the older generation and must be the ones who
quietly provide, while each step forward no longer opens our view of new
prospects of the future, as it once did, but instead reveals hitherto unsuspected
depths in the past, often in a surprising way. Then we must humbly confess
how, despite all our speculation and fancied knowledge, we have often wan-
dered as though blindfolded.

   But in Uncle Søren's case there was also the special situation that he had not
acceded to his father's earnest and long-held wish to see him take his [theologi-
cal] degree. As early as 1835 he [Søren] had written the following in a letter to
Uncle Vilhelm in Brazil (included in *Posthumous Papers: 1833–43*) [draft in
B&A I 36 (*SV* XXV 47) and *Pap.* I A 72, p. 51 (*SKJP* 5092, p. 24)]: "Father
believes that the real Canaan lies on the other side of the theological diploma,
but he has made the ascent, just as Moses did Tabor, and reports back that I will
never reach it." To Grandfather, his apparent inactivity and his strong proclivity
to reading widely could only appear a most worrisome phenomenon. And it
became apparent only later, when he had made his name as an author, that these
years had in no way been wasted. The memory of his father's worries was,
however, a heavy burden for a melancholy nature like Uncle Søren's, a burden
that may have grown with distance, like a shadow. This impression could only
have been strengthened by the fact that death had snatched away the strong old
man so suddenly. Even so, he [Søren] apparently maintained his old habits; he
turned up in the cafés as usual and walked just as eagerly in the streets. It was
only between seven and eleven each evening that visitors were not received.
During these hours he studied diligently, and in the course of a very short time
he had prepared himself for the degree that Grandfather had earlier anticipated
with such longing.

Uncle Peter Kierkegaard was sometimes present at these festivities [at Uncle
Christian's house in Købmagergade], but Uncle Søren came only for the brief
visits that he made at the evening hour when he usually came by to see Uncle

Christian. He would then chat with each of us, but was particularly delighted to see Aunt Jens Lund and Marie Falbe, each of whom was so very lovely in her own way that it would have been difficult to find their equals.

As the children [of Uncle Christian] grew up they were permitted as many parties as they could wish. I remember the first children's ball and how oppressed I felt at my earliest acquaintance with the little ladies of Copenhagen, who (despite their short frocks and the braids that hung down their necks) had about them the air of blasé ballroom ladies. In the beginning, the young gentlemen, friends of my boy cousins, preferred fencing and amusing themselves with Uncle Søren, their declared favorite, to the attractions and joys of the dance.

When, shortly after I had started in school, we were surprised by the news that Uncle Søren had become engaged, I was to meet "the new aunt" for the first time at Uncle Christian's house. She was a pretty young girl of eighteen, extremely loving to us children and eager to win our love in return, which was scarcely difficult under the circumstances. Soon afterward, we were invited to a visit at her home, where everyone, not least Uncle Søren, served up everything for our enjoyment.

Her parents lived in one of the old buildings in Børsgade, and its back yard faced the present Slotsholmsgade. For me, who until then had known hardly anything of Copenhagen aside from the route from Gammeltorv to Kjøbmagergade—my school was in fact also on Kjøbmagergade, just as Uncle Christian's house was, too—it was a great event to walk so frequently through the interesting arcades and on past the castle as well as the beautiful Stock Exchange.

It was through her parents' windows that I also remember having seen the procession when Princess Marianne arrived as the bride of the crown prince, and it would be hard to imagine a more beautifully arranged reception. The day before, my brothers and I had seen the arcade, decked with scarlet cloth, which stretched all the way from the palace down to the pier, where it broadened out onto a richly decorated dais. This was where the king and queen were to receive the young couple, whom I could now see standing in the royal barge, which glided slowly from the harbor into the canal while the crowd cheered, music played, cannons thundered, and the pink-muzzled white horses (which at the time were viewed as something uniquely Danish and indispensable for every royal pageant) shook and trembled with every shot! When I think of it, I can still remember it all like a beautiful picture. The sun shone clearly, and she looked so fine and lovely, dressed from top to toe in rose red, the color of youth and happiness. He stood at her side in an admiral's uniform, a genuinely gallant and manly form with a royal dignity that distinguished him so wonderfully and that irresistibly reminded one that here was the scion of an ancient race of kings. Oh, if only it had not been merely the sun and all the externalities that shed their glory on them! How much better things would have looked for Denmark if only inner reality had corresponded a bit to the external appearances!

On that occasion there was a great gathering in the apartment of Regine's parents. A lot of ladies, in particular, were there, and they all asked eagerly after her sweetheart. But to their great amazement he had chosen precisely that day to take a walk in the woods with her father; her sweetheart had thus not been alone in his eccentricity.

One day during the summer I was allowed to come in from Vesterbro or Bakkehus, where we must have been living at that time, and visit Regine. She was just as loving as always, but it seemed to me that I noticed clouds in the skies which had previously been so bright. When we said goodbye, she followed me through the yard out to the Slotsholm side, where the canal had not yet been filled in at that time, and I remember how surprised I was at coming out of the shade and into the bright bath of light, where the sun played on the water and the many impressive buildings. Here we once again said farewell, and for a long time afterward I could see her at the same spot in the clear sunshine with her hand over her eyes, nodding a last greeting to me—how definitively it was to be "the last" we did not know then, and yet I returned home with a feeling of something sad in the air.

I couldn't give any definite form to this sense of foreboding, nor did I hear the least bit afterward. Thus shortly after we moved back into town in the autumn, when we children were invited over to his house, I didn't know that Uncle Søren had broken off the engagement. He was then living at the old place on Nytorv together with Uncle Peter, who had recently married Henriette Glahn.

I can only faintly remember Uncle Peter's first wife, Marie Boisen. It does not seem to me that she was pretty, but I do have a wonderfully warm impression of something truly lively and warm. She sang beautifully; I remember that one evening on a visit there with my parents I heard her sing Bürger's *Lenore* and that everyone was much taken with her voice. Aunt Henriette, on the other hand, was really beautiful, with something delicate and fine, almost refined, in her looks, and a charming feminine softness in her manner. Her speech was soft but full of grace, and she was a lovely hostess.

When we children from Gammeltorv and those from Kjøbmagergade (who were also invited) arrived there that evening, she [Aunt Henriette Glahn Kierkegaard] received us in a very kindly fashion, happy that we had come to visit her on our own; but she was soon made aware of her mistake when Uncle Søren immediately arrived to take us in to his apartment. He appeared much moved, and instead of his usual playfulness he kissed my hair so gently that I was quite touched. After a moment, he wanted to speak to us, but instead broke into a violent fit of weeping, and without really knowing what there was to cry about—at least this was the case for me—but simply carried along by his suffering, we soon were all sobbing as if burdened with a heavy sorrow.

Uncle Søren quickly pulled himself together, however, and he told us that one day soon he would leave for Berlin, perhaps to stay away for quite a while.

We therefore had to promise to write to him frequently, because he would be anxious to hear how each of us was doing. With many tears, we promised.

Soon after, we returned to the parlor, where we found Uncle Peter busy reading aloud to his wife. In our honor lotto or some other game was taken out, and again every attempt was made to amuse us a bit. It took quite a while before even modest success was achieved, however, and when Uncle Søren just then opened the door to ask about something or other, I remember being cut to the quick by the notion that he might think that we had already stopped thinking of him. He himself looked as if he had been crying ever since we had parted!

I started my twelfth year of life rather inexperienced in handwriting; nonetheless I kept the sacred promise [to write to Uncle Søren] and received regular replies. On one occasion, I remember, I was about to get a bit high-flown in one of my letters. It happened like this. On the way home from school one day, I witnessed a strange event. I suddenly found myself in the midst of swarm of people around a carriage, which was moving slowly from the City Hall toward Nørregade. Every face shone with enthusiasm. At that instant a man put his head out of the window—an interesting head to see—and everyone looked at him while the name "Orla Lehmann" was on everyone's lips. He had just come from having delivered his famous speech in his own defense. That was as much as I heard. I no longer remember how the rest was explained to me.

I had heard absolutely nothing about this affair at home. My parents did not regard the freedom movements of the time with sympathy, and in cases like this Mother behaved as if she believed that the saying "Talk about a thing, and it gains power" was absolutely true. She didn't talk about it at all. It must have been in the air, because in my own way I was instantly familiar with the situation and full of the youthful hatred of oppression—which meant more or less that every existing arrangement of things is oppression and that anyone who rises up against it is a hero.

One fine day, after I had quietly sustained this new passion for some time and had not been able to dampen it by consuming large quantities of Orla Lehmann–brand sweets (as did my schoolmates as well), I decided to confide in Uncle Søren. Unfortunately, it happened that on just this occasion Mother read my effusions, whereupon she remarked, quite curtly, "I would advise you to rewrite that letter because that matter does not interest Uncle Søren." And because previous experience had shown that such "advice" was synonymous with an order, I had to busy myself politely with a new letter, in which, after the strong lyricism [of the previous version], the turns of phrase were indeed a bit forced, but which on the other hand reported the events of our domestic life more accurately. Each letter could perhaps serve as an example of youthful attempts in the "hysterical" and "historical" epistolary styles discussed by Weyse.

I remember another, very different, evening that we children spent at Uncle Søren's, which must have been right after his return home. Yet it was after he had moved out of his old apartment on Nytorv, because I remember that it was in his place on Nørregade. I remember that we arrived, as requested, very early in the evening and were received rather ceremoniously by our host, while Emil Boesen, later archdeacon in Aarhus, who was visiting, quickly removed himself in order not to disturb the event. As we came in, Uncle Søren presented my girl cousin and me each with a bouquet of lilies of the valley, quite a rarity for the season, and then he gave beautiful presents to each of us. We were hardly finished admiring the various things before "Anders," Uncle Søren's faithful servant, the well-known bringer of many a pleasant surprise both at Christmas and on birthdays, informed us that the carriage was at the door. "Oh, then we must be off!" cried Uncle Søren. "Where?" Ah, no one was told before we stopped at the various, prearranged spots of interest, where we were shown the lesser-known sights of the city. Strangely enough, the only thing I remember from this trip is a seal, whose melancholy, humanlike eyes made a deep impression on me.

After our return we played lotto; the prizes consisted of various items, mostly books. Then supper arrived: sandwiches, a marzipan cake covered with the most magnificent flowers, and champagne. Uncle Søren was the attentive, untiring host, and Anders equally diligent as the waiter. But since children in those days were not so pampered as today—so that, for example, wine was a rarity, and champagne, even for the adults, was served only on great occasions—Father and Mother did not approve of this repast, just as they thought the whole evening's event had been rather much. I heard expressions like "spoiling children" used, accompanied by a few sharp remarks about "that preposterous person."

But if they took the party to be just a random impulse, I think they were wrong. To me, at least, it seemed as though he wanted to celebrate some special occasion, which was perhaps important to himself but which remained a secret from us. Not long afterward he wrote: "It is over, my dinghy is afloat. In a moment I will be there again: there, where the ideas roar with elemental force, where thoughts arise noisily like the peoples of the earth in migration; there, where at other times there is a stillness like the deep silence of the Pacific Ocean, so still that one can hear oneself speak, even though the movement takes place only within oneself; there, where every moment life is at risk, where every moment it is lost and won again" [SV III 254 (KW VI 221)]. Perhaps, then, he wanted to gather us together one more time before he went further out onto the lonely deep; despite outward liveliness and joy, it was thus a farewell party, and there was a sadness to his mood.

In fact, he did not invite us to visit him again like that, and never again would we all gather together at his home. We visited him individually; we saw him when he came to visit, mostly at Uncle Christian's; and finally, we also met him on the street, where he always knew how to find us if there was something he wanted to say or if he longed to see us. I have vivid impressions of these meetings, especially from my school days.

Just as at the gathering in Lyngby and a number of earlier visits, these encounters were not always without a little sting. One of my many faults in those palmy days was the bad habit of going out with "tulip fingers" [open, unstitched fingertips] on my gloves. And, as is so often the case, to avoid the trouble of sewing them up, I subjected myself to many other, far greater, inconveniences. Thus I discovered that I could hide my lack of neatness by quickly pulling off my gloves every time I shook hands, and I explained my behavior by pointing out that Christian VIII usually did this out of politeness. While carrying out a similar maneuver with Uncle Søren, however, I had the bad luck of exhibiting a slightly inky finger, at which he immediately cried out, "Oh, if you have become so learned that you have ink spots on your fingers, then I don't dare talk to you anymore!" And he quickly disappeared.

Another time it was even worse, and again it was neglect that caused my downfall. The rule for neatness at school required that we use blotting paper in our notebooks. I was not the only one who frequently forgot this rule, however, and thus had occasion to admire a schoolmate who, when there were drops of ink, adroitly managed to suck them up with her full lips. Once, when I wanted to take the step from admiration to imitation, I was so stricken with disgust at the decisive moment that all the ink (which I couldn't bring myself to suck up) unfortunately remained on my lips. And, because mirrors were viewed as unnecessary in school, the traces had not completely disappeared before I walked home. As fate would have it, I again met Uncle Søren, who this time did not even condescend to say a word, but only gave me a deep bow and walked past me, smiling.

At other times, however, all was happiness and harmony between us. He could even amuse himself by introducing "his little niece" to individuals of whom he was fond: "There goes Prof. Sibbern; come now, you must have a closer look at that man," and so on. In general, the streets of Copenhagen were for him one large reception room, where he moved about all the time and spoke to everyone he wished to. When he was gone, and I was never again to meet his dear and familiar figure, it seemed to me as if the entire city had suddenly become empty and foreign. My wanderings had also expanded from my rather limited school route: the arcades on Sunday mornings; the many sudden twists and turns in the small streets of the neighborhood, on which the afternoon sun casts its brief smile as spring approaches; the ramparts on frosty winter mornings; and untold other places had brought me greetings and conversations with him whom I now missed.

I can still remember a little episode from my school days, where the above-mentioned Anders was obliged to play the tease. It must have been on my twelfth birthday that he brought me a letter from Uncle Søren, which upon being opened turned out to contain only a rather primitive pen-and-ink drawing of a flower, which he was giving me for my birthday. Below, in large letters, was added: "But by all means don't show it to anyone, because it is so silly!"

This referred to an incident shortly before, when I had given him a drawing and had evidently used this genuinely schoolgirlish expression. But my anger at this unexpected treatment had hardly had time to reach its maximum before the trusty Anders returned with a new letter with quite different contents, accompanied by a package that on closer inspection turned out to be Poul Møller's posthumous works.

Just a few days earlier, at my cousins', I had got hold of a book that quickly reduced me to the same state as the man of whom the Spanish king had remarked, "Either he must be mad, or he is reading Don Quixote!" The story of "the frizzy Fritz" had sent me reeling with laughter and hilarity. Now that I had that treasure in my hands as my own rightful property, I was so overwhelmed with ecstasy that I could hardly find words with which to express this to Uncle Søren. Even so, he was somewhat disappointed that chance had placed a book by Poul Møller in my hands before he had managed to do so.

After that he gave me no more books; still less did he send me his own—it was against his principles. On the other hand, I was allowed to borrow freely from his library and to keep the books as long as I pleased.

It seems that he preferred to look after my musical development. Presents like the music from *The White Lady*, *Figaro*, and several others still bring this to mind. Still, these were intended only to teach me to find modest enjoyment in the magic of music, and not out of any interest in my becoming "an advanced musician." He used to say, "Plain bread is best."

When we came home from church [the day Henriette Lund was confirmed], I remember that Uncle Søren was there waiting for us; he actually visited us only rarely after Father's second marriage, nor did he stay very long that day. But the next day he sent with his present a letter in which he expressed his warm wishes for me quite explicitly. Uncle Peter Kierkegaard, who could not come in person, also wrote to me; his wife, Aunt Henriette, came over in the evening, however, where she met representatives from every branch of the Lund family. For some of those concerned, this was a study in the meeting of contrasts! To see Marie Falbe (plump and glowing, in the complete *grande toilette*, with decolleté and short sleeves) next to Aunt Henriette (of the same age and quite lovely, but with her narrow, delicate face modestly wrapped in a matronly cap, a tightly fastened-up, high-necked dress, and with sleeves fitted perfectly to her little hands)—it was almost as if one were looking at that beautiful painting in the Palazzo Sciarra-Colonna by Luini, which depicts two so differently dressed female figures, about whose allegorical meaning opinion is still divided. If they did have a conversation, their thoughts and opinions were probably no less different.

Sometime after my confirmation, my cousin and I were invited to visit the Pedersborg parsonage where Uncle Peter Kierkegaard was then the pastor and where my frail Aunt [Henriette Glahn Kierkegaard] had not yet become so sadly bedridden, as she was later to be for nearly thirty years. Riding in Uncle

Christian's own carriage (which he got rid of for good soon after, when the war broke out in 1848 and he gave the horses to the army), we arrived at the cheerful parsonage together with her [Aunt Henriette's] mother on a lovely summer evening. Situated on mounds that were the remains of ancient ramparts, the parsonage garden still shows clear signs of having belonged to an old baronial castle.

The first Saturday after our arrival, a stagecoach rolled into the courtyard with just one lonely passenger. It quickly became clear that this passenger was Uncle Søren, and now there was much ado. Sunday morning broke with a cloudless sky, and the dinner table was set in the open on one of the little hills in the garden. I still remember with what animation Uncle Søren spoke and the many funny stories and remarks with which he obliged us. But in the evening, when we lay down in the grass by the little lake, this brilliant merriment was cut off as if by a single stroke. He only stared straight ahead in deep silence, dreaming, and not until the moon, like a half-erased death mask, looked down on us from the dull June sky did he break the silence to greet it softly and pathetically with Aladdin's words:

> Oh, pale moon!
> You who measure out time here on earth,
> Why were you so short with me, you cold,
> You sallow miser? Why were you so stingy? Etc.

Despite all our pleas, the next day he was off again on his way back—he never permitted himself any long holidays.

Once, in the last years of Uncle Søren's life, when I met him on the street, he spoke almost with enthusiasm about ladies' needlework. It seemed to him that such a pastime was enviable because of its necessarily restful qualities. But in order to be healthy and natural, rest presupposes work; it will not do as a starting point, or as an unchanging, continual occupation.

And now needlework became the alpha and omega of my existence. For Mother, who not only had lived much longer than I but had also become acquainted with the difficult side of life, it surely was rest, and she must have assumed that I was just fine when sitting comfortably, needle in hand, without any particularly pressing need to finish the work. Her nature was also quite different from mine; it did not occur to her how much healthier for body and soul it can be to use one's abilities, even amid adversity and hardship. There were no worries in our home, but neither was there any use for my abilities. Everything was so well ordered; the one cog fit so perfectly into the next that the movements became almost mechanical, and any changes were unthinkable.

Knowledge was what I strove for as long as there was any vigor left in my soul, but Mother's will and the conventions of the time rose up against this like a double iron wall. Perhaps my aspiration was neither energetic nor self-conscious enough. As a dreamer from childhood on, I in fact needed the help of others so that all my fermenting, self-consuming powers could find a goal in life and my talents could develop appropriately. But even if I had turned to Uncle Søren—who had insightfully noted my needs earlier and arranged that I go to school—he wouldn't have given me any other answer than his favorite principle: "Plain bread is best." Furthermore, seeing me troubled and miserable, he would only have feared that any interference would be inopportune and a hindrance to the beginnings of my possible growth toward eternity and the one thing needful, which was perhaps stirring within me. And truly, what is human sympathy, with its scanty means and shortsighted calculations, when compared to God's mercy, which has another and greater goal than our mere earthly welfare?

No matter how rarely Father saw Uncle Søren, nor how foreign Uncle Søren's intellectual development was to him—something he himself, oddly enough, used to document by telling about a painting that Uncle Søren had given him as a reward "because he had been so sensible as never to have read one jot of his writings"—still it was impossible for this brother-in-law to be other than precious to Father. He [Uncle Søren] had been the favorite brother of his [Father's] late wife, and was in many ways similar to her. And, for his part, Uncle Søren also had warm feelings for Father. I am reminded of this by a brief letter, one that only a fortunate happenstance saved from the flames during one of those sad leave-taking days on Gammeltorv, when much more was burned and destroyed than I would find necessary now in calmer moments. The letter was from Uncle Søren to Father on one of his birthdays, and he expresses in a heartfelt way his appreciation of Father's merits; he found Father's quiet constancy and unchangingness particularly appealing. I later gave the letter to my brother Troels.

As for the painting that had been accompanied by that joking statement of approval, it was actually given in gratitude because Father had taken care of his money matters. This, however, was not a difficult task, because according to Uncle Søren's own arrangement, his fortune had simply been divided into portions, which he gradually used up quite calmly. He did not become wealthy through his writings, but he privately exercised charity toward many needy persons and did nothing to provide for his subsistence and his future. He viewed the security of possessions and what the world calls prosperity as mere hindrances and burdens on his way toward the land of eternity, and in quiet, daily self-denial he sought to realize his ideal of life, which was certainly quite distant from the eager aspirations of most people.

I remember well the day when Father came home from the bank and said that Uncle Søren had been in to see him in order to get his last portion. It was in the winter of 'fifty-five. Father had looked at him sadly and inquiringly, and he had answered with a long serious look. "God knows what Søren has in mind," added father with a sigh.

Despite the fact that Uncle Søren visited Uncle Christian Lund's much more often, his entire nature was foreign to that brother-in-law, and his development incomprehensible to him. Many a time, even when I was a child, I was amused by their good-natured disputes, which almost always ended with Uncle Søren turning his head away from his adversary, staring into empty space, and making a face that gleamed with satire, merely saying just these few words with emphasis on every syllable: "Now, that was a devil of a thing!"

When, many years later, the first volume of the *Posthumous Papers* had appeared, I remember that I listened with a smile to Uncle Christian's remarks on that occasion: "Yes, isn't it a dismal thought that a person who always appeared so happy was so thoroughly melancholy; but how could anyone be in a good mood while he was using up his fortune like that!" Yet this is nothing in comparison to the wrongheaded ideas I have heard from strangers from time to time.

Before I get farther away from the inexplicable things we may encounter in life, I must add that the reason why I am so little willing to deny the possibility of such things on others' behalf may well stem from my having experienced something similar myself. But since all this touches upon only aspects of my life that are not dealt with here, I will not dwell on it.

While on the subject of Uncle Søren, however, I can't help recounting a dream in which he appeared, and which moved me by its great clarity, even though it cannot really be said to contain anything definitely supernatural. Nevertheless, I do not wish to explain further why it necessarily made a particular impression on me. I must, however, preface my remarks by noting that at that time I was troubled, and that a certain disquiet regarding religion had also seized hold of my spirit.

At that point I dreamed one night that I had gone on my usual morning walk, and that Uncle Søren suddenly came walking toward me, just as in the old days and large as life. People say, of course, that after ten years' time not even the best memory can retain an exact picture of someone who has died. This was well over ten years after his death, but not even real life and clear daylight could have brought a more definite likeness to my eyes. While at some distance, he unfolded his large, white handkerchief with a familiar gesture, and with what tenderness and sympathy he gazed at me as he stood there facing me! I cannot say what he said; actually, I don't know if he said anything. But in that spectral way in which such things happen in dreams, I received both assurance that the cause of my sorrow would continue, and yet comfort; and there was also another hint, which suggested that I should talk to Uncle Peter Kierkegaard.

Really and truly, the very first news I got the next morning was a message that Uncle Peter Kierkegaard was expected in Copenhagen from Aalborg that very same evening. I followed the hint, and not only on this occasion but also on many later ones I found comfort and reassurance in a conversation with him.

But back to the time when Uncle Søren was still alive, even if I saw him much less frequently than in my childhood days, when he always arranged to

meet us children every so often. I knew quite well that the reason for this
change was primarily his fear of dragging us into the sort of publicity of which
the lack of understanding by the general public had on several occasions made
him the object. I knew this was so, at least with respect to his concern for me,
because he had said as much to a mutual acquaintance. But how far I was from
understanding at that time what a sacrifice this was for him! First, I myself had
to learn the extent of the tenderness, the almost quivering pain, by which the
heart can be bound to the children in a family. One is not always allowed to take
care of them according to one's own lights, but the mere sight of them is nonetheless a joy and also a comfort in many a lonely moment.

No, at that time I really did not grasp this at all. Nonetheless, when, contrary
to his usual practice, he came walking out to Gammel Bakkehus one summer
evening, I remember how amazed I was at the exactitude with which he apolo-
getically explained that he had not seen me more than three times in the course
of the year. He had had reason to consider the number [of his visits] carefully,
and there had not been as many as he had wanted.

That very evening remains quite clear to me. It had been a warm day, fatigu-
ing for many people. And now it was as if nature herself were resting after the
sun's heat; even the constantly rustling poplars seemed to be quiet for a moment
in a drowsy calm, and the whole of the old farm lay enveloped in a hazy twi-
light, while the inhabitants of the houses and farms round about came out to
enjoy the cooler air. When we accompanied Uncle Søren back to the road to
Copenhagen, a whole group of gentlemen were still sitting outside at the neighboring farm with Mr. Hall, then a minister in the government. "You promised
to look in on us on your way back, Dr. Kierkegaard!" they called after him in
unison. "Yes, and I am looking in, as much I can," was his teasing answer, as he
nodded and swung his thin cane in the air.

I remember that once, when I met Uncle Søren in my early youth, he teased
me by being unwilling to admit my right to have an opinion about some subject or other that was currently popular. In the ensuing dispute, in which I
attempted to demonstrate my dignity and maturity, also with respect to intellectual matters, there was, however, one argument that instantly overpowered
him. I said: "Yes, because I have learned to appreciate love." With a changed
expression, and with a serious tone of voice, he replied just as quickly: "That is
another matter. Then you are right. I realize now that you really are grown up!"
I still remember it. It was as if he had taken off his hat and bowed to me with
enormous respect.

Though I was admitted to be the victor by such a keen observer, I now feel,
with the experience of later years, that my proof had been pulled out of thin air.
My awakening to reality came about so late that it is impossible that at such an
early point I could have had the necessary maturity of mind to express myself in
that way—that is, in such a way that my words were backed up by a serious
idea—which must have been what Uncle Søren thought. Strictly brought up,

as I had been, and accustomed only to rather restrained affection, both my circumstances and my own nature were such that I tended to value intellectual things exclusively. I therefore had to be treated quite roughly by life before I could not merely admit but also feel in my innermost heart that love is the source of life, the roses of which grow for the most part in valleys. It required quite a struggle before I was to learn to respect lesser gifts, the "ordinary minds," which are often like the mortar that holds together the stones of buildings. My understanding of things in those days could be compared to the view I had so often from our summer house, when the haze melted away from distant Copenhagen and the towers and large buildings of the city were the first things one could see. Both in life and in literature, only the great and remarkable managed to arouse my attention.

Once during the last year of his life, when I met Uncle Søren on the street, he expressed amazement over my interest in Shakespeare's *Hamlet*, which had caused me to read and reread it, both in the original and in translation, as well as to follow with great interest the least details of the work's performance. I tried to involve him as a participant by asking him if he himself were not captivated and moved by this strange drama. "Yes, but it is a completely different matter with me," and when I stared at him inquiringly, he added as some sort of explanation, "You cannot understand it now—perhaps someday you will."

Later, when remembering these words, I have thought with sadness about the sympathetic connection there must have been at that period in his life between him and the melancholy prince, for whom the "native hue of resolution" always gave way to the "pale cast of thought" and to whom the ghost from the bowels of the earth continually called out, urging him to speak and to act. It was just such an urging voice that spoke to Uncle Søren, though from the depths of his own soul rather than from those of the earth. Long and faithful practice in the service of the Idea had made him attentive, so that he made no mistake about what it meant but thoroughly understood his mission in life, understood with anxiety that the most difficult part still lay ahead: to assert the truth of the Ideal to a soft and pampered generation in a completely different way, in order to demonstrate pointedly the dangers of thoughtless devotion to the State Church; in a word, to awaken, to awaken all those who slumber and are secure—and human beings love slumber and security. But after the fervor of resolution, he was also tempted by the pale cast of thought. It told him that, from a human point of view, he would be defeated in the struggle. It showed him that he—though equipped by nature with precisely the eminent mental powers with which he could easily avoid such a fate—would be at the mercy of everyone, that both crude and subtle weapons would be directed at him, and, finally, that he himself would also come to strike and to wound, which would cause him profound pain. But a man standing alone on the field of battle cannot be softhearted—which he was by nature to no little degree. He was strengthened in battle by the pure and elevated beauty of the Idea. And who else could

with greater right struggle in the light of that Idea than he, who was so completely disinterested in his relation to his times—he, who was so foreign to all
personal rancor as well as to personal interest?

But in the end he struggled as one for whom time is short and who therefore
uncompromisingly pushes everything to extremes. He felt the earth shake beneath him. No wonder, then, that one can point to errors and one-sidedness.
Yes, one-sidedness is the accusation; but it must be remembered that it is rare
that anything is accomplished without great one-sidedness. The strongest cur-
rents flow through the narrowest chasms. And those whose call it is to recover
the treasure—the moment of truth that has been lost or distorted in the mael-
strom of time—have no eye for anything but this one thing, for which they
humbly and faithfully sacrifice the joys of their days and the peace of their
nights—indeed, even their heart's blood, should it be required. To others is
given the task of putting to right what has been recovered, of putting things in
their places—and of finding the errors in what has been accomplished.

In this last period of struggle, this hard year, Uncle Søren did not fail to think
of those closest to him. I do not know for certain whether it was he who was the
first to suggest to Uncle Christian Lund and my [female] cousin the idea of
taking a trip abroad to Paris and London, where one of my brothers and one of
my [male] cousins had recently traveled. But Uncle Søren was pleased about
this, and I know for certain that it was he who arranged that I go along. He was
troubled by the feeling that we might take the battle too hard, and he was
therefore able to say farewell with a completely satisfied expression. At the
moment of our departure he even took the opportunity to whisper in my ear
with a bit of his old teasing: "And be sure not to forget your native tongue!"

In the beginning of the same autumn, a message suddenly arrived that Søren
Kierkegaard had collapsed, unconscious, on the street; a carriage had been
called and he had been driven to Frederik's Hospital. I was not at home when
the news reached me. I rushed home and was immediately able to join Father,
who was just on his way to him. I don't remember now whether it was on the
way or at the hospital itself that I heard what Uncle Søren had said to those who
had received him, something like what Tasso had said on entering St. Onofrio
Monastery: "I have come out here to die." But when I entered the little room
and was received by the glow that practically shone from his face, I got the
impression that a feeling of victory was mixed in with the pain and sadness.
Never have I seen the spirit break out of its mortal frame and impart its brilliance
in that way, as if it were the very transfigured body on the Day of Resurrection.
On a later occasion, when I went in to see him, his expression was different, and
the misery of his illness was more prominent. But I will not forget that first time
or his loving farewell.

When the last, sorrowful period of illness was followed by death on November 11, 1855, I myself was so concerned with the past that the thought of what
lay immediately ahead made no impression on me. I do not know whether the
others also experienced this. Perhaps no one individual felt any definite call to

make the arrangements. Each person may well have been slightly too disposed to rely on the others, and it was probably in this way that some things were decided by mere chance—for example, the choice of the day of the funeral. This should not have been allowed to fall on a Sunday. The considerable stir that *The Moment* had caused, not least among a class of society which in no way understood how to distinguish the heart of the matter from its outer trappings, made it unfortunate, in any case.

Uncle Peter Kierkegaard was of the same opinion when he arrived in Copenhagen from the parsonage at Pedersborg and discovered that it had been arranged in that way. But when a number of the clergymen of the city came to him and demanded that, as a man of the Church, he ought to change the arrangements, he put forth his own view that a change now, at the last minute, would only be viewed as cowardice and therefore ought to be avoided. And so things remained as planned.

But I will not forget the painful feeling that took hold of me that day in the Church of Our Lady, when from a seat in the gallery I looked out over the nave of the church, where the tightly packed mass of people surged like an angry sea, while a ring of rather unpleasant-looking characters had placed themselves around the flower-decked coffin. Then the church door opened once again, and to my joy in came a compact group of people of a completely different appearance. They wished to follow Denmark's great thinker to his grave and to stand around his coffin as a guard of honor. But could they make their way through? With undivided sympathy I noticed in the foreground a powerful figure who bravely opened the way; the others followed him just as valiantly until they had conquered the space, and their ring replaced the other like a solid wall.

As for clergymen in vestments, aside from Uncle Peter I saw only old Archdeacon Tryde. Had I been in the mood for it, I would probably have smiled at this sight, since he evidently was not in the least comfortable. His little skullcap was pushed back and forth on his head at a feverish pace, while his face, usually so benign, wore an expression of profound annoyance. But now Uncle Peter stood up, and soon the skullcap was allowed to remain at rest. The restless sea of people became still as glass, and I could cry in peace while he reminisced first about the old home in the days when it blossomed with young people, of whom he now was the only one remaining; then he dwelled on the deceased, and in a well-constructed, powerful speech attempted to sketch his significance for the Church.

After the coffin had been carried out and the ceremony was over, I remember that Peter Boisen, now deceased, a brother of Uncle Peter's first wife, came up to me in order to comfort me in his gentle way. But I remember even more clearly, however, the way in which Mother, when I came home, came into my little room, sat down quietly, and with that dignity she possessed—a dignity which also contained something strangely sad, with a fleeting hint of weakness—asked me not to think so much about the dead, and not to cry so much

(Anna) Henriette Lund. Photograph from a visiting card. From the original in the Picture Collection of the Royal Library. Reproduced courtesy of the Royal Library.

over them, since this of course accomplished nothing. It was better to think of the living, those whom we still have with us, and whom one could both help and please. True words and healthy thoughts, which we are all too likely to forget with each new loss. But there is comfort in constantly having a task, however weakly and imperfectly we carry it out each time we try.

　A few years before Uncle Søren's illness and death, I had attended Vartov Church one Sunday, accompanied by several friends. Earlier, I had repeatedly avoided going there with them. It had seemed to me that in order to come into harmony with the spirit of that place I would practically have to violate my own nature and sacrifice my individuality. But I remember well the strangely tranquil mood of that day, and I was so deeply taken with the lively hymn singing (which at that time was something quite unusual) and with the earnestness of the entire church service, that I continued my visits, and I only smiled in return when, on one of my first walks over there, I met Uncle Søren, who in passing remarked with a smile: "It is actually not considered proper to join Vartov!"

Troels Frederik Troels-Lund[43]

As has been mentioned, he was my father's brother-in-law, because in 1828, several months after Søren Kierkegaard had been confirmed by P. Mynster, the curate at the Church of Our Lady (subsequently a bishop), Father had been married by this same minister to his [Søren Kierkegaard's] favorite sister, Petrea Severine Kierkegaard. First as a schoolboy, later as a university student, Søren Kierkegaard had always been a welcome guest in their rural home on Nørrebro Allé and was free to enjoy himself there. It was at their place that he made his first attempts at horseback riding. And later on, when they moved to their newly purchased place on Blegdam Road, with its large garden fronting on Sortedam Lake, their home became even more attractive to him.

In those days the family was gathered for a short, happy time that was like a beautiful autumn day. Then they were torn asunder by autumn storms. Vilhelm Lund departed anew for Brazil, never again to return. Petrea and Søren Kierkegaard's mother became ill and died. During zealous efforts to care for her and save her life, Petrea herself, who was pregnant, became ill and died in December 1834 shortly after having given birth to a son, who was named after her: Peter Severin.

For both brothers-in-law this death was a decisive blow. Within a short time Søren Kierkegaard had lost the two people dearest to him: his mother, the mild, gentle sunbeam of his childhood home, and his sister, the merry, understanding playmate in her bright, new home.

For my father, the loss of his wife and his happy home was at first even more crushing than for the young people, for whom life, with its call to action, still lay open. Supposing himself close to the end of his life, he persuaded his relative of roughly the same age, Anna Cathrine Lund, who was highly respected by all the family, to become a mother for his four children.

This relative aroused Søren Kierkegaard's lively interest even though he had hitherto known her only slightly. He admired the purity and strength of her character and her strong sense of reality. She was neither disputatious, nor dictating, nor weakly submissive, but represented something new and unusual: quiet, purposefully active, or at any rate, with a ready and willing grasp of things, supported by a deep, but simple religiosity and a cheerful courage in the face of life.

Troels Frederik Troels-Lund. Daguerreotype. From the original in the Picture Collection of the Royal Library. Reproduced courtesy of the Royal Library.

There must have been something in her that reminded him of his mother's mild, gentle optimism. But here it was coupled with greater firmness, and there was more resilience in her pliancy. She radiated a quiet strength. Naturally it was his mother's manner that he valued most. But if she had also had Cathrine's strength, wouldn't she have been able to hold his father's peculiarities in check? Remarkably, she had already gently but definitely shown the old man the limits of his authority over the grandchildren. She had the necessary courage and was also capable of doing so without offending him!

In the beginning, her view of Søren Kierkegaard was not entirely positive. She knew him mostly only by reputation, according to which he was a rather irresponsible person. And now she also heard his father speak about him with misgivings. His own slightly exaggerated mode of behavior did more to create amazement than to instill confidence. Even though he often came to their home, was liked by her husband, and was on friendly terms with the children, he was still a puzzle to her. Despite his obvious gifts he must now and then have seemed to her strangely immature, capricious, and ill-mannered.

The brother, Peter Kierkegaard, was indeed easier to understand and accept. On October 21, 1836, a half-year after my parents' marriage, he married a daughter of the late Bishop P. O. Boisen, Elise Marie, of whom they both became very fond. When she died the following summer and Peter Kierkegaard moved in with his father (while Søren from now on lived on his own), the association between the two homes, nearly next door to each other on Gammeltorv and Nytorv, quite naturally became very frequent and warm.

For some time, however, the relationship between Mother and Søren Kierkegaard still remained for the most part one of mere observation. He viewed her with interest and respect. She viewed him with some wonderment and with the uncertainty that a lack of complete understanding often easily entails.

Then there occurred a complete change in 1838. The loving care with which Søren Kierkegaard looked after and nursed his father, after having discovered the reason for his melancholia, could not fail to touch anyone who saw it close at hand. All her life, Mother had been used to caring for both young and old. Her old father was still alive. Almost from her childhood she had had to try to lead him, cajole him, accommodate him, encourage him. Not only did Søren Kierkegaard's new manner strike similar chords in her, but she had a fine ear for the genuineness of these new strains.

And this breakthrough remained a part of him even after the death of his father. Despite a bit of easily forgiven dandyism (in the form of attempts to present himself as if he were a mere idler), he worked with unusual energy and faithfulness to achieve his father's most cherished wish. In July 1840, two years after his father's death, he took his divinity degree with top marks. A couple of months later he became engaged to seventeen-year-old Regina, the daughter of a respected civil servant, Councillor of State Olsen in the Ministry of Finance.

My parents followed the whole of this development with the most intense sympathy. All the best in Søren Kierkegaard had broken through and had almost transformed him. With pride and joy Father watched the unfolding of much of what he had sensed, hoped for, and believed in regarding his favorite. And Mother felt somewhat apologetic that she had not immediately understood how profound and amiable his nature really was. What was still missing was no more than what a good wife could manage to straighten out. With the warmest of feelings, they both welcomed the charming, happy young girl who had now linked her fate to his.

The year 1840 was the period when Søren Kierkegaard's rising star reached its highest point in my parents' firmament. I was born that same year. Perhaps early unconscious impressions prepared my psyche to feel devotion and sympathy for him.

Søren Kierkegaard's star did not long remain at the zenith in my parents' home. Hardly had they become acquainted with and fond of his young bride-to-be before he broke off his engagement with her.

In those days, a step of this sort was much more unusual than it became later on, and it was more likely to cause bitterness than a divorce between married people nowadays. It was an insulting break, which not only called forth curiosity and gossip but also absolutely required that every decent person take the side of the injured party. The time when it occurred was unfavorable, both in the social life of Copenhagen and especially in the small circle of our home.

A later era has reconciled itself with his behavior (understanding it in part as a necessary condition for his development) and has at any rate appreciated the profundity of the feeling with which he viewed her as "his Regina" throughout his life, happy to place the laurels of his fame as an author upon her brow. The gripping words of Christian Winther's poem resound throughout his writings, both as an apology and as a continued declaration of love:

> You may think I have forgotten you,
> But believe me if you can,
> I have hid you in my heart,
> And past the edge of the grave,
> Despite the bitter cold of death,
> Beyond life's shores
> Will carry your fair name
> Stamped deep in my breast.

But his contemporaries suspected nothing of this. They witnessed only Søren Kierkegaard's irritating behavior, the apparently merely egoistic, teasing, and inconsiderate way in which he had thrust her aside and had forced her to be the one who broke off the connection. If at the time anyone had tried to explain his conduct as the self-expression of a smoldering melancholia and of the urge to write, as the strange ways of a suffering and unusually gifted soul, the natural response would have been: "Oh, of course, self-expression—balderdash! It is the height of selfishness, of seeking one's own advantage by being vicious to someone else."

Crushed and torn, Søren Kierkegaard fled to a lonely hiding place in Berlin, while here at home harsh judgment was unanimously voiced against him. Disapproval, anger, and shame were as strong among those closest to him as anywhere. Even from the faraway mountain caves of Brazil was heard: "Give Cousin Troels my congratulations on his engagement and Magister Søren my condolences for his stroke of genius of the opposite sort."

In time things sink into oblivion and are healed. When the sensational book *Either/Or* appeared in February 1843, and Søren Kierkegaard was alleged to be its author, he became a different person in the public eye. The few petty incidents from his engagement that were still being talked about merely became the ornamental foliage framing the piquant final section of the work's first volume, "The Diary of a Seducer." His continuing flood of productivity quickly transformed him into a highly interesting and remarkable author.

When his former fiancée married an earlier admirer, Johan Frederik Schlegel, the head clerk in the consular office, even the most exacting of moral bookkeepers finally declared his past accounts to be settled up and in order. She thus disappeared from the saga and turned up again only many years later. Fate was kind to her. She lived together happily with her husband, who possessed an unusually amiable and harmonious nature. Because of his competence, he acquitted himself well in his position and was promoted far higher than the young couple had dreamed. He became the governor of the Danish West Indies and subsequently was president of the Copenhagen city council, receiving the Order of the Great Cross and the title of councillor of state. At the same time, her past came to blossom in a new form. Through the publication of Søren Kierkegaard's posthumous papers a halo spread out around her as the one he had never forgotten, but to whom he had dedicated his works and his fame. Fresh and youthful in appearance, modest, natural and gentle, she occupied a peculiar double position, until her death in 1904 at the age of eighty-two, as Søren Kierkegaard's fiancée and as Councillor Schlegel's wife.

Søren Kierkegaard's closest family did not forget his broken engagement quite as quickly as did strangers. After his brother Peter Kierkegaard became pastor in Pedersborg-by-Sorø in September 1842, the only two members of his "closest family" in Copenhagen were his brothers-in-law, the merchant Christian Lund and Father.

Christian Lund was the eldest in the family and was respected as such. Now and then he hosted family gatherings, and Søren Kierkegaard was always sure to be among the guests. It was not uncommon for me to encounter him there, because in accordance with the nice custom of the family, the younger as well as the elder were of course invited.

The tone between the two brothers-in-law, Christian Lund and Søren Kierkegaard, was of a special sort, however. I have—perhaps wrongly—an impression that it became sharper after the broken engagement, and that this later intensified when Søren Kierkegaard became a standing joke in *The Corsair*. It consisted of an oddly superior and mocking form of address from the older man and of sharp, witty counterattacks in response from the younger. But clearly it must have been painful for Søren Kierkegaard to be stung by references to the broken engagement. From a few suggestive remarks in his *Posthumous Papers*, it seems to me that I can now detect a sharper eye for the weaknesses of this brother-in-law than I had earlier realized.

In my parents' home the situation was different. Of course my impression of how Søren Kierkegaard was viewed after he had broken off the engagement does not rest on contemporary observation. I was much too little then—only a few years old—to observe and reflect on a situation like that. My impression was formed by inferences drawn from what I later heard now and again from my parents, from my brothers and sisters, and from Mother's sisters. Nevertheless, I believe it gives a fairly reliable picture of the actual situation. It is at any rate the truth for me.

As I mentioned before, my parents strongly disapproved of and deplored the fact that he had broken off the engagement, and especially the manner in which it had happened. Therefore when he returned in the spring of 1842, after half a year's stay in Berlin, his star was descending in our home. He himself undoubtedly had a definite feeling that this was the case, and he stayed away more than he had earlier, which must also have been a necessary consequence of the enormous project he was then working on: from March [1842] to February [1843] he wrote the two volumes of *Either/Or* and prepared them for the press, in all about 850 pages of small print.

After the book had appeared, and public opinion regarding him shifted, a corresponding change did not occur at home, or at any rate not so suddenly. In part this was because my parents scarcely read the book with any particular admiration; it was remote from their taste and background. And in part it was because they assumed that no matter how well the book was written, it hardly changed the moral evaluation of his previous actions. Naturally it pleased them, in a way, that his book was a success, and they did not begrudge him that.

Mother was the strongest and the leader. Søren Kierkegaard's behavior had offended her sense of honor and loyalty, and her sympathy remained with the injured party, the cast-off woman. Father certainly viewed the case as she did, but without Mother's firmness he would probably have withdrawn his verdict and would have allowed himself to be guided by the spontaneous affection he had felt for his old favorite, and despite everything, continued to feel for him until his death.

Strange though it may sound, the coolness that set in does not seem to have offended the person who was its object. Søren Kierkegaard was much too fine an observer not to be aware of both the source and the cause of that coolness, even though the subject was not mentioned. On the contrary, his interest and respect for Mother seems only to have grown. There was something in the firmness of her opinion that attracted him and inspired respect—she did not behave aggressively, but neither did she give in, allow things to be brushed off, or let them evaporate into oblivion. From that moment on she entered his experimental collection as a reliable touchstone for healthy moral feelings—although in certain cases, e.g., his own, one ought to take the religious leap away from those feelings and out into the "Paradox."

Mother's viewpoint indicated a limited and lower sort of verdict, which was without validity for him. But, at the same time, he was moved and touched by her judgment because of its loyalty and sympathy for the woman whom he had had to leave. He shared these feelings himself, wrestled with them, as it were, alternately exalting and ridiculing them. Here again, the calm firmness of Mother's judgment furnished a sort of landmark, a point around which his writings continually circled for years.

He had little understanding or approval of the fact that from the moment when Regina Olsen's engagement with cand. juris. Schlegel in the summer of 1843 became a reality, the affair was viewed as concluded. For him there was something humiliating in this. But he buried himself in the issue all the more eagerly, and made of it a sort of mountain cave, into which, like his brilliant friend and relative Vilhelm Lund in Brazil, he descended untiringly, ever to unearth new discoveries defining the nature of life.

A confidential relationship of an unusual sort developed between our home and Søren Kierkegaard during this period, when he approached my father with a request with which he [Father] found it difficult to comply. It must have been after the autumn of 1841, when Father became a high official at the National Bank, a position that rendered it possible for him to fulfill Kierkegaard's wishes. And it must also have been after the engagement was broken off, because this was not the sort of step that would be taken by someone who was thinking of starting a family. And finally, it must have been after the various mortgages and shares in the house on Nytorv, which Søren Kierkegaard had inherited from his father, had matured and were paid to him, though I do not know any further details concerning this. As a rough guess I would assume it must have been around 1844—though possibly even somewhat later—that Søren Kierkegaard came to Father one day and asked him to keep his money for him.

Father readily agreed to do so. But then it became clear that the request was meant in the most literal sense, namely to keep his money in the form of ready cash, which Kierkegaard had counted out into ten or twelve packets of equal value. Father tried in vain to dissuade him from this strange idea, and counseled him to invest the bulk of it in shares in the National Bank, as he himself and Vilhelm Lund had done; it was sound and easily marketable paper, with the prospect of a steady increase in value as long as the bank's ninety-year charter was in effect. Søren Kierkegaard answered that receiving interest was precisely what he wished to avoid, because this was in conflict with his religious convictions. Father was not successful in convincing him of the unreasonableness of his plan. At the same time, however, Father realized that unless he acceded to his wishes there was the risk that the capital itself could be lost through bad luck or swindling. He accepted the entire arrangement with a heavy heart, promising to tell no one of it as long as Søren Kierkegaard was alive, and then put the money aside, with an appropriate label identifying to whom it belonged, in a locked chest to which he had the only key.

After that Søren Kierkegaard visited his co-conspirator at the bank at certain intervals and removed some of his money. In the beginning there were humorous comments, but later my father was increasingly worried. When the last packet was taken—probably in the autumn of 1854—they both looked at one another seriously and silently shook hands.

My parents' feelings for Søren Kierkegaard did not change particularly during the course of his writing career, which they hardly followed. On the other hand, their old warm feelings were rekindled when, after challenging Goldschmidt and his *Corsair*, he went from being a famous author to being a ridiculed person, hounded by public opinion. In our time it is hard to imagine the chilling vulnerability that could be the lot of a victim of such attacks in those days. He must have felt the lack of a home, and they felt an instinctive need to prepare him a friendly sanctuary for his occasional visits. Whatever their individual assumptions, they all united in worried concern for him, who, in accordance with his own choice, now stood alone. The youngest of the family, alone in battle with a laughing, malicious crowd.

The reason that my sister [Henriette Lund] was a frequent and welcome guest both at Søren Kierkegaard's and at Regina Olsen's, even long after their engagement was broken, was not only because they were both fond of her but surely also because, without her realizing it, they used her as a sort of indirect messenger.

A textile dealer named G. lived in the same building as my uncle. G. was one of the eccentrics of the period and cultivated an odd trait, which was that he did not really greet others when he met them, but merely raised a couple of fingers to the brim of his hat with a condescending smile. This method of greeting was well known in the neighborhood but could occasion irritation among strangers.

Uncle Christian saw G. go out of the gate with great dignity and cross over to the opposite sidewalk. Along came Søren Kierkegaard, walking in a friendly manner with the two Ørsted brothers, one on each arm. Upon seeing G., and expecting his strange greeting, Søren Kierkegaard stopped, faced him, and took off his hat with a deep, sweeping gesture, which was also done by the Ørsted brothers, believing that this must be an extraordinarily important encounter. G. was confused for a moment, and was about to remove his hat, but he got hold of himself and passed by with two fingers raised to the brim of his hat and a gracious smile. Both Ørsteds were visibly impressed.

Another time, it was said that Søren Kierkegaard was walking the lonely path along the revetment, out where the road from the workhouse runs into Farimagsvej. In those days there were still small embankments along the path, and behind one of these stood two inmates from the workhouse to whose conversation he [Søren Kierkegaard] was an invisible witness. The one said: "Isn't it a damned shame that you're never happy!" The other: "Nonsense! What's happiness?" The first: "Well, if an angel were now to fall down from heaven and give me a blue one." Søren Kierkegaard found these words irresistible. He took a five-rixdollar note ("a blue one") out of his wallet, stepped forth unexpectedly, presented it with a deep bow, and disappeared without saying a word.

Now, sixty to seventy years later, my direct personal impression of Søren Kierkegaard during those years has largely faded. But I can still see him clearly one evening, when we were gathered at Uncle Christian's on Købmagergade in the regular dining room. He arrived when we others were almost finished and was seated up at the end of the table, among the grownups, on the side near the street. He was in very high spirits, and to my amazement I even saw a smile from

Miss Dencker, the housekeeper, who always tossed her head in such a strange way and who did not like Doctor Søren. Finally the host made a flank attack, but he parried all assaults with great skill. I did not fully understand what was being talked about, but I followed it with lively interest. When, as it seemed to me, Uncle Christian began to talk self-importantly and to express his opinions on the questions of the day with great emphasis, Uncle Søren answered with a teasing smile: "Was that the speech you did *not* deliver to the city council the other day?" That must have hit the nail on the head, because Uncle Troels (the set designer), who was also a representative on the city council, almost burst into laughter.

After a while, when the host started in with his speechifying again and included some little jibes directed at Søren Kierkegaard, the latter answered only by interrupting—at appropriate intervals and with rhetorical pauses designed to enhance the effect—and saying, "Now *that* was a devil of a thing." This had an irresistible effect upon everyone, child and grownup alike.

My best recollections of him, however, are from one day when he spent some time alone with me. It was a summer day, and I was walking along the ramparts to school. I met him at the bastion at Vesterport, and he accompanied me to the steps down to Nørregade. With a laugh he asked me if I was certain that the school was in its usual location. "Yes, unfortunately." "Yes, but, for example, it could have burned down in the night," because he had heard the watchman blow his horn. That possibility put me in an especially good mood. I confided in him that I was not well prepared for some of my classes. Together we imagined all the pleasant consequences that would ensue if the school had burned down. I spared practically none of the teachers. As the teachers of Latin, French, and German and [Headmaster] Bohr escaped from the door of the burning school, I had them shot down with grapeshot.

We reached the point where the rampart hill came down to Nørregade. I was delighted with all the imagined possibilities but had to say goodbye. While still halfway down the hill I shouted up to him one more time, and said goodbye with a satisfied smile. I was alone and back in reality. The farther I descended the hill the more depressing things seemed. Not a trace of smoke could be scented at the corner of Nørregade. No crowds. Not so much as a single fire hose at the gate to the schoolyard. Only Mr. Bohr, standing inside with his hand on his chest and with a serious demeanor, as was his custom. Taken aback, I removed my cap. Then a slightly rough push on my book pack: "Hurry up, you're late, Troels!" Goodbye to all my vanished glory.

Once, on Gammeltorv, right near Nygade, I was walking behind him and wanted to run up to him to say hello. But just at that moment I heard some passersby say something mocking about him and saw a couple of people on the other side of the street stop, turn around to look at him, and laugh. His one trouser leg really was shorter than the other, and I could now see for myself that he was odd-looking. I instinctively stopped, was embarrassed, and suddenly remembered that I had to go down another street.

Søren Kierkegaard was thoroughly aware of my parents' admiration for Bishop Mynster and of what they both believed they owed him as their religious adviser. For one thing, this had been a point of connection among his own father, my father, and my mother, who raised their children in the old-fashioned way. And this shared point of view had also been endorsed by Søren Kierkegaard himself, who was always sure to be among the listeners when Mynster preached at the Church of Our Lady.

Søren Kierkegaard was aware, furthermore, of my mother's sound judgment and integrity. Indeed, he had earlier used her as a sort of sounding board with respect to the moral aspects of his break with his fiancée. The way I understand the whole matter now is that he thus decided to make use of her and our home in the same way again. He wanted to have a test case of how people, good people whom he respected, would view and react to the business he now had at hand.

For this reason he came to lunch with us every day for a week, which was unusual for him. At lunch he could be sure to meet both of my parents, but no outsiders. It was on Gammeltorv, and I was out of school for at least some of the days and could witness the conversations. I therefore conclude that it must have been during the Easter vacation of 1854, which was a couple of months after Martensen's memorial sermon for Mynster.

Søren Kierkegaard came only in order to carry out a test case under safe circumstances and to see what kind of reception his words might meet with. Therefore he clearly wanted to get past his reception as a cherished guest, questions about whether they could offer him anything, etc., as quickly as possible. He immediately sat down at the table at his customary place, and, no matter what my parents would begin talking about, he quickly got around to his topic: Bishop Mynster and his shortcomings. This behavior necessarily appeared peculiar, inexplicable, and unattractive to my parents. I think that the fact that this nonetheless continued for an entire week demonstrates both how eager my parents were to fulfill their obligations as hosts and how bravely Mother, in particular, withstood the assaults.

I believe I can still remember how amazed my parents were on that first day, to hear the deceased spoken of in such an unexpectedly negative way. They expressed the opposite opinion and referred, among other things, to Søren Kierkegaard's own earlier remarks, which supported their position. Finally the conversation was interrupted, because Father had to go to the bank and time was short. Then Søren Kierkegaard left. The last words I heard Father say when Mother followed him out into the foyer were: "What is it that's eating Søren today?" Mother answered: "Oh, he's just ———." And then they shut the door in my face.

There was no little surprise, but increasing uneasiness, when he returned the next day, the day after, and so on. The purpose of these repeated visits was certainly no desire to retract any ill-considered or exaggerated statements. On the contrary, the remarks became increasingly harsh. I seem to remember that when she sensed that the visits were going to continue, Mother tried to keep us away by asking us to take a walk. I know that in any case I did not hear all the conversations, probably no more than four. I am therefore a poor witness to what went on, all the more so because I had an imperfect understanding of what they were talking about. I am nonetheless the only living witness, and I followed along as best I could.

I do not think I am wrong in my belief that it was at that time that I heard some of the expressions that Søren Kierkegaard later, in December 1854, appended to his original article. In the expressions, "To declaim in the quiet hours on Sundays, and to cover himself in worldly-wise fashion on Mondays," and "He [Mynster] was weak, pleasure-mad, and great only as an orator" [SV XIV 10], I can still hear the sound of the speaker's voice and the shock wave of disapproval and contradiction it aroused.

It is my impression that the week-long battle was divided into three skirmishes. Or, more correctly, I really think that it was resumed daily with many tiresome repetitions, but I noted that my mother took up three defensive positions. The first one sounded to me roughly like this: that none of us, despite what others have said, either can or will surrender, so it is best that everyone stick to his or her own opinion, and that we let the matter drop.

When, despite this, he continued and declared that he could not let the matter drop but would have to attempt to deal with it by attacking, because Mynster had been a misfortune both for [Kierkegaard] himself and for his times, Mother replied that here, as everywhere, it was important to take what one found to be of benefit and leave the rest. When he attacked the deceased in this way, it was his responsibility to make clear to himself his own reasons for action and to be sure that these had validity in themselves and did not have vanity, for example, as their mainspring.

The last position was finally emphasized clearly on the seventh day. Both my parents were depressed at the prospect of another nerve-racking visit. Søren Kierkegaard had already arrived, and I heard my mother say to my father in the other room: "I have so little desire to be at the table today, do you think I can stay away?" Father asked her to remain, however, and lunch began. Søren Kierkegaard sat to the right of Mother, near the wall with the two old family portraits. I sat diagonally across from him. At one end of the table was the polished copper samovar for coffee, from which Cille drew coffee, silent and a little shy. Father tried to strike a cheerful note and said, "Well, Søren, can I tempt you with a little glass of Madeira today?" Mother asked him about something or other and tried to get to a neutral topic. In vain. Immediately: Bishop Mynster. Mother once again tried to deflect this by saying, "Oh Søren, let's not go into that old dispute. We are totally familiar with one another's opinions, and to discuss it further can of course only lead to a quarrel."

Søren Kierkegaard continued, however, more violently and pointedly than before. When he stopped for a moment, as though he expected a reply, there was a very unpleasant silence. Then Mother said, calmly and firmly: "You know that the man of whom you speak so ill is someone for whom we cherish the greatest respect and to whom we are profoundly grateful. I cannot put up with hearing him scorned unceasingly here. Since you will not stop it, I can escape from it only by leaving the room." And with that she stood up from the table and left.

There was an even more oppressive silence after that scene. No one seemed to want anything further, not even Cille's coffee, which, slightly uncertainly, she offered to the guest and to Father. The meal was quickly adjourned, and Søren Kierkegaard left shortly afterward. When he had said goodbye to Father and had left, Mother came into the "salon" to us. Both of them had been greatly distressed by what had taken place. Father thought that there had been a breach of hospitality. Mother thought that it had been a necessary step to have peace in our home.

After the beginning of the struggle he [Søren Kierkegaard] had seen less of them [the Lund children] in order not to involve them in something with which they could not cope. Nevertheless, he attended to them with his usual love. For example, he had arranged that my sister accompany Uncle Christian and his daughter on a trip abroad. When saying farewell he assumed his old playful manner. But after their return home he refused to receive guests for the entire remainder of the summer. Peter, who had seen him one day on the street, thought he looked very weak.

On October 2, with the news that Søren Kierkegaard had collapsed unconscious on the street and had been taken, mortally ill, to Frederik's Hospital, our home was suddenly shaken with every manner of concern and sympathy for him.

Immediately after the news reached our house, Father decided to rush out there [to Frederik's Hospital], and my sister, who had also heard and had hurried home to tell us, joined him. On arrival at the hospital they were told that he was still alive but that he was firmly convinced that he would die soon. They were allowed to go in and see him for a moment, and entered, deeply moved, each with his or her own concerns.

Father was afraid that in addition to his illness he might also be plagued by the thought that he had used up all his assets and that he would now suffer hardship. Therefore he managed to tell him: "Don't worry about money matters. I will take care of everything you need. Now just get a complete rest, let them take care of you, and recover." The sick man replied: "I have enough. Enough to cover things admirably. Just like your old friendship, for which I sincerely thank you."

My sister had been afraid she would see clear signs of the rending battle and perhaps of despair about the failure of his powers. Instead she received a happy smile, a blessed, relieved expression like that of a martyr when the struggle is over. Both visitors were struck by the transfigured glory that shone from the expression of his eyes and from his entire being. Here there was no doubt that the end was near. They said goodbye with gentle, understanding words, each of them feeling that this was the last time.

From the very beginning, the answer given to everyone else who wanted to see the sick man was that he would not receive visitors. This reply was also given to his brother Peter [Christian] Kierkegaard. The reason he was not received was that his visit would probably have been accompanied by overly strong emotions and perhaps by a violent exchange of views. This is because the previous July, at the Pastoral Convention in Roskilde, Peter Kierkegaard had opposed his brother's conduct. And on that occasion Søren Kierkegaard had given vent to his feelings in a very sharp and witty reply, which, however, was not published. Søren Kierkegaard's final, lengthy conversations with Emil Boesen—after, as mentioned above, he had forbidden all other visits—testify to how rough and troubled the waters still were and how suspicious Søren Kierkegaard was of the declarations of friendship by his brother, by Lic. Ferdinand Fenger (chairman of the Pastoral Convention), and by other Grundtvigians.

Nonetheless, Emil Boesen returned on October 25 and brought a copy of Fenger's farewell sermon, given on the occasion of his move from Lynge-by-Sorø to Høje Taastrup. The sick man said: "Send it back to him! I will not accept it!" "It was not for you to read, but he does think kindly of you." "He has spoken publicly. Now he wants to send me this privately, and then it is supposed to be as if it were nothing, despite the fact that there is such a great difference." "Your brother was there on his journey back home." "So the fact that I would not receive him is of course well known, and people are scandalized about it?" "No, I cannot say that. They really think of you with great sympathy. You should not be surprised that each of them has said what they said. It was only in self-defense, you know, and we are all entitled to defend ourselves. Thus they are still really quite capable of thinking of you with great sympathy." "Believe me, this is the sort of thing of which Christ says, 'Get thee behind me, Satan, for you are a stumbling block to me! You think only of earthly things and have no sense for that which is above.'" "No, they speak as they do because they are convinced that they are right and that your sort of attack on existing conditions is wrong. It is possible, of course, that there is a way to salvation leading through the Established Church." "I cannot stand talking about this. It is too much of a strain on me."

It is quite understandable that the prospect of this sort of conversation with clerical friends and relatives prevented the sick man from receiving visits, even from his brother.

Nonetheless, although all visitors were turned away, by an odd coincidence I came to see the sick man and to talk with him.

When my father and my sister had been with him, they quite naturally told my uncle, the businessman [Johan] Christian Lund, about their visit. He felt that he also ought to go out to see him. And Søren Kierkegaard certainly did not want to offend this brother-in-law by refusing to receive him—all the more because his son, the young doctor Henrik [Sigvard] Lund, was serving his residency at the hospital and was tireless in caring for his sick uncle in every way. The visit could of course be scheduled at the least inconvenient time and would naturally be quite brief.

It was thus decided that Uncle Christian, accompanied by his daughter Sophia, should go out there one afternoon (the time of day when the patient tended to be at his best) and be received, if possible, for a very brief visit.

I will not say whether the patient was happy to have this visit by his brother-in-law. It was certainly the case that the brother-in-law and his daughter were none too keen about it. Among [Uncle Christian's] eccentricities, which had developed quite markedly over the years because of too much leisure, was an excessive concern about his own health. As a form of self-protection he was a born opponent and explainer-away of every form of illness. And where this was impossible, he believed that he could certainly demonstrate that the illness was self-inflicted. Under these circumstances it was certainly very unpleasant for him to have to visit someone who was sick, someone whom the doctors and his own son had said was actually sick—and all this in a hospital, where one is exposed to the danger of infection.

His daughter knew her father had this eccentricity. Furthermore, she was also aware of the oddly condescending form of address he tended to use when talking to his brother-in-law. She was afraid that it might perhaps be difficult for him to refrain from this during the visit, and she was even more afraid that on this occasion the sick man would be hurt and offended by it.

Thus, before they went out there, in their distress they turned to us on Gammeltorv in order to ask if anyone from our home would accompany them. No one had the courage to join that risky company. When they had gone around asking all those present, my cousin [Sophia] finally turned to me in her misery and said, "Troels, would you like to come along?" I very much wanted to do so and received my parents' permission, and then we departed immediately.

I had never been to a hospital before. It was thus fascinating for me to go inside, to look in the windows and see people wearing hospital uniforms, and to learn that one looked for someone not by name but only by room number. I think that it made just as depressing an impression on my uncle as it did on me. Finally we found the place: the pavilion on the left, when viewed from Bredgade, private room number thus-and-such, and in corridor such-and-such on the second floor. We were announced and received permission to enter.

The sick man sat in a tall reclining chair, pale, thin, and very bent-over. When he said hello to us, a tired, friendly smile crossed his face. When he saw me I received a little extra wink, which I shyly returned. Uncle Christian spoke up and asked how he was and what was really the matter. The sick man answered: "Things are as you see them. I myself know no more." This summoned Uncle Christian to his usual way of thinking and of expressing himself: "No! Listen. Do you know what, Søren? So help me God, there is nothing wrong with you except your old and unreasonable habit of letting your back slouch over. The position you are sitting in would of course make anybody sick. Just straighten your back and stand up and the sickness will disappear! I can tell you that!"

The explosion had been violent, but spontaneous. The speaker felt it himself and fell into a slightly embarrassed silence. My cousin looked unhappy with downcast eyes. I glanced at the sick man, who spared my cousin by not looking at her, and who looked at me as the only member of the audience present. He did not say a single word, but the look in his eyes spoke volumes. Through the sadness there gleamed a look of gentle tolerance, combined with the playful, provocative glint of a subversive proclivity to laughter, and a sense of fun—this was instantly captivating, and we looked at one another in happy conspiracy. And yet there was something in his look which instinctively kept one at a distance, or rather, which elevated and purified one. It was as if this characteristic ran through the entire gamut of feelings, from a schoolboy's sparkling laughter to a penetrating and all-forgiving glance.

After this, the sick man became livelier and more like his old self. But at the same time, the difference between then and now became clearer. It was as if all expression had been drained from his bodily movements, indeed, even from his facial features, and that it had been concentrated all the more strongly in his eyes alone. They shone with a soulfulness that made an indelible impression.

The visit lasted only a short while, and we said goodbye. I do not remember what words were spoken, but I had the impression that the sick man carefully and helpfully brought his brother-in-law back onto an even keel, so that all three could part under circumstances that no one need regret later on. As the youngest, I extended him my hand last, looked into his incredible eyes one more time, and said, shyly and with emotion, "Good-bye, and a good recovery!"

I think that, given his sensitive nerves, he was somewhat agitated and afflicted by the visit. I think that he liked me as a funny boy with whom he had occasionally and good-naturedly spent some time. I also think it is reasonable to believe that he had seen through the situation and had understood why I had been brought along, and that I had been a bit useful by serving as a sort of audience, which formed a diversion upon which he could fasten his eyes in the hope of finding understanding. And I believe, finally, that his illness (which was undoubtedly spinal tuberculosis) had endowed his eyes with an unusual—if you will, a supernatural—brilliance, which expressed more than what was normally there.

I am saying all this to myself to protect myself against any misunderstanding to the effect that I had been incapable of seeing that what happened was something quite ordinary and straightforward. In other words, I am differentiating sharply between the simple, everyday things that happened and the impression it necessarily made on a young and receptive mind.

When I extended my hand to him, the others had already turned toward the door, so it was as though we were alone. He took my hand in both of his own—how small, thin, and transparently white they were—and said only: "Thank you for coming to see me, Troels! And now live well!" But these ordinary words were accompanied by a look of which I have never since seen the equal. It radiated with an elevated, transfigured, blessed brilliance, so that it seemed to me to illuminate the entire room. Everything was concentrated in the flood of light from these eyes: profound love, beatifically dissolved sadness, an all-penetrating clarity, and a playful smile. For me it was like a heavenly revelation, an emanation from one soul to another, a blessing, which infused me with new courage, strength, and responsibility.

I was silent and withdrawn when I emerged [from the hospital]. I was on my guard to keep from revealing what had happened to me, but my mind grasped [these events] as though with a firm hand, and held onto them in order properly to preserve and understand them. A sick man had said some quite ordinary words to me and had looked at me in a friendly fashion with eyes that had been clarified by illness. That was all.

For me, it was more than that. An inspiring initiation. An encounter with a spirit which was transfigured and ready to depart and which at that very instant became profoundly dear to me—a brief, blissful moment in which I was able to have a glimpse of what life and blessedness could be.

Finally, on the evening of November 11, 1855, Søren Kierkegaard passed away into the peace for which he had so deeply longed.

A practical question, which required an immediate solution, was: under what circumstances should his burial take place? He had wanted to be buried in the family plot at the Assistens Cemetery, and he had himself chosen the verse of the hymn that was to be inscribed on his gravestone. But how should the interment take place?

There were two alternatives. Either to let it take place in the quietest possible way or to proceed in the usual way. By permitting it to take place quietly—i.e., in a clandestine and secret fashion—one would appear to dishonor the deceased, appear to take sides and to declare his life's work (which everyone was talking about at the time) as best served by silence and oblivion. On the other hand, by permitting it to take place in accordance with the usual forms—starting from a church, with a eulogy by a clergyman, etc.—one would strike a strongly discordant note, because everyone knew that the deceased had characterized pastors as "liars, deceivers, perjurers; quite literally, without exception, not one honest pastor" [cf. *SV* XIV 269–70]. Even from the coffin, an audible objection would resound against being used, posthumously, in a theatrical performance that had the effect of making a fool of God. And to everyone present, the message would be: by not participating in what is taking place here, you have one sin fewer on your record [cf. *SV* XIV 85–86].

His brother, parish pastor, Lic. theol. Peter Kierkegaard, made the decision. He chose to allow the burial to take place on a Sunday, beginning at the Church of Our Lady in Copenhagen, and to deliver the eulogy himself.

As might have been anticipated, the church was filled by a throng composed of all sorts of people. The first two pews were reserved for the family, who arrived early and got in without difficulty. Father and Uncle Christian and the oldest cousins and brothers were in the first pew. By chance I came to sit alone in the next pew. A man who I later heard was Prof. Rasmus Nielsen sat in the pew with me and closed the door so hard that it locked shut. So we sat sheltered, while the crowd came in waves like the sea, pushed forward, and was driven out into the center aisle.

I didn't think it was very comfortable there at all, and I exchanged some clandestine glances with my sister, whom I had discovered up in the gallery. All of a sudden there was even more movement and more vigorous pushing than before. I was afraid that some of these angry men, whose expressions showed their excitement, were about to carry off the coffin. But from looking in the eyes of my sister, who had a view of the entire church, I could see that everything was under control. A procession of university students pushed their way forward and formed a circle around the coffin.

Peter Kierkegaard's talk was powerfully delivered and was not disturbed by shouting or interruptions. I heard afterward that my sister thought it was good. I probably understood only a little of it and cannot remember any of it. From the church, our carriage crept behind the hearse, inch by inch, out to Assistens Cemetery. When we alighted, the place was completely packed with people, and it was with difficulty that I saw the coffin borne forward down the broad, straight path to the grave site. Everywhere teemed with the tightly packed crowd, which surged over the graves and the latticework fences, forward to its common goal. I was separated from my family, but I made my way by myself to the grave, where freshly dug earth formed a yellow-gray hill to the left of the fence that had been removed from the grave site. There was less pushing here than I would have expected. In any case I stood in a sheltered spot and had a rather good view of what was going on. I was anxious to see how all this awful business was going to end.

It seemed to me that it lasted a long time. They pushed and shoved over the yellow-gray hill. Then all at once one person broke free from the rest of them and stood in front. This was a very tall, pale young man, dressed in black. He removed his hat, looked around himself with a strangely excited, zealous look, and shouted out over the crowd: "May I be permitted to speak!" Now I recognized him. It was my beloved older cousin, the physician Henrik Lund, who had always been so cheerful and good-natured in his understanding of us younger ones. Not long before, he had written me an amusing letter from Paris with a drawing of one of my old tin soldiers, and just recently he had been serving his residency at the hospital and had attended to and taken care of Søren Kierkegaard. I trembled to see him come forward as a speaker now, in these surroundings.

"Who is *that?*" said people in the crowd, which had suddenly become quieter. "I am Lund, a medical graduate," he replied. "Hear, hear!" shouted someone on the edge of the crowd. Someone else said, "He's pretty good! I have been a patient of his. Just let him speak!" Then he began, approximately as follows: "When he was alive, this man being buried here with full pomp, as if he belonged to the Church, was the most zealous opponent of the Church. It is only by means of a deception that the Church has now appropriated him, has attempted to steal him after his death. But witness must be borne to this at his grave," etc. Using Søren Kierkegaard's own words and phrases, he then demonstrated the incompatibility between the deceased and the Church, and ended by protesting against what had taken place here today.

When the speech was finished there were some signs of approval from various parts of the crowd. Most people, however, stood in tense, silent expectation of what would happen *now*. Something had to happen. Riots, disturbances, something extraordinary. Something, at any rate. But nothing happened.

The speaker was gone. I saw the heavy man from the church pew, Rasmus Nielsen—whom I had again discovered near the grave, and who had probably wanted to speak out there—depart with an annoyed expression on his face. People began to get bored with waiting. A couple of grave-diggers came forward. It caused amusement when a slightly drunk fellow shouted to a friend, "Let's go home, then, Chrishan!" I slipped past the crowd and over the trampled grave sites to where the carriage was waiting. I now noticed that it was cold, and I was freezing. I was lucky enough to find the carriage in which Father and Uncle Christian were sitting, and I got in with them.

Chapter Ten

FIVE PORTRAITS BY CONTEMPORARIES

Andreas Ferdinand Schiødte[1]

[*A. F. Schiødte to H. P. Barfod, September 12, 1869*]
S. Kierkegaard was three years older than I and three years ahead of me in school. But in those days, at least, and in school, a gap of three years was of great significance. Therefore I really cannot be called his contemporary, and I have almost no firsthand memories of him from my school years. I have subsequently asked various of his classmates, including Archdeacon Welding in Viborg, Pastor Anger, and several others, about the impression he made on them. They all agreed that he had not aroused any special expectations of anything great in the future. One trait emphasized by all of them was his delight in jokes—and mockery. He liked to triumph over statements that were simpleminded or a bit ridiculous, and this tendency sometimes awakened indignation against him and brought him a few blows from more robust schoolmates. He did not awaken any particular expectations among his classmates, and that seems to me completely normal and in perfect harmony with his essence, his nature and character, which he subsequently and so notoriously revealed. His strength, of course, consisted not in amassing knowledge but in inwardness—in its extent, clarity, and depth, and in its earnestness. There can be no doubt—he said so himself—that even then he felt himself isolated and thrown back upon himself in melancholia. He could not involve other people in what he obscurely felt to be brewing within him. It had to remain concealed. And he himself concealed it quite deliberately by making use of its opposites, jokes and mockery. Yet there can be no mistaking the fact that his nature also contained a need to mock. He had a great sense of the ridiculous, and this sense was inaugurated and developed quite early, when his own inwardness helped him to discover the lack of inwardness and the emptiness in others. In Latin composition, at any rate, he must have turned in an extraordinary performance, because I remember that when he was quite a young university student Prof. Nielsen appointed him his assistant, with responsibility for correcting essays. I occasionally spoke with him when he was at the school in this capacity, and he pleased me very much with the unaffectedly plainspoken and straightforward manner in which he, the university student, addressed school pupils. There was no contact between us as university students, but I remember a time I was walking in Frederiksberg, deep in thought. I, too, was a melancholic and a hypochondriac, but I did not live under

such favorable external circumstances as did S.K. My outward appearance must certainly have shown clear signs of what was weighing upon my soul and consuming it, because K. suddenly came over to me and, with a look and a voice that trembled with sympathy, he asked me if I knew Prof. Sibbern. I ought to see him; he was a whole person, the very soul of kindness; there was something calming in associating with him. Almost before I could reply, he had left me again. Nor was there any relationship between us after he made his appearance as an author. I was an opponent—which, I might note in passing, I still am—of the way in which he defined the relation of philosophy to religion (Christianity, faith). I was in fact a rather zealous and angry opponent. It seemed to me that he complicated instead of explicated many things, and he was in general too complex and full of digressions for me. I did, however, concede that he was generally correct in his polemics against the speculative thinking that was dominant at the time. On the few occasions I spoke with him, almost the entire time was taken up with my explanations of my own views and reservations. As much as I would have liked it, it was not possible to involve him in a direct discussion of these matters, and he limited himself to listening to me with great patience and gentleness. Therefore I cannot remember any remark of importance by him, except perhaps for the following witticism. We spoke of Grundtvig, whom I valued very highly (without, however, being a real Grundtvigian). K. ridiculed the whole Grundtvigian phenomenon, but conceded that G. was a genius. He was a genius, because a genius is someone who discovers something, and Grundtvig had certainly done that. I attempted to parry his mockery by making a separation between G. and his party. I said that you always see that a founder of something finds himself followed by a party of embarrassing and stupid yes-men. "Yes," K. said, "but I must nonetheless point out that it seems to me that a peculiar position has been reserved for G.: he is himself simultaneously both founder and his own yes-man."

One of S.K.'s peculiarities was that he preferred to involve himself with people whose interests in life were completely different from his own or which were diametrically opposed to his own. The linguist I. Levin, who helped him proofread his writings, has told me of a remark that in my view was very typical. He said to Levin that it was a piece of *good fortune* for him (Levin) that he, as a Jew, was *free of Christ*. If he (K.) were free of Christ, he would enjoy life and make himself comfortable in a completely different way. When he occasionally read Levin something from the New Testament he would break out in tears and sobbing. How strange that in unguarded moments this enormous fervor, which concealed itself carefully from all others, sought a breath of air by revealing itself to a benighted Jew—a man who did not have the least sympathy for this spiritual profundity, the wealth of which poured forth so powerfully, streamed toward him, and threatened to drown him.

He also spoke a great deal and in a very friendly fashion with an atheistic theologian of my acquaintance. The latter had published a philosophical piece in *Fædrelandet*, which was written in the well-known dismissive and decisive tone of Hegelianism. K. thanked him, because now he had learned how to judge the matter; he had been especially impressed to see at the bottom line of the newspaper the words, "Completed at the press at 6:30 o'clock."

With respect to the period when he published *The Moment*, I remember hearing that he once encountered his schoolmate, Pastor E. Lind of Sæby, and that the latter said in passing to K.: "You are a spineless person." I have heard some things about his last hours at the hospital from Boesen, now archdeacon in Aarhus, but I would rather not report on this, because I assume that you will seek out the source yourself.

In Viborg, where I was a pastor at the cathedral, I met a police officer named Vestergaard from Finds District, who had for many years been K.'s trusted servant. He showed me a letter of recommendation that K. had given him at the time that he had sought a position on the police force. There is really no reason to report it here, especially in view of its length, but I will note that I found it worth copying at the time, because that insignificant document seemed to me to have all the characteristic features that are typical of the style of his works as a whole.

One of the more interesting features of his daily life, V. told me, was that the first half-hour or hour of each morning was given over to a solitary pursuit that V. surely understood to be devotional exercises. He stood up and knelt down a great deal, read aloud, etc.

Not infrequently, he came home from town and went straight to his writing desk, where he would stand with his hat and his cane or umbrella and write.

He had ordered V., in case of fire, to save the tin boxes in which he preserved his manuscripts. Everything else was insured.

One time V. asked him whether, as a learned man, he couldn't provide him with a completely firm conviction and assurance of the immortality of the soul. That would please and comfort him a great deal. K. answered that we are all equally ignorant on such points; that one had to choose between the one possibility and the other; and that conviction then comes in accordance with the choice.

In one of his later years, K. had moved out to Østerbro and associated with a carpenter who had been a childhood acquaintance, whose family most likely kept house for him and his servant. A daughter of the family was confirmed, and K. gave her a beautiful outfit, including a shawl, other accessories, etc., and probably some gold ornaments as well. In the afternoon he saw her walking in the garden, flaunting all that finery and putting herself on display with obvious delight. He was terrified by all this and, perhaps also fearing what people would say, instantly decided that the family should move away and rent rooms elsewhere at his expense. This decision was put into effect at once, but it made K. the object of a great deal of anger on the part of the family—especially the somewhat crazy carpenter—who naturally couldn't understand it. I mention this episode, which seems to me to be typical of Kierkegaard, who often found it necessary voluntarily to break ties that were personally dear to him when it seemed to him that higher considerations required it.

I have now, to the best of my ability, gathered together all the personal incidents regarding S.K. which left an impression in my mind. It is not much, but fate has not favored me with any earlier or closer contact with this man, whose entire work has exercised such great influence upon me.

Hans Lassen Martensen[2]

He [Søren Kierkegaard] had his own way of arranging his tutoring. He did not follow any set syllabus, but asked only that I lecture to him and converse with him. I chose to lecture to him on the main points of Schleiermacher's dogmatics and then discuss them. I recognized immediately that his was not an ordinary intellect but that he also had an irresistible urge to sophistry, to hairsplitting games, which showed itself at every opportunity and was often tiresome. I recollect in particular that it surfaced when we examined the doctrine of divine election, where there is, so to speak, an open door for sophists. In other respects he was most attentive to me at that time. My mother has told me that while I was abroad, he quite often came to her for news of me. In addition, she related something I will not fail to mention here, that from time to time he stayed and sat with her a while and that she took great pleasure in his conversation. Once he came in deep sorrow and told her that his mother had died. My mother has repeatedly confirmed that she never in her life (and she had had no little experience) had seen a human being so deeply distressed as S. Kierkegaard was by the death of his mother. From this she felt she could conclude that he must have an unusually profound sensibility. She was not wrong about this. No one can deny him that. The more he developed, the more his life and work developed into a union of sophistry and a profound, although unhealthy, sensibility. In the diaries he left behind (which have now been displayed to the public tactlessly and without consideration for the deceased), he himself has provided the most incontrovertible evidence of the sickly nature of his profound sensibility, which increasingly got the upper hand as the years passed.

Kierkegaard was the inspiring spirit who stood in the background during that first period of the attack [on Martensen by the theologian Rasmus Nielsen]. In the beginning his relation to me had been friendly, but it assumed an increasingly hostile character. He was moved to this in part by the differences in our views and in part by the recognition I enjoyed from the students and the public, a recognition which he clearly viewed—nor did he attempt to conceal it—as an unjustified overestimation. S. Kierkegaard had a natural tendency to find fault, to tear down, and to disparage—something Mephistophelian, something in the nature of Loki. I was now chosen to be the object of his attack, and in many ways he sought to disparage me, my abilities, and my work. He sought to

Hans L. Martensen. Lithograph from a photograph, 1862. From the original in the Picture Collection of the Royal Library. Reproduced courtesy of the Royal Library.

annihilate and extinguish every bit of activity that emanated from me. He did not attack me directly at all. His writings of course contained all sorts of polemical and satirical attacks on speculation, a portion of which were directed at me. But he never attacked me in straightforward and open battle. I also assume that he was unsuited to do scholarly combat in theology, because he was suited to fight only in quasi-poetic, humorous circumstances in which he could make use of playful discourse and flank attacks. He did not have the gift for instructive and dogmatic discourse, which explains why he continually polemicizes against "the teachers," whom he loathed. His high level of cultivation prevented him

Nørreport with the ramparts. Watercolor by C. W. Eckersberg, 1804. From a photograph owned by the Copenhagen City Museum. Reproduced by permission of the
Copenhagen City Museum.

from joining forces with Rasmus Nielsen's coarse assault, but his attack was put
forward in the many conversations he held with an infinite number of people
on the street, where he went about like a Mephistopheles, scattering the seeds
of his hostility. He never showed me any open enmity, however; he was always
friendly to me and always solicited conversation with me on the street. I, however, was stiff and reticent, since I was not fond of associating with someone
whom I knew was always probing into things experimentally, while he himself
was reserved and hid his innermost opinions. In his conversation he often
brought up his own works, upon which I did not engage to speak, among other
reasons because, as I expressed it in my *Explanations of Dogmatics*, I had only
fragmentary knowledge of this long-winded body of literature. Of course I
knew the essence of it and knew what it concerned. But I was immersed in my
own work and was pursuing my own aims, to which I felt myself called, and I
could not devote any of my time to this strange work, while he more or less
demanded that one should shelve one's own work and drop all one's own
concerns in order to devote oneself exclusively to his new wisdom.

It may be that his enmity could have been softened if I had conferred greater
recognition on him. He once came to me in my home and wished to read me
part of his treatise on the concept of irony—as far as I remember, a polemic

against Friedrich Schlegel's one-sided aestheticism. I let him read, but expressed appreciation only rather coolly. A contributing factor was his language and style, with its intolerable discursiveness. The many tiring repetitions, the unendingly long sentences, and the affected and mannered expressions were unpleasant to me, just as they have always disturbed me when I read his works. But he appears not to have forgotten that I failed to display a greater enthusiasm for his opus. And yet it is very possible that I am wrong when I assume that a greater appreciation on my part could have diminished his enmity. Because his pretensions were unbounded and his demands were extremely difficult to satisfy if one refused to make oneself into a blind admirer and a parrot of his views, which some of our literati have undeniably done. Because he had pretensions not only to the unbelievable claim of being one of the world's greatest thinkers (and perhaps the greatest of them) but also to being one of the greatest of poets—this despite the fact that he lacked immediacy and consisted wholly and solely of reflection. As far as I was concerned, he was neither the one nor the other; from my point of view he was only a humorist, who possessed elements both of the poet and of the thinker, by means of which he developed his humor—which in Kierkegaard took on a pessimistic character, the complete opposite of Jean Paul, for whom everything is optimism and love. But even a humorist may certainly have his sort of greatness, and far be it from me to deny the sublime, the many profound and acute insights, which can be found in his writings. Nor should one overlook that there is in him a religiosity which underlies everything, and that his most profound significance is that of a religious author, to which his edifying discourses testify. As is well known, the fundamental idea for which he does battle is individualism, or the individual and the individual's relationship to God. His efforts in the field of religion are entirely deserving of attention, but unfortunately these attempts have gone astray in one-sidedness and morbidity, in half-truths and false paradoxes. It soon became clear that the individual had been entirely torn loose from society, and that the Christian requirement of self-denial and dying away from the world had been presented in such a way that the religious ideal pointed out to us was only a caricature of holiness. It would take us too far afield to delve into this in detail at this point, and I must refer to the detailed presentations I put forth about his views in my *Ethics*. Although at the time there were complaints that I did not take sufficient notice of him and involve myself with his contributions, I do not believe that there can any longer be dissatisfaction on this point. But it has very much surprised me that among his supporters—if any can still be found—there has been no one who has done me or his master [Kierkegaard] the honor of arguing against me or of subjecting my claims to examination.

When I look back on the many conversations I had with him, short or long, most often on the street or on the ramparts (which I could hardly avoid, since I did not wish to break off all social contact), they were on the whole insignificant and without substance, because they were marked by a certain stiffness and reticence that prevented sincere discourse. Only when we spoke of Mynster might something sincere arise, because Kierkegaard showed real enthusiasm in his feelings for Mynster, and I believe Kierkegaard's love for him to have been sincere *for a time*. I will here recall one of my other conversations in particular, because it has some real content, and also because it seems to display a hint of something resembling a rapprochement.

I had walked out toward Christianshavn on a Sunday afternoon. Here I met S. Kierkegaard and could not avoid his conversation. We walked together along the ramparts of Christianshavn, where we talked for a long time about Danish literature, about *The Corsair* and the miserable condition of our literature, to which he often returned and which was of little interest to me. We went back through town and first stopped on Østergade, where I went up to the Athenæum. But he followed me up and we sat down. And here—it came up of itself so to speak—a conversation started about my dispute with Rasmus Nielsen. I expressed unreserved indignation over what I found objectionable in R. Nielsen's behavior, especially the completely distorted, erroneous, and improper way in which he had used Kierkegaard's Johannes Climacus, taking sentences from that work crudely and out of context, investing them with dogmatic significance, and making direct use of them. Kierkegaard did not contradict anything—indeed, not a single word—of what I said, and in general did not make the least effort to defend R. Nielsen. He did, however, find fault with particular expressions in the introduction to my *Dogmatics*, which he believed would better have been omitted. And in the course of the conversation he then said: "The difference between us (between Kierkegaard and myself) is a difference within Christianity." This statement appeared to be something of a rapprochement, because a difference *within* Christianity could perhaps be worked out, and if the difference was within Christianity his opposition to me could of course not be absolute. I tried to get him to explain himself in more detail, and he then explained that in his view we should not try to make use of the Pauline opposition between sin and grace, which most people are not mature enough to make use of. Rather, he felt that we should try to make thorough use of the epistle of James, and that would make us most capable of plowing up what must be plowed up in our souls in order to become receptive to higher influences. There was a lot to this notion, even though it could also be said that the same could be achieved with the proper use of Paul's doctrine about the Law, about which I will not argue here, because if there is anything to argue about here, there are certainly other and larger issues. The use of this contrast did not bring us particularly far into the difference [between us], which lay much deeper. Nonetheless, that hour could perhaps have led further if I had made use of it, that is, if I had really had a deep desire to get closer to him. But I was so opposed to his essential being—experimenting and self-enclosed as it was, and which seemed to me to be unavoidably linked to the danger of some inner falsity in his character—that I was unable to feel any desire for a closer relationship. The shadow of a rapprochement (if one can call it that) that I have just discussed was so faint that it had no further implications, and his explanation of our difference was of course equally feeble. I was unable to come to any confidence in him and had to stick to the view that everyone must hold to his own ideas. When Bishop Mynster died, it became clear what sort of ideas had got the upper hand in him. I do not have sufficient knowledge of his relationship to Bishop Mynster to be able to speak on the subject, but there can be no doubt that there must have come a point when Mynster, who had long liked him, may have demonstrated a certain coolness and dissatisfaction with his works, and that his [Kierkegaard's] love had then transformed itself into hatred.

But I was yet to have an experience of the most unpleasant sort: Søren Kierkegaard's attack on Mynster's posthumous reputation, which was tantamount to an attack on me. Shortly after Mynster's death, I gave a sermon at the Castle Church (where we had so often gathered around his pulpit) in which I included Mynster among the Christian witnesses to the truth that the sermon gave me occasion to discuss. This became the object of a violent attack by Kierkegaard, an attack that would very soon rock the entire country. The blow that was inflicted on me was calculated far in advance, and it was intended to be a mortal blow, to destroy me utterly, and to make it impossible for me to hold the high position that had recently been entrusted to me. If this event is to be understood historically—and in a certain sense its consequences entitle it to be viewed as an event in the ecclesiastical history of our little society—I assume that it may be explained, in part, by the fanatical notion that Kierkegaard had formed about a high mission to which he had been called, and, in part, by simple, personal animosity, not to mention hatred. No matter how much people talk in general about objectivity, about the principle of the thing, and about justice in connection with literary disputes and similar affairs, personal issues nonetheless play an important role, often in the narrowest way, and it is impossible to arrive at an adequate explanation without reference to them. His shamelessness in saying publicly that I had given that sermon about Mynster in order to promote my candidacy for the episcopacy made clear the degree to which there was a personal element involved. One would not have expected that a man of Søren Kierkegaard's spirituality and intelligence would lower himself to that sort of thing, which was appropriate only for scribblers of the lowest and most common sort. Both here and in other cases, however, he has descended to this genre. Sibbern made the very telling comment that S. Kierkegaard had here revealed himself to be a philistine.

I will deal with the unpleasant affair itself as briefly as possible. I must begin by stating, with respect to the phrase "witness to the truth" and to its use apropos of Mynster, that I do not intend to make the least excuse for this term—as though it were less than proper, or something that ought to be retracted. I would use the same term today. When taken in the right sense—that is, in context—my expression was completely proper. But S. Kierkegaard had the dishonesty and the effrontery to tear it out of context, to take it to an extreme, and to assign to the term "witness to the truth" the meaning "blood witness" or "martyr." Naturally, neither I nor anyone else had had this in mind. I had included Mynster among the Christian witnesses to the truth because my sermon emphasized his importance to our fatherland, the desolate times in which he appeared, his battle against unbelief and rationalism, and how he had reintroduced the Gospel into many hearts. Anyone who carefully considers the concept of a witness to the truth must come to the realization that the main thing is that a person so characterized must have witnessed to *the truth*, but that suffering and persecution are in no way a sure sign of a witness to the truth, because fanatics and false teachers have also often been subjected to great suffering and have become martyrs. Furthermore, external suffering and martyrdom belong to certain historical epochs and presuppose particular social conditions and circumstances; they cannot appear during all epochs, while witnesses to the truth may be found at all times and under all social conditions.

Rasmus Nielsen seconded Kierkegaard in several newspaper articles, but this does not seem to have earned him thanks from Kierkegaard, who in general did not appear to value R. Nielsen's help and services. Kierkegaard won support from a number of people who were lacking in judgment and who were in sympathy with those who opposed the Established Church. There were many young people who thought that in any case there was something great and admirable in the daring and fearlessness of Kierkegaard's behavior. And there were many women who had been passionately fond of Mynster but who now entirely abandoned him and went over to Kierkegaard. On this occasion, when so many were falling by the wayside, I gained a vivid sense of human fickleness, which occasionally tempts one to a disdain for the human race. There were, however, also many people who clung to a healthy view of things. They protested against Kierkegaard's false notion of suffering and maintained that Mynster—to whom so many, including Kierkegaard himself, were indebted for their Christianity—was fully entitled to the reputation he had received. They maintained that he had been for us a genuine witness to the truth, and they expressed their indignation at Kierkegaard, who on this occasion revealed his failure to appreciate Mynster's merits and his venerable character. I myself wrote a reply to Kierkegaard's attack, which I published in *Berlingske Tidende* and which many people thought should have been worded more gently. It is possible that they were right, and the only answer I can give to this is that, at that time at least, I was not capable of writing otherwise than as I did. I had been made indignant by the moral vileness. And I have always accepted the notion that there is a righteous anger, an indignation, which has a right to be expressed. Subsequently, Kierkegaard complained a great deal that after that article I observed complete silence instead of involving myself with him, as he demanded, in a fuller polemical debate. I really could not do him the service of appearing with him in a theatrical piece performed for idle and curious spectators. I maintained silence. He deserved no answer other than that which was given to him.

In *The Moment* (of which I read only the first issues) he unleashed his attack on the Established Church. He declared that the Church and its pastors had deviated entirely from the Christianity of the New Testament; that what was called Christianity in this country was an enormous falsification of Christianity, an enormous lie; and that the best advice which could be given to a person was to refrain entirely from participating in the divine services of the Folkekirke, both from the Word and from the sacraments. Here he addressed himself to the masses—he, who had earlier disdained the masses and had sought only a quiet encounter with the individual. His method differed in no way from that of the sects, which attack the Established Church because it is not in accord with what they call the Christianity of the New Testament—which they prove with a number of scriptural passages that have been torn out of context. This was precisely Kierkegaard's course of action, and there was no continuity between *The Moment* and his earlier, more profound writings that had been directed at the individual. He produced great results. The masses could now easily understand what he wrote because the intellectual content was no different from what could be read in the scandal sheets, excepting that here it was done with talent, with wit, and with biting sarcasm, so that *The Moment* became an armory from which people took new weapons. The audience he gained consisted of the sectarians and all those who were hostile to the Church and the clergy, as well as a number of defenseless souls who were unable to appreciate the significance of these attacks. Even among the peasant class his accusations created ill will in many places. Similarly, he found his adherents among the out-and-out atheists and those who deny God, who wanted to have nothing to do with Christianity or religion. I myself have had occasion to hear them elevate his understanding of Christianity to the skies as the only genuine view because his Christianity is inhuman and makes exaggerated, ascetic demands no one can fulfill. They thus feel themselves completely justified and absolved for their refusal to have anything whatever to do with Christianity because they see all other views [except Kierkegaard's] as inadequate. He has contributed in no small measure to the growth and strengthening of unbelief in this country.

To the extent that Kierkegaard thought that he had a mission in his activity, it must certainly be said that he entirely missed his calling. His true calling was to be quietly active as an author, as he had been earlier. And now he wanted to enter into public life actively, as a reformer—or at any rate as some sort of reformer. But here one may ask: what did he really want to accomplish, then? After all, every sect that attacks the Folkekirke as a Babel has itself got a congregation, a society, it wishes to put forward in place of the Folkekirke and within which it wishes to gather together those who leave the Folkekirke. But Kierkegaard did not want to involve himself in any exodus from the Folkekirke. He did not want to found a congregation or establish any new society. He totally denied every notion of society or association, and he looked only to individuals—despite the fact that he now addressed them en masse. He wished to raise a call to arms to abandon the Folkekirke as a den of thieves. But what then? How were things to end? He does not seem to have thought about this at all. The reforming activity was without aim or purpose. And from this point of view one may find it fortunate that he died, because the entire business might otherwise have ended in the greatest tedium. Because it would of course have been impossible to continue to listen ad infinitum to the tautological repetition of this call to arms to abandon the Folkekirke without being provided with any direction concerning where one ought to go. Detached from society, he stood in the midst of society like a hermit who could provide society with only words of condemnation, not words of guidance, of uplift, or of edification.

Although he called forth a great stir with his *Moment*, it was not difficult to perceive that the entire effect would be transient and negligible, precisely because it had been so negative and without plan. I believe that he produced a more profound effect with his work as an author, where he quietly had an influence on many souls. And yet, if we view this meteor, which produced such a strangely mixed impression, both in its ascent and in its fall—if we consider the whole of his activity and ask, What, in the end, has been accomplished with these rich gifts, with these remarkable talents?—then the answer must certainly be, Not very much! It is certainly true that he has awakened a profound and fervent sort of unrest in many souls. But the many half-truths, the many false paradoxes, and false witticisms can hardly have assisted any soul in finding serenity and peace. He has probably given many souls food for thought concerning Christianity's seriousness and concerning what is reprehensible in a merely habitual Christianity, but he has not led any souls to a knowledge of the truth. The effect he produced was essentially only critical. He wanted to winnow us like wheat. If we view him ideally, he comes more and more to resemble an *accusing angel* in his attitude toward the Folkekirke, and it is as such that he is still hailed and invoked by the opponents of the Folkekirke. He himself also seems increasingly to have viewed his mission as that of an accusing angel. His criticism was not that of the Holy Spirit, nor that of the prophets, with whom strictness is always asserted against a background of charity and mercy. It was the criticism of a Mephistopheles; it was a heartless criticism, which looks upon depravity with a certain malicious pleasure, assured that in the end the people will certainly be damned. But this is precisely why the positive result was necessarily so scanty—practically zero.

Certainly one occasionally finds men of letters who praise him to the skies as a thinker and a writer of first rank and as something of a great reformer or a powerful force within the Church. But here one must ask, What are the great truths he has bequeathed us? Is it that the individual's relationship to God is a principal point of religion? We have long known this, but everything depends on how and within what limitations this individualism is understood. Or is it to be the various stages of life that he has sketched: the aesthetic, the ethical, the religious, and the Christian-religious? This, too, we have known for a long time, but surely many people have noted the peculiarly Kierkegaardian element in the way it was presented, i.e., that it is so one-sided and affected that scarcely anyone can make personal use of it. Or do people wish to repeat what has often been repeated, namely, that he asserted the ideal, and that it is his great accomplishment to have kept the ideal unsullied? This is a great untruth. He did not assert it in a manner any different from that of every sect, inasmuch as he puts forth his own one-sidedness and views that as the true ideal. His image of Christ is completely distorted, and his ideal of the imitation of Christ is an ascetic caricature. If these points were discussed in more detail, people would surely have to refrain from uncritical and unthinking praise.

But it would be regrettable if the great wealth of spirit and genius that is to be found in Kierkegaard's writings did not yield some fruit for the future. Until now we have seen only flawed preliminary attempts, but there has yet to appear any writer of significance who shows signs of having been genuinely inspired by the many brilliant details in his writings. Even if these details are one-sided, they are nonetheless suited to provide impulses and to produce ferment. One dare hope that perhaps this may yet come to pass. But it will certainly require great patience and charity in the person who will have to work through this mass of material.

But for my own part, as we take leave of him in this book—and it is not likely that I will ever concern myself with him again—I wish to remember him by repeating a few words, which I find telling and which were spoken by one of my friends, who acknowledged this unique and remarkable literary and religious phenomenon: "He was a noble instrument with a cracked sounding board." Alas, this crack became greater and greater. And under this heading I must reckon his broken health, which increasingly exercised a disturbing influence upon his intellectual life. In my opinion, the disturbing influences that emanated from his physical condition can in no small degree serve to mitigate the judgment of his behavior. No one is able to determine the extent of his sanity.

Israel Levin[3]

[*A. Wolff to H. P. Barfod, December 12, 1869*]

During the years 1857–59 the philologist and linguist I. Levin frequented my father's house, and since your remark on p. liv ("the linguist I. Levin probably helped S.K. for a period") suggests that this source of knowledge about S.K.'s private life has not been accessible to you, I take the liberty of directing your attention to him. This is my real reason for bothering you with this letter. From my conversations with him I got the impression that he must have had extensive knowledge of S.K., even though his judgments need to be tempered a bit. Much of what he told me is now forgotten; I will relate what I remember. L.'s account of the circumstances surrounding the engagement merely coincided with the usual loose, well-known, and inane stories. Similarly, he mentioned the solitary country rides, the heavy use of hot baths, K.'s disdain for money, his charity, his hermitlike life, his extreme fastidiousness with regard to a fixed order of things (which Levin ascribed to the influence of life in his father's house), his wealth of ideas, his strange gestures, and the difficulty of keeping up

Israel Levin. Retouched daguerreotype. From the original in the Picture Collection of the Royal Library. Reproduced courtesy of the Royal Library.

when he dictated (despite the fact that the paper was prepared, i.e., cut, numbered, etc.).

Levin found Kierkegaard's fear of fires striking. When a fire occurred, K. could behave like someone with a case of nerves. When he lit a candle or a cigar he threw the matches into the stove with a remarkable caution. Once when L. lit a candle and then threw the match into the spittoon, K. shouted, "Are you mad? You might set the whole house on fire!" And he bent down on the floor, picked up the match, called for water, laid the match neatly in the spittoon and poured water over it and also onto the floor. It took a quarter of an hour before K. was calm enough that he stopped shaking and the sweat disappeared from his forehead. L. attributed this morbid fear to a fire that occurred during his mother's pregnancy, but that is of course merely a hypothesis.

L. mentioned as an oddity that K. had never written so much as two lines of verse. On the other hand, he mentioned a remarkable draft of a tragedy, from which he described several scenes. I can remember only that it was intended to conform to Aristotle's rules for arousing "fear and pity" and that L.'s summary, vague as it was, made a deep impression on me. The first scene alone was gripping: a dark night like the night on the heath in *King Lear*, an open grave-yard with a freshly dug grave. Ludwig comes in, bows down over the grave and whispers: "Emma, Emma, are you there? Are you sleeping while I keep watch, or are you keeping watch while I sleepwalk here?"

[*A. Wolff to H. P. Barfod, January 9, 1870*]

Remarks by Mr. I. Levin, B.A., Concerning S. Kierkegaard, 1858 and 1869: Anyone who wants to deal with S.K.'s life must take care not to burn his fingers: this is a life so full of contradictions that it will be difficult to get to the bottom of his character. He often refers to double reflections; all his own speech was more than sevenfold reflection. He fought to achieve clarity himself, but he was pursued by all manner of moods and was such a temperamental person that he often alleged things that were untrue, imagining that they were the truth. Thus he never warned Bishop Mynster as he claims he did. When he wrote "Guilty/ Not Guilty" he said: "I should have known that I at some point would write 'Guilty/Not Guilty' when I wrote *Either/Or*." And yet later he wanted to give the impression that everything had been arranged in advance. It is impossible that there could have been room for all that in his head at one time. On the whole, he lived in fantasies and empty reflections in which he seized upon each thing, transformed it in every possible way, looked at it from all sides, and then reflected on it. He never managed to understand himself, and in his mental activity he sought satisfaction for his ceaseless craving. It was enough for him to form a conception: he "poetized himself" into every kind of existence. Thus he lived for eight days with the sole purpose of thinking and feeling like a miser (though all the while using money in the usual way), and he carried this to its most extreme consequences. Once he confessed that he had an enormous desire to carry out an actual theft, and then to live with his bad conscience and in fear of discovery. Thus he gave vent to reveries and poetic images, and with his eloquence and almost demonic imagination he produced surprising effects. We spoke of the tragic. "The tragic," he said, "is not when a soldier appears bleed-ing on the stage; the tragic must have eternity as its background, in this way: it is evening, a cemetery, a grave. A young girl comes in, bows down over the grave, and calls 'Ludwig, Ludwig, are you asleep? I gave you everything. I gave you my honor. Give it back to me.' And then she throws herself onto the grave in desperation." One evening in the Frederiksberg Gardens we spoke of Ander-sen: "Andersen has no idea what fairy tales are. It is enough that he be good-hearted, why should he also attempt poetry? This poor woman, how brutally she drinks, but, dear me, the children get their sweets, they had to have some-thing. All very innocent—but fairy tales?" And then he conjured up six, seven tales that made me very uncomfortable. His imagination was so lively that it was as if he saw the images right before his eyes. It was as though he lived in a spirit world, and with a strange impropriety and eccentricity he could evoke the most frightful things with an explicitness that was terrifying. In similar fashion, he described, from *The Attic Nights*, a Greek pederast and his opposite, an anchorite, in a forest undergoing spiritual temptations, all of which was depicted with a meticulousness that was indecent and demonic. In Gilleleje, where he was called "the crazy student," he confused and frightened chambermaids by the way he looked at them when they entered his room. His soul burned with desire, even though his body was calm. It was his intention with regard to his writing that only lewd thoughts but not daring expressions were to be avoided. He was of the opinion that "literature is not for nursing babes or for half-grown girls, but for mature human beings." This elaborate depiction of situations and the pointedness of his phrasing, which one finds everywhere in his notes, meant that many portions of his books were produced at the cost of an enormous amount of work. What with all the corrections, and yet more corrections, we almost never finished "The Discourse of the Ladies' Tailor." I became extremely useful to him, just by helping him to get beyond the most insignificant of the items upon which he foundered. At times I spent up to eight hours a day with him. Once I ate at his house every day for five weeks. Merely providing nourishment for his hungry spirit was also a source of unending bother. Every day we had soup, frightfully strong, then fish and a piece of melon, accompanied by a glass of fine sherry; then the coffee was brought in: two silver pots, two cream pitchers and a bag of sugar which was filled up every day. Then he opened a cupboard in which he had at least fifty sets of cups and saucers, but only one of each sort, and said: "Well, which cup and saucer do you want today?" It was of no consequence, but there was no way around it; I had to choose a set. When I said which I would take, he asked, "Why?" One always had to explain why, and then at long last we would be finished and get our cups. (He also had an astounding number of walking sticks.) Next he filled the cup with sugar over the rim and then poured coffee on it. It amused him no end every day to see the sugar melt. This really delighted him. The coffee was so extremely strong that he destroyed himself with it. It was excellent coffee; Minni provided the beans at an exorbitant price. The sugar was from Sundorph, and he paid his bill exactly on the first of every month. The account book was found after his death, and his way of life had cost him surprising sums. He inherited the house and ninety-eight thousand rixdollars from his father. At his death nearly everything had been spent; he had gradually consumed his fortune. His father's maidservant, who was married to a carpenter, and his manservant Peter had plenty to do to take care of him. He always lived on the sunny side of his house, but shut out the sun when it shone and closed off the windows, both the inner and the outer, either with white curtains or with paint or blinds. While we were out, everything was opened up and a fire was laid in the stove, so that the air was fresh when we came home. Then K. walked back and forth

Grib Forest with a view over Esrøm Lake to Fredensborg. This was one of Søren Kierkegaard's favorite places, and he owned a copy of this print. Print by S. H. Petersen,
1820. From the original in the Copenhagen City Museum. Reproduced by permission
of the Copenhagen City Museum.

in the room, waved his handkerchief and looked at the thermometer. It read
13¾° [Réaumur], and that made him happy. Goodness knows how they managed it, but it was always just as it was supposed to be, exactly 13¾°. Then we
each took a bottle of eau de cologne, sprayed some on the stove, and went to
work. His peculiarity with regard to fear of fires is well known; it was the result
of a fire in the house during his mother's pregnancy. When Berling's place in
Vimmelskaftet (across from Badstuestræde) burned, I went to his house. Like a
child, he put his arms around his manservant's neck and said, "Peter, Peter, oh
yes, is there any news? Yes, I guess I know." Since he avoided the sun, he always
walked in the shade, and, just as with trolls, it was impossible to get him to walk
over a sunny spot. He had a falling-out with Pastor Spang just because he [Kier-
kegaard] wanted to turn back when a ray of sunshine fell across the road—and
he did so, saying, "But I don't want to bother anyone. Go ahead, do just as
you please." The drives up to northern Zealand had to go at an extremely fast
pace. The "air bath" did him good. The carriage arrived precisely on time. He
himself was always punctual to excess. And then off we drove. We arrived in
Fredensborg. The coachman hurried into the inn and merely said: "The magister." This started everything in motion. K. stepped inside and in his thin voice
said only, "Good mor-ning," and then disappeared into the forest. After we

returned we had soup and chicken or duck. Then K. took out ten rixdollars and said: "Here my little girl, be so kind as to pay everyone." Then home again in a rush. The coachman laughed because he got a five-rixdollar tip. On these trips K. could be amiability itself: so engaging, sparkling with wit, emotion, and thought. Once I said: "That was an excellent outing, only it seemed to me to be too short. I wish I could repeat it." "Done!" said K., "See if the carriage is still there." But the carriage had driven off. "Then come again tomorrow at —— o'clock." I came the next morning. "No, none of that today." "But the enjoyment—I had been looking forward to it." "Ah. You have had all the enjoyment. Pleasure resides in the imagination. You were happy yesterday evening; you dreamed about it last night; you were happy this morning on your way over here; you have had enjoyment enough."

The last evening, it had been at Cand. Giødwad's, he sat on the sofa and had been so merry, playful, and charming. Then he fell down off the sofa, and we helped him up. "Ohh, lemme l-l-l-lie here 'til the girl sweeps up in the mornin'," he stammered, but fainted shortly thereafter. I believe that during the last year of his life he lacked full control of his mental faculties. With him everything was inner emotions. His talk of a prodigal youth, of the sins of youth, etc. can only refer to "sins in thought," because even if he "was always a participant, this was only in order to prove that in his case the entire basis of his life annihilated every thought of debauchery." S.K. was and could be monstrously malicious. He paid court to Mrs. Nielsen, tearing down Mrs. Heiberg, and vice versa. There are notes that testify to this. Nielsen and he became enemies. In the end he despised N. to an extreme degree, and this was the reason: one day he spoke with N. on the Esplanade. It was his wish, of course, that when people spoke with him they should be oblivious to everything else, even an earthquake of the magnitude of that which destroyed Lisbon. A young man walked past and said hello. "Stop," shouted N., "Why don't we see you? My wife and I have very much longed to see you. Remember how much my wife likes you. The other day she called you her one and only. I'm not jealous. So come. *Au revoir.*" And then he kissed the young man on the fingers. "Who was that?" asked K., who had witnessed all this in silence. "Oh, a dull boy, the illegitimate son of ——. He has no understanding of us; he is ill brought up and coarse, without culture." "But you kissed him on the fingers?" "Yes, you must understand that for the sake of his father something must be done for him. But he himself is a very nice and attractive fellow, though only a boy, about whom my wife does not really bother, either." It made a deep impression on K. that people could behave like that. He didn't like Monrad either. When Monrad had gone off to become a bishop, K. said, "Bishop—a minister—bishop, well that's not what he'll really be. It's only a title—but it of course fits him quite well. And, while he's waiting, it is as if I were to say, 'If the coach should come, say that I've gone to the toilet to wait.'" With him, things never had anything to do with reality, and when malice came to the fore, his delight in contentiousness enticed him into defending positions that were entirely at variance with all probability. One time I was somewhere with a Mrs. Boisen, well known as a wild woman with various children, etc. She sat down, "but was unable to speak because she was so moved by a sermon she had heard that day by (Spang?) in (Holy Spirit?) Church, etc." Later a visitor came and was asked what he had thought of the sermon in that church. "He did not preach. In fact, he was sick." Mrs. Boisen became pale and defended herself by saying, "Yes, well, you did not let me say everything. I would have said 'three weeks ago today.'" "Then your memory must fail you," the visitor said, "because then he was in Roskilde." I told K. this story, which might have served as grist for his mill, but he said: "Yes, you see, you are lacking in fantasy. That poor woman—oh, I of course have also heard that they say things about her—perhaps she has a vivid imagination. At one point—who knows when?—she could have read a sermon—by who knows whom?—which made an impression on her. She thought about it, she believed that it was today, etc." I could not figure out whether or not this was really his view of the matter, but another time, when we were speaking of the queen, who was not particularly intelligent, he said, "You are mistaken. Christianity does not bother about the head. It sees only a good heart. It relates itself only to feelings, and the queen has precisely these genuine Christian feelings," whereupon he burst into loud laughter.

His relationship to Christian VIII was the most ridiculous comedy. Christian VIII was enormously vain, and K. was no less so, despite the fact that sometimes it was impossible to determine whether it was pride, justifiable self-importance, or just a desire for amusement that seduced him. Christian VIII wanted to see him, and K. wanted to be pressed in order to show the king that his royal power was unavailing in this case. The go-between was Pastor Ibsen in Lyngby. The matter was much discussed, but K. would not go up to the castle. Otherwise he went to Lyngby only now and then, but now he went there all the time. Finally Pastor I. came right out with the words that this was the will of the king: "Oh, yes, then I must submit to the will of the king—but I have no black tails." The pastor's suit was too large, Christian's was too small, Paul's was not good enough, etc., but the next time it could be done. Finally, the king said, "Oh, nonsense! Just bring him along whether he has gray or green trousers and green or gray tails." This was the king's definite will. "Yes, so I must of course obey." And they went to the castle. The king stood inside, informed of their arrival, and took up his position. Pastor I. and K. came up the stairs. The door was to be opened. "Everything well thought out," said K., "I will not do it." And he ran away. Well, finally he came to the king. Remarks were exchanged. "Now the queen must see you as well." "That cannot be done, Your Majesty." "Of course it can. She's waiting just inside." "But no, it is impossible, Your Majesty," etc. So he was presented the next time. During his conversation with the king, the chamberlain announced that dinner was served. "Magister K. will be dining with us," said the king, and the chamberlain went. "You will surely give us the pleasure of remaining with us for dinner, quite *en famille*," said the king. "No, Your Majesty, I simply cannot. It is impossible," etc. And the king had to dine without K.

The king wanted to give him a position, a professorship at the university. No, K. did not want that. A position as a pastor, yes, that was a fine idea, but preferably on the heath of Jutland, where only two or three people, at most, came to church. K. said it was as if he were standing before Philip II, and he cited *Don Carlos*: "Ein solcher Geist muß man behutsam feiern, man darf ihn nicht in seiner Freiheit lassen" (or however it goes).

K. did not like businessmen or fossilized civil servants. He liked to draw them out. Algreen-Ussing, who still mentions K. with veneration, never noticed how K. got the better of him. He [Kierkegaard] hatched a scheme by which he could catch him, and then when he met him he said: "At last I am so fortunate as to meet you, Mr. Councillor of State. There is no one who is better able to tell me than you," etc. And then he asked him about something that was miles over U.'s head. All of Ussing's resistance was of no use, and he finally gave in. When he really got going, K. took hold and turned his [Ussing's] entire train of thought into a "hollow tube open at both ends." U. held his ground and, to free himself, finally said, "Oh, I know what you have to do—take a hot bath." Then K. jumped up and said, "You see, you were just the man. I knew it. No one but you could have given me that advice. No, only Algreen-Ussing could have done it. A thousand thanks. Goodbye."

After K.'s death, everything in his room was found to be in order, as if he were going to travel, to take a trip to the country. At last a key was found. What was it for? It was for his desk. Inside lay a letter to P. Chr. K. The book dealer Lynge and —— were present. [P.C.]K. took the letter and read it, and so profound was the impression that it made that he had to sit down in a chair and take a couple of minutes to pull himself together. No one knows the contents of the letter. The brothers were not on good terms. A third party was always employed when there were differences between the two of them.

The story of Tardini is amusing. Søren always went about thinking up witticisms, which he often incorporated in conversations, in which his witticisms could appear to be sudden thoughts, intellectual sparks, and thus call forth the admiration he sought. I came in to see him. "Well, what's new?" he exclaimed—he who never cared a bit about the news. "Oh, nothing new." "What has been happening in Copenhagen? What are people talking about?" "What are people talking about? Well, about Tardini. It was pretty sad, too. And his sweetheart was with him in the balloon." "Yes. See, once again I am unable to agree with you. It is like so many other things that happen and that surprise people—the effect is produced only because of the person who is involved. Right now people are surprised both about Tardini and about Grundtvig, about what they did simultaneously. But had Tardini gone and got married and Grundtvig ascended into the heavens, then everything would have been in order."

After K.'s death, thirteen thousand rixdollars in cash were found, and the entire fortune was certainly around twenty thousand rixdollars, but Mrs. Schlegel, to whom it was offered, hates him so much that she refused to receive it.

Søren was in general not very likable. His pupils did not like him. He was sarcastic and could bear a grudge. He did private tutoring for many years because his father would not help him. That was before the reconciliation, which cost his father a couple of thousand rixdollars. His brother did much to facilitate this by taking Søren's side.

Frederik Christian Sibbern[4]

[F. C. Sibbern to A. Sibbern Møller, October 2, 1863]

It is not easy for me to write anything about Kierkegaard that would satisfy myself or others.

He was, inherently and in his innermost being, a very inwardly complicated sort of person. I spoke with him mostly on walks, and he nearly always was only capable of speaking about the things with which he was then engaged in his innermost self. I don't know whether he had a genuinely Christian disposition and temperament, although he certainly must have had something of that sort. There was a period when he always listened to Mynster preach. One summer he was out in Lyngby and came into Copenhagen, a distance of one and one-half Danish miles, every time Mynster preached. But of course zealous polemics about Christian matters can easily undermine Christianity. He wanted to forge closer connections with Mynster, who, however, simply could not approve of a person like Ki. I think there can be no doubt that Kierkegaard owes Mynster a great deal with respect to spiritual and intellectual influences. So it was all the more surprising when, after Mynster's death, he attacked Mynster's memory so vehemently. Mynster once publicly praised his [Kierkegaard's] spiritual discourse upon the words of Job, "The Lord giveth, etc."

Permit me, however, to talk about something that I am particularly suited to discuss, namely, his engagement and how it was broken off. When he became engaged, he brought me along to visit his sweetheart, but on that occasion I only met her and her sisters. One day he got me to come to the Deer Park with both her and himself. As I later came to realize, at that point discord had already arisen in their relationship. Afterward, when he had broken off the engagement, I was the person to whom the pretty and very charming young lady turned, so that I frequently spoke with her in private. The first times she saw him, she felt for him a sort of respect mixed with dread. When he wanted to break off with her—but by compelling her to break off with him—he behaved in such a way that Miss O. said he had mistreated her soul. She used that expression, and she felt deep indignation about it, but she could not stand it when people spoke ill of him, as they did in her parents' home. That she was able to speak otherwise in my presence meant that I became the person who had to give her support. I told her, however, that I had to view the fact that she did not become K.'s as

Frederik C. Sibbern. Drawing by Christen Købke, 1833. The original is in the Royal
Print Collection of the Royal Museum of Fine Arts. Reproduced courtesy of the Royal
Print Collection of the Royal Museum of Fine Arts.

a good thing for her. This was because Kierkegaard's spirit was continually preoccupied with itself, and this man, confined as he was in self-reflection, would
either have tormented her with jealousy or have lived with her as if he were
totally unconcerned with her.

    When the engagement was broken off, I said to K. that he was the sort of
person who ought never be engaged at all, but that the sort of thing which had
happened to him should not have happened to a man of his age. When she later

became engaged to a man who had previously been in love with her, had given her up, and now came back to her—she married him shortly thereafter—K. came to me, not exactly in triumph but at any rate extremely pleased about it. But I knew the state of her soul, and I knew that she would not find it easy either to forget K. or to recover from the violation of her life. I have not seen her since then, and I cannot remember how it happened that I completely stopped seeing her. She appeared to me to be a profound, powerful soul, as well as lovely and charming.

I must say that K. was a thoroughgoing egocentrist, and with respect to his writings—which contain much that is excellent, so that I would certainly like to see a chrestomathy excerpted from them—I must nonetheless say that in general, "In vielen Worten wenige Klarheit."

I did not see him again during the years before his death. In his last years he began to visit A. S. Ørsted, the jurist, who thought very highly of him. But when his attack on Mynster began, this stopped and could not have done otherwise than come to a stop.

[*F. C. Sibbern to A. Sibbern Møller, October 3, 1863*]

I wrote the enclosed letter as soon as I received your letter yesterday morning, when I did not find myself particularly able to give you the information you wished. I will now add a bit.

Mother and Grethe remind me—I myself have forgotten a lot of this sort of thing—that before you were born, when we lived on Chrystalgaden, Kierkegaard came to see me regularly; that he continued to do so subsequently, after you were born, when we lived on Nørregade; and that he often got me to accompany him on walks. He looked to me in those days, but I cannot remember anything we spoke about. But there was one time we met at Gammeltorv that he spoke of something I have not forgotten. It was during the period that he occupied himself with Hegelian philosophy. He wanted me to tell him what the relationship between philosophy and life is in reality. The question astonished me because I did not have, nor do I now have, any other understanding of philosophy than that it is an attempt to penetrate to the very ground of reality and to its most fundamental conditions, or as it has also been expressed, to solve the riddle of existence. But since then, I have come to think that in the case of a philosophy such as Hegel's, which claims to derive all its contents from the inner wellsprings of thought—which is called a priori construction—one may very well ask about its relationship to the world of reality, just as one can ask the same question of mathematics, which draws all its contents solely from within the understanding.

Kierkegaard's father had been a hosier and had given up his business as the result of a sort of hypochondria that had led him to believe that he did not have long to live. But he lived quite a long time nevertheless, another twenty years, I believe. According to what K. told me, he was a very sharp thinker, a dialec-

tician, and it was supposedly from him that his sons had inherited their dialectical acuity—that is to say, their ability to differentiate concepts and think
them through to their consequences, which often degenerated into hairsplitting
subtlety. He undoubtedly also was of a genuinely Christian way of thinking.

When I said earlier that I didn't know whether I really ought to say that he
had a *genuinely* Christian spirit and *temperament*, I probably went too far, and was
thinking in particular of the last part of his life. He had a very Christian *way of
thinking*, but a way of thinking when one talks and reasons is different from a
temperament. Temperament can show itself in one's way of thinking, however,
and did so often with Kierkegaard.

He held his late father in great respect and could not see his father's signature,
"K., former hosier," without being greatly moved. He also had great respect for
Prof. Nielsen, the headmaster of the Borgerdyd School.

He had inherited a great fortune. His manner of living and his lodgings were
those of a man of means. I believe he also used a good deal of his fortune for
charity. When he died there was supposedly nothing left of his fortune. The
publication of his voluminous writings must have cost him something over a
considerable period of time. Toward the end, on the other hand, he must have
earned considerable royalties.

He was fundamentally a very polemical sort of person, inclined to opposition. But during the time I knew him he loathed journalistic agitation. I was
very surprised to see him end up as an out-and-out journalist-agitator.

He had a witty, somewhat sarcastic face and a brisk way of walking. He was
thin and not large of build, with a crookedness that seemed just on the verge of
hunchback, and he also took pleasure in sarcasm, but it was coupled with wit
and humor, as sarcasm generally seems to be.

He wrote quickly and had things printed just as they were written. He once
told me how on the same evening that one of his books was finished at the
printer's he would start on a new book.

It was typical of him to want to look after precisely those people whom the
public did not value.

People said he died paralyzed in his lower body, no doubt of epilepsy. But
epilepsy can put the soul in a very exalted state.

[*F. C. Sibbern to H. P. Barfod, September 19, 1869*]

I am not surprised that you have asked me for information about Kierkegaard's life, because I did exactly the same thing when I had to write sketches
of Melchior and Brorson at Herlufsholm. The Kg. I knew was certainly not a
loner, and I would never label him as such. Early on, he looked to me for advice
and not infrequently came to my house, and I visited him. I often walked with
him or rode with him in a carriage. He traveled by carriage a good deal. I did
not have very many discussions with him—*that is something I do remember*—
because he was one of those people who was continually preoccupied with

himself. That is, he was preoccupied with what stirred inside him and with expressing it. I do remember, however, that once, during his Hegelian period, he met me at Gammeltorv and asked me what relationship obtained between philosophy and actual life, which astonished me, because the gist of the whole of my philosophy was the study of life and reality. But subsequently I of course realized that the question was a natural one for a Hegelianized thinker, because the Hegelians did not study philosophy existentially—to cite the expression used by Welhaven when I once spoke with him about philosophy.

You will surely notice that this is written by the hand of an eighty-four-year-old man. Above, I underlined the words "that is something I do remember," because there is much that I do not remember, especially dates. But my daughter tells me that Kierkegaard was visiting us even as early as when we lived on Chrystalgaden—that is, between 1831 and 1836. These were undoubtedly his early years as a university student, if, as I assume, he entered the university in 1833.

I never knew him to be melancholic. He traveled about a good deal, visited many people, during his last years even the elderly A. S. Ørsted, who took considerable pleasure in seeing him, but who of course ceased to do so after Kierkegaard's attack on Mynster's posthumous reputation.

He visited his brother-in-law, Agent Lund, daily, and from him you could learn how Kierkegaard fared during his great battle. But I know one other person to whom I would advise you to turn for information, namely Pastor Ipsen at the Citadel in Copenhagen. He became a student at the university at the same time that Kg. did, also from the Borgerdyd School.

Kierkegaard turned to me early on and also subsequently, especially during the period of his engagement, about which I could tell you things that only a very few people know. But I dare not entrust the most important of these things to paper.

Come to Copenhagen, visit us, hear what my wife and daughter can tell you, and visit yet another lady to whom I will direct you.

I daresay that he was never melancholic during the long period that I knew him, and it was only during his final two or three years that I no longer saw him.

To bear a cross and to preach the cross are two very different things. The latter can be done in a very satisfying way.

Many of Kierkegaard's writings received a great deal of attention in my house. The whole time I knew him he hated agitation, and it surprised me when he himself became a zealous agitator.

I must still note that it is certainly possible for a man to carry a great melancholia within himself along with a good deal of liveliness and buoyancy.

I take it, on the basis of what Kierkegaard told me, that his father, the "former hosier," had a powerful intellect and a certain profundity, which had its effect upon the son.

In those days, not only did every new university student receive a Latin testimony from the school, but a couple of months before the entrance examination the school's headmaster would send reports (sometimes quite detailed) on the matriculants to the university. Speer, our university porter, could probably look up Nielsen's report on Ki. for you and would probably be happy to do so if you mention my name.

Henrik Hertz[5]

1.

[*June 4, 1836*]
Evening at Hb's [Heiberg's] and said farewell before their trip to Paris. Kierkegaard, Poul Møller, etc. were there.

2.

[*September 6, 1838*]
Visited Heiberg. Said about Kierkegad's book on Andersen: "The Mesopotamian language is a strange language"

3.

[*September–December 1838*]
Kirkegaard's book about H. C. And[ersen] (1838). What a peculiar churchyard! To judge from various clues, it would appear that the trumpets have been sounded for resurrection from the grave—but if that is the case, the dead have not yet recovered their bones, but are lying there quarreling over them. Because the confusion is great. (The Mesopotamian language is a strange language.)

4.

[*March 18, 1839*]
Took a walk with Kierkegd (about his book on And[ersen]).

5.

[*August 8, 1839*]
Met Kierkegaard. Was very happy about the politics in *Moods and Situations*, but probably not about the philosophy in it, I should think. "Now *I* would have done it like this, etc." His egoism.

6.

[*Undated, but most probably from ca. 1840*]
Those who have picked up the German philosophy are completely incapable of practicing it in Danish. Their text teems with words of which no Dane knows the meaning. Kirkegrd's work on Andersen shows what language we can expect from this philosophy.

Henrik Hertz. Lithograph by D. Monies, 1838. From the original in the Picture Collection of the Royal Library. Reproduced courtesy of the Royal Library.

7.

[Undated, but most probably from late 1844]

It is said that when Kg. talks with young people at the Student Union, he speaks very slowly and asks them at every moment whether they have understood him.

8.

[Undated, but most probably after February 19, 1848]

S. Kierkegaard often seems to me, though only in his humorous works, to be nothing more than a very talented and well informed writer of serialized novels. Like one of them, he takes his good time, lets his pen run on about all manner of things, turns molehills into mountains and the reverse, and puts the main emphasis on piquant description, often even on the eccentricity of an idea! His style is quite that of the writer of serialized fiction, though not quite the French

serialist, but a cross between Jules Janin and some young German with an education in philosophy.

9.

[*Undated, but between late 1858 and 1866, most probably 1860*]

S. Kirkeg.'s numerous works are like tall trees in literature. High up in the
treetops, his monkeys sit and eat from the trees. If you attack them, they throw
large Kierkegaardian pieces down at you—rather like monkeys who sit up in
coconut palms and throw down nuts if you attack them with stones. If only the
Kirkegaardian nuts were not so large and tough that you have a difficult time
opening them to get to the relatively small kernel.

10.

[*Undated, but probably from between late 1860 and 1865*]

The story of my life must touch upon my acquaintance with *Søren Kierkegaard*, whom I first met when he was a quite unknown young student. It was
ca. 1836, and he was at the Student Union lying on a sofa in a comfortable
position, from which he addressed me in confidential tones as if we had long
known each other. After that we met often, though only on the street, in public
places, etc., and I was very taken with his cheerful, intelligent conversation, his
own weak, often rather castratolike voice, the sudden transition from something cheerful to a rather serious expression.

My remark concerning his *From the Papers of One Still Living*, which he took
(or seemed to take) quite well: I expressed the opinion that his style had been
taken from Hamann. "I have not read anything by him," he answered. But the
fact is that Hamann haunts the writing of so many in Germany that you can get
him second- and thirdhand.

His engagement to the young, lovely Miss Olsen, whom he practically tor-
tured to death with his peculiarities. One day he fetched her in a landau for a
ride in the country, about which she was indescribably happy. But at the circle
in Vesterbro he turned around and drove her home again, so that she could
become accustomed to denying herself pleasures. He should have been beaten
on his a—— for that.

He sent me a copy of the second printing of *Either/Or* with a fine tribute to
me in a dedication on the outside of the jacket. I sent a book in return, and we
can scarcely have met one another again before we appeared in *100 Years*, which
caused him to send me a little work, *On My Activity as an Author*, in which it is
explained whom and what he meant when he spoke of "one single reader."

I wrote something somewhere about his journalistic style. He does not seem
to me to be an author by whom I can feel strengthened and supported.

11.

[*Undated, but probably from between late 1860 and 1865*]

To what has been said about my acquaintance with S. Kierkeg. can be added
Mad. Hvidb.'s [Madame Hvidberg's] stories about him, including the fact that

he frequently came to them with the extra post, that he climbed out of the carriage in the pouring rain, which he liked, and often brought with him two partridges or two snipe, which he had them roast—always two, one of which he gave to his hosts.

12.

[*Undated, but probably from early 1856*]

In the "Vejle Journey," sketch Johannes Climacus [i.e., Søren Kierkegaard] from nature: of middle height, with broad shoulders and a rather rounded back, a thin lower body; a bit bent-over when he walks; thin, rather long hair; blue? eyes; the voice often breaking into a treble or a bit piping. Also quite easily provoked to laughter, but suddenly switching to seriousness. There was something pleasing about him, not so much the promise of anything special as many different things—not so much in the depth? as in the breadth, or at any rate in depth treated broadly—but in any case there was something entertaining (he took his sweet time). He sits or lies down comfortably, with a certain sense of physical ease. The certainty in him.

13.

[*Undated, but after March 1846*]

In his work on *Two Ages* hasn't Kierkegaard, who is certainly a son of modern philosophy—and be it noted parenthetically that in addition to the infinitely many other things he owes to German culture must also be reckoned his infinite breadth and his wealth of vocabulary—made room for a remark concerning the short stories by the author of *A Story of Everyday Life*, a remark about something that is quite important to him himself? Hasn't he touched upon the fact that from beginning to end these stories remain within the *category of dualism*? That the recurrent and sharply drawn antitheses within human nature which they contain—culture and lack of culture, poetic and prosaic dispositions, aristocracy and cynicism, the most delicate cunning and the coarsest crudity (especially in feminine natures)—continually make it impossible for these stories to solve life's mysteries and saturate their characters with a truly poetic *ruach elohim*. The fact that they do not understand how to depict the intermediate forms of human nature, but one-sidedly present antitheses as units with absolute boundaries. . . . When Poul Møller says in his review of *The Extremes* that "in Theophrastian style, [one] could make a collection of certain profiles of many of the characters sketched in the story," this is true, but a poor recommendation for the character sketches because a literary work of art must not be Theophrastic, not generic, but individual.

14.

[*Undated, but after February 1846 and probably before the end of 1848*]

Overskou to Kierkegaard: "I will be your *one* reader of *everything* you write. You are to be my one stockholder."

In [. . .] "Fifth Monarchy" cannot do without Kirkgd, his thought experiments, his relationship to *Fædrelandet*, the piece that recommended his first work, cf. his quarrel with someone in *Berlingske* and somewhere in the *Postscript*, his book of February (1846), his irritability when criticized, his insatiable urge to write, taking his good time, continual wandering about in the streets, etc. "Have you understood me?" "Well, no . . ." "Then I will repeat it . . ." "No, it is precisely your repetitions that make the words incomprehensible to me." Sitting in a pastry shop in the Deer Park, he states that he is experimenting at seducing the waitress (*malet die Wollust, doch malet der Teufel dabei!*). When someone reproaches him for corrupting the girl and for giving people, especially the young, a bad example, and himself a bad name, he answers, Me? God forbid! I stand quite apart from my writings, with the exception of the 1,118 edifying discourses. All my works are objective (cf. the postscript to the *Postscript*). Each work is by quite a different person from the next one. Just listen! And then he quotes a passage by each of his personae, texts that are all similar in language, etc. He also says (which I then also use against him) that it is not he who has insulted those who are attacked.

"The Fifth Monarchy" . . . Kirkeg. seduces the girl in the tent, but under one of his assumed authorial pseudonyms, and says that he is not responsible for what has been done by that firm.

Pierrot [M. A. Goldschmidt?]: "Yes, I stand here talking to myself. Such excellent thoughts and remarks deserve an audience. Nor is it a good thing to make remarks to oneself. It is as though the thoughts eat into one's flesh and make one callous; the free flow is blocked, as Barfod ? says. Is there no one nearby to whom I can hand over a portion of the troublesome weight of my thoughts! Here comes someone—it's Kirkegd. Now, he will probably pay me back in kind, so that I would collapse under the weight. Then it is better to bear my own cross patiently. (He calls thoughts of solitude that remain unused a cross for the soul.)"

Poesia and Kg or another in conversation about the recent (i.e., German) requirements concerning the relationship between philosophy and a literary work.

(Kg on the author of *A Story of Everyday Life*.) Life is divided between poetry and prose, that is clear. But this is not to be understood in such a way that some people are only poetic, others only prosaic. No one is so poetical that he is without prosaic inclinations and interests, and indeed no one is so prosaic that he is without some poetry, even if it is only that of tears of pain, want, anger, or regret (indignation), or of sighs, light and heavy, which lie upon his breast like dew or fog that has not yet risen, and is perhaps incapable of rising higher, to the region of the eye. It goes without saying that the pearls of these teardrops are so delicate that often only God and the angels—but only rarely human beings—

can collect them and string them into a necklace. Not every lady can string tiny embroidery pearls. But the poet can do it if anyone can; I require it of him. It is the much-spoken-of Day of Poetic Judgment that will determine how large a portion of poetry and prose is given to each: poetry, poetry at one remove, with long fingers, etc.

At the Hill Kierkeg.—but as Climacus, whom it does not concern—states what has been written by the author of the review of *Two Ages*. He can conveniently enter [the stage] with a fat man from the countryside, and explain the part about dualism in everyday life, with an occasional, "Do you understand me? Are you following me?" "Yes, God forbid, Herr Magister, I am following, but my whole body is dripping with sweat at your words. You did not speak in this way at all in your review of *Two Ages*." "Yes, but I ought to have spoken like this. But what it says in that book is irrelevant to me anyway, because what you are now reading and sweating over is Climacus, etc." "But for these last fourteen years my entire family and I have regarded these stories as the soul of all our poetry, and we have nourished ourselves by them. In a sense, they have been our daily bread, our manna in the desert of rural life." "Oh? Well, it hasn't harmed you at all. There is really excellent nourishment in these stories (his gestures allude to fodder cakes, sugar beet sugar, gun cotton). I will explain it to you, if you will walk just a little further with me." "Yes, if we don't go too far." Thus K. states that the yield is the lyrical impressions, the beauty of the language, and the embellishment of so many aspects of everyday life.

Program with Kierkegaard. Pierrot [M. A. Goldschmidt?]: "Immediate! That is such a confounded word to understand!" Kierkegaard: "That is because you are yourself placed on the plane of the immediate and the visible." Pierrot: "No, but my wife, who follows the new philosophers, uses the word constantly and about so many things that I haven't any idea what it is. Philosophy has made great strides in the neighboring market town. When I rode over there last week with my hired man to buy some coffee, since my supply from Copenhagen was used up, the clerk—he wears a goatee and a moustache—asked me if I wanted miniature grind, etc. He has divided up the drawers in his shop in categories. In the category of dried tropical fruits there are seven drawers: raisins and almonds, currants, etc. I hear that philosophy has abated here in Copenhagen, but in the provinces we will still be wearing the hand-me-downs from here for a while longer.

Kg says about the short stories by the author of *A Story of Everyday Life* that they can certainly *move* one, but that they do so by means of the pressure of reality, or because the characters lack cheerfulness, and especially because of their worldview. Suffering and prosaic phenomena appear just as bleak in those stories as in life, and therefore awaken the same melancholia. One does not feel strengthened and uplifted, because one is moved without being purged.

He can also refer to the scene in Poul Møller's *A Danish University Student's Tale*, in which thirteen-year-old Fritz on his romantic escapade wants to earn his bread with his violin, and at a poor peasant farm is addressed prosaically and gruffly by a peasant woman. Now the latter would have been made even coarser by the author of *A Story of Everyday Life* and left at that. He would have sought an antithesis in two personalities: Fritz with poetic, free tendencies—and the peasant woman, sunk *utterly* in the prose of life. But how different is the poetic, radiant clarity that P. Møller sheds upon the situation! The woman discovers that she was Fritz's wet nurse, and now the full strength of the poetry of her existence (which every existence has) breaks through from beneath her hard crust. Fritz is far from being *utterly* absorbed into the poetic.

At the request of the chorus, Kierkegaard or someone else puts forth the case for why the art of drama is the highest. Lyric and epic art produce all their marvelous effects by *depicting* passions or states of the soul in such a way that the listener or reader is utterly transported to empathy, to tears, to laughter, recognizing the whole of his own inner being. But the *epic* poem only *tells about* such conditions, which often belong to an era far in the past. And the *lyric* poet does not appear personally in his poem, nor does he always refer to himself. But the *dramatic* and thus the *theatrical* art possesses the highest degree of the imitative power that poetry has over sensibility. Because here the sufferer, the acting agent, he about whom we hitherto have only heard things related, steps forth *himself* and reveals his life to us. Nothing is concealed from us; we see everything before us clearly and immediately. We see him turn pale, blush, become angry, melt into tears. The poet, the actor, and the stage combine to give us the most remarkable illusion, which grips us with the intensified—poetically intensified—force of reality. And yet it neither wounds nor depresses us as does reality, since all our empathy is silently accompanied by the awareness that we are seated in front of a beautiful play. It is like a gripping scene in a dream, which in all its clarity carries us off into that dream, making the heart pound, the blood rush, and bringing forth tears. But when we awaken, the thought that "it was a dream" leaves us with only a light vibration of the nerves and a quickly calmed rise in blood pressure. (Chorus: "You have explained this admirably, Kg. Never before has it been so obvious to us; but neither have you ever before spoken so briefly and *clearly*, and with so few circumlocutions.)

Chapter Eleven

HANS BRØCHNER ON KIERKEGAARD

Hans Brøchner's Recollections of Kierkegaard[1]

I have wanted to note down some of my recollections of Søren Kierkegaard drawn from a period of many years, which might also be of interest to others. Perhaps some day, when S.K. finds a skillful biographer, they will be able to contribute to making various aspects of his portrait more complete and lifelike. I record my recollections merely as materials for a portrait of K., and thus without any attempt to shape them into a whole or round them off by arranging them in groups. They are presented just as they have been preserved: from the first impression, as *individual* recollections from a faithful memory.

1.

My first meeting with S.K. took place just after I became a student at the university (1836). I then saw him at the home of my old uncle, the merchant M. A. Kierkegaard, at a party held on the occasion of the engagement (or wedding?) of the present Bishop Kierkegaard with his first wife. I saw S.K. there without knowing what he was; I had only been told that he was Dr. K.'s brother. He spoke very little that evening; he primarily played the role of observer. My only definite impression was of his appearance, which I found almost comical. He was then twenty-three years old; he had something quite irregular in his entire form and had a strange coiffure. His hair rose almost six inches above his forehead into a tousled crest that gave him a strange, confused look. Without quite knowing how, I got the impression that he was a shop assistant— perhaps because the family were merchants—and I immediately added to this, from my impression of his strange appearance, that he must work in a dry goods shop. Later on I have often laughed heartily at my perspicacity.

2.

Next, I remember that shortly thereafter I saw S.K. every once in a while in that same place. Now I came there in order to speak with him and soon realized that he belonged elsewhere than behind a counter with a yardstick in his hand. He amused himself among this very ordinary company by making little paradoxical statements. Thus I recollect that he once amazed his relatives by claiming, with the most serious of expressions, that the old ABC that we had used in our childhood was one of the most interesting of books and that he still read it regularly with much profit. One evening he joined a game of Boston. It was played with several variations there, one of which consisted of dealing seventeen cards to three of the players, and only one to the fourth. The first three players then each gave four cards to the latter. In that house, where card playing was regarded with reverential solemnity, the predicament of the fourth player in this game was viewed as extremely pitiable. Again S.K. surprised them greatly by explaining that it was the very finest situation imaginable and that he only wished that he could permanently be the fourth man. That would be the most stimulating of all.

3.

In 1837 I occasionally met K. at a restaurant. At that time he no longer lived at his father's but in a house on Løvstræde; I believe it was the one where Reitzel's bookshop is now (1871). He preferred to eat his evening meal at a restaurant. I can remember how surprised I was, on one of the rare occasions when I indulged myself with "half a steak," at the luxury S.K. displayed when he ate a dinner, with a half bottle of wine, etc. We now conversed more often, and he was very kind to me. One evening he asked me what aestheticians I had read. In that connection I touched on how limited my access to books was and that in many areas there was much of which I was ignorant. He asked if I knew the writings of the German romantics, which I had to admit I did not. He invited me to accompany him home and lent me a book by Eichendorff: *Dichter und ihre Gesellen*. Later, when his books were auctioned off, I bought this book as a memento of this encounter with him. I also remember that when I returned it to him two weeks later, and was about to apologize because I had kept it so long (I was studying theology with a passion at the time), he confounded me by receiving me with the question of whether I had read it *already*. With his sharp eye he had evidently been able to see that the opposite word was on the tip of my tongue, and he amused himself in a friendly way by embarrassing me, which was extremely easy to do in those days. I blushed so easily, and he always found that spectacle charming in "the young person." There are two things I remember from this visit to K. when he lent me the book: the one was my surprise at his large library, which quite impressed me. The other was a peculiarity of K.'s: he went out again when we had fetched the book and, as we left, he blew out a wax candle that he had lit. He explained to me that he always did this with some caution, and at a little distance, since he had the notion that the smoke from the candle was dangerous to breathe and that it might damage his lungs.

4.

In 1838 S.K.'s father died. I only saw him once, at my old Uncle Kierkegaard's. His character was of such consequence that his appearance made a vivid imprint on my memory. He and my uncle walked up and down the length of the floor in my uncle's dining room, conversing. He walked bent slightly forward; his posture corresponded to the thoughtful, serious expression on his face; his facial

Hans Brøchner, age twenty-five. Drawing by J. V. Gertner, 1845. The original is in the National Historical Museum at Frederiksborg. From a photograph of the original in the Picture Collection of the Royal Library. Reproduced courtesy of the National Historical Museum at Frederiksborg.

traits were displayed sharply because his gray hair was combed back behind his ears. The love and veneration that S.K. felt for his father has been vividly expressed in his writings. The old man was a very punctual, exact man in money matters, and, though frugal in everyday matters, he could nonetheless be liberal on certain occasions. S.K. once told me how he had taken a trip in northern Zealand as a young university student, and how the old man had provided him generously with travel money and nonetheless had surprised him by sending him a letter with fifty rixdollars to one of his last stops. S.K. once used this expression in speaking with Magister Adler about his father's punctuality: "My father was born on the due date." When S.K. left his father's house, the old man gave him an annual sum that was very generous for those times; if I am not much mistaken it was eight hundred rixdollars a year.

5.

My late sister Hansine, then a young woman, spent the year 1839 here in the city. Once when I mentioned S.K., she told me that she had seen him [in 1828] when she, as yet unconfirmed, had been on a visit at old Uncle Kierkegaard's. On a day when S.K. was coming to visit, our girl cousins had given her the advice that she shouldn't have anything to do with him, since he was "a fright-fully spoiled and naughty boy who always hung on his mother's apron strings." My sister was then thirteen years old and S.K. was fifteen. She later read with great pleasure some of his devotional writings, in particular *Works of Love*, and could then, with her own special smile, remind me of how our cousins had warned her.

6.

I had a talk with S.K. soon after he had taken his degree in theology in 1840. He told me that his father had always wanted him to take a theology degree and that they had discussed the matter very often. "Nevertheless, as long as Father was alive, I could defend my proposition that I ought not to take the degree. But after he died, and I also had to assume his side in the debate, I could no longer resist and had to make the decision to prepare for my degree." S.K. then did this with great energy. He had chosen "his Brøchner" as tutor, worked his way through the driest of the disciplines, made notes on ecclesiastical history, learned the list of popes by heart, and so on. His tutor was very pleased with him. Soon after S.K. had taken his degree, Peter Stilling (later Dr. phil.) went to "his Brøchner" and wanted to be tutored. He announced that he thought he could be finished in a year and a half; "S.K. did not study any longer than that." "Ah, yes," said old Brøchner, who did not excel in courtesy, "Don't fool yourself! S.K. was something else; he could do everything!" I recollect that in 1839, together with S.K., I attended a writing seminar in theology given by Clausen. But he came to only the first two or three classes. It was said that several years earlier he had participated in Clausen's seminars, and once, instead of doing the written assignment, he had analyzed it and demonstrated that it was mean-ingless. Clausen had been affronted by this, and S.K. had stopped going to class. At the written examinations in theology, S.K. was rated fourth by the outside examiners. Above him were M. Wad, Warburg, and Chr. F. Christens. The outside examiners, however, told these three that K.'s essays showed evi-dence of far greater maturity and development of thought than any of the others, though their essays contained a greater measure of specifically theologi-cal material.

7.

In the same conversation in which S.K. told me how he had come to take his degree in theology, he also mentioned his father's amazing composure and objectivity. Thus the old man had once said to S.K., "It would actually be good for you if I were dead; then you might yet make something of yourself; you won't do that as long as I am alive." (I was told of another incident concerning his father by my late cousin Peter Kierkegaard. When S.K.'s mother died, his father was profoundly saddened. At the funeral, Bishop Mynster came up to him and movingly spoke his words of condolence. Without speaking of his sorrow, the old man listened to Mynster, whom he esteemed greatly, and when Mynster fell silent he said: "Your Reverence, should we not go into the next room and drink a glass of wine?" Mynster, who knew him, did not misunderstand this remark.)

8.

It was while S.K. was in Berlin during the winter of 1841–42 that I applied to take the examinations in theology, but was denied permission because of my unorthodox convictions. I corresponded at the time with Chr. F. Christens, who was also in Berlin, and through him I exchanged greetings with Kierkegaard. Shortly after his return home I met Kierkegaard on the street. He was very kind to me, spoke to me of my situation and my studies, and pleased me very much by telling me that in Berlin he had longed for a number of things here at home, one of which was to see me. He could say that sort of thing with a singularly winning expression. His smile and his look were indescribably expressive. He had his own way of giving a greeting at a distance with just a glance. It was only a small movement of the eye, and yet it expressed so much. There could be something infinitely gentle and loving in his eye, but also something stimulating and exasperating. With just a glance at a passerby he could irresistibly "establish a rapport" with him, as he expressed it. The person who received the look became either attracted or repelled, embarrassed, uncertain, or exasperated. I have walked the whole length of a street with him while he explained how it was possible to carry out psychological studies by establishing such rapport with the passersby. And while he expanded on the theory he realized it in practice with nearly everyone we met. There was no one on whom his gaze did not make a visible impression. On the same occasion he surprised me by the ease with which he struck up conversations with so many people. In a few remarks he took up the thread from an earlier conversation and carried it a step further, to a point where it could be continued again at another opportunity. His reason for demonstrating these experiments for me was that one day I had been walking ahead of him, deep in thought, and had not heard him call to me, nor had I noticed when he tapped me on the shoulder. When I finally noticed him, he said that it was wrong to be so lost in one's own thoughts and fail to make the observations that were so richly available. To demonstrate the method, he took me in tow up and down several streets and surprised me with his talent for psychological experimentation. It was always interesting to accompany him, but there was a difficulty of a sort in walking with him. Because of the irregularity of his movements, which must have been related to his lopsidedness, it was never possible to keep in a straight line while walking with him; one was always being pushed, successively, either in toward the houses and the cellar stairwells, or out toward the gutters. When, in addition, he also gestured with his arms and his rattan cane, it became even more of an obstacle course. Once in a while, it was necessary to take the opportunity to switch around to his other side in order to gain sufficient space.

9.

S.K. met many Danes in the winter he spent in Berlin. Many of them had gone there in order to hear Schelling. Among them was my late friend Christian Fenger Christens. S.K. spoke of him with great appreciation; later he told me that Christens was the brightest of all the Danes who had been in Berlin that winter, and among them were such men as the jurist A. F. Krieger (later cabinet minister) and Judge Advocate Carl Weis (now administrative head of the Ministry of Religion and Culture). Christens told me various little stories about K. One was about his ineptitude when he had to speak German, especially when he had to refer to everyday things: the first evening in Berlin, for example, it was impossible for him to express that he wanted a candlestick. He also told how K.'s landlord squeezed money out of him, and, as he extorted more, repaid K. by promoting him from magister to doctor and then to professor. Kierkegaard himself found this amusing since he suspected the reason. Another story concerned his embarrassment when Weis, who appreciated an elegant dinner, once led him into a first-class restaurant where a number of elegantly dressed gentlemen wearing black evening dress, white scarves, and collars were standing in the corners of the room. After K. had politely greeted them and sat down at a table with W., they leaped into action, making it clear that they were the waiters. Christens also told me how Kierkegaard amused himself in Berlin by setting traps for the theologian Rothe (now an archdeacon). Rothe had already been abroad for a long time, had attended lectures in Strasbourg and other places, and was very self-consciously aware of all the wisdom he had gathered. When they met, S.K. rarely refrained from asking him to present the most significant scholarly results of his foreign travels. When Rothe then formulated some proposition or other to exhibit his newly acquired knowledge, K. always understood either how to demonstrate to him that this was passé, or how to pose little questions about "something that was not quite clear to him," leaving the poor theologian, who was not a very gifted thinker, in such confusion that he was entirely at sea. When K. had brought him to this point, he always suddenly realized he was very busy and had to rush off someplace or other. The theologian [Rothe] was left in all his confusion, to the great amusement of the others. In *Either/Or* K. describes this method, also used on a theologian. I wonder if he wasn't recollecting his acquaintances in Berlin when he wrote those pages?

10.

Not long after K.'s return home, he once talked with me about his studies. I told him what I then was reading of the Greek authors and touched on the increasing interest I had conceived for Greek poetry and philosophy. He encouraged me to continue these studies and spoke with enthusiasm of the significance of the Greeks for our time. He expressed himself in this way: "Greece ought always to have an ambassador in our time, just as one power has an ambassador to another to protect its interests." K. himself had a fine facility with Greek and had read fairly widely. His writings bear witness to how well he understood the Greek spirit.

11.

In 1842 a short pseudonymous pamphlet appeared: "Johan Ludvig Heiberg after Death." I knew about it before its publication and mentioned it once to S.K. He did not like Heiberg being made the object of such a jest. He spoke with warmth of his [Heiberg's] importance as an aesthetician and as the aesthetic educator of his generation in our country. K. ranked H. above all the contemporary aestheticians in Germany. (N.B.: Vischer had not yet appeared then, except for a few brief works.) Later, after *Either/Or* had appeared and Heiberg had written his well-known review of it, S.K. once spoke to me about him and made no secret of his displeasure at H.'s behavior. He recognized H.'s importance as an aesthetician, but now also emphatically emphasized his limitations. "I could name a whole series of aesthetic problems about which H. hasn't a clue." Here he evidently alluded to the problems that were treated in *Stages on Life's Way* and *Concluding Unscientific Postscript*.

12.

In those years I often met S.K. when I went for a walk in the evening. As a rule, Frederiksberg Gardens were the goal for my walk. S.K. also walked that far, but only to the entrance of the gardens, where the small flower beds lined each side of what was at that time a narrow path that led from the gate to the first open area. There he would inhale the fragrance of the flowers for a few moments and then return with the recollection of this "moment." He liked to limit and conclude things in this way. His wanderings had a definite goal, but this goal was, as it were, only just touched upon. There was no lingering by it, and it was as if it were nothing more than a motif of a delight, which could be elaborated on in ideas.

There is a comical recollection related to one of these evening walks. When we returned from the gardens to the allé and had to pass between the posts that mark the end of the path between the trees, it turned out that the posts had just been painted. K. did not notice this, and placed his hand on them for support as he passed between them. He then noticed that his hand was covered with paint, and he made a whole series of unsuccessful attempts to wash the paint off by rubbing his hands on the leaves, which dangled down from the trees and were damp with the dew, all the while continuing his conversation and keeping his indispensable cane under his arm. His efforts called forth many smiles on the lips of the passersby.

13.

In those days, I occasionally saw S.K. on horseback. He had learned to ride in order to get some exercise and to make short outings without having to depend on coachmen and so forth. He did not cut a particularly good figure on a horse. His posture revealed his lack of confidence about being able to do much to control the horse should it take it into its head to rebel. He sat on the horse stiffly and gave the impression that he was constantly recalling the riding master's instructions. He can hardly have had much freedom to pursue his thoughts and fantasies on horseback. He soon gave up this sport and preferred to take a carriage when he wanted to visit his favorite spots in the forests around Copenhagen. In the years of his most intense literary activity, these excursions were one of the means he employed to keep fresh and to bring on the mood required for production.

14.

I will mention a particular expression of K. from that time as typical. K. had a servant who was very reliable and to whom he entrusted the discharge of all sorts of practical matters. Thus when he was going to move, he drove out in the morning, and in the evening proceeded to his new home, where everything had been put in perfect order by the servant—even the library was in order. K. once said of this servant, with respect to his practical talents: "He is, in reality, *my body*."

15.

Just after the publication of *Either/Or* I had frequent conversations with him about the book. As soon as I read the Διαψάλματα I recognized the anonymous author; I had immediately found words that had been spoken earlier, in conversations with K. Naturally, I never attempted in my conversations with K. to get him to reveal himself as the author. But when something was obscure to me, I spoke with him about it as one does with an elder who has more profound insights. In this way I obtained many an explanation, and he spoke candidly about the book, which he would scarcely have done had I been indiscreet. A point on which he dwelled a number of times was the poetic element in the first part. He explained one day in lively fashion how at many points the motif of a poem was indicated, but purposely not carried out. He thus pointed out, as an example, the descriptions of the beauty of woman and said: "In each of these sentences: the little hand, the dainty foot, etc. lies a theme for a sonnet." Now and then he hinted at what appeared to be further developments of the problems treated in *Either/Or*, but most of his allusions were not clear to me until after his later writings appeared. He was not unreceptive to expressions of appreciation of the book's significance. One day I remarked that not since I had read Hegel's *Logic* had any book set my thoughts going as had *Either/Or*. He was obviously pleased by this remark. We stood near the door of his house (on Nørregade) and were each going home; as we parted, he shook my hand kindly and smiled the smile I knew so well.

16.

After I had published my piece against Martensen ("Some Remarks on Baptism"), K. spoke to me about it. He was dissatisfied with a review in *Berlingske Avis*, which had tried to adopt a superior tone and to dismiss the young author by means of such assumed authority. I told him that actually I had been only amused by the review, since its forced Christian tone assumed a slightly comic aspect when one remembered that it was an anonymous article appearing in a paper edited by a Jew. K. pointed out a single remark in my short pamphlet that he wished had been omitted; this was where I ridiculed Martensen's attempt to assert the freedom of the newborn infant, saying that the only act of freedom available to the newborn infant at baptism is to scream when splashed with water. K. thought this remark appeared flippant and that it could easily be exploited by the ill-disposed.

17.

K. often referred to Ludvig Feuerbach in our conversations. It is on the basis of verbal statements by K. that I claim in *The Problem of Faith and Knowledge* (p. [125]) that the quotation cited there was directed at Feuerbach by K. He appreciated the clarity and penetration with which Feuerbach had understood Christianity, precisely because he [Feuerbach] had been offended by it. In conversation, however, K. once emphasized that from Feuerbach's enthusiasm for nature—in particular from *The Essence of Christianity*, where he speaks with pathos (also spiritual pathos) of the strengthening power of water—he had got the impression not only of a strong sensuality in F., but also of a weakening through sensuality. To this he added: "This is an opinion that I naturally would never express in print; but I have not been able to avoid the impression that there is something in Feuerbach's peculiarly passionate pathos, and in his antipathy to Christianity, which this conjecture makes clearer to me." These remarks about F. brought him to talk about figures from classical antiquity who represented sophisticated sensuality. Thus he presented a most imaginative picture of Mæcenas, telling how he "who had exhausted all the pleasures of Rome" sought to drug himself during his insomnia with the quiet splashing of a water fountain in his bedchamber and with weak strains of music from afar.

He was very good at producing such pictures; however, it was not the poetic portrayal, but the psychological analysis—or rather, perhaps, dissection—that interested him.

18.

In those years I once had the opportunity on a longer walk to observe with what expression and force K. could recite passages of works of poetry. He spoke of [Oehlenschläger's] *Aladdin*, of the brilliant boldness that characterized his desires, and of the contrast between the spirited self-confidence of this genius and the cautious calculations of reflection. He then quoted Aladdin's words to the Genie at the point where he bids him build the magnificent palace for the wedding night. Just then we were passing Charlottenborg. K. stopped as he recited these lines, accompanying them with a slight gesture of the arm. His cheeks colored, his eye turned bright and warm, and his voice, though soft, was like that of a ruler who knows that he has the power to give orders.

19.

We once talked about Hegel's presentation of the history of philosophy. K. emphasized what were, in many ways, the subjective aspects in Hegel's point of view, and said: "Actually, geniuses always lack the ability to perceive others' thoughts objectively; they find their own everywhere." In a conversation with me soon after this, he happened to say about himself: "I have never had this ability to perceive others objectively." At that moment he can scarcely have remembered his remark in our earlier conversation; I did, and I smiled to myself as I drew the obvious conclusion of his remark about himself.

20.

Kierkegaard told me about a couple of strange incidents concerning Magister Adler at the time when Adler's mental disturbances began. One day Adler came to K. with a work he had published and talked to him for a long time about both of their activities as religious writers. Adler made it clear to K. that he viewed him [Kierkegaard] as a sort of John the Baptist in relation to himself, who, since he had received the direct revelation, was the genuine Messiah. I still remember the smile with which K. told me that he had replied to Adler that he was completely satisfied with the position that Adler had assigned him: he found it a very respectable function to be a John the Baptist and had no aspirations to be a Messiah. During this same visit, Adler read aloud a large portion of his work to K.; some of it he read in his ordinary voice, the rest in a strange whisper. K. permitted himself to remark that he could not find any new revelation in Adler's work, to which Adler replied: "Then I will come to you again this evening and read all of it to you in *this* voice (the whisper), and then you shall see, it will become clear to you." When he told me the story, K. was much amused by this conviction of Adler's that the variation in his voice could give the writings greater significance. In my first year as a student I once heard a remark by Adler concerning Kierkegaard. He spoke of K.'s brilliant conversation, but advanced the opinion that K. sometimes prepared for his conversations.

21.

When K. was younger, and perhaps even as late as the time when he had finished his dissertation, he considered the possibility of a career at the university. This thought soon faded into the background, however. Once he told me that Sibbern had suggested he apply for a position as a lecturer in philosophy. K. had replied that in that case he would have to insist on a couple of years in which to prepare himself. "Oh! How can you imagine that they would hire you under such conditions?" asked Sibbern. "Yes, of course, I could do like Rasmus Nielsen and let them hire me unprepared." Sibbern became cross and said: "You always have to pick on Nielsen!" This was shortly after Nielsen had been appointed to the university. K. later spoke to me about Nielsen on many occasions. Once during Christian VIII's reign he mentioned how N. had sought the king's protection, and [Kierkegaard] made slightly snide remarks about his [Nielsen's] business sense. "He understands what they say in Jutland, that a person must have something to live off!" At a later point, when N. had allied himself with K., he spoke of him with more interest and acknowledged his talents. Once he said: "Nielsen is the only one of our younger authors of this general tendency who may amount to something." However, it was more N.'s intellectual talents than his character that K. appreciated. From the period in which K. struggled with himself over whether or not he should enter into polemics with the clerical establishment, there is an entry in his diary where he reflects on whether he ought to acquaint anyone with his thoughts. He mentions N., who at that time had attached himself very closely to him, and whom K. saw daily. But he rejects the thought again with these unflattering words about N.: "No! Nielsen is a windbag!"

22.

K. has expressed his opinion of *The Corsair*'s attack on him in several of his works. In these he has primarily considered the matter from an ethical point of view, and he has probably substantially exaggerated the influence the attacks in *The Corsair* had on public opinion in general. In relation to a given phenomenon, K. did not possess a sense of reality—if I may use this expression—which could counterbalance his immensely well developed powers of reflection. He could reflect on a trifle until it assumed world-historical significance, as it were. This is evidently what happened to him with *The Corsair*. In a conversation with me he spoke of *The Corsair*'s general tendency and appraised its wit from a purely aesthetic point of view. His most serious complaint against it was that it destroyed the public's sense of the comic ideal by always attaching ridicule to certain known persons, who were then once and for all identified for its readers as comical figures. The reader then laughed at what was said, not because it really was the stuff of comedy but merely because—without being truly comi-cal—it was said about persons now generally deemed to be comical and objects of derision.

23.

Something similar to *The Corsair*'s attack also happened to him with "Søren Kirk" in Hostrup's play *Gjenboerne*. In the diaries he left behind, K. often re-ferred to Hostrup as having put him on the stage. And he refers to it in such a way that shows that he was affected by it. In the first performance of the play, I played this role, and I remember having spoken with K. about it at the time without noticing that he made anything of it. But as time passed he must have reflected on it until he underwent a change of attitude. Although Hostrup used themes from S.K.'s writings in this little role, in the role itself he apparently had in mind principally the sort of dialectics that flourished among young students after Martensen had stimulated a very superficial interest in philosophy. K. was a master of this form of dialectic in his younger years—when he cared to be. My conversation with K. about the role took place one evening when I was on my way to a rehearsal at the Court Theater. On Højbroplads I met K., who stopped me and asked where I was going. I told him that I was on my way to the rehearsal of Hostrup's play. "Ah, yes, you are of course playing me!" said K. I replied that I wasn't exactly playing *him*, but a dialectician of our domestic variety. We then parted without my having detected that K. had disapproved of my having taken that little part. In any case, he ought to have understood my relationship to him sufficiently to know that I would not try to place him in a comical light by imitating him. I was too devoted to him for that—and much too poor an actor.

24.

At the beginning of the forties K. took a trip to his father's birthplace on the west coast of Jutland. He told me a typical little incident from that trip. He was in his family's native town, where his father had established a generous endow-ment for a school. He had been received with great respect, and the school-teacher in particular had been busy in his official capacity. "I was really afraid they would erect a triumphal arch for me," he said. When he was ready to depart, he drove past the school. There stood the schoolteacher with all the children lined up to sing a song the schoolteacher had written in S.K.'s honor. The teacher, who was to direct the song, had a copy in his hand and was just about to give the signal to begin when K.'s carriage [came to a stop] next to him. S.K. leaned over with his friendliest smile and took the copy from his hand as if to read it through, and at the same moment gave the driver the sign to drive on. At this the whole arrangement fell apart. The teacher, who didn't know his poem by heart, could not get the song started. The children stood silent and surprised, and S.K. rolled down the road, nodding and waving, inwardly amused at the teacher's disappointment.

25.

On the day on which Licentiat Hagen (later professor of theology) had defended his doctoral dissertation, I spoke with K. about Hagen's dissertation ("On Marriage"). I had been one of the official opponents. K. found little in it of which to approve. He found the whole treatment superficial, and he alluded to the fact that the pseudonyms had given a fuller treatment of these ideas. On this occasion he also stressed the much more thorough treatment given such topics by the Germans, and he said, with reference to Hagen's dissertation, that "an effort ought to be made to make a decent show when books of this sort will be read by the Germans."

26.

While I was in Berlin for the summer of 1846, S.K. arrived there. It was one of the short trips he made from time to time when he wanted to work really intensively and sought a change in surroundings in order to put himself in the mood. I met him quite unexpectedly in a restaurant where I was dining. He had gone there to meet his fellow countrymen, since it had been a gathering place for the Danes during his first stay in Berlin. He did not set much store by it as a restaurant; it limited itself, he remarked, to "the crudest notion of fodder." He approached me in a very friendly manner, invited me to eat with him the next day at his hotel, and went on long walks with me for the few days he stayed in Berlin. I was very curious about all the new things to which I was exposed in Berlin and was unflaggingly busy. K. was amused by all this activity, which even included my attendance at meetings of a democratic workers' association. We talked a lot about conditions in Berlin and at home, about my dissertation, and so on. On our walks I noticed that there were several places K. fancied, which it pleased him to seek out. One such place was a beautiful section in the zoo where there was a park surrounded by flower beds. This became the object of his walks just as the flower beds at the entrance to Frederiksberg Gardens had been in Copenhagen. Perhaps this park reminded him of that place and its associations. On a visit to his hotel, I noticed how much ingenuity had been expended on arranging everything in his rooms in order to encourage the mood for his work: the lighting, the connection between the rooms, the placement of the furniture. Everything was arranged according to a definite plan. K. placed very great demands on service, but was also very generous with gratuities. Our little dinner for two was served in his room. We drank a wine for which he had a preference on account of its name: liebfraumilch. This name had given him the impression of something mild and light, and he drank the wine in this belief without noticing that it is in fact one of the stronger Rhine wines. It did me a great deal of good to meet K. in this foreign place. He fortified me in my renewed consideration of returning to Denmark and trying to make my way. K. was always amused by the effusiveness of Berliners, and at one point I sent him from Berlin, through our cousin Mrs. Thomsen (*née* Kierkegaard), a notice I had found in a Berlin newspaper. Under the headline "Query" it read: "Wouldn't it be fitting if the tinkers also formed an association in order to keep in step with the spirit of the times?" This amused Kierkegaard, who saw through their [the Berliners'] little games.

27.

After I had returned home from my first trip to Italy (late in 1847), K. came over to me one day when I was standing on Østergade and looking at some plaster copies of classical statuary in the window of Barsugli, the plasterer. When we came to speak of sculpture, he remarked that he actually had not previously had an eye for it, but that it had now begun to appeal to him because of its tranquility. I do not think that K.'s interest in, or comprehension of, the pictorial arts was at all strongly developed; he nourished his interest in beauty almost exclusively with poetry.

28.

Shortly after the rebellion broke out in 1848 I spoke with K. about the plan I then had of enlisting as a volunteer. I emphasized, in addition to the ordinary motives inherent in the situation, that I, personally, needed to gain experience, in particular, personal experience. K. agreed that the lessons of reality were necessary for many, but he implied that by means of imagination and reflection he had been able to obtain an even greater wealth of experience on the level of the ideal. Apparently he could find a *motif* from reality sufficient; this was processed by his reflection and fantasy, which were in turn directed by the experience he had garnered through the endless workings of his own mental life.

29.

Several years later I talked with K. about a similar subject. I was then dissatisfied with my lack of a specific occupation with definite responsibilities. The complete freedom of a life of private study had begun to become a burden to me. I expressed this in a conversation with K. and said: "I miss practical activity to such an extent that for lack of anything better I could be tempted to become an innkeeper." K. smiled and said: "Then you can have my trade." On this occasion he told of how he had been visited a few years earlier by a German scholar who had probably had been sent by someone to see him as one of our curiosities. He had received the German very politely, but assured him that a misunderstanding must have led to the visit. "My brother, the doctor," he had said, "is an exceedingly learned man, with whom it would surely interest you to become acquainted, but I am a beer dealer."

30.

Dr. P. K. held a series of lectures at the university at some point. I don't remember just exactly when, but it must have been in the 'fifties on one of his occasional visits here in town. They were held in the ceremonial hall at the university for a large and quite varied audience. Søren K. exhibited a rather ironic attitude toward these lectures, and it was with a certain malice that he related to me a fragment of a conversation he had overheard outside the university just as a lecture began. A crowd of men and even more ladies rushed up the university steps. The driver waiting outside with a carriage was addressed by a passerby with the question, Why are all these people going in there? To S.K.'s great delight the coachman answered: "Oh! They must be going to a dance!" The lectures were in the doctor's manner, that is to say, a rather forced cleverness in a prophetic-apocalyptic style. In connection with these lectures, I had occasion to tell S.K. an anecdote about our old uncle who lived in Kjøbmagergade. He attended the lectures regularly, even though they were far beyond him, and he was moreover very deaf. He felt very proud to see "the son of his cousin from Gammeltorv" lecture to such a large crowd. One evening after he came home from one of the lectures he walked up and down the floor in his parlor repeating, without a pause: "Yes! He has no equal, that Peter Kierkegaard! The way he can talk, the way he can talk." His daughter permitted herself to ask him: "Could you in fact follow his lecture? Could you really hear what he said?" "Not *one* word, not *one* word!" said the old Jutlander guilelessly, and his enthusiasm for the peerless speaker was undiminished.

31.

S.K. once told me a curious story regarding this old uncle. The old uncle had a passion for writing verses, which were equally dreadful in both form and content. One day he came up to S.K., and after a brief preamble he brought forth a bundle of his verses, which he asked his nephew to read aloud. They then seated themselves next to each other on the sofa. The old man sat down, leaned back, and put on his glasses in order to follow the reading, evidently to make sure that nothing was skipped. Søren K. sat slightly bent forward with the papers, probably choosing this position in order to keep the old man from observing the treasonous smile on his face. He read the poems to the very end in a raised voice and with great pathos. The old man was completely delighted; touched as he was by the beauty of the verse, tears ran down his cheeks, and he parted from S.K. with his warmest thanks. I have often heard my old uncle's verses; they were altogether peculiar, and had in particular the wonderful property that, with very minor changes, they could be used—or at any rate, they were used—on the most widely differing occasions. Thus the old man had once written a verse on the occasion of a granddaughter's engagement. Not only was it used again for another engagement where, however, the personal situations of those involved were very different, but it was also intended to have been used, with only minor adjustments, on the occasion of my appointment to the university. That it was not used then was only because the old man had not yet learned it by heart on the evening when, a bit earlier than we had expected, my appointment was announced in *Berlingske*, and we happened to be at a party at the old man's house. Sometimes, at his urgent request, the verses were sung by his guests. A melody would then be chosen which, with the use of a Procrustean method, could more or less fit the verses. It was hilarious to hear: first a large number of syllables all had to be swallowed in one mouthful, as it were, and then one single syllable had to be stretched out in accordance with Holberg's prescription. But to the old man's ears it always resounded like the loveliest of harmonies, and his face shone with delight.

32.

Old Kierkegaard sometimes used peculiar word order both in speech and in writing, but especially in writing. Thus when referring to S.K. and his brother in his letters back to his hometown he always wrote: "My cousin's departed son Peter K." or "My cousin's departed son S.K." (instead of: "My departed cousin's son"). This could appear especially comical depending on the context, as when he informed the family that his cousin's departed son Peter Kierkegaard had taken a new wife. I once told S.K. about my uncle's mode of expression. It amused him, but he himself attributed to it a significance of which the old man was unconscious (since he was a poet, the old man was of course naturally inspired!), namely, that he [Søren Kierkegaard] really was the deceased S.K. On this same occasion he happened to speak of my uncle's great age. I said that in a certain sense he could not be called old, if the length of a life were to be measured according to its content, because the old man had in reality "lived" only the least fraction of the time he had existed, and for the most part had just vegetated and slept. Jokingly, I added that actually S.K. was the oldest man I had known. He smiled and made no objection to this mode of calculation.

33.

K. once told me—it occurs to me in referring to his age—that as a young man he had for many years had the firm conviction that he would die when he reached the age of thirty-three. (Was it Jesus' age which also was to be the norm for Jesus' imitator?) This belief was so ingrained in him that when he did reach this age, he even checked in the parish records to see if it really were true; that was how difficult it was for him to believe it.

34.

In the winter semester of 1849–50, when I held lectures at the university for the first time, S.K. spoke with me rather often about the topic of the lectures (Greek philosophy) and about my plan for treating the subject. He told me that at some point he would come and listen, but that he would not specify any definite time. He did not come, however, but the continual prospect of him as a possible auditor gave me the incentive for a careful treatment of my subject. I think in fact it was this he intended. He also knew that I would be easily bothered by his presence were he actually there, and this may have been his reason for staying away.

35.

On the occasion of my lectures he once spoke to me about the definition of virtue in Aristotelian metaphysics as μεσότης. He had correctly seen that this definition was not valid for virtue in general, but only for ethical virtue—something which by no means was generally accepted at that time. He told me that he had sought enlightenment from Madvig and Sibbern on this point and on several others in the *Nichomachean Ethics*. Madvig had told him that it was so long since he had read that work that he no longer could recall it. "And Madvig is otherwise a brick," added S.K. Sibbern, on the other hand, had immediately been able to provide him with the information he sought. S.K. appreciated Sibbern greatly, even though he was not blind to his weaknesses. Among these he once emphasized Sibbern's complete lack of irony, and, from a psychological point of view, his lack of an awareness of the disguised passions, the reduplication [*Fordobbling*] by which the one passion assumes the form of another. In his opinion, this was why Sibbern was often taken in when many people, ladies, in particular, turned to him to consult him as a sort of psychological and spiritual adviser.

36.

S.K. often mentioned Poul Møller, and always with the most profound devotion. Far more than his writings, it was Poul Møller's character that had made an impression on him. He regretted that the time would soon come when—after the vivid memory of his personality had faded, and judgments of him would be based only on his works—his significance would no longer be understood. He once told me of an amusing little episode regarding P. Møller. He [Møller] was to speak as an ex officio opponent at a doctoral defense and had jotted down his remarks on several loose sheets that were placed in the dissertation. He introduced each objection with the phrase *graviter vituperandum est* ["it must be seriously criticized (that)"], but as soon as *Præses* [the doctoral candidate] had given an answer to his objection, he said good-naturedly, *Concedo* ["I yield, I give way to (your argument, your words)"], and moved on to the next objection. After a rather short opposition he closed by expressing his sincere regrets that the time allotted him did not allow him to continue this interesting conversation. As he left he passed S.K., who was standing in the audience, and said in an undertone to him: "Shall we go down to Pleisch?" This was the tearoom he usually frequented. During his service as opponent all his loose sheets of paper had fallen out of the book at once and had floated down onto the floor. Seeing the great man crawling around picking up the scattered sheets had contributed not a little to lifting the mood in the auditorium.

37.

A man with whom I often saw K. walking in those years was Prof. Kolderup-Rosenvinge. They had most likely been brought together by their common interest in aesthetics. K.-R. was a cultivated man who was interested in the literature of southern Europe and had translated a play by Calderón. On the other hand, he was already rather lethargic and in many ways extremely narrow-minded at that point. Once, when I expressed my surprise to S.K. that he could find it interesting to talk with Rosenvinge, he emphasized the man's general cultivation. He set great store by people from the older generation who had retained the humane interests of earlier times and the refined bearing that was so sorely lacking in the younger generation.

38.

K. saw much of the late Pastor Spang for a period (in the years 1841–45?), and almost every day he picked up Spang at his home for a rather lengthy evening walk. (A good number of interesting letters to Spang from S.K. are in the possession of Spang's daughter, Mrs. Rump.) After Spang's death, K. once related to me how overwhelmed with sorrow Spang's widow had been and how by conversing with her he had contributed to restoring her mental balance. On this occasion he used the expression: "I know how one should grieve and how one should give comfort in sorrow." And certainly he understood as few do. He comforted not by covering up sorrow but by first making one genuinely aware of it, by bringing it to complete clarity. Then he reminded that while there is a *duty* to mourn, there is also a duty not to let oneself be crushed by sorrow, but rather, in sorrow, to preserve the strength to do one's work, indeed, even to find in sorrow the challenge to do this task still more thoroughly. In my relationship to S.K. I myself experienced more than once the manner in which he understood how to lift one up when one was discouraged, how to give comfort in grief. He did this without finding it necessary to mention the cause of the discouragement or distress. Thus I remember a period in the autumn of 1850 when I had to stay at an unpleasant inn for a short while because I had been unable to find an apartment at a time when I needed one. Under the influence of my surroundings despondent thoughts gained the upper hand, but one evening while I walked the streets in dejection I met K., who struck up a conversation with me. Without any need for me to speak a word about myself, his sharp eye noticed that I needed to be brought out of my dejected mood. Without ever seeming to aim at this purpose, he understood how to use his conversation to free my mind. I left him, happy and cheerful, and for a long time I was freed from the power of melancholia.

39.

Much of what S.K. accomplished in his writings, I remember, he touched upon in conversations with me while he was thinking them through. And thus because these thoughts were still in their inception, they took on a life and an appeal even greater than they would have when fully formed. Thus I remember that once, while walking with Christens and myself, he developed the theme he so often treated in his devotional writings: that "*all* of life is the time of testing."

He developed the idea in this form: that for the believer there was an "at last!" which seemed to be so close as to be palpable, but which continually retreated until it could finally be grasped at the end of life. Not until death could one say: "At last!" From time to time S.K. expressed his thought in conversation in an even more pointed, more paradoxical form than in his writings. It amused him to express a thought so that it formed the antithesis of conventional wisdom. As opposed to the saying that experience is the best teacher, he used to advance the thesis that "experience makes us fools!" He could then whimsically adduce as proof all the innumerable contradictions of concrete experience.

40.

The differing orientations of our spiritual lives and our fundamentally different relationship to Christianity surfaced explicitly once in a while in our conversations. Once, in 1851, I believe, he asked me what I was working on at the moment. I replied that I was reading the New Testament. That seemed to please him, but it did not please him when I added that I was reading it mostly with this end in view: to find primitive Christianity in the received texts and follow the successive development of the Christian dogmatic concepts. To him such an investigation bordered on the offensive. Although he deals so little with dogma in his writings and adheres everywhere to what is central to Christianity, he was nonetheless unable to relate himself to the Scriptures in such a way that they became the object of critical investigation. He could not do this, in part because the Scriptures were to him a whole, an integral expression of Christianity into which he would not introduce any distinctions, and in part because when made the object of scholarly investigation, the Scriptures became an object of knowledge rather than an object of faith.

41.

I did not conceal from S.K. my differences with him concerning Christianity, but we did not argue about them. There was so very much about which we were in sympathy, and I preferred to be taught by him about a great many things of great importance to me, rather than to carry on a discussion in which he could easily have overwhelmed me with his superiority but could not easily have convinced me. He did most of the communicating in our conversations, and I viewed this as evidence that he was well disposed toward me. He had two modes of conversing: the one was essentially communicative, stimulating, encouraging; the other was questioning, making use of irony and, by means of his dialectics, confounding. He never employed this latter mode against me. Occasionally, when I became zealous, he might throw in a jesting, teasing word. Thus I once spoke quite zealously about how no positive religion could be tolerant, precisely because, with its claim to be revealed religion, it must insist that it is the only true religion, and it would have to consign the others to untruth. From the point of view of positive religion, a general religiousness, "a religion in general," must therefore be a nonentity. As I eagerly developed this idea, I happened to repeat the expression "a religion in general," and adopted as my principle that a religion (i.e., a *positive* religion) in general is a nonentity. "Yes, and so is a chamberpot in general," said K., thus putting a damper on my zeal. That, however, is the only teasing of that sort that I remember from him. He never tried to refute my deviant beliefs directly, but always displayed a completely amicable interest in me which I remember gratefully. The only reason I can find for this was that he knew that I honestly and seriously labored with the cause, which was to him the most important thing of all—and that, furthermore, I was so familiar with what he had written on this and with his whole manner of thinking, that I had sufficient premises to reach a conclusion and would not be brought closer to it by another person, but only by myself.

42.

I once said a word to S.K. about the general effect of his writings, which seemed to make an impression on him. He spoke of how his fate as an author had been peculiar: he had published one work after another without eliciting any real criticism, either attack or praise. Then he mentioned that his writings had from the beginning found a circle of readers, apparently a fixed circle, since the number of copies that sold soon after publication was always about the same (roughly seventy for the works that came after *Either/Or*). I expressed my conviction that a great many people read his writings with genuine seriousness and that the silence of our press, which I more or less interpreted as the critics' sense that the works were beyond their powers of criticism, was by no means a sign that he had encountered indifference among the wider public, among whom, I believed, he had already had significant influence. But I added that, with respect to attitudes toward Christianity, the effect had been just as much negative as positive. Everyone who had been influenced by the works in either the one direction or the other was apparently in agreement that his conception of Christianity was the only one that was truly appropriate, fitting, and worthy of respect. But his definition of Christianity was just the sort that might perhaps repel many people from it. Such had been the case with me, and it was capable of doing so precisely because of the separation it proposed between Christianity [on the one hand] and nature and concrete human life [on the other]. Just as I was saying these words to K. we were in the process of saying goodbye to each other; he became serious, gave me his hand in silence, and left me, but with a kind look on his face.

43.

S.K. expressed himself without hesitation on the significance his works could have for certain specific persons. His old uncle, the merchant M. Kierkegaard, had a son, a couple of years younger than S.K., who was handicapped, wholly paralyzed on the one side, and a complete cripple; mentally, however, he was well endowed. He [Hans Peter Kierkegaard] read his cousin's works with the greatest of interest, visited him from time to time in his home, and received considerable spiritual uplift from these visits. I spoke of him once with S.K. and told him what a great impression one of the works, the confessional discourses [entitled] *Edifying Discourses in a Different Spirit*, had made on his cousin. At one point the book discusses a person who is hindered by physical weakness from performing good works in the external sense. And there is a beautiful and inspiring description of how such a person also has the common human ethical task before him unabridged, and in what special form the task of life presents itself to him. S.K. said: "Yes! For him that essay is a joy." And that it truly was. It had the power to give a person who was sorely burdened the strength to overcome the thought that existence was useless and give him an awareness of being essentially equal to those whom nature had equipped more fortunately. S.K. also understood just how to keep this awareness alive in him through their conversations, and his cousin was therefore quite strengthened by them.

44.

Shortly before the publication of *Practice in Christianity*, I had a conversation with S.K. that I have often recalled since. We were walking together out by the lakes, and he encouraged me to begin writing for publication and not to put it off too long. Jokingly, he added: "There is a space available in our literature *now that I am finished*." This remark, which at the time I did not take very seriously, later came back vividly to my memory when the last portion of S.K.'s written works was completed. At the time that he spoke those words to me, he evidently still clung to the hope that he could avoid the final struggle against the Established Church. Had he not been forced into it [that struggle], his writings would have been essentially completed at the point at which that conversation took place. In reality all the stages that had to be gone through had then been completed; his works formed a remarkably finished whole. But the last stage contained within itself yet another possibility for reduplication [*Fordobbling*], and this possibility became a reality when the attempt was made [by his opponents] to reduce his view of Christianity to an eccentric exaggeration, and to propose mediocrity and spiritlessness as the real norm.

45.

In this same conversation S.K. came to emphasize an aspect of his writings about which he spoke with his characteristic objectivity: namely, the significance of his writings for Danish prose. He said, "In this century our literature has displayed an almost abnormal wealth in the development of poetry; our prose literature, on the other hand, has not kept pace; we lacked a prose with the stamp of art. I have filled this gap, and my works will retain this significance for our literature." In this I believe he is right: his prose is art, not without shadows, but as a whole it is the clearest, most flexible, most extensive and abundant expression of thought, as well as of emotion and passion, known in our literature. It has often reminded me of Plato, the author with whose prose I would most closely compare Kierkegaard's, and who evidently also provided him with a model which he freely imitated.

46.

In S.K.'s writings there are several places where he refers to Grundtvig and Grundtvigianism, virtually always with a comic slant. He frequently expressed himself in the same vein in conversation. The sharp contrast between his conception of the religious and that of Grundtvig arose constantly; and in that contrast the childish spontaneity of Grundtvigianism was placed in a comical light. Only once did S.K. speak to me with interest and appreciation about an episode in Grundtvig's life, and that was the time Gr. came forth as an opponent of Clausen. But what appealed to K. in G.'s behavior at that time was obviously not what was specifically Grundtvigian, least of all the "matchless discovery," which always seemed to K. to be a matchless foolishness—moreover, it was not even an original foolishness. Rather, what appealed to K. about G. was the contrast with rationalism, the inner experience of religious *life*. It was evidently from this point of view that S.K.'s father—whose religious persuasion was quite close to old-fashioned pietism—sympathized with Grundtvig and Lindberg, and S.K.'s sympathy doubtless had the same motivations and the same limitations as his father's.

47.

When I think of Grundtvig, I am reminded of a little anecdote about S.K. The patroness of Grundtvigianism, the dowager queen Caroline Amalie, also set great store by S.K., at least before his attack on Mynster. S.K. was evidently not insensitive to the queen's favor. One day, when I was walking with him on the Lover's Path, he suddenly exclaimed: "Oh! Damn it! Now I can't escape!" I stared at him in amazement—he, a man who otherwise never used words that resembled an oath. I looked up the path, and there, at a considerable distance, I espied a red-liveried servant preceded by two ladies. One of these was the dowager queen, who, when we met her, very graciously stopped S.K. and spoke with him. When he saw her, we were so far away from her that we could easily have turned back without having been noticed. I got the impression that his outburst was not really sincerely meant; his "Oh! Damn it!" was so unlike him and came out rather forced, as if strong language were being used to hide a sense of satisfaction with what was happening. S.K.'s old traditional veneration for royal authority was not unimportant in his relationship to the dowager queen.

48.

In the spring of 1852 I had a conversation with S.K. about Bishop Mynster which I often had occasion to remember afterward, when K. set himself in opposition to him. I went walking one afternoon on the ramparts, on the path up on the parapet, and there I walked past Bishop Mynster. A moment later I met S.K., who was walking below, along the ramparts, and called to me. He had seen Mynster walking ahead of him, and therefore our conversation turned to him. K. spoke first of his impressive and venerable appearance, then of his

intelligent and elegant demeanor and how he, as a man of the world, was superior to most of the young men who had thought for so long that with their
philosophical apparatus they could treat Mynster as an insignificant figure but
who, as soon as they made personal contact with him, were overwhelmed by
him, and then subordinated themselves to him. He mentioned Martensen in
particular as an example of one who, because of his clumsiness and lack of
elegance, had permitted Mynster a great degree of superiority in their personal
relationship. But he stressed very emphatically that Mynster's strong point consisted precisely in his worldly wisdom, and that it was this that determined his
conduct. K. spoke ironically with respect to his own relationship to Mynster.
He told me with a smile that he had once requested permission from Mynster
to seek guidance from his honored Excellency when there were problems he
himself was unable to elucidate—and that Mynster had kindly consented!
Merely the smile that accompanied his words showed me clearly in what little
esteem he actually held Mynster at that time, and the whole manner in which
he characterized Mynster as a worldly person was fully in accord with his later
statements. There had been a time when he had respected Mynster greatly, an
attitude he had adopted largely because of his veneration for his father, who had
set great store by Mynster. I have noticed that this reverential consideration for
his father's judgment determined K.'s views in a number of cases. Thus I remember that he once referred very favorably to a man who by no means deserved respect or could have inspired S.K.'s interest in his own right. S.K.'s
father, however, had cherished great affection for and gratitude to this man,
who had once given good advice that had prevented disturbance of his financial
affairs during the period of fiscal confusion that followed after the threat of war
with England.

49.

When S.K. began his polemics against the establishment, and perhaps even
somewhat earlier, he stopped participating in the church services at which he
had previously been a very constant participant. The late Dr. Frederik Beck
once told me that during that period S.K. came to Athenæum on Sunday mornings at church time; Beck, with his peculiar delight in making snide remarks,
interpreted this as follows: that S.K. wanted to make people notice that he did
not go to church. Once, many years earlier, S.K. had asked me if I went to
church. I answered no, and said that I did not partly because I felt myself a
stranger there and partly because there was so much disturbance at services in
the churches in Copenhagen that I was totally unable to maintain a devout
mood, but was instead annoyed. He replied that it was a *duty* not to let oneself
be disturbed by whatever went on around one; one *ought* to be edified when
one was in church.

50.

The last time I spoke with S.K. was in the summer of 1855 after an unusually
long period during which I had not seen him. It was an evening when I was

walking from Højbroplads up toward Vimmelskaftet. K. approached me and
started a conversation. After touching for a moment on my brief participation
in political life (in the winter of 1854–55 I had been a member of Parliament),
we soon moved on to his polemics against the clerical establishment. I thanked
him warmly for his conduct and told him how I had found many people to be
in profound sympathy with him. With the greatest of clarity and calmness, he
spoke of the situation he had provoked, and it surprised me that during this
ferocious battle, which disrupted his life so thoroughly and made such demands
on his last energies, he was able to retain not only his usual equanimity of mind
and cheerfulness but even his sense of humor. When we got close to his house—
he lived then in Klædeboderne—he said in a joking tone: "Now I'll go home
and go to bed, and then I'll say the same thing to the world that the councillor
did." I asked what the councillor had said. He told me that there had once lived
an eccentric on this same street, who bore the title of councillor, and every
evening he had carried on the following conversation with the watchman.
When the watchman had called ten o'clock, the councillor opened his window
and asked: "Watchman! What time is it?" "It is ten o'clock, Councillor."
"Good! I think I'll go to bed. If anyone should ask for me, Watchman, you can
tell them to lick my arse!" He told this story with his old humor, and I said good
night to him without realizing that on that evening I had spoken to him for the
last time.

(Written down during the period from December 27, 1871, to January 10,
1872) [Hans Brøchner]

Hans Brøchner's and Christian K. F. Molbech's
Correspondence on Søren Kierkegaard[2]

[H. Brøchner to C.K.F. Molbech, January 6, 1855]
   [Bang] has recently been much preoccupied with Søren Kierkegaard's article
on Mynster, which he was naturally unable to understand. In the final analysis
this is also the case for the majority of the public, who see the article only as an
attack on a person and not as a defense of a cause, and in Mynster they see only
a dead man, not a man with cultural significance. Kierkegaard's most recent
reply seems to have ended the discussion: Martensen and I. Levin ("the serious
man from Nørrebro") are probably still smarting over the blows they have
received.

[H. Brøchner to C.K.F. Molbech, May 29, 1855]
   Apropos of witnesses to the truth, now Søren is bringing out the big guns and
has opened up his batteries in an article in *Fædrelandet* and in a sort of journal,
The Moment. But our witnesses to the truth are like those in Sebastopol: as long
as they are not starved out, they don't care at all about anything else; they are

quiet and continue their studies of card games and parish tax rates—the Old and New Testaments of our clergy.

[*C.K.F. Molbech to H. Brøchner, November 8, 1855*]

How are things going with S. Kierkegaard? I see from the papers that now the children and babes are also beginning to write polemics. A young pup named Holten, who two years ago took his Cand. theol. degree with honors and is a curate at his father's church, has let his pen run. I know the fellow from Hammerich's school, and I owe him thanks because his piece gave me a hearty laugh, which I am otherwise rarely granted.

[*H. Brøchner to C.K.F. Molbech, December 2, 1855*]

In addition to everything else, I have lately also written—rather against my will but at the special request of Giødwad—an article "On Søren Kierkegaard as a Religious Author," which appeared in yesterday's issue of *Fædrelandet*. Earlier Giødwad had requested a number of times that I write a comprehensive review of K.'s writings, but I have always shunned the task, both because I value the books and the author so highly and because I felt I could not measure up to the demands that I myself would bring to such a task. This time I let myself be persuaded, essentially because I was annoyed at the misunderstandings the other newspapers had perpetuated in discussing K.'s work. I certainly realized that it would be impossible—working within the constraints of brevity imposed by a newspaper—to write in a popular style, and I do not in fact think that what I wrote will be of use to anyone other than those who know a bit about the books I discuss or who are willing to think a bit about what they read.

You can well imagine that Søren Kierkegaard's death has been an event that has aroused people in a fashion he would not have liked very much. His death has made a painful but not a depressing impression on me. He has meant a great deal to me, both through his works and through the personal relationship I had with him. There is no one whose personality has had such an awakening and encouraging effect on me, and the friendly good will that he always demonstrated toward me often gave me courage when I was about to lose it. It is with joy that I remember him and the long series of years—almost twenty years—during which I knew him: how the gentle and loving side of his personality more and more gained the upper hand over the strongly ironic and polemical element that was in him by nature; and how his thought constantly became richer, more certain, and clearer, so that often a word from him could have a calming and reconciling effect and could clear up a confusion that one could not manage on one's own. I will certainly come to miss him, but when I think of how completely he fulfilled that which was his life's task, how rich and full that life was, in all its brevity, and how much of him remains, I cannot think of his death with any depressing feelings. On the contrary, it seems to me to have been beautiful and fortunate. Through my cousin I have received a fine little portrait of him, a pencil drawing made when he was in his twenty-fifth year.

Despite the fact that he had changed a good deal since that time, one still gets a very vivid picture of him, and it captures him remarkably.

[*C.K.F. Molbech to H. Brøchner, February 7, 1856*]

Now listen, before this letter is finished, I have something to ask of you. I have probably already told you that for a couple of years a translation [into German] of *Either/Or* has been completed in manuscript form but is still lying about for want of a publisher. The translation was done by an intelligent elderly woman, a sister of Prof. Panum—I still don't know how she did it. Because of this [presumably, that the translator is Prof. Panum's sister] it has been difficult for me to avoid promising, for one thing, to look through the manuscript, and for another, to write a general account of Kierkegaard for a German journal in order to call attention to the book and help find a publisher for it. I would naturally never have been able to assume this task if I didn't have your *Fædrelandet* article for support. But *in addition* to this I would very much like to have some brief biographical data on K. as well as some information on his personality to the extent that this could contribute to making such a literary picture fuller and more interesting. This is what I am asking you for, therefore, when you have the time and the desire to do so. Write me a letter and tell me what you know, or whatever you think would serve as good material for me—I mean quite freely, in the form of á letter, solely for my own preparations and use. In doing so you would be doing me a great service. And if you will take the same opportunity to add some words about Kierkegaard's last polemics (which, as far as I can remember, were touched upon only briefly in your article)—that is, to allude to the *main points* against which those polemics were directed—I will be very thankful to you. *Finally*, I want to ask you to get me a copy of your *article* itself, which I have had available only [from someone else] for perusal. Now don't be annoyed at these requests, but take them lightly, as if you were writing another letter to me. I myself feel somewhat inadequate and ill at ease for having made my promise, but because of my relationship to Prof. Panum I could not very well refuse his request. Live well!

[*H. Brøchner to C.K.F. Molbech, February 17, 1856*]

I have been so busy during the past week that it was not until this evening that I had a few extra moments in which to answer your letter. And I actually find answering it a bit awkward, because what can I really report to you about Kierkegaard's life and personality that is of interest and is also something new to you? When one restricts oneself to external events, there is of course very little that can be said about his life at all: he was born May 5, 1813; he became a student at the university in 1830; he took his degree in theology in 1840; he submitted his doctoral thesis in 1841; and he died in 1855. These are of course more or less all the external facts of a biographical nature that can be provided, and they are not interesting. His inner life, his personal development, was certainly very much richer, but it has left its impression in his writings, and the finest contents of that inner life are certainly to be found in these writings. Nor am I able to describe the actual genesis of his personal development. When I became acquainted with him, he was already complete, and I was quite young. In those days I strove only to understand him as he was, and I did not dare to investigate how he had become what he was. It was only later, with continued study of his writings, that I obtained some glimpses into the history of his development, but I never sought personal confirmation of these insights from him. The overwhelming stamp he received in his childhood was religiosity of a strictly orthodox sort, and that formed the basic tenor of his entire life. Living together with his father and his elder brother [Peter Christian Kierkegaard] developed his acute sense of dialectics, which in his youth went off on adventures of its own, so to speak, and which later became the means for his religious development. After his independent studies began, he was especially influenced by German philosophy and poetry. For a long time he was much occupied with Hegelian philosophy, which indeed seems to have overwhelmed him until an ethical respect for the conditions of existence taught him to see the errors in that philosophy. In addition to Hegel, he was influenced by Lessing, Hamann, Jacobi, and Kant, and later by the study of the Greeks, including Socrates, whom he understood in a brilliant and unique fashion and who always represented the *human* ideal to him. The romantic school in Germany was important to him both as a philosopher and as a poet. He was significantly influenced by Friedrich Schlegel's *Lucinde*, which can be detected in the dissertation on irony and in the first part of *Either/Or*. But the reverberation of *Lucinde* is not an echo; it resonates with a deeper note. He followed our own poetic developments [in Denmark] with the most lively interest and with a piety that often probably led him to value them too highly. Heiberg's *Flyvende Post* and the aesthetic disputes of the period contributed to the development of his aesthetic theories.

He always kept himself at a distance from active participation in political life. On the other hand, when he was younger he concerned himself quite a bit with the theoretical aspects of politics, and in the early days he was Lehmann's opponent at the Student Union when the latter defended liberal positions. Kierkegaard was brought up with strictly conservative views, and the subsequent tendency of his entire life led him away from all efforts to change externalities.

You probably knew his personality as well as I did, even if my memory reaches back a bit farther. But you certainly remember him as a young man, when he was feisty and combative and used the keen-edged weapons of dialectic and irony to fight for poetic ideals against prosaic mediocrity. You will remember him a bit older, when with the highest of goals before him, he worked "in the service of divinity" with an energetic will, undaunted by physical weakness, compressing into a few short years the substance of a long and fruitful life. You, as well as I, will have preserved the image of this markedly artistic life, in which everything was in the service of the Idea, bound together in transparent harmony under the lordship of that Idea. You only lack a picture of him from his last period. But I know that during that earnest struggle—when "his wish was death, his longing for the grave, and his desire that this wish and this longing might soon be fulfilled" [cf. *SV* XIV 92]—he retained a loving concern for others, even for life's smallest details; that he retained gentleness, friendliness, even playfulness; that he retained an even-tempered spirit and clarity of thought; and that he retained above all peace and repose in the faith which never failed him, even during the severe suffering of his deathbed.

You will be able to complete this picture from your own memory. I will add only one incident, of which you can scarcely be aware. You know that people have talked a great deal about K.'s great fortune and found fault with him for contradicting his own principles in possessing it. The day he went to the hospital he sent Giødwad three hundred rixdollars so that he could pay a few small bills for him, and certainly also in order to pay for his stay at the hospital. These three hundred rixdollars were the last remains of his fortune, and they sufficed to cover the hospital bills but scarcely the costs of his burial. That was the great fortune. He leaves behind only his books and some modest household furnishings. He must have given away the greater portion of his fortune, because he spent significant sums on himself only while his work as an author was at its most strenuous and most in need of support and of the right atmosphere.

You ask me to indicate the particular targets against which his final battle was directed. They can really be included under a single heading: the fusion of what is Christian and what is worldly. For him, Christianity was unconditionally incompatible with the world; it was absurd to the understanding; it could be embraced only in the passion of faith; its requirement was to die away [from the world]; its hallmark was suffering; its constant companion was the possibility of offense. His polemics were therefore directed against everything that rested upon the fusion of the Christianity and worldliness in an insipid security; against every notion that Christianity was something one came by easily, through birth or by means of ceremonies; against every attempt to falsify the inconceivable by wanting to conceive it, to falsify what must be the goal in the re-formation of life by wanting to relate oneself to that goal impersonally and merely intellectually or through some poetic notion.

This was the essential content of his final polemics. You can find the rest in my article in *Fædrelandet*, which I will obtain for you tomorrow. I do not in fact have a copy myself. Be satisfied with these few remarks, then, which I have written while a little tired and sleepy. God knows if it will do any good if *Either/Or* comes out in German. If someone wants to translate a single work of Kierkegaard, it should be his *Concluding Unscientific Postscript*. Everything else would be easily misunderstood, because it is only a fragment.

Appendix A

THE KIERKEGAARD FAMILY TREE

(On following pages)

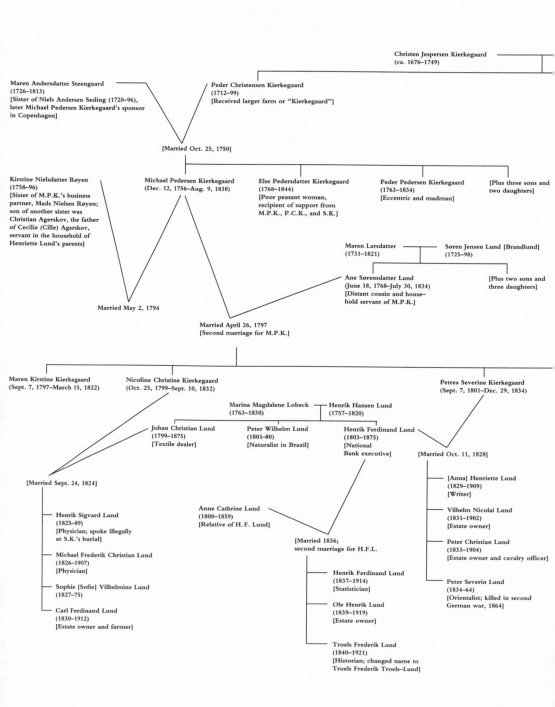

Christen Jespersen Kierkegaard
(ca. 1676–1749)

Maren Andersdatter Steengaard
(1726–1813)
[Sister of Niels Andersen Seding (1720–96),
later Michael Pedersen Kierkegaard's sponsor
in Copenhagen]

Peder Christensen Kierkegaard
(1712–99)
[Received larger farm or "Kierkegaard"]

[Married Oct. 25, 1750]

Kirstine Nielsdatter Røyen
(1758–96)
[Sister of M.P.K.'s business
partner, Mads Nielsen Røyen;
son of another sister was
Christian Agerskov, the father
of Cecilie (Cille) Agerskov,
servant in the household of
Henriette Lund's parents]

Michael Pedersen Kierkegaard
(Dec. 12, 1756–Aug. 9, 1838)

Else Pedersdatter Kierkegaard
(1768–1844)
[Poor peasant woman,
recipient of support from
M.P.K., P.C.K., and S.K.]

Peder Pedersen Kierkegaard
(1763–1834)
[Eccentric and madman]

[Plus three sons and
two daughters]

Maren Larsdatter
(1731–1821)

Søren Jensen Lund [Brandlund]
(1725–98)

Ane Sørensdatter Lund
(June 18, 1768–July 30, 1834)
[Distant cousin and house–
hold servant of M.P.K.]

[Plus two sons and
three daughters]

Married May 2, 1794

Married April 26, 1797
[Second marriage for M.P.K.]

Maren Kirstine Kierkegaard
(Sept. 7, 1797–March 15, 1822)

Nicoline Christine Kierkegaard
(Oct. 25, 1799–Sept. 10, 1832)

Petrea Severine Kierkegaard
(Sept. 7, 1801–Dec. 29, 1834)

Marina Magdalene Lobeck
(1763–1830)

Henrik Hansen Lund
(1757–1820)

Johan Christian Lund
(1799–1875)
[Textile dealer]

Peter Wilhelm Lund
(1801–80)
[Naturalist in Brazil]

Henrik Ferdinand Lund
(1803–1875)
[National
Bank executive]

[Married Oct. 11, 1828]

[Married Sept. 24, 1824]

[Anna] Henriette Lund
(1829–1909)
[Writer]

Henrik Sigvard Lund
(1825–89)
[Physician; spoke illegally
at S.K.'s burial]

Anne Cathrine Lund
(1800–1859)
[Relative of H. F. Lund]

Vilhelm Nicolai Lund
(1831–1902)
[Estate owner]

Michael Frederik Christian Lund
(1826–1907)
[Physician]

[Married 1836;
second marriage for H.F.L.]

Peter Christian Lund
(1833–1904)
[Estate owner and cavalry officer]

Sophie [Sofie] Vilhelmine Lund
(1827–75)

Henrik Ferdinand Lund
(1837–1914)
[Statistician]

Carl Ferdinand Lund
(1830–1912)
[Estate owner and farmer]

Ole Henrik Lund
(1839–1919)
[Estate owner]

Peter Severin Lund
(1834–64)
[Orientalist; killed in second
German war, 1864]

Troels Frederik Lund
(1840–1921)
[Historian; changed name to
Troels Frederik Troels–Lund]

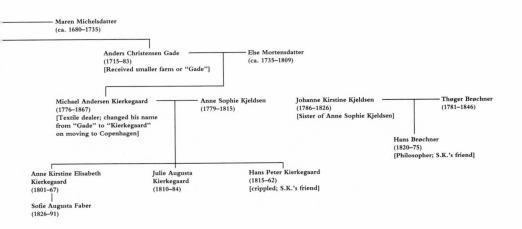

Maren Michelsdatter
(ca. 1680–1735)

Anders Christensen Gade
(1715–83)
[Received smaller farm or "Gade"]

Else Mortensdatter
(ca. 1735–1809)

Michael Andersen Kierkegaard
(1776–1867)
[Textile dealer; changed his name
from "Gade" to "Kierkegaard"
on moving to Copenhagen]

Anne Sophie Kjeldsen
(1779–1815)

Johanne Kirstine Kjeldsen
(1786–1826)
[Sister of Anne Sophie Kjeldsen]

Thøger Brøchner
(1781–1846)

Hans Brøchner
(1820–75)
[Philosopher; S.K.'s friend]

Anne Kirstine Elisabeth
Kierkegaard
(1801–67)

Julie Augusta
Kierkegaard
(1810–84)

Hans Peter Kierkegaard
(1815–62)
[crippled; S.K.'s friend]

Sofie Augusta Faber
(1826–91)

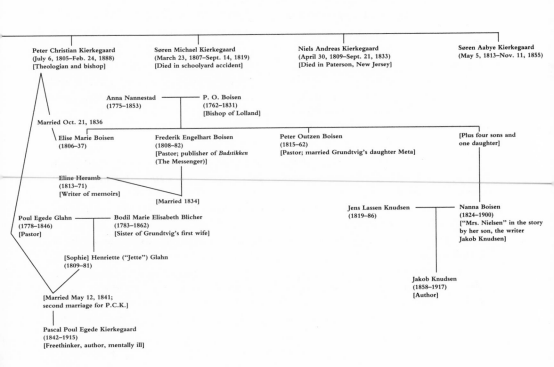

Peter Christian Kierkegaard
(July 6, 1805–Feb. 24, 1888)
[Theologian and bishop]

Søren Michael Kierkegaard
(March 23, 1807–Sept. 14, 1819)
[Died in schoolyard accident]

Niels Andreas Kierkegaard
(April 30, 1809–Sept. 21, 1833)
[Died in Paterson, New Jersey]

Søren Aabye Kierkegaard
(May 5, 1813–Nov. 11, 1855)

Anna Nannestad
(1775–1853)

P. O. Boisen
(1762–1831)
[Bishop of Lolland]

Married Oct. 21, 1836

Elise Marie Boisen
(1806–37)

Frederik Engelhart Boisen
(1808–82)
[Pastor; publisher of *Budstikken*
(The Messenger)]

Peter Outzen Boisen
(1815–62)
[Pastor; married Grundtvig's daughter Meta]

[Plus four sons and
one daughter]

Eline Heramb
(1813–71)
[Writer of memoirs]

[Married 1834]

Poul Egede Glahn
(1778–1846)
[Pastor]

Bodil Marie Elisabeth Blicher
(1783–1862)
[Sister of Grundtvig's first wife]

Jens Lassen Knudsen
(1819–86)

Nanna Boisen
(1824–1900)
["Mrs. Nielsen" in the story
by her son, the writer
Jakob Knudsen]

[Sophie] Henriette ("Jette") Glahn
(1809–81)

Jakob Knudsen
(1858–1917)
[Author]

[Married May 12, 1841;
second marriage for P.C.K.]

Pascal Poul Egede Kierkegaard
(1842–1915)
[Freethinker, author, mentally ill]

Appendix B

PETER CHRISTIAN KIERKEGAARD ON
SØREN KIERKEGAARD

Peter Christian Kierkegaard's October 30, 1849, Talk
at the Roskilde Ecclesiastical Convention[1]

[E]xcuse that I now must offer you something which first came to mind yesterday evening and which I prepared in haste.

My text is II Corinthians 5.13 (εἴτε γὰρ ἐξέστημεν, θεῷ· εἴτε σωφρονοῦμεν, ὑμῖν): "For if we are beside ourselves, it is for God; if we are in our right mind, it is for you. . . ."

[T]he *application* which I now intend to make of our passage concerns two peculiarities of our recent literature, *Magister S. Kierkegaard's* well-known works and *Prof. Martensen's Dogmatics* and his work in dogmatics generally. . . .

[The passage in II Corinthians, in which St. Paul juxtaposes ecstasy and sober-mindedness is] a *generally applicable sketch* of the peculiar sort of ebb and flow that characterizes *the way in which human beings make* Christianity *a part of themselves*—of the Christian life in the entire congregation and in the individual *believer*—in accordance with its two poles, its movement inward and upward [or] outward and downward, toward increasing inwardness and concentration or toward dissemination and broad acceptance. . . . [W]ith *us* [emphasis added], this same genuine duality [between ecstasy and sober-mindedness] can easily seem to be replaced by a genuine contradiction between the two sides, so that we acknowledge only the one condition or mode of embracing [Christianity], and on that basis fail to appreciate the other and [instead] combat it [by viewing] ecstasy as something fantastical from its first awakening, sobriety as worldliness and halfheartedness. . . . And unless I am entirely wrong in what I see, we must view *both the above-mentioned authors*, with their unique characteristics and their mutual opposition, in the context of this *duality* that has just been emphasized.

What *Søren Kierkegaard* investigates with the warmth of a lover and speaks about with the enthusiasm of a poet certainly does not include the work of redemption—and only in part does it include apostolic majesty. On the contrary, he really concerns himself with *only one* part of the order of salvation, with faith, and *exclusively* with faith as *subjective*. . . .

[H]e plunges every day into the sea of light and fullness he has found there, always afraid that, like the son of Thetis, he will retain a tiny dry spot on his heel, where he could be wounded by the arrow of speculation and the poison of proofs, so that he would die the death of spiritlessness. Faith has within itself the *energy of choice and decision*, and is opposed by the world's power and the world's wit, its swords and staves, the strongholds of logism and the snares of method (II Corinthians 104–5 and Ephesians 6.11; cf. 4.14). He has sensed this, and therefore he not only refuses to tolerate any belief because one understands, but absolutely *no "belief because"*—indeed, he consequently has not even any use for an understanding because one believes. . . . Faith is tried in *battle* and is strengthened in *danger*. He has sensed this. And therefore he is *glad* to cool off now and again (especially when the blood rises to his head and the thoughts within crisscross one another with dizzying speed) by a leap from the mainmast of speculation in order to *swim* in "seventy thousand fathoms of water." And, moved by sheer sympathy for our well-being, he gladly makes us take the plunge at the same time. Vainly and with all delicacy, we try to insinuate that just as we are still not yet able to serve only one master, so would we prefer to mediate a little, to unite the refreshing qualities of swimming with the security of a safety belt. He splits hairs as well as we do, if not better, and he flings us out into the water as the gymnastics instructor does the naval cadet, salving his conscience with the thought that when we were on land or wearing our safety belts we were, after all, shamming—and if we are to be saved we must let everything depend upon [the possibility of] drowning. The believer is "someone in love," he says. His cause is the defense of this proposition. But then, what must he not think, when we wish to win people for the faith *by means of proofs*? Moreover, marriages of convenience do not have the best reputation. And, of course, *all these* are pure gems in the crown of *paradox*. And as you know, he says this quite rightly as a man who well knows how to appraise these jewels and the rainbow garland of paradoxes that they produce when expertly placed in proximity to one another. And he values all this not merely as an intellectual game but (in order to push the paradox to its uttermost point) as the immanent categories of the faith of *the simple person*, as moments of the struggle to which everyone is called—even if only a very few choose to engage in it—the struggle for life and peace, the struggle for a garland that will never wither.

Next, with respect to *Prof. Martensen*, it is of course only *with many reservations*, and only in a certain sense, that it would occur to me to portray him as an author whose theological efforts in the service of the congregation present us with sobriety and cautiousness. . . . *[R]ight from the beginning*, he (and here I am of course speaking of the docent and not of the person) had the habit of cutting off the threads of his own line of thinking at certain points and of *breaking with his own assumptions*, in order not to get involved in a conflict with various parts of the Christian faith. . . . [E]very time he stood at the crossroads and embraced an article of faith while his objective logic made ugly grimaces, he concealed his

inconstancy from himself and from others, either by means of clever circumlocutions or with the ambiguity that is the hallmark of Hegelian dialectic. . . . But
despite the fact that it is far from my view that Prof. Martensen ever put himself
forward as a consistent and decisive proponent of a speculation that is independent of faith, nonetheless a *large portion* of his *earlier* works was strongly influenced by that sort of speculation. Indeed, it places so much emphasis on such
speculation that in my view it *absolutely cannot* be included when one speaks of
an exposition of Christianity that is to be in the service of the congregation.
And thus it is only the form that his system has begun to assume in *recent* years
. . . that I have in mind when I here single him out as the most recent Danish
theologian who appears to be joining the countless legion of those who, for
eighteen hundred years now, have worked for growth of the congregation
indeed in the knowledge of our Lord Jesus Christ (cf. II Peter 3.18). . . . Naturally, the Apostle's ecstasies and his calm expositions differ from those of all
subsequent believers, in particular because neither the careful progress of
thought nor bold flights of enthusiasm ever lead him *away* from the living way
of truth (cf. John 10.9 and 14.6 with II Corinthians 2.14–16). But with all those
who come after it is *clear*, and in general quite easy to demonstrate, that there are
deviations to one side or the other.

[I] wish to *express my outspoken wonder* about a phenomenon with respect to
the *effect* that seems to be emanating from *Søren Kierkegaard's* efforts. And then
I will *confide in you* here, *sub rosa*, concerning the manner in which I, for my part,
enjoy and employ the two famous authors—especially the one of whom I first
spoke [i.e., Søren Kierkegaard]. . . .

Thus *Prof. Martensen*, like every other theologian, ought to serve me as a *goad*
. . . in the search for new *acquisitions* in the area of *knowledge* in the service of
life. . . . But then—despite the fact that I continually tell myself that all this
grows only in the soil of faith and draws its nourishment only from the dew of
the heavenly Word—I immediately begin to depend, little by little, upon this
knowledge as a well-earned possession, which I can maintain and defend. I
begin to forget that the faith I had last year or yesterday and from which my
knowledge sprang forth—that I must have that faith now, now, or else the
whole thing is a castle in the air. . . . But I have been delighted to discover in
Søren Kierkegaard's writings a means by which I can remind myself of all this
before it is too late, a *medicine* that protects against *conceptual dizziness*, before the
most powerful of cures must be employed. An hour of reading those writings
has, in fact, almost exactly the same effect upon me that a shower used to have
upon my physical constitution. For a moment it is as though the life in me were
gasping for air, and then I am breathing deeply and freely *again* in the fresh
breezes of *faith*, while the legions of the intellect retreat to their subordinate
position as the servants of life, and the head is again content to be a head instead
of the entire person. . . . Thus I have absolutely *nothing against* the *speculative
tendency*, whoever its spokesman may be, when it repeatedly induces me to

experiment in the sphere of knowledge. And this in spite of the fact that I well know that as soon as I have entered into that territory, puffed-up knowledge, the Hercules of concepts and ideas, immediately begins to take me, like all mortals, into its embrace, to lift me up off the earth, and then to smother me in the air—and that the beginning of the affair is just as seductive as the conclusion is dangerous. But I therefore have *even less against* having an *ecstatic monastery brother* [*ekstatisk Kloster-Broder*] who, when danger is at hand, does not call out to me with a clever expression on his face, saying, "Nachbar, mit Rath"— which could easily make the temptation even more tempting—but who, with all necessary ingenuity, trips me up in order that I might sink to my knees. Because *on our knees and on our faces* we are all invincible to that Hercules, just as was *Antæus* of old.

Peter Christian Kierkegaard's July 5, 1855, Talk at the Roskilde Ecclesiastical Convention[2]

REMARKS ON THE FAMOUS PSEUDONYMS OF THE DAY
AND ON THE THEOLOGY OF THEIR AUTHOR
(NOTES ON A LECTURE AT THE
ROSKILDE ECCLESIASTICAL CONVENTION, JULY 5, 1855)

"The Jews ask for signs, and the Greeks seek wisdom, but we proclaim Christ crucified, for the Jews, of course, an offense and for the Greeks foolishness. But for those who are called, Jews as well as Greeks, we proclaim Christ, the power of God, and the wisdom of God" (I Corinthians 1.22–24). Such, as we all know, is the wording of the testimony that, even in the early days of the congregation, the Apostle Paul felt called upon to speak against two forms of one-sidedness. In doing so he was of course opposing the universal tendency—either from the very beginning or at a later stage—to clutch at the shadow or the appearance of Christianity instead of embracing it in an increasingly ardent and profound manner. But he does this in such a way that he also intimates clearly that this tendency engenders within itself a double deviation, to the right and to the left. And it is clearly incumbent upon him to keep us away from both of them. We must not, like the Jews, choose appearances—appearances that one tries to produce by means of the tangible and piecemeal restructuring of the various external conditions, during which one must conceal the fact that the situation, both as a whole and in itself, remains unchanged. Nor, like the Greeks, may we become infatuated with shadows, that is, with knowledge and insight that is detached from life and from reality, so that people rest easy about all the un-Christian things that are obviously present in them, soothing themselves with the consciousness that the ideal, after all, is only something to be striven for and not something to attain. . . . [T]he Scriptures are unlike ordinary human polemics that, when indicting one sort of one-sidedness, fall prey to another. On the contrary, quite often when the Scriptures voice a strong and emphatic rejection of one error, in a subtler but no less powerful manner, they also preclude and prevent precisely the opposite error as well. . . . [F]rom these [Scriptures], the way lies clear to the judgment and correction of the whole of the pseudonymous theology that has been so influential in our fatherland in recent years. . . .

[B]oth "wisdom" and "signs" will always have their place and justification in Christianity. . . . "[S]igns" and "wisdom" have their great Christian significance, both *as forerunners of the acceptance* of Christian faith and *as experiences* that persist *during the development* of the life of faith in the individual and in the congregation. . . .

[A]s long as the Apostle and all honorable servants of the Word proclaim Christ as God's power and God's wisdom, then the Lord is of course being proclaimed in a manner that is entirely unmistakable and unexceptionable, both as the Sign of signs, to which all other [signs] are related almost as rays to the sun . . . and as the eternally inexhaustible Fount of all wisdom in which are concealed all the treasures of wisdom and knowledge for which any Greek-spirited person has ever asked (cf. Colossians 2.3 and Isaiah 11.2–3). . . . [H]uman power and human wisdom must be counterposed to divine power and wisdom not in an entirely unconditional and straightforward manner but only within the definite boundaries that are implied in the Scriptures—particularly when wisdom, instead of leading to the Lord, wishes to be sufficient unto itself and will not acknowledge itself as foolishness in comparison with him. . . . [A]s long as the Lord's name is proclaimed in the congregation, the genuine and apostolic proclamation of Christ as God's power and God's wisdom includes within itself the uninterrupted and continuing fulfillment of that which was correct and valid in the Jews' desire for signs and the Greeks' search for wisdom.

[B]oth "signs" and "wisdom" have their Christian justification as that which precedes—which *prepares* and *initiates*—the faithful acceptance of Christianity. . . . [I]t is also quite clear in the scriptural passage dealt with here that although he combats the overvaluation of signs and wisdom, the Apostle by no means rejects them or the human heart's searching for them, but he wants them to be sought as "Stages on Life's Way." . . .

[W]hen he confessed publicly, "Thou art Christ, the Son of the living God," Peter certainly had saving faith—at least the Lord says so. And this despite the fact that at that point this faith was so far from being able to leap into the seventy thousand fathoms, that, immediately thereafter, he refused to entertain any notion that the Savior would have to suffer. And even much later—although his growth as a Christian had never come to a halt—he at first fled and then sought, with oaths, to evade even the then-remote possibility of plunging (to keep with our metaphor) with him [Christ] into the terrifying deep. . . . [I]t is only in unconditional submission and in the movement of a spirituality that has entered into the power of the Spirit, that [this faith] makes its appearance. Precisely because a human being is subject to temporal development, it [faith] may have been present for a long time; it could have been present as such and nonetheless have vacillated; it could have apparently disappeared and only come to its genuine and full presence within us after all manner of struggle. It is Abraham, the Father of the faithful, upon whom the pseudonymous literature focused an especially penetrating scrutiny quite early. Yet what Christian would not want to see a clear demonstration and an energetic exposition of that which the Holy Scriptures so often imply and presuppose, namely that he had really become the great man of faith long before the great day of faith dawned on the earth—that he had been the great, exemplary Christian long before the name of Christ was heard here on earth? . . . But in the brilliant treatment of this matter in one of the first works of this literature, it seems to me that I have always sensed the lack of two things which concern us—and it seems to me that I cannot acquiesce in their absence. . . . [What is needed is a] strong statement and a clear assertion of the fact that Abraham's life of faith was longer than three days. Just as when we speak of other plants, when we are speaking of the plant called faith, the fruit and the flower remain its essence in the clearest and fullest sense, but one cannot deem them the entire plant and abstract entirely from the root and the stalk. Or am I really wrong in believing that Abraham already had faith, that he had already made the leap and was in many fathoms of water when, in his seventy-fifth year, he left his family and his native land in order (expressing it in a worldly manner) to go on an adventure in an unknown land? [Am I wrong in believing] that his faith was subsequently tested in many ways, and that it had indeed occasionally failed him (when he disowned his wife, and when he yielded to her and took Hagar), and that through all this his faith matured to pass the test of Isaac's sacrifice? And if this is correct, then how can what is consciously or unconsciously present in a large part of that [pseudonymous] literature be defended in its desire to frighten and punish all those who, perhaps in all honesty, are on their way from Haran in Mesopotamia and are drawing nigh to the land of Canaan? Who perhaps stumble [?] every day but who also make daily progress in their pilgrimage? Doesn't the manner in which the Savior accepts the beginnings of faith, whose frailty he can see a great deal more clearly than can any pseudonym, form a striking contrast? . . . The literature that I here am examining wishes to argue for the Christianity of the New Testament, and this phrase is supposed to signify the Christianity that is taught in the Holy Scriptures of the New Testament. But how can it be correct, this wish to acknowledge as faith and as the life of faith only those cases in which the highest has been attained (or in which movement in that direction is so striking and tangible that the pseudonyms find themselves obligated to accept it as valid)? The greater part of the scriptures of the New Testament of course consists of letters and of church history. In almost every case—in part because of whom they are addressing and, at many points, in part because of the context—the above-mentioned letters depict and speak to their readers as believers. And of course it is almost impossible to read two chapters in a row without becoming convinced that these first readers not only were far from the goal and from perfection, but were far from the sort of situation that the pseudonymous literature would even acknowledge as movement in that direction.

[I]f it is being argued that the Christianity of the New Testament is really only that Christianity which can be derived from a number of tendentiously emphasized utterances of the Lord himself, as we encounter them in the four Gospels, then real Christianity has never actually existed, excepting in the Lord's demand for it, a demand that even the apostolic congregations did not fulfill or move toward fulfilling. Thus undoubtedly the first thing that ought to be done is to direct specific attention to this arbitrary division within what are customarily accounted to be the contents of the New Testament. . . .

If I remember correctly, an Anti-Climacus says that Christianity is not what the sniveling pastors would like to make it into, or at any rate say that it is. It is in fact the Absolute, the infinite requirement. I am too lowly to oppose this Anti-Climacus, and yet, praise God, I am not so utterly devoid of Christian experience and of all understanding of things Christian that I will weep over the obstacle that this word [the Absolute] is of course destined to constitute for all the speakers and listeners who do not know—or do not want to know—of any difference between sentimental preaching and the proclamation of the Gospel. But, on the other hand, I would like to ask a little question about the extent to which there is any difference at all between Judaism and Christianity, and if there is, wherein it consists. That Judaism is in fact also the absolute requirement is something which is completely beyond dispute—at any rate as long as there is no way to deny or to conceal the fact that when the Lord himself wishes to assert the absolute requirement, he borrows the words from the Old Testament, and says, Thou shalt love the Lord thy God with all thy heart, all thy soul, and all thy might. Concerning this absolute requirement, Christianity (if Christ himself has proclaimed it correctly) is therefore entirely in agreement with Judaism (if one will grant that the true Judaism is that propounded by Moses from the beginning of the people and propounded without the least deviation, one and the same, by the scribes just prior to the destruction of the people). Thus if Christianity is to differ somewhat from Judaism, there is no alternative except for us, with Paul and Luther, to posit the difference in the fact that in Christianity the Absolute has made itself relative. . . . But if this is the case, then it can[not] be viewed as anything other than a very serious error to speak repeatedly of faith, not only in all its strength and at the highest tension of the struggle, but from that plane to denounce with very pointed antitheses and to cast frequent mocking glances at the faith that is starting out and is making preparations; the faith that is still childlike and untested; the faith that scarcely suspects the least bit of the terrors to which its decisions will lead; the faith that has doubts and becomes weak during the struggle; the faith that longs after refreshment and support; and that in all Christian experience receives it again and again from the Lord, in whom we dare believe; from him who took Peter by the hand when they walked on the roaring waves; from him who many times called out to Paul that no one will harm you—in brief, from him who is unspeakably merciful, and with whom, therefore, we will scarcely become acquainted if we accept at face value everything that the pseudonyms would like to demand of us on his behalf.

[T]oday [I] wish to venture to put forth some of the misgivings that I, for my part, have long felt in relation to the theology—or, as it probably prefers to be called, the nontheology—which an academy of pseudonyms has in recent years developed as a part of the literature of our fatherland. . . . [B]oth according to what it claims to be and in conformity with what has been confirmed by the experiences of all ages, Christianity [is] essentially life—that is, a renewal of genuine human life, both in individuals and in the race. This is the case precisely to the degree and to the extent that each person honestly embraces it, but always and everywhere within the customary human category of development and of unfolding, from the earliest beginnings to a condition of complete maturity. . . . The entire pseudonymous academy seems to wish to conclude with a wholly new and profound message about "the Christianity of the New Testament"—which must of course be that for which Johannes Climacus in his time searched with his Diogenes lamp, when he wanted to know definitively how a thirty-odd-year-old man of private means, etc., could acquire a share in a good called "an eternal salvation." I must, however, permit myself to remark that a person would have a difficult time finding mention of "an eternal salvation" in the New Testament one single time. But on the other hand one will find that the Scriptures speak all the more often about "an eternal life"—and this not merely as the Christians' hope for the future (as in the officially authorized catechisms, where it is indeed situated "after death"), but as the experience and possession of Christians, here in a happy beginning, hereafter in all its fullness. . . . I shall . . . ask each of you only to consider carefully how the New Testament scriptures speak constantly and repeatedly of conception and birth, childhood and youth, growth and maturity, mother's milk and solid food, all in a Christian sense, all as experiences and conditions through which the seeds of eternal life appear and develop in believers. . . . But in its detailed and many-faceted treatment of this subject, [this] body of literature (whose particular virtue consists in emphasizing the existential) does not touch at all upon this principal truth, the Christian authority and vital significance of which I have just pointed out. Or at any rate it does not do so very often or with express emphasis upon the fact that the existential, of which we are speaking, absolutely cannot live without the basic form of human life. And the basic form of human life is development and unfolding, from the beginnings of conception to the maturity of man. In this case, there can be no mistaking that only one of two things is possible: that is, either the pseudonymous thinkers, who have been carrying on a public conversation about the existential for some time now, have not taken any notice of this truth, or, to use their own expression, they have intentionally glossed over and deemphasized it. . . .

As the mystical-ascetic literature that I am discussing has frequently emphasized, all those who wish to have a living experience of faith are invited to a swimming exercise without safety belts over seventy thousand fathoms of water, and are therefore advised to leap head-first. . . . [I] myself, praise God, have experienced a bit of the beneficial effects of a shower, in the spiritual sense perhaps even more than in the physical. Beyond this, however, I will not allow myself to be deprived, either by cunning or by force, of my joy that—despite the infinite requirement, and as consequence of his patience with our weaknesses—the Lord also accepts us when the first beginnings of faith begin to stir within us; that he also recognizes this beginning faith and rewards it by allowing it to sense his blessing. This is something that I myself have experienced and that can be seen quite clearly in the scriptural depiction of Christianity. . . . [W]hen we really come to him as those who honestly surrender ourselves and all else— when, as unconditionally as we can, we surrender ourselves to him in faith— then, first of all, in his [unreadable word omitted] acceptance, he faithfully and gently keeps to himself the knowledge that, despite the fact that we ourselves do not know it, we are as yet entirely incapable of surrendering ourselves to him unconditionally. And, further, he does not mock us or chase us away from him because when we are tested for the first time, we know no better than that our lives are in danger and that the seventy thousand fathoms are already closing over us—while in reality . . . we have perhaps just barely begun to splash a bit in the shallow water with its sandy bottom, right near the land, and nonetheless are almost screaming in terror. Or am I perhaps wrong in this assertion? Is what I am arguing for perhaps only an experience of a Christianity which I myself have dreamed up, which is of course wanting when "the Christianity of the New Testament" speaks up and immediately cries out: "Stop thief!" . . . ? In a large number of express statements, Scripture itself . . . acknowledges a faith that exists even within the limits of frailty, and thus entitles us to speak of such a faith. . . . [F]or example, in the words of the Apostle John—who certainly can hardly be supposed to smack of any Copenhagen laxity in [stating] the requirement or of any State-Churchly falsification of the task—the disciples believed in the Lord as soon as, and because, he gave them a sign at Cana in Galilee. . . . But I . . . will merely point out what is found over and over again in the Scriptures with respect to the faith which is beginning and germinating, weak and untested—indeed, which is not yet ready for the truly serious test—but which nonetheless, in the "New Testament" account, is spoken of, praised, encouraged, and blessed as being included within the definition of the faith which has received great promises for time and for eternity. And therefore no reasonable person would blame me for preferring this, the original "Christianity of the New Testament," over the pseudonyms' edition of same, in which from the very beginning, as far as I have been able to see, there was no room for a friendly word about that faith with which, as the Scriptures demonstrate, the Apostles were obliged to begin, and with which, as all experience has taught us, every subsequent believer must also begin. . . . Here, however, if anywhere, it must be strikingly obvious to everyone who knows the arguments advanced by the pseudonyms—and their later results, pronounced and proclaimed, so far as I can see, in consistency with those arguments—what a difference there is between [the pseudonyms'] ideas and the Lord's ideas concerning the faith that saves us. . . . [I]n a solitary, quiet hour with a circle of friends at Cæsarea Philippi, Peter quite boldly and outspokenly declared himself a believer (Matthew 16.16). But, according to the pseudonyms' point of view, because of his fear of the cross, which erupted immediately thereafter, he must undoubtedly be counted among the good people who feel something in "quiet hours," who declaim something in "ceremonial hours," who thus play at being believers among all those who themselves are "part of the affair," and who therefore do not betray the secret that "on Monday"—much less on market day, or on fast days, or on Good Friday—it is of no further importance. . . . [I]f this suspiciousness [on the part of the pseudonyms] is to be unconditionally recognized as well founded— and not merely as a suggestion for self-examination, but (as has been the case explicitly in recent years) as a judgment passed upon all those who say they have faith, but whose faith has not yet been grounded in the sorts of trials that are visible or tangible to the pseudonyms—then one ought to argue not that Christianity has perished but that Christianity has never existed. . . . I have no wish to pass judgment upon the particular talents of anyone in other respects, and I especially have no desire to deny that in our times there is a great need to bear witness quite earnestly and terribly against the self-deceptive Christianity fostered by the muddle within the State Church, a Christianity that is Christian in name only, and that is based upon numbers. And I therefore permit myself to think that this sort of testimony (about how the Lord condescends to take account of our weakness and of the conditions of our temporal development) will occasionally be more likely to win him an honest friend among human beings than will the most terrifying demands of the infinite requirement, of which not the least bit can be remitted. . . . I have indeed been poorly understood if it is thought that I, like so many others, am really complaining over an exaggeration or exaggerations on the part of the pseudonyms. Of course, these undoubtedly do occur in the pseudonyms. But, for one thing, it actually requires a great deal more than most people think before one can presume to indict, as exaggerated, enthusiastic language about the glory of the Lord or the glory of faith. Therefore in this respect I prefer to stay with what I said a number of years ago and to limit myself to saying that the matter itself—and the depth of the riches of God's grace and power and wisdom and love—is both the cause and the justification of the ecstatic speech of everyone who truly beholds it and who is not, out of concern for others, occasioned to curtail and moderate, as it were, his remarks about it. For another thing, there is a laxity that reigns in our times and that once in a while opens its eyes halfway, so to speak, when a new clamor intrudes above the ordinary street-symphony of omnibus signals. This laxity is a great extenuation that explains why everyone who really has something to say either prefaces it with trumpets or accompanies it with cannon fire. And in all modesty, this is how I view some of the pseudonyms' paradoxes: now and then they shock polite society by swearing like sailors. Thus it is not exaggerations about which I wish to complain. Rather, it is the disorder, so that most of what is said about faith in these pieces can be said, in New Testament fashion, about love. And, it is the incompleteness, so that the path to strong and powerful faith—a path that is itself faith—is in part concealed and placed in the shadows, and is in part denied. . . .

[I]n my view, throughout the entire pseudonymous literature [there is] an inclination (as mentioned above) which not merely wishes to limit recognition exclusively to the faith that has completed its development and which is actually, so to speak, disappearing into love—but also, in the faith which finally is acknowledged, this tendency demands or wants to see demonstrated the presence of a strength and elasticity that, to judge from appearances, exceeds what we encounter in the scriptural conception of faith. . . . I know of no faith among mere humans—there is of course no question here of speaking of the faith of the Lord in the extreme darkness of his self-sacrifice—which has not been supported in the manner which I have demonstrated above in the case of Abraham. And, to refer yet again to the exposition of I Corinthians 1.22ff. [I know of no human faith that has not been supported], indeed, *either* by an intimation of insight into the special characteristics of Divine Providence and by what the Greeks would call "wisdom" (but what the pseudonyms, if I am not mistaken, call dim vision, which they mock as an ill-timed jest), *or* by situations of an analogous sort, which have been triumphantly experienced, and which in Jewish terminology would certainly be called "signs" (but which, when discussed by the pseudonyms, are also surely rejected as expressions of a philistine and self-satisfied way of thinking that says: "Since I converted, praise God, everything has gone fortunately for me, grain prices have gone up, servants' wages have gone down, etc.").

Another thing the absence of which I noted earlier in Johannes de Silentio, and which I still note, is information to the effect that the journey to Moriah lasted much longer than those three days which are mentioned in Genesis and on which he [Johannes de Silentio] focuses his attention exclusively. . . . Should one therefore desist from protesting against it [the theology of the pseudonyms] because of the danger that for many individuals, who would otherwise be awakened, such a protest will be a comfort and a better slumber-pillow than any which are commercially available? Yes, I was indeed restrained by that consideration as long as I could console myself with the thought that these results—which, in my view, were the consistent consequences of the earlier pseudonymous works—were not consciously intended and would in fact not be noticed by a great many people on whom so much of the other material could exercise an awakening influence. But it seems to me that this consideration is no longer valid, because the pseudonymous academy has itself acknowledged, in a summary and clear fashion, the results of its own entire debate. . . . But, assuming that they [the pseudonyms] are not omniscient, how then can they manage to conclude that a good portion of previous generations of the human race—or, precisely as a consequence of their [the pseudonyms' own] taunts, a good number of *us* [emphasis added]—are not in fact beginning upon the narrow path of the life of faith? And in that case [i.e., if a good number of people *are* in fact on the path of faith], of course, Christianity has not yet disappeared. Or how do they know that no one in this country has begun—as Abraham in days of yore—to abandon his dreamed-up domestic Christianity, with its parishes and its sexton's books and its statistical tables, in order to make a pilgrimage to the holy land? Or that on that pilgrimage absolutely no one—even if, because of hunger and persecutions, a person occasionally deviates in the direction of the Egyptians and the Philistines or occasionally proclaims his relation to the congregation with less intensity—has, in fact, by the grace of God advanced a bit in the experience that the Lord is our shield and our very great reward? . . . [P]erhaps after closer consideration, however, they [the pseudonyms] will not find it so entirely un-Christian if someone were to cry: "Oh, how hasty are men, and how slow is the Lord, in passing judgment." And oh, when we can still hear the Lord say, "Judge not," it is not so much a commandment to us as it is much more a pleasant echo of the amnesty decree that was issued at Golgotha, which is undoubtedly proclaimed by a great angel throughout all the heavens every day, for as long as the hour has not yet struck when the heavenly heralds will proclaim the Day of the Lord—and at that time surely no one else will be tempted to come forward to join in passing judgment. . . .

Yes, to be sure, Christianity is not what the sniveling pastors say that it is. Except that from this it of course does not follow that it [Christianity] is more likely to be what jesting or damning prophets seek to make it into. Rather, it is characterized much more by a striking likeness to him from whom it comes, and who calls himself "I become what I am." So it thus becomes what it is, namely the life of the God-Man which, by means of the Word and of faith, is continually born and continually grows in the little flock, which in the beginning he accepts as his own, and which at the end he transforms into likeness with himself. . . . And now the Absolute. Yes, if we finally must come to speak of the eternal life in dead and empty phrases, abstract philosophical forms, which every temporal philosophy coins and uses in its own way, Christianity is quite certainly the Absolute, but only insofar as it still remains entirely identical with Judaism. . . .

Therefore, if the Christianity of Anti-Climacus is not to become entirely identical with "official" Judaism—and Judaism is indeed something official; this was set forth in the books of Moses and was repeatedly emphasized fifteen hundred years later by the scribes, precisely when they wanted to combat Christianity as something new and unjustified—then surely something else must be added to the information that Christianity is the Absolute. And what could that be other than that, in Christianity, the Absolute—I wish indeed to remain for a moment longer with this philosophical language, which I now find rather distant and foreign—has made itself relative, both with respect to the content of its message and with respect to the acceptance of that message?

Notes

━━━━▶◉◀━━━━

Chapter One
"The Fork": Childhood and School

1. From Troels-Lund, *Bakkehus og Solbjerg* [Hill House and Sun Mountain], vol. 3 (Copenhagen: Gyldendal, 1922), pp. 37–38.

Troels Frederik Troels-Lund (1840–1921), an author and historian, was born Troels Frederik Lund and later changed his name to Troels Frederik Troels-Lund. Though not a blood relative, he was related to Søren Kierkegaard by marriage in that he was the son of Henrik Ferdinand Lund (1803–75) by his marriage after the death of his first wife, Kierkegaard's sister Petrea Severine (1801–34). In this connection and in connection with all subsequent references in these notes to members of the extended Kierkegaard family, see the Kierkegaard family tree in Appendix A of this book for details. **That sort of attitude**: Troels-Lund believes that Kierkegaard's childhood taught him the art of caustic polemics and made him a more intellectually combative and acute thinker. On the nickname "**the Fork**," see also Henriette Lund in chapter 9 of this book.

2. From P.F.A. Hammerich's autobiography, *Et Levnedsløb* [A Life], vol. 1 (Copenhagen: Forlagsbureauet i Kjøbenhavn, 1882), pp. 58–59.

[Peter] Frederik [Adolph] Hammerich (1809–77), a follower of Grundtvig and a friend of Peter Christian Kierkegaard, was a church historian and professor. Hammerich's father's sister, Sophie Hammerich Boesen, was the mother of Kierkegaard's lifelong friend **Emil Boesen**. The Boesens, the Hammerichs, and the Kierkegaards were all members of the Brødremenighed [Congregation of Brothers], a pietistic Herrnhuter or Moravian congregation in Copenhagen. For more information on Emil Boesen, see the note accompanying his entry in chapter 2 of this book; see also Boesen's entries in chapter 8 of this book. **His father's mood in 1848** is obviously an erroneous recollection on Hammerich's part, because Michael Pedersen Kierkegaard died in 1838; it has been suggested that this may be a reference to M. P. Kierkegaard's patriotism during the British attack on Copenhagen in 1807. It is also possible that the recollection is about M. P. Kierkegaard's younger cousin, Michael Andersen Kierkegaard (1776–1867). Like M. P. Kierkegaard, M. A Kierkegaard was a textile merchant in Copenhagen, and he apparently had a histrionic bent to his personality, which would accord with this recollection. (For more information on Michael Andersen Kierkegaard, see the note to the first entry by Hans Brøchner in chapter 11 of this book.)

3. From M. Bojesen, *Generalpostdirektør Christen Svendsens Slægttavle* [The Genealogical Table of General Postal Director Christen Svendsen] (Helsingør: J. M. Welsch's Bogtrykkeri, 1925), p. 4. I am grateful to Harry Christensen of Oregon City, Oregon, for supplying this reference.

Christian Julius Svendsen (1810–81) and his brother **Thomas Wilhelm Severin Svendsen** (1818–95) were not blood relations of Søren Kierkegaard, but, like him, they were nephews of Michael Andersen Kierkegaard (1776–1867), at whose home they met Søren, who was about their age; for more information on Michael Andersen Kierkegaard, see the note to the first entry by Hans Brøchner in chapter 11 of this book.

4. From F.V.B. Meidell's letter to H. P. Barfod, dated November 7, 1869, in which we learn that some of Meidell's information comes from Hans Peter Kierkegaard, the son of Kierkegaard's father's cousin, Michael Andersen Kierkegaard. The original is in **KBHA** (**SKA** D. Pk. 5).

Frederik Vilhelm Berg Meidell (1833–1913), naval officer and historian.

5. From H. P. Ipsen's letter to H. P. Barfod, dated September 24, 1869. The original is in **KBHA (SKA** D. Pk. 5).

Harald Peter Ipsen (1813–76) was a pastor in Frederikshavn in northern Zealand and, subsequently, in Gentofte, a suburb of Copenhagen. He states that he entered the university in 1832, but his name is not to be found in the printed list of students. Ipsen's sister was married to Prof. Frederik Christian Sibbern.

6. From F. L. Liebenberg's memoirs, *Nogle Optegnelser om mit Levned* [Some Notes on My Life] (Copenhagen: Gyldendal, 1894), p. 11.

F[rederik] L[udvig] Liebenberg (1810–94), attended the Borgerdyd School and in 1828 enrolled in the University of Copenhagen, where his initial intention to become a theologian was abandoned after he read D. F. Strauss's *Leben Jesu*. Liebenberg became a literary scholar and editor and evolved considerably over his lifetime, beginning as a worshiper of Oehlenschläger and ending up as an admirer of Brandes.

7. The first portion of the present entry is translated from the archivist Eiler Nystrøm's book *Biografiske Efterretninger om Peter Munthe Bruns og Ane Munchs Slægt paa Fædrene og Mødrene Side* [Biographical Information on the Family of Peter Munthe Brun and Ane Munch on the Paternal and Maternal Lines] (Copenhagen: privately published, 1910), pp. 1–2. The second portion is also said to stem from the Munthe Brun family, but is cited without specific attribution in Sejer Kühle, *Søren Kierkegaard. Barndom og Ungdom*, p. 42, from which the present passage is translated.

Peter Munthe Brun [or Bruun] (1813–1904), jurist, was a childhood friend of Kierkegaard and entered the university upon graduation from the Borgerdyd School in 1831. According to Sejer Kühle ("Søren Kierkegaard og den heibergske Kreds" [Søren Kierkegaard and Heiberg's Circle], *Personalhistorisk Tidsskrift*, 1947, vols. 1–4, p. 2, and *Søren Kierkegaard. Barndom og Ungdom* [Søren Kierkegaard: Childhood and Youth] [Copenhagen: Aschehoug Dansk Forlag, 1950], p. 91), in 1831–33 Munthe Brun and Kierkegaard were members of a small debating society at the university founded by Peter Engel Lind (see the entry by Lind later in this chapter). The society survived for two years but left no literary remains; besides Kierkegaard, Munthe Brun, and Lind, the other members of the society were C.C.V. Silfverberg (subsequently an educator in Jutland), Ludvig Heckscher (subsequently a jurist and civic leader in Copenhagen), S.D.E. Schrader (subsequently pastor at Christiansborg Castle Church), and J.M.G. Bondesen (subsequently a pastor in western Zealand). **Michael Nielsen** (1776–1846) was a titular professor and headmaster of the Borgerdyd School from 1813 until 1844. **He and his father walked around the living room, etc.**: the imaginary walks that Kierkegaard supposedly took with his father in the family home are the apparent source for the accounts in *Johannes Climacus eller De omnibus dubitandum est* (published posthumously in *Pap.* IV B 1 pp. 106f. [*KW* VII, see especially pp. 119–20]); see also Kierkegaard's 1844 letter to his sister-in-law, Henriette Glahn Kierkegaard (*B&A* I 137 [*KW* XXV 174]).

8. From F. P. Welding's letters to H. P. Barfod, dated September 3 and October 23, 1869, in **KBHA (SKA** D. Pk. 5).

Frederik Peter Welding (1811–94), matriculated from the Borgerdyd School into the University of Copenhagen in 1830; a follower of Mynster, he became pastor and archdeacon at Viborg cathedral and elsewhere. See Per Krarup, *Søren Kierkegaard og Borgerdydskolen* [Søren Kierkegaard and the Borgerdyd School] (Copenhagen: Gyldendal, 1977) for more details about the school and its staff. With respect to the nickname **Choirboy**: a few centrally located schools in Copenhagen were obligated to maintain boys' choirs, whose members were required (both during actual church ceremonies and at other times) to wear long black gowns. By the time of Kierkegaard's childhood these uniforms had been somewhat altered; see Michael Neiiendam, *Københavns Kirkeskolers Krønike* [Chronicles of Copenhagen Church Schools] (Copenhagen: Gad, 1941), pp. 120ff. Vilhelm Andersen's mention of Kierkegaard's "orphanage uniform" (in Carl S. Petersen and Vilhelm Andersen, *Illustreret dansk Litteraturhistorie* [Illustrated History of Danish Literature], vol. 3: *Det nittende Aarhundredes første Halvdel* [The First Half of the Nineteenth Century] [Copenhagen: Gyldendal, 1924], p. 696) is incorrect. **H. P. Holst**: see the note accompanying the entry by him in this chapter. **His brother the [later] bishop** is Kierkegaard's older brother, Peter

Christian Kierkegaard (1805–88). **Children are the only reasonable human beings**: cf. *Either/ Or*, vol. 1: "I prefer to talk with children, because one dare hope that they can become reasonable beings" (*SV* I 4 [*KW* III 19]). Johan Frederik **Storck** (1799–1854) was an instructor of religion and Danish and later became a pastor on Zealand. **Charlottenlund** is a palace to the north of Copenhagen. It is surrounded by a park and has long been a favorite place for walks and picnics.

9. From E. J. Anger's letter to H. P. Barfod, dated September 15, 1869, in **KBHA (SKA** D. Pk. 5).

Edvard J. Anger (1813–95) matriculated into the University of Copenhagen from the Borgerdyd School in 1830 and subsequently became a pastor. **Welding's letter**: Barfod had earlier solicited a letter from Frederik Welding (see above in this chapter) and had apparently sent a copy of Welding's letter to Anger when asking for the latter's recollections of his school days with Kierkegaard. Prof. Nielsen's **school testimony** concerning Søren Kierkegaard, which is included in this chapter, is published in *B&A* I 5–6 (*KW* XXV 5–7). **Ludvig Christian Müller** (not "Møller") (1806–51) later became a highly respected pastor, seminary principal, philologist, and historian. Vilhelm August **Heger** (1811–35) studied philology at the University.

10. From P. E. Lind's letter to H. P. Barfod, dated September 16, 1869, in **KBHA (SKA** D. Pk. 5).

Peter Engel Lind (1814–1903) matriculated into the University of Copenhagen in 1831 and was one of Kierkegaard's friends at the university; subsequently he became a pastor and succeeded Peter Christian Kierkegaard as bishop of Aalborg. According to Sejer Kühle ("Søren Kierkegaard og den heibergske Kreds," p. 2), Lind was the founder of a small debating society at the university that included himself, Kierkegaard, P. Munthe Brun, and four others; for Munthe Brun, see the entry earlier in this chapter. For further information concerning Lind, see *B&A* I 37–39 and II 27 (*KW* XXV 48–50, 452). **[Emil] Boesen** (1812–79), a pastor in Jutland and subsequently archdeacon in Aarhus, was a schoolmate, close confidant, and lifelong friend of Kierkegaard. For more information on Kierkegaard and Boesen, see Carl Koch, *Søren Kierkegaard og Emil Boesen. Breve og Indledning* [Søren Kierkegaard and Emil Boesen: Letters and an Introduction] (Copenhagen: Karl Schønbergs Forlag, 1901). See also chapter 2 of this book for Boesen's letter to H. P. Barfod and chapter 8 for Boesen's accounts of his conversations with Kierkegaard when the latter lay dying in the hospital. Their correspondence has been reprinted in *B&A* I (*KW* XXV). **L[udvig] C[hristian] Müller**: see the note accompanying the entry by Edvard Anger, earlier in this chapter.

11. From Martin Attrup, *En Landsbydegns Erindringer. Afsluttet med en Samling gode Ord til Vejledning og Berigelse* [Memoirs of a Rural Parish Clerk, Concluded with a Collection of Sayings for Guidance and Enrichment] (Copenhagen: Det folkelige Forlag, 1938), pp. 74f.

Martin Attrup (born 1854) was parish clerk and schoolteacher in Hørby on Tuse Næs in northern Zealand. **The dean** was apparently **Christian Albrecht Ravn** (1822–1912), who entered the University of Copenhagen after being graduated from the Borgerdyd School in 1839, later becoming a pastor in rural Zealand, and as such was the official visitor to the school. In the present memoir by Attrup, Ravn is referred to as "Peder Ravn"; this is probably an error of memory on Attrup's part. **The Metropolitan School**: a preparatory school in Copenhagen, an error for the Borgerdyd School, from which Ravn and both Kierkegaard brothers were graduated. **Peter Christian Kierkegaard** had been graduated from the school in 1822 and **Søren** Kierkegaard in 1830. Therefore none of the three who are mentioned in this story were in the same class. But one should not necessarily conclude from this that the recollection has merely been fabricated by Attrup, because much of it appears to bear the mark of authenticity. Since Attrup seems to have remembered other things very well, the errors may stem from the above-mentioned Dean Ravn.

12. The first paragraph of H. P. Holst's recollections is from his letter to H. P. Barfod, dated September 11, 1869, and the remainder is from his letter to Barfod, dated September 13, 1869. Both are in **KBHA (SKA** D. Pk. 5).

H[ans] P[eter] Holst (1811–93), author, was Kierkegaard's classmate at the Borgerdyd

School, from which he was graduated in 1829, when he enrolled at the University of Copenhagen. "**Literary Quicksilver,**" which has been ascribed to Kierkegaard, is printed in *SV* XIII 471–85 (*KW* XIII 73–86). Concerning the authorship of this pseudonymous article, see Alastair McKinnon, "Could Kierkegaard Have Written 'Literary Quicksilver'?" in *International Kierkegaard Commentary: The Corsair Affair,* ed. Robert L. Perkins (Macon, Ga.: Mercer University Press, 1990), pp. 163–78. **His first written work on Andersen** was *From the Papers of One Still Living* (*SV* XIII 41–92 [*KW* I 53–102]), Kierkegaard's first book, published in 1838; it was a review of Hans Christian Andersen's *Kun en Spillemand* [Only a Fiddler] (Copenhagen: 1837). **De mendacio** [About Lies]: an abbreviated version of the title of P. C. Kierkegaard's doctoral dissertation; the full Latin title is *De notione atque turpitudine mendacii commentatio.* **Prof. Nielsen made use of him, etc.**: this should probably be understood to mean that even before Kierkegaard became a university student Michael Nielsen used him to correct Latin compositions for the higher grades. Although it is well known that during a part of his time as a university student Kierkegaard was a teacher, composition grader, and outside examiner at the school, the full extent of this activity is not known. In this connection, see the entries by Benjamin Feddersen and Holger Lund, with their accompanying notes, in chapter 2 of this book. **I[Jens] E[mil] Damkier** (1811–58) was graduated from the Borgerdyd School in 1829 and enrolled in the University of Copenhagen. The playwright, critic, and aesthetician **I[Johan] L[udvig] Heiberg** (1791–1860) was the editor of *Kjøbenhavns flyvende Post* [Copenhagen's Flying Post] in 1827, 1828, and 1830. **Mrs. Gyllembourg** was Thomasine Buntzen Heiberg Gyllembourg-Ehrensvärd (1773–1856), J. L. Heiberg's mother and an important prose author in her own right. [Carl Holger] **Visby** (1801–71) was pastor at the prison as well as at the Church of Our Savior and was later a member of the Rigsdag and involved in numerous social causes. Kierkegaard's knowledge of Visby began at least as early as the beginning of the 1830s. On Easter Sunday 1831, Visby, who had supported H. N. Clausen in his dispute with Grundtvig in the 1820s, preached a sermon in which he appeared to deny the orthodox Christian notion of eternal damnation. This in turn aroused a great debate in which Clausen was on Visby's side, and the Grundtvigians, including Peter Christian Kierkegaard, attacked Visby. In this connection, in May 1835 Søren helped his brother proofread a contribution to this debate by T. V. Oldenburg, who was a Grundtvigian and a friend of P. C. Kierkegaard (see Sejer Kühle, "Nogle Oplysninger om Søren Kierkegaard, 1834–38" [Some Information on Søren Kierkegaard, 1834–38], *Personalhistorisk Tidsskrift* [in five parts: I, 9. Række, 4. Bind, 4. Hæfte (1931): 1–11; II, 9. Række, 5. Bind, 2. Hæfte (1932): 150–56; III, 9. Række, 5. Bind, 3.–4. Hæfte (1932): 1–17; IV, 9. Række, 6. Bind, 3.–4. Hæfte, (1933): 1–10; V, 56. Aargang, 10. Række, 2. Bind (1935): 1–7], I, p. 3, and *Pap.* I A 60, p. 30 [*SKJP* 5089]). Kierkegaard's subsequent preference for Visby, a preference he expressed both publicly and privately (see the many entries in his journals, e.g., *Pap.* X^1 A 437) is perhaps best understood in this context. Kierkegaard's approval of Visby does not necessarily reflect any leaning toward Visby's ally Clausen, but is more likely rooted in an appreciation of Visby's social endeavors as prison chaplain—and perhaps also in a desire to annoy his brother and the Grundtvigians, who had so opposed Visby in the 1830s.

13. From Frederik Hammerich's memoirs, *Et Levnedsløb,* vol. 1, pp. 308f.

Frederik Hammerich: see the note accompanying the entry by Hammerich earlier in this chapter. **"Hebrew Müller"** was Ludvig Christian Müller: see the note accompanying the entry by Edvard J. Anger earlier in this chapter.

14. From letters by Juliane and Christiane Rudelbach to their brother A. G. Rudelbach, dated June 5 and July 9, 1830. The original letters are in **KBHA** (NkS 1543, 2^0), and portions of them have been reprinted in Carl Weltzer, *Peter og Søren Kierkegaard* [Peter and Søren Kierkegaard] (Copenhagen: G.E.C. Gad, 1936), p. 32.

Juliane and **Christiane Rudelbach** were sisters of Andreas Gottlob Rudelbach (1792–1862), an older friend of Peter Christian Kierkegaard, a respected theologian, and an early supporter of Grundtvig. As his views made it impossible for him to obtain a suitable post in Denmark, Rudelbach accepted a position in Saxony where he remained from 1828 to 1845, after which he returned to Denmark, distanced himself from Grundtvig, and, failing to obtain a university appointment, ultimately accepted a pastorate in the provinces. Rudelbach's sisters were frequent guests at the Kierkegaard home on Nytorv, and their letters to their brother contain references to the Kierkegaard family, including young Søren.

15. School reports such as the present one from Michael Nielsen, headmaster of the Borgerdyd School, were submitted annually with respect to each group of pupils who intended to matriculate into the University of Copenhagen. The pupils were ranked in order of overall performance. Kierkegaard ranked second, after Edvard Anger (see above in this chapter), in a group of ten students from the Borgerdyd School; the only other classmate who figures in the present volume was Frederik Welding (see above in this chapter), who ranked eighth. The original of the present document is in the National Archives (**RA**, Københavns Universitet, Det filosofiske Fakultet, KU 35.20.03). It has previously been published, with minor errors and omissions, in *B&A* I 4f. (*KW* XXV 4–5); these versions give no source and were not based on the original document, but were apparently taken from Valdemar Ammundsen, *Søren Kierkegaards Ungdom. Hans Slægt og hans Religiøse Udvikling* [Søren Kierkegaard's Youth: His Family and Religious Development] (Copenhagen: Universitetsbogtrykkeriet, 1912), pp. 66–67, where the source is given incorrectly.

His oldest brother: Peter Christian Kierkegaard; see the note to the entry by Martin Attrup in this chapter. **Anger** is Edvard J. Anger, who was ranked number one in his class (Kierkegaard was number two); see the note to the entry by Anger, earlier in this chapter. **The same as no. 1**: for all his pupils excepting Anger, Nielsen refers to the reading list for Anger, noting only how each student deviated from what Anger had studied. Thus to obtain a fuller idea of what Kierkegaard studied in school it is necessary to append Nielsen's list for Anger:

IN LATIN

Horace, *The Odes*, the first three books of the *Epistles*, and the *Ars poetica*
Virgil, *The Æneid*, the first six books
Terence, *Andria* and *Phormio*
Cicero, first book of *de Officiis*; all three books of *de Oratore*; *de Amicitia*; *de Senectute*; from the
    Catilinean Orations: "pro Roscio Amerino," "Lege Manilia," "Archia poeta," "Milone,"
    "Ligario," and "Dejotaro"; the first sixty letters in Weiske's edition
Livy, the first *Pentade*
Caesar, *Bellum civile*
Sallust, both the *Wars*
Cornelius Nepos

IN GREEK

Homer, *Odyssey*
Plato, the *Crito* and *Euthyphro*
Xenophon, *Memorabilia Socratis*
Herodotus, *Urania* and *Calliope*
the Gospel of John

IN PLACE OF HEBREW

Homer, the first ten books of the *Iliad*

Both he [Anger] and the others have used the following textbooks and grammars: Nikolai Fogtmann, *Lærebog i den christelige Religion. Til Brug for den studerende Ungdom* [Textbook of the Christian Religion, for the Use of Young Students] (Copenhagen: 1823); Svend Borchmann Hersleb, *Lærebog i Bibelhistorien* [Textbook of Bible History] (Copenhagen: 1832); Abraham Kall, *Den almindelige Verdens Historie til Skolernes Brug* [Universal World History for Use in Schools] (Copenhagen: 1776, 1780, 1793); Hans Ancher Kofod, *Almindelig Verdenshistorie i Udtog* [Outline of Universal World History] (Copenhagen: 1813, 1817, 1821, 1828); Jacob Riise, *Lærebog i Geographien for den studerende Ungdom* [Textbook of Geography for Young Students] (Copenhagen: 1821, 1824, 1830); Georg Frederik Krüger Ursin, *Lærebog i den rene Mathematik, især med Hensyn til dem, der forberede sig til Universitetet* [Textbook of Pure

Mathematics, Especially for Those Who Are Preparing for the University], vols. 1–2 (Copenhagen: 1822 and 1824); Jacob Christian Lindberg, *Hebraisk Grammatik* [Hebrew Grammar] (Copenhagen: 1822); Johan Nicolai Tileman, *Kortfattet tydsk Sproglære* [Brief German Grammar] (Copenhagen: 1798, 1803, 1816, 1819, 1823); Jens Deichmann, *Jens Deichmanns franske Grammatik, paa ny udgivet og bearbejdet af Laur. Chr. Ditl. Westengaard* [Jens Deichmann's French Grammar, Newly Reedited by Laur. Chr. Ditl. Westengaard] (Copenhagen: 1821, 1827). [Nielsen listed only the authors and vague titles of these textbooks; full titles and other bibliographic information have been supplied by the present editor].

16. Originally written in Latin. Published in Holger Lund, *Borgerdydskolen i Kjøbenhavn, 1787–1887. Et Mindeskrift* [The Borgerdyd School in Copenhagen, 1787–1887: A Commemoration] (Copenhagen: Wroblewski, 1887), pp. 162–65, in a Danish translation that is probably by Lund. This Danish translation is reprinted in *B&A* II 4–5, and is the source for the present version. Another English translation has been published in *KW* XXV 5–7. The original document is in **KBHA (SKA** D. Pk. 6).

Chapter Two
A Young Intellectual: The University Years

1. From the Rudelbach sisters' letter, dated May 7, 1831, to their brother Andreas. The original letter is with the Rudelbach correspondence in **KBHA (NkS** 1543, 2^0), and a portion of the letter is reprinted in Weltzer, *Peter og Søren Kierkegaard*, p. 40.

Juliane and Christiane Rudelbach: see the note accompanying their entry in chapter 1 of this book. **The Doctor**: Peter Christian Kierkegaard, recently returned from his study travels in Germany, where he had earned a doctorate at the University of Göttingen. **Stupid brother-in-law**: presumably Johan Christian Lund (1799–1875), married to Nicoline Christine Kierkegaard.

2. From letters by Augusta Sibbern Møller (then in Oslo) to Harald Høffding, dated November 20 and December 7, 1912; in **KBHA (NkS** 4620, 4^0, "Nogle Sibberniana").

Augusta Sibbern Møller (born 1838) was the daughter of Prof. F. C. Sibbern, with whom Kierkegaard became personally acquainted in his early student years. For more information on F. C. Sibbern, see below in this chapter for the notes accompanying the comments on Kierkegaard's dissertation.

3. From a letter from Niels Lindberg to Peter Christian Kierkegaard, dated March 14, 1866; the original is in **KBHA (NkS** 3174, 4^0, kasse VII, fasc. 4, nr. 61).

Niels Lindberg (1829–86), the son of the theologian and Kierkegaard family friend Jacob Christian Lindberg, became himself a theologian and supporter of Grundtvig; for information on Jacob Christian Lindberg, see the notes accompanying the entries by Peter Christian Kierkegaard in chapter 9 of this book. **Your Reverence**: Søren Kierkegaard's older brother, Peter Christian Kierkegaard.

4. From a letter from Peter Rørdam to his brother Hans, dated December 4, 1834, published in H. F. Rørdam, ed., *Peter Rørdam. Blade af hans Levnedsbog og Brevvexling fra 1806 til 1844* [Peter Rørdam: Pages from His Biography and Correspondence from 1806 to 1844] (Copenhagen: Karl Schønbergs Forlag, 1891), p. 75.

Peter Rørdam (1806–83), follower of Grundtvig, teacher at the Borgerdyd School, and subsequently pastor, first in the village of Mern, in southern Zealand, and later at Lyngby, near Copenhagen. **Prof. Clausen**: H[enrik] N[icolai] Clausen (1793–1877), moderate rationalist theologian and liberal politician, taught New Testament theology at the University of Copenhagen beginning in 1825, and later served several terms as rector of the university. Though widely respected, Clausen had little in common with the principal Danish religious thinkers of his time, i.e., Grundtvig (who libeled Clausen in a notorious case in 1826), Mynster, Martensen (against whom Clausen competed unsuccessfully to succeed to Mynster's bishopric in 1854), and Kierkegaard.

5. From Vilhelm Birkedal, *Personlige Oplevelser i et langt Liv* [Personal Experiences from a Long Life], vol. 1 (Copenhagen: Karl Schønbergs Forlag, 1890), pp. 188–89.

Vilhelm Birkedal (1809–92) was pastor in Ryslinge on Funen, a staunch Danish nationalist, and a leader in the Grundtvigian movement. **Prof. H. N. Clausen**: see note accompanying the entry by Peter Rørdam in this chapter. **The custom of the king of the Persians**: Kierkegaard uses this image in *The Concept of Anxiety* (*SV* IV 312 [*KW* VIII 40]) to criticize the German theologian Leonhard Usteri. It is possible that Kierkegaard used this image in conversation with Birkedal to criticize Clausen, but it is also possible that this is a confused recollection by Birkedal.

6. From a letter from J. A. Ostermann to H. P. Barfod, dated May 28, 1867, now in **KBHA** (**SKA** D. Pk. 5). It is also published in Teddy Petersen, *Kierkegaards polemiske debut* [Kierkegaard's Polemical Debut] (Odense: Odense Universitetsforlag, 1977), pp. 53–54. Another English translation is available in *KW* I 200–201.

Johannes A. Ostermann (1809–88) was a fellow university student with Kierkegaard in the 1830s, and in speeches at the Student Union they set forth opposing views concerning the politics of the day. He was later head teacher at the Frederiksborg Learned School. Kierkegaard mentions Ostermann in *Pap.* I B 2 (*SKJP* 5116). As can be seen from the letter reprinted here, on November 14, 1835, Ostermann gave a lecture at the Student Union in defense of freedom of the press. It was subsequently published in *Fædrelandet* [The Fatherland] on January 22, 1836, and has been reprinted in Teddy Petersen, *Kierkegaards polemiske debut*, pp. 29–37. On November 28, 1835, Kierkegaard gave an address at the Student Union in reply to Ostermann's. The address was entitled "Our Journalistic Literature: A Study from Nature in Noonday Light" (*Pap.* I B 2 pp. 157–78 [*KW* I 35–52]). Barfod had found the manuscript of Kierkegaard's address among his papers; this occasioned the query to Ostermann that elicited the present reply. **The essay by Kierkegaard** is the manuscript of Kierkegaard's talk, "Our Journalistic Literature." **My essay** is Ostermann's above-mentioned defense of freedom of the press. **Joh[annes] Hage** (1800–1837) was editor and co-founder (in 1834) of *Fædrelandet*. His death by suicide in 1837 came shortly after the government imposed a sentence of lifelong censure upon him for having published several liberal articles in his newspaper. **The essay was read aloud**: that is, it was not presented as an informal talk. **Lehmann**: Peter Martin Orla Lehmann (1810–70) was a future leader of the National Liberal Party and was at that time a leading student spokesman for liberalism; he subsequently became head of the Student Union.

7. From a letter from Peter Rørdam to his brother Hans, dated February 23, 1836, as published in H. F. Rørdam, ed., *Peter Rørdam. Blade af hans Levnedsbog og Brevvexling fra 1806 til 1844*, p. 79. It has been reprinted in Teddy Petersen, *Kierkegaards polemiske debut*, pp. 158–59.

Peter Rørdam: see the note accompanying the entry by Peter Rørdam earlier in this chapter. **Homeward went brave Peter, etc.** is from Dick's song in the first act of *Ludlams Hule* [Ludlam's Cave], a musical drama by Adam Oehlenschläger (see *Oehlenschlägers samlede Værker* [Oehlenschläger's Collected Works], vol. 17 [Copenhagen: Høst, 1845], p. 100); Kierkegaard had cited the same passage at the beginning of the first of his two articles alluded to in this entry. **The younger Kierkegaard who now writes in the *Flyvende Post* under the pseudonym B.**: the *Flyvende Post* was J. L. Heiberg's paper, and Kierkegaard published two articles in that journal under the pseudonym "B." The first was entitled "The Morning Observations in *Kjøbenhavnsposten* [The Copenhagen Post], no. 43" and was published in the *Flyvende Post* on February 18, 1836. The second article by "B." was entitled "On the Polemic of *Fædrelandet*" and appeared in the *Flyvende Post* on March 12, 1836. Kierkegaard also wrote a third article directed against Lehmann, which he signed with his own name and published in the *Flyvende Post* on April 10, 1836; it was entitled "To Mr. Orla Lehmann," who had also been writing under a pseudonym. The fact that Rørdam's letter clearly identifies "B." as Kierkegaard only two days after the publication of the first of his pseudonymous articles is testimony to how transparent this sort of pseudonymity in fact was. (Kierkegaard's three articles from the *Flyvende Post* are available in *SV* XIII 9–39 [*KW* I 6–34].)

8. From a letter from Johan Hahn to Peter Christian Kierkegaard, dated May 17, 1836. The

original letter is with Peter Christian Kierkegaard's papers in **KBHA** (**NkS** 3174, 4⁰, kasse V, fasc. 3, nr. 30²), and has been published in Weltzer, *Peter og Søren Kierkegaard*, p. 98.

Johan [Gottfried Wilhelm] Hahn (1804–40) was a friend of Peter Christian Kierkegaard, a follower of Grundtvig, and a pastor in the rural parish of Hyllested in southwest Zealand.

9. From B. J. Feddersen's article, "Smaa Oplevelser" [Minor Experiences], which was published in *Illustreret Tidende* [Illustrated Times], vol. 41, no. 25, March 18, 1900.

Benjamin Johan Feddersen, a younger literary figure from the 1890s, now quite forgotten. He presumably has his knowledge from his father, the civil servant Henry George Feddersen (1811–71), a schoolmate of Kierkegaard who was graduated from the Borgerdyd School and entered the university in 1831. Andreas Ferdinand Schiødte (see his entry in chapter 10 of this book), who entered the University of Copenhagen in 1833, says that as a young university student Kierkegaard came to teach Latin at the Borgerdyd School; this dates Kierkegaard's teaching activity as having begun in the early part of the 1830s. Thus it is not impossible that as a first-year university student, in 1830–31, Kierkegaard could have taught the elder Feddersen, who was one year behind Kierkegaard in school. We know from a letter by Michael Pedersen Kierkegaard (see the entries from the journals and correspondence of Peter Christian Kierkegaard in chapter 9 of this book) that Søren Kierkegaard was teaching at the Borgerdyd School in 1836, and according to Sejer Kühle (*Søren Kierkegaard. Barndom og Ungdom*, p. 155) he taught there in 1837–38. In a letter of 1840, Michael Nielsen, headmaster of the Borgerdyd School, attested to Kierkegaard's skill in Latin (see below in this chapter, as well as *B&A* I 12 [*KW* XXV 16–17]), stating that Kierkegaard had taught Latin at the Borgerdyd School "for several years" and most recently in 1840. Thus it seems likely that Kierkegaard's teaching activity, in various capacities, at the Borgerdyd School extended over a period beginning as early as 1831–33 and ending in 1840. **The examiner**: on Kierkegaard as a Latin examiner at the Borgerdyd School, see also the note to the entry by H. P. Holst in chapter 1 of this book as well as the entry by Holger Lund in this chapter.

10. From Holger Lund, *Borgerdydskolen i Kjøbenhavn, 1787–1887. Et Mindeskrift*, p. 236.

Holger Lund (1853–86), whose history of the Borgerdyd School was published in 1887 on the occasion of the one hundredth anniversary of the school's founding, was aware that Søren Kierkegaard was one of the institution's most famous graduates. Lund sought out graduates of the school who had been Kierkegaard's pupils some fifty years earlier when Kierkegaard, then a university student, had taught at the school, and he summarized their testimony in his book.

11. From J. H. Lorck's memoirs, *Femoghalvfjerdsindstyve Aar. Erindringer nedskrevne for Venner og Bekjendte* [Seventy-Five Years: Memories Written Down for Friends and Acquaintants] (Copenhagen: Gyldendal, 1885), pp. 108–9.

J[ørgen] H[enrik] Lorck (1810–95), physician, amateur musician, and composer, moved in Copenhagen artistic and intellectual circles in the the 1830s when Kierkegaard was a student at the university. **The above-mentioned performance on Weyse's birthday**: on March 5, 1836, there was a gala performance at the Royal Theater on the occasion of the birthday of C.E.F. Weyse (1774–1842), one of Denmark's leading composers.

12. From Angul Hammerich, *Festskrift i Anledning af Musikforeningens Halvhundredaarsdag* [Festschrift on the Occasion of the Fiftieth Anniversary of the Music Society] (Copenhagen: Udgivet af Musikforeningen [Published by the Music Society], 1886), p. 6.

Angul Hammerich (1848–1931), music historian, son of [Peter] Frederik [Adolph] Hammerich (see the note on Frederik Hammerich accompanying the entry by him in chapter 1 of this book).

13. From a letter by Eline Heramb Boisen, as published in P. Bojsen, *Budstikkens Udgiver, Præsten F. E. Bojsens Liv og Levned* [The Publisher of "The Messenger": The Story of Pastor F. E. Boisen's Life] (Horsens: C. Schønberg, 1883), p. 94; for a similar account of this episode, taken from Eline Heramb Boisen's memoirs, see her entry in chapter 9 of this book.

Eline Heramb Boisen, born in Norway, was F. E. Boisen's wife and P. C. Kierkegaard's sister-in-law; see the note accompanying her memoirs in chapter 9 of this book. **Bojsen**: Frederik Engelhart Boisen (1808–87), a nationally known pastor and editor of the journal *Budstikken* [The Messenger], was the brother of Peter Christian Kierkegaard's first wife, Elise Marie Boisen (1806–37), to whom P. C. Kierkegaard was married from October 1836 until her death less than a year later. In 1837 **Peter Rørdam** (see the note to the entry by Peter Rørdam earlier in this chapter) was living at the home of his widowed mother, Mrs. Catrine Rørdam, in Frederiksberg, a suburb of Copenhagen, which was where Kierkegaard first met Regine Olsen (cf. *Pap.* X⁵ A 149:3 [*SKJP* 6472 p. 191]). According to Goldschmidt's account (see chapter 5 in this book) this was also where Kierkegaard first met Goldschmidt. See Elise Lindberg's entry and the accompanying note in chapter 4 of this book regarding Kierkegaard's attendance at Rørdam's farewell party on the occasion of the latter's departure to take up his pastorate. On Peter Rørdam see H. F. Rørdam, ed., *Peter Rørdam. Blade af hans Levnedsbog og Brevvexling fra 1806 til 1844.*

14. From Jakob Knudsen, *Jyder. Sytten Fortællinger* [Jutlanders: Seventeen Tales] (Copenhagen and Kristiania: Gyldendal, 1915), pp. 218–23. The story is based on a recollection by the author's mother, Nanna Knudsen (*née* Boisen) (1824–1900), apparently recounted to her son Jakob, who subsequently used it in the story "Et Mindedrag" [A Recollection], which was first published in a Christmas supplement to the *Kolding Folkeblad* [Kolding People's Paper] December 24, 1908. Later Jakob Knudsen incorporated it in *Jyder* [Jutlanders], this time entitled simply "Mindedrag" [Recollection]. Jakob Knudsen changed the names in the story; see Aug. F. Schmidt's essay "Mindedrag," which appeared in the yearbook published by Galtrup High School for 1927, pp. 44–47, and Schmidt's book *Jakob Knudsen. Randbemærkninger til nogle af hans Arbejder samt et bibliografisk Tillæg* [Jakob Knudsen: Marginal Notes to Some of His Works, plus a Bibliographical Appendix] (Aarhus: privately published, 1936), pp. 13–17.

Jakob Knudsen (1858–1917), author. The present passage is Knudsen's poetic rendering of what his mother experienced as a very young girl during a carriage ride in the **Deer Park** and across the clearing near the **Hermitage** (a park and a royal hunting lodge north of Copenhagen, popular destinations for country outings) with a group that included Peter and Søren Kierkegaard. In 1898 the author's mother took part in a carriage ride from Lyngby by way of Fortunen to the Hermitage Plain. The trip awakened a great number of memories for the old and very alert lady, and among the things she remembered was a similar carriage ride along the same route that she had taken sixty-one years earlier, in 1837, as a fourteen-year-old confirmand accompanied by family members including Peter and Søren Kierkegaard. **Her grandmother, the bishop's wife**: Anna Nannestad Boisen (1775–1853), the widow of Bishop P. O. Boisen (1762–1831), was Nanna Boisen Knudsen's grandmother and hence author Jakob Knudsen's great grandmother; she was also the mother of Elise Marie Boisen (1806–37), Peter Christian Kierkegaard's first wife (see the note accompanying the entry by P. Bojsen in this chapter), and thus Peter Christian Kierkegaard's mother-in-law. **Aunt Marie**: Elise Marie Boisen, later Peter Christian Kierkegaard's first wife.

15. From Hans Christian Andersen's *Mit Livs Eventyr* [The Fairy Tale of My Life], in *H. C. Andersens Samlede Skrifter* [H. C. Andersen's Collected Writings], 2d ed., vol. 1 (Copenhagen: Reitzel, 1876), p. 188.

Hans Christian Andersen (1805–75), poet, novelist, writer of fairy tales. His novel *Kun en Spillemand* [Only a Fiddler] came out in 1837, and Kierkegaard's review of it, *From the Papers of One Still Living*, came out in September 1838 (*SV* XIII 41–92 [*KW* I 53–102]). For further information on Andersen's relation to Kierkegaard, see Bruce H. Kirmmse, "A Rose with Thorns: Hans Christian Andersen's Relation to Kierkegaard," in *International Kierkegaard Commentary. Early Polemical Writings*, ed. Robert E. Perkins (Macon, Ga.: Mercer University Press, forthcoming).

16. From a letter by Michael Nielsen; the original is in **KBHA** (**SKA** D. Pk. 6.) and is reprinted in *B&A* I 12 (*KW* XXV 16–17).

As mentioned in the note accompanying the entry by Peter Munthe Brun in chapter 1 of this book, **Michael Nielsen** (1776–1846) was the headmaster of the Borgerdyd School where Kierkegaard had helped teach Latin, both while he was an advanced student at the school and, subsequently, as a university student. This testimonial letter was written to attest to Kierkegaard's great skill with Latin. Kierkegaard intended to write and publish his dissertation in Danish, which was in conflict with the regulations that generally required that such works be written in Latin. Kierkegaard received permission, and the dissertation, *On the Concept of Irony, with Continual Reference to Socrates*, was published in Danish in September 1841 (*SV* XIII 93–393 [*KW* II 1–329]).

17. From a letter by Emil Boesen to H. P. Barfod, dated May 22, 1868. The letter is now in **KBHA** (**SKA** D. Pk. 5).

Emil Boesen: see the note on Boesen accompanying the entry by P. E. Lind in chapter 1 of this book. **While he was writing** *On the Concept of Irony* **and during the period of his engagement**: these periods of time were virtually identical. Kierkegaard wrote his dissertation *On the Concept of Irony* in 1840 and the first half of 1841, and his oral defense took place on September 29, 1841. He became engaged to Regine Olsen on September 10, 1840, and their engagement was finally broken off on October 11, 1841.

18. From comments on Kierkegaard's doctoral dissertation by professors at the University of Copenhagen. The passages that have been included are those that shed light on how Kierkegaard was perceived as a person. The comments were written on several sheets of paper fastened together. Prof. Sibbern wrote his comments first, and the pages were then passed from one professor to the next, so that each could see the comments of the previous readers; this explains the consistency of metaphor demonstrated in these selections, which are here reproduced in the order they were written. The original documents are located in the archives of the University of Copenhagen, which are at the National Archives (**RA**, Københavns Universitet. Det filosofiske Fakultet. KU. 35. 02. 17); excerpts have been published in Carl Weltzer, "Omkring Søren Kierkegaards Disputats" [About Søren Kierkegaard's Dissertation], *Kirkehistoriske Samlinger*, 6. Række, bd. 6 (1948–50): 292, 293–94, 296, 297–98, and 300.

Prof. Frederik Christian Sibbern (1785–1872): a professor of philosophy who wrote works on ethics, psychology, metaphysics, politics, and religion. Sibbern was one of Kierkegaard's teachers at the University of Copenhagen and subsequently his valued confidant. They had serious differences, however. See also Holger Frederik Rørdam's entry, with accompanying note, in chapter 4, and Sibbern's entry, with accompanying note, in chapter 10 of this book. At the time of the submission of Kierkegaard's dissertation, Sibbern was the dean of the philosophical faculty at the university and hence responsible for shepherding the dissertation through the university machinery. **Prof. Johan Nicolai Madvig** (1804–86): a classicist at the University of Copenhagen and one of Kierkegaard's teachers. Madvig's textbook of Latin grammar appeared in many editions and was used all over the world long after his death. **Prof. Frederik Christian Petersen** (1786–1859): professor of classical philology at the University of Copenhagen. **Prof. Peder Oluf Brøndsted** (1780–1842): professor of classical philology and archeology at the University of Copenhagen and an expert on Greek tragedy. **Hans Christian Ørsted** (1777–1851), discoverer of electromagnetism and the most famous Danish scientist of the age, was rector of the University of Copenhagen at the time Kierkegaard submitted his dissertation.

Chapter Three
Søren and Regine: The Engagement and Afterward

1. From Regine Olsen Schlegel's recollections, as recorded by Hanne [or Hanna] Mourier, *née* Weilbach (1824–1918). Hanne Mourier was the sister of the art historian Philip Weilbach (1834–1900) and was married to the jurist and mayor of Odense, Louis E. Mourier (1805–77). There was a personal connection between Philip Weilbach and Regine Schlegel, which was due, among other things, to Weilbach's work on the second edition of his *Kunstnerleksikon* [Encyclopedia of Artists] (published in 1877–78), for which Frederik Schlegel was a principal financial backer, as is explained in the work's introduction. Later, as an old woman (after Schlegel's death in 1896), Hanne Mourier visited her friend Regine and subjected her to a cross-examination concerning her relationship to Søren Kierkegaard. Hanne Mourier's report was subsequently deposited in the Søren Kierkegaard Archives, at that time located at the University of Copenhagen Library. Hjal-

mar Helweg published Mourier's account in his *Søren Kierkegaard. En psykiatrisk-psykologisk Studie* [Søren Kierkegaard: A Psychiatric-Psychological Study] (Copenhagen: H. Hagerups Forlag, 1933), pp. 385–92. In his introductory remarks on p. 385 Helweg informs us:

> The following document has been generously given to me by Librarian J. C. Kall, M.A., and I take this opportunity to convey my great thankfulness for this interesting document, thanks which must be conveyed further to the authoress Miss Hanne Mourier, with whose consent the report has been given to me. With the conveyance of the document came the right of publication as well as obligation to publish it in its entirety. Miss Mourier, who was a close associate of the late Mrs. Regine Schlegel, wrote down the fruits of her conversations with Mrs. Schlegel, who read them through and approved the account as written.

The Søren Kierkegaard Archive has long since been incorporated into the Manuscript Department of the Royal Library, but Hanne Mourier's original manuscript is not to be found there; its whereabouts are not known, and the present entry is translated from the document as published in Helweg's book.

Regine Schlegel (1822–1904) was the daughter of Terkild Olsen (1784–1849), councillor of state and department head in the Finance Ministry, and his wife, Regine Frederikke Malling Olsen (1778–1856). On her gravestone in Assistens Cemetery in Copenhagen, Regine Olsen Schlegel's given name is spelled "Regina"; see Peter Parkov and Gert Posselt, *Troskab—og Tilgivelse* [Faithfulness—and Forgiveness] (Copenhagen: Danmarks Nationalleksikon A/S, 1992), pp. 8 and 22–24, where it is pointed out that Regine spelled and signed her name both "Regine" and "Regina." **Your husband**: [Johan] Frederik ("Fritz") Schlegel (1817–96) was a high-ranking civil servant who served as governor of the Danish West Indies (after 1917 the U.S. Virgin Islands) from 1855 to 1860 and subsequently held important posts in the Copenhagen city administration; Schlegel was also a man of literary interests, an art connoisseur, and a philanthropist. **Mrs. Rørdam**: Mrs. Catrine Rørdam, widow of Pastor Thomas Schatt Rørdam and mother of Pastor Peter Rørdam, lived in the Copenhagen suburb of Frederiksberg, where Kierkegaard and other young people came for social gatherings; see also the note to the entry by P. Bojsen in chapter 2 of this book. **Your home**: the Olsen family home was in Børsgade, behind the Stock Exchange and near Knippelsbro, a drawbridge in Copenhagen. **"Gathering of the Holy" (The Moravians?) in Stormgade** is a reference to the pietistic Herrnhuter or Moravian *Brødremenighed* [Congregation of Brothers], whose meeting hall was on Stormgade at the site of the present National Museum. Moravianism offered an alternative to the rationalist theology that was still dominant among much of the clergy in the first part of the nineteenth century, and the congregation, which met for devotions in the evening, attracted such families as the Olsens, the Boesens, the Hammerichs, and the Kierkegaards. Michael Pedersen Kierkegaard was a pillar and a leading financial supporter of the congregation and was the chairman of the building fund when it was necessary to build a new meeting hall—which could seat six hundred people! **Paulli**: Just Henrik Paulli (1809–65), later chaplain at the royal palace chapel; Paulli was Bishop J. P. Mynster's son-in-law and a good friend of the later Bishop H. L. Martensen, but was also open to influence from Grundtvig. **F. C. Sibbern**: Frederik Christian Sibbern (1785–1870); see the note accompanying the comments on Kierkegaard's dissertation in chapter 2 of this book; cf. also the passage in Sibbern's entry in chapter 10 of this book, where he refers to his role as Regine Olsen's spiritual and psychological confidant after her engagement to Kierkegaard was broken off, as well as entry number 35 in chapter 11 of this book, where Hans Brøchner relates Kierkegaard's skepticism about Sibbern's ability to play just such a role. In letters dated October 31, 1841, and November 18, 1841, to Emil Boesen and P. J. Spang, respectively, Kierkegaard vents his annoyance with Sibbern for getting involved in the aftermath of his broken engagement to Regine Olsen (*B&A* I 71–73 and 75–77 [*KW* XXV 89–92 and 95–98]). **His will**: for Kierkegaard's will and the exchange of letters it occasioned between the Schlegels and Kierkegaard's relatives, see below in this chapter. **Kierkegaard's diaries . . . together with his letters to you . . . are preserved at the University Library**: since the letters and diaries that had been in Regine Schlegel's possession were not delivered to the University Library until late 1898 (see Henriette Lund's letter to Regine Schlegel, dated November 1, 1898, cited in the note accompanying Henriette Lund's entry later in this chapter), this fact cannot have been a part of Hanne Mourier's interview with Regine Schlegel, which is described in the document as having taken place in 1896. Since the entire document is followed by a postscript dated March 1, 1902, it seems likely that Hanne Mourier added this detail (and possibly others) between the time of the interview in 1896 (if that is in fact when the interview took place) and 1902. **Inspector Ottesen at Refsnæs** was in charge of the Coast Hospital on Refsnæs [Røsnæs] in northwest Zealand (established 1874–75), of which Frederik Schlegel was one of the founders and chief supporters. The conversation here alluded to must have taken place on October 17, 1875, when the new hospital was dedicated and Ottesen took the Schlegels on a tour of the establishment.

   2. In 1904 Raphael Meyer (1869–1925), a librarian, philologist, and literary scholar, published *Kierkegaardske Papirer, Forlovelsen. Udgivne for Fru Regine Schlegel* [Kierkegaardian Papers: The Engagement. Published on Behalf of Mrs. Regine Schlegel] (Copenhagen: Gyldendal, 1904), a volume containing a wealth of material, including reprints of many letters, etc., and which has for many years served as a principal source for the study of Kierkegaard's engagement. It was translated into German in 1904 and into Japanese in 1974. In his introduction (pp. i and vii), Meyer recounts:

> Mrs. Schlegel, who had known me since I was a child, approached me in October 1898 and, without any beating around the bush, asked me to listen to what "an old lady" had to tell. And she requested that after her death, when the matter of *Søren Kierkegaard's engagement* would again become a burning issue, I should use the information I had obtained in conversations with her. All that winter and spring, until mid-May, I generally visited her once a week at her home in Frederiksberg. Immediately following our meetings, I took notes on the contents of our conversations. . . . After S.K.'s death, Henrik Lund, who was the first to look after Kierkegaard's estate, sent most of the papers published in the present volume to Mrs. Schlegel in the West Indies in two sealed packages. These packages also contained Mrs. Schlegel's letters to S.K. "Luckily, however, I burned them," she said, because she was very reluctant to grant them any public significance. The remainder she hid away as a valuable treasure. According to her testimony, later, during her husband's final illness, when she herself was very much affected, partly by sorrow and partly by repeated attacks of influenza, she presented the letters [from Kierkegaard to herself] to S.K.'s niece Miss Henriette Lund [see Henriette Lund's entry in this chapter] to do with as she saw fit. Miss Lund could burn them or do whatever else she wished. The papers remained with Miss Lund until November 12, 1898, when in accordance with Mrs. Schlegel's wishes they were delivered by me to the University Library in a sealed package, which she wished to have opened and published after her death.
>   In publishing this material it has has been my duty to reproduce the text as faithfully as possible.

The present text is a translation of the greater part of the book's introduction (Meyer, *Kierkegaardske Papirer, Forlovelsen. Udgivne for Fru Regine Schlegel*, pp. i–vii), which Raphael Meyer says is an unedited account of his conversations of 1898–99 with the widowed Mrs. Schlegel.

   Schlegel: Regine Olsen's husband, Frederik Schlegel; see the note accompanying Hanne Mourier's account of Regine Schlegel's memoirs in this chapter. **Prof. Rudin**: the Swedish theologian, Waldemar Rudin, who made use of his correspondence with Regine Schlegel in his book *Sören Kierkegaards Person och Författarskap. Ett försök* [Søren Kierkegaard's Personality and Authorship: An Essay], vol. 1 (Stockholm: A. Nilsson, 1880). **Mrs. Catrine Rørdam**: see the note accompanying Hanne Mourier's account of Regine Schlegel's memoirs in this chapter. **The Olsens' [home]**: see the note accompanying Hanne Mourier's account of Regine Schlegel's memoirs in this chapter. **"The gatherings of the Holy" in Stormgade**: see the note accompanying Hanne Mourier's account of Regine Schlegel's memoirs in this chapter. **Inspector**

Ottesen at Refsnæs: see the note accompanying Hanne Mourier's account of Regine Schlegel's memoirs in this chapter.

3. From Eiler Nystrøm, *Biografiske Efterretninger om Peter Munthe Bruns og Ane Munchs Slægt paa Fædrene og Mødrene Side*, pp. 34–35.

Peter Munthe Brun: see the note to the entry by Brun in chapter 1 of this book.

4. From Henriette Lund's account of Kierkegaard's engagement, *Mit Forhold til hende* [My Relationship to Her], (Copenhagen: Gyldendal, 1904), pp. 17–20, 22–23, 66–69, 69–70, 97–99, and 128. She was about eleven years old during the period of Kierkegaard's engagement. As an eyewitness Henriette Lund would not have been able to report much. Her much later portrayal of the engagement rests for the most part on information in Kierkegaard's *Posthumous Papers*, and here and there on a few valuable pieces of information from Regine Olsen Schlegel herself, which is the reason for the inclusion of the present selections. A word is in order concerning the provenance of this account and Henriette Lund's custodianship of the Kierkegaard manuscripts on which it is based. According to the account she gives in the foreword of *Mit Forhold til hende*, Henriette Lund had been approached at least as early as 1893 by Regine Schlegel, who asked that after her death, Henriette Lund take custody of the Kierkegaard papers in Regine Schlegel's possession. Regine Schlegel subsequently decided to surrender the papers earlier, however, and in the autumn of 1895 she gave the papers to Henriette Lund, who quickly set to work to produce the commented set of excerpts, which was finally entitled *Mit Forhold til hende* and which she read aloud to Regine Schlegel in the autumn of 1896. But the matter did not rest there. Although Henriette Lund had already decided that the papers would eventually be turned over to the University of Copenhagen Library, two years later both women met and, apparently at Regine Schlegel's insistence, agreed to deliver the papers to the library immediately, as is clear from a letter from Henriette Lund to Regine Schlegel, dated November 1, 1898 (in **KBHA** [**SKA** D. Pk. 4]). This development seems to have caused Henriette Lund some concern: she had invested a great deal in her presentation of the documents depicting Kierkegaard's relationship to Regine Olsen, and she seems not to have been pleased at the prospect of competing interpretations. Thus Henriette Lund induced Regine Schlegel to agree to several conditions attaching to the deposition of the papers in the University Library. Henriette Lund's above-mentioned letter lists the conditions and the reasons motivating them as follows:

> Since everything [i.e., the Kierkegaardian letters and papers in question] had already been given to me "as my rightful property," as the expression goes, it will not surprise you if I now remind you of the promises you made when we parted earlier today: 1) that you yourself will remove none of the materials upon which I have in good faith based my presentation; and 2) that the package will be sealed in your presence for preservation in the Library. As number 3, I would like to ask if you would agree to add the condition that the package remain unopened for the first ten years after your death? That is what I had intended, and I have very much wished that it could be arranged in this fashion. *After all, everything about which people might want to know is set forth in my presentation.* But even though I carefully and conscientiously adhered to the truth, a certain caution was nonetheless necessary. I am not delighted at the thought that everyone—thus also including the crudest hands—could get hold of his posthumous papers so quickly and perhaps distort them *from the very beginning* [emphasis in original].

Thus from whatever motive, Henriette Lund appears to have had a strong interest in seeing her version of Kierkegaard prevail. Further, as is clear from an undated (apparently spring 1904) letter from Henriette to her half-brother Troels-Lund, the latter also participated in the preparation of the "Lund" account; he helped write and rewrite the draft of Henriette's foreword and gave the volume the title it bears (Henriette Lund's letter to Troels-Lund and the accompanying draft are in **KBHA** (**NkS** 3883, 4°). Nonetheless, despite the fact that Henriette Lund's account appeared shortly following Regine Schlegel's death in 1904, it is clear that Regine did not acquiesce in the third of the conditions set forth in Henriette's letter of November 1, 1898. With the assistance of

Raphael Meyer (see his entry earlier in this chapter) Regine Schlegel made certain that the documents on which Henriette Lund's account was based would in fact be made public shortly after her death, more or less simultaneously with Henriette Lund's volume—both volumes were published in 1904—which thus failed to gain monopoly status.

[Anna] Henriette Lund (1829–1909), was Søren Kierkegaard's niece; see the note accompanying the entry by Henriette Lund in chapter 9. **Trip to Jutland**: Kierkegaard's travels to Sædding, his father's native village, lasted from July 19 to August 6, 1840 (see *Pap*. III A 14–84 [most of this is available in *SKJP* 5437–76, 880–82, 3282, 38–39, 1026–27, 1321–23, 3382, 2178, 1589–90, 1099–1100, 1983, 1721, 1240, 1722, 2387, 2276, 2796, 2829–30, 2585]). For more information on Kierkegaard's trip to Jutland, see Arthur Dahl, *Søren Kierkegaard's Pilgrimage to Jutland* (Copenhagen: Danish Tourist Association, 1948). **The councillor** refers to Regine's father, Terkild Olsen, who bore the title of councillor of state [*Etatsraad*]. **The festive procession**: see also Henriette Lund's other account of this same procession in her entry in chapter 9 of this book.

5. In his notes on Kierkegaard's will, Niels Thulstrup makes the assumption (*B&A* II 14) that the document was probably written in 1849 at the same time that he wrote the various drafts of the letters he contemplated sending to Regine and Frederik Schlegel (*B&A* I 253–64 [*KW* XXV 322–37]). Kierkegaard's will is in **KBHA (SKA** D. Pk. 3). It has been previously published in *B&A* I 25 (*KW* XXV 33) and in Raphael Meyer, ed., *Kierkegaardske Papirer, Forlovelsen. Udgivne for Fru Regine Schlegel*, p. 139. Another English translation is also available in T. H. Croxall, ed. and trans., *Glimpses and Impressions of Kierkegaard* (Digswell Place: James Nisbet, 1959), p. 130). The letter from Schlegel to Peter Christian Kierkegaard is in **KBHA (SKA** D. Pk. 3), and the other two letters are also in **KBHA (SKA** D. Pk. 4), from which the present translations have been made. The three letters have been published in Raphael Meyer, ed., *Kierkegaardske Papirer, Forlovelsen. Udgivne for Fru Regine Schlegel*, pp. 140–47, and were subsequently reprinted in Thulstrup, ed., *B&A* II 14–18. Portions of these letters exist in another English translation in T. H. Croxall, *Glimpses and Impressions of Kierkegaard*, pp. 131–34.

After his death, Søren Kierkegaard's will was found among his papers by his brother Peter Christian Kierkegaard. After reading the will, Peter Christian wrote the Schlegels in St. Croix in the Danish West Indies, where Frederik Schlegel was governor. Peter Christian Kierkegaard's letter to the Schlegels has not been found. The three letters reprinted in this volume—one of them incomplete—are all the correspondence known to exist regarding this matter. The first is a reply by Frederik Schlegel to Peter Christian Kierkegaard, and the latter two are addressed from Regine Schlegel to Søren Kierkegaard's nephew, the physician **Henrik** Sigvard Lund (1825–89)—the same Henrik Lund who gave an illegal speech at Kierkegaard's burial—see chapter 8 in this book. **St. Jean** and **Søllerød**: we know from Troels-Lund's memoirs *Et Liv. Barndom og Ungdom* [A Life: Childhood and Youth] (Copenhagen: H. Hagerups Forlag, 1924), p. 241, that not long after Kierkegaard's death, Henrik Lund, deeply distressed, tried to commit suicide and was nursed back to health by his father, who bought him a house in Søllerød, a suburb north of Copenhagen, after which he made a trip to the Danish West Indies, but apparently did not visit St. Jean, where Regine Schlegel was then living.

6. From Georg Brandes, *Levned* [Life], vol. 1 (Copenhagen and Kristiania: Gyldendal, 1905) p. 207.

Georg Brandes (1842–1927), major intellectual figure and literary critic. The place mentioned in the text as being in **Nørrebro** was number 8 Nørrebrogade, the home of Frederik Schlegel and his wife Regine. Brandes provides a little glimpse of the aging Schlegel couple during one of their evening receptions, when they held open house for friends and acquaintances.

7. From Julius Clausen's memoirs, *Mennesker paa min Vej. Minder fra de unge Dage* [People on My Way: Memories from My Youth] (Copenhagen: Gyldendal, 1941), pp. 86–89.

Julius Clausen (1868–1950), librarian and author. After the death of her husband on June 8, 1896, Mrs. Regine Schlegel decided to sell her husband's large collection of books at auction. When Clausen says that Mrs. Schlegel had become a widow "about a year ago" his memory is mistaken. Frederik Schlegel died June 8, 1896, and the auction was held in October 1896. Clausen assisted her in preparing a catalog. The catalog was published (printed by Græbe under the title *Fortegnelse over afd. Gehejmekonferensraad J. F. Schlegels efterladte Bogsamling bestaaende af c. 7,000 Bind* [Catalog of the Book Collection Left by Privy Councillor J. F. Schlegel, Consisting of ca. 7,000 Volumes] (1896). It was an all-around collection of books from the humanities—history, biography, geography, etc. Only a few books by Kierkegaard were among them, including six or seven of the best-known works, but not the *Posthumous Papers*. After her husband's death, Mrs. Schlegel moved to Alhambravej 10 in Frederiksberg. **The Rørdam family**: see the notes accompanying the entry by Peter Bojsen in chapter 2 of this book and Hanne Mourier's account of Regine Schlegel's memoirs earlier in this chapter. **How good it had been for her to be "out there" in the years of Kierkegaard's crisis, 1854–55**: Clausen is in error here, for the Schlegels did not travel to the West Indies until March 1855, by which time Kierkegaard's attack had already been under way for several months; see the accounts by Raphael Meyer and Henriette Lund earlier in this chapter. **His will**: see above in this chapter and *B&A* I 25 (*KW* XXV 33).

8. From Robert Neiiendam's memoirs, *Robert Neiiendam fortæller* [Robert Neiiendam Speaks] (Copenhagen: Branner og Korch, 1953), pp. 48–49, which contain a short summary of Neiiendam's conversations with Regine Schlegel.

Robert Neiiendam (1880–1966), theater historian, museum director, and actor. As a young man, Neiiendam was for three years (1895–98) an apprentice of the bookseller and publisher Albert Sørensen at Gammel Kongevej 125, not far from Alhambravej in Frederiksberg, where Regine Schlegel had moved after her husband's death. During her visits to this nearby bookshop she made the acquaintance of young Neiiendam, and this led to conversations and walks, in the course of which he learned a great deal about her relationship with Kierkegaard. **One evening, when they sat in the theater, he got up after the overture and said, "Now we are leaving"**: see earlier in this chapter for Julius Clausen's account of this same story, in which he reports that Regine Schlegel told a different version. **That he took her with him into history**: cf. e.g., *B&A* I 258 (*KW* XXV 329); *Pap.* X² A 3 p. 6 (*SKJP* 6488), and especially X⁵ A 150:4 (*SKJP* 6473: 4): "I am taking her with me into history."

Chapter Four
The Young Writer (ca. 1840–45)

1. From p. 43 of Elise Lindberg's unpublished manuscript entitled *Oplevelser nedskrevne af Elise Lindberg 1899 Kolding* [Experiences: Written Down by Elise Lindberg, 1899, in Kolding], **RA** (Privatarkiv no. 5887, kasse 3, C, nr. 5).

Elise [Christiane] Lindberg (1832–1913) was the daughter of the very well known Pastor Jacob Christian Lindberg (1797–1857); see the notes accompanying the entries by Peter Christian Kierkegaard in chapter 9 of this book for further information on Jacob Christian Lindberg. The farewell party mentioned was in honor of Pastor **Peter Rørdam** in the late summer of 1841 on the occasion of his appointment as pastor in Mern; concerning Peter Rørdam, see the note accompanying the entry by Peter Bojsen in chapter 2 of this book. The party took place in the Lindberg home at number 5 Allégade in the Copenhagen suburb of Frederiksberg. **Christensen** is the theologian P[eter] V[ilhelm] Christensen (1819–63), who was at the time a private tutor for Jacob Christian Lindberg's children.

2. From Holger Frederik Rørdam, *En gammel Præsteslægts Historie* [The History of an Old Clerical Family], vol. 2 (Copenhagen: G.E.C. Gad, 1878), pp. 63–64 and 64n.

Holger Frederik Rørdam (1830–1913), church historian and pastor. **My grandmother, Catrine Rørdam**: for the Rørdam family and their home in Frederiksberg, see the note accompanying the entry by P. Bojsen in chapter 2, the entry by Elise Lindberg in this chapter, as well as the first entry (with the accompanying note) by Meïr Goldschmidt in chapter 5 of this book.

Peter R.: Peter Rørdam; see the notes accompanying entries by him and by P. Bojsen in chapter 2 of this book. In his biography and edition of the collected correspondence of his uncle Peter Rørdam (*Peter Rørdam. Blade af hans Levnedsbog og Brevvexling fra 1806 til 1844*, pp. 208–9), H. F. Rørdam gives a brief summary of Peter Rørdam's relationship to Søren Kierkegaard:

> Among those with whom he [Peter Rørdam] associated was *Søren Kierkegaard*, who frequently accompanied him out to his mother's home in Frederiksberg. With his lively talk and his uncommon talent for debating intellectual problems, he was a very stimulating element in the family circle. Of course he and P. Rørdam were in many respects complete opposites, but it is reasonable to assume that the latter's open and immediate nature was a good object for Kierkegaard's experimental psychological studies. Finally, however, the relationship between them was abruptly terminated. The occasion for this was that while on a walk with R., S.K. spoke of Grundtvig in mocking tones. This touched P.R. in his most sensitive spot, because he loved Grundtvig as his greatest benefactor. Instantly, the vehemence of his passion flared up against the mocker, so that the latter shrank back in fear. The relationship between them was ruptured and was never subsequently reestablished.

He became pastor in Mern: see the note accompanying the entry by Elise Lindberg earlier in this chapter. **Sibbern**: see the note accompanying the comments on Kierkegaard's dissertation in chapter 2 of this book. **Goldschmidt**: Meïr Goldschmidt (1819–87), author and journalist; see chapter 5 of this book. **Fr. Barfod**: [Povl] Frederik Barfod (1811–96), a "Scandinavianist" historian and politician who was a follower of Grundtvig; coincidentally he was also the uncle of H. P. Barfod, the first editor of Kierkegaard's *Posthumous Papers*.

3. From A. D. Jørgensen's diary as published in "A. D. Jørgensens Dagbog Gammelt og Nyt for Aarene 1884–96" [A. D. Jørgensen's Diary "Old and New," for the Years 1884–96], Troels G. Jørgensen, ed., *Danske Magazin, indeholdende bidrag til den danske histories oplysning*, 7. Række, Femte Bind, Udgivet af det kongelige danske selskab for fædrelandets historie (Copenhagen: Rosenkilde og Bagger, 1949–53), p. 26.

A[dolph] D[etlef] Jørgensen (1840–97) historian and archivist at the National Archives. **Giödvad**: Jens Finsen Giødvad (or Gjødwad or Gjødvad) (1811–91) was editorial secretary and administrator of *Fædrelandet*. **Either/Or**: according to Alastair McKinnon and Niels Jørgen Cappelørn, "The Period of Composition of Kierkegaard's Published Works" in *Kierkegaardiana* IX (1974), p. 138, *Either/Or* was published on February 20, 1843.

4. From Hother Ploug's biography of his father, *Carl Ploug. Hans Liv og Gerning* [Carl Ploug, His Life and Work], vol. 1 (1813–48) (Copenhagen: Gyldendal, 1905), pp. 110f.

Hother Ploug (1856–1932), author, civil servant, and son of the nineteenth-century nationalist poet **Carl Ploug** (1813–84), who was also the well-known editor of the National Liberal newspaper *Fædrelandet*. In the 1840s the editorial offices of that newspaper were at number 35 Købmagergade, next to the post office. **Gjødwad**: see the note accompanying the entry by A. D. Jørgensen earlier in this chapter. **Carl Weis** (1809–72), and his brother **Ernst Weis** (1807–73) were jurists and intellectuals who were especially noted for their love of music. **Christian Winther** (1796–1876) was one of the most popular and respected poets of the Danish Golden Age. Kierkegaard wrote several journal entries about *Fædrelandet*, e.g., *Pap.* X³ A 88–90 (*SKJP* 6619–21), and he published quite a number of articles in that newspaper, including the first portion of his attack on the Church; see the note accompanying the entry by Henrik Hertz in chapter 10 of this book for more information on Kierkegaard's *Fædrelandet* articles.

5. From a letter by Henriette Wulff to Hans Christian Andersen, dated February 20, 1843; the original letter is in **KBHA** (Den collinske Brevsamling, XII, fasc. 14, nr. 202), and it has been published in *H. C. Andersen og Henriette Wulff. En Brevvexling* [Correspondence of Hans Christian Andersen and Henriette Wulff], ed. H. Topsøe-Jensen, *I. Indledning. Breve 1826–48* [I: Introduction. Letters 1826–48] (Odense: Flensteds Forlag, 1959), pp. 315–16.

[Hanna] Henriette [Frideriche] Wulff (1804–58): friend and admirer of Hans Christian Andersen, known for her correspondence with him.

6. From a letter from Signe Læssøe to Hans Christian Andersen, dated April 7, 1843; it has been published in *Breve til Hans Christian Andersen* [Letters to Hans Christian Andersen], ed. C. St. A. Bille and Nikolaj Bøgh (Copenhagen: C. A. Reitzels Forlag, 1877), pp. 466–67.

[Margrethe Juliane] Signe [Abrahamson] Læssøe (1781–1870), was Hans Christian Andersen's friend and informal literary advisor. **"There is no bliss except in despair; hurry up and despair, you will find no happiness until you do"**; **"One's happiness can only consist in choosing oneself,"** and **"Happy the man who dies; happier still the child who dies; happiest of all he who is never born"** are all paraphrases of well-known passages from *Either/ Or*; cf. *SV* II 189, 193, and *SV* I 195 [*KW* IV 211, 215, and *KW* III 221]. **Heiberg wrote a glowing review in the *Intelligensblade*** [Intelligenser]: Heiberg's review "Litterær Vinter-Sæd" [Literary Winter Seed] appeared in his *Intelligensblade*, no. 24 (March 1, 1843), pp. 285–92.

7. From a letter from Hans Christian Andersen, then in Paris, to Signe Læssøe, dated April 21, 1843. The original letter is in **RA** (Niels Frederik Læssøe og Signe Læssøes Privatarkiv, privatarkivnr. 5917, A. II); it has been published in Poul Høybye, "Om Søren Kierkegaard i H. C. Andersens Correspondence" [On Søren Kierkegaard in Hans Christian Andersen's Correspondence] in *Meddelelser fra Søren Kierkegaard Selskabet* [Communications from the Søren Kierkegaard Society], third year, no. 1 (March 1951) (Copenhagen: Ejnar Munksgaard, 1951), p. 86.

8. From the letters of Caspar Wilhelm Smith, which are in the State Library, Århus, Denmark (Håndskrift nr. 842, C. W. Smiths Arkiv); they have been published, with minor variants, in "Filologen Caspar Wilhelm Smiths Rejsebreve 1841–1845" [Correspondence of the Philologist Caspar Wilhelm Smith from his Travels, 1841–45], ed. H. D. Schepelern, *Danske Magazin, indeholdende bidrag til den danske histories oplysning*, 7. Række, Femte Bind, Udgivet af det kongelige danske selskab for fædrelandets historie (Copenhagen: Rosenkilde og Bagger, 1949–53), pp. 81– 172.

Caspar Wilhelm Smith (1811–81): scholar of Slavic languages. **Johannes Fibiger** (1821–97): pastor and writer, Smith's half-brother by his mother's second marriage. **Spargnapani** (or Sparganapani): owner of a fashionable coffee shop in Berlin. In a letter from Berlin to P. J. Spang, dated November 18, 1841, Kierkegaard calls Sparganapani's "my coffee shop, the best I have found in Berlin, a coffee shop which has better coffee than one gets in Copenhagen, more newspapers, excellent service. As long as he [Sparganapani] is here in Berlin, I will never suffer from homesickness" (*B&A* I 77 [*KW* XXV 97]). Smith's accuracy in this detail lends credibility to the rest of his report. **His monster of a book on Socrates**: Kierkegaard's dissertation, *On the Concept of Irony, with Constant Reference to Socrates* (*SV* XIII 93–393 [*KW* II 1–329]). **Christian [Emanuel August] Fibiger** (1819–73): a physician, was Smith's half-brother by his mother's second marriage.

9. From the entry for September 1, 1843, in C. J. Brandt's unpublished "Dagbøger (1835–55)" [Diaries: 1835–55], which are the property of Anders Monrad Møller, who has generously given permission for their use.

C[arl] J[oachim] Brandt (1817–89) was a pastor and a historian of Danish literature. Brandt was an important supporter of Grundtvig; he was an editor of the principal organ of the Grundtvigian movement, *Dansk Kirketidende* [Danish Church Times], and ended his career by succeeding Grundtvig as pastor of Vartov Church in Copenhagen. Kierkegaard apparently knew Brandt reasonably well: see Henriette Lund's entry in chapter 3 of this book for a reference to Kierkegaard and Brandt in the autumn of 1841. Kierkegaard subscribed to the *Dansk Kirketidende*, and the auction catalog of his library shows that he owned Brandt's study of Danish hymnology. **Rudelbach's volume of Christian consolation**: undoubtedly Andreas Gottlob Rudelbach's anthology *Christelig Trøstebog, samlet af Kirkens Fædres og fromme Bekjenderes Skrifter* [Book of Christian Consolation, Collected from the Writings of the Church Fathers and the Pious Confessors] (1827). For A. G. Rudelbach, see the note to the entry by Christiane and Juliane Rudelbach in chapter 1 of this book.

10. From Frederik Benedikt Møller, *En gammel Præst fortæller. Pastor Frederik Benedikt Møllers Optegnelser 1832–1864 ved Hans Degen* [An Old Pastor Speaks: Pastor Frederik Benedikt Møller's Journal Entries, 1832–64, with Hans Degen] (Copenhagen: Haase, 1953), pp. 54–55.

Frederik Benedikt Møller (1832–1914) was a pastor in a number of places, ending his career in a parish on the island of Funen. Møller's comments concerning stories told about Kierkegaard in the period following the breakoff of his engagement (1841) and the publication of *Either/Or* (1843) are of specific interest because they demonstrate the extent to which Kierkegaard was the object of remarkable gossip.

11. From a letter from Hans Brøchner to H. P. Barfod, dated November 10, 1871. Barfod published it in *SKEP 1844–46* pp. 329f., and it is currently in **KBHA** (**SKA** D. Pk. 5). Brøchner again discusses the incident mentioned in this letter in his recollections about Kierkegaard; see entry number 23 in chapter 11 of this book. Kierkegaard mentions this incident in *Pap.* VII^1 A 154 (*SKJP* 5940) and VIII^1 A 654 (*SKJP* 6089).

Hans Brøchner (1820–75): philosopher. In 1857 he became a lecturer and in 1860 a professor at the University of Copenhagen. He was distantly related to Søren Kierkegaard, in that his mother's sister was married to Michael Andersen Kierkegaard (1776–1867), a very well-to-do silk and clothing merchant in Copenhagen, who was thus Brøchner's uncle by marriage. Søren Kierkegaard's father Michael Pedersen Kierkegaard (1756–1838) was a hosier in Copenhagen, and *his* father was the brother of the father of the above-mentioned Michael Andersen Kierkegaard. Thus Michael Andersen Kierkegaard and Michael Pedersen Kierkegaard were first cousins. The relationship between Søren Kierkegaard and Hans Brøchner was therefore as follows: Søren Kierkegaard was the son of the one cousin, while Hans Brøchner was the nephew of the other cousin, and they were thus at most very distant cousins and not blood relations at all. **Kirk**, i.e., not "Kierkegaard." After the first two performances of *Gjenboerne*, which took place on February 20 and March 9, 1844, the author, C. [Jens Christian] Hostrup (1818–92, playwright and pastor) subsequently changed the name of the character to "Søren Torp." Kierkegaard was not the only one offended by Hostrup's caricature. When Hostrup's next "student comedy," *Spurv i Tranedands* [A Sparrow among Hawks], also featured a Kierkegaard-like figure who bore the first name "Søren," the well-known poet B. S. Ingemann (see the note accompanying the entry by Vilhelm Birkedal, later in this chapter) wrote his younger friend Hostrup on December 14, 1847, admonishing him,

> I saw your *Spurv i Tranedands*, which was presented here by our students. Something was lacking, however, something which would undoubtedly have been of great importance for an understanding of your views about the relation of the bright and breezy intellectual life of university students to the various intellectual currents of our times. Throughout the entire piece, you employ real humor and merriment in dealing with the extremist and caricaturist tendencies of these currents. I saw clearly that you let your students appreciate the fact that there is something in life and in these times which is not merely an object of ridicule. But there was something missing, or I felt the absence of something important. The Aristophanean presentation of well-known personalities (namely Søren K.) conflicts with my principle of poetic freedom, and I believe that what you gain in immediate effect is offset by a loss in the higher artistic sphere. All my complaints on this score would disappear if you would simply omit allusions to names and to the accidental externalities of personal peculiarities. [From *Breve fra og til C. Hostrup* (Letters from and to C. Hostrup), ed. Elisabeth Hostrup (Copenhagen: Gyldendal, 1897), pp. 105–6]

In May 1871 Hostrup wrote H. P. Barfod, insisting that he had never intended to caricature Søren Kierkegaard himself:

> *Gjenboerne* was performed for the first time in the Student Union, February 20, 1844, and "Søren Torp," who was played by Mr. Brøchner (now a professor), once had the name "Søren Kirk" on the playbill. On the other hand, when the piece was performed at the Royal Theater for the first time, he was called Søren Torp, and the role was played by Mr. Pätges, actor at the Royal Theater. I do not need to tell you that I had never thought of this figure as anything other than a young university student who had been overwhelmed by

Kierkegaard, an imitator like Hutter [a character in the play, a law student who aped the fashionable liberal politicians of the day], and I chose the name, which was similar to the name of Ole Kirk, who was then an assembly representative, in order to make my point easily understood. Later, however, when I became afraid of being misunderstood to the effect that I had wanted to make fun of Kierkegaard himself, I changed the name, which had only been appropriate for a private performance. [From a letter from Hostrup to H. P. Barfod, dated May 22, 1871, in **KBHA** (**SKA** D. Pk. 5); published in part and with errors in *SKEP 1844–46* 329]

A few weeks later, in another letter to Barfod, Hostrup again explained that "it is obvious that with Søren Torp (or Kirk) I had in mind nothing more than a young university student who spoke Kierkegaardian, just as a bit earlier the language of the student world had been Hegelian" [letter from Hostrup to H. P. Barfod, dated June 12, 1871, in **KBHA** (**SKA** D. Pk. 5); published in part and with errors in *SKEP 1844–46* 329].

Even twenty years later, in 1891, this was still a sensitive subject for Hostrup, who discusses it in his memoirs:

[A] famous author became very angry about *Gjenboerne*, something which I learned only many years later. This was Søren Kierkegaard, and I have also heard that several of his closest admirers were quite annoyed with me because of Søren Kirk or *Torp*, as he was later called. I find this very unreasonable and will explain why. I needed several supporting characters for the general meeting at Regensen [a university residence], and I chose one from each of the three major faculties: one from medicine, one from law, and one from theology. I had noticed that young medical students had a tendency to notice in themselves all the disease symptoms about which they had read or heard, and that they therefore went through a phase when they were very preoccupied with their own health; this was the origin of [the character] Klemme. During that period lawyers were of course the most powerful political speakers, and I thus came up with Hutter. But what was I to do with my theologian? At that point the rage for Hegel was over, and, in addition, [Carl] Ploug had dealt with it humorously in *Kontubernalene* [The Roommates]. So I thought of the latest thing—of Kierkegaard and his many books from the previous year, which had aroused extraordinary interest—and my theologian was thus a young student who was carried away with the style of the first part of *Either/Or*. This was absolutely not a case of any genuine appropriation [of Kierkegaard's ideas]: my *Søren Kirk* (which is what I had originally called him in order to put the public on the right track) is a parrot and a yes-man, just like those who have parroted Grundtvig, [Bjørnstjerne] Bjørnson, and, most recently, J. P. Jacobsen. But to say that I attacked Søren Kierkegaard's books in my *Gjenboerne* is just as foolish as to claim that it was he himself whom I put on the stage as a garrulous young student at Regensen. . . .

[I] once came to exchange words with Søren Kierkegaard. One day when I was walking on the street with [Emil] Boesen, who was Kierkegaard's personal friend, I was introduced to him by Boesen. The strange thing about this meeting was that he proved to be extremely friendly toward me, despite the fact that—according to his journals—he was extremely embittered about *Gjenboerne*. I looked at this strange man with the greatest of interest, and both before and since I have been deeply moved by several of his books, but especially by his *Practice in Christianity* from 1850. [From C. Hostrup, *Erindringer fra min Barndom og Ungdom* (Memories of My Childhood and Youth) (Copenhagen: Gyldendal, 1891), pp. 142–43 and 155–56]

12. From Julie Weber Sødring, *Erindringer fra min Barndom og Ungdom* [Memories from My Childhood and Youth], vol. 1. (Copenhagen: Gyldendal, 1894), p. 138.

Julie Weber Sødring (1823–94): actress and daughter of the actor Christen Niemann Rosenkilde (1786–1861). **One day**: in the fall of 1844, when Sødring was twenty-one years old.

13. From Carit Etlar, *Carit Etlars Minder fortalte af ham selv. I biografisk Ramme af hans Hustru*

[Carit Etlar's Reminiscences as Told by Himself. Placed in a Biographical Framework by His Wife] (Copenhagen: Nordisk Forlag, 1896), pp. 92–93. ("His Wife" refers to Brosbøll's second wife, Augusta Carit Etlar, as she called herself.)

[Johan] **Carl Brosbøll** is the real name of the pseudonymous author Carit Etlar (1816–1900); see also the note for the entry by Anna Brosbøll in chapter 6 of this book. For a time during his youth, Brosbøll was part of a circle of friends centering around P. L. Møller, Poul Chievitz, Meïr Goldschmidt, et al. In the mid-1840s, the young author Carl Brosbøll lived at number 24 Kloster-stræde, where the conversation here recorded must have taken place. The conversation can be dated as having taken place on December 6, 1844, because it includes an allusion to the premiere of Brosbøll's play *Eiaghs Sønner* [The Sons of Eiagh], which took place the following day. (This allusion is not included here.) Brosbøll's verse, which is cited here, was published in the 1846 issue of *Gæa*, p. 91. (In Etlar/Brosbøll's book of memoirs, cited here, the verse is reproduced with slight inaccuracies.) Goldschmidt lived at number 32 Købmagergade in 1846, but not in 1844, and Kierkegaard lived on Nørregade from 1840 to 1844, and again in 1850–51 but not in 1846. As can be seen, Brosbøll has bungled the chronology a bit.

14. From W. I. Karup, *Mit Livs Roman* [The Novel of My Life] (Copenhagen: Cohens Bog-trykkeri, 1864) pp. 22–24.

W[ilhelm] I[gnatius] Karup (1829–70), writer, controversialist, and a convert to Roman Catholicism, emigrated to Germany in 1864. The incident described here probably took place in 1844 or 1845.

15. From Nanna Videbech, *Nanna Videbech født Wanscher: Minder fra min Barndom og Ungdom* [Nanna Videbech, *née* Wanscher: Memories of My Childhood and Youth] (Copenhagen: privately published, 1912), p. 33.

The country estate **"Dodecagon,"** which was north of Copenhagen on the Strand Road in Hellerup, was owned by **Agent Lund**, i.e., Kierkegaard's brother-in-law, the businessman Johan Christian Lund (1799–1875), who had been married to Kierkegaard's sister Nicoline Christine (1799–1832). Among Lund's circle of friends were the paper merchant Wilhelm Wanscher (1802–82) and his wife, Johanne Juliane Wegener Wanscher; in the winter of 1845 they bought the nearby country place referred to in this passage. Wanscher's daughter was **Nanna [Wanscher] Videbech** (1838–1915). **His other sister** refers to Kierkegaard's sister Petrea Severine (1801–34), who had been married to Johan Christian Lund's brother, National Bank director [Henrik] **Ferdinand** Lund (1803–75). The phrase "his other sister" must be understood as meaning "his other *surviving* sister"; there had been a third, and eldest, sister, Maren Kirstine Kierkegaard (1797–1822) who had died unmarried.

16. From Vilhelm Birkedal, *Personlige Oplevelser i et langt Liv*, vol. 2 (Copenhagen: Karl Schønbergs Forlag, 1890), p. 67.

Vilhelm Birkedal: see the note accompanying the entry by Birkedal in chapter 2 of this book. **Sorø** was the site of Sorø Academy, a royally supported institution of higher learning in central Zealand, which was a focal point of much intellectual and artistic life from the 1820s until it closed in 1849. **Ingemann**: Bernard Severin Ingemann (1789–1862), a poet and author, was a friend of many of the period's writers, particularly Grundtvig and Hauch, and was known principally for his hymns and historical romances; in the 1840s Ingemann was director of Sorø Academy. **Hauch**: [Johannes] Carsten Hauch (1790–1872), poet, novelist, and playwright. **Wilster**: Christian [Frederik] Wilster (1797–1840), minor poet and literary critic. **Hjort**: Peter Hjort (1793–1871), literary critic.

17. From a letter from J. A. Ostermann to H. P. Barfod, dated April 25, 1868, now in **KBHA** (**SKA** D. Pk. 5); portions of the letter have been published in Valdemar Ammundsen, *Søren Kierkegaards Ungdom. Hans Slægt og hans religiøse Udvikling* [Søren Kierkegaard's Youth: His Family and His Religious Development] (Copenhagen: Universitetsbogtrykkeriet, 1912), pp. 109–10.

Johannes A. Ostermann (1809–88): see the note accompanying Ostermann's entry in chapter 2 of this book. The **lakes** were parts of the defensive works around Copenhagen, in Kierkegaard's time on the outskirts of the city. For **Gjødvad**, see the note to the entry by A. D. Jørgensen earlier in this chapter. **[Israel] Levin** (1810–83): linguist, lexicographer, and man of letters, was Kierkegaard's personal secretary for a number of years; see the entry by Levin in chapter 10 of this book. **My letter of last year**: see Ostermann's letter to H. P. Barfod, dated May 28, 1867, in chapter 2 of this book. **The bishop** refers to Søren Kierkegaard's brother, Bishop Peter Christian Kierkegaard, who along with Ostermann had been a member of the **Rigsdag**, or Parliament, of Denmark, which had been established as a result of the constitutional changes of 1848 and 1849. **[Meïr Aron] Goldschmidt** (1819–97), author and journalist; see chapter 5 in this book. For a short period, Goldschmidt was imprisoned on bread and water, a common punishment for censorship violations.

Chapter Five
Goldschmidt and the *Corsair* Affair

1. From a letter of early February 1846 from Henriette Collin to Hans Christian Andersen. The date of the letter is in dispute. The actual letter is undated. The editors of the published correspondence between Andersen and the Collins date the letter as February 2, 1846, while the Manuscript Department of the Royal Library dates it February 6, 1846. The manuscript is damaged and is here presented in the form in which it has been reconstructed by the editors of the published version. The original letter is in **KBHA** (Den collinske Brevsamling, XIII, fasc. 3, nr. 42), and it has been published in *H. C. Andersens Brevveksling med Edvard og Henriette Collin* [Hans Christian Andersen's Correspondence with Edvard and Henriette Collin], ed. C. Behrend and H. Topsøe-Jensen, vol. 2 (1844–60) (Copenhagen: Levin og Munksgaards Forlag, 1934), pp. 59–60.

Henriette Collin: Henriette [Oline Thyberg] Collin (1813–94) was the wife of Edvard Collin (1806–86), a high official in the Ministry of Finance, a scholar and bibliophile of Danish literature; both husband and wife were lifelong friends of Hans Christian Andersen.

2. From a letter by V. Fohlmann to P. L. Møller, dated June 3, 1846; the original is in **KBHA** (Additamenta 697, 4⁰ [P. L. Møller Arkiv]).

V. Fohlmann: most probably August Vilhelm Fohlmann (ca. 1813–70) who matriculated into the University of Copenhagen from the Metropolitan School in 1831 and subsequently became a physician; see **RA** (Københavns Universitet, 12.16.04 [Konsistorium, Studentermatrikel 1829–1901]) and P. M. Plum, ed., *Hundrede Aars Metropolitanere. Tillæg til Metropolitanskolen gennem 700 Aar* [One Hundred Years of Metropolitan School Graduates: Supplement to Seven Centuries of the Metropolitan School] (Copenhagen: Gyldendal, 1916), p. 114 . Fohlmann's letter is addressed to **P[eder] L[udvig] Møller** (1814–65), Danish writer, poet, and literary critic. Møller was for a time closely associated with Goldschmidt and *The Corsair*, particularly during that journal's attack on Kierkegaard. Møller had hoped for a professorship in aesthetics at the University of Copenhagen but failed to obtain this post, in part, perhaps, because of doubts about his character that had arisen during the *Corsair* dispute. Disappointed, he left Denmark in 1847, never to return. *KW* XIII contains a useful discussion of Møller in the introduction. An interesting novel based on Møller's life has been written by Henrik Stangerup, *Det er svært at dø i Dieppe* (Copenhagen: Gyldendal, 1985), published in English as *The Seducer: It Is Hard to Die in Dieppe*, trans. Sean Martin (London: Marion Boyars, 1990).

3. From Meïr Aron Goldschmidt, *Livs Erindringer og Resultater* [Memories and Results of My Life], vol. 1 (Copenhagen: Gyldendal, 1877), pp. 214–16 (cf. *KW* XIII 138).

Meïr Aron Goldschmidt (1819–87): author and journalist, editor of *Corsaren* [The Corsair] from October 1840 to October 1846, with whom Kierkegaard had a well-known collision in 1845–46. **Summer of 1837** is an error by Goldschmidt for 1838, because he refers to Kierkegaard's book *From the Papers of One Still Living*, which appeared in September 1838 (*SV* XIII 41–92 [*KW* I 53–102]). **P. Rørdam** is Peter Rørdam: see the note accompanying the entry by P. Bojsen in chapter 2, as well as the notes accompanying Hanne Mourier's account of Regine Schlegel's memoirs and Julius Clausen's entry, both in chapter 3 of this book. When Goldschmidt speaks of his time as an editor, he must mean the period from October 1837 to December 1838, when he edited *Næstved Ugeblad, eller Præstø Amts Tidende* [Næstved Weekly, or the Præstø County Times]. **People in the Lyngby area believed that he was in love with, or was quite taken with, a young lady (who later married one of his cousins)**: this may refer to Bolette Rørdam (1815–87), who was the daughter of the pastor Thomas Schatt Rørdam (1776–1831) and his widow, Mrs. Catrine Rørdam (1777–1842); she was thus the sister of Pastor Peter Rørdam. The Rørdams regularly held open house at their home in the Copenhagen suburb of Frederiksberg, which is where Kierkegaard reportedly met Regine Olsen for the first time. Henning Fenger (in *Kierkegaard-Myter og Kierkegaard-Kilder* [Kierkegaard Myths and Kierkegaard Sources] (Odense: Odense Universitetsforlag, 1976), pp. 123–28) argues that Bolette Rørdam, and not Regine Schlegel, was Kierkegaard's first love. Goldschmidt's testimony here would seem to support Fenger's position. There are counterarguments, e.g., in *KW* XXV 459, n. 2 to letter 47. (Most of Fenger's book has been published in English translation as *Kierkegaard: The Myths and Their Origins*, trans. George Schoolfield [New Haven: Yale University Press, 1980].) If Goldschmidt's informants were correct with respect to "the young lady's" subsequent marriage to "one of his [Kierkegaard's] cousins," there may have been a *third* young lady in Kierkegaard's life in the later 1830s. As Fenger points out (*Kierkegaard-Myter og Kierkegaard-Kilder*, p. 128) with respect to this possible third young lady, since neither Regine Olsen nor Bolette Rørdam later married a cousin of Kierkegaard, this unknown young woman (if she existed) would probably have had some connection to the Lyngby area, most likely because she was somehow associated with the parish of Lyngby Church, of which the pastor, Peter Diderik Ibsen (1793–1855), was a friend of Kierkegaard. Even as a child, Kierkegaard came on visits to Lyngby as a guest of the Agerskov family, to which he was distantly related. See also Johanne Sandfeld, *Træk af Lyngbys Historie* [Incidents in the History of Lyngby] (Copenhagen: Forlaget Zac, 1968), p. 37, where it is mentioned that among the linden trees in the parsonage garden, people still point out the tree under which Kierkegaard preferred to sit.

4. From Goldschmidt's memoirs, *Livs Erindringer og Resultater*, vol. 1, pp. 275–80; portions are available in another English translation in *KW* XIII 139–41.

At that time was the late summer or early autumn of 1841. The phrase **a review was sent to me** should be understood as meaning "I was sent the manuscript of a review" (to be published in *The Corsair*). This was the review of Kierkegaard's doctoral thesis. It appeared anonymously in *The Corsair* on October 22, 1841. It has been conjectured that this very jovial review was written by the writer P. L. Møller. (The little postscript appended to that review is Goldschmidt's, however.) **Madame Rørdam**: see the note accompanying the entry by P. Bojsen in chapter 2 of this book. In Goldschmidt's time, as in our own day, **Østergade** was a very fashionable street and the site of some of the finest clothing shops in town. Østergade, along with **Amagertorv** and **Vimmelskaftet** are now parts of "Strøget," Copenhagen's central walking street. **Købmagergade** runs through the center of the city of Copenhagen, where it meets "Strøget" at Højbro Plads (see map). **Pastor [Carl Holger] Visby** was pastor at the Church of Our Savior and was also pastor at the prison; see the note accompanying the entry by H. P. Holst in chapter 1 of this book. *Japhet in Search of a Father* is the title of a novel published in 1836 by Captain [Frederick] Marryat (1792–1848), English author of maritime adventure novels popular in Denmark.

5. From Goldschmidt's memoirs, *Livs Erindringer og Resultater*, vol. 1, p. 297; another English translation is available in *KW* XIII 141.

P. L. Møller: see the note to the letter by V. Fohlmann in this chapter.

6. From Goldschmidt's memoirs *Livs Erindringer og Resultater*, vol. 1, pp. 305–6; most of this selection is available in another English translation in *KW* XIII 141.

In *The Corsair* for February 2, 1843, Goldschmidt had published a piece written in the style of James Fenimore Cooper, which his friend P. L. Møller had praised as **comic composition**, which, as we have seen above, Kierkegaard had earlier proposed as Goldschmidt's *métier*.

7. From Goldschmidt's memoirs, *Livs Erindringer og Resultater*, vol. 1, pp. 318–20; portions of this material are available in another English translation in *KW* XIII 141–42.

S. Kierkegaard published *Either/Or*: the book was published on February 20, 1843.

8. From Goldschmidt's memoirs, *Livs Erindringer og Resultater*, vol. 1, pp. 323–24; another translation is available in *KW* XIII 142–43.

Goethe, who had cast aside Frederikke in Sesenheim: Frederikke Brion, a daughter of a pastor in Sesenheim, was an early love of Goethe's. **He was once supposed to have taken his fiancée to the theater to hear Mozart's *Don Giovanni***: see the conflicting accounts of this incident in chapter 3 of this book, where Robert Neiiendam reiterates the story as true, while Julius Clausen denies that this is the case, citing what he says is Regine Schlegel's version of the story.

9. From Goldschmidt's memoirs, *Livs Erindringer og Resultater*, vol. 1, pp. 371–73; another English translation is available in *KW* XIII 143–44.

The book refers to Goldschmidt's brilliant breakthrough novel *En Jøde* [A Jew] (Copenhagen: published by M. Goldschmidt, 1845), published pseudonymously in 1845 under the name Adolph Meyer. A recent English-language version of the novel is available in a translation by Kenneth H. Ober, *A Jew* (New York: Garland Press, 1990). **P. L. Møller**: see the note to the letter by V. Fohlmann in this chapter.

10. From Goldschmidt's memoirs, *Livs Erindringer og Resultater*, vol. 1, pp. 411–14; part of this selection is available in another English translation in *KW* XIII 144–45.

Sorø Academy: see the note accompanying the entry by Vilhelm Birkedal in chapter 4 of this book. P. L. Møller cultivated friendships among the intellectuals at Sorø, including the poet and novelist Carsten Hauch, who was a friend of Oehlenschläger. *Gæa*, i.e., *Gæa, æsthetisk Aarbog 1846, udg. af P. L. Møller* (Udgiverens Forlag, 1846) [Gæa: Aesthetic Almanac for 1846, ed. P. L. Møller. Published by the Author's Press] (Copenhagen: privately published, 1846 [actually published in December 1845]), in which Møller had published a long sketch (pp. 144–87) with the title "Et Besøg i Sorø" [A Visit to Sorø]. Møller's piece contained detailed accounts of supposed conversations from a little party held one evening, concerning among other things Kierkegaard's written work, so different from all other writing, as well as his peculiar style, his "experiments," etc. (A selection of this long piece is reprinted in *S. Kierkegaards Bladartikler med Bilag samlede efter Forfatterens Død, udgivne som Supplement til hans øvrige Skrifter* [S. Kierkegaard's Newspaper Articles, with an Appendix Collected after the Author's Death: Published as a Supplement to His Other Writings], ed. Rasmus Nielsen (Copenhagen: C. A. Reitzels, 1857), pp. 224–30, and appears in English translation in *KW* XIII, 96–104.) Kierkegaard assumed that *The Corsair* was principally edited by P. L. Møller, and the *Gæa* article led him to break with *The Corsair* and thus with Goldschmidt. He *demanded* to be abused by *The Corsair* (see *SV* XIII 433 [*KW* XIII 47]). The editors of *The Corsair* accepted the challenge, and in the first three months of 1846 appeared the many caricatures of Søren Kierkegaard that have subsequently become so well known and have been reproduced so often.

11. From Goldschmidt's memoirs, *Livs Erindringer og Resultater*, vol. 1, pp. 421–30; another English translation is available in *KW* XIII 145–50.

The entire book: *Gæa* for 1846. **"Min Onkels Tømmerplads"** [My Uncle's Lumberyard] was a short story by Goldschmidt published in *Gæa*, pp. 110–29, under the pseudonym "Adolph Meyer," the same transparent pseudonym he had used for his successful first novel *En Jøde* and for subsequent short stories. **Then he identified himself publicly as Victor Eremita, Frater Taciturnus, etc.**: Kierkegaard acknowledged these and other pseudonyms in "A First and Final Declaration," which was an appendix to *Concluding Unscientific Postscript*, published February 27, 1846 (see *SV* VII 545–49 [*KW* XII 625–30]). **Skamlingsbanke** was the site of large Danish nationalist gatherings in 1844 and 1845 during the controversy over Slesvig and Holstein. Goldschmidt had made a speech at the gathering of July 4, 1844, in which, responding to a challenge from the person he mentions here, he boldly referred to himself as a Jew who supported the Danish cause in southern Jutland, and called for Old Testament-style "eye-for-an-eye" revenge upon German nationalists.

12. From Goldschmidt's memoirs, *Livs Erindringer og Resultater*, vol. 1, pp. 433–36; another English translation is available in *KW* III 150–52.

At that time was in the autumn of 1847, after Goldschmidt's return from his trip. **Cited by Bishop Mynster**: in the first issue of his new journal *Nord og Syd* [North and South], vol. 1 (1848), pp. 12–13, Goldschmidt had lavish praise for the historical influence of Christianity. As Møller had predicted, in 1851 Bishop Mynster did in fact praise Goldschmidt in return, referring to him as "one of our most talented authors"; see "Yderligere Bidrag til Forhandlingerne om de kirkelige Forhold i Danmark" [Further Contributions to Negotiations on the Ecclesiastical Situation in Denmark] (1851), reprinted in Jakob Peter Mynster, *Blandede Skrivter* [Miscellaneous Writings], vol. 2 (Copenhagen: Gyldendal, 1853), p. 60. **A pact that we had made**: see entry number 5, earlier in this chapter.

13. The first passage is from a letter dated February 28, 1870; the second is from a letter dated March 9, 1870, both from Goldschmidt to H. P. Barfod, the editor of Kierkegaard's posthumous papers; and the third is from a letter by Barfod to Goldschmidt, dated May 18, 1872. The originals of these three letters are in **KBHA** (**SKA** D. Pk. 5). The fourth passage is from a letter dated March 18, 1878, to illustrator and engraver Frederik Hendriksen, who had formerly worked for Goldschmidt and subsequently worked for the writer and journalist Otto Borchsenius; the original is in **KBHA** (**NkS** 4659, 4⁰). The remaining passages are from Goldschmidt's letters dated March 25, April 22, and December 25, 1878, and January 8, 1879, to Borchsenius himself; the originals are in **KBHA** (**NkS** 4656, 4⁰, I). The letters from which passages 4 through 8 have been excerpted have been published in *Breve fra og til Meïr Goldschmidt* [Letters from and to Meïr Goldschmidt], ed. Morten Borup, vol. 2 (1853–85) (Copenhagen: Rosenkilde og Bagger, 1963), pp. 207, 208–10, 211–12, 218–19, and 224–25.

The phrases **stinging bitterness** and **the challenge to Goldschmidt** are in Barfod's introductory notes, **p. xiii** of *SKEP 1833–43*. **Prof. Rasmus Nielsen** (1809–84): professor of philosophy at the University of Copenhagen. For a time Kierkegaard entertained the notion that Nielsen might be his disciple and popularizer, but he subsequently abandoned the idea, while Nielsen did not. See also entry number 21, with its accompanying note, in Brøchner's memoirs in chapter 11 of this book. *Nefas*: a Latin term for an act of impiety. **Your words**: it seems clear that before Goldschmidt wrote the second letter he had received Barfod's reply to his first letter, but this reply has not been found in the Manuscript Department of the Royal Library. **S. Kierkegaard's papers**: Barfod is alluding to the second volume of Kierkegaard's posthumous papers, *SKEP 1844–46*, which would appear late in 1872 and for which he is preparing Goldschmidt in this letter. In the late 1870s Otto Borchsenius published a series of literary sketches of the 1840s in the form of journal articles, several of which presented the battle between Kierkegaard and *The Corsair* largely from the point of view of Kierkegaard's *Posthumous Papers*, which had recently been published. (Borchsenius's articles were subsequently collected and reprinted in book form in *Fra Fyrrene* [From the Forties], 2 vols. (Copenhagen: C. A. Reitzels og Otto Wroblenskys Forlag, 1878 and 1880). The section on Goldschmidt and *The Corsair* is in vol. 2, pp. 231–325.) Borchsenius's sketches upset Goldschmidt, who believed that his point of view as presented in his memoirs (which had been published in 1877) had been neglected; the letters excerpted in passages 4 through 8 were written to protest Borchsenius's treatment of *The Corsair* affair. For information pertaining to Goldschmidt, P. L. Møller, Kierkegaard, and *The Corsair*, see above, especially the notes accompanying entries 1, 2, and 3 in this chapter. **Indian-style**: Goldschmidt uses the word *indiansk*, which is not an ordinary Danish word, and which he apparently intends as a synonym for "fanatical." **Nemesis**: in the latter part of his life, Goldschmidt became obsessed with the idea that our lives are ruled by "Nemesis," by which he meant a sort of cosmic justice. He traced the origins of this idea to ancient Egypt, corresponded on the subject with learned men, and dedicated the second volume of his memoirs, significantly entitled *Livs Erindringer og Resultater* [Memories and Results of My Life], to propagating his rediscovery of the Nemesis theory as his life's greatest "result." **Hep! Hep!** is a term of abuse that was shouted at Jews and reportedly is an acronym for "Hierosalem est perdita!" [Jerusalem is lost]. **Sharpen the point upon which he was later impaled**: see entry number 2 in this chapter. **Some literary criticism**: an allusion to P. L. Møller's critique of Kierkegaard in *Gæa* in December of 1845. *To acknowledge* **the order of**

things and to bring ourselves to order is taken from Goldschmidt, *Livs Erindringer og Resultater*, vol. 2, p. 11. **My father's talk about the secret law (at the burning field of rape plants)**: see Goldschmidt, *Livs Erindringer og Resultater*, vol. 1, pp. 40–42.

14. The original of the present selection is with Goldschmidt's papers, now in **KBHA** (NkS 4252⁵, 4⁰); it has been published as an appendix entitled "Varianter" [Variants] in the 1965 edition of Goldschmidt's memoirs, *Livs Erindringer og Resultater*, ed. Morten Borup, vol. 1 (Copenhagen: Rosenkilde and Bagger, 1965), pp. 275–76.

15. The original of the present selection is with Goldschmidt's papers, now in **KBHA** (NkS 4252⁵, 4⁰); it has been published as an appendix entitled "Varianter" [Variants] in the 1965 edition of Goldschmidt's memoirs, *Livs Erindringer og Resultater*, Morten Borup, ed., vol. 1, pp. 271–74.

On S.K.'s Physiognomy: a good deal has been written about what Kierkegaard actually looked like; cf. especially Rikard Magnussen, *Søren Kierkegaard set udefra* [Søren Kierkegaard Seen from Without] (Copenhagen: Ejnar Munksgaard, 1942), and Aage Kabell, *Kierkegaardstudiet i Norden* [Kierkegaard Studies in Scandinavia] (Copenhagen: H. Hagerup, 1948), pp. 289–300. **A very gifted attorney**: undoubtedly Goldschmidt's friend, Prokurator Jens Emil Damkier (1811–58), who was Kierkegaard's classmate, cf. Sejer Kühle, *Søren Kierkegaard. Barndom og Ungdom*, p. 43. **Stages on Life's Way**: unreadable in original; Morten Borup, editor of the 1965 edition of Goldschmidt's memoirs, suggests the present reading, but adds a question mark. **(p. 96)**: p. 96 of the original edition of *Repetition* [*Gjentagelsen* (Copenhagen: Reitzel, 1843)] corresponds to *SV* III 224 (*KW* VI 189); on that page, the relevant text by Kierkegaard reads, "[A]t times I believe that you are mentally disordered" [*sindssvag*]. Goldschmidt would substitute "unloving" [*ukjærlig*] for "mentally disordered."

16. The original of the present selection is with Goldschmidt's papers, now in **KBHA** (NkS 4252⁵, 4⁰); it has been published as an appendix entitled "Varianter" [Variants] in the 1965 edition of Goldschmidt's memoirs, *Livs Erindringer og Resultater*, ed. Morten Borup, vol. 1, pp. 274–75.

A small part: unreadable in original; Morten Borup, editor of the 1965 edition of Goldschmidt's memoirs, suggests the present reading, but adds a question mark.

Chapter Six
After *The Corsair*: The Peripatetic and Controversialist of the Later 1840s

1. From Anna Brosbøll, *Træk af Carl Brosbølls og hans Hustru Hansine Thorbjørnsens Liv og Hjem* [Features of the Life and Home of Carl Brosbøll and His Wife Hansine Thorbjørnsen] (Copenhagen: V. Pio, 1909), p. 53.

Anna Brosbøll was the daughter of Johan Carl Brosbøl (1816–1900), a prolific writer who wrote under the pen name Carit Etlar; see the note to Carl Brosbøll's entry in chapter 4 of this book. The encounter referred to here presumably took place in 1846. Kierkegaard certainly was one of Brosbøll's circle of acquaintances, but only marginally.

2. From Frederik Nielsen's memoirs, *Minder. Oplevelser og Iagttagelser* [Memories: Experiences and Observations] (Aalborg: M. M. Schultz, 1881), pp. 44–45.

Frederik Nielsen (1818–89) was a pastor on Funen.

3. From the second of Arthur Abrahams's volumes of memoirs, *Minder fra min Barndom og tidlige Ungdom* [Memories from My Childhood and Early Youth] (Copenhagen: Schubothe, 1895), pp. 54f.

Arthur Abrahams (1836–1905) was a language teacher, author, and dilettante actor. He is nearly forgotten now, though he is remembered for his three interesting volumes of memoirs. **My father**: Arthur Abrahams's father was N[icolai] C[hristian] L[evin] Abrahams (1798–1870), a professor of French literature at the University of Copenhagen. There is no mention of N.C.L. Abrahams in Kierkegaard's papers, though Kierkegaard did own a copy of Abrahams's translation of a play by Scribe (see *Pap.* X¹ A 320, p. 211), and it is not unlikely that a man like Abrahams (and his son Arthur) could have accompanied Kierkegaard on walks. **Whether he really had one**

short and one long trouser leg: belief in the supposed difference in the length of Kierkegaard's trouser legs was very widespread, even in Kierkegaard's own time; see, for example, the accounts by Willy Schorn, in this chapter, and by Troels-Lund, in chapter 9 of this book, where Troels-Lund states that "one trouser leg really was shorter than the other." The Grundtvigian cleric Thomas Skat Rørdam (1832–1909) wrote that Kierkegaard's "imaginary martyrdom" could have been avoided: "If he had worn trousers like other people, nobody would have been able to see how thin his legs were" (letter of April 6, 1880, in *Otto Møller og Skat Rørdam. En Brevveksling* [Otto Møller and Skat Rørdam: Correspondence], edited and annotated by H. Skat Rørdam, vol. 1 (Copenhagen: G.E.C. Gad, 1915), p. 347.

4. From Willy Schorn's first volume of memoirs, *Da Voldene Stod* [When the Ramparts Stood] (Copenhagen: Gyldendal, 1905), pp. 195f.

Willy Schorn (1834–1912), author, teacher, and artist. **My father**: Peter Theodor Schorn (1796–1879), writer and translator. Although Peter Theodor Schorn is not mentioned in Kierkegaard's papers, it is quite plausible that Schorn (and his son Willy) could have walked with Kierkegaard. **The doctor**: Søren Kierkegaard's *magister* degree was later converted into a doctorate. **Sibbern** is the philosopher F. C. Sibbern; see the note accompanying the comments on Kierkegaard's dissertation in chapter 2, as well as the entry by Holger Frederik Rørdam in chapter 4 and the entry by Sibbern, with accompanying notes, in chapter 10 of this book.

5. From the opening lines of August Bournonville's notes for a speech he made at a farewell party given for him on October 10, 1861, on the occasion of his departure to accept a new position in Stockholm. The original document is with Bournonville's papers in **KBHA** (NkS 3285, 4^0, kapsel 9, fasc. 3). The entire document will be included in Knud Arne Jürgensen's forthcoming book *The Bournonville Tradition: The First 50 Years, 1829–1879* (publication expected 1996). I am grateful to Knud Arne Jürgensen for bringing this passage to my attention prior to the publication of his own study.

[Antoine] August Bournonville (1805–79): dancer, choreographer, and ballet master at the Royal Danish Theater; he was the principal founder of the Danish ballet tradition. **A lengthy dissertation on the concept of irony**: Kierkegaard's dissertation *On the Concept of Irony* (*SV* XIII 93–393 [*KW* II 1–329]).

6. From Frederik Hammerich's memoirs, *Et Levnedsløb*, vol. 2, pp. 51–53.

For **Hammerich**, see the note in chapter 1 of this book. The **ramparts** were the ancient fortifications of Copenhagen; they were surrounded by a moat and topped by a broad pathway that was very popular for walks and outings. **His brother** refers to Søren Kierkegaard's brother, Peter Christian Kierkegaard. **Bellevue** is a pretty spot on the coast north of Copenhagen. **Ten miles** means ten Danish miles, the equivalent of ca. forty-seven English miles or seventy-five kilometers. **Poor people**: on Kierkegaard's accessibility to the poor, see Frithiof Brandt and Else Rammel, *Kierkegaard og Pengene* [Kierkegaard and Money] (Copenhagen: Levin & Munksgaard/ Ejnar Munksgaard, 1935), pp. 94–97. **Emil Boesen**: see the note accompanying the entry by Boesen in chapter 2 of this book. **Visby**: Pastor Carl Holger Visby; see the note accompanying the entry by H. P. Holst in chapter 1 of this book.

7. From Julie Sødring's memoirs, *Erindringer fra min Barndom og Ungdom*, pp. 183 and 222f.

Julie Weber Sødring: see the note accompanying the entry by Sødring in chapter 4 of this book. **Father went to a poor woman and gave her a five-rixdollar bill, whereupon he and Kierkegaard delighted in her surprise**: see also the similar story by Troels-Lund in chapter 9 of this book as well as the story in *Either/Or* (*SV* II 12 [*KW* IV 12]). The incident described in the first selection probably took place in 1846 or 1847, whereas that recounted in the second selection took place on Sødring's wedding day, May 25, 1849.

8. From F. L. Liebenberg's memoirs, *Nogle Optegnelser om mit Levned*, pp. 38–39.

F. L. Liebenberg: see the note accompanying the entry by Liebenberg in chapter 1 of this book.

9. From Carl Koch, *Grundtvigske Toner* [Grundtvigian Notes] (Copenhagen: Det schønbergske Forlag, 1925), p. 7.

Carl Koch (1866–1925), pastor and author. **There was someone who told me**: according to personal communication from Carl Weltzer to Steen Johansen, the person who recounted this episode to Carl Koch was surely Emil Boesen. In his journals, Kierkegaard comments on the motives that underlay his warm public association with Grundtvig:

> The individual is what I am fighting for, and it is true that the Kingdom of Denmark has provided and continues to provide a very inhospitable climate for this—because here everything is coteries. But wherever there is a coterie, I am careful to choose one member, whom I venerate or draw close to me—simply in order to weaken the coterie. The most amusing case is that of Grundtvig. Among the reasons he has been attacked is because of his party. And nonetheless I have been successful in maintaining a sort of high-spirited relationship with him—which very much embitters his party. [*Pap.* IX A 206, p. 104]

10. From O. P. Sturzen-Becker, *Hinsidan Sundet* [On the Other Side of the Sound], vol. 2 (Stockholm: A. Bonniers Förlag, 1846), pp. 233–38.

O[scar] P[atrick] Sturzen-Becker (1811–69) was a Swedish author and journalist who wrote under the pseudonym Orvar Odd. He lived in Copenhagen in 1844–47.

11. From Frederikke Bremer, *Liv i Norden* [Life in Scandinavia] (Copenhagen: F. H. Eibes Forlag, 1849), pp. 37–38. Part of this passage is available in another English translation in *KW* XXV 482–83.

Frederikke Bremer (1801–65) was a Swedish writer, traveler, and literary critic who visited Denmark in 1848–49. She developed unorthodox religious views under the influence of D. F. Strauss and became a pioneer of feminism. Kierkegaard refused to be interviewed by Bremer for her survey of the Scandinavian literary world and disliked her portrait of him; cf. *Pap.* X¹ A 658 p. 412 and X² A 25 p. 22 [*SKJP* 6493].

12. From Clara Bergsøe, *Camilla Collett. Et Livsbillede* [Camilla Collett: A Picture of Her Life] (Copenhagen: Gyldendal, 1902), pp. 91–92. A similar account is contained in Ellisiv Steen, *Diktning og Virkelighet. En Studie i Camilla Colletts Forfatterskap* [Poetry and Reality: A Study of Camilla Collett's Works] (Oslo: Gyldendals Norske Forlag, 1947), p. 230.

Camilla [Wergeland] Collett (1813–95): Norwegian author and campaigner for women's rights, most remembered for her novel *Amtmandens dötre* [The Prefect's Daughters] (1854–55); she visited Copenhagen literary circles several times, and this particular incident took place during her visit from October 1852 until the summer of 1853.

13. From Andrew Hamilton, *Sixteen Months in the Danish Isles* (London: Richard Bentley, 1852), vol. 2, pp. 268–70.

Andrew Hamilton was a Briton who lived in Denmark ca. 1850. He was fluent in Danish and familiar with Danish literary and cultural life. He dedicated his book to Bishop Mynster.

14. From William and Mary Howitt, *The Literature and Romance of Northern Europe. Constituting a Complete History of the Literature of Sweden, Denmark, Norway and Iceland*, vol. 2 (London: Colburn and Co., 1852), pp. 239–40.

William and Mary Howitt: William Howitt (1795–1879) and his wife, Mary [Botham] Howitt (1799–1888), were English authors. The Howitts wrote a great many works, both individually and jointly, and Mary Howitt produced many English translations of Scandinavian writers, including Hans Christian Andersen and Frederika Bremer.

15. From Otto Zinck, *Fra mit Studenter- og Teaterliv* [From My Life as a Student and in the Theater] (Copenhagen: Gyldendal, 1906)], pp. 25f.

Otto Zinck (1824–1908) was an actor. **When he lived on Nørregade** could refer either to the period from April (or October) 1840 to October 1844, when Kierkegaard lived at Nørregade 230A (now number 38), or to the period from April 1850 to April 1851, when Kierkegaard lived at number 43 (now number 35) Nørregade. Kierkegaard's comment **I never have parties** is not quite accurate, inasmuch as Henriette Lund reports on a family gathering at his home; see her report in chapter 9 of this book, but see also Georg Brandes's account below in this chapter.

16. From Georg Brandes, *Søren Kierkegaard. En kritisk Fremstilling i Grundrids* [Søren Kierke-

gaard: Outlines of a Critical Presentation], originally published in 1877, as reprinted in Georg Brandes, *Samlede Skrifter. Danmark* [Collected Writings: Denmark], 2d ed., vol. 2 (Copenhagen: Gyldendal, 1919), pp. 237–38.

Georg Brandes (1842–1927): see also the note for the entry by Brandes in chapter 3 of this book. Brandes was born in 1842 and was thus thirteen years old when Kierkegaard died. Consequently much of his sketch of Kierkegaard's life in Copenhagen can scarcely be based upon his personal observations, but must have been based on knowledge acquired later. It may well be that the only genuine eyewitness memory is the account of the illuminated windows in Kierkegaard's lodgings.

Chapter Seven
The Moment Comes: Final Opposition

1. From an undated (1870) letter from Johannes C. Barth to H. P. Barfod, in **KBHA** (**SKA** D. Pk. 5).

Johannes C. Barth (1833–88), graduate of the Polytechnic Institute and son of Colonel Søren Christian Barth, a cavalry officer. **The Spangs' home** refers to the home of Peter Johannes Spang, a friend of Kierkegaard; see the entry by Tycho E. Spang and its accompanying note in this chapter. **E/O** refers to *Either/Or*. **The place in which E/O was found** is an allusion to the foreword of *Either/Or*, where Kierkegaard's fictive narrator, Victor Eremita, pretends that he had gone to a secondhand furniture dealer and purchased a desk in which he found the manuscript of *Either/Or* (see *SV* I vi–viii [*KW* III 4–6]). The German poetry cited near the end of the passage—*so dumm*, etc.—is taken from the so-called study scene in Goethe's *Faust*, verses 1946f. For another version of the **anecdote** concerning Kierkegaard's sense of obligation to his father in finishing his university education, see entry number 6 by Hans Brøchner in chapter 11 of this book.

2. From three letters from Emil Boesen to his wife, Louise Sophie Caroline Holtermann Boesen (1815–79), written at two-day intervals in the autumn of 1851; translated from Carl Koch, ed., *Søren Kierkegaard og Emil Boesen*, p. 35.

Emil Boesen: see the note accompanying the entry by Boesen in chapter 2 of this book. **Out in Østerbro**: from April 1851 until April or October 1852 Kierkegaard lived at Østerbro 108A. *For Self-Examination* [*SV* XII 291–370 (*KW* XXI 1–87)] was published in September 1851. **Over there**: Boesen and his wife lived in Horsens, Jutland.

3. From August Bournonville's unpublished diaries in **KBHA** (**NkS** 747, 8⁰, Dagbøger, bind 13, December 29, 1854). I thank Knud Arne Jürgensen for bringing this passage to my attention prior to the publication of his forthcoming book (see the note accompanying the entry by Bournonville in chapter 6 of this book).

[Antoine] August Bournonville (1805–79): see the note accompanying Bournonville's entry in chapter 6 of this book. **[Frederik Ludvig] Høedt** (1820–85): theatrical director and a leading actor at the Royal Danish Theater; he was a devoted reader of Kierkegaard and had many clashes with the Royal Theater's two leading figures, Johan Ludvig and Johanne Luise Heiberg. **Paullis**: presumably Simon Holger Paulli (1810–91) and his wife. S. H. Paulli was a musician, conductor, and composer; he composed much of the ballet music for Bournonville's creations. S. H. Paulli's elder brother, Pastor Just Henrik Paulli (1809–65) was Bishop Mynster's son-in-law; see the note accompanying Hanne Mourier's account of Regine Schlegel's memoirs in chapter 3 of this book. **S. Phiseldeck**: presumably Carl Otto von Schmidt-Phiseldeck (1812–79), a pastor who was married to Bournonville's sister.

4. From a letter by Petronella Ross to F. C. Sibbern, dated January 6, 1855; the original is in **KBHA** (Additamenta 1040, 4⁰).

Petronella [or Petronelle] [Margrethe] Ross (1805–75): born to a genteel but impoverished family, she was obliged to become a housekeeper for Bishop Rasmus Møller (1763–1842) (father of the philosopher Poul Martin Møller). She became deaf at an early age and entered

Nykøbing Hospital, on the island of Falster, a home for older maiden ladies of gentle birth. **F. C. Sibbern**: see the note accompanying the comments on Kierkegaard's dissertation, in chapter 2 of this book. Under a pseudonym, Ross published four collections of *Fortællinger for simple Læsere* [Tales for Simple Readers] with the assistance of her friend and confidant F. C. Sibbern, with whom she carried on an extensive correspondence. Ninety-one letters by Ross to Sibbern are preserved in **KBHA** (Additamenta 1040, 4⁰), and a number of letters by Sibbern to Ross have been printed in *Breve til og fra F. C. Sibbern*, ed. C.L.N. Mynster, vol. 2 (Copenhagen: Gyldendal, 1866), pp. 214–19, 220, 224–31, and 232–38, where the editor preserved Ross's anonymity, naming her only as "the author of *Tales for Simple Readers*." Ross wrote Sibbern in connection with many matters, especially the books she was reading. Ross seems to have taken a particular interest in Kierkegaard in the period 1850–51, when she mentions Kierkegaard's works several times. In a letter dated December 19, 1850, Ross reports on her reading, which included, in addition to Sibbern's own *Gabrielis Breve* [Letters of Gabrielis], "some of Tholuck's and Martensen's works, and that odd S. Kirkegaard's *Works of Love*, of which I have read a little for a moment and have both marveled at it and been pleased by it. I own Mynster's *Betragtninger* [Observations], and I will never be done with reading them" (in **KBHA** [Additamenta 1040, 4⁰, letter dated December 19, 1850]). Sibbern replies, "One finds much that is good in Kierkegaard's writings: I would mention to you his "Gospel of Sufferings" [the seven discourses included in "The Gospel of Sufferings," constituting the third and final portion of Kierkegaard's *Edifying Discourses in a Different Spirit* from 1847 (*SV* VIII 297–416 [*KW* XV 213–341])]. Among his edifying discourses is one that is very fine: it is a discourse on Job's famous words, "the Lord giveth etc." [a reference to the first of Kierkegaard's *Four Edifying Discourses* from 1843 (*SV* IV 9–23 [*KW* V 109–24])]" (*Breve til og fra Sibbern*, vol. 2, p. 215, letter dated January 7, 1851). Later that year, in a letter of November 5, 1851, Ross tells of what she has been reading:

> [A]nd part of Søren Kirkegaard's *Edifying Discourses* [i.e., *Edifying Discourses in a Different Spirit* (*SV* VIII 107–416 [*KW* XV 1–341])] is my favorite reading material just now. . . . Dear Councillor of State, it is a pleasure for me to read Kirkegaard; he provides me with both a crutch and staff. And if I don't get very far, it isn't his fault: I stand where I stand all the more steadfastly and can survey him from that standpoint. But when it sometimes gets to be too much for me, I put the book aside and knit or do some mending, taking pleasure in completing a little piece of work. [In **KBHA** (Additamenta 1040, 4⁰, letter dated November 5, 1851)]

Sibbern immediately replied, seconding Ross's approval of Kierkegaard: "I can imagine that Kierkegaard affords you spiritual nourishment and comfort; there is much that is good in his writings, especially with respect to religion" (*Breve til og fra Sibbern*, p. 218, letter dated November 8, 1851). On at least one occasion, Ross wrote directly to Kierkegaard (*B&A* I 304–5 [*KW* XXV 387–88], letter dated July 12, 1851), briefly outlining her situation and indicating some points of connection with him, e.g., that she was a childhood friend of his brother Peter Christian's first wife, Marie Boisen, and that her brother (whom she would shortly be visiting) resides at Østerbro 107A, quite near where Kierkegaard was then living. Ross praises Kierkegaard's work and asks if he would be so kind as to lend her a copy of his *Christian Discourses* or, failing that, another of his works. Kierkegaard's reply, if any, is not preserved, but the fact that Ross specifically and repeatedly mentions Kierkegaard's *Christian Discourses* in her subsequent correspondence with Sibbern could indicate that Kierkegaard did reply, perhaps sending Ross a copy of the book she requested. Ross had wide-ranging tastes, however: not only was she a great admirer of Kierkegaard but, as can be seen from the passages cited here, she was also very fond of Bishop Mynster, and wrote Sibbern a letter of condolence on learning of "your friend Bishop Mynster's unexpected departure from this life" (in **KBHA** [Additamenta 1040, 4⁰, letter dated February 12, 1854]). Even after Kierkegaard had been dead for years, Ross could invoke his name casually to indicate a particular personality type, e.g.: "Your friend has the spirit of S. Kirkegaard—things went unhappily for him in this world" (letter from Ross to Ludvig Schröder dated April 9, 1859, in **KBHA** [NkS 3550,

4⁰]). **Arndt**: Johann Arndt (1555–1621), a German Lutheran pietist author whom Kierkegaard also read. **Blædel**: Nicolai Gottlieb Blædel (1816–79), an influential pastor, distinguished himself with his service as pastor at Copenhagen's General Hospital during the cholera epidemic of 1853 and subsequently became pastor at the Garrison Church in Copenhagen; he was the author of two collections of sermons. **That article of his in *Fædrelandet* about Bishop Mynster**: Kierkegaard's article of December 18, 1854 (*SV* XIV 5–10), with which he began his attack on the Church.

5. From letters from B. S. Ingemann to J. Paludan-Müller, dated January 15, 1855, and to H. L. Martensen, dated January 28, 1855; both letters are published in *Breve til og fra Bernh. Sev. Ingemann* [Letters to and from Bernh. Sev. Ingemann], ed. V. Heise (Copenhagen: C. A. Reitzels Forlag, 1879), pp. 485 and 489–90.

Bernhard Severin Ingemann: see the note accompanying the entry by Vilhelm Birkedal in chapter 4 of this book. **J[ens] Paludan-Müller** (1813–99): a pastor and theologian; in church politics he was a centrist with connections to Mynster and Martensen, but was also open to Grundtvigian influence. He was married to the daughter of Eggert Tryde, archdeacon of the Church of Our Lady (for Tryde, see the note accompanying the entry by K. Arentzen later in this chapter). **What you wrote in defense of Mynster's reputation**: Paludan-Müller's *Dr. Søren Kierkegaards Angreb paa Biskop Mynsters Eftermæle belyst* [Clarification of Dr. Søren Kierkegaard's Attack on the Reputation of Bishop Mynster] (Copenhagen, 1855). **His brother**: Peter Christian Kierkegaard. **H[ans] L[assen] Martensen**: see the note accompanying Martensen's entry in chapter 8 of this book. **Your rebuke**: Martensen's reply to Kierkegaard was published in *Berlingske Tidende* on December 28, 1854 (no. 302), and is reprinted in Rasmus Nielsen, ed., *S. Kierkegaards Bladartikler med Bilag samlede efter Forfatterens Død, udgivne som Supplement til hans øvrige Skrifter*, pp. 242–46. **Jacobi's phrase about a "thrashing"**: Bishop Martensen quoted Jacobi as follows: "Mir fallen gleich Maulschellen ein, wenn ich Leute mit erhabenen Gesinnungen herankommen sehe, die nicht einmal nur rechtschaffene Gesinnungen beweisen." **Graveyard**: in Danish, "Kirkegaard," apparently intended by Ingemann as a pun on "Kierkegaard."

6. From a letter by Hans Rørdam to his brother Peter, dated February 28, 1855; published in *Peter Rørdam. Blade af hans Levnedsbog og Brevvexling* [Peter Rørdam: Pages from His Biography and Correspondence], vol. 2 (Copenhagen: Karl Schønbergs Forlag), pp. 295–96.

Hans Rørdam (1803–69): a pastor and brother of **Peter Rørdam**; see the note accompanying the entry by P. Rørdam in chapter 2 of this book. **I know my own and my own know me**: John 10.14.

7. From a letter from B. S. Ingemann to Carsten Hauch, dated March 9, 1855. The original letter is in **KBHA** (**NkS** 3751, 4⁰, I, fasc. 8, no. 108); published in *Hauch og Ingemann. En Brevveksling* [Hauch and Ingemann: Correspondence], edited and annotated by M. Hatting (Copenhagen: Gyldendal, 1933), p. 108.

[Johannes] Carsten Hauch: see the note accompanying the entry by Vilhelm Birkedal in chapter 4 of this book. **The graveyard scandal**: see the note accompanying Ingemann's letter to H. L. Martensen, earlier in this chapter.

8. From a letter from Petronella Ross to F. C. Sibbern, dated March 20, 1855; the original is in **KBHA** (Additamenta 1040, 4⁰).

Petronella Ross: see the note accompanying the entry by Ross earlier in this chapter. **The councillor of state**: F. C. Sibbern.

9. From a letter from Carsten Hauch to B. S. Ingemann, dated March 25, 1855, and written in reply to Ingemann's letter of March 9, 1855, included earlier in this chapter. The original letter is in **KBHA** (**NkS** 3751, 4⁰, II, fasc. 2, no. 204); published in *Hauch og Ingemann. En Brevveksling*, p. 111.

10. From a letter from F. C. Sibbern to Petronella Ross, dated March 26, 1855, and written in reply to Ross's letter of March 20, 1855, cited earlier in this chapter. Sibbern's letter has been published in *Breve til og fra F. C. Sibbern*, vol. 2, pp. 224–26.

F[rederik] C[hristian] Sibbern: see the note accompanying Sibbern's comments on Kierkegaard's dissertation in chapter 2 of this book. **Petronella Ross**: see the note accompanying the first entry by Ross, earlier in this chapter. **Lindbergians**: followers of the preacher and theologian Jacob Christian Lindberg; see the notes accompanying the entries by Peter Christian Kierkegaard in chapter 9 of this book for information on Lindberg.

11. From a letter from C. T. Engelstoft to Ludvig Müller, dated March 30, 1855. The original letter is in **KBHA (NkS** 3748, 4⁰).

C[hristian] T[horning] Engelstoft (1805–89) was professor of church history and later bishop of Funen; in ecclesiastical politics he was a supporter of the Mynster-Martensen line. **[Carl] Ludvig Müller** (1809–91) was a numismatist and archeologist.

12. From a letter from Hans Rørdam to his brother Peter, dated May 4, 1855; published in *Peter Rørdam. Blade af hans Levnedsbog og Brevvexling*, vol. 2, p. 299.

Hans Rørdam: see the note accompanying Hans Rørdam's letter earlier in this chapter. **Peter Rørdam**: see the note accompanying Peter Rørdam's letter in chapter 2 of this book. **Shoemaker of Jerusalem**: an allusion to the legend of the Wandering Jew, Ahasuerus, a shoemaker of Jerusalem, who refused to give Christ a resting place on his way to Calvary, and who, despite subsequent repentance, was punished by being forced to live until the end of time as a wandering witness to Christianity. Interestingly, Kierkegaard himself not only was very fascinated by the tale of the Wandering Jew but at one point in his papers speculates about someone, perhaps himself, whose fate is like that of the Wandering Jew, i.e., a person condemned to directing others to Christianity without being able to embrace it himself; see *Pap.* VI B 40:33 [*SKJP* 5797] as well as Bruce H. Kirmmse, "Kierkegaard, Jødedommen og Jøderne" [Kierkegaard, Jews, and Judaism], in *Kirkehistoriske Samlinger* (1992), pp. 77–107. Coincidentally, in his letter to his brother, dated February 28, 1855 (see earlier in this chapter), Hans Rørdam says much the same thing, namely that Kierkegaard "stood outside of Christianity and spoke with the greatest virtuosity about the beauty of heavenly things."

13. From F. C. Sibbern's papers in **KBHA** (Additamenta 8⁰, 287, II, Notebog V, p. 13); published, in slightly different form, in Jens Himmelstrup, *Sibbern* (Copenhagen: Schultz, 1934), p. 269.

Kierkegaard calls upon us to refrain from attending church: presumably a reference to Kierkegaard's pamphlet "This Must Be Said, so Let It Be Said," which appeared on May 25, 1855, in which Kierkegaard writes: "*Whoever you are, whatever your life might be, my friend, by ceasing to participate (if you do) in public worship as it presently is (with its claim to being the Christianity of the New Testament) you will continually be guilty of one fewer transgression, and a major one: You will not be making a fool of God . . .*" (*SV* XIV 85 [emphasis in original]). This was Kierkegaard's first public call for people to stop attending church.

14. From a letter from Magdalene Hansen to Elise Stampe, dated June 20 [1855]; the original is in **KBHA (NkS** 2744 II², 2⁰). I thank the historian Tinne Vammen of Copenhagen for bringing this letter to my attention and for providing biographical data on its author and recipient.

Magdalene Barbara Købke Hansen (1825–98) was the wife of the artist [Carl Christian] Constantin Hansen (1804–80) and an active supporter of Grundtvig. **Baroness Karen Marie Elisabeth (Elise) Stampe** (1824–83) was a follower of Grundtvig and a religious mentor of Magdalene Hansen. **Constantin**: the painter Constantin Hansen, the husband of the author of this letter. **Mrs. Monrad**: Emilie Nathalie Lütthans Monrad (1815–71), the first wife of the National Liberal politician and churchman D. G. Monrad (1811–87).

15. From Vilhelm Birkedal, *Personlige Oplevelser i et langt Liv*, vol. 2, pp. 84–87.

Vilhelm Birkedal: see the note accompanying the entry by Birkedal in chapter 2 of this book. **When I came to his brother to study**: P. C. Kierkegaard took on Birkedal as a private student in 1833 (see Weltzer, *Peter og Søren Kierkegaard*, p. 66). Henrik Johan Matthiesen (born 1815), who was graduated from the Borgerdyd School in 1834 and later became a physician, tells a similar story in a letter to Peter Christian Kierkegaard, dated May 19, 1879:

My Right Reverend old and dear teacher: I have a faint little hope that you will be able to remember one of your students, who struggled with you in your study on Gammeltorv [*recte*

Nytorv] on the ground floor at the desk by the window, while your late blessed brother Søren lay on the sofa and made occasional remarks. I struggled with you on matters pertaining to the [Christian] faith and on another occasion had my Latin composition corrected. I can still see it before my eyes. [Matthiesen's letter is in **KBHA** (**NkS** 3174, 4⁰, VIII, fasc. 13, nr. 23), and has been published in Otto Holmgaard, *Peter Christian Kierkegaard* (Copenhagen: Rosenkilde og Bagger, 1953), p. 26]

Corns [on the foot]: at the beginning of *Either/Or* Kierkegaard has an aphorism that includes the phrase "Now I have corns" (*SV* I 12 [*KW* III 28]). **Gjødwad**: Jens Gjødwad; see the note accompanying the entry by Hother Ploug in chapter 4 of this book.

16. From the "Dagbog" [Diary] passages for April 15, 1855, and September 1, 1855, published on September 15, 1855, in Goldschmidt's journal *Nord og Syd*, Ny Række, 8de. Bind, Nr. 1, pp. 42 and 78–81.

Meïr Aron Goldschmidt: see the notes accompanying Goldschmidt's entries in chapter 5 of this book. **R. Nielsen's fine work *Om Skjæbne og Forsyn*** [On Fate and Providence]: by Rasmus Nielsen, published 1853.

17. From H. C. Rosted, *Den gamle Postgaard i Hørsholm* [The Old Mailcoach Inn at Hørsholm] (Hørsholm: O. Cohn and E. Hasfeldt, 1925), p. 27.

H. C. Rosted (1891–1968), assistant school inspector and local historian, author of historical works about Hørsholm, a town north of Copenhagen. Rosted does not tell us how he obtained his knowledge of Kierkegaard's visit. An inn was connected to the post office in Hørsholm, and **Regine Reinhard** was the proprietress of the inn, while Jens Madsen **Hvidberg** was director of the post office. The author Henrik Hertz also frequented the inn; see Hertz's entry in chapter 10 of this book for his recollection of Hvidberg's account of Kierkegaard's visits there.

18. From Otto B. Wroblewski, *Ti Aar i C. A. Reitzels Boglade* [Ten Years in C. A. Reitzel's Bookshop] (Copenhagen: privately published, 1889), pp. 22–23.

Otto B. Wroblewski (1827–1907), book dealer. For ten years, from 1843 to 1853, Wroblewski was the book dealer at C. A. Reitzel's, which was housed at that time in the orphanage building at number 44 Købmagergade. Wroblewski subsequently became a book dealer in Roskilde.

19. From an account published in *SKEP* 1844–46 pp. 870–74, which stems, according to H. P. Barfod, "from written and oral communication from a pastor [Tycho E. Spang], who approved the present written version and agreed to its publication."

Tycho E. Spang (1830–1907), pastor and the son of Peter Johannes Spang (1796–1846), pastor at the Church of the Holy Spirit in Copenhagen. There is surviving correspondence between Kierkegaard and Peter Johannes and Christiane Philippine Spang (1797–1865), the latter's wife; see *B&A* I 75–77, 91–93, 160–63, and 329 (*KW* XXV 95–98, 117–19, 203–6, and 421). **G.** refers to the editor J. F. Giødwad; see the note accompanying the entry by Ploug in chapter 4 of this book. **He often had powerful attacks from his ailments when he was with G., so that he would fall to the floor**: see Levin's entry in chapter 10 of this book for an account of one such attack. Another attack is reported by Henriette Lund from the period of Kierkegaard's engagement to Regine Olsen; see the entry by Henriette Lund in chapter 3 of this book. At about that same time, in a letter dated April 2, 1841, Henrik Ferdinand Lund wrote to Peter Wilhelm (or Vilhelm) Lund in Brazil:

> As for ourselves, we are all very well, despite the fact that there is sickness everywhere. The one who is somewhat ill is Uncle Søren. He has got engaged to a young and quite pretty girl, a daughter of Councillor Olsen. That is not what ails him, however. Rather, it is his chest which is affected, and he has begun to spit blood again. [**KBHA** (**NkS** 3261, 4⁰, IV, fasc. 54, nr. 365); published in Weltzer, *Peter og Søren Kierkegaard*, p. 162]

As a young university student: Tycho Spang became a university student in 1850.

20. From Peter Christian Zahle, *Til Erindring om Johan Georg Hamann og Søren Aabye Kierke-*

gaard [In Memory of Johan Georg Hamann and Søren Aabye Kierkegaard] (Copenhagen: privately published, 1856), pp. 7–10 and 44.

Peter Christian Zahle (1825–98), politician, author, editor, and subsequently pastor in Vallensved in southern Zealand. **Mini's**: Mini's café, a popular meeting place. **[H]ow Søren Kierkegaard looked**: Zahle gives us a clear picture of Søren Kierkegaard as an older man—he aged strikingly early. The question of portraits of Kierkegaard and the accuracy of various representations of his physical appearance is discussed in detail in Rikard Magnussen, *Søren Kierkegaard set udefra*, and in Aage Kabell, *Kierkegaardstudiet i Norden*, pp. 289–300.

21. From the first edition of M. A. Sommer's autobiography, *Stadier paa Livets Vei* [Stages on Life's Way], vol. 1 (Aalborg: Bechske Bogtrykkeri, 1868), p. 23.

Mogens Abraham Sommer (1829–1901) was a widely traveled lay preacher and politician whose sectarian agitation frequently involved him in difficulties with the authorities. He claimed that Kierkegaard's attack on the Folkekirke was the inspiration for his own coarse and radical assaults on all established religion. For details see Emil Larsen, *Mogens Abraham Sommer* (Copenhagen: Gad, 1963), where it is explained, among other things, that on one of his last trips to America Sommer fell ill and supported himself by drawing and selling pictures of "Dr. Martin Luther, . . . Søren Kierkegaard, . . . Crown Prince Frederik, . . . Frederik VII, Benjamin Franklin, William Penn, Christ—and myself" (p. 166). Sommer had a son, born in 1865, whom he named "Mogens Søren Aabye Kierkegaard Sommer."

22. Both passages are from Niels Johansen's journal *Brevbærer mellem Kristne*. The first is from *Brevbærer*, no. 6, second Sunday after Trinity [i.e., June 17], 1855, pp. 55–56, and the second passage is from *Brevbærer*, 5. Aargang, nos. 4–5, February 2, 1859, p. 33.

Niels Johansen (1815–99) was a lay preacher. His career began in the 1830s, and he was subsequently strongly influenced by Kierkegaard's attack on the Folkekirke. Johansen published the journal *Brevbærer mellem Kristne* from 1855 to 1860.

23. From Kristian Arentzen's memoirs, *Fra yngre og ældre Dage. Livs-Erindringer* [From Younger and Older Days: Life Memories] (Copenhagen: Wroblewsky, 1886), pp. 122f.

Kristian Arentzen (1823–99), author, historian of literature, subsequently a teacher. **Athenæum**: a private library and reading room, founded in 1824 and located in the center of Copenhagen at Østergade 68; many intellectuals, including Arentzen, Kierkegaard, and H. L. Martensen, were members; cf. entry number 49 in Hans Brøchner's memoirs in chapter 11 of this book, where Brøchner cites Frederik Beck as saying essentially the same thing as here reported by Arentzen. δοῦλος Χριστοῦ Ἰησοῦ: "a servant (or slave) of Jesus Christ"; the phrase appears in many variants in the New Testament, especially in Paul's epistles, and it appears in this particular form in Colossians 4.12. **A relative, a young physician** was Henrik Sigvard Lund (1825–89), Kierkegaard's nephew by his sister Nicoline Christine and her husband, Johan Christian Lund. For Lund's graveside speech and for more information concerning Kierkegaard's burial and the events at the cemetery, see chapter 8 of this book. **Tryde**: Eggert Christopher Tryde (1781–1860), a Mynsterian centrist who nonetheless maintained good relations with the Grundtvigians, was archdeacon of the Church of Our Lady and hence responsible for officiating at Søren Kierkegaard's funeral and burial.

Chapter Eight
Illness, Death, and Burial

1. From Mathilde Reinhardt, *Familie-Erindringer 1831–1856* [Family Memoirs, 1831–1856] (Copenhagen: privately published, 1889), pp. 214–17.

Mathilde Reinhardt (1820–1900), writer, now remembered mostly for her two volumes of family memoirs. **Mrs. B.**: Mrs. Borries, Kierkegaard's landlady, 1852–55. 1849 cannot be correct; the actual year was 1852, though it is not known whether Kierkegaard moved in on the April or the October moving day. **Rosenvinge**: J.L.A. Kolderup-Rosenvinge (1798–1850): legal historian at the University of Copenhagen and friend of Kierkegaard. The friendship between Kierkegaard and Kolderup-Rosenvinge reached its zenith in 1848–49. They regularly took walks every Monday at 2:00 P.M. Their correspondence is published in *B&A* I 179, 191, 196–98, 200–216, 230–34, 235–38, 239–42, and 282 (*KW* XXV 226, 240–41, 246–49, 252–75, 292–98, 299–303, 304–308, and 358–59). See also the mention of Kolderup-Rosenvinge in entry 37 of Hans Brøchner's memoirs in chapter 11 of this book. **A particularly harsh reply from Martensen**: see *Berlingske Tidende* for December 28, 1854, reprinted in Rasmus Nielsen, ed., *S. Kierkegaards Bladartikler med Bilag samlede efter Forfatterens Død, udgivne som Supplement til hans øvrige Skrifter*, pp. 242–46. **The Moment** came out in nine issues from late May to late September 1855; a tenth issue, which lay ready for press when Kierkegaard was admitted to the hospital, was published posthumously. **The day on which he was supposed to depart** was October 2, 1855, the day on which, according to Kierkegaard's hospital record (*B&A* I 21 [*KW* XXV 28]), he was admitted to Frederik's Hospital.

2. From a letter from Carsten Hauch to B. S. Ingemann, dated October 6, 1855. The original letter is in **KBHA** (**NkS** 3751, 4⁰, II, fasc. 2, nr. 206); published in *Hauch og Ingemann. En Brevveksling*, pp. 113–14.

B. S. Ingemann: see the note accompanying the entry by Vilhelm Birkedal in chapter 4 of this book. **A nobler, milder spirit speaks up**: Hauch is alluding to Ingemann's work *Tankebreve fra en Afdøde* [Philosophical Letters from a Deceased Person] (Copenhagen: C. A. Reitzel, 1855), which Ingemann had recently sent to Hauch as a gift. **According to his own admission he is not a Christian**: see, e.g., Kierkegaard's articles in *Fædrelandet* of March 26, 1855 ("I am not a Christian in the New Testament sense" [*SV* XIV 42]), March 31, 1855 ("I do not dare to call myself a Christian" [ibid., p. 55]), and *The Moment*, no. 10 ("I am not a Christian" [ibid., p. 351])—this last article had not yet been published at the time Hauch wrote this letter, however. It is interesting to note that Hauch's strongly negative judgment of Kierkegaard changed over time. In an undated letter (apparently ca. 1870) to H. P. Barfod, Hauch subsequently wrote that "over the years my views of Kierkegaard and his important work have certainly changed a great deal" (**KBHA** [**SKA** D. Pk. 5]).

3. From H. P. Kofoed-Hansen's introduction to his edition of *Prædikener af Johan Nikolai Lange* [Sermons of Johan Nikolai Lange] (Copenhagen: Gyldendal, 1866), pp. xxiv–xxv.

H. P. Kofoed-Hansen (1813–93), pastor, author, adherent of Kierkegaard. **Johan Nikolai Lange** (1814–65), pastor at the Copenhagen General Hospital. He visited Kierkegaard during the debate about "witnesses to the truth," and he later obtained permission to visit Kierkegaard at Frederik's Hospital; Kierkegaard routinely turned away many other prospective visitors.

4. From a letter from Hans Christian Andersen to Henriette Wulff, dated October 10, 1855, originally published in *Breve fra Hans Christian Andersen* [Letters from Hans Christian Andersen], ed. C.St.A. Bille and Nicolaj Bøgh (Copenhagen: C. A. Reitzels Forlag, 1878), p. 324, and reprinted in *H. C. Andersen og Henriette Wulff. En Brevveksling* [Hans Christian and Henriette Wulff: Correspondence], ed. H. Topsøe-Jensen, *II. Breve 1849–58* [II: Letters, 1849–58] (Odense: Flensteds Forlag, 1959), p. 244.

Henriette Wulff: see the note accompanying the letter by Wulff to H. C. Andersen in chapter 4 of this book. **A theologian named Thura has written a *coarse* poem against him**: theological student Christian Henrik de Thurah (1830–98), later a pastor, was one of Kierkegaard's most outspoken opponents during the attack on the Church, and is particularly remembered for his crude poem "Riimbrev til Johannes Forføreren alias Dr. Søren Kierkegaard" [Epistolary Verse to Johannes the Seducer, alias Dr. Søren Kierkegaard], published in late September 1855, and which, it has been speculated, led to Kierkegaard's collapse. We know from the auction catalog of Kierkegaard's library (H. P. Rohde, ed., *Auktionsprotokol over Søren Kierkegaards Bogsamling* [The Auctioneer's Sales Record of the Library of Søren Kierkegaard] [Copenhagen: Det kongelige Bibliotek, 1967]) that Kierkegaard owned a copy of Thurah's scurrilous book. In his notes on his hospital conversations with Kierkegaard (see below in this chapter), Emil Boesen states that he and Kierkegaard discussed "Thurah and Martensen" on October 15, 1855.

5. From an entry in Hansine Andræ's diaries dated October 18, 1855; published in *Geheim-raadinde Andræs politiske Dagbøger* [The Political Diaries of Madame Privy Councillor Andræ], ed. Poul Andræ, vol. 1 (Copenhagen: Gyldendal, 1914), p. 111.

Hansine Andræ (1817–98): active in the women's rights movement and known for her very valuable political diaries; she was the wife of the politician and mathematician C. G. Andræ (1812–93).

6. From a letter, dated October 7, 1855, from Michael Lund to Kierkegaard's brother Peter Christian, who was at that time a parish pastor in Pedersborg-by-Sorø in west-central Zealand. The original letter is with Peter Christian Kierkegaard's correspondence in **KBHA** (NkS 3174, 4⁰, VIII, fasc. 8, nr. 333). A portion of it has been published in Carl Weltzer, *Peter og Søren Kierkegaard*, p. 266; another English translation of a portion of this letter is available in T. H. Croxall, *Glimpses and Impressions of Kierkegaard*, p. 101.

Michael [Frederik Christian] Lund (1826–1907), a physician, was the son of Kierkegaard's sister Nicoline Christine Kierkegaard Lund and her husband Johan Christian Lund.

7. From Johan Christian Lund's letters to Peter Christian Kierkegaard, dated October 10 and October 16, 1855. The original letters are with Peter Christian Kierkegaard's correspondence in **KBHA** (NkS 3174, 4⁰, VIII, fasc. 3, nos. 255 and 256). Portions of these letters have been published in Carl Weltzer, *Peter og Søren Kierkegaard*, pp. 266–67; another English translation of a portion of this letter is available in T. H. Croxall, *Glimpses and Impressions of Kierkegaard*, pp. 101–2.

Johan Christian Lund (1799–1875), husband of Kierkegaard's sister Nicoline Christine Kierkegaard Lund. **Henrik and Michael** are Johan Christian Lund's sons, Henrik Sigvard Lund (1825–89) and Michael Frederik Christian Lund (1826–1907), both physicians. **Peter** is Johan Christian Lund's nephew Peter Severin Lund (1834–64), the youngest son of Johan Christian Lund's brother Henrik Ferdinand Lund and his wife, Kierkegaard's sister, Petrea Severine Kierkegaard Lund. **[L]ast Sunday, when I visited him with Sophie**: Sophie (or Sofie) Vilhelmine Lund (1827–75) was another child of the marriage of Johan Christian and Nicoline Christine Lund; for another account of this hospital visit by Johan Christian Lund, his daughter Sophie, and her cousin Troels, see Troels-Lund's account in chapter 9 of this book.

8. From Henrik Ferdinand Lund's letter to Peter Christian Kierkegaard, dated October 23, 1855. The original letter is with Peter Christian Kierkegaard's correspondence in **KBHA** (NkS 3174, 4⁰, VII, fasc. 9, nr. 160). A portion of it has been published in Carl Weltzer, *Peter og Søren Kierkegaard*, p. 267; another English translation is available in T. H. Croxall, *Glimpses and Impressions of Kierkegaard*, p. 102.

Henrik Ferdinand Lund (1803–75) had been married to Kierkegaard's sister Petrea Severine Kierkegaard Lund (1803–34). **He would not permit you to come in and see him . . . your literary dispute**: on his deathbed Søren Kierkegaard refused to see his brother Peter Christian. See Peter Christian Kierkegaard's diary entry for October 1855 and his 1881 article, with accompanying notes, in chapter 9 of this book; see also his notes on his July 5, 1855, talk in Appendix B of this book as well as Emil Boesen's hospital conversations with Søren Kierkegaard in this chapter.

9. From Carl Lund's letter to Peter Christian Kierkegaard, dated October 24, 1855. The original letter is with Peter Christian Kierkegaard's correspondence in **KBHA** (NkS 3174, 4⁰, VII, fasc. 6, nr. 99). A portion of it has been published in Carl Weltzer, *Peter og Søren Kierkegaard*, pp. 268–69; another English translation is available in T. H. Croxall, *Glimpses and Impressions of Kierkegaard*, pp. 102–3.

Carl [Ferdinand] Lund (1830–1912), a landowner and farmer, was Søren Kierkegaard's nephew, the son of Søren Kierkegaard's sister Nicoline Christine Kierkegaard Lund (1799–1832) and the businessman, textile merchant Johan Christian Lund (1799–1875). **Monday** was October 22, 1855, and since we know that this letter is dated October 24, 1855, two days elapsed between the two visits reported here. **Michael and Henrik**: see the reference to Henrik and Michael Lund in the note accompanying Johan Christian Lund's letters of October 10 and 16, 1855, earlier in this chapter.

10. From Peter Severin Lund's letter to Peter Christian Kierkegaard, dated October 25, 1855. The original letter is with Peter Christian Kierkegaard's correspondence in **KBHA** (**NkS** 3174, 4⁰, VIII, fasc. 10, nr. 352). A portion of it has been published in Carl Weltzer, *Peter og Søren Kierkegaard*, pp. 267–68; another English translation of a portion of this letter is available in T. H. Croxall, *Glimpses and Impressions of Kierkegaard*, p. 103.

Peter Severin Lund (1834–64), the youngest son of Henrik Ferdinand Lund and Kierkegaard's sister Petrea Severine Kierkegaard Lund. **A letter from Father**: a reference to the letter dated October 23, 1855, from H. F. Lund to P. C. Kierkegaard, in which Lund states that Søren Kierkegaard had sent "a friendly and brotherly greeting" to Peter Christian Kierkegaard; see earlier in this chapter for this letter.

11. The first portion of this entry is from Emil Boesen's letters of October 15 and 17, 1855, to his wife; they are translated from Carl Koch, *Søren Kierkegaard og Emil Boesen*, pp. 35–36 and 36–37. The remainder of this entry is Boesen's account of his hospital conversations with Kierkegaard, translated from *SKEP 1854–55*, pp. 593–99; another English translation is available in Alexander Dru, ed., *The Journals of Søren Kierkegaard* (London: Oxford University Press, 1938), pp. 548–53.

Emil Boesen (1812–81), a pastor, was Kierkegaard's closest friend, and they carried on an extensive correspondence. (See also Boesen's entry with its accompanying note in chapter 2 of this book.) Their relationship is explored in Carl Koch, *Søren Kierkegaard og Emil Boesen*. (The Kierkegaard-Boesen correspondence has subsequently been reprinted in *B&A* I and is published in English translation in *KW* XXV.) **[Carl] Emil Fenger** (1814–84), politician and physician, was a professor of medicine at the University of Copenhagen and was in charge of Frederik's Hospital, which was the university's first teaching hospital. **Martin [Johannes] Hammerich** (1811–81), a brother of Peter Frederik Adolph Hammerich (see the entry by the latter, with its accompanying note, in chapter 1 of this book), was a philologist and educator who was influenced by National Liberalism, Grundtvig, and the Scandinavianist movement; he became headmaster of the Christianshavn Borgerdyd School and bore the rank of titular professor. **Pray for me**: this line by Kierkegaard is quoted in letters by the Grundtvigian pastor Gunni Busck (1798–1869) to Peter Christian Kierkegaard, dated November 1, 1855 (in **KBHA, NkS** 3174, 4°; cited in Weltzer, *Peter og Søren Kierkegaard*, pp. 269–70), and to another friend (in Henr. Bech, ed., *Gunni Busck, et Levnedsløb i en Præstegaard* [Gunni Gusck: A Life in a Parsonage] [Copenhagen: Karl Schønbergs Forlag, 1878], p. 326), dated November 14, 1855. This proves that Boesen communicated at least some of the contents of his hospital conversations with Kierkegaard while the latter was still alive. **I did not receive him when he last came to me after his speech in Roskilde**: in August 1855, in the wake of his speech at the Roskilde Ecclesiastical Convention, Peter Christian Kierkegaard appears to have attempted to visit his brother in Copenhagen, but was rebuffed, returned home, and soon thereafter fell ill and took to bed, as was not unusual for him in periods of stress; cf. the discussion in Weltzer, *Peter og Søren Kierkegaard*, p. 255, as well as Peter Christian Kierkegaard's 1881 attempt at reconstructing his eulogy of his brother, in chapter 9 of this book. For the July 1855 Roskilde Convention speech, see Peter Christian Kierkegaard's 1881 statement about this, with accompanying notes, in chapter 9, and see also the selections from his notes on that speech, included in Appendix B of this book. **I wrote a piece against him, very harsh**: see *Pap.* XI³ B 154; 155; 156. **Miss Fibiger**: the writer and philanthropist Ilia Marie Fibiger (1817–67), who served as an attendant at Frederik's Hospital from 1854 to 1860. **Gjødwad**: Jens Gjødvad [or Gjødwad] (1811–91) who served on the editorial staff of *Fædrelandet* in the 1840s and who also served as a sounding board for Kierkegaard, particularly during the writing of *Either/Or*; see the entry by Hother Ploug in chapter 4 of this book. **Mynster**: Jakob Peter Mynster (1775–1854), bishop of Zealand and primate of Denmark from 1834 until his death. Mynster was the most important representative of the Established Church and was particularly popular among the upper and upper-middle classes in Copenhagen. Mynster was on relatively close terms with the Kierkegaard family, and initially Søren Kierkegaard had the highest respect for him. After the mid-1840s, however, Kierkegaard began to see Mynster in an increasingly negative light, and came to view him as personally self-serving and as the lynchpin of an all-too-comfortable Established Church, which served as the guarantor of bourgeois "Christendom." H. L. Martensen, in many ways Mynster's protégé, preached a remarkable sermon memorializing Mynster after the latter's death, and was himself subsequently appointed as Mynster's successor. This served as the signal for Kierkegaard to launch his attack—which began publicly and unambiguously on December 18, 1854—on Mynster's posthumous reputation, on Martensen, and, most important, on the entire set of arrangements that constituted Danish Christendom. For a further discussion of this in its historical context, see Bruce H. Kirmmse, *Kierkegaard in Golden Age Denmark* (Bloomington: Indiana University Press, 1990). **Thurah**: see the note accompanying the letter by H. C. Andersen to Henriette Wulff in this chapter. **Martensen**: Hans Lassen Martensen; see the note accompanying Martensen's entry in this chapter, as well as the above note on Mynster, and Kirmmse, *Kierkegaard in Golden Age Denmark*. **Fenger's farewell sermon**: [Johannes] Ferdinand Fenger (1805–61), brother of the above-mentioned Emil Fenger, was a theologian and pastor, a founder of the Roskilde Ecclesiastical Convention (see Peter Christian Kierkegaard's entries in chapter 9 and Appendix B of this book), and a disciple of Grundtvig. **Get thee behind me, Satan, etc.** is freely adapted from Matthew 16.23. **The bedroom you had before**: Kierkegaard's lodgings at Mrs. Borries's house in Klædeboderne, where he had lived before coming to the hospital; see the entry by Mathilde Reinhardt in this chapter. **Horsens**: a medium-sized town in Jutland, where Boesen was a pastor.

12. From a letter from Peter Severin Lund to his uncle Peter Christian Kierkegaard, dated November 4, 1855; with Peter Christian Kierkegaard's correspondence in **KBHA** (**NkS** 3174, 4⁰, VIII, 10, nr. 353.).

Peter Severin Lund: see the note accompanying his letter to P. C. Kierkegaard, dated October 25, 1855, earlier in this chapter. **Jette**: Peter Lund's sister (Anna) Henriette Lund. **Father**: Peter Lund's father, Henrik Ferdinand Lund.

13. From a letter from Johan Christian Lund to Peter Christian Kierkegaard, dated November 10, 1855. The original letter is with Peter Christian Kierkegaard's correspondence in **KBHA** (**NkS** 3174, 4⁰, VIII, fasc. 3, nr. 257). A portion of it has been published in Carl Weltzer, *Peter og Søren Kierkegaard*, pp. 270–71; another English translation is available in T. H. Croxall, *Glimpses and Impressions of Kierkegaard*, p. 105.

14. From a letter from Henrik Lund to Emil Boesen, dated November 11, 1855, translated from Carl Koch, ed., *Søren Kierkegaard og Emil Boesen*, pp. 42–43.

Henrik [Sigvard] Lund (1825–89) was serving his residency as a physician at Frederik's Hospital when his Uncle Søren was dying.

15. The first passage is from a letter from Michael Lund to his father, Johan Christian Lund, dated November 12, 1855. The original of this letter is in **KBHA** (**NkS** 1994, Fol.). The second passage is from a letter from Michael Lund to his uncle, Peter Christian Kierkegaard, also dated November 12, 1855. The original of this letter is with Peter Christian Kierkegaard's correspondence in **KBHA** (**NkS** 3174, 4⁰, VIII, fasc. 8). A portion of this second letter has been published in Carl Weltzer, *Peter og Søren Kierkegaard*, p. 272, and another English translation is available in T. H. Croxall, *Glimpses and Impressions of Kierkegaard*, p. 105.

Michael [Frederik Christian] Lund (1826–1907) was a brother of Henrik Lund and, like him, a physician at Frederik's Hospital at the time of Kierkegaard's illness and death. **Uncle Ferdinand**: Michael Lund's uncle, Henrik Ferdinand Lund (1803–75); see the note accompanying his entry in this chapter. **Uncle Peter**: Peter Christian Kierkegaard; see Michael Lund's letter to him in this entry. **Carl**: Carl Ferdinand Lund (1830–1912), Michael Lund's younger brother; see Carl Lund's entry in this chapter. **Father** is the textile merchant Johan Christian Lund (1799–1875), who had been married to Kierkegaard's sister Nicoline Christine (1799–1832). **A letter from Father, sent the day before yesterday**: see earlier in this chapter for Johan Christian Lund's letter to Peter Christian Kierkegaard, dated November 10, 1855.

16. From Frederik Hammerich's autobiography, *Et Levnedsløb*, vol. 1, p. 145.

Frederik Hammerich: see the note accompanying the entry by Hammerich in chapter 1 of this book.

17. From the "Dagbog" section in Goldschmidt's journal *Nord og Syd*, Ny Række, 8de. Bind, Nr. 2, p. 224, which was published November 15, 1855.

18. From a letter from Henrik Ferdinand Lund to his son Vilhelm Nicolai Lund (1831–1902), dated November 18, 1855. The original letter is in **KBHA** (**NkS** 1994, Fol.). A portion of it has been published in Carl Weltzer, *Peter og Søren Kierkegaard*, pp. 272–73; another English translation is available in T. H. Croxall, *Glimpses and Impressions of Kierkegaard*, pp. 106–7.

Henrik Ferdinand Lund (1803–75) was a director of the National Bank and was Kierkegaard's brother-in-law by his first marriage to Kierkegaard's sister Petrea Severine (1801–34). **Uncle Peter** is Søren Kierkegaard's brother, Peter Christian Kierkegaard. **Cousin Carl** is Carl Ferdinand Lund (1830–1912), the son of Kierkegaard's sister Nicoline Christine (1799–1832) and H. F. Lund's brother, the textile merchant Johan Christian Lund (1799–1875). **Uncle Christian** is the above-mentioned Johan Christian Lund, H. F. Lund's brother. **He disposed of his money**: H. F. Lund is dispatching the myth of the fortune Kierkegaard was said to possess by invoking other myths concerning the expenses Kierkegaard supposedly incurred in publishing his books and in allegedly showing great generosity to the poor. See Brandt and Rammel, *Kierkegaard og Pengene*, for a more accurate account.

19. From Frederik Benedikt Møller's memoirs, *En gammel Præst fortæller. Pastor Frederik Benedikt Møllers Optegnelser 1832–1864 ved Hans Degen*, p. 80.

Frederik Benedikt Møller: see the note accompanying Møller's entry in chapter 4 of this book. **[H]e died without allowing his brother Peter Christian to visit him**: see the note accompanying the entry by Emil Boesen earlier in this chapter. **His brother, kneeling, offered a moving prayer for him**: for Peter Christian Kierkegaard's attempt at reconstructing his eulogy of his brother, see his 1881 statement, with the accompanying note, in chapter 9 of this book. **A medical graduate named Lund**: Henrik [Sigvard] Lund (1825–89), Kierkegaard's nephew; see his graveside speech later in this chapter.

20. From a letter from F. Sodemann to his future father-in-law, Pastor Peter Marius Barfod of Næstved (1813–89), dated November 18, 1855, in **KBHA** (**SKA** D. Pk. 5).

F. Sodemann: Kristian [or Christian] Frantz Henrik Sodemann (1832–1911), then a theological student at the University of Copenhagen, subsequently a pastor on Bornholm. **Archdeacon Tryde**: see the note accompanying the entry by Kristian Arentzen in chapter 7 of this book. **The eulogy**: see Peter Christian Kierkegaard's 1881 statement in chapter 9 of this book for his attempt at reconstructing his eulogy of his brother. **Dr. Lund from Frederik's Hospital**: Henrik [Sigvard] Lund (1825–89), Kierkegaard's nephew; see his graveside speech later in this chapter. **Revelations 3 (Laodicea)**: Revelations 3.14–22 is directed to the church at Laodicea, and the pertinent section is probably verses 15–16: "I know your works: you are neither cold nor hot! Would that you were cold or hot! So, because you are lukewarm, and neither cold nor hot, I will spew you out of my mouth." **Apoc. 18**: Revelations 18 is a lamentation over the fall of Babylon, featuring such typical language as in verses 2–3: "Fallen, fallen is Babylon the great! It has become a dwelling place of demons, a haunt of every foul spirit, a haunt of every foul and hateful bird; for all the nations have drunk the wine of her impure passion, and the kings of the earth have committed fornication with her, and the merchants of the earth have grown rich with the wealth of her wantonness." **"To Bury with Full Honors"**: the phrase was used not in any of the issues of *The Moment* but rather in Kierkegaard's article entitled "There the Matter Rests," which was published in *Fædrelandet*, no. 304, December 30, 1854 (*SV* XIV 15–21). **Prof. Clausen**: Henrik Nicolai Clausen (1793–1877), professor of New Testament at the University of Copenhagen; see the notes accompanying Peter Rørdam's entry in chapter 2 and entries 6 and 46 in Hans Brøchner's memoirs in chapter 11 of this book. **Dagbladet**: see *Dagbladet*, November 17, 1855, no. 272, p. 1.

21. From Henrik Lund's graveside speech, as published in *Fædrelandet* (16. Aargang, no. 273, [November 22, 1855], pp. 1144–45).

Henrik [Sigvard] Lund (1825–89), physician and Kierkegaard's nephew; see the notes to other entries by him in this chapter. Henrik Lund's speech at the cemetery was in violation of the law, which forbade unauthorized persons from speaking at such events. In a case decided on June 5, 1856, Lund was fined one hundred rixdollars plus court costs and had to make an apology to Archdeacon Eggert C. Tryde of the Church of Our Lady, who had been officially in charge of the ceremony. **My mother, who died young**, i.e, Nicoline Christine Lund *née* Kierkegaard (1799–1832). **The Revelation of St. John 3.14–end**: the key passage here is verses 15–16; see the note to the previous entry, by F. Sodemann. **God's Kingdom and His Righteousness** is from Matthew 6.33; cf. Matthew 6.24–end, which begins with "No one can serve two masters. . . . You cannot serve God and Mammon," etc., and constitutes the context of the cited phrase. **"The great whore Babylon, with whom all the kings of the Earth have fornicated,"** etc.: cf. Rev. 17.1–2. **Chapter 18 of the Revelation of St. John**: cf. Rev. 18.2. **What must be said**, i.e., "This Must Be Said, So Let It Be Said," a pamphlet dated "December 1854" but published on May 24, 1855; the passage cited is a close paraphrase of *SV* XIV 85. **"Come out of her, my people,"** etc.: Rev. 18.4. The sensation caused by Lund's speech led to a great deal of debate in the newspapers, and Lund therefore felt it necessary to reprint the text of his remarks in *Fædrelandet*.

22. From a letter by Hans Lassen Martensen to his friend and follower, the cleric Ludvig J. M. Gude (1820–95), dated November 18, 1855; the letter is in **KBHA** (**NkS** 3450, 4⁰, II) and has been published in *Biskop H. Martensens Breve* [The Letters of Bishop H. Martensen], ed. Bjørn Kornerup, vol. 1: *Breve til L. Gude, 1848–1859* [Letters to L. Gude, 1848–59] (Copenhagen: G.E.C. Gad, 1955), pp. 151–52.

Hans Lassen Martensen (1808–84), theologian, professor at the University of Copenhagen, and subsequently bishop of Zealand, had been Kierkegaard's tutor during the latter's years as a university student. **Tryde**: Archdeacon Eggert Christopher Tryde (1781–1860); see the note accompanying the entry by Kristian Arentzen in chapter 7 of this book. **R. Nielsen**: see the note accompanying the letter of February 28, 1870, from M. A. Goldschmidt to H. P. Barfod, in chapter 5 of this book; see also entry number 21, with its accompanying note, in Brøchner's memoirs in chapter 11 of this book. **Magister Stilling**: Peter Michael Stilling (1812–69), a writer on philosophy and theology whom Kierkegaard influenced. **Lund**: see earlier in this chapter for Henrik Lund's graveside speech and the details of the legal case against him.

23. From an entry in Hansine Andræe's diaries, dated November 18, 1855; published in *Geheimeraadinde Andræs politiske Dagbøger*, vol. 1, p. 125.

A memorial address for Bishop Mynster: this was Martensen's second "eulogy" of Bishop Mynster, *Til Erindring om J. P. Mynster* [In Memory of J. P. Mynster] (Copenhagen: Gyldendal, 1855), which was delivered in lecture form to the Videnskabernes Selskab [Scientific Society] on November 23, 1855, only five days after Kierkegaard's burial, and issued in print the following month. Hansine Andræ appears to draw the not unreasonable inference that the timing of Martensen's second eulogy of Mynster was quite deliberate, i.e., that he had prepared the piece somewhat earlier, that he held it in readiness until immediately after Kierkegaard's death, and that he then presented it in the hope that it would be the last word in the whole affair. This surmise appears to be confirmed by Martensen's letter to his friend Gude, dated November 18, 1855, in which he wrote: "On Friday [November 23, 1855] I intend to read a memorial piece for Mynster to the Scientific Society. The portion I read to you has been partly reworked and also significantly expanded. After the lecture I intend to publish it immediately, so that it will be out in time for Christmas" (from the letter cited in the previous entry; in **KBHA** [**NkS** 3450, 4⁰, II] and published in *Biskop H. Martensens Breve*, vol. 1, p. 152).

24. From a letter from Hans Christian Andersen to August Bournonville, dated November 24, 1855; published in *Breve fra Hans Christian Andersen*, pp. 329–30. Andersen sent a very similar letter

to Henriette Wulff on November 26, 1855; see *H. C. Andersen og Henriette Wulff. En Brevveksling. II (Breve 1849–58)*, p. 247, and *Deres broderligt hengivne. Et udvalg af breve fra H. C. Andersen* [Yours in Brotherly Devotion: A Selection of Letters from Hans Christian Andersen], ed. Niels Birger Wamberg (Gyldendal: Copenhagen, 1975), p. 169.

August Bournonville: see the note accompanying the entry by Bournonville in chapter 6 in this book. **Ladies in red and blue hats**: Andersen notes two improprieties: 1) in accordance with the custom of the time, it was not proper for women (excepting family members) to be present at public funerals, and 2) their hat colors were inappropriate—apparently just as inappropriate as the presence of dogs! **Tryde**: see the note accompanying the entry by Kristian Arentzen in chapter 7 of this book.

25. From a letter from Frederikke Bremer to Hans Christian Andersen, dated December 14, 1855; published in *Breve til Hans Christian Andersen*, p. 674.

Frederikke Bremer: see the note accompanying the entry by Frederikke Bremer in chapter 6.

Chapter Nine
Søren and the Family

1. The present selections are translated from a copy of the original manuscript of Eline Heramb Boisen's memoirs, which was kindly made available by Anna Bojsen-Møller. Another version of these memoirs, containing a number of errors, has been published as *—men størst er kærligheden. Eline Boisens erindringer fra midten af forrige århundrede* [—but the greatest of these is love: Eline Boisen's Memoirs from the Middle of the Last Century], ed. Anna, Elin, Gudrun, and Jutta Bojsen-Møller and Birgitte Haarder (Copenhagen: Gyldendal, 1985).

Eline [Birgitte Heramb] Boisen (1813–71): see the note to the entry by P. Bojsen in chapter 2 of this book, where a portion of a letter by Eline Heramb Boisen is cited in paraphrase. Eline Heramb Boisen married Pastor F[rederik] E[ngelhart] Boisen (1808–87) in 1834. The latter was the brother of Elise Marie Boisen (1806–37), who was Peter Christian Kierkegaard's first wife. Eline Boisen was thus the wife of Søren Kierkegaard's sister-in-law's brother. **While I was out at the Boisens**: in the winter of 1833–34, while engaged to F. E. Boisen, Eline Heramb visited her fiancé and his widowed mother at the family home on the island of Lolland. **Aunt Würzen**: a relative of Eline Heramb's. **A sister of Kierkegaard, married to a Lund**: Petrea Severine Kierkegaard (1801–34), who married Henrik Ferdinand Lund in 1828 and died in December 1834. **Kierkegaard**: Peter Christian Kierkegaard. **An older sister had been married to this Lund's brother**: Nicoline Christine Kierkegaard (1799–1832), who married Johan Christian Lund in 1824 and died in September 1832. **During that time, before he became a university student, Søren wrote some articles against Orla Lehmann**: actually, the articles were written in 1836, while Kierkegaard was enrolled as a student at the university; they are reprinted in *SV* XIII 9–39 (*KW* I 6–34). See also Teddy Petersen, *Kierkegaards polemiske debut*, and the entries by Peter Rørdam and Johan Hahn in chapter 2 of this book. **The elder Kierkegaards**: Michael Pedersen Kierkegaard (1756–1838) and Ane Sørensdatter Lund Kierkegaard (1768–1834). **Mrs. Teilmann**: a relative of Mrs. Catrine Rørdam (cf. the entries by P. Bojsen and H. F. Rørdam in chapters 2 and 4, respectively, of this book), who was the mother of Peter and Bolette Rørdam (cf. the first entry by Goldschmidt in chapter 5 of this book). Eline Heramb was a longtime friend of Bolette Rørdam, who was possibly an early romantic interest of Kierkegaard's. **Boisen**: F. E. Boisen (1813–71), Eline Heramb Boisen's husband. **He became engaged shortly thereafter**: in another passage, reproduced later in this entry, Eline Heramb Boisen makes it clear that she believes this episode took place during the winter of 1835–36. In any event, since Eline Heramb Boisen dates this episode as taking place "shortly after" her marriage (November 12, 1834), and since Kierkegaard did not become engaged to Regine Olsen until September 10, 1840, which was almost six years later, Eline Boisen appears to confuse the dates of this account. Either Kierkegaard was not engaged at the time, or the assignment of a date is incorrect. **Many years later**: perhaps during one of F. E. Boisen's frequent visits to Copenhagen in 1848. **The rocket**: probably an error for "comet"; in the January 9, 1846, issue, (no. 277) of *The Corsair*, Kierkegaard is described as a "comet," and *The Corsair* then has Kierkegaard define a comet as "an eccentric, illuminated body that appears to us mortals at irregular intervals." **On that occasion . . . his engagement**: elsewhere in her text Eline Heramb Boisen makes it clear that this was during the winter of 1835–36. Assuming that she is correct in her statement that Kierkegaard was engaged at the time of this episode, this date is incorrect; see above in this note.

2. From Vilhelm Birkedal's memoirs, *Personlige Oplevelser i et langt Liv*, vol. 2, p. 78.

Vilhelm Birkedal: see the note accompanying the entry by Birkedal in chapter 4 of this book.

3. From Marguerite Lund Løfting's memoirs as reproduced in Anders Uhrskov, *Landsmænd. Tre Livsbilleder* [Compatriots: Three Life Portraits] (Copenhagen: G.E.C. Gad, 1957), p. 8.

[Catharine Marie Caroline] Marguerite [Lund] Løfting (born 1871) was the daughter of the younger Henrik Ferdinand Lund (1837–1914), who was in turn the son of the elder Henrik Ferdinand Lund (1803–75), and his first wife, Søren Kierkegaard's sister Petrea Severine (1801–34). Marguerite Lund Løfting was thus Søren Kierkegaard's grandniece. **Augusta**: Sofie Augusta Faber (1826–71), a distant cousin of Søren Kierkegaard. She was the daughter of Friedrich Faber (1796–1828) and Anne Kirstine Elisabeth Kierkegaard Faber (1801–67) and, on her mother's side, the granddaughter of Michael Andersen Kierkegaard (1776–1867) and Anne Sophie Kjeldsen (1779–1815).

4. From "'En Undtagelse'" [An Exception], a memoir about Hans Peter Kierkegaard by his friend Frederik Meidell, which was published in the journal *For Ide og Virkelighed* [For Idea and Reality], ed. R. Nielsen, B. Bjørnson, and Rud. Schmidt, vol. 1 (1870) (Copenhagen: Chr. Steen & Søns Forlag, 1870), pp. 53–55.

Hans Peter Kierkegaard (1815–62) was the son of Michael Andersen Kierkegaard (1776–1867), a textile dealer who lived at Købmagergade 45 and was Kierkegaard's father's first cousin. Søren and Hans Peter Kierkegaard were thus first cousins, once removed. Hans Peter Kierkegaard (known as "Peter" to his friends and relatives, including his cousin Søren) was crippled from birth but his mental faculties were unimpaired. He was one of Søren Kierkegaard's favorite relatives. **The house where Peter lived**: the home of Peter's father Michael Andersen Kierkegaard, who was an elderly and somewhat pompous eccentric whom Søren Kierkegaard tended to avoid. Michael Andersen Kierkegaard was also the uncle of Hans Brøchner; see Brøchner's memoirs on Kierkegaard, entry numbers 30, 31, and 32 in chapter 11 of this book, for Brøchner's comments on the relationship between Søren and Michael Andersen Kierkegaard. **One of his edifying discourses, which really seemed to have been written specifically for me**: this could refer either to one of the discourses in *Edifying Discourses in a Different Spirit* (see the note accompanying entry 43 in chapter 11 of this book) or to one of the discourses that constitute *Works of Love*, "Mercifulness, a Work of Love, Even if It Cannot Give Anything and Is Incapable of Doing Anything" (*SV* IX 300–314 [*KW* XVI 315–30]).

5. From a letter by Michael Pedersen Kierkegaard to his son Peter Christian Kierkegaard, dated July 29, 1826; the original is in **KBHA** (Troesgaards Autografsamling, I. 1); part of the letter has been previously published in Kühle, *Søren Kierkegaards Barndom og Ungdom*, p. 29.

Søren Kierkegaard's elder brother **Peter Christian Kierkegaard** (1805–88) was a theologian, a follower of Grundtvig, a pastor in the Danish Church, bishop of Aalborg (1856–75), and briefly a cabinet minister (1867–68). **In Frederiksborg**: in the Hillerød area of northern Zealand, ca. twenty miles (thirty kilometers) north of Copenhagen.

6. From Peter Christian Kierkegaard's journal, in **KBHA** (NkS 2656, 4°, vol. 1, p. 3 at end of volume); published (in slightly different form) in Weltzer, *Peter og Søren Kierkegaard*, p. 24.

Søren was confirmed on the 20th: see Søren Kierkegaard's confirmation certificate (*B&A* I 4 [*KW* XXI 4]).

7. From a letter from P. C. Kierkegaard to H. F. Lund, dated January 2, 1829. The original letter is in **KBHA** (NBD IX, fasc. 12, nr. 7); published (in slightly different form) in Weltzer, *Peter og Søren Kierkegaard*, p. 26.

When he wrote this letter, twenty-three-year-old Peter Christian Kierkegaard was on an academic stay in Germany, where he earned his theological doctorate. The recipient of the letter was Henrik Ferdinand Lund, a brother-in-law of the Kierkegaard siblings, having married Petrea Severine Kierkegaard in 1828.

8. From a letter by T. V. Oldenburg to P. C. Kierkegaard, dated May 17, 1829. The original letter is in **KBHA** (**NkS** 3174, 4⁰, IX, fasc. 5, nr. 9); published in Weltzer, *Peter og Søren Kierkegaard*, p. 16.

Theodor Vilhelm Oldenburg (1805–42), a pastor, hymn writer, and follower of Grundtvig, was a good friend of Peter Christian Kierkegaard and in the 1820s was a frequent visitor at the Kierkegaard family home at Nytorv 2. When Peter Christian was in Germany in the early part of 1829, Oldenburg reminded Søren to write to his brother. By the time Oldenburg wrote Peter Christian, Søren had in fact already written his brother; that letter, dated March 8, 1829 (*B&A* I 29–31 [*KW* XXV 37–39]), is the earliest surviving writing from his hand, and in it Søren expresses displeasure at being reminded to write by a third party.

9. From a letter from P. C. Kierkegaard to Henrik Ferdinand Lund, dated July 3–4, 1829. The original letter is in **KBHA** (**NBD** IX, fasc. 12, nr. 9); also published in Weltzer, *Peter og Søren Kierkegaard*, p. 27.

Christian was Henrik Ferdinand Lund's brother, the businessman Johan Christian Lund (1799–1875); see the letters by him, with accompanying notes, in chapter 8, as well as the entries by Henriette Lund and Troels-Lund later in this chapter. **Wilhelm** is Henrik Ferdinand Lund's brother, Peter Wilhelm (or Vilhelm) Lund (1801–80). P. W. Lund traveled to Brazil in 1832 and remained there for most of his adult life, becoming a well known and widely respected natural scientist. See Henrik Stangerup's novel *Vejen til Lagoa Santa* (Copenhagen: Gyldendal, 1981)— available in English translation as *The Road to Lagoa Santa*, trans. Barbara Bluestone (New York and London: Martin Boyars, 1984)—for an imaginative treatment of P. W. Lund's life. See also Henriette Lund's mention of P. W. Lund later in this chapter. **Niels** is Niels Andreas Kierkegaard (1809–33), who emigrated to America as a young man and died there; see the note to the next entry in this chapter. **My dear sisters** are Nicoline Christine Kierkegaard (1799–1832) and Petrea Severine Kierkegaard (1801–34), who were married to Johan Christian and Henrik Ferdinand Lund, respectively.

10. From a letter from Michael Pedersen Kierkegaard to his son Peter Christian Kierkegaard, dated July 15, 1829; the original is in **KBHA** (**NkS** 3174, 4⁰, VI, fasc. 7, nr. 37). It has been published in Valdemar Ammundsen, *Søren Kierkegaards Ungdom*, pp. 62–63; excerpts have also been published in *B&A* I 32 and II 24 (*KW* XXV 41 and 451).

Young Søren Kierkegaard had the task of copying his father's letters into a copybook and thus had the opportunity to read these speculations by his father concerning his reluctance to write to his brother. Michael Pedersen allowed Søren to append, in his own hand, the following remark to this letter sent to Peter Christian: "I (Søren) will soon write to you in order, among other things, to refute Father."

11. From a letter from Niels Andreas Kierkegaard to his brother Peter Christian, dated February 26, 1833. The original letter is in **KBHA** (**NkS** 3174, 4⁰, VI, fasc. 7, nr. 48); also published in Weltzer, *Peter og Søren Kierkegaard*, p. 64.

Niels Andreas Kierkegaard (1809–33) was destined by his father, Michael Pedersen Kierkegaard, to be trained for the business world and thus did not attend the university; see also the entry by Henriette Lund in this chapter. In 1832 he set off for America to seek his fortune. The present letter was written while Niels was staying with acquaintances in Boston. Later in 1833 he fell ill, and he died, in Paterson, New Jersey, on September 21, 1833. **In the same fashion**, i.e., correcting the grammatical and stylistic errors in Niels's Danish prose.

12. From Peter Christian Kierkegaard's journals, located in **KBHA** (**NkS** 2656, 4⁰, bd. I, p. 52); also published (in slightly different form) in Weltzer, *Peter og Søren Kierkegaard*, p. 79, and Sejer Kühle, "Nogle Oplysninger om Søren Kierkegaard 1834–38," I, p. 2.

Matthew 5.23–24: "So if you are offering your gift at the altar, and there remember that your brother has something against you, leave your gift at the altar and go; first be reconciled to your brother, and then come and offer your gift." Two things should be noted here. First of all, participating in the Eucharist was a relatively infrequent event for members of the Danish Church during this period. Second, the very rarity of the event helps bring into focus Peter Christian Kierkegaard's scruples with respect to his relationship with his brother Søren, a source of trouble and regret to him during his entire life. (For an examination of Søren Kierkegaard's relation to the Eucharist, see Michael Plekon, "Kierkegaard and the Eucharist," *Studia Liturgica*, vol. 22 (1992), no. 2, pp. 214–36.)

13. From Peter Christian Kierkegaard's journals, located in **KBHA** (**NkS** 2656, 4⁰, bd. I, p. 52); also published (in slightly different form) in Weltzer, *Peter og Søren Kierkegaard*, p. 79, and in Sejer Kühle, "Nogle Oplysninger om Søren Kierkegaard 1834–38," II, pp. 151–52.

The young Bornemann: presumably either Georg Bernhard Bornemann (1815–84), who entered the University of Copenhagen in 1832 and subsequently became an attorney for the Danish military, or his brother Johan Alfred Bornemann (1813–90), who entered the university in 1830 and subsequently became a theologian and an ally of Martensen.

14. From Peter Christian Kierkegaard's journals, located in **KBHA** (**NkS** 2656, 4⁰, bd. I, p. 58); also published (in slightly different form) in Weltzer, *Peter og Søren Kierkegaard*, pp. 80–81 and in Sejer Kühle, "Nogle Oplysninger om Søren Kierkegaard 1834–38," I, p. 4.

Things were significantly worse with Mother: Ane Sørensdatter Lund Kierkegaard died ca. 10:30 P.M. on the evening of July 30, 1834, and as can be seen from this entry Søren was not able to return home from Gilleleje until the following morning, by which time his mother had died.

15. From Peter Christian Kierkegaard's journals, located in **KBHA** (**NkS** 2656, 4⁰, bd. I, p. 63); also published (in slightly different form) in Weltzer, *Peter og Søren Kierkegaard*, p. 87, and in Sejer Kühle, "Nogle Oplysninger om Søren Kierkegaard 1834–38," I, p. 2.

16. From Peter Christian Kierkegaard's journals, located in **KBHA** (**NkS** 2656, 4⁰, bd. I, p. 64); also published (in slightly different form) in Weltzer, *Peter og Søren Kierkegaard*, p. 89, and in Sejer Kühle, "Nogle Oplysninger om Søren Kierkegaard 1834–38," I, p. 5.

17. From Peter Christian Kierkegaard's journals, located in **KBHA** (**NkS** 2656, 4⁰, bd. I, p. 67); also published in Weltzer, *Peter og Søren Kierkegaard*, p. 91, and in Sejer Kühle, "Nogle Oplysninger om Søren Kierkegaard 1834–38," I, p. 5.

His letters: in the summer of 1835 Søren Kierkegaard was on his momentous vacation stay at the resort town of Gilleleje; the letters referred to are not collected in *B&A* and are apparently lost.

18. From a letter from Michael Pedersen Kierkegaard to Peter Christian Kierkegaard, dated July 15, 1836. The original is in **KBHA** (**NkS** 3174, 4⁰, fasc. 7, nr. 39); also published (in slightly different form) in Weltzer, *Peter og Christian Kierkegaard*, p. 102, and (partially) in Kühle, "Nogle Oplysninger om Søren Kierkegaard 1834–38," I, p. 7.

Peter Christian Kierkegaard was on vacation in Jutland, where he was visiting the family of his fiancée, Elise Marie Boisen, whom he married in October 1836.

19. From Peter Christian Kierkegaard's journals, located in **KBHA** (**NkS** 2656, 4⁰, bd. I, p. 90); also published in Weltzer, *Peter og Søren Kierkegaard*, p. 115, and in Kühle, "Nogle Oplysninger om Søren Kierkegaard 1834–38," I, p. 8.

The very day of the burial: Elise Marie Boisen Kierkegaard (1806–37), Peter Christian Kierkegaard's first wife, died on July 18, 1837, and was buried four days later.

20. From Peter Christian Kierkegaard's journals, located in **KBHA** (**NkS** 2656, 4⁰, bd. I, p. 94); also published in Weltzer, *Peter og Søren Kierkegaard*, p. 120, and in Kühle, "Nogle Oplysninger om Søren Kierkegaard 1834–38," I, p. 9.

21. From Peter Christian Kierkegaard's journals, located in **KBHA** (**NkS** 2656, 4⁰, bd. I, p. 98); also published in Weltzer, *Peter og Søren Kierkegaard*, p. 121, and in Kühle, "Nogle Oplysninger om Søren Kierkegaard 1834–38," I, p. 9.

P. Købke: a young theologian and the fiancé of Bolette Rørdam; for Bolette Rørdam, see the note to the second entry by Goldschmidt in chapter 5 of this book. **Lindberg**: Jacob Christian Lindberg (1797–1857), a renowned scholar of Hebrew, respected Bible translator, sharp-witted and charismatic controversialist on the "antirationalist" side in theological matters, ally of Grundtvig, and pastor. Lindberg was a frequent visitor at the Kierkegaard family home on Nytorv and was respected by Michael Pedersen Kierkegaard and both his sons. See Kaj Baagø, *Magister Jacob Christian Lindberg* (Copenhagen: G.E.C. Gad, 1958) and Jørgen Bukdahl, *Søren Kierkegaard og den menige Mand* [Søren Kierkegaard and the Common Man] (Copenhagen: Gyldendals Ugle-bøger, 1970), pp. 24–31.

22. From Peter Christian Kierkegaard's journals, located in **KBHA** (NkS 2656, 4⁰, bd. I, p. 102); also published in Weltzer, *Peter og Søren Kierkegaard*, p. 128, and (partially) in Kühle, "Nogle Oplysninger om Søren Kierkegaard 1834–38," I, p. 10.

Michael Pedersen Kierkegaard died on August 9, 1838, and Peter Christian here recounts the old man's attitude toward Søren shortly before his death. **M.'s death**: the death of Elise Marie Boisen Kierkegaard, Peter Christian Kierkegaard's first wife, had taken place the previous summer on July 18, 1837. **Monday**: Monday, August 6, 1838.

23. From a letter from Johan Hahn to Peter Christian Kierkegaard, dated August 18, 1838. The original is with the letters to Peter Christian Kierkegaard in **KBHA** (NkS 3174, 4⁰, V, fasc. 3, nr. 13); also published in Weltzer, *Peter og Søren Kierkegaard*, pp. 129–30, and (partially) in Kühle, "Nogle Oplysninger om Søren Kierkegaard" V, pp. 1–2.

Johan [Gottfried Wilhelm] Hahn (1804–40): see the note accompanying the entry by Hahn in chapter 2 of this book.

24. From a letter from Peter Hansen to Peter Christian Kierkegaard, dated November 7, 1867. The original is with the letters to Peter Christian Kierkegaard in **KBHA** (NkS 3174, 4⁰, V, fasc. 8, nr. 113); published (in a slightly different form) in Weltzer, *Peter og Søren Kierkegaard*, pp. 153–54, and (partially) in Sejer Kühle, *Søren Kierkegaard. Barndom og Ungdom*, p. 175.

Peter Hansen, a university student from southern Jutland, shared an apartment at Kultorvet 11 with Søren Kierkegaard in 1839–40; he subsequently became a government official; see Sejer Kühle, *Søren Kierkegaard. Barndom og Ungdom*, p. 175. **Nathanael** means "gift of God"; in John 1.47 Jesus says of Nathanael, "Behold, an Israelite indeed, in whom is no guile." **Israel** and **God's true warrior** are allusions to the fact that the name "Israel" means "he who strives with God" (Genesis 32.28–29).

25. From Peter Christian Kierkegaard's journals, located in **KBHA** (NkS 2656, 4⁰, bd. I, p. 118); also published in Weltzer, *Peter og Søren Kierkegaard*, p. 163.

On the 10th (?): Kierkegaard actually broke off his engagement to Regine Olsen on October 11, 1841; see chapter 3 of this book. **Em. Boesen**: Emil Boesen; see the note accompanying Boesen's entry in chapter 2, as well as Boesen's entry in chapter 8 of this book.

26. From Peter Christian Kierkegaard's journals, located in **KBHA** (NkS 2656, 4⁰, Bd. I, p. 118); also published in Weltzer, *Peter og Søren Kierkegaard*, p. 163.

The first proper letter from Søren: this letter does not appear in *B&A* and is apparently lost.

27. From Peter Christian Kierkegaard's journals, located in **KBHA** (NkS 2656, 4⁰, bd. I, p. 119); also published (in slightly different form) in Weltzer, *Peter og Søren Kierkegaard*, p. 167.

I wrote Søren in Berlin and **his [Søren's] letter of January 27**: neither of these letters is collected in *B&A*, and they are apparently lost.

28. From a letter from Else Pedersdatter Kierkegaard to her nephew Peter Christian Kierke-gaard, dated July 1, 1842. The original is with the letters to Peter Christian Kierkegaard in **KBHA** (NkS 3174, 4⁰, VI, fasc. 6, nr. 33); also published in Weltzer, *Peter og Søren Kierkegaard*, p. 170.

Else Pedersdatter Kierkegaard (1768–1844) was the younger sister of Michael Pedersen Kierkegaard. She remained in Sædding, the Jutland village from which Michael Pedersen came, but corresponded by mail with her brother and his children, from whom she received occasional financial assistance. The letters she addressed to Søren or jointly to Søren and Peter Christian Kierkegaard have been collected in *B&A* (*B&A* I 43–44, 46–47, 101–2 [*KW* XXV 55–56, 59–60, 130–31]); the editors of *B&A* point out that at least two of those three letters bear the mark of an educated letter writer who assisted in their composition, and this seems to be case with the present letter as well.

29. From a letter from Peter Christian Kierkegaard to his wife, Henriette, dated December 11, 1842. The original is in **KBHA** (**NkS** 3013, 4⁰, II); also published in Weltzer, *Peter og Søren Kierkegaard*, p. 173.

[Sophie] Henriette ["Jette"] Glahn Kierkegaard (1809–81) was Peter Christian Kierke-gaard's second wife; she was the daughter of pastor Poul Egede Glahn, curate of the Garrison Church in Copenhagen and his wife, Bodil Maria Elisabeth Blicher, who was the sister of Grundtvig's first wife. Jette Glahn was thus Grundtvig's niece and had lived part of her childhood in Grundtvig's home as a member of his family. At the time of the writing of this letter Peter Christian was at his parish at Pedersborg-by-Sorø in west-central Zealand, while his wife was living in Copenhagen at the family home at Nytorv 2 with her infant son; Søren Kierkegaard was also living at Nytorv 2.

30. From Peter Christian Kierkegaard's journals, located in **KBHA** (**NkS** 2656, 4⁰, bd. I, p. 128); also published in Weltzer, *Peter og Søren Kierkegaard*, p. 185.

Either/Or was published on February 20, 1843. The book's putative author-editor was Victor Eremita, but many pieces of evidence make clear how transparent this pseudonymity was; e.g., in addition to this journal entry by Peter Christian Kierkegaard, the following excerpt from a letter, dated February 27, 1843, from Henrik Ferdinand Lund to Peter Wilhelm (or Vilhelm) Lund in Brazil: "At my first opportunity I will send you a book that has attracted much attention and is being read 'by almost every cultured person.' The title of the book is *Either/Or*, and people assume that Søren is the author" (**KBHA** [**NkS** 3261, 4⁰, fasc. 55, nr. 372]), published in Weltzer, *Peter og Søren Kierkegaard*, p. 185). Other evidence attesting to early knowledge of the actual authorship of *Either/Or* includes two letters to Hans Christian Andersen, one dated February 20, 1843, by Henriette Wulff (**KBHA** [Den collinske Brevsamling, XII, fasc. 14, nr. 202]) and one from Signe Læssøe, dated April 7, 1843 (*Breve til Hans Christian Andersen*, pp. 466–67); see chapter 4 of this book for these letters.

31. From a letter by Carl Lund to his uncle Peter Christian Kierkegaard, dated January 12, 1850; the original letter is in **KBHA** (**NkS** 3174, 4⁰, VII, fasc. 6, nr. 92).

32. From a letter from Johan Christian Lund to Peter Christian Kierkegaard, dated May 2, 1851. The original letter is in **KBHA** (**NkS** 3174, 4⁰, VIII, fasc. 3, nr. 245); also published in Weltzer, *Peter og Søren Kierkegaard*, pp. 241–42.

Your brother is now living in Østerbro: in April 1851 Søren Kierkegaard moved out of Copenhagen proper to Østerbro, then a suburb; see the list of Kierkegaard's residences in the introduction to this book.

33. From a letter from Carl Lund to his uncle Peter Christian Kierkegaard, dated May 20, 1851. The original letter is in **KBHA** (**NkS** 3174, 4⁰, VII, fasc. 6, nr. 94); it is cited, with errors, in Weltzer, *Peter og Søren Kierkegaard*, p. 242.

In Østerbro: see the note to the previous entry, by J. C. Lund.

34. From a letter from Carl Lund to his uncle Peter Christian Kierkegaard, dated February 2, 1855; the original letter is in **KBHA** (**NkS** 3174, 4⁰, VII, fasc. 6, nr. 96).

Uncle Søren's battle now seems to be dying down: Kierkegaard's attack on the Church was in fact interrupted by a pause that lasted from January 29 until March 20, 1855. If Carl Lund's date on the letter can be trusted, Kierkegaard's pause was only three days old when Lund wrote the letter, and it is not clear how Lund was able to say so quickly that Kierkegaard's battle was "dying down."

35. From Peter Christian Kierkegaard's journals, located in **KBHA** (**NkS** 2656, 4⁰, bd. II, p. 14); also published in Weltzer, *Peter og Søren Kierkegaard*, p. 254.

"This Must Be Said" (i.e., "This Must Be Said, So Let It Be Said") (*SV* XIV 83–92) appeared on May 24, 1855. *The Moment* nos. 1 and 2 (*SV* XIV 103–38) appeared on May 26 and June 4, 1855, respectively. The **articles in *Fædrelandet*** (*SV* XIV 5–81 and 93–100) appeared between December 18, 1854, and May 26, 1855.

36. From Peter Christian Kierkegaard's journals, located in **KBHA** (**NkS** 2656, 4⁰, bd. II, p. 14); also published in Weltzer, *Peter og Søren Kierkegaard*, p. 254.

On July 5, 1855, Peter Christian Kierkegaard spoke on the subject of his brother Søren at the **Roskilde [Ecclesiastical] Convention**, a gathering of pastors who came from the Grundtvigian wing of the Danish Church. See further mention of this talk later in this chapter, in P. C. Kierkegaard's 1881 statement, with its accompanying note. See also Appendix B of this book, which includes selections from Peter Christian Kierkegaard's notes on the talk itself.

37. From a letter by Carl Lund to his uncle Peter Christian Kierkegaard, dated July 9, 1855; the original letter is in **KBHA** (**NkS** 3174, 4⁰, VII, fasc. 6, nr. 97).

The business at the convention: the Roskilde Ecclesiastical Convention, where Peter Christian Kierkegaard had strongly criticized his brother in an address he delivered on July 5, 1855 (see mention of this in the present chapter as well as in Appendix B of this book). Since Bishop Martensen was informed that P. C. Kierkegaard would speak on this subject even before he did so (see the notes accompanying P. C. Kierkegaard's 1881 article, later in this chapter), it is not unlikely that, four days after the speech in question, a family member such as Carl Lund also knew that P. C. Kierkegaard had spoken in opposition to his brother. In this context Carl Lund's mention of "peace" is quite understandable. In this letter Carl Lund is apparently alluding to Søren Kierkegaard's attack on the church, concerning which he otherwise tended to observe a tactful silence. In this connection it is worth noting that in an earlier letter to his uncle P. C. Kierkegaard, Carl Lund had informed him of the death of Bishop Mynster, describing the latter as "a very excellent man" who despite his "stiffness and unbounded conservatism" had nonetheless "called many people to Christianity" (letter of January 30, 1854; in **KBHA** [**NkS** 3174, 4⁰, VII, fasc. 6, nr. 95]). The only other mention of Søren Kierkegaard's attack on the church in Carl Lund's rather extensive correspondence with P. C. Kierkegaard is a line in his letter of February 2, 1855, cited later in the present chapter. Søren Kierkegaard (but not his attack on the church) is also discussed in Carl Lund's letter to P. C. Kierkegaard of October 24, in which Lund describes his hospital visit (see that letter in chapter 8 of this book). Otherwise, however, Uncle Søren is not mentioned again in Carl Lund's letters to P. C. Kierkegaard (with the exception of brief mention, in 1859, of P. C. Kierkegaard's intent to publish Søren Kierkegaard's *The Point of View for My Activity as an Author*) until a letter of June 2, 1876, in which Lund informs his uncle Peter that his wife has given birth to a baby boy whom he has named "Søren Aabye Kierkegaard Lund"! (the letter is in **KBHA** [**NkS** 3174, 4⁰, VII, fasc. 8, nr. 128]). (Søren Aabye Kierkegaard Lund was born August 28, 1875, and was to be the father of yet another Søren Aabye Kierkegaard Lund, born April 21, 1910.) In the more than twenty years that had passed since Søren Kierkegaard's attack on the Church, Carl Lund's attitude toward his uncle Søren appears to have undergone a remarkable transformation, perhaps in the same tempo as the change that had taken place in public opinion. It would be interesting to know P. C. Kierkegaard's reaction to the naming of his newborn grandnephew!

38. From Peter Christian Kierkegaard's journals, located in **KBHA** (**NkS** 2656, 4⁰, bd. II, p. 15); also published in Weltzer, *Peter og Søren Kierkegaard*, p. 266.

J. C. Lund: Johan Christian Lund (1799–1875), a brother-in-law of Søren and Peter Christian Kierkegaard; see letters by him, with accompanying notes, in chapter 8, as well as the entries by Henriette Lund and Troels-Lund elsewhere in this chapter. **Tried to see him at Frederik's Hospital, but in vain**: see also the entry in Peter Christian Kierkegaard's account books for October 1855: "Traveled in and out (18 & 20 Oct.) in connection with Søren's illness" (**KBHA** [**NkS** 3005, 4⁰, II, p. 86]) and Emil Boesen's notes on his hospital conversations with Kierkegaard in chapter 8 of this book. It was without doubt Peter Christian's remarks at the Roskilde Ecclesiastical Convention in July 1855 that led to the complete break between the brothers. See P. C. Kierkegaard's 1881 statement, with accompanying notes, later in this chapter; see also the selections from his notes on his 1855 talk in Appendix B of this book.

39. Peter Christian Kierkegaard's obituary notice for his brother; published in the "Tillæg" [Supplement] to *Berlingske Tidende* (no. 267), Friday, November 16, 1855.

40. From an article written by Peter Christian Kierkegaard in mid-March of 1881; cf. his introductory note: "The communication below was written March 14–16 of this year [1881], after I had been asked to do so in terms that had led me to believe that it would be included in the conclusion of the final volume of Søren Kierkegaard's *Posthumous Papers*, which, however, the editor decided against." It was thus first published in *Dansk Kirketidende* 1881, nr. 22, cols. 337–45, and reprinted in *Peter Christian Kierkegaards Samlede Skrifter* [The Collected Writings of Peter Christian Kierkegaard], ed. Poul Egede Glahn and Lavrids Nyegård, vol. 4 (Copenhagen: Karl Schønbergs Forlag, 1903), pp. 120–28. Another English translation of P. C. Kierkegaard's attempt at reconstructing his funeral oration has been published in T. H. Croxall, *Glimpses and Impressions of Kierkegaard*, pp. 127–29.

The words of the Psalmist: Psalm 38.13. **The first time I came to speak publicly**: this depends in part upon how Peter Christian Kierkegaard defines "publicly"; in May 1846 he had spoken critically about his brother Søren's work at the Sydvestsjællandske Broderkonvent [Southwest Zealand Convention of Brothers], emphasizing the importance and validity of faith in its beginning stages and taking to task in particular the volumes by Johannes Climacus (*Philosophical Fragments* and *Concluding Unscientific Postscript*); see J. F. Fenger, *Det sydvestsjællandske Broderkonvent (1837–1854)* [The Southwest Zealand Convention of Brothers: 1837–1854] (Copenhagen: Karl Schønbergs Forlag, 1890), pp. 222–23. **The meeting of the Roskilde Ecclesiastical Convention at Ringsted on October 30, 1849**: see Appendix B for selections from this talk. Although Peter Christian Kierkegaard seems to be correct in characterizing his 1849 talk as generally favorable to his brother, Søren Kierkegaard was remarkably thin-skinned, and his journals are filled with angry reactions to it (cf. *Pap.* X² A 256 [*SKJP* 6550]; 273 [*SKJP* 6553]; 275 [*SKJP* 6554]; 280 [*SKJP* 6557]; 285 [*SKJP* 6562]; 286; 295; 415 [*SKJP* 6581]; 589 p. 421; X³ A 38; X⁶ B 125 p. 167; 130 [*SKJP* 6558]; 131 [*SKJP* 6559]; 132 p. 177; XI¹ A 47 [*SKJP* 6857]; XI² A 307 p. 334); these entries include the draft of an article (*Pap.* X⁶ B 130 and 131 [*SKJP* 6558 and 6559]), never published, in which Søren Kierkegaard attacked his brother's appearance at the convention. Søren Kierkegaard's principal objections were as follows: first of all, he objected to the characterization of his works with the term "ecstasy," which he regarded as a code word for "madness" [*galskab*, a word that occurs with great frequency in the writings from the last years of Kierkegaard's life, when it is almost always used in an ironic or sarcastic sense]; second, he objected to a comparison that put him on the same plane as Martensen; and finally, he was bothered by the fact that the criticism was from his *brother* and thus might take on increased credibility in the eyes of the public. In view of Peter Christian's subsequent characterization of his younger brother as an "Ølver" figure (see later in this entry and in this note), perhaps Søren's fears that "ecstasy" was a polite word for "madness" were not entirely out of place. When he performed his heroic deeds, Ølver was apparently either somewhat mad or intoxicated or both. **The summer meeting of the Roskilde Convention, July 5, 1855**: see Appendix B for selections from Peter Christian Kierkegaard's notes on this talk. In contrast to his 1849 talk at the Roskilde Convention, Peter Christian Kierkegaard's July 1855 talk was scathingly critical of Søren Kierkegaard's work, not only of the attack on Christendom that had begun in December 1854, but of his brother's entire oeuvre, in which Peter Christian saw that attack prefigured. Despite the urging of Archdeacon Eggert C. Tryde (see Friis Berg, in *Nationaltidende* [The National Times] [Copenhagen], August 5, 1942), P. C. Kierkegaard's 1855 talk was never published. It is thus not clear what Søren Kierkegaard knew of its contents. He must have learned something, however, because he wrote of it quite angrily in his journals (*Pap.* XI³ B 154; 155; 164 pp. 270–72); the first two of these entries are a draft of an article Kierkegaard never published but that served as the source for the little piece called "Convent Beer," which was published on the last page of the final, posthumously published issue of *The Moment* (*SV* XIV 363). In any event, Peter Christian Kierkegaard's remarks on his brother's works were very widely known, and it appears that people were aware of the critique even *before* Peter Christian made it. See, for example, Bishop H. L. Martensen's letter to his friend Gude: "At the Roskilde Ecclesiastical Convention, Dr. P. C. Kierkegaard will hold a lecture about the situation in our Church and in it will discuss his brother's behavior" (in **KBHA** [**NkS**

3450, 4°, II]; published in *Biskop H. Martensens Breve*, vol. 1, p. 148). Martensen's letter is dated July 5, 1855, i.e., the same day as Peter Christian Kierkegaard's talk, and it refers in the future tense to the latter's intention to speak, thus indicating that Martensen in fact had advance knowledge of the talk. Since Martensen was not in the inner circle of Grundtvigians, it is reasonable to assume that his advance knowledge was shared by many. As mentioned in an earlier note in this chapter, Peter Christian Kierkegaard's talk at the July 1855 Roskilde Convention was certainly the event that resulted in the final rupture between the two brothers. Søren appears to have refused to receive his brother in August 1855, and as has been seen in this chapter and chapter 8 of this book, even when Søren lay dying in Frederik's Hospital he again refused to allow his brother to visit. **Which I never wrote down . . . I had only begun an attempt to jot down the contents**: this is a matter of interpretation; P. C. Kierkegaard's notes on his July 5, 1855, talk are quite extensive; see Appendix B for selections from these notes. **A slightly hostile or clumsy summary that appeared in a newspaper**: P. C. Kierkegaard is apparently referring to the account that appeared in the *Berlingske politiske og Avertissements-Tidende*, evening edition, for Monday November 19 (no. 270); the newspaper's account in fact is quite close to P. C. Kierkegaard's version. **The old man**: Michael Pedersen Kierkegaard (1756–1838). **Ølver**: a form of "Qlvir miklimunnr," meaning literally "Qlvir Bigmouth." He is a hero who appears in Magnus Blinde's saga in Snorri Sturluson's account of the history of the kings of Norway; see *Heimskringla. Nóreg Konunga Sǫgur* [Heimskringla: Sagas of the Kings of Norway], ed. Finnur Jónsson (Copenhagen: G.E.C. Gad, 1911), pp. 563–64. The story of Qlvir is told in connection with an actual historical event, namely an attack by pagan Wends on southern Norway in the year 1135. Despite lack of support from his fellows, a peasant named Qlvir left a party at which he and his friends had been drinking beer, and went to the defense of the local townsmen. Incredibly, he fought eight Wends simultaneously, and, although surrounded, he killed six and succeeded in putting the other two to flight. Qlvir was himself gravely wounded in his heroic struggle and was taken away by his countrymen and nursed back to health. Peter Christian Kierkegaard presumably has his version of the story from one or both of the two translations that were current in his time, namely *Snorre Sturlesons norske Kongers Sagaer* [Snorri Sturluson's Sagas of the Norwegian Kings], trans. Jacob Aall, vol. 2 (Kristiania: Guldberg & Dzwonkowskis Officin, 1839), p. 145, and N.F.S. Grundtvig's translation, *Norges Konge-Krønike af Snorro Sturlesøn* [Snorro Sturleson's Chronicle of the Kings of Norway], vol. 3 (Copenhagen: Schultz, 1822) pp. 259–60. Good arguments can be made for P. C. Kierkegaard's acquaintance with either or both versions. He was interested in Scandinavian history and was a supporter of Grundtvig, so it is not unreasonable to suppose he owned Grundtvig's version. Similarly, Aall's translation was published in Kristiania (now Oslo) in 1839, the same year that P. C. Kierkegaard spent time in that city. In both translations the name is spelled "Ølver," with an Ø and an *e*, though in Aal's translation his full name is given as "Ølver Stormund" whereas in Grundtvig's it is the more colloquial "Ølver Gabmund." Both mean "Ølver Bigmouth." In any event, not only is P. C. Kierkegaard's choice of the story—a brave but foolhardy hero who singlehandedly fights off a pagan horde—quite revealing, but the hero's nickname of "bigmouth" also seems aimed at his brother Søren, whether in a complimentary or less-than-complimentary sense.

41. From Peter Christian Kierkegaard's journals, located in **KBHA** (**NkS** 2656, 4°, bd. II, p. 222); also published in Weltzer, *Peter og Søren Kierkegaard*, p. 358.

Wrote to the probate court: Peter Christian Kierkegaard's letter to the probate court apparently contained some sort of statement of conscience about his relation to his brother Søren. During the last years of his life, Peter Christian, whose relation to his brother had never been comfortable, was increasingly haunted by a sense of guilt. As the heir to Søren's estate, Peter Christian received the royalties from the various editions of his brother's works over a thirty-year period. Toward the end of his life, from 1879 to 1883, he donated these sums to charity; the rather incoherent record of these donations is in Peter Christian Kierkegaard's account book (**KBHA** [**NkS** 3005, 4°, bd. II, pp. 143–58]; see the discussion in Weltzer, *Peter og Søren Kierkegaard*, pp. 358–59). Peter Christian Kierkegaard gave up his bishopric in 1875, returned his royal decorations to the government in 1879, consented to being declared the equivalent of *non compos mentis* [*borgerlig Umyndiggørelse*] in 1884, and died on February 24, 1888, at age eighty-two, "in the darkness of insanity" (Weltzer, *Peter og Søren Kierkegaard*, p. 359). **I John 3.15**: "Any one who hates his brother is a murderer, and you know that no murderer has eternal life abiding in him." Interestingly, in his lecture notes on this same text from the winter of 1836–37, P. C. Kierkegaard writes: "Just as, in the Old Testament, [a murderer] is subject to the death of the body, . . . in the New Testament he is naturally expelled from the Church, i.e., the Kingdom of God is closed to him. . . . And here the Apostle says this same punishment is reserved for the person who commits murder in his heart, i.e., hates" (**KBHA [NkS** 3013, 4⁰, I]). It should also be noted that the text of I John 3.15 is an amplified version of Matthew 5.23–24 ("If you are offering your gift at the altar, and there remember that your brother has something against you, leave your gift and go," etc.), which, as has been seen earlier in this chapter, P. C. Kierkegaard had cited in a journal entry of February 1834 as an explanation of why he had been unable to receive the Eucharist. **Dahlstrøm**: Frederik Christian Emil Dahlstrøm (1815–89), prefect of the Aalborg district.

42. From Henriette Lund's memoirs, *Erindringer Fra Hjemmet* [Recollections from Home] (Copenhagen: Gyldendal, 1909), pp. 16–26, 51–52, 81–83, 102, 105–7, 109, 110, 111–20, 145–46, 150–51, 166–67, 168–77. Originally published privately in 1880. Portions of this material have appeared in earlier English translations in T. H. Croxall, *Glimpses and Impressions of Kierkegaard*, pp. 49–77, and in Dru, *The Journals of Søren Kierkegaard*, pp. 555–61. The apparent authenticity of Henriette Lund's recollections of Kierkegaard is attested to by a letter to her, dated September 25, 1880, from Kierkegaard's lifelong friend Emil Boesen, to whom she had sent a privately printed copy of her book:

> Dear Jette Lund,
>
> Many thanks for *Recollections from Home*. One of the reasons I didn't return it earlier is that I didn't know where you were. I don't know that now, either, but I will send this little note to Rosenvænget and then see whether it finds you.
>
> It has been a great pleasure for me to read the book. At times there was also something sad. It summoned up many memories and often reminded me of "Uncle Sören," even when you didn't mention him directly. It seems to me that the atmosphere in the book was often like that in his room when I would visit him. Reading the book certainly brings pleasure to your family and friends, but I believe that many more could benefit from it, and I wish that the portrait of Uncle Sören could be taken out and made available to people who otherwise often have a very distorted and incorrect picture of him. You know from experience that he could frequently say something that was loving and sweet, succinct but well-considered in form and therefore very pertinent. If he were still living on Nørregade or Østerbro and met you the day after having read the book, I think he would have said something of this sort to you, something loving and sweet.
>
> You will certainly come out here some time and look in on me, and I will then thank you again for the happiness I have derived from reading the book.
>
> Your devoted,
> E. BOESEN
>
> [In **KBHA (NkS** 3883 4⁰ III)]

As was the case with her publication of the papers pertaining to Kierkegaard's engagement to Regine Olsen (see the note accompanying Henriette Lund's entry in chapter 3 of this book), Henriette Lund's volume of memoirs was crafted with the particular purpose of producing a revisionist portrait of her Uncle Søren. After he met with Henriette Lund, H. Gottsched, the editor of the later volumes of *SKEP*, wrote to H. P. Barfod in a letter dated November 7, 1880, stating that "Miss L. would very much like to help give people a different impression of her beloved Uncle Søren" (**KBHA [NkS** 3866, 4⁰]). To this end, Henriette Lund made sure that copies of the privately published edition of her memoirs reached various individuals who were influential in molding received opinion regarding her uncle. In addition to Pastor Emil Boesen, these included Pastors Peter Christian Zahle and A. F. Schiødte, both followers of Kierkegaard within the Danish Church; such influential foreign scholars of Kierkegaard's work as A. Bärthold in Germany, Frederik Petersen in Norway, and Waldemar Rudin in Sweden; Sophus Birket-Smith, librarian of the Royal Library (Copenhagen); and H. Gottsched, then the editor of Kierkegaard's posthumous papers, who included lengthy excepts from Henriette Lund's memoirs, without attribution, in the final volume of *SKEP* (see H. Gottsched's letter to H. P. Barfod, dated November 27, 1880, in **KBHA** [**NkS** 3866, 4⁰]). Henriette Lund's memoirs were publicly issued after her death in 1909.

[Anna] **Henriette Lund** (1829–1909), a writer, was the daughter of Kierkegaard's sister Petrea Severine and Henrik Ferdinand Lund. **Living outside of town**: Henriette Lund's parents' first home was outside the city proper, next to Sortedam Lake, one of the lakes that lie just beyond Nørreport. **Father and Mother**: Henrik Ferdinand Lund and Petrea Severine Kierkegaard Lund. **Grandmother**: Henrik Ferdinand Lund's mother, Marina Magdalene Lobeck Lund (1763–1830). **Grandfather**: Henrik Ferdinand Lund's father, Henrik Hansen Lund (1757–1820). **Nicoline** and **Christian**: Nicoline Christine Kierkegaard Lund (1799–1832), Søren Kierkegaard's sister, and [Johan] Christian Lund (1799–1875), the brother of Henriette Lund's father, Henrik Ferdinand Lund. **Grandfather [Kierkegaard]**'s: Michael Pedersen Kierkegaard (1756–1838). **Councillor Boesen**: Johannes Boesen (1768–1859), was a secretary in the Treasury, with the title of councillor of justice. He was married to Sophie Hammerich, and they were the parents of Kierkegaard's closest friend, Emil Boesen (1812–81), subsequently archdeacon in Aarhus. See Emil Boesen's entries with accompanying notes in chapters 2 and 8 of this book. **Congregation of Brothers**: see the note to Hanne Mourier's account of Regine Schlegel's memoirs, in chapter 3 of this book. **Two professors of that name** [i.e., Hammerich]: [Peter] Frederik [Adolph] Hammerich (1809–77) was a theologian and professor of theology at the University of Copenhagen (see the note accompanying the entry by him in chapter 1 of this book), and Martin [Johannes] Hammerich (1811–81), author and educator (see the note accompanying the entry by Emil Boesen in chapter 8 of this book). **Grandmother Kierkegaard**: Ane Sørensdatter Lund Kierkegaard (1768–1834), the wife of Michael Pedersen Kierkegaard and the mother of Søren Kierkegaard, of Henriette Lund's mother Petrea, and of five other children. **My brother Vilhelm**: Vilhelm Nicolai Lund (1831–1902), councillor of state and owner of the estate Annisegaard. **My second mother**: Henriette's mother, Petrea Severine Kierkegaard, died in 1834, and in 1836 Henriette's father, Henrik Ferdinand Lund, married his cousin Anna Cathrine Lund (1800–59), who bore him three children. He already had four children from his first marriage. **Gammeltorv** and **Nytorv**: the old and new market squares, located in the heart of Copenhagen and immediately adjacent to one another. The home of Michael Pedersen Kierkegaard was situated on the portion of Nytorv that abuts Gammeltorv, where the Lund family lived. The two dwellings cannot have been separated by more than 100–150 meters. **When his house was engulfed in flames**: on the night of April 1–2, 1826, there was a great fire in the neighborhood of the Kierkegaard home, which suffered serious damage but was saved. **The decree of January 1813**: in January 1813 the Danish state declared bankruptcy and the revaluation of the rixdollar, which devastated many wealthy people. Acting on good advice, Michael Pedersen Kierkegaard had put much of his fortune into guaranteed-convertible bonds, which were not affected by the general devaluation. (See entry number 48 of Hans Brøchner's recollections, with its accompanying note, in chapter 11 of this book.) **Kjøbmagergade** and **Gammeltorv**: Kjøbmagergade [Købmagergade] was where the family of Johan Christian Lund and Nicoline Christine Kierkegaard Lund lived; their children (Henrik Sigvard Lund, Michael Frederik Christian Lund, Sophie Vilhelmine Lund, and Carl Ferdinand Lund) were the first cousins of Henriette Lund and her siblings, who, as mentioned above, lived on Gammeltorv, which was not far away. **Prof. Brøchner**: the quotation in question has not been found in Brøchner's articles on Kierkegaard. **The little pencil drawing of him that I own**: a pencil sketch in profile, dated January 15, 1838, and believed to be by [Niels] Christian Kierkegaard (1806–82), an artist and a teacher of drawing, who was a distant cousin of Søren Kierkegaard. It is among the illustrations reproduced in this volume. **Grandfather was eighty-four years old**: Michael Pedersen Kierkegaard in fact died at the age of eighty-one. **The doctor no longer thought it advisable, etc.**: but see Carl Weltzer, *Peter og Søren Kierkegaard*, p. 127, where Peter's diary is quoted as saying that the emetic was prescribed by the doctor. **Uncle Søren bought the place after Grandfather's death**: in fact, Søren and Peter Christian Kierkegaard owned Nytorv 2 jointly for a time, though Søren spent more time living there, subsequently bought out his brother's interest, and ultimately sold the house. See Brandt and Rammel, *Kierkegaard og Pengene*, pp. 65–79, for details. **Marie Boisen**: [Elise] Marie Boisen Kierkegaard (1806–37), Peter Christian Kierkegaard's first wife; see the entry by P. Bojsen, with its accompanying note, in chapter 2 of this book. **Henriette Glahn**: [Sophie] Henriette ["Jette"] Glahn Kierkegaard (1809–81), Peter Christian Kierkegaard's second wife; see the notes accompanying the entries by Peter Christian Kierkegaard, earlier in this chapter. **The Agerskov family**: Niels Madsen Røyen was a business companion of Michael Pedersen Kierkegaard, whose first wife, Kirstine Nielsdatter Røyen Kierkegaard (1758–96), was Røyen's sister. The son of another of Røyen's sisters was Christian Agerskov (1783–1853), who was thus M. P. Kierkegaard's nephew, and a sort of "cousin" (by M. P. Kierkegaard's first, childless marriage to Kirstine Røyen) of the Kierkegaard children. The Agerskov family lived at Buddinge Mark in northern Zealand, ca. five to seven miles (eight to ten kilometers) north of Copenhagen, and it was here that Søren Kierkegaard is said to have had his childhood fall from a tree. Cecile ("Cille") Agerskov was a daughter of Christian Agerskov and became a domestic servant in the household of Henriette Lund's parents ca. 1833. **Mother, then a young married woman**: since Petrea Kierkegaard was married to Henriette's father in October 1828, when Søren was fifteen years old, there appears to be something wrong with the dates in this account. Troels-Lund, in *Bakkehus og Solbjerg*, vol. 3, p. 68, states that "as far as is known" this incident took place in 1825, when Kierkegaard was twelve years old and his sister Petrea was on a visit at the Agerskovs. But this of course contradicts Troels-Lund's older sister Henriette's claim that Petrea was already married at the time of the alleged incident. **Uncle Christian's children . . . my girl cousin and the "big boy cousins"**: see above (under "Kjøbmagergade") for the children of Johan Christian and Nicoline Christine Lund. **Miss Dencker**: Johan Christian Lund's housekeeper. **Uncle Vilhelm in Brazil**: [Peter] Wilhelm (or Vilhelm) Lund (1801–80); see the note accompanying the letter from P. C. Kierkegaard to H. F. Lund, dated July 3–4, 1829, earlier in this chapter. **Aunt Jens Lund and Marie Falbe**: the former was a widowed aunt in Henriette Lund's family, and the latter (whose full name was Bolette Marie Lund Falbe [1807–69]) was a cousin of remarkable beauty. **The procession**: see also Henriette Lund's other account of this same procession in her entry in chapter 3 of this book. **Princess Marianne** and **the crown prince**: in 1841 Crown Prince Frederik [later King Frederik VII] married Princess Caroline Charlotte Mariane of Mecklenburg-Strelitz (1821–76); it proved to be an unfortunate match for both parties and the marriage ended in divorce in 1846. Frederik was an eccentric man, and, in an action that was viewed as scandalous by the respectable bourgeoisie of Copenhagen, he subsequently married Louise Rasmussen, a commoner with a checkered past. **Vesterbro**: the neighborhood that lay immediately west of the city proper and was quite rural at that time. **Bakkehus** ["Hill House"]: a country estate, earlier the home of the literary critic K. L. Rahbek; Bakkehus lay in Valby, then a small village just beyond Vesterbro, ca. two to three miles (three to four kilometers) from the center of Copenhagen. Henriette Lund's family had a summer place in Vesterbro for the summers 1836–40 and rented Bakkehus for the summers from 1841 to 1861. **He was then living at the old place on Nytorv**: Søren Kierkegaard was in fact living at Nørregade 230A at that time. **He would leave for Berlin**: Kierkegaard left for Berlin on October 25, 1841. **I kept the sacred promise [to write to Uncle Søren] and received regular replies**: none of Henriette Lund's letters to Kierkegaard during his stay in Berlin in 1841–42 is known to have survived, but two of Kierkegaard's replies are extant and have been published in *B&A* I 79–80, 85–86 [*KW* XXV 100–101, 108–9]. **Orla Lehmann**: [Peter Martin] Orla Lehmann (1810–70); see the note accompanying the entry by Johannes Ostermann in chapter 2 of this book. In a celebrated case, Lehmann was sentenced in January 1842 to three months' imprisonment for having impugned royal authority in a speech a year earlier, when he had expressed skepticism that absolute monarchy was in the best interests of the peasantry. Lehmann became a hero to many people, and his face was on the packaging of such everyday items as matches and candy. **Right after his return home**: Kierkegaard returned to Copenhagen from Berlin on March 6, 1842. **After he had moved out of his old apartment on Nytorv** and into **his place on Nørregade**: Kierkegaard had moved from his childhood home at Nytorv as early as 1837, and lived various places, including Nørregade 230A (present-day number 38) from April or October 1840 until October 1844, i.e., during the entire period in question, after which he moved back to Nytorv 2 until April 1848; see the list of Kierkegaard's residences in the introduction to this book. Note that Henriette Lund situates the meeting of Kierkegaard and his nieces and nephews immediately prior to his departure for Berlin (in October 1841) at Nytorv 2, while she situates the meeting just after his return from Berlin (in March 1842) at his place on Nørregade. The former may be an erroneous recollection; she may be remembering the wrong apartment or perhaps another meeting with Kierkegaard or his departure for another trip to Berlin. Yet the account has vividness of detail and the ring of truth, so it is not impossible that Søren could have managed deliberately to have his farewell at the family home at Nytorv 2, even though his principal residence at the time was on Nørregade. **Lotto**: Chr.K.F. Molbech mentions Kierkegaard's love of children and children's games in a newspaper article from 1870:

> As everyone who knew him could testify, S. Kierkegaard . . . had a special love for children and a gift for getting along with them. He could take joy in their games, their questions, their smiles. He could come down to the level of their imagination. He could awaken and satisfy their thirst for knowledge. He could enliven them and be enlivened by them. Indeed, he could be merry and mischievous in their company. . . . [It is known that] in his loneliness he invited children in and held a Christmas party for them. . . . [From *Dagbladet* (The Daily News), no. 47, February 25, 1870]

Ramparts: see the note accompanying the entry by Frederik Hammerich in chapter 6 of this book. **A letter from Uncle Søren**: *B&A* I 110–11 (*KW* XXV 142–43); from the date assigned this letter by the editors of *B&A*, it would appear that it was in fact sent to Henriette Lund on her thirteenth rather than her twelfth birthday, as she reports. **A new letter**: this second letter does not appear in *B&A* and is not in the Søren Kierkegaard Archive. **"The frizzy Fritz"** [*den krøllede Fritz*]: the chief character in *En dansk Students Eventyr* [A Danish University Student's Tale], a posthumously published comic tale by Kierkegaard's mentor and favorite professor, the philosopher and author Poul Martin Møller (1794–1838). **The White Lady** [*La Dame blanche*]: an opera written in 1825 by François Adrien Boieldieu (1775–1834). **The day Henriette Lund was confirmed . . . the next day he sent with his present a letter**: the letter is in *B&A* I 153–54 (*KW* XXV 195); according to the editor's notes in *B&A* II 71 (*KW* XXV 472), Henriette Lund's confirmation day was April 26, 1846; however, Kierkegaard's letter is dated April 23, 1846, and clearly refers to Henriette Lund's confirmation in the past tense. Thus one or the other of the dates must be in error. Since the supposed date of the confirmation, April 26, 1846, was in fact a Sunday, and thus a normal confirmation day, it seems likely that that date is correct and that Kierkegaard dated his letter incorrectly. **Aladdin's words**: from Adam Oehlenschläger's verse drama *Aladdin* (near the end of act 4), which formed the second part of his romantic breakthrough work *Poetiske Skrifter* [Poetic Writings] (Copenhagen: Schubothe, 1805). **A brief letter**: this letter is apparently lost; it is not included in *B&A*, nor is it in the Søren Kierkegaard Archive. **His fortune had simply been divided into portions**: Brandt and Rammel (*Kierkegaard og Pengene*) demonstrate that for most of his life, at any rate, Kierkegaard managed most of his assets much more conventionally than this. **He privately exercised charity toward many needy persons**: Brandt and Rammel (*Kierkegaard og Pengene*, pp. 94–123), however, demonstrate that this was on a more limited scale than Henriette Lund implies. **Mr. Hall**: C[arl] C[hristian] Hall (1812–88), a prominent moderate liberal politician; he served as Cultus Minister during Kierkegaard's attack on the Church from late 1854 to 1855. **The roses . . . grow in valleys**: an allusion to "Den yndigste Rose er funden" [The loveliest rose was found], a much-loved Christmas hymn by the great Danish poet and hymnwriter Hans Adolph Brorson (1694–1764); Kierkegaard also favored Brorson, and chose a verse from one of Brorson's hymns for his epitaph. **Archdeacon Tryde**: see the note accompanying the entry by Kristian Arentzen in chapter 7 of this book. **Peter Boisen**: Peter Outzen Boisen (1815–62), Grundtvigian priest and Grundtvig's assistant; he was the son of Bishop P. O. Boisen, the brother of Elise Marie Boisen Kierkegaard (Peter Christian Kierkegaard's first wife), and the husband of Meta Grundtvig (1827–87), N.F.S. Grundtvig's daughter. **Vartov Church**: a minor church in a Copenhagen home for elderly women. Beginning in 1839, with the partial lifting of the censorship to which he had been subjected (in the wake of H. N. Clausen's 1826 libel judgment against him), N.F.S. Grundtvig was permitted to preach at Vartov, which soon became the center and symbol of the flourishing Grundtvigian movement—a movement to which Søren Kierkegaard, of course, was profoundly opposed.

43. From Troels Frederik Troels-Lund's memoirs, *Et Liv. Barndom og Ungdom*, pp. 207–13, 215, 217, 218, 218–19, 220, 222–25, 232, 234, 235–41. Portions of Troels-Lund's memoirs are available in another English translation in T. H. Croxall, *Glimpses and Impressions of Kierkegaard*, pp. 108–15.

Troels Frederik Troels-Lund: see the note accompanying Troels-Lund's entry in the first chapter of this book. **P. Mynster**: Jakob Peter Mynster (1775–1854), became resident curate at the Church of Our Lady in Copenhagen in 1811 and was bishop of Zealand and primate of Denmark from 1834 until his death. **Nørrebro Allé**, **Blegdam Road**, and **Sortedam Lake** are all located in the Nørrebro neighborhood, which lies north of the lovely lakes that once formed a part of Copenhagen's defensive works; in the mid-nineteenth century Nørrebro was still a semirural area just outside the city proper. **Vilhelm Lund**: i.e., Troels-Lund's uncle, Peter Wilhelm (or Vilhelm) Lund (1801–80); see the note accompanying Henriette Lund's entry, earlier in this chapter. **Peter Severin**: Troels-Lund's half-brother, Peter Severin Lund (1834–64). **Anna Cathrine Lund**: see the note on "my second mother" that accompanies the entry by Henriette Lund, earlier in this chapter. **Elise Marie [Boisen Kierkegaard]**: see the entry by P. Bojsen, with its accompanying note, in chapter 2 of this book. **Gammeltorv and Nytorv**: see the note accompanying the entry by Henriette Lund, earlier in this chapter. **Christian Winther's poem**: Christian Winther (1796–1876), Danish poet; the lines quoted form the last portion of Winther's "Længsel" [Longing], first published in his 1840 collection *Sang og Sagn* [Song and Legend] and subsequently collected in his *Samlede Digtninger* [Collected Poetry], vol. 1 (Copenhagen: Gyldendal,1905), pp. 140–41. **Berlin**: Kierkegaard departed for Berlin on October 25, 1841, and returned to Copenhagen on March 6, 1842. **Cousin Troels**: Troels-Lund's uncle, Troels Lund (1806–67), a "scenery painter" or set designer for the Royal Theater, was the cousin of naturalist Peter Vilhelm Lund, then in Brazil, who is the author of the letter cited here. **Johan Frederik Schlegel**: see the note accompanying Hanne Mourier's account of Regine Schlegel's memoirs, in chapter 3 of this book. **Christian Lund**: [Johan] Christian Lund (1799–1875), Troels-Lund's uncle and Kierkegaard's brother-in-law by virtue of his marriage to Kierkegaard's sister Nicoline Christine (1799–1832). **A few suggestive remarks in the *Posthumous Papers***: see *Pap.* X^1 A 234 p. 156 (*SKJP* 6379). **Goldschmidt and his *Corsair***: see chapter 5 of this book. **Ørsted brothers**: Hans Christian Ørsted (1777–1851) (see the note accompanying the comments on Kierkegaard's dissertation in chapter 2 of this book), and Anders Sandøe Ørsted (1778–1860) a Kantian legal scholar and one of Denmark's leading statesmen, who on several occasions served as prime minister. **He took a five-rixdollar bill**: see also the account of Julie Weber Sødring in chapter 7 of this book as well as the story in *Either/Or* (*SV* II 12 [*KW* IV 12]). **Uncle Troels**: Troels-Lund's "Uncle Troels" was of course the same person as Peter Vilhelm Lund's "Cousin Troels" mentioned earlier in this note. **Ramparts**: see the note accompanying the entry by Frederick Hammerich in chapter 6 of this book. **He had arranged that my sister accompany**

Uncle Christian and his daughter on a trip abroad: see Henriette Lund's entry earlier in this chapter. **Peter**: Troels-Lund's brother Peter Severin Lund. **"I have enough"**: see Kierkegaard's conversation of October 25, 1855, with Emil Boesen, in chapter 8 of this book. **At the Pastoral Convention in Roskilde, Peter Kierkegaard had opposed his brother's conduct**: see Peter Christian Kierkegaard's 1881 statement, with its accompanying note, earlier in this chapter; see also P. C. Kierkegaard's notes on his 1855 talk in Appendix B and Søren Kierkegaard's hospital conversations with Emil Boesen, with accompanying notes, in chapter 8 of this book. **A very sharp and witty reply**: see the entry by Emil Boesen, with accompanying notes, in chapter 8 of this book. **[Johannes] Ferdinand Fenger**: see the note accompanying Emil Boesen's entry in chapter 8 of this book. **Grundtvigians**: Kierkegaard was rightly suspicious of the Grundtvigians' offer of friendship and of the initial inclination on the part of some of them to lend partial support to his attack on the Church; see P. G. Lindhardt, *Konfrontation* [Confrontation] (Copenhagen: Akademisk Forlag, 1974) for a convincing account of how Grundtvig repeatedly framed his Sunday sermons in 1855 as clear rebuttals of the positions Kierkegaard adopted in his journal *The Moment*. **Get thee behind me, Satan, etc.**: see the entry by Emil Boesen, with accompanying notes, in chapter 8 of this book. **The young doctor Henrik [Sigvard] Lund** (1825–89) was the son of Johan Christian Lund (1799–1875) and Kierkegaard's sister Nicoline Christine (1799–1832); Henrik Lund was thus the brother of Johan Christian Lund's daughter **Sophia**, i.e., Sophie [or Sofie] Vilhelmine Lund (1827–75). **Uncle Christian, accompanied by his daughter Sophia, should go out there one afternoon**: this must be the same hospital visit mentioned by Johan Christian Lund in his letter of October 16, 1855, in chapter 8 of this book, and must therefore have taken place on Sunday, October 14, 1855. **Prof. Rasmus Nielsen**: see the note accompanying the letter of February 28, 1870, from M. A. Goldschmidt to H. P. Barfod, in chapter 5 of this book; see also entry number 21, with its accompanying note, in Brøchner's memoirs in chapter 11 of this book.

Chapter Ten
Five Portraits by Contemporaries

1. From A. F. Schiødte's letter to H. P. Barfod, dated September 12, 1869; in **KBHA** (**SKA** D. Pk. 5).

Andreas Ferdinand Schiødte (1816–87), pastor in Århus, journalist, and author. He was graduated from the Borgerdyd School and became a student at the University of Copenhagen in 1833. In his letter to Barfod of September 3, 1869 (in **KBHA** [**SKA** D. Pk. 5]), F. P. Welding describes Schiødte as "one of S.K.'s most zealous adherents for a period of time," who "had studied S. Kirkegaard's works carefully and thoroughly as have few others." According to Welding, when Schiødte sought out Kierkegaard's one-time servant, Anders Westergaard (see below), he not only received information from the latter regarding Kierkegaard's life but went so far as to purchase from Westergaard a hat that had previously belonged to Kierkegaard—which Schiødte then proceeded to wear about town! **Welding** and **Anger**: see their recollections of Kierkegaard in the first chapter of this book. **Prof. Nielsen** was Michael Nielsen, headmaster of the Borgerdyd School, who was a titular professor; see the note accompanying the entry by Peter Munthe Brun in chapter 1, other entries by or about Nielsen or his school in chapters 1 and 2 of this book, as well as Per Krarup, *Søren Kierkegaard og Borgerdydskolen*. **Sibbern** is the philosopher Prof. F. C. Sibbern; see the note accompanying Sibbern's comments on Kierkegaard's dissertation in chapter 2 of this book, as well as Sibbern's recollections and the accompanying note, later in this chapter. For **I[srael] Levin**, see his recollections and the accompanying note, later in this chapter, where it is clear both that Levin was angry about not having been consulted about the use of this anecdote, which Barfod recounted in the first volume of *SKEP*, and that he confirmed its veracity. **An atheistic theologian** is probably a reference to Hans Brøchner, whose recollections of Kierkegaard are included in chapter 11 of this book. **Pastor E. Lind** is Peter Engel Lind, who was graduated from the Borgerdyd School and became a student at the University of Copenhagen in 1833; see his recollections, with the accompanying note, in the first chapter of this book. **I have heard some things about his last hours at the hospital from Boesen**: Emil Boesen was Kierkegaard's closest friend and confidant; see the entry by him, with its accompanying note, in chapter 2, and see also Boesen's entries, with accompanying notes, in chapter 8 of this book for his account of his hospital visits to Kierkegaard. It seems clear that Boesen communicated Kierkegaard's hospital conversations orally to various people; cf. the remark by Gunni Busck in the note accompanying Boesen's account in chapter 8 of this book. **Vestergaard**: Anders Christensen Westergaard (1818–67) was Kierkegaard's servant from 1844 until 1851 or 1852, although he was absent for at least part of the duration of the war of 1848–51; see Robert J. Widenmann, "His Servant: A. C. Westergaard," in *Kierkegaard as a Person*, ed. Niels Thulstrup and Maria Mikulová Thulstrup, vol. 12 of *Bibliotheca Kierkegaardiana* (Copenhagen: C. A. Reitzel, 1983), pp. 109–18. **A letter of recommendation that K. had given him**: Kierkegaard wrote a letter of recommendation for Westergaard that is printed in *B&A* II 55, as well as in *SKEP 1833–1844*, p. lv and in Frithiof Brandt and Else Rammel, *Kierkegaard og Pengene*, pp. 135f., but is not included in *KW* XXV. It is not known whether the original letter survives. Kierkegaard's letter of recommendation reads as follows:

The applicant has been in my service since May 1844. Since that time he has satisfied even my most fastidious demands so completely that I can truthfully and emphatically recommend him in every respect. Sober, moral, always mentally alert, unconditionally dependable, used to keeping quiet, not without a certain degree of intelligence, which enables one to allow him to take care of things a bit on his own: he has been so indispensable to me that I would truly be delighted to keep him in my service. To my way of thinking, that is the highest recommendation I could give anyone. If it is possible that any of these qualities, to which I have truthfully testified, could render him suited to the particular requirements of the position for which he has applied, and that these qualities could direct favorable attention to the applicant; and if my recommendation, which is admittedly from someone whom you do not know, could have any favorable influence on decisions regarding the applicant's future, this would be a source of genuine joy to me, because I feel myself highly obligated to recommend him in every way.

Copenhagen, September 1847
S. KIERKEGAARD, M.A.

Østerbro: the address was Østerbro 108A, where Kierkegaard lived from April 1851 until April or October 1852.

2. From H. L. Martensen's autobiography, *Af mit Levnet* [From My Life] (Copenhagen: Gyldendal, 1882–83), vol. 1, pp. 78–79; vol. 2, pp. 140–48; vol. 3, pp. 12–23.

H[ans] L[assen] Martensen: see the note accompanying Martensen's entry in chapter 8 of this book. **His mother had died**: Kierkegaard's mother died July 30, 1834. **First period of the attack**: Prof. Rasmus Nielsen began his attack on Martensen in 1849. *Explanations of Dogmatics*: *Dogmatiske Oplysninger. Et Lejlighedsskrift* [Explanations of Dogmatics: An Occasional Piece] (Copenhagen: C. A. Reitzel, 1850). **His treatise on the concept of irony**: *On the Concept of Irony* (1841) (*SV* XIII 93–393 [*KW* II 1–329]). **Jean Paul**: pseudonym for Johan Friedrich Richter (1763–1825), German romantic writer. **Ethics**: *Den christelige Ethik* [Christian Ethics], vol. 3: *Den almindelige Deel* [The General Section] (Copenhagen: Gyldendal, 1871), pp. 275–300. **Ramparts**: see the note accompanying the entry by Frederik Hammerich in chapter 6 of this book. **Christianshavn** is an artificial island immediately adjacent to the city of Copenhagen proper, built in the seventeenth century during the reign of King Christian IV as part of the fortifications of the city. **Athenæum**: see the note accompanying the entry by Kristian Arentzen in chapter 7 of this book. **Johannes Climacus** is the pseudonymous author of two of Kierkegaard's works, *Philosophical Fragments* and *Concluding Unscientific Postscript*. **Particular expressions in the introduction to my *Dogmatics***: Martensen is undoubtedly referring to the first part of the introduction to *Den christelige Dogmatik* [Christian Dogmatics] (Copenhagen: C. A. Reitzel, 1849), pp. ii–iii, where he notes that he has "the conviction" that

> coherent theological thought, indeed theological speculation, is both possible and neces- sary. . . . And those who do not feel the tendency toward coherent thought but are able to satisfy themselves by thinking in random thoughts and aphorisms, sudden discoveries and hints, can also be within their rights in viewing coherent knowledge as unnecessary for themselves. But when, as in recent times, it begins to be put forth as a sort of dogma that *the* believer can have absolutely no interest in seeking coherent knowledge of that which is of greatest importance for him, . . . that *the* believer must view the concept of systematic knowledge about faith as a self-contradiction that abolishes true Christianity, etc.—then I confess that such statements, even when I have heard and seen them put forth with ingenious paradoxicality, are not capable of convincing me. Indeed, I can see them only as containing a great misunderstanding and a new or, rather, old error. . . . As far as I can see, there is only one person who corresponds perfectly to the concept of *the* believer, namely the entire Universal Church. As individuals, each of us possesses the faith to only a certain limited degree, and we must certainly be on guard against making our own individual, perhaps rather one-sided, perhaps even rather sickly life of faith into a rule for all believers.

A reply to Kierkegaard's attack, which I published in *Berlingske Tidende*: Martensen's reply to Kierkegaard was published in *Berlingske Tidende* on December 28, 1854 (no. 302), and is re- printed in *SV* XIV 11–14 and in Rasmus Nielsen, ed., *S. Kierkegaards Bladartikler med Bilag samlede efter Forfatterens Død, udgivne som Supplement til hans øvrige Skrifter*, pp. 242–46.

3. From August Wolff's letters to H. P. Barfod, dated December 12, 1869, and January 9, 1870, reporting Israel Levin's recollections of Kierkegaard; the original letters are in **KBHA** (**SKA** D. Pk. 5). In view of the fact that doubt has been cast on the reliability of Levin's remarks by other scholars and in view of the complexity (and indeed duplicity!) of the manner in which Levin's remarks were obtained by Barfod, the details of their provenance will be recounted here. The first portion of Levin's remarks, consisting of the first three paragraphs, is contained in an account by First Lieutenant August Wolff, who had known Levin from his father's home. According to his letter to Barfod, dated December 12, 1869, Wolff had been profoundly influenced by Kierkegaard in his youth, an influence that continued into Wolff's later years, so that he wrote, "What I am as a person I am because of Søren Kierkegaard, . . . and when he was buried and I was the very last person to leave the grave, I felt . . . that I now stood alone in the world, that now my father was dead." Wolff's great interest in Kierkegaard and in Levin had been awakened (or reawakened) by the publication of the first volume of *SKEP* in 1869, and in particular by an anecdote on p. liv of the foreword, where the editor, H. P. Barfod, passed on a report, from an unnamed source, that Kierkegaard had congratulated Levin on his good fortune in not being a Christian. (This source was Andreas Ferdinand Schiødte; see his entry earlier in this chapter.) Barfod's reply to Wolff's letter of December 12, 1869, appears to be lost, but he must have requested that Wolff visit Levin, which Wolff promptly did. In his reply to Barfod, dated December 18, 1869, Wolff gives an account of the visit that took place some time between December 12 and December 18, 1869:

> Dear Sir!
> After thanking you for your kind answer, I have the following to report:
> I visited Mr. Levin, but was careful not to mention my intention with a single word. He became angry because no one had come to him, and he found it improper to repeat at second hand *an anecdote* [this is the anecdote referred to above] about him. He also found it improper that P. Chr. K. [Peter Christian Kierkegaard] had not come to him.
> Mr. Levin is quite certainly a bit difficult to get on with. He has a chronic sense of having been pushed aside, overlooked, used, and then kicked away. "I have slaved enough for others without recognition"; "How people treat me"; etc. were his words. I tried to encour- age in him the notion that he should write a life of S.K. He said: "No, I won't. I have enough

to do. I would approach the task with much uneasiness, many doubts. No one could do it better than I. Merely the collection of manuscripts I have is invaluable. Why hasn't P. Chr. K. visited me and asked me if he could borrow the letters?" etc.

For the good of the cause, I would therefore advise you—without mentioning my humble person with a single word—to send Mr. I. Levin a copy of the book and write him something to chase away his injured pride, such as: that since the book is only a printed version of S.K.'s posthumous papers, you had not wished to approach him, despite the fact that he had certainly been closely connected to the deceased; but that at the conclusion, when a supplement containing other written materials will be published, you will count upon his friendly assistance, etc. Perhaps you could advise him to write a biography. Or whatever you prefer.

The most important thing is to show him some attention—without mentioning me. Later I will probably succeed in getting him to go along.

I do not feel myself justified in recounting everything he told me in a four-hour conversation. But I have written it down [in note form] and hope to be able to send it to you some time after the New Year.

Naturally, Editor Gjødvad is in possession of valuable information, both written and verbal.

Yours faithfully
A. WOLFF

N.B.: Your anecdote was true, but no one had asked L. about it, and it was an insult, etc.

[Letter from August Wolff to H. P. Barfod, dated December 18, 1869
(in KBHA [SKA D. Pk. 5])].

Another letter to Barfod, dated January 9, 1870, accompanied Wolff's promised notes from his four-hour conversation with Levin:

Your Honor:

I enclose two sets of notes for you to copy and to use as it suits you, but I would like to have them returned after, as I assume, you have copied them.

I do not need to say that they are truthful and in many places literal renderings. In the event that you make use of them in more or less unaltered form, I must reserve the right to permit mentioning I. Levin by name, because he has not given me express permission, and he is a stickler with respect to his name.

I have been to Levin's. He received your book and your letter but was not conciliated. He does not suspect my mediation and thus expressed himself unreservedly, asking me what he should do. I advised him to put aside his personal grievances for the good of the cause, but he would not agree to this, as he could not keep from bringing up S.K.'s unpleasant characteristics, and he felt that it was only with difficulty that one could deal with this semi-inscrutable person. He was angry at P. Chr. K., who had once denied him an audience. He said that you ought to have come to him before you told stories about him, and he mentioned that the dedication copy of the *Edifying Discourses* intended for Gjødwad was never sent, "because, as ever, Søren Kierkegaard always rewrote it twenty-seven times," but that he (Levin) and Gjødvad had the real dedication.

We were interrupted by a visitor. I had most success at the end, when I was able to promise to do him a literary favor, upon which he promised me notes on S.K. in return, etc. That is something, anyway, but I must be wary, as there were indications that too forward a posture on my part and too much familiarity could easily lead to too much familiarity from him in the future.

But however all that may be, I suggest that this matter be allowed to rest completely. I will not lose sight of it, and I am convinced that if the fish is to bite on the hook, I must be the fisherman.

As for the notes, it is clear that Mrs. Rump's recollections [Mrs. Benedicte Sophie Rump was the daughter of Kierkegaard's friend Pastor P. J. Spang; see the entry by T. E. Spang in chapter 7 of this book as well as Brøchner's mention of Mrs. Rump in chapter 11 of this book; the location of the memoir alluded to is not known] are in a sympathetic vein, but that Levin has definite views. I have had no desire to alter anything in his presentation or in hers, and they must speak for themselves. I will not tire you with my own comments, but I will conclude by saying that I am always, as now, at your service in this matter.

[Letter from August Wolff to H. P. Barfod, dated January 9, 1870
(**KBHA** [**SKA** D. Pk. 5])]

Levin's promise that he himself would write down something about Kierkegaard was a promise he apparently never kept. Thus all we have is Wolff's letter of December 12, 1869, containing Levin's earlier recollections about Kierkegaard (which constitute the first section of the present entry, consisting of three paragraphs), and Wolff's letter of January 9, 1870, containing the notes from his four-hour conversation with Levin in December 1869 (which constitute the second section of the present entry). Wolff's original manuscript appears to be lost, but the Søren Kierkegaard Archive in the Royal Library has preserved a fair copy, by an unknown hand (not Barfod's), with the following title: "Hr. Cand. I. Levins Udtalelser om S. Kierkegaard 1858 og 1869" [Remarks by Mr. I. Levin, B.A., Concerning S. Kierkegaard, 1858 and 1869]. A portion of Levin's recollections is available in another English translation in Alexander Dru, *The Journals of Søren Kierkegaard*, pp. 561–63; for some unknown reason Dru has arranged his excerpts in an order that differs considerably from the original.

Israel Levin: see the note accompanying the entry by Johannes Ostermann in chapter 4 of this book. **Hypothesis**: a more plausible hypothesis about the origin of Kierkegaard's alleged fear of fire might be found in his experience of the fire that damaged the Kierkegaard family home in 1826; see Henriette Lund's entry in chapter 9 of this book. **"Guilty?/Not Guilty?"**: the title of the third section of *Stages on Life's Way* (1845) (*SV* VI 175–370 [*KW* XI 185–397]). **Andersen**: Hans Christian Andersen; see the entry by Andersen with its accompanying note in chapter 2 of this book. **Frederiksberg Gardens**: a large park area not far to the west of Copenhagen proper; many people, including Søren Kierkegaard, enjoyed walking there. *The Attic Nights*: a reference to Gellius, *Noctes atticae*, to which Kierkegaard nowhere refers, nor does it appear in the auction catalog of his library. **Anchorites** are mentioned in the second part of *Either/Or*, (*SV* II 215 [*KW* IV 240]). Levin must be referring to the section in the second part of *Either/Or* entitled "The Equilibrium between the Aesthetic and the Ethical in the Composition of the Personality." Here we learn that the book title *Either/Or* refers to the choice not only between good and evil, between the aesthetic and the ethical ways of life, but also between choosing or willing, as opposed to not making a choice—which is of course also a choice (cf. *SV* II 153–54 [*KW* IV 168–69]). **Gilleleje**: a resort town on the north coast of Zealand, where Kierkegaard took a famous and meditative vacation in the summer of 1835, when he was a university student. **"The Discourse of the Ladies' Tailor [or Fashion Designer]"**: a section in *Stages on Life's Way* (*SV* VI 65–70 [*KW* XI 65–71]). **Minni [Mini]**: Mini's café, like Reitzel's bookshop, was frequently used as a meeting place by journalists and authors; see also the entry by Peter Christian Zahle in chapter 7 of this book. **Ninety-eight thousand rixdollars**: this figure has no connection with reality; cf. Frithiof Brandt and Else Rammel, *Kierkegaard og Pengene*. **His father's maidservant, who was married to a carpenter**: there is more detailed information on the carpenter F. C. Strube in *B&A* II 91 (*KW* XXV 481); cf. also the entry by Schiødte in this chapter. **13 3/4⁰ Réaumur**: ca. 17⁰ Celsius or 63⁰ Fahrenheit. **Berling's place**: number 38 Vimmelskaftet, where Louise Rasmussen (Lord Chamberlain Carl Berling's mistress and later Countess Danner, wife of King Frederik VII), had established a women's clothing shop in November 1844. It was called "Berling's Place" for her lover, Berling, who had provided the money. The shop burned on January 23, 1846, and then moved to 16 Amagertorv, though only for a short while. **Pastor Spang**: Peter Johannes Spang (1796–1846); see the entry by Tycho E. Spang, with accompanying notes, in chapter 7 of this book. **The drives up to northern Zealand**: for a list of Kierkegaard's carriage rides, see Brandt and Rammel, *Kierkegaard og Pengene*, pp. 140ff., as well as the chronologies given in *Pap.* VII¹ pp. xvii–xxv, and VIII¹ pp. xi–xxi. He usually drove with a coachman and a servant, and most often no one else. In a fictionalized account in *SV* III 188 (*KW* VI 147–48) he tells of an exception, when a female passenger accompanied him on a drive into town. **Fredensborg**: a picturesque village on the shore of Esrøm Lake in northern Zealand; it was one of Kierkegaard's favorite destinations for carriage excursions. **Giødvad**: see the note accompanying the entry by A. D. Jørgensen in chapter 4 of this book; see also Tycho E. Spang's entry in chapter 7 of this book for a description of an attack of illness suffered by Kierkegaard while at Giødvad's. **Mrs. Nielsen**: actress Anna Nielsen (1803–56). **Mrs. Heiberg**: actress Johanne Luise Heiberg (1812–90). **There are notes that testify to this**: see *B&A* I 189–90, and 306–7 (*KW* XXV 238–40 and 389–90). **Nielsen**: this must refer to the actor N. P. Nielsen (1795–1860). D[itlev] G[othard] **Monrad** (1811–87): a liberal politician and cabinet minister; he became bishop of Lolland and Falster in February 1849, but was forced to resign for political reasons in April 1854. He was subsequently made a bishop again in 1871. **Holy Spirit Church** is in the center of Copenhagen. **Roskilde**: a cathedral town ca. thirty kilometers west of Copenhagen. **Christian VIII** and Queen Caroline Amalie: concerning Kierkegaard's relationship with them (audiences, etc.) see his journal entries in *Pap.* X¹ A 41–43 (*SKJP* 6309–11). **Pastor Ibsen**: Peter Diderik Ibsen (1793–1855) was pastor of **Lyngby** Church and a friend of Kierkegaard's; see the first entry by Goldschmidt, with its accompanying note, in chapter 5 of this book. **"Ein solcher Geist muß man behutsam feiern, man darf ihn nicht in seiner Freiheit lassen"**: in the manuscript containing Levin's remarks, the words *feiern* and *lassen* are written in a different hand than the rest of the document and must therefore have been added later. Wolff was thus unable to remember the cited text accurately (and we can see that Levin was likewise unable to do so). It can immediately be seen that the word *feiern* (to celebrate or pay homage to) is meaningless here, and that the context makes it clear that the word *fesseln* (to bind in chains) ought to be here instead. *Ein solcher Geist* ought to read *Einen solchen Geist*. But the entire passage cited does *not* occur in Schiller's *Don Carlos* and has not yet been traced. Tage **Algreen-Ussing** (1797–1872): a politican and jurist. **P. Chr. K.**: Kierkegaard's elder brother, Peter Christian Kierkegaard. **Lynge**: Hermann Henrik Julius Lynge (1822–97) was an important book dealer in Copenhagen, specializing in scholarly antiquarian books; Lynge probably prepared the auction catalog of Kierkegaard's library, and his shop was the largest single purchaser of Kierkegaard's books at the auction itself (cf. H. P. Rohde, *Auktionsprotokol over Søren Kierkegaards Bogsamling*, pp. xviii and 177–78). The unnamed third person present at the reading of the letter was probably Levin himself. **The story of Tardini**: the aeronaut Tardini, a balloonist, had three successful balloon flights in August 1851; on his fourth flight, however, which took off from the Royal Riding Grounds on September 14, 1851, he had an accident and drowned, although the passengers were rescued. **"What has been happening in Copenhagen?"**: Kierkegaard can ask about this because in 1851–52 he was living in Østerbro, outside the fortifications, i.e., outside the city proper. **Grundtvig** had married his second wife on October 24, 1851, not long after Tardini met his fate. **Thirteen thousand rixdollars** and **twenty thousand rixdollars**: like the sums cited earlier, these are completely erroneous figures. **The reconciliation**: Kierkegaard went quite deeply into debt in 1837; his father paid his debts for him on July 5, 1837, and in the same month Kierkegaard moved out of the family home and took up lodgings in Løvstræde (see Sejer Kühle, *Søren Kierkegaard. Barndom og Ungdom*, p. 155).

4. From three letters from F. C. Sibbern. The first two letters, dated October 2 and October 3, 1863, were written by Sibbern to his daughter, Augusta Sibbern Møller, and are translated from a copy of the original made by Harald Høffding in 1912, which is now in **KBHA** (NkS 4620, 4⁰ [Nogle Sibberniana]). The final passage is from a letter from Sibbern to H. P. Barfod, dated September 19, 1869, portions of which were published in *SKEP 1833–43* p. liii; the letter is now in **KBHA** (SKA D. Pk. 5).

Frederik Christian Sibbern (1785–1872): see the note accompanying the comments on Kierkegaard's dissertation in chapter 2 of this book. **One and one-half Danish miles** is the equivalent of seven English miles or eleven and one-quarter kilometers. **[Kierkegaard's] spiritual discourse upon the words of Job, "The Lord giveth, etc."**: see the note accompanying the first entry by Petronella Ross in chapter 7 of this book. **"I was the person to whom the pretty and charming young lady turned"**: see Hanne Mourier's account of Regine Schlegel's memoirs, with the accompanying note, in chapter 3 of this book. Hans Brøchner records Kierkegaard's reactions to Sibbern in this role; see entry 35 in Brøchner's memoirs, in chapter 11 of this book, as well as Kierkegaard's letters on this subject to Emil Boesen and P. J. Spang (*B&A* I 71–73 and 75–77 [*KW* XXV 89–92 and 95–98]). **In vielen Worten wenige Klarheit** is cited (with slight inaccuracies) from the "Vorspiel" to Goethe's *Faust*, "In bunten Bildern wenig Klarheit" (line 170). **A. S. Ørsted**: see the note to the entry by Troels-Lund in chapter 9 of this book. **Before you were born** refers to Sibbern's daughter, Augusta Sibbern Møller (born 1838), to whom the letter was addressed. **Chrystalgaden**: from 1832–36 Sibbern lived at number 24 Krystalgade. **A great fortune**: on Kierkegaard's inheritance and his expenditures, see Brandt and Rammel, *Kierkegaard og Pengene*. **Melchior and Brorson at Herlufsholm**: a reference to two published memorial lectures by Sibbern on Hans Bøchman Melchior (1834) and Anders Winding Brorson (1836), both of whom, like Sibbern himself, were alumni of the preparatory school Herlufsholm. **Agent Lund**: Kierkegaard's brother-in-law Johan Christian Lund (1799–1875). An entry by **Pastor Ipsen**, the **Latin testimony**, and the [school] **report** are all included in the first chapter of this book.

5. All entries are taken from Henrik Hertz's papers in **KBHA**. Entries 1, 2, 4, and 5 are from Hertz's diaries, which are dated. All the other entries are from Hertz's notebooks and commonplace books; he began each of these volumes in chronological order, but often left himself space for continuing his notes at a later date, and he would frequently return to an older entry and add more material. This makes it very difficult (and sometimes impossible) to date these entries more than very approximately. The final entry (number 14) is of particular interest; it is an assemblage of notes drawn together from one of these volumes, all dealing with Hertz's planned (but never completed) play "The Fifth Monarchy." Most entries are in a difficult hand, with occasional dubious or illegible passages and lacunae. Entry 1: **NkS** 3179, 4^0 I (Henrik Hertz's dagbøger 1831–40, bind 6: 1. juni 1835, 1836 og 1837); entry 2: **NkS** 3179, 4^0 I (Henrik Hertz's dagbøger 1831–40, bind 7: 1838–40); entry 3: **NkS** 2807, 4^0 (Henrik Hertz's optegnelsesbøger og efterladte papirer, I: Optegnelsesbøger A–J, bind G, p. 11); entry 4: **NkS** 3179, 4^0 I (Henrik Hertz's dagbøger 1831–40, bind 7: 1838–40); entry 5: **NkS** 3179, 4^0 I (Henrik Hertz's dagbøger 1831–40, bind 7: 1838–40); entry 6: **NkS** 2807, 4^0 (Henrik Hertz's optegnelsesbøger og efterladte papirer, I: Optegnelsesbøger A–J, bind F, unpaginated pages immediately following p. 36); entry 7: **NkS** 2807, 4^0 (Henrik Hertz's optegnelsesbøger og efterladte papirer, II: Optegnelsesbøger K–N, bind M, p. 29); entry 8: **NkS** 2807, 4^0 (Henrik Hertz's optegnelsesbøger og efterladte papirer, II: Optegnelsesbøger K–N, bind N, p. 188); entry 9: **NkS** 2807, 4^0 (Henrik Hertz's optegnelsesbøger og efterladte papirer, III: Optegnelsesbøger O–Q, bind P, p. 164); entry 10: **NkS** 2807, 4^0 (Henrik Hertz's optegnelsesbøger og efterladte papirer, III: Optegnelsesbøger O–Q, bind P, pp. 243–45); entry 11: **NkS** 2807, 4^0 (Henrik Hertz's optegnelsesbøger og efterladte papirer, III: Optegnelsesbøger O–Q, bind P, p. 303); entry 12: **NkS** 2807, 4^0 (Henrik Hertz's optegnelsesbøger og efterladte papirer, II: Optegnelsesbøger K–N, bind N, pp. 155–56); entry 13: **NkS** 2807, 4^0 (Henrik Hertz's optegnelsesbøger og efterladte papirer, II: Optegnelsesbøger K–N, bind M, pp. 213–14); entry 14: (all from notes for "The Fifth Monarchy") **NkS** 2807, 4^0 (Henrik Hertz's optegnelsesbøger og efterladte papirer, I: Optegnelsesbøger A–J, bind H, p. 28 and subsequent pages; n; v; y; bb; (paper scrap) r + j^3–k^3; n^3–o^3; l^4; x^4–y^4; $ö^4$–a^5). Approximately one-third of this material has been published earlier (with some minor differences) by Sejer Kühle in his series of articles "Nogle Oplysninger om Søren Kierkegaard 1834–38" and his book *Søren Kierkegaard. Barndom og Ungdom*.

Henrik Hertz (1797–1870), Danish poet, playwright, aesthetician. **At Heiberg's**: in the draft of her memoirs, Johanne Luise Heiberg writes that Søren Kierkegaard was among those who could come by in the evening without having to be invited; see *Et Liv gjenoplevet i Erindringen*

[A Life Relived in Recollection], 4th ed., ed. Aage Friis (Copenhagen: Gyldendal, 1944), vol. 4, p. 95. **Book on Andersen**: Kierkegaard's first published book, *From the Papers of One Still Living* (*SV* XIII 41–92 [*KW* I 53–102]), had been published on September 7, 1838. **"The Mesopotamian language is a strange language"**: from Holberg, *Ulysses von Ithacia*, act 1, scene 14; a reference to the difficulties of Kierkegaard's style in *From the Papers of One Still Living*. **Churchyard**: in Hertz's Danish, "Kirkegaard," a pun on "Kierkegaard." **The politics in *Moods and Situations*** [*Stemninger og Tilstande*]: an 1839 roman à clef by Hertz, in which one of the characters, the Translator, is based in part on Kierkegaard. [Johan Georg] **Hamann** (1730–88) was a German philosopher whom Kierkegaard did, in fact, read quite avidly. **Miss Olsen** is Kierkegaard's fiancée Regine Olsen. **A fine tribute to me in a dedication**: the second printing of *Either/Or* appeared in May 1849; Kierkegaard's dedication to Hertz is in *B&A* I 340 (*KW* XXV 432). **"We can hardly have met one another again before we met in *100 Years*,"** is a reference by Hertz to his work *One Hundred Years*, a long, rhymed, satiric comedy that was written on the occasion of the hundredth anniversary of the Royal Theater, December 18, 1848, and was published anonymously in 1849. A "night guest" (presumably Kierkegaard) who recites a long monologue appears in the work. Hertz's supposition that *One Hundred Years* prompted Kierkegaard to send him *On My Activity as an Author* in return is probably an erroneous recollection, as the piece by Kierkegaard appeared only in August 1851. No copy of *On My Activity as an Author* containing Kierkegaard's dedication to Hertz has been found. **Madame Hvidberg**: presumably the wife of Jens Madsen Hvidberg, postmaster in Hørsholm at a mailcoach stop to which was attached an inn frequented both by Kierkegaard and by Hertz; see the entry by H. C. Rosted in chapter 7 of this book. (In *Søren Kierkegaards Barndom og Ungdom* [p. 136], Sejer Kühle states, without giving a source, that Kierkegaard and Hertz were both at Hvidberg's inn at Hørsholm on July 28, 1851, when there was a solar eclipse; Kierkegaard did not come out to observe the eclipse, however, but remained in his room, eating his dinner.) **"Vejle Journey"** [Vejle-Rejsen]: Hertz's planned (but never completed) play about the events of the war of 1848–50. **His work on *Two Ages***: Kierkegaard's *A Literary Review*, (*SV* VIII 3–105 [*KW* XIV 1–112]), a review of Mrs. Gyllembourg's *Two Ages* [*To Tidsaldre*]. **A Story of Everyday Life** [*En Hverdagshistorie*]: the novella that made the reputation of Thomasine Gyllembourg (1773–1856), an author and the mother of Johan Ludvig Heiberg; for the rest of her writing career she remained anonymous, and was referred to only as "the author of *A Story of Everyday Life*." **Ruach elohim**: "spirit of God" (Hebrew). **Poul [Martin] Møller** (1794–1838): poet, author, and professor of philosophy, published his review of Mrs. Gyllembourg's 1835 novella *The Extremes* [*Extremerne*] in *Maanedskrift for Litteratur* [Monthly Journal of Literature] in 1836. The review was reprinted in Møller's *Efterladte Skrifter* [Posthumous Writings], vol. 2 (Copenhagen, 1842), pp. 126–58; Hertz does not cite Møller quite correctly, but the passage in question is found on page 155. **[Thomas] Overskou** (1798–1873): dramatist, historian of the theater, and, like Hertz, a member of Johan Ludvig Heiberg's circle. **Fifth Monarchy** [Det 5te Monarchie]: a planned (but never completed) play by Hertz; from Hertz's surviving notes, it is clear that the play takes place on "The Hill" (see below) in the Deer Park north of Copenhagen, that it is a satire on the theater criticism of the period (cf. **KBHA [NkS** 2807, 4⁰, II, bd. M, p. 10]), and that Kierkegaard and Goldschmidt (apparently as the Pierrot figure) appear in it. **His relationship to *Fædrelandet***: between 1842 and 1846 Kierkegaard published seven letters to the editor in *Fædrelandet*, primarily dealing with his pseudonymous works (*SV* XIII 397–435 [*KW* XIII 3–27 and 38–46]), and it is probably these to which Hertz refers; later Kierkegaard chose *Fædrelandet* as the newspaper in which to publish other pieces, including his reply to Rudelbach (*SV* XIII 436–44 [*KW* XIII 51–59]) and the articles that opened the attack on the Church (*SV* XIV 5–81 and 93–100). **His quarrel with someone in *Berlingske***: Hertz is apparently alluding to Kierkegaard's letter, "An Explanation and a Little More" (*SV* XIII 418–21 [*KW* XIII 24–27]), which appeared in *Fædrelandet* on May 9, 1845, and was a reply to a review of *Three Discourses on Imagined Occasions* and *Stages on Life's Way*, which had appeared in *Berlingske Tidende* on May 6, 1845. **The Deer Park**: see the note accompanying the entry by Jakob Knudsen in chapter 2 of this book. **M. A. Goldschmidt**: see the note accompanying the entry by H. F.

Rørdam in chapter 4 of this book; see also chapter 5 of this book. **The Hill**: an amusement center located in the Deer Park. *A Danish University Student's Tale* [*En dansk Students Eventyr*]: see the note to Henriette Lund's memoirs in chapter 9 of this book.

Chapter Eleven
Hans Brøchner on Kierkegaard

1. From Hans Brøchner's recollections of Søren Kierkegaard. As is made clear at the conclusion of these memoirs, Brøchner wrote them in the period December 1871–January 1872, a time when Søren Kierkegaard was very much in vogue. The first volume of Kierkegaard's *Posthumous Papers* had just appeared in 1869, and it was doubtless in connection with this that Brøchner was asked to write *his* recollections of his famous relative, though we do not know who requested him to do so. They were published for the first time, posthumously, in the March 1877 issue of Georg and Edvard Brandes's journal *Det nittende Aarhundrede* [The Nineteenth Century], vol. 5, pp. 337–74. Formally, the editor of Brøchner's memoirs was Harald Høffding, because he was viewed as Brøchner's philosophical successor. Georg Brandes, however, was probably the actual editor because the corrections written on the manuscript are in Brandes's hand. These memoirs were published for a second time as Hans Brøchner, *Erindringer om Søren Kierkegaard* [Recollections about Søren Kierkegaard], ed. Steen Johansen (Copenhagen: Gyldendal, 1953), and for a third time in *Erindringer om Søren Kierkegaard. Samlet Udgave ved Steen Johansen* [Recollections about Søren Kierkegaard: Collected Edition by Steen Johansen] (Copenhagen: C. A. Reitzel, 1980), pp. 91–117, in which earlier errors were corrected. The present translation is from the original manuscript, which is in **KBHA** (Additamenta 415d, 4⁰). Another English translation of Brøchner's recollections is available in T. H. Croxall, *Glimpses and Impressions of Kierkegaard*, pp. 7–39; a few brief selections are also available in English translation in Alexander Dru, *The Journals of Søren Kierkegaard*, pp 563–64.

Hans Brøchner: see the note accompanying Brøchner's letter to H. P. Barfod in chapter 4 of this book. When Brøchner became a student at the University of Copenhagen, he came to lodge with his uncle Michael Andersen Kierkegaard, who lived at Købmagergade 45, and he met Søren Kierkegaard at social gatherings. Despite the difference in age, they spent a good deal of time together.

Entry 1. Hans Brøchner became a university student in October of 1836 at the age of sixteen, and the **party** which is mentioned as taking place at the home of his uncle Michael Andersen Kierkegaard must therefore have been a celebration on the occasion of the wedding of Søren Kierkegaard's brother, Peter Christian Kierkegaard, which took place on October 21, 1836. Brøchner lived with his uncle for ten years, until 1846. A pencil sketch that was first published in the *Ny Illustrerad Tidning* [New Illustrated Times] (Stockholm), November 25, 1876 (included among the illustrations in the present volume), gives an impression of Kierkegaard's appearance as a young student; it confirms what Brøchner writes about Kierkegaard's **coiffure**. Brøchner writes that he saw Kierkegaard **without knowing what he was**. This is understandable enough, because at that point Brøchner was a brand-new student from the provinces, and he could not have known that even then Kierkegaard had already made a name for himself in the academic world of Copenhagen, not only by means of his newspaper articles and lectures—see Teddy Petersen, *Kierkegaards polemiske debut*, pp. 9–14 and 152–57—but also with his wit and his dialectical ability, which he exhibited at gatherings with fellow students, during walks, or at cafés or tea shops.

Entry 2. That same place means Michael Andersen Kierkegaard's home at Købmagergade 45. With respect to Kierkegaard's **paradoxical statements**, see, for example, chapter 2 of this book, where J. A. Ostermann comments on Kierkegaard's love of political dialectic for its own sake, apart from any actual content. Brøchner discusses Kierkegaard's love of paradoxes again below, in entry number 39 of these memoirs.

Entry 3. Kierkegaard moved away from home ca. July 1837 and took up lodgings in **Løvstræde**, probably at number 7, where the publisher Reitzel later moved in. Incidentally, this residence for Kierkegaard is known only from Brøchner's account. (A listing of all Kierkegaard's places of residence in Copenhagen, so far as they can be determined, can be found on the map of Copenhagen in 1844 at the front of this book.) The book by **Eichendorff** mentioned here was a long novella published in 1834. See H. P. Rohde, *Gaadefulde Stadier paa Kierkegaards Vej* [Mysterious Stages on Kierkegaard's Way] (Copenhagen: Rosenkilde og Bagger, 1974), pp. 12–38, for information on Kierkegaard's copy of Eichendorff's book, which, as Brøchner notes, he purchased at the auction of Kierkegaard's library, and which is still extant. It cannot be demonstrated from Kierkegaard's journal entries in the fall of 1837 that he was particularly preoccupied with Eichendorff's book (however, see *Pap.* II A 405, dated May 3, 1839, for mention of it), but during that period he did study many German poets, theologians, philosophers, etc., including, e.g., Hoffmann, Arnim, and Chamisso. Kierkegaard's psychological acumen was well known by his associates, and Brøchner cites numerous examples of this; see especially entry number 8 below. **The young person**: in this entry Brøchner hints that he served as the model of "The Young Man" in the section of *Stages on Life's Way* entitled "In vino veritas" (cf. *SV* VI 13–83 [*KW* XI 7–86]). It was, however, at most the externalities, the appearances, which Kierkegaard took from Brøchner; cf. Knud Jensenius, " 'Det unge Menneske' hos Søren Kierkegaard" [" 'The Young Man' in Søren Kierkegaard"], *Nordisk Tidsskrift* (Stockholm), 1930, pp. 340ff. **His large library**: according to the auction catalog, at his death Søren Kierkegaard's library comprised 2,748 volumes, which, in comparison to the collections possessed by some of his scholarly or bibliophile contemporaries, can scarcely be called a "large library." The library was large enough to impress the young Brøchner, however. (For more on Kierkegaard's library, see H. P. Rohde, "Søren Kierkegaard as a Collector of Books," in H. P. Rohde, ed. *Auktionsprotokol over Søren Kierkegaards Bogsamling*, pp. xlvii–xlviii.) See also Sejer Kühle, "Søren Kierkegaards Bibliotek" [Søren Kierkegaard's Library], *Berlingske Aftenavis*, February 24, 1943, and Carl Koch, "Søren Kierkegaard og Eventyret" [Søren Kierkegaard and Fairy Tales], *Dansk Tidsskrift*, 1899, pp. 146–60. At the auction of Kierkegaard's library in 1856, Brøchner purchased not only the volume of Eichendorff that he mentions but also several others; cf. the information in Rohde's essay in *Gaadefulde Stadier paa Kierkegaards Vej*, pp. 33–35.

Entry 4. Kierkegaard's father died on August 9, 1838, at the age of eighty-one. When Brøchner writes that Kierkegaard's veneration for his father **has been vividly expressed in his [Søren Kierkegaard's] writings** he is presumably referring to, e.g., the conclusion of *Concluding Unscientific Postscript*, where Kierkegaard writes of "my late father, the person to whom I owe the most, also with respect to my work" (*SV* VII 548 [*KW* XII 629]); see also "my father, the person whom I have loved the most" (*SV* XIII 565); "my beloved, deceased father" (*SV* XIV 324). Kierkegaard published no fewer than eight collections of edifying and other discourses with dedications to his deceased father. **A trip in northern Zealand** (Gilleleje) took place in June and July 1835. See the note to entry number 20 for information on **Magister Adler. The due date** refers to the specific times during the year (i.e., June 11 and December 11) when mortgage notes and other obligations fell due. Kierkegaard received five hundred, not eight hundred, rixdollars annually from his father after he moved away from home in 1837; cf. Carl Weltzer, *Peter og Søren Kierkegaard*, p. 115, and Kühle, *Søren Kierkegaard. Barndom og Ungdom*, p. 155.

Entry 5. My late sister Hansine is Brøchner's sister Hansine Brøchner Obel (1815–69). **Our girl cousins** refers to Michael Andersen Kierkegaard's three daughters of which two (born in 1803 and 1810, respectively) were still living at home at the time under discussion (1828). **Thirteen years old**: the manuscript has "nineteen years old," which is an error of memory or a slip of the pen.

Entry 6. On July 3, 1840, Kierkegaard received the degree of Cand. theol. with first-class honors. **As long as Father was alive, I could defend my proposition that I ought not to take the degree**; for a similar version of the same anecdote, see the entry by Johannes C. Barth in chapter 7 of this book. **His Brøchner** means Hans Brøchner (1796–1843), a theological tutor in Copenhagen and a cousin of Brøchner's father. The fact that Kierkegaard called him "his Brøchner" fits in very well with what else we know of Kierkegaard's habits. He in fact tended to use "my" with respect to everyone who served him: "my shoemaker," "my fruit dealer," "my coachman," etc., which, incidentally, his fiancée's brother criticized him for; see *B&A* I 49–50 (*KW* XXV 63). **Peter Stilling**: see the note accompanying the entry by H. L. Martensen in chapter 8 of this book. **A writing seminar** refers to seminars held by Prof. H. N. **Clausen** (1793–1877) during the winter semester of 1839–40 every Friday from 9:00 to 11:00 A.M. **[Kierkegaard's] degree in theology**: during the April–July examination period in 1840, sixty-three students passed the theological examination; twenty-seven of these received first-class honors, among whom Kierkegaard was fourth best. Information on Kierkegaard's performance on the oral portion of his theological examination is reported by the author Sophus Schandorph: "I once heard a bishop say, 'Søren Kierkegaard, hmm, the honors he got at his theological examination were really not very spectacular'" (Sophus Schandorph, *Oplevelser* [Experiences] [Copenhagen: C. A. Reitzel, 1889], p. 275). Of the three whom Brøchner mentions as being ahead of Kierkegaard: **M[athias] Wad** (1816–97) ended up as a pastor in Korsør; **[Emil Fr. Vil.] Warburg** (1817–86) as pastor in Asminderød; and **Chr[istian] F[lenger]** Christens (1819–55) as a schoolteacher and pedagogical author.

Entry 7. The words **It would actually be good for you, etc.** were varied by Kierkegaard's father from time to time, e.g.: "Nothing will ever become of you as long as you have money" (*Pap.* VIII[1] A 640 p. 289 [*SKJP* 6131]). **My late cousin Peter Kierkegaard**, i.e., Hans Peter Kierkegaard (1815–62), the youngest child of Michael Andersen Kierkegaard; see his entry in chapter 9 of this book and entry number 43 in this chapter. **When S.K.'s mother died**: Kierkegaard's mother died on July 30, 1834, and was buried on August 4 at Assistens Cemetery.

Entry 8. **It was while S.K. was in Berlin during the winter of 1841–42 that I applied to take the examinations in theology, but was denied permission**: on October 25, 1841, Kierkegaard left Copenhagen to travel to Berlin where he heard (among other things) Schelling's lectures. His references to Schelling's lectures are in *Pap.* III C 27 (in *Pap.* XIII pp. 253–329 [*KW* II 331–412]). Kierkegaard was back in Copenhagen again on March 6, 1842. In his petition to take the theological examination that same fall (1841), Brøchner had confessed his conviction that the Christian faith was incompatible with modern thinking, which led to the rejection of his application by the theological faculty. This was something previously unheard of in a theological student, and it caused quite a sensation. See S. V. Rasmussen, *Den unge Brøchner* [The Young Brøchner] ed. Justus Hartnack (Copenhagen: Gyldendal, 1966), pp. 16–26. The text of Brøchner's petition and the documents connected with that case are printed in the *Universitets Aarbog* [University Yearbook] for 1841, pp. 72–75. **Christens**: see entry number 6, with its accompanying note, in this chapter. **The irregularity of his movements**: there is an entire literature written about Kierkegaard's external appearance; see Kabell, *Kierkegaardstudiet i Norden*, pp. 289–300, and K. Bruun Andersen, "Søren Kierkegaards Udseende" [Søren Kierkegaard's Appearance], *Personalhistorisk Tidsskrift*, 1949–50, pp. 117–21, where his manner of walking receives minor discussion. Julie Weber Sødring and Arthur Abrahams also mention Kierkegaard's unusual and uneven gait; see their entries in chapter 6 of this book. The English scholar Roger Poole has reported that Kierkegaard was not alone in his erratic, weaving manner of walking; the "romantic gait" was also known among English poets of the early nineteenth century.

Entry 9. **The winter he spent in Berlin**: see the note to entry number 8 in this chapter. **Christens**: see the note to entry number 6 in this chapter. **A[ndreas] F[rederik] Krieger** (1817–93), jurist, later a leading politician and cabinet minister; in 1841–43 he studied law abroad. **Carl Weis**: see the note to the entry by Hother Ploug in chapter 4 of this book; Weis was on a lengthy foreign trip at the time, studying law and music. **Rothe**: Peter Conrad Rothe (1811–1902) became a licentiate in theology in 1840, after which he took a two-year study trip abroad and attended Schelling's lectures in Berlin. He was appointed to the Church of Our Lady in Copenhagen in 1843, where he eventually advanced to archdeacon. **In *Either/Or* K. describes this method**: see *SV* I 270–71 (*KW* III 299).

Entry 10. K.'s return home: see the note to entry number 8 in this chapter. **Greek poetry and philosophy**: after the university refused Brøchner's petition to be permitted to take the theological examinations despite his unorthodox views, Brøchner immersed himself in the study of philosophy and oriental languages and in June 1845 took the Magisterkonferens examination in "Semitic languages, Latin, Greek, and the history of philosophy" (cf. *Univeritets Aarbog* [University Yearbook], 1845, p. 87).

Entry 11. A short pseudonymous pamphlet: the full title of the pseudonymous work mentioned here is *J. L. Heiberg efter Døden. Apokalyptisk Komedie i fire Akter* [J. L. Heiberg after Death: Apocalyptic Comedy in Four Acts], by Adam Howitz, and behind that pseudonym hid Christian K. F. Molbech and Hans Brøchner. Brøchner, however, was only an assistant; the real author of this parody of Heiberg's *En Sjæl efter Døden* [A Soul after Death] was Brøchner's friend Molbech. The portion of the text that begins with **K. ranked** and concludes with **works** was added in the margin of the manuscript. **Vischer**: Friedrich Theodor Vischer (1807–87), a German aesthetician whose principal aesthetic works came out in the period 1846–57. *Either/Or* was published on February 20, 1843, and Heiberg's **well-known review** was published in vol. 2, pp. 288–92, of his *Intelligensblade* [Intelligenser] (March 1, 1843) as the conclusion of an article entitled "Vintersæd" [Winterseed]; it is reprinted in Rasmus Nielsen, ed., *S. Kierkegaards Bladartikler med Bilag samlede efter Forfatterens Død, udgivne som Supplement til hans øvrige Skrifter*, pp. 208–10, but is not reprinted in Heiberg's *Prosaiske Skrifter* [Prose Writings]. Kierkegaard's notes concerning that review are published in *Pap.* IV A 162 (*SKJP* 5697) and B 25–58; his public reply was the ironic "Taksigelse" [Thank You], published in *Fædrelandet*, March 5, 1843 (*SV* XIII 411–15 [*KW* XIII 17–21]).

Entry 12. His wanderings had a definite goal; cf. Brøchner's sketch of Kierkegaard in Berlin in entry number 26 in this chapter.

Entry 13. S.K. on horseback: it is known that Kierkegaard learned to ride a horse in 1840; cf. a letter from the autumn of 1840 (*B&A* I 54 [*KW* XXV 68]), where Kierkegaard uses expressions borrowed from riding. Although Brøchner says that **he soon gave up this sport**, *The Corsair* seems to have remembered it for a long time; cf. the cartoon in the issue for January 16, 1846! Troels-Lund reports that Kierkegaard made his first attempts at horseback riding at his (Troels-Lund's) parents' home in Nørrebro in the early 1830s (see chapter 9 in this book). Johannes C. Barth reports that his father advised Kierkegaard to take up riding as a cure for his stomach pains (see chapter 7 in this book).

Entry 15. For the period surrounding the publication of *Either/Or*, see the note for entry number 11 in this chapter. Διαψάλματα ("diapsalmata") is the name of the collection of aphorisms with which *Either/Or* begins. The word means "interlude"; for further explanation of the term see *SV* I, 2d ed. (Copenhagen: Gyldendal, 1920), appendix, p. 8. **These sentences, etc.**: cf. passages such as *SV* I 286 (*KW* II 314), ("that lovely little foot"); 287 (*KW* II 314) ("that little foot"); 288 (*KW* II 316) ("a . . . hand as white and well-formed as an antique"), all taken from "The Diary of a Seducer." **His house (on Nørregade)**: from 1840 to 1844 Kierkegaard lived at Nørregade 230A (now number 38).

Entry 16. My piece against Martensen: Brøchner's *Nogle Bemærkninger om Daaben* [Some Remarks on Baptism] (Copenhagen: 1843), was occasioned by Prof. Martensen's work *Den christelige Daab betragtet med Hensyn paa det baptistiske Spørgsmaal* [Christian Baptism Examined in the Light of the Baptist Question] (Copenhagen: C. A. Reitzel, 1843); it was published ca. June 26, 1843, and reviewed anonymously in *Berlingske Tidende* on July 29. *Berlingske Tidende* was **a paper edited by a Jew**, namely Mendel Levin Nathanson (1780–1868), formerly a figure in the world of finance, who had turned to journalism and social reform.

Entry 17. Ludwig Feuerbach (1804–72), a German philosopher whose best-known work, *Das Wesen des Christentums*, came out in 1841. **The Problem of Faith and Knowledge**, i.e., Hans Brøchner's book *Problemet om Tro og Viden. En historisk-kritisk Afhandling* [The Problem of Faith and Knowledge: A Historical and Critical Essay] (Copenhagen: P. G. Philipsens Forlag, 1868); the passage in Kierkegaard referred to on p. 125 of Brøchner's book and alluded to in this entry is from *Concluding Unscientific Postscript* (*SV* VII 535 [*KW* XII.1 614]): "On the other hand, a scoffer attacks Christianity and at the same time expounds it so creditably that it is a pleasure to read him, and a person who has difficulties in presenting Christianity properly and definitely is almost compelled to resort to him." **Pathos**: see the above-mentioned book by Feuerbach, pp. 321–23, especially p. 322.

Entry 18. *Aladdin*: another example of Kierkegaard's delight in declaiming can be found in Henriette Lund's memoirs in chapter 9 of this book (which also involves a passage from Oehlenschläger's *Aladdin*). **Charlottenborg** is a mansion in Copenhagen that houses the Royal Academy of Art.

Entry 19. Geniuses always lack: compare this to Kierkegaard's oft-cited journal entry from 1837 (*Pap.* II A 26 [*SKJP* 1288]): "A thesis: great geniuses cannot really read books because while reading they will develop themselves more than they will understand the author"; cf. *Pap.* II A 46 (*SKJP* 131).

Entry 20. Magister Adler was Adolph Peter Adler (1812–69), a theological and philosophical author. He took his Cand. theol. degree in 1836, his doctorate in 1840, and became pastor at Hasle on the island of Bornholm in 1841. In January 1844 he was suspended from his post and in 1845 was retired with pension. He subsequently returned to Copenhagen. His suspension from his pastorate was occasioned primarily by the preface he wrote to his *Nogle Prædikener* [Some Sermons] (Copenhagen: C. A. Reitzel, 1843), in which he claimed to have received personal revelations from Jesus Christ. This was seen as a sign of insanity or of heresy. The statement about **the time when Adler's mental disturbances began** must refer to 1843, not long after Adler's purported revelations, when he came from Bornholm on a visit to Copenhagen. **A work he had published**: Adler published two books in 1843 and four in 1846, and it is not possible to determine to which of these Brøchner is referring. Adler's authorship and his fate was of such great interest to Kierkegaard that in the summer of 1846 Kierkegaard planned and began work on a major book about him. It was never published, however, but various materials (drafts, fragments, etc.) have been printed in *Pap.* VII^2 and have been separately published as *Nutidens religieuse Forvirring. Bogen om Adler* [The Religious Confusion of Modern Times: The Book on Adler], ed. Julia Watkin (Copenhagen: C. A. Reitzel, 1984), and will appear in English translation as *KW* XXIV. Adler's remark to Brøchner in 1836–37 to the effect that Kierkegaard prepared for his conversations lends weight to other testimony of this sort.

Entry 21. Shortly after Nielsen had been appointed to the university: for information on Prof. Rasmus Nielsen, see the note accompanying the letter of February 28, 1870, from M. A. Goldschmidt to H. P. Barfod, in chapter 5 of this book. In the winter of 1840–41 Rasmus Nielsen lectured at the university as a private tutor; his topics were Church history and New Testament exegesis. On April 22, 1841, he was appointed professor of moral philosophy as the successor to Poul Martin Møller, who had died in 1838 but whose position had not been filled for want of a qualified candidate. In the summer semester of 1841, his first semester as a professor, Nielsen lectured on metaphysics. He cannot have had much time in which to prepare for these lectures. **Christian VIII's reign**: December 3, 1839–January 20, 1848. In the original manuscript, the remark, **He understands what they say in Jutland, that a person must have something to live off!** is a marginal note. **When N. had allied himself with K.**: this happened ca. 1846–47, and in the years 1848–50 the friendship was at its high point. **Nielsen is a windbag**: the passage in Kierkegaard's writings in which these words are supposed to occur has not been found. There are, incidentally, many places in his papers where Kierkegaard talks about Nielsen (cf. e.g., *Pap.* IX A 229 [*SKJP* 6239], 231; X^2 A 580; X^3 A 681, 701; X^6 B 83–102 [partly in *SKJP* 6403 and 6663], 121 [*SKJP* 6574]).

Entry 22. *The Corsair*'s attack on him was occasioned by an article by Kierkegaard, published in *Fædrelandet* on December 27, 1845. In January 1846 *The Corsair*'s editor, M. A. Goldschmidt, (and others) began to tease, parody, and caricature Kierkegaard; this lasted about six months. See chapter 5 of this book for Goldschmidt's recollections about this affair. **He could reflect on a trifle until it assumed world-historical significance**: cf. Brøchner's entry in chapter 4, where he makes a similar remark regarding Kierkegaard's reaction to Hostrup's comedy *Gjenboerne*.

Entry 23. "Søren Kirk": cf. *Pap.* VII¹ A 154 (*SKJP* 5940) and VIII¹ A 654 (*SKJP* 6089) for Kierkegaard's references to Brøchner's appearance as "Søren Kirk" in *Gjenboerne*. See also Brøchner's other account of this incident, with its accompanying note, in chapter 4 of this book.

Entry 24. K. took a trip: Kierkegaard's trip to Jutland took place ca. July 19–August 6, 1840. For Kierkegaard's notes on this journey, see *Pap.* III A 14–84 (most of this is available in *SKJP* 5437–76, 880–82, 3282, 38–39, 1026–27, 1321–23, 3382, 2178, 1589–90, 1099–1100, 1983, 1721, 1240, 1722, 2387, 2276, 2796, 2829–30, 2585), especially A 81 (*SKJP* 5474), for a much briefer and less colorful account. Cf. also Arthur Dahl, *Søren Kierkegaard's Pilgrimage to Jutland*. **His family's native town**, i.e., Sæding (or Seding, Sedding, or Sædding), which is about six or seven miles (ten kilometers) north of Skjern. In 1821 Kierkegaard's father had founded a trust fund called "Niels Sedings Minde" [Niels Seding Memorial Fund]; for information on this and on the relation of Kierkegaard's father and the Kierkegaard family to the town of Sæding, see *SKEP 1833–1843* pp. xxxi–xxxiii and Thorkild Andersen, "Kierkegaard-Slægten og Sædding" [The Kierkegaard Family and Sædding], *Hardsyssel Årbog* [Hardsyssel Yearbook], 27. Bind (1933), pp. 26–40. **K.'s carriage [came to a stop] next to him**: in the manuscript the text reads "carriage next to him."

Entry 25. Licentiat Hagen is Johan Frederik Hagen (1817–59), who received his theological doctorate on July 14, 1845. The title of his dissertation was *Ægteskabet, betragtet fra et ethisk-historisk Standpunkt* [Marriage Regarded from an Ethical-Historical Point of View] (Copenhagen: Wahlske Boghandels Forlag, 1845); see Kierkegaard's comments in *Pap.* VI A 92 (*SKJP* 921). Hans Brøchner was one of the opponents *ex auditorio* at Hagen's doctoral defense. **The pseudonyms had given a fuller treatment of these ideas** is to be understood as meaning that a more complete understanding of the role of love in marriage is provided by the pseudonyms. Hagen discusses the issue in his dissertation on pp. 149–50, and on p. 150 he refers specifically to Victor Eremita's work, i.e., *Either/Or*, vol. 1. Hagen published reviews of several of Kierkegaard's works, namely, *Either/Or*, *Fear and Trembling*, and *Philosophical Fragments*.

Entry 26. While I was in Berlin for the summer of 1846: Kierkegaard left Copenhagen for Berlin at the beginning of May 1846 and was away until May 16. If Brøchner is correct in claiming that this journey marked the beginning of work on a book, then it must have been *The Book on Adler* (cf. the note for entry number 20 in this chapter), which Kierkegaard worked on during the next six months. **My dissertation**: in November 1845 Brøchner defended his doctoral thesis *Om det jødiske Folks Tilstand i den persiske Periode* [On the Situation of the Jewish People during the Persian Period]. See also the note to entry 12 in this chapter for more on Kierkegaard's preference for specific goals in his walks. **Our cousin Mrs. Thomsen** is Michael Andersen Kierkegaard's daughter, Mrs. Julie Augusta Kierkegaard Thomsen, who was Brøchner's cousin. The advertisement mentioned is reproduced in *Det nittende Aarhundrede*, vol. 5 (1876–77), p. 176, as a footnote in a letter from Kierkegaard to Mrs. Thomsen (see *B&A* II 75 [*KW* XXV 473]). Brøchner had sent him the advertisement in February 1847.

Entry 27. My first trip to Italy: beginning in April 1846, Brøchner studied in Berlin for a year (see entry number 26 in this chapter) and departed for Rome at the beginning of 1847, returning to Denmark in November of the same year. According to the city directory, the plasterer B. **Barsugli** lived at Store Købmagergade 7 (now Købmagergade 42). He had display windows and a shop on Østergade, though it is unclear exactly where. Prior to the opening of Thorvaldsen's Museum in 1848, Barsugli's gallery was one of the only public places in Copenhagen where one could get a sense of classical sculpture. "The plasterer in Østergade" is also mentioned in *Pap.* II A 200 (*SKJP* 5279) in connection with admiration for Greek antiquity.

Entry 28. Shortly after the rebellion broke out in 1848: the rebellion broke out in Rendsborg and Kiel on March 24, 1848; rumors concerning this reached Copenhagen on March 27. **Needed to gain some experience**: see entry 29 and its accompanying note in this chapter.

Entry 29. Dissatisfied with my lack of a specific occupation: Brøchner had been a student at the university for nine years (1836–45), had subsequently studied abroad for another year and a half, lived on grants, travelled, and served as a private tutor at the university. Starting in 1853 he taught Greek at the Borgerdyd School, and obtained a university appointment only in 1857, becoming a professor in 1860.

Entry 30. Dr. P. K.: Peter Christian Kierkegaard. **Lectures**: in December 1850 Peter Christian Kierkegaard held a series of six public lectures at the university, of which the final five were held in the ceremonial hall (cf. Weltzer, *Peter og Søren Kierkegaard*, p. 241). He subsequently published them in his journal, *Fortsættelser fra Pedersborg* [Continuations from Pedersborg], vol. 3 (Copenhagen, 1853), pp. 1–132; the first three lectures were republished in his *Peter Christian Kierkegaards Samlede Skrifter* [The Collected Writings of Peter Christian Kierkegaard], ed. Poul Egede Glahn and Laurids Nyegård, vol. 2 (Copenhagen: Karl Schønbergs Forlag, 1902), pp. 24–155, under the title "Belysning af vigtige politiske og kirkelige Spørgsmaal, knyttet til en udførlig Forklaring over Matth. 1,8.9" [Illumination of Important Political and Ecclesiastical Questions in Conjunction with a Detailed Explanation of Matthew 9.1,8]. Søren Kierkegaard refers to these lectures in *Pap.* X^2 A 415 pp. 295–96 (*SKJP* 6581) and X^3 A 38. **Our old uncle** refers to Michael Andersen Kierkegaard, Brøchner's uncle; see above in this note. **His daughter** is certainly a reference to Mrs. Julie Augusta Kierkegaard Thomsen, mentioned in entry number 26 in this chapter, who became a widow in 1845 and presumably lived with her father.

Entry 31. This old uncle: see the note to entry number 30 in this chapter. **A granddaughter's engagement**: Michael Andersen Kierkegaard had three daughters and four granddaughters; of the latter, the youngest remained unmarried, while the other three were married in 1858, 1863, and 1868, respectively. **My appointment to the university**: it was reported in *Berlingske Tidende* for February 6, 1857, that Brøchner had been appointed as an adjunct tutor at the University of Copenhagen. **Holberg's prescription** is a reference to the Harlequin's Song in *De Usynlige* [The Invisible], act 2, scene 6.

Entry 32. Old Kierkegaard: Brøchner's uncle Michael Andersen Kierkegaard. **Peter Kierkegaard had taken a new wife**: Peter Christian Kierkegaard married for the second time on June 12, 1841. His second wife was [Sophie] Henriette ["Jette"] Glahn; see the notes accompanying the entries by Peter Christian Kierkegaard in chapter 9 of this book. **Great age**: Michael Andersen Kierkegaard lived to the age of ninety-one (February 6, 1776–April 12, 1867).

Entry 33. With respect to Kierkegaard's **firm conviction that he would die when he reached the age of thirty-three**, see Hans Brix, *Analyser og Problemer* [Analyses and Problems], vol. 3 (Copenhagen: Gyldendal, 1936), pp. 300–308. See *Pap.* VIII^1 A 100 p. 49 (*SKJP* 5999), where Kierkegaard expresses surprise that he has attained the age of thirty-four. Brøchner's supposition about this being Jesus' age seems a highly plausible explanation of Kierkegaard's attachment to this idea. The Kierkegaard family, not only old Michael Pedersen Kierkegaard but also his sons Peter Christian and Søren, tended to be quite superstitious; cf. Kühle, *Søren Kierkegaard. Barndom og Ungdom*, pp. 56–57.

Entry 34. When I held lectures at the university for the first time: as a private tutor Brøchner gave public lectures during the winter of 1849–50 on the history of Greek philosophy, and he simultaneously gave private interpretive exercises on Aristotle's metaphysics and on the "Theaetetus" and "Sophist" of Plato.

Entry 35. μεσότησ ("mesotes"): meaning "the center, the middle way," is a concept that plays an important role in Aristotle's definition of ethical virtue in his *Nichomachean Ethics* (book 2, chapter 5); cf. e.g., Brøchner, *Philosophiens Historie i Grundrids I. Den græske Philosophies Historie* [Outline of the History of Philosophy: Book 1, The History of Greek Philosophy] (Copenhagen: P. G. Philipsens Forlag, 1873), pp. 187f. **Madvig**: Prof. J. N. Madvig; see the notes accompanying the comments on Kierkegaard's dissertation in chapter 2 of this book. **Sibbern**: Prof. F. C. Sibbern; see the notes accompanying the comments on Kierkegaard's dissertation in chapter 2 and Sibbern's recollections in chapter 10 of this book. **Ladies, in particular, turned to him to consult him as a sort of psychological and spiritual adviser**: on Sibbern's role as a psychological and spiritual counselor to Regine Olsen after the breaking off of her engagement with

Kierkegaard, see Sibbern's account in chapter 10 and Hanne Mourier's account of Regine Olsen's memoirs in chapter 3 of this book.

Entry 36. Poul Møller was Poul Martin Møller (1794–1838), author and professor of philosophy at the university. Møller was Kierkegaard's teacher and, along with Emil Boesen, perhaps his closest friend. See Frithiof Brandt, *Den unge Søren Kierkegaard* [The Young Søren Kierkegaard] (Copenhagen: Levin & Munksgaard, 1929), pp. 336ff. for a discussion of their relationship. Kierkegaard's feelings for Poul Martin Møller are perhaps best expressed in the dedication to *The Concept of Anxiety* (*SV* IV 277 [*KW* VIII 5]). The episode depicted took place on October 25, 1836, during the doctoral defense of F. O. Lange (later Headmaster of the Vordingborg Learned School and titular professor). **Pleisch** had his tea shop at Amagertorv 4.

Entry 37. Prof. [J.L.A.] Kolderup-Rosenvinge (1798–1850): see the note accompanying the entry by Mathilde Reinhardt in chapter 8 of this book.

Entry 38. Pastor Spang is Pastor P. J. Spang (1796–1846), pastor of the Church of the Holy Spirit. See the note on Pastor Spang accompanying the entry by Tycho E. Spang in chapter 7 of this book. **Spang's daughter, Mrs. Rump**, was Benedicte Sophie Spang, who married the landscape painter Godtfred Rump in 1868. In *Pap.* VIII[1] A 658 Kierkegaard discusses dedicating "one or another book to the late Spang." With respect to Kierkegaard's ability to comfort others in their sorrow, see also the entry by Tycho E. Spang in chapter 7 of this book.

Entry 39. Christens: see the note for entry number 6 in this chapter. The theme of **At last!**: cf. *SV* III 33 (*KW* V 28); *SV* V 122 (*KW* V 345); and especially *SV* XII 181 (*KW* XX 195–96) (in *Practice in Christianity*), which is surely the place to which Brøchner alludes. According to Brøchner (in *Fædrelandet*, December 1, 1855), that work, which came out in 1850, was composed in 1848. See also Alastair McKinnon and Niels Jørgen Cappelørn, "The Period of Composition of Kierkegaard's Published Works," *Kierkegaardiana*, vol. 9 (1974), pp. 132–46.

Entry 41. Chamberpot in general is actually a slightly vulgar and untranslatable pun. The Danish equivalent of "in general" is *overhovedet* (cognate of the German *überhaupt*) which literally means "over the head." So Kierkegaard's remark means that a generic religion is the equivalent of a "chamberpot in general," which can also be taken to mean "a chamberpot over one's head."

Entry 42. Without eliciting any real criticism: Kierkegaard is only partially correct in this assertion; cf. Kabell, *Kierkegaardstudiet i Norden*, pp. 13–18 and 49–90, for an account of the critical reception given Kierkegaard's work during his lifetime. **The number of copies that sold**: the assertion that seventy copies of his book sold quickly should not be understood as meaning that that was the total number sold. See Frithiof Brandt and Else Rammel, *Kierkegaard og Pengene*, pp. 11–25, for information on the number of copies Kierkegaard's books sold.

Entry 43. A son, a couple of years younger than S.K., who was handicapped refers to Hans Peter Kierkegaard (1815–62), the crippled son of Michael Andersen Kierkegaard; see the entry by Hans Peter Kierkegaard in chapter 9 of this book and the note to entry number 7 in the present chapter. *Edifying Discourses in a Different Spirit* were published in 1847 (*SV* VIII 107–416 [*KW* XV 1–341]); the passage alluded to is found on pp. 211f. [pp. 116f.]; the word "crippled" appears on p. 207 [p. 112].

Entry 44. *Practice in Christianity* was published on September 27, 1850. **The lakes**: see the note accompanying the entry by Johannes A. Ostermann in chapter 4 of this book. **When the attempt was made etc.** probably refers to H. L. Martensen's *Dogmatiske Oplysninger. Et Lejlighedsskrift*, pp. 29ff. and 39, where Martensen strongly protested both against Kierkegaard's view of faith as a passion and against treating Kierkegaard's version of Christianity as normative. In this connection, see also the note accompanying Martensen's remarks in chapter 10 of this book.

Entry 45. The significance of his writings for Danish prose: see *Pap.* VII[1] A 150 (*SKJP* 5939), where Kierkegaard discusses this.

Entry 46. Grundtvig and Grundtvigianism: the principal passage in which Kierkegaard sets forth his disagreements with Grundtvig and Grundtvigianism is in the first part of *Concluding*

Unscientific Postscript; see *SV* VII 23–34 (*KW* XII 34–46), but there are also many points in his journals and papers where Kierkegaard concerns himself with Grundtvig. Kierkegaard felt attracted to the young Grundtvig, "the solitary warrior for the Bible" and opponent of rationalism, but he neither could nor would understand Grundtvig's "congregational" Christianity. See also Carl Weltzer, *Grundtvig og Søren Kierkegaard* [Grundtvig and Søren Kierkegaard] (Copenhagen: Gyldendal, 1952), for further information on the personal relationship between the two men, their mutual friends, etc. **Clausen** was the theologian and liberal politician H. N. Clausen; see also the note to entry number 6 in this chapter and the note to Peter Rørdam's entry in chapter 2 of this book. The **matchless discovery** was Grundtvig's claim that he had discovered that the true and continuing source of Christianity lies not in the Bible (which he sometimes called "the dead word") but in the oral, congregational transmission of "the living words"—the Lord's Prayer, the words of institution of the sacraments, and the Apostle's Creed—which, Grundtvig asserted, were direct utterances from Jesus Christ. **Lindberg**: Jacob Christian Lindberg (1797–1857); see the notes accompanying the entries by Peter Christian Kierkegaard in chapter 9 of this book.

Entry 47. Queen Caroline Amalie: both the Queen and King Christian VIII valued Kierkegaard very highly. For Kierkegaard's journal notations on King Christian VIII, see *Pap.* X[1] A 41–43 (*SKJP* 6309–11). On Queen Caroline Amalie's faulty understanding of *Either/Or*, which she called "Either and Or," see *Pap.* X[1] A 42 p. 34 (*SKJP* 6310 p. 95). For another account of Kierkegaard's relationship to King Christian VIII and Queen Caroline Amalie, see the entry by Israel Levin, with accompanying note, in chapter 10 of this book.

Entry 48. A conversation with S.K. about Bishop Mynster: as late as 1846 Kierkegaard's respect for Bishop Mynster was still remarkably great (cf. *SV* VII 542 [*KW* XII 622]). In 1851 Kierkegaard declared publicly that he and Mynster want the same things, but that he (Kierkegaard) wants them "only one note stronger" (*SV* XII 311 [*KW* XXI 21]). *Officially* the relationship between them was thus very honorable, and it therefore came as a great shock to the reading public in December 1854 when Kierkegaard made his violent attack on Mynster—an attack not only on what Mynster represented but on Mynster personally. Kierkegaard had prepared for this attack over a long period; see his journals and papers. The major shift in Kierkegaard's view of Mynster seems to have come in 1848, which was a decisive year with respect to Kierkegaard's inner development in general. **Ramparts**: see the note accompanying the entry by Frederik Hammerich in chapter 6 of this book. **Good advice**: prior to the government bankruptcy of 1813, Kierkegaard's father had invested his fortune in bonds that were not affected by the general devaluation.

Entry 49. When S.K. began his polemics, etc.: Kierkegaard's attack on the church began December 18, 1854. Dr. **[Andreas] Frederik Beck** (1816–61), a philosopher and theologian, was, like Brøchner, influenced by the German theologian David Friedrich Strauss. The **Athenæum**: see the note accompanying the entry by Kristian Arentzen in chapter 7 of this book, where Arentzen, who was decidedly sympathetic with Kierkegaard's cause, says essentially the same thing that Beck is here cited as saying.

Entry 50. My brief participation in political life: Brøchner was a member of Parliament from December 1, 1854, until June 14, 1855, as one of the two representatives of Fredericia, his native city. **Klædeboderne** was until 1879 the name of the part of Skindergade that runs from Skoubogade to Gammeltorv. Kierkegaard lived in Klædeboderne nos. 5–6; see the list of Kierkegaard's residences in the introduction to this book. **Lick my arse**: Kierkegaard's papers from 1847 (*Pap.* VIII[1] A 412) record almost exactly the same story that he told Brøchner in 1855.

2. From the correspondence of Hans Brøchner and Christian K. F. Molbech; the letters are in **KBHA** (Additamenta 877, 4[o]) and have been published in *Hans Brøchner og Christian K. F. Molbech. En Brevvexling (1845–1875)* [Hans Brøchner and Christian K. F. Molbech: Correspondence, 1845–1875], edited and with an introduction by Harald Høffding (Copenhagen: Gyldendal, 1902), pp. 153, 164, 172, 173–74, 185–86, and 186–89. A portion of Brøchner's letter of December 2, 1855, and his letter of February 17, 1856, are available in another English translation in T. H. Croxall, *Glimpses and Impressions of Kierkegaard*, pp. 40–44.

The philosopher, **Hans Brøchner** (1820–75), and the poet, Dante translator, dramatist, and professor of Danish, **Christian K. F. Molbech** (1821–88), were lifelong friends who carried on an extensive correspondence. **Bang**: probably Oluf (Ole) Lundt Bang (1788–1877), Mynster's stepbrother and Kierkegaard's personal physician. **Kierkegaard's most recent reply**: Kierkegaard's article "There the Matter Rests!" dated December 28, 1854, and published in *Fædrelandet*, no. 304, December 30, 1854 (*SV* XIV 15–21). **Martensen**: Bishop Hans Lassen Martensen; see the note accompanying Martensen's entry in chapter 8 of this book. **I. Levin**: it is generally believed that Israel Levin (see note accompanying the entry by Levin in chapter 10 of this book) was the author of a piece published in *Flyveposten* on December 27, 1854, in which the author, who signed himself "J.L." and called himself "a serious man from Nørrebro," accused Kierkegaard of lacking seriousness (cf. *Pap.* XI³ B 211:14). **Sebastopol**: during the Crimean war, Sebastopol was the object of a lengthy siege in 1854–55, and ultimately capitulated in September 1855. **Holten**: [Hans] Nicolai Holten (1829–71) was a young theological student who had been to some extent an admirer and follower of Kierkegaard. He published two pamphlets against Kierkegaard during the latter's attack on the Church: *"Det er fuldbragt." Langfredagsprædiken Dr. Kierkegaard helliget i Kjærlighed* ["It Is Finished": A Good Friday Sermon Lovingly Dedicated to Dr. Kierkegaard] (Copenhagen: C. G. Iversen, 1855), transparently attributed to "NH"; and *Polemiske Smuler eller en Smule Polemik mod Dr. S. Kierkegaard* [Polemical Fragments or a Fragment of a Polemic against Dr. S. Kierkegaard] (Copenhagen: C. G. Iversen, 1855), which was published under Holten's own name. **Giødwad**: Jens Giødwad [or Giødvad] (1811–91), editor of *Fædrelandet*; see the entry by Hother Ploug, with its accompanying note, in chapter 4 of this book. **An article "On Søren Kierkegaard as a Religious Author," which appeared in yesterday's issue of** *Fædrelandet*: Brøchner's article "Om Søren Kierkegaards Virksomhed som religieus Forfatter" [On Søren Kierkegaard's Activity as a Religious Author] appeared in *Fædrelandet*, 16de Aargang, no. 281, December 1, 1855, pp. 1179–80, signed by the pseudonym "r." It is a brilliant and very concise summary of the content and import of Kierkegaard's written work, illustrated with many well-chosen quotations. **A pencil drawing** must be one of the two known pencil drawings done by Søren Kierkegaard's cousin [Niels] Christian Kierkegaard, dated 1838. N. C. Kierkegaard (1806–82) was the son of Anders Andersen Kierkegaard, who was a brother of Michael Pedersen Kierkegaard's first cousin, Michael Andersen Kierkegaard. See also chapter 9 of this book for Henriette Lund's mention of "a little pencil sketch of him that I own." **Prof. Panum**: Peter Ludvig Panum (1820–85), one of the greatest medical researchers in Danish history, was at the time professor of medicine at the University of Kiel, where Molbech was professor of Danish. **Lehmann**: [Peter Martin] Orla Lehmann (1810–70) was a liberal political leader with whom Kierkegaard debated during his student years in the 1830s (see *SV* XIII 9–15 and 28–39 [*KW* I 6–11 and 24–34]); see also the entries by J. A. Ostermann and Peter Rørdam, with their accompanying notes, in chapter 2 of this book. **He must have given away the greater portion of his fortune**: see Frithiof Brandt and Else Rammel, *Kierkegaard og Pengene*, where this myth is convincingly dispelled.

Appendix B
Peter Christian Kierkegaard on Søren Kierkegaard

1. This article by Peter Christian Kierkegaard, which is the published text of his October 30, 1849, address to the Roskilde Ecclesiastical Convention, appeared in the organ of Grundtvigian movement, the *Dansk Kirketidende*, no. 219, vol. 5 (no. 11) (December 16, 1849), cols. 171–93, from which the present selections have been translated; it was subsequently republished in Poul Egede Glahn and Lavrids Nyegård, eds., *Peter Christian Kierkegaards Samlede Skrifter*, vol. 4, pp. 99–120. The Roskilde Ecclesiastical Convention was a gathering of pastors who were generally allied with Grundtvig. Peter Christian Kierkegaard spoke on the subject of the writings of his brother, Søren Kierkegaard, and those of Hans Lassen Martensen (later bishop of Zealand and

primate of Denmark). See also P. C. Kierkegaard's 1881 statement and its accompanying note in chapter 9 of this book. This apparently literal account of his October 1849 Roskilde Convention speech was not in fact written down until December 1849, by which time P. C. Kierkegaard had had an opportunity to modify it somewhat. According to Søren Kierkegaard (Pap. X² A 280 [SKJP 6557]), "God knows what what he really said at the convention."

[W]ith *us* [emphasis added] **this same genuine duality [between ecstasy and sober-mindedness] can easily seem to be replaced by a genuine contradiction between the two sides**: later in his talk, Peter Christian Kierkegaard enlarges upon this theme, labeling the problem one of "deviations," and in his journals, Søren Kierkegaard made it clear that he was annoyed at being labeled by his brother as a representative of one of these "deviations." In his July 1855 Roskilde Convention talk about his brother Søren's writings, Peter Christian would again attack "two forms of one-sidedness," and this time it is made very clear that he believes that Søren has in fact fallen into this sort of error. See the latter part of Appendix B for selections from Peter Christian Kierkegaard's notes on his 1855 talk. **Marriages of convenience**: the Danish is *Fornuft-Giftermaal*, which literally means "a marriage based upon reason," a shade of meaning appropriate to P. C. Kierkegaard's message here.

2. The notes pertaining to Peter Christian Kierkegaard's July 5, 1855, talk to the Roskilde Ecclesiastical Convention are in two sections, the second of which is principally a variant of the latter portion of the first. They are somewhat fragmentary, contain lacunae and illegible words, and are written in a style even more prolix than usual for P. C. Kierkegaard. It is clear from internal evidence that they were written down after the talk, as an attempt at reconstruction, and not before, as speaker's notes. The present selections include the most important criticisms of the work of Søren Kierkegaard contained in those notes. The original documents are with P. C. Kierkegaard's papers in **KBHA** (**NkS** 3005, 4⁰, VII, læg 1) and have been published in Otto Holmgaard, *Exstaticus. Søren Kierkegaards sidste Kamp, derunder hans Forhold til Broderen* [Exstaticus: Søren Kierkegaard's Final Struggle, Including His Relationship With His Brother] (Copenhagen: Nyt Nordisk Forlag/Arnold Busck, 1967), pp. 23–84. See also Peter Christian's 1881 statement and its accompanying note in chapter 9 of this book.

"Thou art Christ, the Son of the living God": Matthew 16.16. **The sniveling pastors**: cf. *SV* XII 59 (*KW* XX 62). **Thou shalt love the Lord thy God with all thy heart, all thy soul, and all thy might**: original locus Deuteronomy 6.5; cited by Jesus in Mark 12.30. **Took Peter by the hand when they walked on the roaring waves**: Matthew 14.28–31. **Called out to Paul that no one will harm you**: Acts 18.9–10. **Intentionally glossed over it over and deemphasized it**: cf. *SV* XIV 6, Søren Kierkegaard's *Fædrelandet* article of December 18, 1854, with which he opened the attack on Christendom. **"Stop thief!"**: cf. *SV* XIV 337, *The Moment*, no. 9, September 24, 1855; this is the only place in which Søren Kierkegaard uses this phrase, and it appeared several months *after* P. C. Kierkegaard's talk of July 1855. This is evidence that these notes were at least somewhat influenced by hindsight and cannot be an entirely accurate account of what Peter Christian Kierkegaard in fact said on July 5, 1855. **"Quiet hours" . . . "on Monday"**: cf. *SV* XIV 10, Søren Kierkegaard's *Fædrelandet* article of December 18, 1854. **What I said a number of years ago . . . ecstatic speech**: a reference to Peter Christian Kierkegaard's October 30, 1849, address to the Roskilde Ecclesiastical Convention; see above in this appendix. **The amnesty decree that was issued at Golgotha**: cf. Luke 23.34, "Father forgive them, for they know not what they do." **"I become what I am"**: cf. Exodus 3.14. P. C. Kierkegaard's Danish is "jeg bliver den, jeg er" and is translated literally here. The authorized Danish version at the time was *Jeg skal være den, som Jeg skal være*, which translates into English as "I shall be that which I shall be." The original Hebrew is perhaps best translated "I will become that which I will become." P. C. Kierkegaard's emphasis on process rather than stasis is important to his argument and is quite correct as a translation. In light of the criticisms contained in the above address and in light of other materials that illuminate the tortuous relationship of the two brothers, it is interesting to note an account of P. C. Kierkegaard's remarks on another occasion, eleven years later, in 1866. The situation was the following: Peter Christian Kierkegaard, bishop of Aalborg, was being harassed, both in private correspondence and in public writings and speeches, by the agitator and religious zealot Mogens Abraham Sommer (see the entry by Sommer, with its accompanying note, in chapter 7 of this book). Sommer claimed to be the true "Kierkegaardian" and charged that P. C. Kierkegaard, as a bishop in the Danish Folkekirke, did not represent the "Christianity of the New Testament" as his brother Søren had. This criticism apparently stung P. C. Kierkegaard, who in early 1866 delivered a public rebuttal to a packed meeting in Aalborg. *Aalborgposten* [The Aalborg Post] summarized P. C. Kierkegaard's remarks on the topic as follows:

> Then the bishop took the occasion to touch upon his relationship to his brother *Søren*, from whose last writings the above-mentioned speaker and writer [M. A. Sommer] had taken his weapons. And he noted that just as Søren—albeit via a third party—had sent him a fraternal greeting in his last days, despite the dispute their convictions had led them to during the final years of his life, he [Peter Christian] still understood himself to be in agreement with him in his deathbed prayer for more light, for courage in death, for the forgiveness of sins, and for eternal salvation. And he also understood himself to be in agreement with him in the struggle for Christianity not as a doctrine but as existence—except that he would have added that existence ought to be life. That is, it begins, germinates, grows, and matures, and one may not use the yardstick of maturity to measure everyone who confesses the Christian faith in order to find a pretext upon which to deny him that faith [from *Aalborgposten*'s pamphlet containing a reprint of its articles of February 21–22, 1866, p. 7; in P. C. Kierkegaard's archive in **KBHA** (**NkS** 3005, 4⁰, VII)].

Two points are of particular interest. First of all, it is clear that P. C. Kierkegaard had been both personally hurt and publicly weakened by the widely known scandal stemming from brother Søren's deathbed refusal to receive him in October 1855. (See, e.g., Emil Boesen's account of this in chapter 8 and P. C. Kierkegaard's own account in chapter 9 of this book.) This made it necessary for P. C. Kierkegaard publicly to make much of the farewell message that, according to H. F. Lund, Søren had sent him notwithstanding his refusal to receive him personally. (See the October 23, 1855, letter from H. F. Lund to P. C. Kierkegaard in chapter 8 of this book.) Second, as part of his rebuttal of Sommer, P. C. Kierkegaard proceeded from mention of his brother's farewell to a somewhat vague catalog of points of supposed agreement between Søren and himself. But to these points of supposed agreement P. C. Kierkegaard appended a major point about Christianity as "growth" and "germination," about the error of using the strict yardstick of "maturity" on all who call themselves Christians, etc. P. C. Kierkegaard's emphasis on this point recalls strikingly his profound disagreement with his brother in the July 1855 Roskilde Convention address, the very address that had led to Søren's deathbed refusal to see him. Thus even in his attempt to smooth over the breach with his brother, P. C. Kierkegaard seems unavoidably drawn to the flame of their discord.

Bibliography

Archives

Nyere Brevsamling Dansk [New Collection of Danish Letters] in the Manuscript Department of the Royal Library, Copenhagen.

Ny kongelige Samling [New Royal Collection] in the Manuscript Department of the Royal Library, Copenhagen.

Søren Kierkegaard Arkiv [Søren Kierkegaard Archive] in the Manuscript Department of the Royal Library, Copenhagen.

Rigsarkivet [National Archives], Copenhagen.

Material by Søren Kierkegaard

Danish Editions

Breve og Aktstykker vedrørende Søren Kierkegaard [Letters and Documents Pertaining to Søren Kierkegaard]. Edited by Niels Thulstrup. 2 vols. Copenhagen: Munksgaard, 1953–54.

Kierkegaardske Papirer, Forlovelsen. Udgivne for Fru Regine Schlegel [Kierkegaardian Papers: The Engagement. Published on Behalf of Mrs. Regine Schlegel]. Edited by Raphael Meyer. Copenhagen: Gyldendal, 1904.

Mit Forhold til hende [My Relationship to Her]. Edited by Henriette Lund. Copenhagen: Gyldendal, 1904.

S. Kierkegaards Bladartikler med Bilag samlede efter Forfatterens Død, udgivne som Supplement til hans øvrige Skrifter [S. Kierkegaard's Newspaper Articles, with an Appendix Collected after the Author's Death: Published as a Supplement to His Other Writings]. Edited by Rasmus Nielsen. Copenhagen: C. A. Reitzel, 1857.

Søren Kierkegaards Efterladte Papirer [The Posthumous Papers of Søren Kierkegaard]. Edited by H. P. Barfod and H. Gottsched. 8 vols. Copenhagen: C. A. Reitzel, 1869–81.

Søren Kierkegaards Papirer [The Papers of Søren Kierkegaard]. Edited by P. A. Heiberg, V. Kuhr, and E. Torsting. 2d augmented ed. by Niels Thulstrup. Index by N. J. Cappelørn. 22 vols. Copenhagen: Gyldendal, 1968–78.

Søren Kierkegaards Samlede Værker [The Collected Works of Søren Kierkegaard]. Edited by A. B. Drachmann, J. L. Heiberg, and H. O. Lange. 1st ed. 14 vols. Copenhagen: Gyldendal, 1901–06.

With Emil Boesen. *Søren Kierkegaard og Emil Boesen. Breve og Indledning* [Søren Kierkegaard and Emil Boesen: Letters and an Introduction]. Edited by Carl Koch. Copenhagen: Karl Schønbergs Forlag, 1901.

English Translations

Kierkegaard's Writings. Howard V. Hong, general editor. 26 vols. [19 vols. published as of April 1996]. Princeton: Princeton University Press, 1978–.

Søren Kierkegaard's Journals and Papers. Edited and translated by Howard V. Hong and Edna H. Hong. 7 vols. Bloomington: Indiana University Press, 1968–78.

Other Works

Abrahams, Arthur. *Minder fra min Barndom og tidlige Ungdom* [Memories from My Childhood and Early Youth]. Copenhagen: Schubothe, 1895.

Ammundsen, Valdemar. *Søren Kierkegaards Ungdom. Hans Slægt og hans religiøse Udvikling* [Søren Kierkegaard's Youth: His Family and His Religious Development]. Copenhagen: Universitetsbogtrykkeriet, 1912.

Andersen, Hans Christian. *Breve fra Hans Christian Andersen* [Letters from Hans Christian Andersen]. Edited by C.St.A. Bille and Nicolaj Bøgh. Copenhagen: C. A. Reitzel, 1878.

————. *Breve til Hans Christian Andersen* [Letters to Hans Christian Andersen]. Edited by C.St.A. Bille og Nikolaj Bøgh. Copenhagen: C. A. Reitzel, 1877.

————. *Mit Livs Eventyr* [The Fairy Tale of My Life]. *H. C. Andersens Samlede Skrifter* [H. C. Andersen's Collected Writings]. 2d ed. Vol. 1. Copenhagen: C. A. Reitzel, 1876.

————, and Edvard and Henriette Collin. *H. C. Andersens Brevveksling med Edvard og Henriette Collin* [Hans Christian Andersen's Correspondence with Edvard and Henriette Collin]. Edited by C. Behrend and H. G. Topsøe-Jensen. Vol. 2 (1844–60). Copenhagen: Levin og Munksgaards Forlag, 1934.

————, and Henriette Wulff. *H. C. Andersen og Henriette Wulff. En Brevveksling* [Correspondence of Hans Christian Andersen and Henriette Wulff]. Edited by H. Topsøe-Jensen. 2 vols. Odense: Flensteds Forlag, 1959.

Andersen, Thorkild. "Kierkegaard-Slægten og Sædding" [The Kierkegaard Family and Sædding]. *Hardsyssels Årbog,* 27. Bind (1933): 26–40.

Andræ, Hansine. *Geheimeraadinde Andræs politiske Dagbøger* [The Political Diaries of Madame Privy Councillor Andræ]. Edited by Poul Andræ. Vol. 1. Copenhagen: Gyldendal, 1914.

Arentzen, Kristian. *Fra yngre og ældre Dage. Livs-Erindringer* [From Younger and Older Days: Memoirs]. Copenhagen: Wroblewsky, 1886.

Attrup, Martin. *En Landsbydegns Erindringer. Afsluttet med en Samling gode Ord til Vejledning og Berigelse* [Memoirs of a Rural Parish Clerk, Concluded with a Collection of Sayings for Guidance and Enrichment]. Copenhagen: Det folkelige Forlag, 1938.

Baagø, Kaj. *Magister Jacob Christian Lindberg.* Copenhagen: G.E.C. Gad, 1958.

Berg, Friis. "Dansk Præsteskikkelser for hundrede Aar siden" [Danish Clerics of One Hundred Years Ago]. *Nationaltidende* (Copenhagen). August 5, 1942.

Bergsøe, Clara. *Camilla Collett. Et Livsbillede* [Camilla Collett: A Picture of Her Life]. Copenhagen: Gyldendal, 1902.

Birkedal, Vilhelm. *Personlige Oplevelser i et langt Liv* [Personal Experiences from a Long Life]. 2 vols. Copenhagen: Karl Schønbergs Forlag, 1890.

Boisen, Eline. *—men størst er kærligheden. Eline Boisens erindringer fra midten af forrige århundrede* [—but the greatest of these is love: Eline Boisen's Memoirs from the Middle of the Last Century]. Edited by Anna, Elin, Gudrun, and Jutta Bojsen-Møller and Birgitte Haarder. Copenhagen: Gyldendal, 1985.

Bojesen, M. *Generalpostdirektør Christen Svendsens Slægttavle* [The Genealogical Table of

General Postal Director Christen Svendsen]. Helsingør: J. M. Welsch's Bogtrykkeri, 1925.

Bojsen, P. *Budstikkens Udgiver, Præsten F. E. Bojsens Liv og Levned* [The Publisher of "The Messenger": The Story of Pastor F. E. Boisen's Life]. Horsens: C. Schønberg, 1883.

Borchsenius, Otto. *Fra Fyrrene* [From the Forties]. 2 vols. Copenhagen: C. A. Reitzels og Otto Wroblenskys Forlag, 1878–80.

———. *Hjemlige Interiører. Bidrag til dansk Literaturs Historie* [Domestic Interiors: A Contribution to the History of Danish Literature]. Copenhagen: Gyldendal, 1894.

Brandes, Georg. *Levned* [Life]. Vol. 1. Copenhagen and Kristiania: Gyldendal, 1905.

———. *Søren Kierkegaard. En kritisk Fremstilling i Grundrids* [Søren Kierkegaard: Outlines of a Critical Presentation]. In *Samlede Skrifter. Danmark* [Collected Writings: Denmark]. 2d ed. Vol. 2. Copenhagen: Gyldendal, 1919.

Brandt, Frithiof. *Den unge Søren Kierkegaard* [The Young Søren Kierkegaard]. Copenhagen: Levin & Munksgaard, 1929.

———, and Else Rammel. *Kierkegaard og Pengene* [Kierkegaard and Money]. Copenhagen: Levin & Munksgaard/Ejnar Munksgaard, 1935.

Bremer, Frederikke. *Liv i Norden* [Life in Scandinavia]. Copenhagen: F. H. Eibes Forlag, 1849.

Brix, Hans. *Analyser og Problemer* [Analyses and Problems]. Vol. 3. Copenhagen: Gyldendal, 1936.

Brøchner, Hans. *Erindringer om Søren Kierkegaard* [Recollections about Søren Kierkegaard]. Edited by Steen Johansen. Copenhagen: Gyldendal, 1953.

———, and Christian K. F. Molbech. *Hans Brøchner og Christian K. F. Molbech. En Brevvexling (1845–1875)* [Hans Brøchner and Christian K. F. Molbech: Correspondence, 1845–1875]. Edited by Harald Høffding. Copenhagen: Gyldendal, 1902.

Brosbøll, Anna. *Træk af Carl Brosbølls og hans Hustru Hansine Thorbjørnsens Liv og Hjem* [Features of the Life and Home of Carl Brosbøll and His Wife, Hansine Thorbjørnsen]. Copenhagen: V. Pio, 1909.

Bruun Andersen, K. "Søren Kierkegaards Udseende" [Søren Kierkegaard's Appearance]. *Personalhistorisk Tidsskrift* (1950): 117–21.

Bukdahl, Jørgen. *Søren Kierkegaard. Hans Fader og Slægten i Sædding* [Søren Kierkegaard, His Father, and the Family in Sædding]. Ribe: Dansk Hjemstavns Forlag, 1960.

———. *Søren Kierkegaard og den menige Mand* [Søren Kierkegaard and the Common Man]. Copenhagen: Gyldendals Uglebøger, 1970.

Busck, Gunni. *Gunni Busck. Et Levnedsløb i en Præstegaard* [Gunni Busck: A Life in a Parsonage]. Edited by Henr. Bech. Copenhagen: Karl Schønbergs Forlag, 1878.

Clausen, Julius. *Mennesker paa min Vej. Minder fra de unge Dage* [People on My Way: Memories from My Youth]. Copenhagen: Gyldendal, 1941.

Croxall, T. H., ed. and trans. *Glimpses and Impressions of Kierkegaard*. Digswell Place: James Nisbet & Co., 1959.

Dahl, Arthur. *Søren Kierkegaard's Pilgrimage to Jutland*. Copenhagen: Danish Tourist Association, 1948.

Etlar, Carit. *Carit Etlars Minder fortalte af ham selv. I biografisk Ramme af hans Hustru* [Carit Etlar's Reminiscences as Told by Himself. Placed in a Biographical Framework by His Wife]. Copenhagen: Nordisk Forlag, 1896.

Feddersen, Benjamin. "Smaa Oplevelser" [Minor Experiences]. *Illustreret Tidende* 41, no. 25 (March 18, 1900): 394.

Fenger, Henning. *Kierkegaard-Myter og Kierkegaard-Kilder* [Kierkegaard Myths and Kierkegaard Sources]. Odense: Odense Universitetsforlag, 1976. [Most of this volume is available in English translation as *Kierkegaard: The Myths and Their Origins*. Translated by George C. Schoolfield. New Haven: Yale University Press, 1980.]

Fenger, J. F. *Det sydvestsjællandske Broderkonvent (1837–1854)* [The Southwest Zealand Convention of Brothers: 1837–1854]. Copenhagen: Karl Schønbergs Forlag, 1890.

Goldschmidt, Meïr Aron. *Breve fra og til Meïr Goldschmidt* [Letters from and to Meïr Goldschmidt]. Vol. 2 (1853–85). Edited by Morten Borup. Copenhagen: Rosenkilde og Bagger, 1963.

————. [Adolph Meyer, pseud.]. *En Jøde* [A Jew]. Copenhagen: published by M. Goldschmidt, 1845. [Available in English translation as *A Jew*. Translated by Kenneth H. Ober. New York: Garland Press, 1990.]

————. *Livs Erindringer og Resultater* [Memories and Results of My Life]. 2 vols. Copenhagen: Gyldendal, 1877.

————. *Livs Erindringer og Resultater* [Memories and Results of My Life]. Edited by Morten Borup. Vol. 1. Copenhagen: Rosenkilde and Bagger, 1965.

————. *Nord og Syd*, Ny Række, 8de. Bind, Nr. 1 (September 1855): 42, 78–80.

————. *Nord og Syd*, Ny Række, 8de. Bind, Nr. 2 (November 1855): 224.

Hamilton, Andrew. *Sixteen Months in the Danish Isles*. London: Richard Bentley, 1852.

Hammerich, Angul. *Festskrift i Anledning af Musikforeningens Halvhundredaarsdag* [Festschrift on the Occasion of the Fiftieth Anniversary of the Music Society]. Copenhagen: Udgivet af Musikforeningen, 1886.

Hammerich, Frederik. *Et Levnedsløb* [A Life]. Vol. 1. Copenhagen: Forlagsbureauet i Kjøbenhavn, 1882.

Hauch, Carsten, and B. S. Ingemann. *Hauch og Ingemann. En Brevveksling* [Hauch and Ingemann: Correspondence]. Edited and annotated by M. Hatting. Copenhagen: Gyldendal, 1933.

Heiberg, Johanne Luise. *Et Liv gjenoplevet i Erindringen* [A Life Relived in Recollection]. Edited by Aage Friis. 4. vols. 4th rev. ed. Copenhagen: Gyldendal, 1944.

Helweg, Hjalmar. *Søren Kierkegaard. En psykiatrisk-psykologisk Studie* [Søren Kierkegaard: A Psychiatric-Psychological Study]. Copenhagen: H. Hagerups Forlag, 1933.

Hendriksen, F[rederik]. *Mennesker og Oplevelser* [People and Experiences]. New revised and illustrated edition. Copenhagen: privately published, 1932.

Himmelstrup, Jens. *Sibbern*. Copenhagen: J. H. Schultz, 1934.

Holmgaard, Otto. *Exstaticus. Søren Kierkegaards sidste Kamp, derunder hans Forhold til Broderen* [Exstaticus: Søren Kierkegaard's Final Struggle, Including His Relationship with His Brother]. Copenhagen: Nyt Nordisk Forlag/Arnold Busck, 1967.

————. *Peter Christian Kierkegaard*. Copenhagen: Rosenkilde og Bagger, 1953.

Hostrup, [Jens] C[hristian]. *Breve fra og til C. Hostrup* [Letters from and to C. Hostrup]. Edited by Elisabeth Hostrup. Copenhagen: Gyldendal, 1897.

————. *Erindringer fra min Barndom og Ungdom* [Memories of My Childhood and Youth]. Copenhagen: Gyldendal, 1891.

Howitt, William and Mary. *The Literature and Romance of Northern Europe. Constituting a Complete History of the Literature of Sweden, Denmark, Norway and Iceland*. Vol. 2. London: Colburn, 1852.

Høybye, Paul. "Om Søren Kierkegaard i H. C. Andersens Correspondence" [On Søren

Kierkegaard in H. C. Andersen's Correspondence]. *Meddelelser fra Søren Kierkegaard Selskabet*, 3d year, no. 1 (March 1951): 86.

Ingemann, Bernhard Severin. *Breve til og fra Bernh. Sev. Ingemann* [Letters to and from Bernh. Sev. Ingemann]. Edited by V. Heise. Copenhagen: C. A. Reitzel, 1879.

Jensenius, Knud. "'Det unge Menneske' hos Søren Kierkegaard" ["The Young Man" in Søren Kierkegaard]. *Nordisk Tidsskrift* (1930): 330ff.

Johansen, Niels. *Brevbærer mellem Kristne*, no. 6 (second Sunday after Trinity [i.e., June 17], 1855): 55–56.

———. *Brevbærer mellem Kristne*, 5. Aargang, nos. 4–5 (February 2, 1859): 33.

Johansen, Steen, ed. *Erindringer om Søren Kierkegaard. Samlet Udgave ved Steen Johansen* [Recollections about Søren Kierkegaard: Collected Edition by Steen Johansen]. Copenhagen: C. A. Reitzel, 1980.

Jørgensen, A. D. "A. D. Jørgensens Dagbog Gammelt og Nyt for Aarene 1884–96" [A. D. Jørgensen's Diary "Old and New," for the Years 1884–96]. Edited by Troels G. Jørgensen. *Danske Magazin, indeholdende bidrag til den danske histories oplysning*, 7. Række, Femte Bind. Udgivet af det kongelige danske selskab for fædrelandets historie (1949–53): 26.

Kabell, Aage. *Kierkegaardstudiet i Norden* [Kierkegaard Studies in Scandinavia]. Copenhagen: H. Hagerup, 1948.

Karup, W[ilhelm] I[gnatius]. *Mit Livs Roman* [The Novel of My Life]. Copenhagen: Cohens Bogtrykkeri, 1864.

Kierkegaard, Olaf, and P. F. Parup. *Fæstebonden i Sædding Christen Jespersen Kierkegaards Efterslægt* [The Descendents of Christen Jespersen Kierkegaard, Copyholder of Sædding]. Copenhagen: Thorsøe-Olsen's Bogtrykkeri, 1941.

Kierkegaard, Peter Christian. *Peter Christian Kierkegaards Samlede Skrifter* [The Collected Writings of Peter Christian Kierkegaard]. Vol. 4. Edited by Poul Egede Glahn and Lavrids Nyegård. Copenhagen: Karl Schønbergs Forlag, 1903.

Kirmmse, Bruce H. *Kierkegaard in Golden Age Denmark*. Bloomington: Indiana University Press, 1990.

———. "Kierkegaard, jøderne og jødedommen" [Kierkegaard, Jews, and Judaism]. *Kirkehistoriske Samlinger* (1992): 77–107.

Knudsen, Jakob. "Mindedrag" [Recollection]. In *Jyder. Sytten Fortællinger* [Jutlanders: Seventeen Tales], pp. 218–33. Copenhagen and Kristiania: Gyldendal, 1915.

Koch, Carl. *Grundtvigske Toner* [Grundtvigian Notes]. Copenhagen: Det schønbergske Forlag, 1925.

———. "Søren Kierkegaard og Eventyret" [Søren Kierkegaard and Fairy Tales]. *Dansk Tidsskrift* (1899): 146–60.

Krarup, Per. *Søren Kierkegaard og Borgerdydskolen* [Søren Kierkegaard and the Borgerdyd School]. Copenhagen: Gyldendal, 1977.

Kühle, Sejer. "Nogle Oplysninger om Søren Kierkegaard, 1834–38" [Some Information on Søren Kierkegaard, 1834–38]. *Personalhistorisk Tidsskrift*. [In five parts: I, 9. Række. 4. Bind. 4. Hæfte. (1931): 1–11; II, 9. Række. 5. Bind. 2. Hæfte. (1932): 150–56; III, 9. Række 5. Bind. 3.–4. Hæfte. (1932): 1–17; IV, 9. Række 6. Bind. 3.–4. Hæfte. (1933): 1–10; V, 56. Aargang, 10. Række, 2. Bind. (1935): 1–7.]

———. *Søren Kierkegaard. Barndom og Ungdom* [Søren Kierkegaard: Childhood and Youth]. Copenhagen: Aschehoug Dansk Forlag, 1950.

———. "Søren Kierkegaard og den heibergske Kreds" [Søren Kierkegaard and Heiberg's Circle]. *Personalhistorisk Tidsskrift* (1947) I–IV: 1–13.

Lange, Johan Nikolai. *Prædikener af Johan Nikolai Lange* [Sermons by Johan Nikolai Lange]. Edited by H. P. Kofoed-Hansen. Copenhagen: Gyldendal, 1866.

Larsen, Emil. *Mogens Abraham Sommer.* Copenhagen: G.E.C. Gad, 1963.

Liebenberg, F[rederik] L[udvig]. *Nogle Optegnelser om mit Levned* [Some Notes on My Life]. Copenhagen: Gyldendal, 1894.

Lindhardt, P. G. *Konfrontation* [Confrontation]. Copenhagen: Akademisk Forlag, 1974.

Lorck, J[ørgen] H[enrik]. *Femoghalvfjerdsindstyve Aar. Erindringer nedskrevne for Venner og Bekjendte* [Seventy-Five Years: Memories Written Down for Friends and Acquaintances]. Copenhagen: Gyldendal, 1885.

Lund, Henriette. *Erindringer Fra Hjemmet* [Recollections from Home]. Copenhagen: Gyldendal, 1909.

Lund, Henrik. "Min Protest: hvad jeg har sagt og ikke sagt" [My Protest: What I Said and What I Didn't Say]. *Fædrelandet*, 16. Aargang, no. 273 (November 22, 1855), pp. 1144–45.

Lund, Holger. *Borgerdydskolen i Kjøbenhavn, 1787–1887. Et Mindeskrift* [The Borgerdyd School in Copenhagen, 1787–1887: A Commemoration]. Copenhagen: Wroblewski, 1887.

Magnussen, Rikard. *Søren Kierkegaard set udefra* [Søren Kierkegaard Seen from Without]. Copenhagen: Ejnar Munksgaard, 1942.

Martensen, Hans Lassen. *Af mit Levnet* [From My Life]. 3 vols. Copenhagen: Gyldendal, 1882–83.

―――. *Biskop H. Martensens Breve* [The Letters of Bishop H. Martensen]. Vol. 1. *Breve til L. Gude, 1848–1859* [Letters to L. Gude, 1848–59]. Edited by Bjørn Kornerup. Copenhagen: G.E.C. Gad, 1955.

McKinnon, Alastair. "Could Kierkegaard Have Written 'Literary Quicksilver'?" In Robert L. Perkins, ed., *International Kierkegaard Commentary: The Corsair Affair*, pp. 163–78. Macon, Ga.: Mercer University Press, 1990.

―――, and Niels Jørgen Cappelørn. "The Period of Composition of Kierkegaard's Published Works." *Kierkegaardiana* 9 (1974): 132–46.

Meidell, Frederik. "En Undtagelse" [An Exception]. *For Ide og Virkelighed*, vol. 1 (1870): 43–67.

[Molbech, Christian K. F.] "Søren Kierkegaards literaire Efterladenskaber" [Søren Kierkegaard's Literary Remains]. *Dagbladet*, no. 47 (February 25, 1870).

Møller, Frederik Benedikt. *En gammel Præst fortæller. Pastor Frederik Benedikt Møllers Optegnelser 1832–1864 ved Hans Degen* [An Old Pastor Speaks: Pastor Frederik Benedikt Møller's Journal Entries, 1832–64, with Hans Degen]. Copenhagen: Haase, 1953.

Møller, Otto, and Skat Rørdam. *Otto Møller og Skat Rørdam. En Brevveksling* [Otto Møller and Skat Rørdam: Correspondence]. Edited and annotated by H. Skat Rørdam. Vol. 1. Copenhagen: G.E.C. Gad, 1915.

Neiiendam, Michael. *Københavns Kirkeskolers Krønike* [Chronicles of Copenhagen Church Schools]. Copenhagen: G.E.C. Gad, 1941.

Neiiendam, Robert. *Robert Neiiendam fortæller* [Robert Neiiendam Speaks]. Copenhagen: Branner og Korch, 1953.

Nielsen, Frederik. *Minder. Oplevelser og Iagttagelser* [Memories: Experiences and Observations]. Aalborg: M. M. Schultz, 1881.

Nystrøm, Eiler. *Biografiske Efterretninger om Peter Munthe Bruns og Ane Munchs Slægt paa Fædrene og Mødrene Side* [Biographical Information on the Family of Peter Munthe

Brun and Ane Munch on the Paternal and Maternal Lines]. Copenhagen: privately published, 1910.

Odd, Orvar [pseud. for Oscar Patrick Sturzen-Becker]. *Hinsidan Sundet* [On the Other Side of the Sound]. Vol. 2. Stockholm: A. Bonniers Förlag, 1846.

Parkov, Peter, and Gert Posselt. *Troskab—og Tilgivelse* [Faithfulness—and Forgiveness]. Copenhagen: Danmarks Nationalleksikon A/S, 1992.

Petersen, Carl S., and Vilhelm Andersen. *Illustreret dansk Litteraturhistorie* [Illustrated History of Danish Literature]. Vol. 3. *Det nittende Aarhundredes første Halvdel* [The First Half of the Nineteenth Century]. Copenhagen: Gyldendal, 1924.

Petersen, Teddy. *Kierkegaards polemiske debut* [Kierkegaard's Polemical Debut]. Odense: Odense Universitetsforlag, 1977.

Plekon, Michael. "Kierkegaard and the Eucharist." *Studia Liturgica* 22, no. 2 (1992): 214–36.

Ploug, Hother. *Carl Ploug. Hans Liv og Gerning* [Carl Ploug, His Life and Work]. Vol. 1 (1813–48). Copenhagen: Gyldendal, 1905.

Plum, P. M., ed. *Hundrede Aars Metropolitanere. Tillæg til "Metropolitanskolen gennem 700 Aar"* [One Hundred Years of Metropolitan School Graduates: Supplement to "Seven Centuries of the Metropolitan School"]. Copenhagen: Gyldendal, 1916.

Rasmussen, S. V. *Den unge Brøchner* [The Young Brøchner]. Edited by Justus Hartnack. Copenhagen: Gyldendal, 1966.

Reimann-Hansen, A., V. Bendtsen, and P. Bendtsen. "Søren Kierkegaards Forfædre her paa Skjernegnen og deres nærmeste Efterkommere" [The Ancestors of Søren Kierkegaard Here in the Skjern Area, and Their Most Closely Related Descendants]. *Hardsyssels Årbog*, 33. Bind (1939): 17–27.

Reinhardt, Mathilde. *Familie-Erindringer 1831–1856* [Family Memoirs: 1831–1856]. Copenhagen: privately published, 1889.

Rohde, H. P. *Gaadefulde Stadier paa Kierkegaards Vej* [Mysterious Stages on Kierkegaard's Way]. Copenhagen: Rosenkilde og Bagger, 1974.

———, ed. *Auktionsprotokol over Søren Kierkegaards Bogsamling* [The Auctioneer's Sales Record of the Library of Søren Kierkegaard]. Copenhagen: Det kongelige Bibliotek, 1967.

Rørdam, Holger Frederik. *En gammel Præsteslægts Historie* [The History of an Old Clerical Family]. Vol. 2. Copenhagen: G.E.C. Gad, 1878.

Rørdam, Peter. *Peter Rørdam. Blade af hans Levnedsbog og Brevvexling* [Peter Rørdam: Pages from His Biography and Correspondence]. 2 vols. Edited by H. F. Rørdam. Copenhagen: Karl Schønbergs Forlag, 1891–92.

Rosted, H. C. *Den gamle Postgaard i Hørsholm* [The Old Mailcoach Inn at Hørsholm]. Hørsholm: O. Cohn and E. Hasfeldt, 1925.

Rudin, Waldemar. *Sören Kierkegaards Person och Författarskap. Ett försök* [Søren Kierkegaard's Personality and Writings: An Essay]. Vol. 1. Stockholm: A. Nilsson, 1880.

Sandfeld, Johanne. *Træk af Lyngbys Historie* [Incidents in the History of Lyngby]. Copenhagen: Forlaget Zac, 1968.

Schandorph, Sophus. *Oplevelser* [Experiences]. Copenhagen: C. A. Reitzel, 1889.

Schmidt, Aug. F. *Jakob Knudsen. Randbemærkninger til nogle af hans Arbejder samt et bibliografisk Tillæg* [Jakob Knudsen: Marginal Notes to Some of His Works, plus a Bibliographical Appendix]. Aarhus: privately published, 1936.

Schorn, Willy. *Da Voldene Stod* [When the Ramparts Stood]. Copenhagen: Gyldendal, 1905.

Sibbern, Frederik Christian. *Breve til og fra F. C. Sibbern* [Letters to and from F. C. Sibbern]. Edited by C.L.N. Mynster. Vol. 2. Copenhagen: Gyldendal, 1866.

Smith, Caspar Wilhelm. "Filologen Caspar Wilhelm Smiths Rejsebreve 1841–1845" [Correspondence of the Philologist Caspar Wilhelm Smith from His Travels, 1841–45]. Edited by H. D. Schepelern. *Danske Magazin, indeholdende bidrag til den danske histories oplysning*, 7. Række, Femte Bind. Udgivet af det kongelige danske selskab for fædrelandets historie (1949–53): 81–172.

Sødring, Julie Weber. *Erindringer fra min Barndom og Ungdom* [Memories from My Childhood and Youth]. Copenhagen: Gyldendal, 1894.

Sommer, Mogens Abraham. *Stadier paa Livets Vei* [Stages on Life's Way]. Vol. 1. Aalborg: Bechske Bogtrykkeri, 1868.

Stangerup, Henrik. *Det er svært at dø i Dieppe*. Copenhagen: Gyldendal, 1985. [Available in English translation as *The Seducer: It Is Hard to Die in Dieppe*. Translated by Sean Martin. London: Marion Boyars, 1990.]

———. *Vejen til Lagoa Santa*. Copenhagen: Gyldendal, 1981. [Available in English translation as *The Road to Lagoa Santa*. Translated by Barbara Bluestone. New York and London: Martin Boyars, 1984.]

Steen, Ellisiv. *Diktning og Virkelighet. En Studie i Camilla Colletts Forfatterskap* [Poetry and Reality: A Study in Camilla Collett's Works]. Oslo: Gyldendals Norske Forlag, 1947.

Troels-Lund, Troels Frederik. *Bakkehus og Solbjerg* [Hill House and Sun Mountain]. Vol. 3. Copenhagen: Gyldendal, 1972.

———. *Et Liv. Barndom og Ungdom* [A Life: Childhood and Youth]. Copenhagen: H. Hagerups Forlag, 1924.

Uhrskov, Anders. "Fru Marguerite Løfting fortæller" [Fru Marguerite Løfting Tells]. In *Landsmænd. Tre Livsbilleder* [Compatriots: Three Portraits from Life], pp. 7–39. Copenhagen: G.E.C. Gad, 1957.

Videbech, Nanna. *Nanna Videbech født Wanscher: Minder fra min Barndom og Ungdom* [Nanna Videbech, *née* Wanscher: Memories of My Childhood and Youth]. Copenhagen: privately published, 1912.

Weltzer, Carl. *Grundtvig og Søren Kierkegaard* [Grundtvig and Søren Kierkegaard]. Copenhagen: Gyldendal, 1952.

———. "Omkring Søren Kierkegaards Disputats" [About Søren Kierkegaard's Dissertation]. *Kirkehistoriske Samlinger*, 6. Række, bd. 6 (1948–50): 284–311.

———. *Peter og Søren Kierkegaard* [Peter and Søren Kierkegaard]. Copenhagen: G.E.C. Gad, 1936.

———. "Stemninger og Tilstande i Emil Boesens Ungdomsaar" [Moods and Situations from the Time of Emil Boesen's Youth]. *Kirkehistoriske Samlinger*, 7. Række, Bd. 1–2 (1952): 379–441.

———. "Søren Kierkegaard karrikeret, kopieret og kanoniseret" [Søren Kierkegaard Caricatured, Copied, and Canonised]. *Dansk teologisk Tidsskrift*, 11. årg. (1948): 105–32, 158–85, 213–26.

———. "Søren Kierkegaard kvindelig set" [Søren Kierkegaard as Seen by a Woman]. *Kirkehistoriske Samlinger*, 7. Række, Bd. 1–2 (1952): 442–57.

Widenmann, Robert J. "His Servant: A. C. Westergaard." In *Kierkegaard as a Person*, edited by Niels Thulstrup and Maria Mikulová Thulstrup, pp. 109–18. *Bibliotheca Kierkegaardiana*, Vol. 12. Copenhagen: C. A. Reitzel, 1983.

Wroblewski, Otto B. *Ti Aar i C. A. Reitzels Boglade* [Ten Years in C. A. Reitzel's Bookshop]. Copenhagen: privately published, 1889.

Zahle, Peter Christian. *Til Erindring om Johan Georg Hamann og Søren Aabye Kierkegaard* [In Memory of Johan Georg Hamann and Søren Aabye Kierkegaard]. Copenhagen: privately published, 1856.

Zinck, Otto. *Fra mit Studenter- og Teaterliv* [From My Life as a Student and in the Theater]. Copenhagen: Gyldendal, 1906.

Index

⇒►◦◄⇐

Page numbers of passages authored by persons listed in this index are set in **boldface type** at the beginning of the entry and are separated by a semicolon from any additional page numbers. Page numbers of letters of which persons listed in this index are recipients are set in *italic type* and are integrated in the sequence of other page numbers of references to that person, but prior to any listing for subentries. Portions of the given names of individuals that are not generally used when they are referred to in the main text have been placed in square brackets. If familiar or shortened versions of given names are used in the main text, they are given in quotation marks within parentheses. All references to the writings of Søren Kierkegaard are grouped under the rubric Kierkegaard's Writings. The following rubrics are ordered chronologically rather than alphabetically: Kierkegaard, Peter Christian; Kierkegaard, Søren Aabye, physical appearance; Kierkegaard's Writings; Schlegel, Regine.

Aalborgposten, **341n.2**
Abrahams, Arthur, **89**
Adler, Adolph Peter, 228, 234–35
Agerskov family, 158–59
Aladdin (Adam Oehlenschläger), 167, 234
Algreen-Ussing, Tage, 212
Andersen, Hans Christian, **28**, **58**, **118**, **136**; 57, 57–58, 65, 66, 95, 136, 207–8. *See also* Kierkegaard's Writings, *From the Papers of One Still Living*
Andræ, Hansine, **118–19**, **135**
Anger, Edvard Julius, **9–10**, 14
Arentzen, Kristian, **115**
Attrup, Martin, **11–12**

Bang, Oluf ("Ole") Lundt, 248
Barfod, Hans Peter, **78**; 4–5, 5, 6–9, 9–10, 11, 12–13, 20–22, 29, 60–61, 63–64, 77–78, 78, 80, 99–100, 193–96, 205–13, 216–18, 286–87, 287, 324–25n.3, 325–26n.3
Barfod, Peter Marius, 132–33
Barth, Johannes C., **99–100**
Barth, Søren Christian, 99–100
Beck, Frederik, 247
Bergsøe, Clara, **95**
Birkedal, Vilhelm, **20**, **63**, **106–8**, **139**
Boesen, Emil, **29**, **100–101**, **121–28**, **317n.42**; 129, 295n.9, 317n.42; as friend of Kierkegaard, 3, 11, 46, 91, 144, 151, 164, 287n.11;

hospital conversations with Kierkegaard, 121–28, 187, 195
Boesen, Johannes, 151
Boesen, Louise Sophie Caroline Holtermann, 100–101, 121
Boesen, Sophie Hammerich, 151
Boisen, Eline [Heramb], 24–25, **137–39**
Boisen, Frederik Engelhart, 24–25, 138–39
Boisen, [Elise] Marie. *See* Kierkegaard, [Elise] Marie (*née* Boisen)
Boisen, Peter [Outzen], 173
Borchsenius, Otto, 79, 79–83
Borries, Mrs. ("Mrs. B."), 116–17
Bournonville, August, **90**, **101**; 136
Brandes, Georg, **51–52**, **97–98**
Brandt, Carl Joachim, **59**; 46n
Bremer, Frederikke, **94–95**, **136**
Brøchner, Hans, **60–61**, **225–48**, **248–49**, **249–50**, **250–52**; 157, 249, 250, 286n.11, 322n.1
Brøndsted, Peder Oluf, **32**
Brosbøll, Anna, **89**
Brosbøll, [Johan] Carl (pseud. Carit Etlar), **61–62**; 89
Brun, Peter Munthe, **6**, **42–43**
Busck, Gunni, 148, 304n.11

Caroline Amalie (Queen), 246; and Christian VIII, 211–12

Clausen, Henrik Nicolai, 20, 133, 228, 246, 272n.12
Clausen, Julius, **52–54**
Collett, Camilla, 95
Collin, Edvard, 24
Collin, Henriette, **65**
Corsair affair, 73–75, 138, 179, 181–82, 235–36; *Corsair* caricatures of Kierkegaard, 89, 90, 97, 156; Goldschmidt's departure from *The Corsair*, 76

Damkier, Jens Emil, 13, 293n.15

Engelstoft, Christian Thorning, **105**
Etlar, Carit. *See* Brosbøll, Carl

Faber, [Sofie] Augusta, 140
Fædrelandet, 20, 56, 194–95, 222. *See also under* Kierkegaard's Writings
Feddersen, Benjamin, **23**
Fenger, Emil, 121
Fenger, [Johannes] Ferdinand, 127, 148, 187
Feuerbach, Ludwig, 233–34
Fibiger, Cathrina, *58, 59*
Fibiger, Christian, *58–59*
Fibiger, Ilia, 124, 126, 127
"Fifth Monarchy" (Henrik Hertz), notes for, 221–24
Fohlmann, V., **65**

Gjenboerne (Jens Christian Hostrup), 60–61, 236, 286–87n.11
Gjødwad, Jens Finsen, 56–57, 64, 107, 112, 125, 249, 325n.3
Goldschmidt, Meïr Aron, **65–78, 79–88, 108–9, 130**; 61–62, 64, *78*; and Borchsenius, 79–83; and *Corsair* affair, 181–82; in "Fifth Monarchy," 222, 223; on Kierkegaard's attack on Mynster and the Church, 108–9; on Kierkegaard's concluding assessment, 84–88; on Kierkegaard's death, 130; and Kierkegaard's *Posthumous Papers*, 77–78, 80–81; Nemesis theory of, 80, 83, 86–87
Gottsched, H., 317–18n.42
Grundtvig, Nikolai Frederik Severin, 38, 41, 55, 93, 272n.12; and Kierkegaard's attack on Mynster and the Church, 322n.43; Kierkegaard's views of, 106, 187, 194, 212, 246, 284n.2, 295n.9
Gude, Ludvig Jacob Mendel, *135, 307n.23, 315n.40*
Gyllembourg, Thomasine (pseud. "Author of

'A Story of Everyday Life' "), 13, 100, 221–24

Hage, Johannes, 20
Hagen, Johan Frederik, 237
Hahn, Johan, **23, 143**
Hall, Carl Christian, 170
Hamann, Johann Georg, 220, 251
Hamilton, Andrew, **95–96**
Hammerich, Angul, **24**
Hammerich, [Peter] Frederik [Adolph], **3, 14, 90–91, 130**
Hammerich, Martin [Johannes], 121
Hansen, Magdalene [Barbara], **106**
Hansen, Peter, **143–44**
Hauch, Carsten, **103, 117–18**; *63, 103, 291n.10*
Hegel, G.W.F., and Hegelianism, 28, 58, 72, 195, 215, 217, 233, 234, 251
Heiberg, Johan Ludvig, 13, 57–58, 218, 231, 251
Helweg, Hjalmar, **279n.1**
Hendriksen, Frederik, *79*
Hertz, Henrik, **218–24**
Høffding, Harald, *19*, 330n.1
Holst, Hans Peter, **12–13**; *8*
Holten, [Hans] Nicolai, 249
Hostrup, [Jens] Christian, **286–87n.11**; *61, 236, 286n.11*
Howitt, William and Mary, **96**
Hvidberg, Jens Madsen, 109–10

Ingemann, Bernhard Severin, **101–2, 103, 286n.11**; *63, 103, 117–18*
Ipsen, Harald Peter, **5**; 217

Johansen, Niels, **114**
Jørgensen, Adolph Detlef, **56**

Kant, Immanuel, 251
Karup, Wilhelm Ignatius, **62–63**
Kierkegaard, Ane Sørensdatter (*née* Lund) (Søren Kierkegaard's mother), 152–53; death of, 142, 175, 196, 229; Søren's relationship with, 14, 25, 137, 196, 228
Kierkegaard, [Niels] Christian (Søren Kierkegaard's cousin), 153
Kierkegaard, Else Pedersdatter (Michael Pedersen Kierkegaard's sister), **144**
Kierkegaard, Henriette ("Jette") (*née* Glahn) (Peter Christian Kierkegaard's second wife), *144*, 158, 162, 166–67

Kierkegaard, Maren Kirstine (Søren Kierke-
    gaard's sister), 152
Kierkegaard, [Elise] Marie (*née* Boisen) (Peter
    Christian Kierkegaard's first wife), 26, 158,
    162, 177, 297n.3
Kierkegaard, Michael Andersen (Michael
    Pedersen Kierkegaard's first cousin), 140,
    225, 239–40
Kierkegaard, Michael Pedersen (Søren Kierke-
    gaard's father), **141**, **142**; 3, 6, 149, 151–57,
    176–77, 215–16, 246; death of, 143, 157,
    160; debates with his sons, 25, 137; and
    Søren, 17–18, 100, 139, 143, 160, 217,
    226–28, 228–29
Kierkegaard, Nicoline Christine. *See* Lund,
    Nicoline Christine (*née* Kierkegaard)
Kierkegaard, Niels [Andreas] (Søren Kierke-
    gaard's brother), **141**; 141, 151–53
Kierkegaard, [Hans] Peter (Søren Kierke-
    gaard's first cousin, once removed), 140,
    229, 244–45
Kierkegaard, Peter Christian (Søren Kierke-
    gaard's brother), **141–50**, **256–68**, **314n.38**,
    317n.41; 13, 19, *19, 23*, 24–25, *47–48, 119–*
    21, 128, 130, 130, 137, 139, *141, 142, 143,*
    144, 145, 151, 152, 156, 157–58, 160, 162,
    166–67, 169, 176–77, 179, 225, *299–*
    300n.15, 310n.10, 314n.37; and Søren, 90–
    91, 102, 141–50, 316–17n.41; comparisons
    with Søren by Headmaster M. Nielsen, 14,
    17; teasing and criticism by Søren, 8, 26–
    27, 64, 106, 238–39; public criticism of
    Søren, 146–50, 256–68, 315n.40; rebuffed
    by Søren in 1855, 119, 122, 125, 127, 131,
    187, 314n.38; "brotherly greeting" from
    Søren, 119–20, 120–21, 131, 341n.2; obitu-
    ary notice for Søren, 145–46; eulogy of
    Søren, 115, 131, 132, 135, 173, 191
Kierkegaard, Petrea Severine. *See* Lund,
    Petrea Severine (*née* Kierkegaard)
Kierkegaard, Søren Aabye, **47–48**, **295n.9**,
    310n.10, **323n.1**
    attack on Mynster and the Church, 118–
        19, 171–72, 184–86, 201–5, 213, 215,
        217, 248 (*see also* Martensen, Hans;
        Mynster, Jakob)
    Berlin, visit in 1841–42, 58, 144, 162–63,
        178, 180, 229–31
    Berlin, visit in 1846, 65, 237
    Borgerdyd School, 193, 273–74n.15
    carriage drives, 109–10, 112, 143, 159–60,
        164, 167, 216
    and writing, 13, 97, 209–10, 232
    comforter in time of sorrow, 111–12, 242
    and *The Corsair* (see Corsair affair; chap-
        ter 5)
    dialectician and debater, 24, 56, 64, 101,
        236, 243
    engagement of (*see* Schlegel, Regine [*née*
        Olsen])
    funeral and burial of, 172–73, 190–92
    and *Gjenboerne* (see *Gjenboerne*)
    Greek philosophy, interest in, 231, 240,
        241
    horseback riding, attempts at, 99, 175, 232,
        333n.13
    illness and death of, 172, 186–90
    on Jews, 62–63, 91, 194
    last will and testament of, 38, 47–48, 213
    as a Latinist, 9, 12, 13, 28–29, 193
    manservant Anders Christensen Wester-
        gaard, letter of recommendation for,
        323n.1
    melancholia of, 36, 40, 41, 44–45, 54, 66,
        83–84, 142–43
    ordinary people, ability of to associate
        with, 8–9, 98, 109–10, 111
    physical appearance of
        in school, 5, 6, 7, 8, 12, 15
        as a young man, 54, 56, 65, 156–57, 225,
            249–50
        as an adult, 84, 89, 90, 97, 106, 111, 112,
            184, 216, 221, 230
        trouser legs of, 23, 89, 90, 92, 97, 138,
            183
        in final years, 107, 110, 113, 115, 116
        in hospital, 120, 172, 187, 189–90
    Sædding, Kierkegaard's visit to, 43, 236
    satirical wit, 3, 55, 64, 85, 92, 140, 151,
        182, 212, 216, 225 (*see also* [within this
        rubric] teasing)
    as a teacher, 23, 23–24, 28–29, 142,
        276n.9
    teasing
        in school, 4, 6, 7, 8, 9, 10, 11, 193
        as an adult, 26–27, 56, 63, 89, 100, 170,
            178, 182, 197, 212, 225, 230–31, 236,
            238
        of Brøchner, 226, 243–44
        of Henriette Lund, 159, 165, 170, 172,
            175
        of Johan Christian Lund, 169, 183, 189
    See also (within this rubric) satirical wit;
        youthful immaturity

KIERKEGAARD, SØREN AABYE (*cont.*)
walks, 89, 94, 96, 97–98, 112, 113, 160
  with Brøchner, 230, 231–32, 237, 246–
    47, 248
  with Sibbern, 19, 213, 216
  with specific persons, 89, 90, 91–92, 107,
    110–11, 111, 137, 165, 199–200, 241,
    242
and writing, 13
works, assessment of by critics, 93, 94–95,
  95–96, 96 (*see also* Birkedal, Vilhelm;
  Boisen, Eline; Brøchner, Hans; Goldschmidt, Meïr; Hammerich, Frederik;
  Martensen, Hans; Sibbern, Frederik)
works, assessment of by self, 113, 244–45
youthful immaturity of, 3, 9, 11, 14, 228
  (*see also* teasing)
KIERKEGAARD'S WRITINGS (listed here in
  order of publication)
early polemical pieces, 21–23, 137
From the Papers of One Still Living, 12, 28,
  65–66, 218, 220
On the Concept of Irony, 29–32, 58, 59, 67,
  90, 198–99
Either/Or, 55, 56–58, 59, 59–60, 61, 69, 74,
  89, 91, 92, 93, 95, 96, 99–100, 144, 178,
  180, 207, 220, 231, 232–33, 250
Fædrelandet, reply to Heiberg's critique of
  Either/Or, 333n.1 (entry 11)
Edifying Discourses, 96 ("Instructive Tales")
Four Edifying Discourses, 297n.3
Fear and Trembling, 95 ("Anxiety and Trem-
  bling"), 96, 261, 266
Repetition, 85–86, 96 ("Reiteration"), 97,
  137, 164
Stages on Life's Way, 85, 89, 207–8, 231,
  331n.1 (entry 3)
Fædrelandet, attack on *Corsair* in, 65, 71, 73,
  75
Concluding Unscientific Postscript, 222, 231,
  252, 263, 331n.1 (entry 4), 334n.1 (entry
  17), 337–38n.1 (entry 46)
Two Ages: A Literary Review, 221, 222–23
Edifying Discourses in a Different Spirit, 245,
  297n.3, 309n.4
"The Gospel of Sufferings" (part of *Edifying
  Discourses in a Different Spirit*), 95, 96,
  297n.3
Works of Love, 95, 228, 297n.3, 309n.4
Christian Discourses, 103, 297n.3
The Sickness unto Death, 95
Practice in Christianity, 245, 262, 267,
  287n.11

On My Activity as an Author, 220
*The Point of View for My Activity as an Au-
  thor*, 138
For Self-Examination, 100–101
Fædrelandet, attack on Mynster and the
  Church in, 101, 105, 114, 134, 145, 248,
  264, 265, 302n.2, 306n.20, 339n.2,
  340n.2
This Must Be Said, So Let It Be Said, 145,
  299n.13, 307n.21
The Moment, 106, 107, 108–9, 110–11, 114,
  115, 117, 125, 127, 130, 133, 134, 135,
  145, 146, 147, 173, 195, 202–4, 248, 264,
  302n.2, 315n.40, 340n.2
Kierkegaard, Søren Michael, 152
Knudsen, Jakob, **25–27**
Knudsen, Nanna Boisen ("Mrs. Nielsen"),
  25–27
Koch, Carl, **93**
Kofoed-Hansen, Hans Peter, **118**
Kolderup-Rosenvinge, Janus Lauritz Andreas,
  116, 241–42

Lange, Johan Nikolai, 118
"Længsel" (Christian Winther), 178
Læssøe, [Margrethe Juliane] Signe, **57–58**; *58*
Lehmann, [Peter Martin] Orla, 22–23, 137,
  163, 251
Levin, Israel, **205–13**; 64, 194, 248
Liebenberg, Frederik Ludvig, **6**, **92–93**
Lind, Peter Engel, **11**; 195
Lindberg, Elise, **55**
Lindberg, Jacob Christian, 19, 143, 246,
  299n.10
Lindberg, Niels, **19**
Løfting, Marguerite, **140**
Lorck, Jørgen Henrik, **24**; 24
Lucinde (Friedrich Schlegel), 251
Lund, Ane Sørensdatter. *See* Kierkegaard,
  Ane Sørensdatter (*née* Lund)
Lund, Anna Cathrine (Henrik Ferdinand
  Lund's second wife), 159, 163, 164, 167,
  173; Søren Kierkegaard's relation to, 175–
  80, 181–82, 184–86
Lund, Carl (Søren Kierkegaard's nephew),
  120, **144**, **145**, **314n.37**; 130, 131
Lund, [Johan] Christian (Søren Kierkegaard's
  brother-in-law), **119**, **128**, **145**; 19, 63, *129–
  30*, 137, 141, 142, 151, 160–61, 172, 179,
  186, 192, 217; differences with Kierkegaard, 169, 179, 183, 188–89, 321n.43
Lund, [Henrik] Ferdinand (Søren Kierkegaard's brother-in-law), **119–20**, **131**,

300n.19, 313n.30; 63, 137, 150–51, 164,
175, 179, 191, 192; and Søren Kierkegaard, 128, *141*, 168, 172, 180, 181, 184–86,
186
Lund, [Anna] Henriette ("Jette") (Søren Kierkegaard's niece), **43–47**, **150–75**, **281n.4**;
182, 186, 191, 317n.42
Lund, Henrik [Sigvard] (Søren Kierkegaard's
nephew), **129**, **133–35**; *48–51*, 119, 120,
128, 188; graveside speech, accounts of,
115, 131, 133, 135, 136, 191–92
Lund, Holger, **23–24**
Lund, Michael (Søren Kierkegaard's
nephew), **119**, **129–30**; 119, 120, 128
Lund, Nicoline Christine (*née* Kierkegaard)
(Søren Kierkegaard's sister), 63, 137, 141,
151–53
Lund, Peter [Severin] (Søren Kierkegaard's
nephew), **120–21**, **128**; 175, 186
Lund, Peter Wilhelm (brother of H. F. and
J. C. Lund), **178**; *141*, *160*, 175, 181,
300n.19, *313n.30*
Lund, Petrea Severine (*née* Kierkegaard)
(Søren Kierkegaard's sister), 63, 137, 141,
150–53, 158, 175
Lund, Sophie Vilhelmine (Søren Kierke-
gaard's niece), 172, 186, 188
Lund, Troels (scenery designer, uncle of
Troels-Lund), 178,183
Lund, Vilhelm [Nicolai] (Søren Kierkegaard's
nephew), *131*, 153

Madvig, Johan Nicolai, **29–31**; 241
Martensen, Hans Lassen, **135**, **196–205**,
307n.23, **315n.40**, **324n.2**; *102*, 126; attack
on, by Kierkegaard, 118, 147; Brøchner's
criticism of, 233; *Christian Dogmatics*, 147,
200, 324n.2; comparisons to Kierkegaard,
94, 146–47, 256–59; and Kierkegaard's funeral, 132, 135; Kierkegaard's view of, 247;
and P. C. Kierkegaard, 135, 256–59, 315–
16n.40; reply to Kierkegaard's attack on
Mynster and the Church, 108, 116–17,
248; as tutor to Kierkegaard, 196
Matthiesen, Henrik Johan, **299–300n.15**
Meidell, Frederik [Vilhelm Berg], **4–5**, **140**
Meyer, Raphael, **39–42**, **280n.2**
Molbech, Christian Knud Frederik, **v**, **249**,
250, **320n.42**; *248–49*, *249–50*, *250–52*
Møller, Augusta Sibbern, **19**; *213–16*
Møller, Frederik Benedikt, **59–60**, **131–32**
Møller, Peder Ludvig, 61–62, 65, 69–77, 79,
82–84

Møller, Poul Martin, 58, 166, 218, 221, 224,
241
Monrad, Ditlev Gothard, 210
Monrad, Emilie Nathalie, 106
Mourier, Hanne, **33–39**
Müller, Ludvig, *105*
Mynster, Jakob Peter, 76, 101, 135, 148–
49n, 175, **314n.37**; Kierkegaard's positive appreciation of, 11, 64, 90, 104,
199–200, 213, 229; Kierkegaard's private
criticisms of, 125, 184–86, 207, 246–47;
Kierkegaard's public attack on, 101–5,
108–9, 118–19, 147, 201–5, 213, 215, 217,
248

Neiiendam, Robert, **54**
Nielsen, Frederik, **89**
Nielsen, Michael, **14–15**, **15–18**, **28–29**, **273–**
74n.15; 6, 9, 10, 11, 13, 193, 216
Nielsen, Rasmus: and Goldschmidt, 77, 108;
and Kierkegaard, 191–92, 202; Kierkegaard's opinion of, 235; and Martensen,
135, 196, 198, 200

Odd, Orvar. *See* Sturzen-Becker, Oscar
Patrick
Oldenburg, Theodor Vilhelm, **141**, **272n.12**
Olsen, Regine. *See* Schlegel, Regine (*née*
Olsen)
Olsen, Terkild, 35, 36, 37, 43, 44, 46
Ølver (hero of Norwegian saga), 150,
316n.40
Ørsted, Anders Sandøe, 182, 215, 217
Ørsted, Hans Christian, **32**; 182
Ostermann, Johannes A., **20–22**, **63–64**

Paludan-Müller, Jens, *101–2*
Paulli, Just Henrik, 36
Petersen, Frederik Christian, **32**
Plato, 9, 100, 245, 273n.15
Ploug, Carl, 56–57
Ploug, Hother, **56–57**

Ravn, Christian Albrecht ("Peder Ravn"),
11–12
Reinhard, Regine ("Tagine"), 110
Reinhardt, Mathilde, **116–17**
Reitzel, Theodor, 110
Rørdam, Catrine, 34, 39, 52, 55, 67
Rørdam, Hans, **102–3**, **105**; *20*, *22–23*
Rørdam, Holger Frederik, **55–56**, **284n.2**
Rørdam, Peter, **20**, **22–23**; *24*, 34, 55, 65,
102–3, *105*, 284n.2

Ross, Petronella [Margrethe], **101**, **103**, **297n.4**; *103–5*, *297n.4*, *296–97n.4*

Rosted, H. C., **109–10**

Rothe, Peter Conrad, 230–31

Rudelbach, Andreas Gottlob, *14*, *19*

Rudelbach, Juliane and Christiane, **14**, **19**

Rudin, Waldemar, 39, 318n.42

Schiødte, Andreas Ferdinand, **193–96**

Schlegel, Johan Frederik ("Fritz"), **48**; engagement and marriage to Regine Olsen, 33–34, 37, 41, 51, 52, 122, 178–79; as Kierkegaard's rival, 35, 40, 53; opinion of Kierkegaard, 38, 41–42

Schlegel, Regine (*née* Olsen), **48–51**, 33–47, *281n.4*; first meeting with Kierkegaard, 34, 39, 52; Kierkegaard proposes marriage to, 35, 40, 42–43, 43, 52; engaged to Kierkegaard, 36, 44, 53, 54, 161–62, 220; on Kierkegaard's melancholia, 36, 40, 41, 44–45, 54; religiosity of, 35–36, 40; engagement to Kierkegaard broken off, 36–37, 41, 43, 45–46, 121–22, 137, 144, 162–63, 177–81, 213–15; Kierkegaard's attempt to reestablish relations with in 1849, 37–38, 42, 47, 49, 53; and Henriette Lund, 182, 281–82n.4; last encounter with Kierkegaard, 38, 42, 47; as beneficiary in Kierkegaard's will, 47–48, 53, 213; as an older woman, 51–54; final assessment of her relationship to Kierkegaard, 33, 38–39, 54

Schorn, Willy, **90**

Sibbern, Frederik Christian, **29**, **103–5**, **105**, **213–18**, **297n.4**; *101*, *103*, *297n.4*; comments on *On the Concept of Irony*, 29; critical appreciation of, by Kierkegaard, 241; as friend and confidant of Kierkegaard, 19, 90; on Kierkegaard's attack on Mynster and the Church, 103–5, 105; on Kierkegaard

and Rasmus Nielsen, 235; as spiritual counselor, 37, 194, 213, 215, 241

Smith, Caspar Wilhelm, **58–59**

Socrates, 58, 59, 93, 251

Sodemann, [Kristian] Frantz [Henrik], **132–33**

Sødring, Julie Weber, **61**, **91–92**

Sommer, Mogens Abraham, **114**, **301n.21**; 341n.2

Sorø Academy, 63, 72. *See also* Hauch, Carsten

Spang, Peter Johannes and Christiane, 111–12, 242

Spang, Tycho E., **111–13**

Stampe, Karen Marie Elisabeth ("Elise"), *106*

Stilling, Peter Michael, 135, 228

Sturzen-Becker, Oscar Patrick (pseud. Orvar Odd), **93–94**

Svendsen, Christian Julius, and Thomas Wilhelm Severin, **3**

Thurah, Christian Henrik de, 118, 126

Troels-Lund, Troels Frederik, **3**, **175–92**; 168, 281n.4, 319n.42

Tryde, Eggert, 115, 132–33, 133n, 135, 136, 173, 298n.5, 315n.40

Videbech, Nanna, **63**

Visby, Carl Holger, 13, 68, 91

Welding, Frederik, **6–9**

Westergaard, Anders Christensen, 195, 322–23n.1

Winther, Christian, 56, 95; poem by, 178

Wolff, August, **324–26n.3**

Wroblewski, Otto Bernhard, **110–11**

Wulff, [Hanna] Henriette [Frideriche], **57**; *118*

Zahle, Peter Christian, **113–14**

Zinck, Otto, **96–97**

JUL 1 6 1996

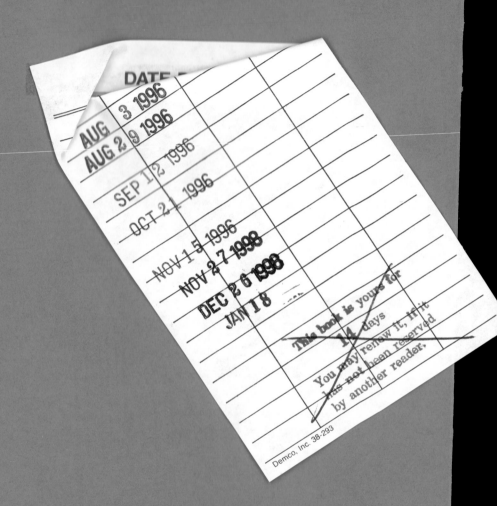

DATE

AUG 3 1996
AUG 2 9 1996
SEP 12 1996
OCT 2 1996
NOV 1 5 1996
NOV 2 7 1998
DEC 2 6 1998
JAN 18

This book is yours for
14 days
You may renew it, if it
has not been reserved
by another reader.

Demco, Inc. 38-293